Fundamentals of Neural Network Modeling

Computational Neuroscience
Terrence J. Sejnowski and Tomaso A. Poggio, editors

Fundamentals of Neural Network Modeling

Neuropsychology and Cognitive Neuroscience

edited by Randolph W. Parks, Daniel S. Levine, and
Debra L. Long

A Bradford Book
The MIT Press
Cambridge, Massachusetts
London, England

This book was set in Palatino on the Monotype "Prism Plus" PostScript Imagesetter by Asco Trade Typesetting Ltd., Hong Kong, and was printed and bound in the United States of America.

Library of Congress Cataloging-in-Publication Data

Fundamentals of neural network modeling : neuropsychology and
 cognitive neuroscience / edited by Randolph W. Parks, Daniel S.
 Levine, and Debra L. Long
      p.   cm. — (Computational neuroscience)
   "A Bradford book."
   Includes bibliographical references and index.
   ISBN 0-262-16175-3 (hc : alk. paper)
   1. Neural networks (Neurobiology) 2. Neuropsychology.
 3. Neuropsychiatry. 4. Cognitive neuroscience. I. Parks, Randolph W.
 II. Levine, Daniel S. III. Long, Debra L. IV. Series.
   [DNLM: 1. Neuropsychology. 2. Neural Networks (Computer)
 3. Models, Neurological. 4. Cognition. 5. Dementia. WL 103.5
 F981   1998]
 QP363.3.F86   1998
 612.8—DC21
 DNLM/DLC
 for Library of Congress   97-34792
                                                                CIP

Contents

Series Foreword

Computational neuroscience is an approach to understanding the information content of neural signals by modeling the nervous system at many different structural scales, including the biophysical, the circuit, and the systems levels. Computer simulations of neurons and neural networks are complementary to traditional techniques in neuroscience. This book series welcomes contributions that link theoretical studies with experimental approaches to understanding information processing in the nervous system. Areas and topics of particular interest include biophysical mechanisms for computation in neurons, computer simulations of neural circuits, models of learning, representation of sensory information in neural networks, systems models of sensory-motor integration, and computational analysis of problems in biological sensing, motor control, and perception.

Terrence J. Sejnowski
Tomaso A. Poggio

Preface

Neural networks began to be the object of serious research in the 1940s. They did not become widely known or popular until the 1980s when several academic centers published articles and distributed software that enabled individuals with modest mathematical and computing skills to learn computational network principles and apply them to broad ranges of projects inside university settings as well as in extramural domains. At first, neural networks were predominantly applied to industrial problems in areas such as pattern recognition and signal processing. However, many active neural network researchers were guided by insights from neuroscience and psychology, and believed that neural networks could become an important computational technique for furthering our understanding of brain and cognitive processes. This belief was borne out by significant progress in the field during the 1990s when substantial improvements in computer architecture, software design, and computing speed occurred. In particular, interest in applying neural networks to understanding neuropsychology and mental function and dysfunction has increased dramatically. Other colleagues such as neurologists, psychiatrists, and cross-disciplinary neuroscientists also have facilitated interest in this new field. The feasibility of making connections between models and clinical data has also increased, calling for a textbook that brings together much of this growing body of work in a single volume. This book is the first of its kind that is specifically intended for neuropsychologists and related disciplines.

Our book has models of many widely used neuropsychological tests and tasks, including the Wisconsin Card Sorting, Stroop, verbal fluency, Tower of Hanoi, Line Cancellation, and many other tests. It covers a wide range of syndromes, including Alzheimer's disease, Parkinson's disease, schizophrenia, epilepsy, alcoholism, stroke, attention deficit/hyperactivity disorder, and frontal lobe disorders. The modeling techniques utilized are not dominated by one "school" of modeling; rather, they include widely used modeling paradigms, such as backpropagation and adaptive resonance, and models designed for a systems approach to interacting brain regions implicated in cognitive tasks. In addition, some chapters have been included to facilitate a better understanding of the neurobiological and neuroanatomical basis of cognitive network models.

Prerequisites of a technical nature are minimized in this book. The mathematics involved in the network models are deemphasized, and in most cases the theoretical basis for the model's structure can be discerned from the diagrams combined with the text. Hence, the aim is to present neural network techniques as theoretical tools that can be readily learned and applied by neuropsychologists and other neuroscientists (including neurologists, psychiatrists, clinical psychologists, mathematicians, and computer scientists) with particular interest in clinical patient applications. We hope that this will contribute to the accessibility of neural networks and to an intensification of the ongoing dialogue between the clinical and theoretical communities.

Contributors

J. Wesson Ashford, M.D., Ph.D.
Department of Psychiatry and
Neurology
University of Kentucky College of
Medicine
Lexington, Kentucky

Rajendra D. Badgaiyan, Ph.D.
Department of Psychology
University of Oregon
Eugene, Oregon

Jean P. Banquet, M.D., Ph.D.
CREARE, Neuroscience and
Modeling
Institute of Neurosciences
Pierre and Marie Curie University
Paris, France

Yves Burnod, Ph.D.
INSERM-CREARE, Neuroscience
and Modeling
Institute of Neurosciences
Pierre and Marie Curie University
Paris, France

Nelson Butters, Ph.D. (deceased)
Department of Neurosciences
University of California, San Diego
San Diego, California

John Cardoso, M.A.
Department of Psychology
University of New Brunswick
Fredericton, New Brunswick, Canada

Agnes S. Chan, Ph.D.
Department of Neurosciences
University of California, San Diego
San Diego, California and
Departmment of Psychology,
Chinese University of Hong Kong
Shatin, New Territories
Hong Kong

Jean-Pierre Changeux, Ph.D.
Molecular Neurobiology
Pasteur Institute
Paris, France

Kerry L. Coburn, Ph.D.
Department of Psychiatry
Mercer University School of
Medicine
Macon, Georgia

Jonathan D. Cohen, M.D., Ph.D.
Department of Psychology
Carnegie Mellon University and
Department of Psychiatry
University of Pittsburgh
Pittsburgh, Pennsylvania

Laurent Cohen, M.D., Ph.D.
Department of Neurology
Salpêtrière Hospital
Paris, France

Jose L. Contreras-Vidal, Ph.D.
Department of Exercise Science
Arizona State University
Tempe, Arizona

Antonio R. Damasio M.D., Ph.D.
Department of Neurology
University of Iowa College of
Medicine
Iowa City, Iowa

Hanna Damasio, M.D.
Department of Neurology
University of Iowa College of
Medicine
Iowa City, Iowa

Stanislas Dehaene, Ph.D.
INSERM Unité, SHFJ-CEA
Orsay, France

Martha J. Farah, Ph.D.
Department of Psychology
University of Pennsylvania
Philadelphia, Pennsylvania

Joaquin M. Fuster, M.D., Ph.D.
Department of Psychiatry
UCLA School of Medicine
Los Angeles, California

Philippe Gaussier, Ph.D.
ETIS ENSEA
University of Cergy-Pontoise
Cergy-Pontoise, France

Angelika Gissler, M.S.
CREARE, Neuroscience and
Modeling
Institute of Neurosciences
Pierre and Marie Curie University
Paris, France

Dylan G. Harwood, M.A.
Department of Educational and
Psychological Studies
University of Miami
Miami, Florida

Michael E. Hasselmo, D.Phil.
Department of Psychology and
Program in Neuroscience
Harvard University
Cambridge, Massachusetts

J. Allan Hobson, M.D.
Laboratory of Neurophysiology
Department of Psychiatry
Massachusetts Mental Health Center
Harvard Medical School
Boston, Massachusetts

Sam Leven, Ph.D.
Scientific Cybernetics
Chery Chase, Maryland

Daniel S. Levine, Ph.D.
Department of Psychology
University of Texas at Arlington
Arlington, Texas

Debra L. Long, Ph.D.
Department of Psychology
University of California, Davis
Davis, California

Roderick K. Mahurin, Ph.D.
Battelle Research Center and
Department of Psychiatry
University of Washington
Seattle, Washington

Raymond L. Ownby, M.D., Ph.D.
Department of Psychiatry
University of Miami School of
Medicine
Miami, Florida

Randolph W. Parks, Ph.D., Psy.D.
Neuropsychology Program,
Department of Psychiatry
Southern Illinois University School
of Medicine
Springfield, Illinois

Michael I. Posner, Ph.D.
Department of Psychology
University of Oregon
Eugene, Oregon

David P. Salmon, Ph.D.
Department of Neurosciences
University of California, San Diego
San Diego, California

David Servan-Schreiber, M.D., Ph.D.
Department of Psychiatry
University of Pittsburgh
Medical Center
Shadyside Hospital
Pittsburgh, Pennsylvania

Chantal E. Stern, D.Phil.
Department of Radiology
Massachusetts General Hospital
Harvard University
Charlestown, Massachusetts

Jeffrey P. Sutton, M.D., Ph.D.
Neural Systems Group, Department
of Psychiatry
Massachusetts General Hospital
Harvard Medical School
Charlestown, Massachusetts

Lynette J. Tippett, Ph.D.
Department of Psychology
The University of Auckland
Auckland, New Zealand

Daniel Tranel, Ph.D.
Department of Neurology
University of Iowa College of
Medicine
Iowa City, Iowa

Bradley P. Wyble, M.A.
Department of Psychology and
Program in Neuroscience
Harvard University
Cambridge, Massachusetts

I Introduction to Neural Networks

function could be duplicated by a suitable network of all-or-none neurons with thresholds. Biological underpinnings of neural network theory were added by two researchers in particular: Hebb (1949), who formally proposed that learning depends on synaptic weight changes in response to paired pre- and postsynaptic stimuli; and Rashevsky (1960), who proposed methods for averaging the all-or-none behavior of single neurons into continuous dynamics of large neural ensembles. Rosenblatt (1962), Werbos (1974), and others combined McCulloch and Pitts's insights with Hebb's in developing the ancestors of current error-correcting learning networks, such as Rumelhart and McClelland's (1986) backpropagation network. Grossberg (e.g., 1969) pioneered the development of continuous dynamical system networks that embodied psychological principles such as associative learning and lateral inhibition. Such principles were also explored by several other researchers who are still leaders in the neural network field, such as Amari (1971), Anderson (1968, 1970), and Kohonen (1977).

Our purpose in this book is to make the neural network approach accessible to practicing neuropsychologists, clinical psychologists, neurologists, psychiatrists, and research neuroscientists (including mathematicians and computer scientists) who may have little substantive knowledge of the topic. The chapters gathered here describe recent advances in the application of neural network modeling to a wide range of topics. Part I provides an overview of neural network modeling. The chapters in part I describe the basic architecture of neural networks and discuss some of the assumptions that underlie this approach. In addition, the chapters describe the application of these models to theoretical topics such as attention and hippocampal contributions to memory. The chapters in part II describe neural network models of behavioral states, such as alcohol dependence, learned helplessness, depression, and waking and sleeping. Part III is devoted to neural network models of neuropsychological tests such as the Stroop, Tower of Hanoi, and Line Cancellation tests. In addition, the chapters in this section describe the application of these models to syndrome-specific topics such as schizophrenia, acalculia, neglect, attention deficit/hyperactivity disorder, and lexical retrieval. The final section, part IV, describes the application of neural network models to dementia. These chapters describe models of acetycholine and memory, frontal lobe syndrome, Parkinson's disease, and Alzheimer's disease. The Wisconsin Card Sorting and verbal fluency tests are modeled within the dementia framework.

Our goal in this first chapter is to provide a comprehensive introduction to principles of neural network modeling. In the first section, we describe the basic architecture of neural networks and contrast these models with the traditional symbolic models used in artificial intelligence (AI). In addition, we provide details about two of the most popular classes of network models, *backpropagation networks* and networks based on *adaptive resonance theory* (ART). In the second section, we discuss some of the controversies surrounding the neural network approach. Should cognition be modeled using

1 An Introduction to Neural Network Modeling: Merits, Limitations, and Controversies

Debra L. Long, Randolph W. Parks, and
Daniel S. Levine

Many researchers in cognitive psychology and neuropsychology have described human mental activity in terms of abstract information-processing models. Still other researchers have focused on regional brain areas associated with hypothesized neuropsychological test performance without an appreciation of multiple brain regions' contributions to cognitive test performance. However, these traditions have been supplemented in recent years by efforts to develop models of cognitive processes that are better founded in our understanding of neural circuitry. Researchers who have adopted a neural network approach attempt to model cognition as patterns of activity across simple computing elements or units (Feldman & Ballard, 1982; Grossberg, 1982, 1988; McClelland, Rumelhart, & the PDP Research Group, 1986; Rumelhart & McClelland, 1986). Such models have been used to investigate theoretical claims about the nature of various cognitive processes (e.g., pattern recognition, attention, semantic memory, natural language processing) and to solve a wide range of applied problems (e.g., machine vision, medical diagnosis, speech recognition and production).

In this chapter, we use the term *neural network* broadly to refer to a large class of models that share certain architectural and processing features: (1) these models contain many simple processing elements or units that operate in parallel; (2) the units in these models communicate activation along connections (weights) of varying strength; and (3) the models learn by adjusting their weights as they gain experience in some environment. Models of this type have also been called *connectionist models* and *parallel distributed processing models*.

Neural network models were introduced to mainstream psychologists and computer scientists in several influential publications, including Feldman and Ballard (1982), Hopfield (1982), and Rumelhart and McClelland (1986). Since that time, these models have been the topic of substantial theoretical and computational interest and the source of considerable controversy.

The main ideas involved in neural network modeling have a substantial history (see Anderson & Rosenfeld, 1988; Levine, 1983, 1991; and Parks et al., 1991, for partial accounts). An influential article in the field was published by McCulloch and Pitts in 1943. They demonstrated that any logical principles of language and logical reasoning, or principles of the underlying neural architecture? Should neural network models be viewed as simulations of cognitive theories? Can behaviors that appear functionally modular (e.g., visual vs. semantic processing, lexical vs. syntactic processing) be performed by a system that is not modular in the same way? In the final section, we describe some of the theoretical and computational limitations of current neural network models.

AN ALTERNATIVE TO TRADITIONAL SYMBOL-PROCESSING MODELS

Traditionally, cognitive psychologists have formulated their theories by analogy to computers and computer programs (Newell, 1980, 1982; Newell, Rosenbloom, & Laird, 1989; Pylyshyn, 1989). This analogy has led to a symbolic- or information-processing view of human cognition. In the symbolic approach, goals, beliefs, and knowledge are represented as abstract symbols. These symbols are semantically interpretable elements; that is, they can be described in terms of ordinary concepts relevant to the domain. Intellectual tasks are performed in these systems by means of explicit rules, such as the rules of formal or sentential logic (Fodor, 1976; Fodor & Pylyshyn, 1988; Newell et al., 1989). These rules specify how symbols are to be manipulated and concatenated. In this approach, symbols and the rules that operate on them are discussed in the absence of assumptions about brain location or brain processes.

In contrast, the neural network approach is an attempt at "brain-style" computation. Here are a few of the properties that distinguish neural networks from traditional symbolic models:

1. Neural networks incorporate the basic properties of neural circuitry. Processing takes place in a system of connected modules. Each module consists of a population of interconnected computational units. Each unit is a simple information-processing device that (a) computes a numerical activation value from the input of other units and (b) communicates this activation value to other units along connections of varying strengths (Feldman & Ballard, 1982; Feldman, Ballard, Brown, et al., 1985; Rumelhart & McClelland, 1986). A unit may correspond to a single neuron, a population of neurons, or a feature of an object or concept. Some units receive input from outside the system; other units produce output or responses that exit the system. Several classes of neural network models contain "hidden" units. Hidden units have connections to other units in the system, but do not send or receive information from outside the system.

2. The individual units in neural networks perform computations in parallel. The activation of each unit changes constantly in response to the activity of the other units to which it is connected. The massively parallel nature of neural networks corresponds to an important feature of brain organization

and processing (Anderson & Hinton, 1989; Pellionisz & Llinas, 1982; Sejnowski, 1986). Although an individual biological neuron is a slow processing device, large numbers of neurons operating in parallel can accomplish a task very quickly (Feldman & Ballard, 1982).

3. Neural networks encode knowledge very differently than do traditional symbolic models (Feldman & Ballard, 1982; Rumelhart & McClelland, 1986; Smolensky, 1988, 1989). In neural networks, knowledge is encoded in the strengths of the connections between individual processing units. Representations consist of patterns of activation across large populations of connected units. An individual unit may participate in several distinct representations.

4. Neural network models also perform mental computations differently than do symbolic models. The rules in a neural network operate at the level of the individual units (Rumelhart & McClelland, 1986; Smolensky, 1988, 1989). These rules specify how units compute their activation value, how activation is passed to other units, and how connection strengths are modified. Intelligent behavior arises from the way in which interacting units are connected.

5. Neural networks learn from experience. The models discover a set of connection strengths (weights) that capture the internal structure of a domain. These connection strengths are typically found by means of error-driven adjustments in the connections among units (Grossberg, 1976; Hebb, 1949; Hinton & Sejnowski, 1986; Rolls & Treves, 1998; Rumelhart, Hinton, & Williams, 1986; Widrow & Hoff, 1960). Once a neural network has discovered a set of weights that results in appropriate behavior, the model can repeat a pattern of activity at some later time or produce a pattern of activity when given some portion of it as a cue. Thus, these systems "program themselves" to perform extraordinarily complex tasks.

These features of the neural network architecture give rise to properties that make neural networks an attractive alternative to traditional symbol-processing models. First, neural networks have distributed representations; thus, they seem well suited to model processes that appear to operate on analog-like representations, such as the mental rotation of objects (Cooper, 1976; Shepard & Cooper, 1982; Shepard & Metzler, 1971). In addition, neural networks have knowledge that is distributed in the connections between units. Thus, these networks have little difficulty modeling nonverbal or intuitive processes.

Second, neural networks provide good accounts of pattern recognition, motor control, and associative learning. Such tasks appear to require mechanisms for processing massive amounts of information in parallel while satisfying large sets of probabilistic constraints. Neural networks are appropriate for these tasks because they implement "soft constraints" (Smolensky, 1988, 1989). The connection between two units is a constraint in that it determines whether or not one unit should be active when the other is active. This constraint is "soft" because it can be easily overridden by the input of other units. The network behaves in a way that balances a massive number of these soft constraints. Thus, the network "settles" into stable representational patterns. As a consequence, neural network models tend to be less brittle and rigid than traditional symbolic models.

Third, neural networks are attractive alternatives to traditional AI models because they exhibit spontaneous generalization. These models can respond appropriately to novel stimuli once they have learned the internal structure of a domain. Similar representations typically have many units in common. Thus, a new item can be classified in the network's existing representational scheme when its features activate representations that share similar features. This is an advantage for tasks that require generalizations from large sets of stored exemplars or tasks that involve degraded input.

Finally, neural networks are attractive because they exhibit "graceful degradation." A representation consists of a pattern of activation that is distributed over a population of units. The pattern of activation representing an entity is distinctive; therefore, different entities can be represented using the same set of units. This feature of neural networks makes them resistant to damage. A distinct pattern of activation may still occur even if the system has lost some portion of its units. In addition, graceful degradation allows for relearning after damage. A damaged network may retain a subset of the weights that produced appropriate behavior before the damage. To the extent that these weights capture some of the internal structure of the domain, the network should readily relearn associations that it previously knew.

So far, we have discussed some of the characteristics that are common to a variety of neural networks. Next, we describe in some detail two of the most popular classes of neural network models.

Backpropagation Networks[1]

Since the middle of the 1980s, backpropagation networks became popular with the publication of a collection of articles from diverse fields and accompanying software (McClelland et al., 1986). The simplified, though powerful, software release enabled university neuroscientists and other researchers with moderate computer skills to program rudimentary cognitive processes with relatively little assistance. Previously, these programming techniques were largely confined to supercomputer centers, such as the large government facility at Los Alamos. In this section, we examine some of the tenets of backpropagation by first describing the basic components of a neural network at the cellular level. This is followed by a brief discussion of how the terms *parallel* and *distributed* are essential to this process. We then describe some of the important neural network principles of backpropagation in training a neural network. We illustrate these principles using a standard neuropsychological test of executive functioning in humans, Tower of Hanoi. A more detailed in vivo demonstration of backpropagation with the

Tower of Hanoi in a clinical population of left frontal lobe patients can be found in chapter 9 by Cardoso and Parks. Ownby utilizes backpropagation in chapters on alcohol dependence (chapter 5), cortical neglect (chapter 11) and attention deficit/hyperactivity disorder (chapter 11). Servan-Schreiber and Cohen in chapter 8 describe the use of backpropagation to model the Stroop test in schizophrenia. Finally, a hypothetical model of basal ganglia function in chapter 14 by Mahurin is applied to human movement sensorimotor dysfunction (e.g., Parkinson's disease).

Artificial Neural Networks: Computer Architecture at the Cellular Level In order to understand some of the essentials of backpropagation, the reader first needs to appreciate how a computer neuroscientist translates principles of dynamic living tissue into a language that the computer understands. Historically, we draw on such pioneers such as Hebb (1949) and his Learning Law, and McCulloch and Pitts's (1943) M-P neuron. Another pioneer was Rosenblatt (1962) who invented the Perceptron, a simple computational learning device. He wrote, "Perceptrons are not intended to serve as detailed copies of an actual nervous system. They are simplified networks, designed to permit the study of lawful relationships between the organization of a nerve net, the organization of its environment, and the *psychological* performances of which it is capable."

Currently, one may describe a neural net as made up of very simple computational units. These units are also called neurons, neurodes, processing elements, cells, nodes, and various other names depending on the theoretical preferences of the neuroscientist. The seminal concepts behind the creation of artificial neural nets, along with the conceptual foundations of the computational sciences which deal with the properties of these units, give rise to the current essential features of a computational neuron. Thus, the artificial neuron is a crude eclectic simulation of its biological counterpart. By adapting language from the biological sciences, the artificial neuron is said to consist of its own dendrites, synapses, cell body, and axon terminals. It receives stimulation from nearby cells, or from its environment, and generates a modified action potential or nerve signal. A frequently used model of a neuron is shown in figure 1.1.

This model neuron (Parks & Cardoso, 1997) has three inputs: x_1, x_2, and x_3. These inputs potentially receive their stimulation from the output (axons) of other neurons, or directly from sensory cells monitoring the environment. Input signals (stimulation) reach the body of the neuron through coupling synapses. The efficacy of these synapses, known as *weights* of the connections, are represented here respectively as w_1, w_2, and w_3. The signals from inputs x_1 and x_3 reach the neuron through inhibitory synapses (synapses with negative weights). The signal from input x_2 reaches the neuron through an excitatory synapse (synapse with a positive weight). Before the input signals reach the neuron, they are scaled by the weights of their respective coupling synapses and added together so that the net-value of

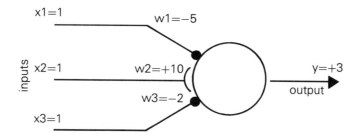

Figure 1.1 A simple model of an artificial neuron.

stimulation I (or weighted sum) reaching the neuron will be, assuming that each input has one unit of stimulation,

$$I = x_1 * w_1 + x_2 * w_2 + x_3 * w_3 = 1 * (-5) + 1 * 10 + 1 * (-2) = 3$$

Since the input net-value I, in this simple case, is transferred directly without experiencing any loss of transformation to the output of the neuron, its output y is also equal to 3. This is an overly simplified model, but it may give readers unfamiliar with this material an idea of how a biological neuron can be simulated. Ordinarily, in a working model, there are other parameters such as a bias, an input threshold, an input (fan-in) function that further reshapes the input signal, an activation function that determines the activation (or excitation) of the neuron, and an output (fan-out) function that changes its activation value to the final value that will eventually reach the postsynaptic neuron(s) or the output of the network.

An artificial neural network is made up of many of these simple units, highly interconnected and generally organized by layers with each neuron in a given layer connected to every neuron in the succeeding layer. Signals travel through these connections from unit to unit and finally generate an output. Some nets are capable of learning by themselves (unsupervised learning). The neurons in these types of nets continually monitor their inputs and keep adjusting their weights trying to mirror the signals they receive. A well-known type of unsupervised-learning net is the Kohonen network (Kohonen, 1984). These types of networks (self-organizing) are capable of modeling the probability distribution function of the input data. Other nets need an executor (supervised learning) to tell them whether they are correct in their responses, and, if not, by how much they are wrong. The difference between the expected (correct) response and the actual response given by a unit is used, as feedback, to readjust the weights of the connections and further to reduce the error until the unit eventually generates the correct response. This is a gradual process which usually takes many iterations to accomplish.

After a neural net is trained, we say that the net has *learned* and that the acquired *knowledge* has been stored (as values) in the weights of its connections. For example, if the correct output that we expected from the neuron in figure 1.1 was a value other than 3, we could *teach* the neuron by gradually adjusting the values of w_1, w_2, and w_3 so that the unit eventually generates the desired output. Two important fundamental features of network organization, the parallelism of neural nets, and the distribution and storage of information in these networks, are described in more detail in the next section.

Parallel Distributed Processing   The term *parallel* refers to the type of network architecture (Koch & Segev, 1998; Parks et al., 1991). It identifies the way the neural net is organized and processes information. In a parallel system, information is not processed sequentially, one step at a time, or by one unit at a time, but simultaneously by many units. This is an important feature of artificial neural networks because it seems also to be a feature of neural systems in the human brain. The *computational* architecture of the brain appears to be highly parallel. Biological neurons are slow devices and the traveling speeds of nerve signals are slow. The brain is capable of achieving its rapid processing speed only through the massive parallelism of its neurons. Similarly to the brain, when an input signal reaches a neural net, the signal is simultaneously distributed throughout many neurodes. Depending on the type of network, one whole layer or even the whole network may be involved at the same time and every unit processes the signal concurrently. The gains in speed, efficiency, and computational power are enormous. However, all of these gains substantially increase the complexity of the process.

The term *distributed* refers to the way in which information is stored and represented internally in the network. An intelligent system, whether natural or artificial, can only learn, remember, and recognize if it is capable of keeping some *internal representation* of what it has learned. AI has utilized rule-based methods and symbolic programming techniques as its main tools to represent and manipulate knowledge in a computer. Semantic networks (Quillian, 1968), schemas, scripts, and frames (Schank & Abelson, 1977), among others, are powerful knowledge tools, but they have not proved to be sufficient to advance substantially the study of *learning*. Connectionism offers a very different approach. In artificial neural networks, learning and knowledge representations are hard to differentiate as two independent processes. It is generally accepted that, in neural nets, it is the weights (the strength of the connections) that do the representing. The weights encode whatever knowledge the network has acquired during its learning phase.

Two main types of representation are possible in neural nets: local and distributed (Rumelhart & McClelland, 1986). In local representations, individual units stand for some unique concept or feature of the input; a particular feature of the input causes one single unit to become active. In distributed representations, one concept or feature of the input is represented by the activation of a set of units. In other words, a single input causes many hidden units to become active (Hanson & Burr, 1990). The multilayer neural net

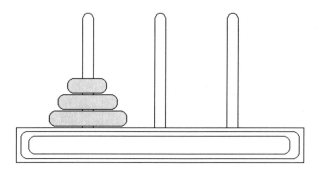

Figure 1.2 The Tower of Hanoi test as used in clinical practice by neuropsychologists.

that was used in the current experiment contained distributed knowledge representations. Many units become active for a given input. However, we have not strictly adhered to how the distributed knowledge representations are programmed nor to how they are interpreted. For example, we do ascribe some computer architecture elements to frontal functions, attentional factors, and visual processing. A more detailed discussion of the controversies of localization and modularity of brain functions is addressed later in this chapter.

Backpropagation with a Complex Human Neuropsychological Test   In this section, we define some of the features needed to model a well-validated neuropsychological test, Tower of Hanoi (TOH). In its classic form, the TOH puzzle consists of three vertical pegs mounted on a board and a set of disks or rings graded in size (Cardoso, 1991; Anderson & Kushmerick, 1992; Shallice, 1982). Initially, all of the rings are stacked in order of size on one peg, with the largest ring at the bottom and the smallest at the top (figure 1.2). The TOH requires the ability to anticipate subroutine steps to achieve the desired final position of the rings. The backpropagation network has three layers (figure 1.3): input, hidden, and output. The input layer has twenty-seven neurodes, the hidden layer has fifteen, and the output layer has twenty-seven. The sizes of the input and output layers were selected to match the number of features that we wanted to represent. The size of the hidden layer was based on the number of statistically significant factors in the input data. A more comprehensive description of subroutine and programming parameters is provided in chapter 9.

In our training of this feedforward multilayer network, the backpropagation (BP) program utilizes an algorithm that is based on the generalized delta rule (Caudill & Butler, 1990; Chauvin & Rumelhart, 1995; Pao, 1989; Rolls & Treves, 1998). Briefly, without discussing the mathematical principles that underlie the rule, BP requires two steps. In the first step, the input is presented and propagated forward through the net to activate the output units. The output value of each of these units is then compared with

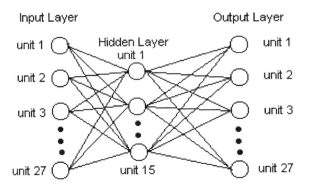

Figure 1.3 Architecture of the Tower of Hanoi network used to study the results of degradation in the output-layer connections.

the expected (target) value and an error δ is computed. The second step is a backward pass through the net to compute the δ for each unit in the network. Once these two steps are completed, we compute the weight error derivatives, and then compute the required weight changes. Users of this rule must be aware that the BP algorithm is a gradient descent procedure. Gradient descent procedures minimize the error function by following the contour of the error surface, always moving downhill and settling at the bottom. In complex error surfaces, the process may settle into a local minimum (which is a low point, but not the lowest point on the surface) rather than into the desired global minimum (the surface's lowest point). Gradient descent methods require very small steps to succeed. One of the parameters used in training the network is the learning rate, ε, a constant of proportionality that determines the magnitude of the weight changes at every step. Large ε-values mean larger steps. Large steps can cause oscillations during learning. In other words, one can easily visualize the system trying to settle into a valley, but always bouncing from hill to hill. Choosing the largest possible value that does not cause oscillations leads to the fastest learning (Chauvin & Rumelhart, 1995; Pao, 1989).

Another important BP parameter is momentum. This parameter has the effect of a high-frequency filter. Filtering out the high-frequency variations in the error surface permits the use of relatively large ε-values, and allows for faster learning. As in the brain, a distributed representation protects the system from forgetting all that it has learned in the case of injury or mutilation (in programming language). In such cases, the system's performance suffers little or no degradation, and the system is not rendered totally useless. This gradient-descent methodology allows the system to process very large data sets, as well as detect very subtle changes during cognitive modeling. This methodology may potentially clarify the multiple-system neuropathological changes of insidious neuropsychiatric conditions, such as the gradual cognitive decline seen in Alzheimer's disease.

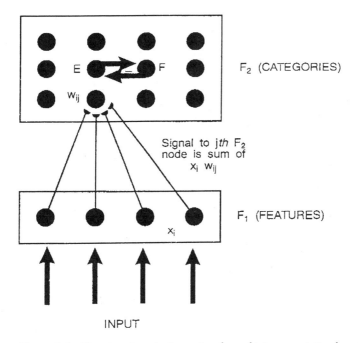

Figure 1.4 Generic categorization network combining associative learning and competition. (Modified from Levine, 1989, with permission of Miller Freeman Publishers.)

Adaptive Resonance Theory (ART)

Backpropagation networks have achieved remarkable success not only in simulating a wide range of neuropsychological data, as will be seen in later chapters of this book, but in a wide range of engineering applications that require "intelligent" systems. Such networks are fairly homogeneous in structure and in mathematical properties. They do not, therefore, capture much of the richness and diversity of the structures of actual brains. Also, backpropagation networks rely on outside "supervision," in the form of an input "telling" the network what the desired or target response should be.

There is another long tradition in neural network theory (Levine, 1991) based on networks that are self-organizing and decomposable into smaller networks that have specialized cognitive properties themselves. Of these, one of the best known is the *adaptive resonance theory* (ART) network for classifying patterns, introduced by Carpenter and Grossberg (1987). ART is built on earlier networks developed by Grossberg and his colleagues (Grossberg, 1976, 1982) that embody principles such as competition and associative learning.

A generic categorization network, examples of which appear in von der Malsburg (1973) and Grossberg (1982), is shown in figure 1.4 (Levine, 1989). The nodes at the F_1 level represent sensory features; the nodes at the F_2 level represent categories. When an input arrives from the outside environment, it activates the corresponding nodes at the F_1 level, which thereupon sends

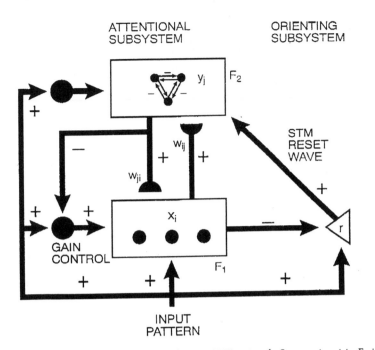

ATTENTIONAL
SUBSYSTEM

ORIENTING
SUBSYSTEM

STM
RESET
WAVE

GAIN
CONTROL

INPUT
PATTERN

Figure 1.5 Adaptive resonance theory (ART) network. Sensory input to F_1 is stored as a vector of node activities. The F_1 node activities are multiplied by the "bottom-up" connection weights w_{ij}, then transmitted to F_2, where the one node receiving the largest signal wins. Then the input is compared with that node's stored prototype, as represented by the "top-down" connection weights w_{ji}. Gain control is a mathematical fine-tuning device, not essential to the discussion herein. Orienting is a response to novel inputs. Reset is a response to inputs that are compared with a prototype and mismatch it. (Adapted from Carpenter and Grossberg, 1987, with permission of Academic Press.)

bottom-up signals (weighted by the connection strengths) to the F_2 level. Whichever F_2 node receives the largest signal determines the category in which the input is classified. The signal to the appropriate category node inhibits activities of the other nodes (as indicated by the minus sign in figure 1.4).

However, Grossberg (1976) showed mathematically that a categorization network such as the one in figure 1.4 can lead to instabilities in coding if the same set of input patterns is presented repeatedly. He showed that such instability can be prevented by supplementing the bottom-up signals from F_1 to F_2 with top-down feedback signals from F_2 to F_1, leading to the ART model shown in figure 1.5. These top-down signals allow for comparison of the input with previously learned category prototypes (see Posner & Keele, 1970; or Mervis & Rosch, 1981, for relevant psychological data) stored at the F_2 nodes. If an input is close enough to a prototype, it resonates with the category (hence the word *resonance*) and is stored at the corresponding node. The term *adaptive* means that the prototype is updated by means of a time-weighted average with the new input: for example, one's mental prototype of the category "bird" might look like a sparrow until one has seen many robins, and then changes to some sort of weighted average of a sparrow and a robin. Thus, in the ART model the top-down feedback connection weights, as well as the bottom-up connection weights, are changed by paired activities of the two interconnected nodes, which is a variant of a learning principle enunciated by Hebb (1949).

Adaptive resonance is one of the principles used by Grossberg and his colleagues (Grossberg, 1988) in models of a wide range of cognitive phenomena including classical conditioning, preattentive vision, word recognition, and many others. It combines with other principles that are suggested by both physiological and psychological data. One of these principles, which also plays a role in ART, is lateral inhibition as a means of modeling decisions between activations of competing entities, whether they be percepts, categories, drives, beliefs, or motor plans. Another principle is opponent processing, which models selective enhancement of novel stimuli or changing reinforcement contingencies. More recently, a variety of researchers have applied different combinations of all of these network principles to model aspects of neuropsychological functioning and mental illness (Hestenes, 1998; Levine, 1996; and chapters 4 and 15 in this book).

CURRENT DEBATES IN NEURAL NETWORK MODELING

In this section, we discuss a few of the controversies surrounding the neural network approach. These controversies relate to three issues: (1) Does a theory of cognition require symbolic representations and rules? (2) Are neural networks simulations of cognitive theories? (3) Is the functional modularity of many cognitive activities reflected in the underlying architecture?

The Need for Symbolic Representations and Rules

Neural network models cannot be distinguished from traditional symbolic models on the basis of a belief in the existence of representations (Fodor & Pylyshyn, 1988; Smolensky, 1989). Representations exist in both types of models, although they are realized somewhat differently. In symbolic models, representations are semantically interpretable in that they correspond to the mental states that we ascribe to persons (e.g., beliefs, thoughts, desires, etc.). Symbolic representations are viewed as purely formal objects. This means that symbolic representations can be manipulated by virtue of their form or syntax without regard to their semantics.

In neural network models, representations are not primitive computational elements (Smolensky, 1988, 1989); rather, representations are patterns of activation across individual units. Although these patterns also correspond to the mental states that we ascribe to persons, the individual units that participate in a representation may or may not be semantically interpretable.

The distributed nature of representation in neural network models is the source of one objection to this approach. Some critics have argued that the absence of semantic interpretations for the units that participate in a representation leads to models that are as inscrutable as the inner workings of the brain itself (Burton & Bruce, 1994; Fodor & Pylyshyn, 1988; Massaro, 1988; McCloskey, 1991; Suppes, 1990). However, proponents of the approach have argued that individual units do have interpretations in the sense that they represent microfeatures of a domain (Hinton, McClelland, & Rumelhart, 1986). Although these microfeatures may not correspond to "namable" entities, they have meaning in the sense that they map onto some property of the domain. One of the challenges faced by neural network modelers is to discover how microfeatures combine to represent semantically interpretable concepts.

The property that truly distinguishes neural networks from symbolic models concerns the manner in which representations are manipulated and transformed. In symbolic systems, representations are governed by rules that are themselves represented symbolically (Newell et al., 1989; Pylyshyn, 1989). These rules take the form of "if A, then B." In a typical AI model, these rules are implemented serially to make inferences. Thus, representations interact with (i.e., causally affect) other representations in a manner specified by the rules. The rules in a symbolic system operate on representations in a manner that is sensitive to their constituent structure. That is, symbolic representations can have a complex structure in that they are composed of symbols that stand in syntactic relations to other symbols. Rules can operate on a symbolic representation by virtue of its structure alone (Fodor & Pylyshyn, 1988).

In neural network models, the relation between representations and rules is very different. Representations are not viewed as formal objects; therefore, they are not subject to direct manipulation. The rules in a neural network operate at the level of individual processing units. They specify how units compute their activation, how activation is transmitted to other units, and how connection weights are modified. Thus, representations do not act as a unit to affect other representations. Rather, individual processing units interact with and causally affect other units. Intelligent behavior emerges from the way in which interacting units are connected; it does not arise from the direct interaction and transformation of representations.

This distinction between neural network and symbolic models has given rise to controversy over the need for explicit symbolic rules to account for certain cognitive activities. In particular, the controversy has centered around the need for explicit rules in models of natural language processing (Fodor & Pylyshyn, 1988; Pinker & Prince, 1988). The study of language processing has been viewed as a crucial test of the adequacy of neural network models.

Traditionally, language has been viewed as the prototypical example of a rule-governed, combinatorial system. The system consists of a finite number of discrete elements (e.g., phonemes, words, phrases). These elements are combined systematically to create larger hierarchical structures (e.g., phonemes combine to form words, words combine to form phrases, etc.). The rules that operate to create these larger structures are sensitive to the syntax of their constituent elements (Fodor & Pylyshyn, 1988). This can be seen in a complex sentence such as "The classes that the professor teaches are canceled." This sentence has a constituent structure such that words combine to form phrases (e.g., noun and verb phrases). These phrases combine further to form a sentence embedded within a sentence. That is, the sentence "the professor teaches the classes" is embedded in the sentence "the classes are canceled." The rules that operate to construct this embedding must be sensitive to the structural relations between the two sentences. For example, the verb "teaches" must agree in number with the noun in the embedding (i.e., professor), not the noun in the main clause (i.e., classes).

The challenge in neural networks has been to implement complex structural relationships such as constituency in a system that lacks explicit rules specifying how structures are to be combined (Lachter & Bever, 1988; Fodor & Pylyshyn, 1988; Pinker & Prince, 1988; Prince & Smolensky, 1997). Although progress has been made in modeling aspects of language performance such as morphology, word recognition, and lexical semantics, it is far from clear that these models can learn to represent complex syntactic relations.

Recently, Elman (1993) has attempted to meet this challenge by training a neural network to represent sentences containing relative clauses. He found that a simple recurrent network learned to represent the hierarchical structure of such sentences under certain conditions. In particular, success was achieved only when the network learned to represent simple sentences before it learned to represent complex ones. Elman's results are extremely promising. They suggest that neural networks have the representational power necessary to capture complex structural relationships (Elman, 1990, 1993). However, the neural network approach does not yet provide the systematic overview of language processing that would make it a satisfactory alternative to generative linguistics.

The Nature of Neural Network Simulations

As we discussed above, one of the attractive properties of neural networks is their ability to discover a set of connection strengths that captures the internal structure of a domain. As an example, consider a reading model, called NETtalk, developed by Sejnowski and Rosenberg (1987, 1988). NETtalk was trained to produce phonemes in response to input in the form of English text. The network was constructed in three layers. It contained a level of input units, a level of output units, and an intervening level of "hidden units." The hidden units were densely connected to both the input and output units. The network received a string of seven letters and spaces of text as input and was trained to produce the phoneme corresponding to the letter in the center of the string. With sufficient training, the model discovered the implicit rules that govern the transformation of visual letters to sounds. This enabled the model to generalize beyond the set of training words and produce the appropriate phonemic output for a large corpus of novel English words.

Exactly what did NETtalk learn that enabled it to perform the reading task? Sejnowski and Rosenberg (1987) examined the pattern of activity distributed across NETtalk's hidden units. They found that some units were activated by vowels; others were activated by consonants. However, the model had so many connections among units (more than 18,000) that it was impossible to be more specific about how the network actually performed the task.

The NETtalk model illustrates a problem that has led some researchers to question whether neural network models should be viewed as simulations of cognitive theories (Estes, 1988; Fodor & Pylyshyn, 1988; Massaro, 1988; McCloskey, 1991; van Hezewijk & de Haan, 1994). For example, McCloskey (1991) has argued that neural network modeling is very different from traditional simulation. In a traditional computer simulation, the modeler specifies how each feature of a theory is to be implemented. The modeler knows that the simulation instantiates the theory's assumptions, because the modeler has specified these assumptions explicitly.

The situation is very different in a neural network simulation. The modeler does not specify how the system is to implement the features of the theory. Rather, the system discovers its own implementation by means of the learning algorithm. According to McCloskey (1991), a neural network "modeler 'grows' the network rather than building it" (p. 391). This causes a tremendous problem in assessing the performance of networks as complex as NETtalk. Neural networks of any significant size are hugely underconstrained (Bullinaria, 1994; Fodor & Pylyshyn, 1988; Massaro, 1988; Reeke & Sporns, 1993). The model discovers a solution that produces the desired output from the specified input. However, it is likely that this solution is one of an infinitely large number of solutions to the problem. Does NETtalk's particular solution have theoretical implications that are different from alternative solutions? Is the knowledge encoded in the weights specific to the details of this particular implementation (e.g., seven character input strings, output constrained to the middle letter)? Which features of the model implement the theory and which are idiosyncratic to this particular simulation? At present, our knowledge of neural network functioning is insufficient to answer such questions.

Given the difficulty in understanding how a complex network accomplishes a particular task, McCloskey (1991) has argued that neural networks should not be viewed as cognitive theories or simulations of cognitive theories; rather, they should be viewed as tools for theory development. In particular, he has argued that networks can be thought of as analogs to animal models of cognitive activities and disorders. Animal models are not simulations of cognitive theories; rather, the animal system is an object of study. The goal is to develop a theory of its functioning that can then be extended to the human system. The theory may need to be modified significantly when it is applied to human functioning. However, the two systems may share enough crucial features such that a systematic analysis of the animal system aids in the development of a theory of the human system. Similarly, neural networks can be studied to develop a theory of their structure and functioning. This theory can then be examined to determine the extent to which it can be applied to the human system.

Viewed from this perspective, animal systems and neural networks share some advantages and disadvantages as models of human functioning. An advantage of these systems is that they can be manipulated in ways that the human system cannot. For example, these models can be subjected to tightly controlled training regimens or they can be lesioned to examine the effects of different types of damage. A disadvantage of these systems is that they may contain critical features that have no counterpart in the human system. The challenge will be to understand neural networks in sufficient detail to determine whether the processes that determine their performance are similar to those that underlie human performance.

Modular vs. Interactive Architectures

Many neuroscientists and psychologists believe that the architectural system underlying human cognitive performance is functionally modular. That is, the system is composed of a number of dedicated processing components (i.e., modules). Each component has a proprietary database and is informationally encapsulated (Fodor, 1983, 1985). This means that each component (a) contains knowledge that is specific to the operations that it performs and (b) this knowledge is available only to the component responsible for these operations. In addition, the partial results of operations that are specific to one component are unavailable to other components.

According to this view of the functional architecture, interaction among modules is severely limited (Fodor, 1983, 1985). In particular, a module interacts with other modules in the system only to receive the computational end product from other modules or to communicate its own end product to these modules. For example, a module that is responsible for lexical analysis (i.e., identifying words from phonemic input) will receive input from a module dedicated to phonetic analysis. Once the lexical module has received this input, it will perform its own operations. As the lexical module performs its function, it will be unaffected by information available from other modules (Fodor, 1983; Forster, 1979; Garrett, 1981). This includes information that may be potentially useful, such as information about the semantic context in which a word appears. Once the module has completed its function, it will present its product to the modules to which it is connected (e.g., a syntactic module). Thus, modules receive input from a small set of other modules and produce a completed product in discrete stages.

The assumption of modularity has implications for how neuropsychologists interpret the effects of brain damage (see Farah, 1994, and Nachson & Moscovitch, 1995, for a review). Brain damage can have very selective effects on cognitive abilities. Neuropsychologists often use information about the selective effects of damage to make inferences about the underlying functional architecture (Allport, 1985; Caplan, 1981; Shallice, 1988). These inferences are based on an assumption of "locality." Damage to one component of the architecture should have relatively local effects to the extent that the components in the system are modular, that is, informationally encapsulated. Processing in undamaged components should be affected only to the extent that they receive degraded input from a damaged module. Because undamaged components continue to function normally, the patient's impairment should relate in a fairly straightforward way to the behavior of the damaged component.

Researchers who work with neural network models have begun to question whether a dissociation of behavior after damage to the architecture implies a dissociation of mechanism (Farah, 1994; Farah & McClelland, 1991; Hinton & Shallice, 1991; Tippett & Farah, 1994). This question has arisen because many neural network models do not contain informationally encapsulated components. The central properties of neural networks contrast directly with the properties of modular systems. First, the knowledge contained in a neural network is distributed across a set of connection weights; it is not localized to a particular component. Second, neural networks are interactive and process information in a graded and continuous fashion. Representations can be partially active either because some subset of the units that comprise a representation are fully active or all of the units in a representation have some subthreshold level of activation. This partially active information can influence the activation of units elsewhere in the network. Thus, interaction is not limited to the endpoints of processing. Rather, the partial products of one part of the network are available to other parts continuously during processing.

As the earlier section on adaptive resonance models suggested, many networks of that type exhibit a greater degree of modularity, with components that have distinct informational significance. For example, Levine and Prueitt (1989) modeled effects of prefrontal cortex damage on Wisconsin Card Sorting Test performance. Their model included components that were labeled as "features" (color, shape, and number of card designs), "categories" (of cards), "reinforcement," "attentional biases," and "habits." The model did not specify in detail exactly which parts of the brain corresponded to which components of the network. However, the network's theoretical structure was rich enough to provide some potential hypotheses about what types of brain connections, and in which regions, might be present and account for the simulated behaviors (Hestenes, 1998; Levine, 1996).

Do neural network models exhibit functional dissociations of behavior after damage even when they are not modular systems? Recent work suggests that they do. For example, Hinton and Shallice (1991) trained a network to produce the appropriate semantic output for a word when it received letter strings as input. The network learned to discriminate visually similar input (e.g., *cat* vs. *cap*, *horse* vs. *hoarse*) as well as semantically similar input (e.g., *peach* vs. *apricot*, *cap* vs. *hat*). The network was fully interactive in the sense that it did not contain modules dedicated to a particular process (e.g., visual processing, semantic processing). Hinton and Shallice found that a lesion anywhere in the network produced an impairment similar to that seen in deep dyslexia. The model produced both visually based (e.g., *cap* read as *cat*) and semantically based errors (e.g., *cap* read as *hat*). In addition, the model produced more combined visual and semantic errors (e.g., *cat* read as *rat*) than would be expected by the base rates of each type of error alone.

Farah and her colleagues have argued that damage to one part of a system can have profound effects on the functioning of undamaged parts of the system (see Farah, 1994, for a review). This claim is supported by simulations of the effects of damage on network models of semantic memory (Farah & McClelland, 1991), visual attention (Cohen, Romero, Servan-Schreiber, et al., 1994), and visual face recognition (Farah, O'Reilly, & Vecera 1993). For example, Tippett and Farah (1994) trained a network to produce semantic output in response to visual input. They then damaged the network's semantic representations to simulate the type of damage suffered in Alzheimer's disease. They found that the performance of the model as a whole was affected when factors such as word frequency or visual degradation increased the processing difficulty of any of its components.

The simulations discussed above suggest that (a) damage to one part of a system can affect the functioning of undamaged parts and (b) behaviors that are functionally modular (e.g., visual vs. semantic processing) can be performed by a system whose structure is not modular in the same way. These findings are controversial partly because they have such profound implications for cognitive neuropsychology. They suggest that it may be misleading to make inferences about the function of a damaged component on the basis of a patient's symptoms. Dissociations of behavior may tell us little about the underlying functional architecture.

CURRENT LIMITATIONS OF NEURAL NETWORK MODELS

Current network technology limits the application of neural networks to small versions of real problems. Restricting the size of a network to the minimum number of units and connections needed to solve the problem allows training to occur in a reasonable period of time, improves generalization, and makes it easier to understand the model's representational and processing properties. However, small systems are likely to differ from large systems in important ways. In order to scale up networks to sizes comparable to those found in the brain, several theoretical and computational limitations must be overcome (Bullinaria, 1994; Bullinaria & Chater, 1993; Feldman, Fanty, & Goddard, 1988).

The Problem of Internal Structure

The first challenge in solving the scaling problem involves finding ways to constrain the search space during learning. Systems that lack built-in knowledge about the world learn incredibly slowly and are overly dependent on particular input-output representations, a knowledgeable tutor, or carefully sequenced training trials (Bullinaria, 1994; Hinton, Sejnowski, & Ackley, 1984). Shepard (1989), in particular, has claimed that nontrivial learning can occur only in a system with an internal structure that captures the regularities in its environment (Shepard, 1987a). Without this structure, a system will have no basis for generalizing information from one context to another. Presumably, this internal structure is acquired as organisms evolve in an environment that is invariant across certain dimensions. Shepard (1989) suggests several general constraints that may be acquired by terrestrial species; these include knowledge that "material objects are conserved, that space is locally Euclidean and three-dimensional with a gravitationally conferred unique upright direction, and that periods of relative light and warmth alternate with periods of relative dark and cold in a regular cycle" (p. 107).

Organisms that come equipped with knowledge about the universal constraints of the world have an adaptive advantage (Shepard, 1987b). These constraints narrow the set of behaviors that must be learned by trial and error. Shepard (1989) provides several examples of the functions that may be served by such internalized constraints. One of these functions may be the ability to recognize an object regardless of its position in space. Consider a system with sensory or input units that become activated in response to light reflected off an object in space. The system also has a set of "hidden units" that will come to represent the object after it has been presented repeatedly in more or less the same position. Now imagine that the object is moved in space such that it no longer functions to activate the same set of sensory units. In current network models, the system may no longer recognize this as the object that it had learned previously. That is, information learned about the object in one location in space may not transfer when the object is moved to a new location.

One solution to this problem is to train the system by presenting the object in all possible spatial locations and orientations. However, this would require a prohibitive amount of training. This solution is even less desirable when you consider that such training would be required for each class of object that the system might be required to recognize.

Shepard (1989) suggests two possibilities of how neural networks might be designed with the internal structure necessary for effective generalization from learning. First, the internal constraints may be hardwired into the system prior to any learning experience. Second, neural networks may be evolved over time to capture the invariant properties of their environments. However, we face enormous obstacles in implementing either of these suggestions given our current knowledge of the microarchitecture of the human system and the evolutionary principles that have guided its development.

The Problem of Biological Plausibility

The second challenge in neural network modeling is to develop network architectures and learning mechanisms that better represent those found in real biological systems (Crick, 1989; Eagleson & Carey, 1992). Modelers generally agree that input-output relations found at one level of organization can be simulated by an infinite variety of models at lower levels of organization (Fodor & Pylyshyn, 1988; Pylyshyn, 1984; Reeke & Sporns, 1993; Shepherd, 1990). For this reason, it is important that neural networks represent properties found in real biological systems.

Currently, neural network models often incorporate features that are known to be biologically questionable. For example, many models have excitatory and inhibitory processes realized in the same set of connections. That is, a unit may be capable of sending either activating or inhibitory output to other units in the system. This is not a property found in real neural anatomy. A neuron may receive both excitatory and inhibitory input, but it sends only one type of signal. In addition, many networks incorporate backpropagation as a learning mechanism, a mechanism that has been criticized repeatedly for its biological implausibility (Crick, 1989; Eagleson & Carey, 1992). The backpropagation learning mechanism requires that the connections between units be able to convey signals in two directions. This is the equivalent of an axon with the capability of both sending messages to other neurons and receiving messages in return. Grossberg (1987) has shown that the neural hardware needed to implement such a mechanism contradicts our knowledge of brain organization and processes.

Developing network structures and processes that better reflect our understanding of real biological systems should help neural network modelers develop a priori answers to questions such as: (1) How many units and how many layers should a network contain to perform a particular task? (2) Which learning rule should be implemented? (3) How many training trials should the network receive? (4) What characteristics of the domain should be captured by the input-output representations?, and (5) If the model is to be damaged, which units should be damaged and how many?

The Problem of Catastrophic Interference

A third limitation of current network models is that they tend to exhibit a phenomenon called "catastrophic interference" (McCloskey & Cohen, 1989; McClelland, McNaughton, & O'Reilly, 1995; Ratcliff, 1990). Catastrophic interference occurs when a model exhibits rapid forgetting for well-learned items when it is trained on a new set of items. This occurs primarily in situations involving the rapid acquisition of arbitrary associations between inputs and outputs. Such associations are required to model a wide variety of memory phenomena (e.g., memory for items in a list, memory for names, memory for telephone numbers).

McCloskey and Cohen (1989) demonstrated catastrophic interference in a neural network model of a paired-associate learning task. In the paired-associate task, participants learn associations between arbitrarily paired words or nonsense syllables. They begin by learning one list of associations called the AB set. The AB set is a stimulus-response pair of words (e.g., book-pear, drawer-car). Participants are trained on the AB items until they accurately produce B (e.g., pear) when they are given A (e.g., book). A typical interference manipulation is to present participants with a second set of words (AC) once their performance on the AB set has reached asymptote. The AC set involves the same list of stimulus words now paired with a different list of response words (e.g., book-mouse, drawer-church). Participants exhibit a gradual loss of the ability to retrieve the AB list after training on the AC list. However, AC learning does not completely interfere with AB retrieval. Participants exhibit about 50 percent correct performance on the AB items even after AC learning has reached asymptote.

McCloskey and Cohen (1989) modeled the paired-associate learning task in a backpropagation network. The network consisted of three layers: a layer of input units, a layer of output units, and an intervening layer of hidden units. A subset of the input units represented A items; another subset represented the B and C items. The network was trained first on the AB items and then on the AC items. They found that the model's performance differed dramatically from the performance of human participants. In particular, the model lost all ability to retrieve the AB items after only a few trials on the AC list. Ratcliff (1990) observed similar catastrophic interference in a neural network model of recognition memory. The model tended to track the information presented last in a list, exhibiting rapid forgetting of well-learned items that had been presented earlier.

Researchers have found that catastrophic interference can be avoided by adjusting the connection weights to reduce the overlap between competing responses (French, 1991, 1992; Hetherington & Seidenberg, 1989; Sloman & Rumelhart, 1992). However, French (1991) has argued that reducing overlap to avoid catastrophic interference comes at the expense of generalization. Generalization occurs in neural network models precisely because patterns that represent similar information overlap. The challenge will be to develop means of reducing interference that do not also reduce the exploitation of shared structure. Carpenter (1997) has developed a mathematical theory suggesting that the appropriate choice of learning laws for connection weights can markedly reduce catastrophic interference without modifying the architecture of the network.

CONCLUSIONS

The neural network field has matured rapidly since it was introduced to mainstream neuroscientists and psychologists in the early 1980s. The field has moved from exploring the properties of different classes of neural network models to testing these models as alternatives to existing theoretical frameworks. We have briefly described some of the basic principles of neural network modeling and the properties that make them an attractive alternative to other approaches.

We have also reviewed some of the theoretical and computational limitations of current models. As we discussed, neural network modelers face enormous problems in developing models that are more biologically plausible, have the preexisting structure necessary to engage in nontrivial learning, and provide adequate accounts of higher-level cognitive processes such as language and reasoning. Although these are formidable obstacles, they provide an exciting set of theoretical and computational challenges to current and future researchers. In spite of methodological and theoretical differences between backpropagation and adaptive resonance programming, preliminary modifications in describing programming parameters have produced some overlap in how processing elements and measures may be interpreted. For example, Cardoso and Parks in chapter 9 use backpropagation, whereas Parks and Levine (in chapter 15) utilize adaptive resonance programming. Yet the outcomes described in both chapters have produced significant advances in neurocomputational and neuropsychological understanding of *executive functioning* (Rabbitt, 1998).

We hope to encourage clinicians to begin their own exploration of computational neuropsychology. An essential step, particularly for those clinicians who are unfamiliar with the methodology, is to acquire backpropagation or ART software, or both. Clinicians may choose to be part of a team of investigators. Such teams typically consist of a mathematician or computer scientist fluent in computer programming techniques, a neuropsychologist, and a physician (psychiatrist or neurologist). Access to clinical populations (e.g., Alzheimer's, head trauma, discrete lesions, and others) and control subjects, both of whom have undergone quantitative neuropsychological batteries, is needed to integrate a priori theories with empirical psychometric data. Neural network modeling of complex neuropsychological data is still at an early stage of development. Current research involving clinical populations attempts to approximate, or in some cases replicate, patients' performance relative to the performance of a control group. Institutions that have access to large databases of neuropathological conditions with corresponding neuropsychological data can, with the appropriate personnel and computing infrastructure, begin utilizing computational methodology. Institutions with access to neuroimaging data (computed tomography, magnetic resonance imaging, functional MRI, single photon emission computed tomography, electroencephalography) are at a particular advantage, since these data may both guide in the development of computer models and provide validation when the computer program results are consistent with neurophysiological and neurostructural information.

NOTES

1. Substantial portions of this section were adapted from Parks and Cardoso (1997). Used with permission.

REFERENCES

Allport, D. A. (1985). Distributed memory, modular subsystems, and dysphasia. In S. K. Newman & R. Epstein (Eds.), *Current perspectives in dysphasia* (pp. 421–452). New York: Churchill Livingstone.

Amari, S. I. (1971). Characteristics of randomly connected threshold element networks and network systems. *Proceedings of the IEEE, 59*, 35–47.

Anderson, J. A. (1968). A memory storage model utilizing spatial correlation functions. *Kybernetik, 5*, 113–119.

Anderson, J. A. (1970). Two models for memory organization using interacting traces. *Mathematical Biosciences, 8*, 137–160.

Anderson, J. A., & Hinton, G. E. (1989). Models of information processing in the brain. In G. E. Hinton & J. A. Anderson (Eds.), *Parallel models of associative memory* (pp. 23–62). Hillsdale, NJ: Erlbaum.

Anderson, J. R., & Kushmerick, N. (1992). Tower of Hanoi and goal structures. In J. R. Anderson (Ed.), *Rules of the mind* (pp. 121–142). Hillsdale, NJ: Erlbaum.

Anderson, J. A., & Rosenfeld, R. (Eds.) (1988). *Neurocomputing: Foundations of research*. Cambridge, MA: MIT Press.

Bullinaria, J. A. (1994). Simulating nonlocal systems: Rules of the game. *Behavior and Brain Sciences, 17*, 61–62.

Bullinaria, J. A., & Chater, N. (1993). Double dissociation in artificial neural networks: Implications for neuropsychology. In *Proceedings of the fifteenth annual conference of the Cognitive Science Society* (pp. 227–264). Hillsdale, NJ: Erlbaum.

Burton, A. M., & Bruce, V. (1994). Local representations without the locality assumption. *Behavioral and Brain Sciences, 17*, 62–63.

Caplan, D. (1981). On the cerebral localization of linguistic functions: Logical and empirical issues surrounding deficit analysis and functional localization. *Brain and Language, 14*, 120–137.

Cardoso, J. (1991). Revisiting the Towers of Hanoi. *AI Expert*, October, 49–53.

Carpenter, G. A. (1997). Spatial pattern learning, catastrophic forgetting, and optimal rules of synaptic transmission. In D. S. Levine & W. R. Elsberry (Eds.), *Optimality in biological and artificial networks?* (pp. 288–316). Mahwah NJ: Erlbaum.

Carpenter, G. A., & Grossberg, S. (1987). A massively parallel architecture for a self-organizing neural pattern recognition machine. *Computer Vision, Graphics, and Image Processing, 37,* 54–115.

Caudill, M., & Butler, C. (1990). *Naturally intelligent systems.* Cambridge, MA: MIT Press.

Chauvin, Y., & Rumelhart, D. E. (1995). *Backpropagation: Theory, architectures, and applications.* Hillsdale, NJ: Erlbaum.

Cohen, J. D., Romero, R. D., Servan-Schreiber, D., & Farah, M. J. (1994). Mechanisms of spatial attention: The relation of macrostructure to microstructure in parietal neglect. *Journal of Cognitive Neuroscience, 6,* 377–387.

Cooper, L. A. (1976). Demonstration of a mental analog of an external rotation. *Perception and Psychophysics, 19,* 296–302.

Crick, F. (1989) The recent excitement about neural networks. *Nature, 337,* 129–132.

Eagleson, R., & Carey, D. P. (1992). Connectionist networks do not model brain function. *Behavioral and Brain Sciences, 15,* 734–735.

Elman, J. L. (1990). Finding structure in time. *Cognitive Science, 14,* 179–212.

Elman, J. L. (1993). Learning and development in neural networks: The importance of starting small. *Cognition, 48,* 71–99.

Estes, W. K. (1988). Toward a framework for combining connectionist and symbol-processing models. *Journal of Memory and Language, 27,* 196–212.

Farah, M. J. (1994). Neuropsychological inference with an interactive brain: A critique of the "locality" assumption. *Behavioral and Brain Sciences, 17,* 43–61.

Farah, M. J., & McClelland, J. L. (1991). A computational model of semantic memory impairment: Modality-specificity and emergent category-specificity. *Journal of Experimental Psychology: General, 120,* 339–357.

Farah, M. J., O'Reilly, R. C., & Vecera, S. P. (1993). Dissociated overt and covert recognition as an emergent property of lesioned neural networks. *Psychological Review, 100,* 571–588.

Feldman, J. A., & Ballard, D. H. (1982). Connectionist models and their properties. *Cognitive Science, 6,* 205–254.

Feldman, J. A., Ballard, D. H., Brown, C. M., & Dell, G. S. (1985). *Rochester connectionist papers: 1979–1985. Technical report 172.* Rochester, NY: Department of Computer Science, University of Rochester.

Feldman, J. A., Fanty, M. A., & Goddard, N. (1988). Computing with structured neural networks. *IEEE Computer, 21,* 91–103.

Fodor, J. A. (1976). *The language of thought.* Sussex, U.K.: Harvester Press.

Fodor, J. A. (1983). *The modularity of mind.* Cambridge, MA.: MIT Press.

Fodor, J. A. (1985). Précis of the modularity of mind. *Behavioral and Brain Sciences, 8,* 1–42.

Fodor, J. A., & Pylyshyn, Z. (1988). Connectionism and cognitive architecture: A critical analysis. *Cognition, 28,* 3–71.

Forster, K. (1979). Levels of processing and the structure of the language processor. In W. Cooper & E. Walker (Eds.), *Sentence processing: Psycholinguistic studies presented to Merrill Garrett* (pp. 27–85). Hillsdale, NJ: Erlbaum.

French, R. M. (1991). Using semi-distributed representations to overcome catastrophic forgetting in connectionist networks. In *Proceedings of the thirteenth annual cognitive science conference* (pp. 173–178). Hillsdale, NJ: Erlbaum.

French, R. M. (1992). Semi-distributed representations and catastrophic forgetting in connectionist networks. *Connection Science, 4,* 365–377.

Garrett, M. (1981). Objects of psycholinguistic inquiry. *Cognition, 10,* 97–101.

Grossberg, S. (1969). Embedding fields: A theory of learning with physiological implications. *Journal of Mathematical Psychology, 6,* 209–239.

Grossberg, S. (1976). Adaptive pattern classification and universal recoding: Part I. Parallel development and coding of neural feature detectors. *Biological Cybernetics, 23,* 121–134.

Grossberg, S. (1982). *Studies in mind and brain.* Dordrecht, Netherlands: Reidel Press.

Grossberg, S. (1987). Competitive learning: From interactive activation to adaptive resonance. *Cognitive Science, 11,* 23–63.

Grossberg, S. (1988). *Neural networks and natural intelligence.* Cambridge, MA: MIT Press.

Hanson, J. S., & Burr, D. J. (1990). What connectionist models learn: Learning and representation in connectionist networks. *Behavioral and Brain Sciences, 13,* 471–518.

Hebb, D. O. (1949). *The organization of behavior.* New York: Wiley.

Hestenes, D. O. (1998). Modulatory mechanisms in mental disorders. In D. J. Stein & J. Ludik (Eds.), *Neural networks in psychopathology* (pp. 132–164). Cambridge, U.K.: Cambridge University Press.

Hetherington, P. A., & Seidenberg, M. S. (1989). Is there "catastrophic interference" in connectionist networks? In *Proceedings of the Cognitive Science Society* (pp. 26–33). Hillsdale, NJ: Erlbaum.

Hinton, G. E., McClelland, J. L., & Rumelhart, D. E. (1986). Distributed representations. In D. E. Rumelhart & J. L. McClelland (Eds.), *Parallel distributed processing: Explorations in the microstructure of cognition,* Vol. 1 (pp. 77–109). Cambridge, MA: MIT Press.

Hinton, G. E., & Sejnowski, T. J. (1986). Learning and relearning in Boltzmann machines. In D. E. Rumelhart & J. L. McClelland (Eds.), *Parallel distributed processing: Explorations in the microstructure of cognition,* Vol. 1 (pp. 282–317). Cambridge, MA: MIT Press.

Hinton, G. E., Sejnowski, T. J., & Ackley, D. H. (1984). Boltzmann Machines: Constraints satisfaction networks that learn. *Technical Report CMU-CS-84-119,* Pittsburgh: Department of Computer Science, Carnegie-Mellon University.

Hinton, G. E., & Shallice, T., (1991). Lesioning an attractor network: Investigations of acquired dyslexia, *Psychological Review, 98,* 74–95.

Hopfield, J. J. (1982). Neural networks and physical systems with emergent collective computational abilities. *Proceedings of the National Academy of Sciences, 79,* 2554–2558.

Koch, C., & Segev, I. (1998). *Methods in neuronal modeling: From ions to networks* (2nd ed.). Cambridge, MA: MIT Press.

Kohonen, T. (1977). *Associative memory: A system-theoretical approach.* New York: Springer-Verlag.

Kohonen, T. (1984). *Self-organization and associative memory.* Springer-Verlag.

Lachter, J., & Bever, T. G. (1988). The relation between linguistic structure and theories of language learning: A constructive critique of some connectionist learning models. *Cognition, 28,* 195–247.

Levine, D. S. (1983). Neural population modeling and psychology: A review. *Mathematical Biosciences, 66,* 1–86.

Levine, D. S. (1989). The third wave in neural networks. *AI Expert, December,* 26–33.

Levine, D. S. (1991). *Introduction to neural and cognitive modeling.* Hillsdale, NJ: Erlbaum.

Levine, D. S. (1996). Modeling dysfunction of the prefrontal executive system. In J. Reggia, E. Ruppin, & R. Berndt (Eds.), *Neural modeling of brain disorders* (pp. 413–439). River Edge, NJ: World Scientific.

Levine, D. S., & Prueitt, P. S. (1989). Modeling some effects of frontal lobe damage: Novelty and perseveration. *Neural Networks, 2,* 103–116.

Massaro, D. (1988). Some criticisms of connectionist models of human performance. *Journal of Memory and Language, 27,* 213–234.

McClelland, J. L., McNaughton, B. L., & O'Reilly, R. C. (1995). Why there are complementary learning systems in the hippocampus and neocortex: Insights from the successes and failures of connectionist models of learning and memory. *Psychological Review, 102,* 419–457.

McClelland, J. L., Rumelhart, D. E., & the PDP Researeh Group (1986). *Parallel distributed processing: Explorations in the microstructure of cognition,* Vol. 2: *Psychological and biological models.* Cambridge, MA: MIT Press.

McCloskey, M. (1991). Networks and theories: The place of connectionism in cognitive science. *Psychological Science, 2,* 387–395.

McCloskey, M., & Cohen, N. J. (1989). Catastrophic interference in connectionist networks: The sequential learning problem. In G. H. Bower (Ed.), *The psychology of learning and motivation,* Vol. 24 (pp. 109–165). New York: Academic Press.

McCulloch, W.S., & Pitts, W. (1943). A logical calculus of the ideas imminent in nervous activity. *Bulletin of Mathematical Biophysics, 5,* 115–133.

Mervis, C. B., & Rosch, E. (1981). Categorization of natural objects. *Annual Review of Psychology, 32,* 89–115.

Nachson, I., & Moscovitch, M. (Eds.). (1995). Modularity and the brain [special issue]. *Journal of Clinical and Experimental Neuropsychology, 17.*

Newell, A. (1980). Physical symbol systems. *Cognitive Science, 4,* 135–183.

Newell, A. (1982). The knowledge level. *Artificial Intelligence, 18,* 87–127.

Newell, A. Rosenbloom, P. S., & Laird, J. E. (1989). Symbolic architectures for cognition. In M. I. Posner (Ed.), *Foundations of cognitive science.* Cambridge, MA: MIT Press.

Pao, Y. H. (1989). *Adaptive pattern recognition and neural networks.* New York: Addison-Wesley.

Parks, R. W., & Cardoso, J. (1997). Parallel distributed processing and executive functioning: Tower of Hanoi neural network model in healthy controls and left frontal lobe patients. *International Journal of Neuroscience, 89,* 217–240.

Parks, R. W., Long, D. L., Levine, D. S., Crockett, D. J., McGeer, E. G., McGeer, P. L., Dalton, I. E., Zec, R. F., Becker, R. E., Coburn, K. L., Siler, G., Nelson, M. E., & Bower, J. M. (1991). Parallel distributed processing and neural networks: Origins, methodology and cognitive functions. *International Journal of Neuroscience, 60,* 195–214.

Pellionisz, A., & Llinás, R. (1982). Space-time representation in the brain: The cerebellum as a predictive space-time metric tensor. *Neuroscience, 7,* 2249–2970.

Pinker, S., & Prince, A. (1988). On language and connectionism: A parallel distributed processing model of language acquisition. *Cognition, 28,* 73193.

Posner, M. I., & Keele, S. W. (1970). Retention of abstract ideas. *Journal of Experimental Psychology, 83,* 304–308.

Prince, A., & Smolensky, P. (1997). Optionality: from Neural networks to universal grammar. *Science, 275,* 1604–1610.

Pylyshyn, Z. (1984). *Computation and Cognition.* Cambridge, MA: MIT Press.

Pylyshyn, Z. W. (1989). Computing in cognitive science. In M. I. Posner (Ed.), *Foundations of cognitive science* (pp. 51–91). Cambridge, MA: MIT Press.

Quillian, M. R. (1968). Semantic memory. In M. Minsky (Ed.), *Semantic information processing* (pp. 227–270). Cambridge, MA: MIT Press.

Rabbitt, P. (1998). *Methodology of frontal and executive function.* Bristol, PA: Taylor & Francis.

Rashevsky, N. (1960). *Mathematical biophysics,* Vol. 2. New York: Dover Press.

Ratcliff, R. (1990). Connectionist models of recognition memory: Constraints imposed by learning and forgetting functions. *Psychological Review, 97,* 285–308.

Reeke, G. N., Jr., & Sporns, O. (1993). Behaviorally based modeling and computational approaches to neuroscience. *Annual Review of Neuroscience, 16,* 507–623.

Rolls, E., & Treves, A. (1998). *Neural networks and brain function.* New York: Oxford University Press.

Rosenblatt, F. (1962). *Principles of neurodynamics: Perceptrons and the theory of brain mechanisms.* Washington, DC: Spartan Books.

Rumelhart, D. E., Hinton, G. E., & Williams, R. J. (1986). Learning internal representations by error propagation. In D. E. Rumelhart & J. L. McClelland (Eds.), *Parallel distributed processing: Explorations in the microstructure of cognition,* Vol. 1 (pp. 318–362). Cambridge, MA: MIT Press.

Rumelhart, D. E., & McClelland, J. L. (1986). *Parallel distributed processing: Explorations in the microstructure of cognition,* Vol. 1: *Foundatons.* Cambridge, MA: MIT Press.

Schank, R. C., & Abelson, R. P. (1977). *Conceptual structures: Information processing in mind and machine.* Mahwah, NJ: Erlbaum.

Sejnowski, T. J. (1986). Open questions about computation in cerebral cortex. In J. A. McClelland, D. E. Rumelhart, & the PDP Research Group (Eds.), *Parallel distributed processing: Explorations in the microstructure of cognition,* Vol. 2: *Psychological and biological models* (pp. 372–389). Cambridge, MA: MIT Press.

Sejnowski, T. J., & Rosenberg, C. R. (1987). Parallel networks that learn to pronounce English text. *Complex Systems, 1,* 145–168.

Sejnowski, T. J., & Rosenberg, C. R. (1988). Learning and representation in connectionist models. In M. Gazzaniga (Ed.), *Perspective in memory research and training.* Cambridge, MA: MIT Press.

Shallice, T. (1982). Specific impairments in planning. *Philosophical Transactions of the Royal Society of London, 298,* 199–209.

Shallice, T. (1988). *From neuropsychology to mental structure.* Cambridge, U.K.: Cambridge University Press.

Shepard, R. N. (1987a). Toward a universal law of generalization for psychological science. *Science, 237,* 1317–1323.

Shepard, R. N. (1987b). Evolution of a mesh between principles of the mind and regularities of the world. In Dupré, J. (Ed.), *The latest on the best: Essays on evolution and optimality* (p. 110). Cambridge, MA: MIT Press.

Shepard, R. N. (1989) Internal representation of universal regularities: A challenge for connectionism. In L. Nadel, L. A. Cooper, P. Culicover, & R. M. Harnish (Eds.), *Neural connections, mental computations* (pp. 104–134). Cambridge, MA: MIT Press.

Shepard, R. N., & Cooper, L. A. (1982). *Mental images and their transformations*. Cambridge, MA: MIT Press.

Shepard, R. N., & Metzler, J. (1971). Mental rotation of three-dimensional objects. *Science, 171*, 701–703.

Shepherd, G. M. (1990). The significance of real neuron architectures for neural network simulations. In E. L. Schwartz (Ed.), *Computational neuroscience* (pp. 105–118). Cambridge, MA: MIT Press.

Sloman, S. A., & Rumelhart, D. E. (1992). Reducing interference in distributed memories through episodic gating. In Healy, S. Kosslyn, & R. Shiffrin (Eds.), *Essays in honor of W. K. Estes*, Vol. 1, (pp. 227–248). Hillsdale, NJ: Erlbaum.

Smolensky, P. (1988). On the proper treatment of connectionism. *Behavioral and Brain Sciences, 11*, 1–23.

Smolensky, P. (1989). Connectionist modeling: Neural computation/mental connections. In L. Nadel, L. A. Cooper, P. Culicover, & R. M. Harnish (Eds.), *Neural connections, mental computations* (pp. 49–67). Cambridge, MA: MIT Press.

Suppes, P. (1990). Problems of extension, representation, and computational irreducibility. *Behavioral and Brain Sciences, 13*, 507–508.

Tippett, L. J., & Farah, M. J. (1994). A computational model of naming in Alzheimer's disease: Unitary of multiple impairments? *Neuropsychology, 8*, 3–13.

Van Hezewijk, R., & de Haan, E. H. F. (1994). The symbolic brain or the invisible hand? *Behavior and Brain Sciences, 17*, 85–86.

Von der Malsburg, C. (1973). Self-organization of orientation sensitive cells in the striate cortex. *Kybernetik, 14*, 85–100.

Werbos, P. J. (1974). Beyond regression: New tools for prediction and analysis in the behavioral sciences. Unpublished Ph.D. dissertation, Harvard University, Cambridge, MA. Reprinted in Werbos, P. J. (1993). *The roots of backpropagation: From ordered derivatives to neural networks and political forecasting*. New York: Wiley.

Widrow, G., & Hoff, M. E. (1960). Adaptive switching circuits. In *Institute of Radio Engineers, Western Electronic Show and Convention, convention record, part 4*. pp. 96–104

2 Functional Cognitive Networks in Primates

J. Wesson Ashford, Kerry L. Coburn, and
Joaquin M. Fuster

The information-processing capability achieved by the human brain is a
marvel whose basis is still poorly understood. Recent neural network models
invoking parallel distributed processing have provided a framework for
appreciating how the brain performs its tasks (McClelland, Rumelhart, & the
PDP Research Group, 1986; Parks et al., 1989, 1992; Bressler, 1995). The
concepts of parallel distributed processing developed in nonhuman primates
provide useful models for understanding the extraordinary processing capability achieved by the human brain (Ashford, 1984; Goldman-Rakic, 1988).
The field of neuropsychology can use this understanding to improve the
capability of assessing specific human cognitive functions such as perception,
memory, and decision making.

The nervous systems of nonhuman primates provide clues to the brain
systems which support human cognition. Monkeys can learn sophisticated
cognitive tasks, and in doing so they use structural and functional brain systems highly similar to those used by humans. The functions of these systems
are revealed through depth electrode recording of single or multiple neuronal unit activity and event-related field potentials, and the anatomical distributions of the systems may be seen using high-resolution structural
scanning and histological techniques. However, the neural bases of cognitive
function become more clear when these techniques are applied in a context
in which a specific neuropsychological function is occurring. For example,
when neurons in a monkey's visual association cortical region are observed
to respond in the context of a visual memory task, the roles of both the neurons in that region and the region as a whole neural network appear to fall
into a comprehensible framework. In turn, models of information processing
developed in regions of the nonhuman primate brain have direct applica-
bility to the function of analogous structures in the human brain (for reviews,
see Fuster, 1995, 1997a,b).

BUILDING BLOCKS OF THE NERVOUS SYSTEM

Several basic principles of nervous system organization form the basis for
understanding higher primate brain function (Jones, 1990). The adaptive

sequence from sensation of the environment to initiation of reflexive movement is the fundamental operation that the nervous system provides. Neural pathways have developed redundant and parallel channels to assure the reliability and fidelity of transmitted information, as well as to increase the speed and reliability of processing. Neurons and neural networks also have developed means for abstracting, retaining, and later retrieving information—the basic time-spanning operations of memory. Progressively more complex levels of analysis form a hierarchy, with higher levels of neurons and networks performing progressively more complex information analyses and more refined response productions (Hayek, 1952). However, one general principle is: the more neurons involved in processing, the more complex the potential analysis of the information (Jerison, 1991). But a larger number of neurons also has a larger energy cost that must be borne by the organism and species, and hence a large brain must have a cost-benefit justification. Further, there is a need for both functional specialization (e.g., analysis of line orientation or color) and generalization (e.g., determining abstract relations between stimuli) of networks.

NEURONS AND NEUROTRANSMITTER SYSTEMS

The fundamental computational building block of the brain is the neuron, which contains dendrites for the input of information and an axon for the dissemination of the results of the neuron's analysis. Typical invertebrate neural systems control muscle fibers by an excitatory acetylcholine neuron opposed by an inhibitory γ-aminobutyric acid (GABA) neuron. In the vertebrates, acetylcholine neurons also work as activators throughout the nervous system, exciting muscle fibers and other effectors peripherally and activating numerous other systems centrally, including motor pacing systems in the basal ganglia and memory storage systems in the cortex. The GABA neurons of vertebrates presently are found only in the central nervous system where they still play the major inhibitory role from the spinal cord up to the cortex. Serotonin neurons appear to mediate sensitization conditioning in the invertebrate (Bailey & Kandel, 1995), and serotonin neurons, with the most widely distributed axons in the vertebrate brain, are retained in vertebrates for a variety of central functions which require a conditioning component (Jacobs & Azmitia, 1992). Similarly, catecholamine neurons developed in invertebrates, and play a role in reward-related learning in vertebrates (Gratton & Wise, 1988).

The principal neuron in the cerebral cortex is the pyramidal cell, which uses the amino acid glutamate as its neurotransmitter. Glutamate mechanisms are highly active in the olfactory system (Kaba, Hayashi, Higuchi, et al., 1994; Trombley & Shepherd, 1993), and play a role in the analyses of chemical stimulants. Olfactory functions include attending to and identifying a particular scent pattern, evaluating its significance, and retaining a memory trace of the scent in its context. The major structural basis for information processing in the cortex may initially have developed in the olfactory system to serve this function. Hence, glutamate neurons developed their central role in the cortex, perceiving and retaining sensory information and making decisions about approach responses in the olfactory system.

The olfactory system may be thought of as a long-range component of the gustatory system, and the interaction of olfaction and gustatation can produce what is perhaps the most powerful form of learning. The olfactory system itself can mediate aversive learning, but it is not particularly powerful. Aversive learning mediated by the gustatory system, however, can be extremely powerful. A taste avoidance response can be conditioned in a single trial and is unusually resistant to extinction. The interaction of olfactory and gustatory systems is seen when odor and taste stimuli are combined; the taste-potentiated odor stimulus then acquires the same extraordinary one-trial conditioning and resistance to extinction as the taste stimulus (Coburn, Garcia, Kiefer, et al., 1984; Bermúdez-Rattoni, Coburn, et al., 1987). Although these phenomena were discovered and have been studied in animals, both taste aversion and taste-potentiated odor aversion learning are seen in humans undergoing chemotherapy for cancer. They probably represent a very specialized form of learning in a situation where the organism must learn to avoid poisonous foods after a single exposure. Although taste-potentiated odor aversion conditioning is an extreme example of rapid acquisition, most odor conditioning appears to be acquired gradually over repeated trials. This form of associative conditioning may serve as an important mechanism of higher learning in the human cortex.

Another essential principle which appears to have originally appeared in the olfactory system is parallel distributed processing (Kauer, 1991). The mammalian olfactory epithelium contains sensory cells each of which has one of about one thousand genetically different odor receptors (Axel, 1995). The axons from these sensory neurons project into the olfactory bulb to terminate on the approximately two thousand glomeruli, with primary olfactory neurons expressing a given receptor terminating predominantly on the same glomeruli (Axel, 1995). However, environmental scents stimulate numerous specific olfactory receptors with different strengths, with each odor causing a spatially (Kauer, 1991; Shepherd, 1994) and temporally (Freeman & Skarda, 1985; Cinelli, Hamilton, and Kauer, 1995; Laurent, 1996) unique pattern of activity in the olfactory bulb which is broadly distributed. Thus, the olfactory circuitry converts an environmental chemical stimulus through a broad range of receptors into a complex pattern of activity in a large neuronal network which is capable of recognizing approximately ten thousand scents (Axel, 1995). This pattern of parallel organization (Sejnowski, Kienker, and Shepherd, 1985; Shepherd, 1995) and broad distribution of activity (Freeman, 1987) serves as a template that is adapted by the cortex of the vertebrate mammalian brain.

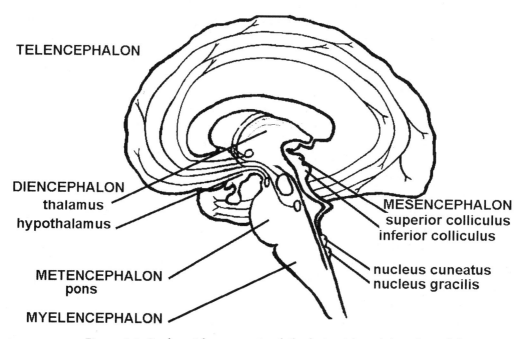

TELENCEPHALON

DIENCEPHALON
thalamus
hypothalamus

MESENCEPHALON
superior colliculus
inferior colliculus

nucleus cuneatus
nucleus gracilis

METENCEPHALON
pons

MYELENCEPHALON

Figure 2.1 Fundamental components of the brain—telencephalon, diencephalon, mesencephalon, and metencephalon, and myelencephalon. For the brain stem, ventral is left and dorsal is right. The cerebellum is not shown.

VERTEBRATE BRAIN ORGANIZATION

Certain principles of vertebrate brain organization have been established, such as sensory analyses occurring dorsally, motor direction occupying a ventral position, and autonomic function lying in an intermediate position. Also, segmentation developed, so that local sensation led to local motor activation. A later development specialized the anterior segments for more complex analysis (Rubenstein, Martinez, Shimamura, et al., 1994). In the vertebrate, the anterior five segments—the telencephalon (most anterior), diencephalon, mesencephalon, metencephalon, and myelencephalon—develop into the brain (figure 2.1), while the posterior segments become the spinal cord.

In the higher vertebrate brain there is a further specialization for sensory information analysis. The dorsal myelencephalon is specialized for somatosensory event detection (nucleus cuneatus for upper limbs and nucleus gracilis for lower limbs) and the dorsal mesencephalon is specialized for auditory (inferior colliculus) and visual (superior colliculus) event detection. These structures receive information through large, rapid transmission fibers and, therefore, serve as sentinels to analyze the sudden occurrence of change in the environment. In contrast, the more anterior diencephalon (thalamus) receives information from these modalities along direct, separate, slower pathways for fine detail analysis.

Movement is regulated by several structures, including the metencephalic cerebellum, the ventral red nucleus and substantia nigra of the mesencephalon, and the basal ganglia of the telencephalon. The cerebellum generates fast ramp movements, while the mesencephalic nuclei and the basal ganglia pace slow ramp movements (Kornhuber, 1974). Accordingly, the brain divides motor activity functionally into fast ballistic movements and slow deliberate actions.

Throughout the vertebrate brain, autonomic function continues to be regulated intermediately between dorsal sensory systems and the ventrally connected motor systems. In the autonomic nervous system, several brain levels coordinate cardiopulmonary function, temperature regulation, and sleep. The anterior apex of the autonomic system is the hypothalamus in the ventral diencephalon. The hypothalamus is largely responsible for coordinating complex drives such as appetite, thirst, territoriality, and reproduction, and for fear and stress reactions. The hypothalamus is controlled in part by the amygdala, the frontolimbic loop (Nauta, 1971), and other telencephalic structures. A particularly important issue for the autonomic system is the conservation of energy, an issue relating to a variety of factors including ecological niche, sleep, predator/prey status, strategies for reproduction, and brain size (Berger, 1975; Allison & Cicchetti, 1976; Armstrong, 1983). The other sensory systems—visual, auditory, and somatosensory—have developed pathways into the cortex to take advantage of the information-processing power of this structure (Nauta & Karten, 1970; Freeman & Skarda, 1985; Karten, 1991; Shepherd, 1995). This invasion has also brought other neurotransmitter systems into the telencephalon to play a role in activation and information processing, including acetylcholine and GABA neurons, and projecting axonal processes from serotonin, norepinephrine, and dopamine neurons whose cell bodies lie in diencephalic, mesencephalic, and metencephalic structures (figure 2.2).

THE ROLE OF THE CORTEX IN INFORMATION PROCESSING

The medial temporal lobe structures in primates are considered nontopographically organized (Haberly & Bower, 1989; Kauer, 1991; Axel, 1995; Shepherd, 1995). These regions have no direct input from somatosensory, auditory, or visual systems, but do receive activating inputs from the brain stem and diencephalon.

In mammals, the lateral telencephalon developed a specialized structure with six lamina referred to as neocortex (Killackey, 1995), the principal structure in the primate brain for processing complex information. As other sensory systems have invaded the cortex, primary regions with specialized topographic organization have developed (somatotopic organization for somatic sensation, cochleotopic organization for audition, and retinotopic organization for vision). As the sensory systems established their primary

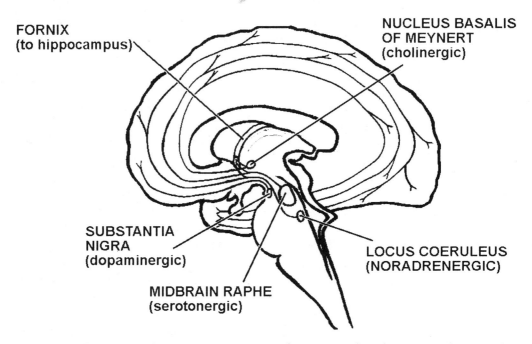

FORNIX
(to hippocampus)

NUCLEUS BASALIS
OF MEYNERT
(cholinergic)

SUBSTANTIA
NIGRA
(dopaminergic)

LOCUS COERULEUS
(NORADRENERGIC)

MIDBRAIN RAPHE
(serotonergic)

Figure 2.2 Neurotransmitter systems and projections from brainstem nuclei. Note that cholinergic, noradrenergic, and serotonergic axons course upward through the fornix to the hippocampus.

entry regions behind the central sulcus, elaboration of the sensory processing regions pushed cerebral volume development posteriorly. As the sensory systems developed, they also established close relationships with the medial temporal lobe structures for the evaluation of the importance of sensory information to the well-being of the animal (amygdala) and spatial categorization (hippocampus) of information (figure 2.3). Somatomotor function invaded the neocortex just anterior to the central sulcus and in conjunction with the somatosensory region, which formed just posterior to this sulcus. Consequently, the primary motor cortex has a somatotopic organization which is closely coordinated with the primary somatosensory region. The somatomotor cortex established a close relationship with the basal ganglia (caudate, putamen, globus pallidus) for pacing and directing movements (figure 2.4). Elaboration of motoric activity for vocalization (Preuss, 1995), and presumably thought and planning (Matthysse, 1974), pushed cortical volume development anteriorly in primates, with the prefrontal cortex coordinating with the nucleus accumbens for pacing speech and abstract thought. Thus, the neocortex of mammals plays a role in all sensory and motor function, the telencephalon expanding over the lower brain regions both anteriorly and posteriorly to accommodate the increased processing demands.

An important and long-standing controversy has addressed the question of the organization of information processing beyond the primary cortical regions. Though topographic organization has developed several levels of

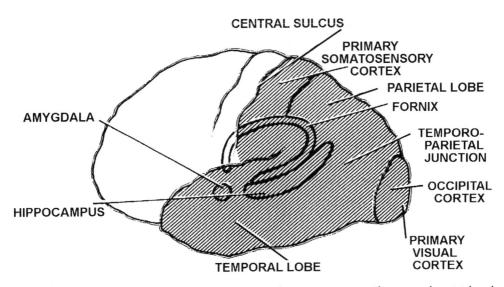

Figure 2.3 Posterior sensory, perception, and memory systems. The temporal, parietal, and occipital lobes process sensory information and are in bidirectional communication with the medial temporal lobe, including the hippocampus and amygdala. These regions also project to the basal ganglia, but are probably less dominant in their influence on this structure than they are on the medial temporal lobe structures or than the frontal lobe is on the basal ganglia.

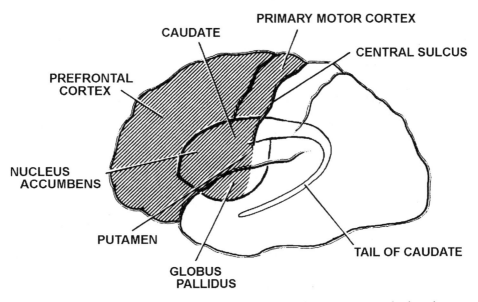

Figure 2.4 Anterior motor-, speech-, and thought-coordinating systems. The frontal cortex projects heavily into the basal ganglia, in particular the nucleus accumbens, which constitutes the large anterior portion of the basal ganglia. However, the frontal lobe seems to have less direct influence on the medial temporal lobe structures.

complexity in primary and secondary neocortical regions (Felleman & Van Essen, 1991; Van Essen, Anderson, and Felleman, 1992), large areas of the neocortex still seem to lack such organization, even as they have expanded to meet the processing demands of complex environmental niches (Lashley, 1950). For example, the temporal lobe has pushed anteriorly in primates to meet the need for more elaborate analysis of visual information (Allman, 1990). Yet the anterior temporal lobe has no significant retinotopic organization (Desimone & Gross, 1979; Tanaka, Saito, Fukada, et al., 1991; Tanaka, 1993; Nakamura, Mikami, & Kubota, 1994).

Important considerations for understanding information processing in the brain are timing and coordination. The primary thalamic nuclei relay detailed information to the primary sensory regions of the cortex. However, relevant broad cortical association regions are activated synchronously with the primary regions, presumably by the occurrence-detecting neurons of the brain stem acting through the pulvinar of the thalamus or by the reticular activating system (Moruzzi & Magoun, 1949), which includes ascending mono-aminergic and cholinergic pathways and the reticular nuclei of the thalamus (Robbins & Everitt, 1995). Also, some modulation of input may occur through "efferent control" (Pribram, 1967). Cortical activation in response to a stimulus is evidenced by electrical field potentials recordable at the scalp. Following cortical activation and receipt of detailed information, analysis of stimulus particulars occurs in the cortex with reciprocal communication occurring between all of the activated cortical regions (for reviews, see Kuypers, Szwarcbart, Mishkin, et al., 1965; Ashford & Fuster, 1985; Coburn, Ashford, & Fuster, 1990; Ungerleider, 1995).

PRIMATE CORTICAL SENSORY, PERCEPTUAL, AND MEMORY SYSTEMS

Visual System

Many of the inferences regarding neuropsychological information processing in the human brain are derived from studies of the monkey. The most widely studied models involve the visual system. In primates, there is a unique crossing of retinal hemifields to both the contralateral superior colliculus and the primary visual cortex (Allman, 1982). Primary visual cortex is activated retinotopically by photic stimuli, and neurons are found there which preferentially respond to bars of light with unique orientations. These neurons are organized in slabs alternately serving inputs from the left and right eyes (Hubel & Wiesel, 1977). The monkey cortex contains at least twenty additional visual areas surrounding the primary visual cortex which are responsible for analyzing a variety of discrete aspects of visual information. Injury to a discrete area can cause loss of a specific neuropsychological analysis capability. The areas most closely connected to the primary visual cortex have a high degree of retinotopic organization, which diminishes at

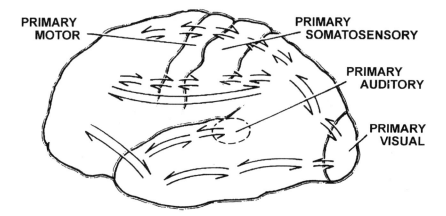

Figure 2.5 Information transmission between different regions of the brain. The dorsal and ventral pathways leading forward from the occipital cortex are shown connecting all the way to specific frontal cortical regions. Short and long fibers connect the sensory regions across the central sulcus. The auditory region's connections with the temporal lobe are shown. Each of these regions has many other connections which are not shown.

higher organizational stages within the secondary visual areas (Felleman & Van Essen, 1991). Beyond the primary and secondary visual areas, retinotopic influence on neuronal responses becomes difficult to detect (Desimone & Gross, 1979; Nakamura et al., 1994). The alternative considerations are whether the specific pattern of analysis is yet to be determined or the mode of distributed processing provided by the olfactory model is utilized.

As processing proceeds forward from the primary and secondary visual areas, information is processed along two separate functional pathways (Ungerleider & Mishkin, 1982) (figure 2.5). One pathway leads ventrally toward the inferior temporal lobe. This ventral pathway abstracts such visual details as color, shape, and texture for identification of objects (Kuypers et al., 1965). In monkeys, a specialized region in the posterior inferior temporal region seems to play a role in the analysis of faces (e.g., Desimone, Albright, Gross, et al., 1984; Mikami, Nakamura, & Kubota, 1994; Ungerleider, 1995), though the intensity of neuron response to faces in this region may simply indicate the general importance of face analysis, even in the monkey (Desimone, 1991). So even in this unusual case, it is unclear whether an association region is specialized. Farther forward in the inferior temporal cortex, neurons respond to many stimuli (Desimone & Gross, 1979). At the anterior tip of the temporal lobe, neurons respond predominantly to abstract stimulus aspects (Nakamura et al., 1994), without any clear evidence of topographic organization, whether retinotopic, classificational, or otherwise. An important question regarding the nature of neuron responses along this path from primary visual cortex to the tip of the inferior temporal lobe concerns the selectivity of individual neurons for specific environmental items or characteristics. In the primary and secondary regions, individual neurons show a broad range of responses between high selectivity and nonselectivity (Van

Essen & Deyoe, 1995). Inferior temporal neurons also have certain degrees of stimulus selectivity, but most neurons can readily be found to respond to one member of any limited set of stimuli, and neurons rarely show highly exclusive selectivity (Tanaka, Saito, Fukada, et al., 1991; Tanaka, 1993; Nakamura, Mikami, & Kubota, 1992; Nakamura et al., 1994). The range of selectivity in the inferior temporal cortex suggests that a stimulus which activates a neuronal field will elicit responses from many neurons rather than a few unique neurons, implying a broadly distributed analysis of information, a pattern of stimulus representation analogous to that of the olfactory system.

These findings concerning visual perception in monkeys are relevant to humans. However, in humans, there is clear evidence of hemispheric specialization. The left hemisphere is usually specialized by encoding verbal information. Regarding recognition of faces, Milner (1974) found that in humans, right temporal lobe lesions interfere with the ability to remember faces and irregular line drawings, but did not affect memory for (perhaps easily verbally encoded) geometric shapes.

The second visual pathway leads dorsally from the secondary visual cortex toward the parietal cortex and is responsible for analysis of spatial relationships. In the dorsal pathway, spatial analysis of visual information is performed in conjunction with posteriorly projecting connections from the somatosensory cortex which monitors the animal's own position. Both animals and humans show deficits in learning tasks requiring perception of the body in space, following lesions of the posterior parietal cortex. In humans, body image and perception of spatial relationships are often severely abnormal following parietal injury.

In addition to the two specific visual pathways described above, projecting from the retina to the primary visual cortex and then anteriorly, neurons at all levels of the visual cortex receive activating input from the pulvinar (e.g., Benevento & Rezak, 1976; Macko, Sarvis, Kennedy, et al., 1982). The pulvinar, receiving visual information from a rapid retinal projection through the superior colliculus, activates the visual cortex broadly, priming neurons at all levels of both visual pathways to analyze informational details arriving through the retinal geniculostriate pathway.

Neurons of the inferior temporal visual cortex are sensitive to behavioral state, including attention (Maunsell, 1995). Neurons in this region have a substantial background level of activity, respond to stimuli with approximately the same latency as the neurons of the primary visual cortex, and remain elevated in the level of activity for several hundred milliseconds following visual stimulation (Ashford & Fuster, 1985). Further, they respond differentially to stimuli presented as a repetition after less than two intervening stimuli (Baylis & Rolls, 1987). While neurons in this region can be classified to some extent according to the range of objects to which they respond (Bayliss, Rolls, & Leonard, 1987), the selectivity of different neurons' responses to a wide variety of stimuli can vary considerably (Nakamura et al., 1992, 1994). Nearly half of the neurons in the inferior temporal region will respond to one of two simple visual stimuli in the context of a behavioral paradigm which requires attention to each stimulus when it is presented (Ashford & Fuster, 1985; Coburn et al., 1990) (figure 2.6). This suggests the existence of an extensive functional neural network (ensemble) comprised of roughly half the inferior temporal neurons, within which analysis of the behaviorally relevant stimulus takes place. The 50 percent response rate is a level which mathematically allows the most powerful analysis of any stimulus (John, 1972; Coburn et al., 1990). The lower limit of the response rate would be one neuron responding to a single environmental configuration, requiring a unique neuron for each configuration. Clearly, this situation is an inadequate explanation and even a small number of responding cells could not provide adequate information-processing power to account for information encoding (Gawne & Richmond, 1993; Singer, 1995b). To achieve maximal encoding capability, the optimal response level is 50 percent of neurons in a field being activated by an environmental stimulus. Higher proportions would give less power, as do smaller proportions. Approximating a transient 50 percent response rate would also allow cortical modulating processes to ensure maximal distribution of processing across cortical regions, while maintaining stability of neuronal excitation (figure 2.7). Further gradation of neuronal responses, for example by modulation of response frequency, would provide additional analytic power.

An important issue in the mode of information analysis of environmental events in the cortex is the nature of the temporal sequencing of the analytic processes. Early anatomical investigations suggested that information processing was serial, following the hierarchy from primary to secondary to association regions of the cortex. The presumption was that processing at each level took some finite amount of time before the results of that processing could be relayed to the next higher level. However, the discovery of reciprocal anatomical connections (Kuypers et al. 1965; Rockland & Pandya, 1979), simultaneously supported the concept of efferent control along the visual cortical hierarchy (Pribram, 1967). Thus, it became apparent that information processing could involve reciprocal communication along the identified processing pathways, even as far as the medial temporal lobe (Mishkin & Aggleton, 1981). When concurrent processing was discovered at the initial and terminal ends of the ventral visual cortical pathway (Ashford & Fuster, 1985) (see figure 2.6), and as far as the hippocampus (Coburn et al., 1990), the notion of simultaneous hierarchical processing was introduced, suggesting that quite complex methods of analysis were possible, including parallel distributed processing.

Individual neuronal responses are organized into temporally brief bundles (Ashford & Fuster, 1985), which have a statistical distribution (Bair, Koch, Newsome, et al., 1994). Additionally, some information may be encoded in the temporal structure of the spike trains (McClurkin, Optican, Richmond, et al., 1991; Eskandar, Richmond, & Optican, 1992; Ferster & Spruston, 1995;

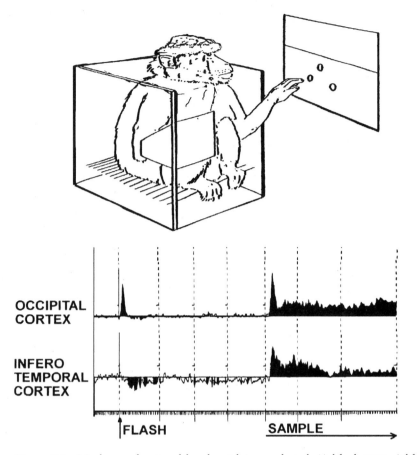

Figure 2.6 Monkey performing delayed match-to-sample task (Ashford, 1984; Ashford & Fuster, 1985). In this task, after a 20-second waiting period, a flash from the upper stimulus panel illuminates the monkey's visual field. Exactly 2.0 seconds later, the top button of the triangle is illuminated either red or green. The monkey must not touch any of the three stimulus buttons for at least 0.5 second prior to the flash, until the top stimulus light is illuminated. Then the monkey must press the top button for the trial to continue. The light is darkened after 1.5 seconds, then the monkey must wait 10 seconds for the two lower lights of the triangle to be illuminated, either red and green or green and red. The monkey must push the button whose color matches the sample to get a juice reward. Then the waiting period begins again. Shown below are composites of several neuronal unit responses recorded from either the occipital or inferior temporal cortex for a trial in which the stimulus button was illuminated red. Note that the occipital cortex units respond to the flash while the inferior temporal units are largely inhibited. However, units from both the occipital and inferior temporal cortex respond to the sample stimulus, and over a similar time course. Vertical dashed lines separate 0.5-second epochs, and the small hashmarks represent 20 ms.

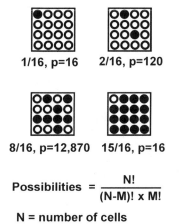

1/16, p=16   2/16, p=120

8/16, p=12,870   15/16, p=16

$$\text{Possibilities} = \frac{N!}{(N-M)! \times M!}$$

N = number of cells
M = activated cells ●

Figure 2.7 Matrix showing the mathematical power of the 50 percent response rate. A darkened circle could represent a responding neuron, while an open circle could represent a nonresponding neuron. For very large N, if M is approximately one half of N, the number of possibilities is about 2^N.

Singer & Gray, 1995), or spatiotemporal firing patterns (Abeles, Prut, Bergman, et al., 1994; Singer, Engel, Kreiter, et al., 1997). However, reciprocal information transfer forward and backward across numerous cortical processing stages (see figure 2.5) is probably required for memory storage (Rolls & Treves, 1994), and can include coherent neuronal activity occurring across widely distributed sites (Bressler, Coppola, & Nakamura, 1993; Bressler, 1995).

Independent of potentially complex temporal response patterns of cortical neuron ensembles, the massively parallel anatomical architecture of the cortical system provides great power for storing and recognizing images using a vector convolution and correlation approach (Murdock, 1982). In this construct, each neuron's response represents a component of the vector occupying a huge N-dimensional abstract mathematical space, with N representing the number of neurons in the brain. In this model, the total number of potentially encodable environmental configurations approximates 2^N (see figure 2.7; for large N, if M approximates $\frac{1}{2} \times N$, the number of possibilities approaches 2^N), a satisfactorily large number. Recent studies have supported the concept that memories of details about the various attributes of a discrete visual object are stored in a distributed fashion in the respective multiple regions responsible for the sensory analysis and perception of those specific attributes (Ungerleider, 1995). This approach for storing information at the neuronal level can be viewed as a vector convolution operation (Murdock, 1982), using the NMDA receptor (McClelland et al., 1986) or other long-term potentiating mechanisms, and involving the establishment of new connections between different neuronal systems (Alkon, 1989), as well as the altering of the efficiency of existing synaptic connections to change their weighting. Recognition occurs if there is a significant correlation between the vector of a perceived image and the vector which describes the current state of the cerebral system.

The implications of this model of reciprocal, hierarchical information processing can be examined in the monkey in the visual processing pathway. Early electrical activity in the cortex (as early as 20 ms in the monkey cortex in response to a flash, but over 40 ms for a discrete visual detail) represents initial visual processing. Unit and field responses can be modified by alertness (e.g., Arezzo, Pikoff, & Vaughan, 1975) and attention to specific detail (Ashford & Fuster, 1985; Maunsell, 1995), as field potentials in the 200 ms latency neighborhood are in the human. The initial neuronal response suggests that information about the visual stimulus is carried both to the primary visual processing area to begin detailed analysis, and more widely to the entire visual system where it serves an alerting function, preparing the larger system for the synchronous and reciprocal analysis of visual information between the primary, secondary, and associational sensory processing areas and the medial temporal lobe. Electrical signals corresponding to selective attention, the analysis of discrete stimulus features, and the detection of a variety of types of unexpected events can be recorded from both primates and humans. For example, in the human, recognition of information as discordant from expectation (Donchin, 1981) or containing details which are to be retained (Fabiani, Karis, & Donchin, 1986) will generate a late positive electrical signal (P300, positivity at 300 ms), which is likely to indicate that the cortex has perceived the incoming information and has initiated a storage operation on the perceived information (Fabiani, Karis, & Donchin, 1990). While much of the work on gross electrical activity following environmental events has been done using electrical recordings from scalp electrodes in the human, studies in monkeys have shown comparable gross electrical events, while also allowing microelectrode analysis of concurrent local activity in deep brain structures. Microelectrode analysis has shown, for example,that the P300 is not just localized to the temporal lobe (Paller, Zola-Morgan, Squire, et al., 1988), further supporting the concept that information processing occurs over broad cortical regions, probably using a parallel distributed processing mode. Work with monkeys looking at the responses of single neurons to behaviorally relevant stimulus dimensions shows the relationship between individual neuronal activity and cognition and also gives direct evidence that a single neuron can participate in a variety of functional networks (Fuster, 1995). Furthermore, these functional networks are widespread (Goldman-Rakic, 1988) and can adapt to task (i.e., environmental) demands over short periods of time (Bayliss & Rolls, 1987).

With regard to detail memory function, two systems have been identified in the monkey (Mishkin, 1982), one involving the hippocampus and Papez circuit through the anterior nucleus of the thalamus and the cingulate cortex (Papez, 1937), and the other involving the amygdala and the Nauta circuit through the dorsomedial nucleus of the thalamus and the orbitofrontal cortex (Nauta, 1971). The hippocampus seems to involve place memory (O'Keefe & Nadel, 1978), and recent studies suggest that hippocampal neurons in the monkey code for specific geographic directions which can be associated with visual information for storage organization (O'Mara, Rolls, Berthoz, et al., 1994; Ono, Nakamura, Nishijo, et al., 1993; Rolls, Robertson, & Georges-Francois, 1995). In contrast, the amygdala codes for emotions, including fear (in rodents; LeDoux, 1995; Killcross, Robbins, & Everitt, 1997) and alimentary, emotional (in dogs: Fonberg, 1969), sexual (in monkeys: Kling & Steklis, 1976), and social factors (in monkeys: Brothers & Ring, 1993), and these factors can also serve to index visual information for retrieval (LeDoux, 1994, 1995). Classic studies of monkeys with lesions of the amygdala revealed disruptions of social behavior (Kling & Steklis, 1976; Pribram, 1961; Rolls, 1995) deriving from failures to perceive or retain social cues relating to dominance or sexual hierarchies. The visual cortex connects broadly with the hippocampus (Van Hoesen & Pandya, 1975a,b; Van Hoesen, Rosene, & Mesulam, 1979; Rosene & Van Hoesen, 1987), allowing the hippocampus to facilitate information storage throughout the visual cortex (Ungerleider, 1995). However, only the anterior portion of the temporal cortex connects with the amygdala (Krettek & Price, 1977; Turner, Mishkin, & Knapp, 1980; Mishkin & Aggleton, 1981), allowing the amygdala to focus on facilitation of the analysis, encoding, and retention of more abstract visual information, particularly that information related to function such as food and sexual appeal and poison and danger signals. This model is consistent with electrical stimulation experiments with the human amygdala which evoke memories associated with emotions (Penfield, 1958).

Auditory System

The auditory system of the monkey is considered to process information using principles akin to those of the visual system (see figure 2.5). While it has been more difficult to train monkeys to perform tasks in response to auditory information, neurons of the auditory cortex are particularly responsive to the vocalizations of other monkeys. Further, there are multimodal cells between the visual and auditory regions within the temporal cortex.

Somatosensory System

The somatosensory system analyzes information in the parietal cortex, but in close association with the motor system and the frontal cortex anterior to the central sulcus (Pandya & Kuypers, 1969; Jones & Powell, 1970; Pandya & Yeterian, 1985) (see figure 2.5). The parietal cortex shows neuronal responses when monkeys perform touch discrimination tasks that are comparable to visual discrimination tasks. In a haptic delayed match-to-sample task (a tactile discrimination task with a delay), neurons in rhesus primary somatosensory cortex (S1) exhibit memory properties by firing during the delay. Also, units in monkey parietal association cortex discharge during perception and mnemonic retention of tactile features (Zhou & Fuster, 1992).

THE FRONTAL LOBE AND ATTENTION AND ACTIVE MEMORY SYSTEMS

Historically, there has been considerable effort to define the systems of the frontal lobe, particularly with regard to attention, thought, and decision-making processes. The "working memory" concept was introduced by Carlyle Jacobsen (1935) to explain the effects of principal sulcus lesions in monkeys, and was later shown to apply only to visuospatial tasks. Lesions of the inferior prefrontal convexity interfere with delayed response tasks, whether or not there is a spatial component, by decreasing the ability to inhibit incorrect responses. Lesions of the arcuate concavity leave delayed response behavior unaffected, but decrease the ability to choose between specific responses when presented with specific stimuli. Orbitofrontal lesions reduce emotionality and emotional arousal. This last finding led Egas Moniz to attempt the treatment of psychiatric patients with prefrontal lobotomy. Patients with prefrontal lobotomy show an inability to change response strategies on the Wisconsin Card Sorting test (Milner, 1974), which appears to be the same inhibition deficit seen in monkeys with inferior frontal convexity lesions. However, these patients show little diminishment on measures of intelligence. Thus, an important function of the frontal lobes appears to be weighing the consequences of various actions, and selection of some actions with the inhibition of others, within the repertoire of all learned or possible behaviors.

The frontal cortex manages information by coordinating activity in the sensory and perceptual regions posterior to the central sulcus. The frontal cortical regions form a functional executive network with the dorsomedial nucleus of the thalamus and the basal ganglia (Alexander, DeLong, & Crutcher, 1992) to generate smooth motor acts (Kornhuber, 1974) and behavioral sequences (Fuster, 1997b), which include thinking and planning (Matthysse, 1974). The frontal cortex makes reciprocal connections with both the ventral and dorsal visual pathways as well as the auditory and somatosensory systems (see figure 2.5). Neurons in the frontal regions are active during tasks requiring visual attention, particularly during the period when short-term retention of information is required for spanning a delay interval before a response can be produced (Fuster, 1973). The prefrontal cortex can selectively analyze face information (O Scalaidhe, Wilson, & Goldman-Rakic, 1997) and integrate the detail and spatial information analysis performed by the posterior cortical regions (Rao, Rainer, & Miller, 1997). Presumably, the prefrontal cortex serves to organize and sequence responses in posterior perceptual regions (Goldman-Rakic, 1988; Fuster, 1997b). In this fashion, the frontal cortex participates in the attentive aspects of perception and active short-term memory, also referred to as "working memory"

(Goldman-Rakic, 1995), as well as facilitating the encoding of relevant information and orchestrating retrieval from long-term storage (Fuster, 1995, 1997a).

Development of Monkey Tasks for Attention and Active Memory

The early paradigms which were developed for testing behavior in the monkey used tasks such as delayed alternation. As an example of this task, the monkey might be required to push one button, then several seconds later, push a different button. Behavior in such tasks is impaired by lesions of the frontal lobes. Early explanations of the cognitive requirements for performing this task focused on memory. However, the performance of this task and others like it are more dependent on attention, or active short-term memory, than the long-term storage of information (Fuster, 1997b).

In a modification of the delayed alternation task, the delayed match-to-sample task, the correct button choice depends on matching to a previously displayed sample (see figure 2.6). In this task, it is clear that it is attention to detail, then maintaining in an active state an internal representation of that now-absent sample stimulus image, which is critical to correct performance. Further studies of the brain regions involved in performance of this task have shown that the inferior temporal lobe is required for the analysis of the information detail component of the task. However, performance of the match when a significant delay is introduced depends on the frontal lobes, indicating that the capability of maintaining attention over time to an internal mnemonic representation of the stimulus detail is critically dependent on frontal lobe function. This dichotomy also demonstrates the behavioral interaction between the temporal and frontal lobes (Fuster, 1997b).

Tasks to Distinguish Active Memory and Retentive Memory

A critical issue in the understanding of memory function was the development of tasks which would demonstrate the storage of information after distraction (beyond the limits of attention, active short-term memory, or "working memory"). An important early demonstration by Gaffan (1977a,b) showed that monkeys could perform recognition tasks involving complex pictures, multiple colors, and multiple spatial positions. Gaffan also demonstrated that the fornix (see figure 2.2), presumably because of its critical anatomical role in connecting the basal forebrain to the hippocampus, was critical to the function of retentive memory, a form of memory frequently impaired in human amnesic patients (Scoville & Milner, 1957).

The role of the medial temporal lobe was further clarified by Mishkin (1982) using the delayed non-match-to-sample task with trial unique objects. This task showed impairment from medial temporal lobe lesions or cholinergic inhibitors, which both produce pronounced deficits of long-term memory in humans. For example, in the case of H.M., who had surgical ablation of both medial temporal lobes for epilepsy control, he is profoundly impaired in the ability to acquire most forms of new information, but can recall information learned prior to the surgery, and he can learn new motor skills (Scoville & Milner, 1957). In Mishkin's initial experiments, lesions of either the hippocampus or amygdala impaired the performance of this task, and lesions of both systems rendered the monkey incapable of retaining the critical information. Later studies by Mishkin's group suggested that the rhinal cortex, which is close to both the amygdala and hippocampus but projects more widely, plays the most pivotal role in the retention of information (Meunier, Bachevalier, Mishkin, et al., 1993). Of note, the rhinal cortex includes the entorhinal cortex, which is the region of the human brain that seems to be the initial site of attack of the Alzheimer's process (Braak & Braak, 1991).

More recently, efforts have been made to computer-automate memory tasks for monkeys so that a computer screen can deliver the stimuli, and responses can be registered using a joystick or touch-screen technology. Use of a joystick keeps the animal's hand out of the visual field, which is important since the hand itself can represent a visual stimulus. Computer control of response-reward contingencies allows teaching of considerably more complex tasks. For example, rhesus monkeys can be taught to read and associate responses with individual letters of the alphabet and retain those associations for up to an hour (figure 2.8) (Ashford & Edwards, 1991). Accordingly, such tasks can be used to test reaction times and brain wave components, and both are comparable to human measures. Also, memory tasks can be applied

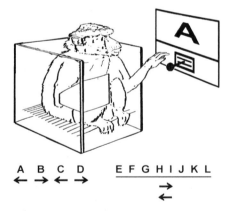

Figure 2.8 Monkey reading letters and performing joystick responses (Ashford & Edwards, 1991). The monkey could push the joystick to either the left or right. This task was taught to the monkey by reinforcing responses with sweetened juice rewards. the letters A, B, C, D always required the same direction for reward. However, the remaining eight letters were associated with a different pattern of correct directions each day. One monkey could learn each of these letters after a single trial (reward would mean correct direction; no reward would mean that the other direction was correct). Then it could recall the correct pattern for the letters, often flawlessly, after up to a half-hour delay, interspersed with trials of the other letters.

to other modalities, such as the sensorimotor system (Murray & Mishkin, 1984; Zhou & Fuster, 1992).

RELATION BETWEEN PROCESSING CAPABILITIES AND ENERGY REQUIREMENTS

In the course of understanding the relations between the volume of the cerebral cortex, information-processing power, and the need for energy-providing nutrients, the focus of attention must be on the neuron with its dendritic and axonal processes. There are about 50,000 pyramidal neurons under each square millimeter of cortical surface area. Each neuron may have up to 100,000 inputs arranged along a dendritic tree which may extend over 6 mm in many directions. Its axon has a comparable number of outputs which may extend as far as the base of the spinal cord, but commonly several centimeters to a target cortical region. The surface area of a pyramidal neuron may average 1 mm^2, but may reach 1 cm^2. Therefore, the total neuronal membrane surface area under a square millimeter of cortex surface is about 50,000 mm^2. This equals about 10,000 m^2 for the 2000 cm^2 of the human cortex. About 40 percent of the metabolism of the brain is devoted to maintaining the resting potential across this huge amount of neuronal surface membrane. The remainder of brain metabolism is devoted to active cell activity (Magistretti & Pellerin, 1996), 10 percent for recovering from action potentials and 50 percent for synaptic activity. The brain consumes 20 percent of the energy resources of the body; maintaining cerebral function is clearly a major energy cost to the individual.

If a single unique stimulus were coded by a single neuron, the brain would indeed be quiet, and the demands of repolarization and synaptic activity would be minimized. However, the stimulated neuronal assemblies, whether they are hard-wired primary cortical connections or plastic networks in association cortex, include large proportions of the cortical neurons. Observations of monkey cortical units responding to relevant stimuli suggest that a functional network of about half of the neurons in a field can manifest a response to a stimulus and that individual neurons may respond with several discharges to a single stimulus (Ashford & Fuster, 1985; Coburn et al., 1990; Mikami et al., 1994; Nakamura et al., 1994). During intense neuronal activity neurons depolarize frequently, creating a major metabolic expense in repolarization demand. The large proportion of cerebral cortex that is activated by environmental stimuli demands a heavy supply of energy, particularly in the primate (Armstrong, 1983). The physiological demands of processing in relation to cognition on a regional cortical basis can be visualized clearly by techniques which measure local cerebral blood flow (single photon emission computed tomography and functional magnetic resonance imaging) and metabolism (positron emission tomography). However, when the brain does achieve its maximum processing power, it may also achieve its point of optimal processing efficiency and actually minimize its metabolic demand (Parks et al., 1989).

One important question is, How do neurons in the brain stem regulate the activity of neuronal ensembles in the cortex? (Woolf, 1996). For example, acetylcholine neurons project to limited cortical patches as small as a few square millimeters (Saper, 1984; Wainer & Mesulam, 1990), presumably calling them into action for relevant processing requirements. Serotonin neurons, whose processes are the most widely distributed in the brain, presumably activate broad regions of the cortex during a variety of waking behaviors (Jacobs & Azmitia, 1992). In relation to neural network models, catecholamines may play a unique role describable as adjusting the gain of logistic activation functions in the network (Servan-Schreiber & Cohen, 1992). Thus, the projections from the brain stem seem to play the role of efficiently orchestrating the processing of the distributed neural networks to assimilate and respond to the environment.

DEVELOPMENT OF INFORMATION-PROCESSING CAPACITY

In early development, primary cortical regions undergo critical periods when environmental input directs the formation of neuronal connections (Hubel & Wiesel, 1977) and the development of functional assemblies (Singer, 1995b). Higher-order association (e.g., perceptual) regions also pass through critical periods of time early in life (Webster, Bachevalier, & Ungerleider, 1995). In one example, neonatal damage to the inferior temporal cortex of the monkey was nearly fully compensated, as measured by multiple memory tasks in four- to five-year-old animals (Malkova, Mishkin, & Bachevalier, 1995). Yet, while the primary regions become relatively hard-wired early in life, higher-order association perceptual regions appear to retain some plasticity, forming new connections to accommodate the learning of new information throughout life (Diamond, 1988; Singer, 1995a) or until disabled by injury or a neurodegenerative process (Ashford, Shan, Butler, et al., 1995). By contrast, the medial temporal region, which is more primitive in its development, does not seem to be able to recover from injury at either early or late stages of life (Malkova et al., 1995). The frontal cortex seems to function less than optimally in immature animals (as the adjective implies when referring to human childlike behavior), but this region undergoes a critical period in humans with massive changes in connections in late adolescence and early adulthood (Feinberg, 1987). Subsequent to this, less flexibility (e.g., for personality change) is present.

As applied to neural networks, most cortical regions seem to have an early quiescent period, followed by a critical period in which the network undergoes intense learning and revision of connections, followed by maturity, after which the region achieves a particular pattern of function that is less modifiable. However, some brain regions, such as the middle temporal lobe and the inferior parietal lobe, may retain high levels of plasticity throughout the animal's life and maintain maximum ability to store complex information. (This maintained elevated level of plasticity may predispose these brain regions to the pathological changes seen in Alzheimer's disease; Ashford & Zec, 1993; Ashford et al., 1995). It is the task of the whole brain working in concert to perceive the environment, analyze relevant information, store critical new information, and develop plans for the future which facilitate the survival and reproductive success of the organism in a complex world. The important aspect of development is the formation of connectivities and the coordination of processing within and between brain regions.

FUTURE PRIMATE MODELS FOR NEUROPSYCHOLOGY AND NEURAL NETWORKS

A central theme of this chapter is the value of nonhuman primates as models of human cognitive processes. Important information about human cognition has been obtained from human studies, such as brain imaging and recording brain electrical activity from scalp electrodes. However, such studies are limited in the amount they can tell us about the structural substrates of information processing. When functional principles and more details are needed, valuable information can be obtained from animal studies. In humans, there is a constant challenge to study ever smaller and deeper components of neuronal networks. Animal research extends the inquiry to progressively more basic levels. Studies of animals provide meaningful answers to questions about human brain structure and function. Moreover, comparative analysis can reveal clues to the development of functions.

The approach of studying the brain of a monkey performing a cognitive task will continue to be a valuable model for neuroscience. Monkeys appear to enjoy playing simple video games for extended periods of time, as do humans, and those games can be designed to test the capabilities of the animals. Brain function can be monitored using minimally invasive electrode recordings or scanning techniques. Perturbations can include administration of drugs with reversible effects or transient lesions such as those achieved by cooling. Using such approaches, the role of specific brain structures, chemical systems, and neuropsychological functioning can be explored relatively noninvasively in nonhuman primates.

An important future direction is the better understanding of how so many neurons work together within specific brain regions and across many different brain regions. Implantation of multiple indwelling electrode arrays, which can be monitored in concert with imaging procedures, and massive computer analysis of the interactions between the individual neurons, regional activations, and complex behavior, will reveal more information about how the brain functions in health and disease. The development of neural network and massive parallel distributed processing models based on empirical data obtained from across the primate order perhaps will reveal insights into human brain function that will transcend models developed using computers, lower animals, or humans alone.

REFERENCES

Abeles, M., Prut, Y., Bergman, H., & Vaadia, E. (1994). Synchronization in neuronal transmission and its importance for information processing. *Progress in Brain Research, 102*, 395–404.

Alexander, G.E., Delong, M.R., & Crutcher, M.D. (1992). Do cortical and basal ganglia motor areas use "motor programs" to control movement? *Behavioral Brain Research, 15*, 656–665.

Alkon, D. L. (1989). Memory storage and neural systems. *Scientific American*, July, 42–50.

Allison, T., & Cicchetti, D. V. (1976). Sleep in mammals: Ecological and constitutional correlates. *Science, 194*, 732–734.

Allman, J. (1982). Reconstructing the evolution of the brain in primates through the use of comparative neurophysiological and neuroanatomical data. In E. Armstrong, & D. Flak (Eds.), *Primate brain evolution: Methods and concepts* (pp. 13–28). New York: Plenum Press.

Allman, J. (1990). Evolution of neocortex. In E. G. Jones, & A. Peters (Eds.), *Cerebral cortex*, Vol. 8A (pp. 269–283). New York: Plenum Press.

Arezzo, J., Pikoff, A., & Vaughan, H. G. (1975) The sources and intracerebral distribution of auditory evoked potentials in the alert rhesus monkey. *Brain Research, 90*, 57–73.

Armstrong, E. (1983). Relative brain size and metabolism in mammals. *Science, 220*, 1302–1304.

Ashford, J. W. (1984). *Cortical electrophysiology of visual encoding in the monkey*. Ph.D. dissertation. Ann Arbor, MI: University Microfilms International.

Ashford, J. W., & Edwards, H. (1991). Memory in the monkey: An automated paradigm and the effect of nicotine. *Society for Neuroscience Abstracts, 17*, 1236.

Ashford, J. W., & Fuster, J. M. (1985). Occipital and inferotemporal responses to visual signals in the monkey. *Experimental Neurology, 90*, 444–466.

Ashford, J. W., Shan, M., Butler, S., Rajasekar, A., & Schmitt, F. A. (1995). Temporal quantification of Alzheimer's disease severity: "Time index" model. *Dementia, 6*, 269–280.

Ashford, J. W., & Zec, R. F. (1993). Pharmacological treatment in Alzheimer's disease. In R. Parks, R. Zec, & R. Wilson (Eds.), *Neuropsychology of Alzheimer's disease and other dementias* (pp. 589–614). New York: Oxford University Press.

Axel, R. (1995). The molecular logic of smell. *Scientific American*, October, 154–159.

Bailey, C. H., & Kandel, E. R. (1995). Molecular and structural mechanisms underlying long-term memory. In M. S. Gazzaniga (Ed.), *The cognitive neurosciences* (pp. 19–36). Cambridge, MA: MIT Press.

Bair, W., Koch, C., Newsome, W., & Britten, K. (1994). Power spectrum analysis of bursting cells in area MT in the behaving monkey. *Journal of Neuroscience, 14*, 2870–2892.

Baylis, G. C., & Rolls, E. T. (1987). Responses of neurons in the inferior temporal cortex in short term and serial recognition memory tasks. *Experimental Brain Research, 65*, 614–622.

Baylis, G. C., Rolls, E. T., & Leonard, C. M. (1987). Functional subdivisions of the temporal lobe neocortex. *Journal of Neuroscience, 7*, 330–342.

Benevento, L. A., & Rezak, M. (1976). The cortical projections of the inferior pulvinar and adjacent lateral pulvinar in the rhesus monkey (*Macaca mulatta*): An autoradiographic study. *Brain Research, 108*, 1–24.

Berger, R. J. (1975). Bioenergetic functions of sleep and activity rhythms and their possible relevance to aging. *Federation Proceedings, 34,* 97–102.

Bermúdez-Rattoni, F., Coburn, K. L., Fernández, J., Chávez, A. F., & Garcia, J. (1987). Potentiation of odor by taste and odor aversions in rats are regulated by cholinergic activity of dorsal hippocampus. *Pharmacology, Biochemistry and Behavior, 26,* 553–559.

Braak, H., & Braak, E. (1991). Neuropathological staging of Alzheimer-related changes. *Acta Neuropathology, 82,* 239–259.

Bressler, S. L. (1995). Large-scale cortical networks and cognition. *Brain Research Reviews, 20,* 288–304.

Bressler, S. L., Coppola, R., & Nakamura, R. (1993). Episodic multiregional cortical coherence at multiple frequencies during visual task performance. *Nature, 366,* 153–156.

Brothers, L., & Ring, B. (1993). Mesial temporal neurons in the macaque monkey with responses selective for aspects of social stimuli. *Behaviovral Brain Research, 57,* 53–61.

Cinelli, A. R., Hamilton, K. A., & Kauer, J. S. (1995). Salamander olfactory bulb neuronal activity observed by video rate, voltage-sensitive dye imaging. III. Spatial and temporal properties of responses evoked by odorant stimulation. *Journal of Neurophysiology, 73,* 2053–2070.

Coburn, K. L., Ashford, J. W., & Fuster, J. M. (1990). Visual response latencies in temporal lobe structures as a function of stimulus information load. *Behavioral Neuroscience, 104,* 62–73.

Coburn, K. L., Garcia, J., Kiefer, S. W., & Rusiniak, K. W. (1984). Taste potentiation of poisoned odor by temporal contiguity. *Behavioral Neuroscience, 98,* 813–819.

Desimone, R. (1991). Face-selective cells in the temporal cortex of monkeys. *Journal of Cognitive Neuroscience, 3,* 1–8.

Desimone, R., Albright, T. D., Gross, C. G., & Bruce, C. (1984). Stimulus-selective properties of inferior temporal neurons in the macaque. *Journal of Neuroscience, 4,* 2051–2062.

Desimone, R., & Gross, C. G. (1979). Visual areas in the temporal cortex of the macaque. *Brain Research, 178,* 363–380.

Diamond, M. C. (1988). *Enriching heredity.* New York: The Free Press.

Donchin, E. (1981). Surprise? . . . Surprise! *Psychophysiology, 18,* 492–513.

Eskandar, E. N., Richmond, B. J., & Optican, L. M. (1992). Role of inferior temporal neurons in visual memory, I. Temporal encoding of information about visual images, recalled images, and behavioral context. *Journal of Neurophysiology, 68,* 1277–1295.

Fabiani, M., Karis, D., & Donchin, E. (1986). P300 and recall in an incidental memory paradigm. *Psychophysiology, 23,* 298–308.

Fabiani, M., Karis, D., & Donchin, E. (1990). Effects of mnemonic strategy manipulation in a Von Restorff paradigm. *Electroencephalography and Clinical Neurophysiology, 75,* 22–35.

Feinberg, I. (1987). Adolescence and mental illness. *Science, 236,* 507–508.

Felleman, D. J., & VanEssen, D. C. (1991). Distributed hierarchical processing in the primate cerebral cortex. *Cerebral Cortex, 1,* 1–15.

Ferster, D., & Spruston, N. (1995). Cracking the neuronal code. *Science, 270,* 756–757.

Fonberg, E. (1969). The role of the hypothalamus and amygdala in food intake, alimentary motivation and emotional reactions. *Acta Biologica Experimentia, 29,* 335–358.

Freeman, W. J. (1987). Simulation of chaotic EEG patterns with a dynamic model of the olfactory system. *Biological Cybernetics, 56,* 139–150.

Freeman, W. J., & Skarda, C. A. (1985). Spatial EEG patterns, non-linear dynamics and perception: The neo-Sherringtonian view. *Brain Research Reviews, 10,* 147–175.

Fuster, J. M. (1973). Unit activity in prefrontal cortex during delayed-response performance: Neuronal correlates of transient memory. *Journal of Neurophysiology, 36,* 61–78.

Fuster, J. M. (1995). *Memory in the cerebral cortex: An empirical approach to neural networks in the human and nonhuman primate.* Cambridge, MA: MIT Press.

Fuster, J. M. (1997a). Network memory. *Trends in Nenrosciences, 20,* 451–459.

Fuster, J. M. (1997b). *The prefrontal cortex: Anatomy, physiology and neuropsychology of the frontal lobe,* 3rd ed. New York: Raven Press.

Gaffan, D. (1977a). Monkeys' recognition memory for complex pictures and the effect of fornix transection. *Quarterly Journal of Experimental Psychology, 29,* 505–514.

Gaffan, D. (1977b). Recognition memory after short retention intervals in fornix-transected monkeys. *Quarterly Journal of Experimental Psychology, 29,* 577–588.

Gawne, T. J., & Richmond, B. J. (1993). How independent are the messages carried by adjacent inferior temporal cortical neurons? *Journal of Neuroscience, 13,* 2758–2771.

Goldman-Rakic, P. S. (1988). Topography of cognition: Parallel distributed networks in primate association cortex. *Annual Review of Neuroscience, 11,* 137–156.

Goldman-Rakic P. S. (1995). Cellular basis of working memory. *Neuron, 14,* 477–485.

Gratton, A., & Wise, R. A. (1988). Comparisons and refractory periods for medial forebrain bundle fibers subserving stimulation-induced feeding and brain stimulation reward: a psychophysical study. *Brain Research, 438,* 256–263.

Haberly, L. B., & Bower, J. M. (1989). Olfactory cortex: Model circuit for study of associative memory? *Trends in Neuroscience, 12,* 258–264.

Hayek, F. A. (1952). *The Sensory Order: An inquiry into the foundations of theoretical psychology.* Chicago: University of Chicago Press.

Hubel, D. H., & Wiesel, T. N. (1977). Functional architecture of macaque monkey visual cortex. *Proceedings of the Royal Society of London, Series B, 181,* 1–59.

Jacobs, B. L., & Azmitia, E. C. (1992). Structure and function of the brain serotonin system. *Physiological Reviews, 72,* 165–229.

Jacobsen, C. F. (1935). Functions of frontal association areas in primates. *Archives of Neurology and Psychiatry, 33,* 558–569.

Jerison, H. J. (1991). *Brain size and the evolution of mind.* New York: American Museum of Natural History.

John, E. R. (1972). Switchboard versus statistical theories of learning and memory. *Science, 177,* 850–864.

Jones, E. G. (1990). Modulatory events in the development and evolution of primate neocortex. In E. G. Jones and A. Peters (Eds.), *Cerebral cortex,* Vol. 8A (pp. 311–362). New York: Plenum Press.

Jones, E. G., & Powell, T. P. S. (1970) An anatomical study of converging sensory pathways within the cerebral cortex of the monkey. *Brain, 93,* 793–820.

Kaba, H., Hayashi, Y., Higuchi, T., & Nakanishi, S. (1994). Induction of an olfactory memory by the activation of a metabotropic glutamate receptor. *Science, 265,* 262–264.

Karten, H. J. (1991). Homology and evolutionary origins of the "neocortex." *Brain Behavior and Evolution, 38,* 264–272.

Kauer, J. S. (1991). Contributions of topography and parallel processing to odor coding in the vertebrate olfactory pathway. *Trends in Neuroscience, 14,* 79–85.

Killackey, H. P. (1995). Evolution of the human brain: A neuroanatomical perspective. In M. S. Gazzaniga (Ed.), *The cognitive neurosciences* (pp. 1243–1253). Cambridge, MA: MIT Press.

Killcross, S., Robbins, T. W., & Everitt, B. J. (1997). Different types of fear-conditioned behavior mediated by separate nucleii within amygdala. *Nature, 388,* 377–380.

Kling, A., & Steklis, H. D. (1976). A neural substrate for affiliative behavior in nonhuman primates. *Brain Behavior and Evolution, 13,* 216–238.

Kornhuber, H. H. (1974). Cerebral cortex, cerebellum, and basal ganglia: An introduction to their motor functions. In F. O. Schmitt & F. G. Worden (Eds.), *The neurosciences. Third study program* (pp. 267–280). Cambridge, MA: The MIT Press.

Krettek, J. E., & Price, J. L. (1977). Projections from the amygdaloid complex to the cerebral cortex and thalamus in the rat and cat. *Journal of Comparative Neurology, 172,* 687–722.

Kuypers, H. G. J. M., Szwarcbart, M. K., Mishkin, M., & Rosvold, H. E. (1965). Occipitotemporal corticocortical connections in the rhesus monkey. *Experimental Neurology, 11,* 245–262.

Lashley, K. S. (1950). In search of the engram. *Symposium, Society for Experimental Biology, 4,* 454–482.

Laurent, G. (1996). Odor images and tunes. *Neuron, 16,* 473–476.

LeDoux, J. E. (1994). Emotion, memory and the brain. *Scientific American,* June, 50–57.

LeDoux, J. E. (1995). In search of an emotional system in the brain: Leaping from fear to emotion and consciousness. In M. S. Gazzaniga (Ed.), *The cognitive neurosciences* (pp. 1049–1061). Cambridge, MA: MIT Press.

Macko, K., Jarvis, C. D., Kennedy, C, Miyaoka, M., Shinohara, M., Sokoloff, L., & Mishkin, M. (1982). Mapping the primate visual system with (2C14) deoxyglucose. *Science, 281,* 394–396.

Magistretti, P. J., & Pellerin, L. (1996). Cellular mechanisms of brain energy metabolism: Relevance to functional brain imaging and to neurodegenerative disorders. *Annals of the New York Academy of Sciences, 777,* 380–1387.

Malkova, L. Mishkin, M., & Bachevalier, J. (1995). Long-term effects of selective neonatal temporal lobe lesions on learning and memory in monkeys. *Behavioral Neuroscience, 109,* 212–226.

Matthysse, S. (1974). Schizophrenia: Relationships to dopamine transmission, motor control and feature extraction. In F. O. Schmitt & F. G. Worden (Eds.), *The neurosciences, Third study program* (pp. 733–737). Cambridge, MA: The MIT Press.

Maunsell, J. H. R. (1995). The brain's visual world: Representation of visual targets in cerebral cortex. *Science, 270,* 764–769.

McClelland, J. L., Rumelhart, D. E., & the PDP Research Group. (1986). *Parallel distributed processing: Explorations in the microstructure of cognition,* Vol. 2: *Psychological and biological models.* Cambridge, MA: MIT Press.

McClurkin, J. W., Optican, L. M., Richmond, B. J., & Gawne, T. J. (1991). Concurrent processing and complexity of temporally encoded neuronal messages in visual perception. *Science, 253,* 675–677.

Meunier, M., Bachevalier, J., Mishkin, M., & Murray, E. A. (1993). Effects on visual recognition of combined and separate ablations of the entorhinal and perirhinal cortex in rhesus monkeys. *Journal of Neuroscience, 13,* 5418–5432.

Mikami, A., Nakamura, K., & Kubota, K. (1994). Neuronal responses to photographs in the superior temporal sulcus of the rhesus monkey. *Behavioural Brain Research, 60,* 1–13.

Milner, B. (1974). Hemispheric specialization: Scope and limits. In F. O. Schmitt, & F. G. Worden (Eds.), *The neurosciences. Third study program* (pp. 75–89). Cambridge, MA: MIT Press.

Mishkin, M. (1982). A memory system in the monkey. *Philosophical Transactions of the Royal Society of London. Series B. 298*, 85–95.

Mishkin, M., & Aggleton, J. (1981). Multiple functional contributions of the amygdala in the monkey. In Y. Ben-Ari (Ed.), *The amygdaloid complex* (pp. 409–420). Amsterdam: Elsevier.

Moruzzi, G., & Magoun, H. W. (1949). Brain stem reticular formation and activation of the EEG. *Journal of Electroencephalography and Clinical Neurophysiology, 1*, 455–473.

Murdock, B. B. (1982). A theory for the storage and retrieval of item and associative information. *Psychological Review, 89*, 609–626.

Murray, E. A., & Mishkin, M. (1984). Severe tactual as well as visual memory deficits follow combined removal of the amygdala and hippocampus in monkeys. *Journal of Neuroscience, 4*, 2565–2580.

Nakamura, K., Matsumoto, K., Mikami, A., & Kubota, K. (1994). Visual response properties of single neurons in the temporal pole of behaving monkeys. *Journal of Neurophysiology, 71*, 1206–1221.

Nakamura, K., Mikami, A., & Kubota, K. (1992). Activity of single neurons in the monkey amygdala during performance of a visual discrimination task. *Journal of Neurophysiology, 67*, 1447–1463.

Nauta, W. J. H. (1971). The problem of the frontal lobe: A reinterpretation. *Journal of Psychiatric Research, 8*, 167–187.

Nauta, W. J. H., & Karten, H. J. (1970). A general profile of the vertebrate brain, with sidelights on the ancestry of the cerebral cortex. In F. O. Schmitt, & F. G. Worden (Eds.), *The neurosciences. Third study program* (pp. 7–26). New York: Rockefeller University Press.

O'Keefe, J., & Nadel, L. (1978). *The hippocampus as a cognitive map*. New York: Oxford University Press.

O'Mara, S. M., Rolls, E. T., Berthoz, A., & Kesner, R. P. (1994). Neurons responding to whole-body motion in the primate hippocampus. *Journal of Neuroscience, 14*, 6511–6523.

Ono, T., Nakamura, K., Nishijo, H., et al. (1993). Monkey hippocampal neurons related to spatial and nonspatial functions. *Journal of Neurophysiology, 70*, 1516–1529.

O Scalaidhe, S. P., Wilson, F. A. W., & Goldman-Rakic, P. S. (1997). Areal segregation of face-processing neurons in prefrontal cortex. *Science, 278*, 1135–1138.

Paller, K. A., Zola-Morgan, S., Squire, L. R., & Hillyard, S. A. (1988). P3-like brain waves in normal monkeys and in monkeys with medial temporal lesions. *Behavioral Neuroscience, 102*, 714–725.

Pandya, D. N., & Kuypers, H. (1969). Cortico-cortical connections in the rhesus monkey. *Brain Research, 13*, 13–36.

Pandya, D. N., & Yeterian, E. H. (1985). Architecture and connections of cortical association areas. In A. Peters, & E. G. Jones (Eds.), *Cerebral cortex, 4*, (pp. 3–61). New York: Plenum Press.

Papez, J. W. (1937). A proposed mechanism of emotion. In R. L. Isaacson (Ed.), *Basic readings in neuropsychology* (pp. 87–109). Huntington, NY: Krieger.

Parks, R. W., Crockett, D. J., Tuokko, H., Beattie, B. L., Ashford, J. W., Coburn, K. L., Zec, R. F., Becker, R. E., McGeer, P. L., & McGeer, E. G. (1989). Neuropsychological "systems efficiency" and positron emission tomography. *Journal of Neuropsychiatry, 1*, 270–282.

Parks, R. W., Levine, D. S., Long, D. L., Crockett, D. J., Dalton, I. E., Weingartner, H., Fedio, P., Coburn, K. L., Siler, G., Matthews, J. R., & Becker, R. E. (1992). Parallel distributed processing and neuropsychology: A neural network model of Wisconsin card sorting and verbal fluency. *Neuropsychology Review, 3*, 213–233.

Penfield, W. (1958). Functional localization in temporal and deep sylvian areas. *Research Publishing Association for Research in Nervous and Mental Disease, 36*, 210–226.

Preuss, T. M. (1995). The argument from animals to humans in cognitive neuroscience. In M. S. Gazzaniga (Ed.), *The cognitive neurosciences* (pp. 1227–1241). Cambridge, MA: MIT Press.

Pribram, K. H. (1961). Limbic system. In D. E. Sheer (Ed.), *Electrical stimulation of the brain* (pp. 311–320). Austin: University of Texas Press.

Pribram, K. H. (1967). The limbic systems, efferent control of neural inhibition and behavior. *Progress in Brain Research, 27*, 318–336.

Rao, S. C., Rainer, G., & Miller, E. K. (1997). Integration of what and where in the primate prefrontal cortex. *Science, 276*, 821–824.

Robbins, T. W., & Everitt, B. J. (1995). Arousal systems and attention. In Gazzaniga, M. S. (Ed.), *The cognitive neurosciences* (pp. 703–720). Cambridge, MA: The MIT Press.

Rockland, K. S., & Pandya, D. N. (1979). Laminar origins and terminations of cortical connections of the occipital lobe in the rhesus monkey. *Brain Research, 179*, 3–20.

Rolls, E. T. (1995). A theory of emotion and consciousness, and its application to understanding the neural basis of emotion. In M. S. Gazzaniga (Ed.), *The cognitive neurosciences* (pp. 1091–1106). Cambridge, MA: The MIT Press.

Rolls, E. T., Robertson, R. G., & Georges-Francois, P. (1995). The representation of space in the primate hippocampus. *Society for Neuroscience Abstracts, 21*, 1494.

Rolls, E. T., & Treves, A. (1994). Neural networks in the brain involved in memory and recall. *Progress in Brain Research, 102*, 335–341.

Rosene, D. L., & Van Hoesen, G. W. (1987). The hippocampal formation of the primate brain: A review of some comparative aspects of cytoarchitecture and connections. In E. G. Jones, & A. Peters (Eds.), *Cerebral cortex*, Vol. 6 (pp. 345–356). New York: Plenum Press.

Rubenstein, J. L. R., Martinez, S., Shimamura, K., & Puelles, L. (1994). The embryonic vertebrate forebrain: The prosomeric model. *Science, 266*, 578–580.

Saper, C. B. (1984). Organization of cerebral cortical afferent systems in the rat. II. Magnocellular basal nucleus. *Journal of Comparative Neurology, 222*, 313–342.

Scoville, W. B., & Milner, B. (1957). Loss of recent memory after bilateral hippocampal lesions. *Journal of Neurology, Neurosurgery and Psychiatry, 20*, 11–21.

Sejnowski, T. J., Kienker, P. K., & Shepherd, G. M. (1985). Simple pattern recognition models of olfactory discrimination. *Society for Neuroscience Abstracts, 11*, 970.

Shepherd, G. M. (1994). Discrimination of molecular signals by the olfactory receptor neuron. *Neuron, 13*, 771–790.

Shepherd, G. M. (1995). Toward a molecular basis for sensory perception. In M. S. Gazzaniga (Ed.), *The cognitive neurosciences* (pp. 105–118). Cambridge, MA: MIT Press.

Servan-Schreiber, D., & Cohen, J. D. (1992, March). A neural network model of catecholamine modulation of behavior. *Psychiatric Annals, 22*, 125–130.

Singer, W. (1995a). Time as coding space in neocortical processing: A hypothesis. In Gazzaniga, M. S. (Ed.), *The cognitive neurosciences* (pp. 91–104). Cambridge, MA: MIT Press.

Singer, W. (1995b). Development and plasticity of cortical processing architectures. *Science, 270*, 758–764.

Singer, W., & Gray, C. M. (1995). Visual feature integration and the temporal correlation hypothesis. *Annual Review of Neuroscience, 18*, 555–586.

Singer, W., Engel, A. K., Kreiter, A. D., Munk, M. H. J., Neuenschwander, S., & Roelfsema, P. R. (1997). Neuronal assemblies: necessity, signature and detectability. *Trends in Cognitive Sciences, 1*, 252–261.

Tanaka, K., Saito, H. A., Fukada, Y., & Moriya, M. (1991). Coding visual images of objects in the inferotemporal cortex of the macaque monkey. *Journal of Neurophysiology, 66*, 170–188.

Tanaka, K. (1993). Neural mechanisms of object recognition. *Science, 262*, 685–688.

Trombley, P. Q., & Shepherd, G. M. (1993). Synaptic transmission and modulation in the olfactory bulb. *Current Opinion in Neurobiology, 3*, 540–547.

Turner, B. H., Mishkin, M., & Knapp, M. (1980). Organization of the amygdalopetal projections from modality-specific cortical association areas in the monkey. *Journal of Comparative Neurology, 1991*, 515–543.

Ungerleider, L. G. (1995). Functional brain imaging studies of cortical mechanisms for memory. *Science, 270*, 769–775.

Ungerleider, L. G., & Mishkin, M. (1982). Two cortical visual areas. In D. J. Ingle, R. J. W. Mansfield, & M. A. Goodale (Eds.), *Analysis of visual behavior* (pp. 549–586). Cambridge, MA: MIT Press.

Van Essen, D. C., Anderson, C. H., & Felleman, D. J. (1992). Information processing in the primate visual system: An integrated systems perspective. *Science, 255*, 419–423.

Van Essen, D. C., & Deyoe, E. A. (1995). Concurrent processing in primate visual cortex. In M. S. Gazzaniga (Ed.), *The cognitive neurosciences* (pp. 383–400). Cambridge, MA: MIT Press.

Van Hoesen, G. W., & Pandya, D. N. (1975a). Some connections of the entorhinal (area 28) and perirhinal (area 35) cortices of the rhesus monkey. I. Temporal lobe afferents. *Brain Research, 95*, 1–24.

Van Hoesen, G. W., & Pandya, D. N. (1975b). Some connections of the entorhinal (area 28) and perirhinal(area 35) cortices of the rhesus monkey. III. Efferent connections. *Brain Research, 95*, 39–59.

Van Hoesen, G. W., Rosene, D. L., & Mesulam, M. M. (1979). Subicular input from temporal cortex in the rhesus monkey. *Science, 205*, 608–610.

Wainer, B. H., and Mesulam M. M. (1990). Ascending cholinergic pathways in the rat brain. In M. Steriade & D. Biesold (Eds.), *Brain cholinergic systems* (pp. 65–119). New York: Oxford University Press.

Webster, M. J., Bachevalier, J., & Ungerleider, L. G. (1995). Transient subcortical connections of inferior temporal areas TE and TEO in infant macaque monkeys. *Journal of Comparative Neurology, 353*, 213–226.

Woolf, N. J. (1996). Global and serial neurons form a hierarchically arranged interface proposed to underlie memory and cognition. *Neuroscience, 74*, 625–651.

Zhou, Y., & Fuster, J. M. (1992). Unit discharge in monkey's parietal cortex during perception and mnemonic retention of tactile features. *Society for Neuroscience Abstracts, 18*, 706.

3 Attention and Neural Networks

Michael I. Posner and Rajendra D. Badgaiyan

OVERVIEW

About a hundred years ago, William James (1890) characterized attention as a distinct psychophysiological phenomenon. In *The Principles of Psychology*, he described attention as "taking possession of by the mind, in clear and vivid form, of one out of what seem several simultaneously possible objects or trains of thought. Focalization, concentration of consciousness are of its essence. It implies withdrawal from some things in order to deal effectively with others" (pp. 403–404). Much of James's description of attention is still appropriate.

Despite the familiarity of attention as a concept, until recently there was almost complete lack of understanding about the brain mechanisms underlying attentional control. This is not so surprising if one considers the fact that an understanding of attention depends on understanding of brain physiology, its mechanism of information processing, and more significantly, objective understanding and assessment of a cognitive process like attention.

As our understanding of human brain physiology develops, cognitive functions like consciousness and attention are no longer regarded as philosophical or theological entities. We have come to recognize them as independent psychological domains, intimately related to brain networks. This view has led to neurophysiological characterization of cognition in terms of the real-time activation of brain areas involved in cognitive processing, using the tools employed for functional exploration of the human brain. In recent years, use of positron emission tomography (PET) and functional magnetic resonance imaging (fMRI) techniques in conjunction with the scalp or depth event-related potentials (ERPs) have allowed us to view the activity of brain areas in real time (Posner & Raichle, 1994).

Our current progress in this area involves the combined use of brain imaging methods and analysis of the cognitive operations involved in complex human tasks. Currently available methods based on hemodynamics such as PET and fMRI lack capability for real-time analysis at the speed needed for cognitive operations (tens to hundreds of milliseconds) and there is only limited success in directly localizing sources of scalp potentials. However, taken together, these methods have begun to allow us to observe the operation of networks in real time. These networks consist of anatomical areas that have been related to cognitive operations. The identification of these operations is itself a difficult part of the problem of defining brain networks.

Current attempts to integrate information available in various fields to formulate a common strategy for understanding cognitive processes have led to the realization that the brain has an independent, anatomically identifiable attentional system. Attention-specific areas of the brain are selectively activated when the organism is engaged in a task and they interact with the sensory, semantic, and motor systems. Because our understanding of the visual system is the best developed, studies of the attentional system have most often concerned visual attention. Attention, however, involves all modalities and higher-order networks of control. This chapter emphasizes visual attention, but we examine other attentional networks as well and seek common principles of operation. In this chapter we consider some of the work involving neuroimaging, ERP, and cognitive techniques in the area of attention in order to provide a background for the construction of more detailed models that involve the brain's attention system.

ATTENTIONAL SYSTEM

Attention involves three major functions: orienting to sensory stimuli; executive functions, including detection of target events and control of cognitive operations; and maintaining the alert state. Though knowledge of the precise neural mechanisms responsible for these operations is still inconclusive, many of the concerned brain areas and networks have been identified. Thus, the orienting network for visual attention is believed to involve posterior structures such as the parietal lobe, pulvinar, and superior colliculus. The executive network is located more anteriorly, and includes frontal midline areas and basal ganglia, while the attentive alert state is maintained by the brain vigilance network operating through the norepinepherine system arising in the locus ceruleus (Posner & Petersen, 1990; Posner & Raichle, 1994).

Orienting Network

Anatomically, this network is located posteriorly, and for the visual system it is largely responsible for operations needed to bring attention to a location or object and to shift attention from an unattended to a target location. It serves to enhance information at the attended location in comparison with that that occurs at relatively unattended locations (Posner & Presti, 1987). In terms of cognitive theories, this network mediates disengagement, engagement, and amplification of the attentional target.

Parietal Lobe   The ability to disengage attention from an unattended location in favor of an attended location is a necessary component of the attentional system. In a study in which PET scanning of subjects was done while they were engaged in attentional tasks, increased blood flow was observed in the area of the pulvinar when subjects were required to separate a target location from surrounding noise (LaBerge, 1995; LaBerge & Buchsbaum, 1990). However, when attention was shifted from one location to the other, the main increase in activity was in the right and left superior parietal lobe (Corbetta, Miezin, Shulman, et al., 1993). These studies suggest that attentional operations are quite specialized within the overall network.

The function of the parietal lobe was clarified by studying patients having lesions in this part of the cerebral cortex. It was found (Posner, 1988) that patients with unilateral lesions have no problem in orienting to the target presented on the lesioned side, but when the target is presented on the contralateral field, it is either neglected or attended following a long response time. The reaction time of these patients for contralateral field targets was two to three times longer than that of normal control subjects. However, before presenting the target, when a cue indicating possible location was given, the response of these patients was similar for ipsilateral and contralateral target locations. These findings indicate that the poor performance on the contralesional side is not due to a sensory deficit and that the role of the parietal lobe can be rather specific to a disengage operation.

Laboratory studies and clinical data suggest that there are differences in attentional functions of the right and left parietal lobes. The right lobe shows increased blood flow when the task requires attentional shifts either in the right or left visual field, where the left parietal lobe is involved only in right visual field shifts (Corbetta et al., 1993). Another difference between right- and left-lesioned parietal lobe patients is in their ability to detect local or global features. When patients are shown a large figure consisting of smaller figures, patients with left parietal damage neglect small figures and report large figures, whereas those with right hemisphere damage report small figures and neglect the large ones (Robertson, Lamb, & Knight, 1988). Moreover, right-lesioned parietal patients are generally slow compared with those with left parietal lesions (Ladavas, Pesce, & Provinciali, 1989). Finally, left-lesioned parietal patients appear to be influenced by object boundaries much more than right-lesioned parietal patients. These findings help to explain the clinical observation that right hemisphere lesions produce greater attention deficit than those on the left and "neglect" as a clinical syndrome is more prevalent with right than with left hemisphere damage (Heilman & Van Den Abell, 1980; Mesulam, 1981).

Superior Colliculus   Besides the parietal cortex, a midbrain structure, the superior colliculus is also involved in the process of attentional shifts (LaBerge, 1995). The superficial layer of the superior colliculus receives input from retinal ganglion cells. It has been estimated that about 10 percent of the ganglion cells project to this layer (Van Essen, Anderson, & Felleman, 1992). The deep layer has extensive connections with the frontal eye field

(Leichnetz, Spencer, Hardy, et al., 1981), prefrontal cortex (Goldman & Nauta, 1976), and posterior parietal lobe (Lynch, Greybriel, & Lobeck, 1985). Stimulation of the cells of this layer produces movements of the eye and the head (Hikosaka & Wurtz, 1983), and these cells show increased firing just prior to saccadic eye movement (Goldberg & Wurtz, 1970). It has been suggested that the movement component of attention shifts involves a network within the superior colliculus and the disengagement and engagement components involve networks in the posterior parietal lobe and pulvinar, respectively (Posner & Raichle, 1994). There is direct evidence of involvement of pulvinar nuclei of the thalamus in visual attention in several PET studies (Corbetta, Miezin, Dobmeyer, et al., 1991; LaBerge & Buchsbaum, 1990).

Amplification Information from the attended object or location is amplified in comparison with other locations or objects. This relative amplification allows preferential higher-order processing of the target by the brain. When a target is attended, activity of the brain areas which specialize in its processing are selectively enhanced. Thus, in a PET study, wherein the subjects were required to attend to different aspects of a stimulus—its motion, form, or color—different prestriate brain areas were activated in each condition (Corbetta et al., 1991, 1993). For example, while attending to a moving object, significant increases in blood flow were found in a prestriate area of the midtemporal lobe. This area might be the human equivalent of the V5 area of the monkey, which contains cells with a strong selectivity for moving stimuli. Further, there was increased blood flow in the motor area when subjects attended to motor movement (Roland, 1984). In general, attention to sensory information appears to increase blood flow in the specific brain areas which process that event. These activations appear to give relative priority to the event to which one is attending. However, it is still not clear exactly how this amplification is accomplished. It may involve mainly reduction of unattended areas in some cases and enhancement of attended areas in other cases.

At neural and cellular levels, there are theories (Van Essen, Anderson, & Olshausen, 1994) suggesting that the amplification is relative and that it results from suppression of information from unattended objects and locations (Chelazzi, Miller, Duncan, et al., 1993; Moran & Desimone, 1985). Thus, when monkeys were trained to attend to a particular location to respond to a color change, cells in area V4, representing a nontarget location, stopped responding to an otherwise adequate stimulus (Moran & Desimone, 1985). Similar suppression has been observed in inferior temporal cortex during a visual search task. Cells that initially fired strongly to a visual object suddenly stopped responding when the monkey attended to a different object at another location (Chelazzi et al., 1993).

Suppression of nontarget information makes sense, particularly in visual tasks. In fact, early visual cells are stimulated to maximum even during passive viewing, so there is little room for target enhancement, but ample scope for suppression of nontarget objects. As the information ascends, there is enhancement of activation for target and suppression for nontarget objects. Thus, neurons of the retina, the lateral geniculate nucleus, and area V1 fire strongly to both attended and nonattended objects while the cells of extrastriate areas such as V4 show greater activity for the attended object (Moran & Desimone, 1985). It has been proposed (Felleman & Van Essen, 1991) that early visual cells have narrow receptive fields and respond mechanically to all stimuli, but as one moves up, the receptive fields widen and cells become more sensitive to the attentional targets and react less effectively to the unattended stimuli.

Executive Network

An anteriorly located attentional network is involved in attentional recruitment and it controls the brain areas that perform complex cognitive tasks. It exerts general control over the areas involved in target detection and response. This network is more active when the task involves complex discrimination (Pardo, Pardo, Janer, et al., 1990) and the degree of activation depends on the number of targets presented (Posner, Petersen, Fox, et al., 1988). The network is also responsible for anticipation of the target location (Murtha, Chertkow, Dixon, et al., 1995). Areas involved in this network are the midprefrontal cortex, including the anterior cingulate gyrus and supplementary motor area (Posner & Petersen, 1990). It may also involve areas of the basal ganglia which supply dopamine to the frontal lobe.

Norman and Shallice (1986) have presented a cognitive model that specifies some of the operations involved in this supervisory function for attention. Norman and Shallice assume that the first level of cognitive control operates via a "contention-scheduling" mechanism which uses a "schema" to coordinate well-learned behaviors and thoughts. The contention-scheduling mechanism is involved when the task demands routine selection. However, when the situation is novel or highly competitive and conflicting, a second level of control mechanism called the "supervisory system" intervenes. This system provides additional inhibition or activation to the target signal for better perception and discrimination.

Generate Uses Task It has been observed that in attentional tasks involving conflict conditions, there is activation of the anterior cingulate gyrus. One such condition is the generate uses task in which the subject is required to think of the proper use of a visual or auditory word. When the ERP evoked by this task was subtracted from that elicited by passive repeating of the words, three cortical areas of activation were observed. The first activation was located in the anterior cingulate, the second in a frontal area anterior to Broca's area, and the third in Wernicke's area (Petersen, Fox, Posner, et al., 1988, 1989; Posner, Sandson, Dhgwan, et al., 1989). Since the second and third areas are classic language areas, the first one, that is, the cingulate, should be related to attention. To further examine the supervisory function of the cingulate, subjects were allowed to practice the same uses for the words over and over again to make the task simpler and less competitive. According to the Norman-Shallice model, this procedure should not use supervisory control for execution and should be mediated by the contention-scheduling mechanism. That was exactly what was observed in a PET study (Raichle, Fiez, Videen, et al., 1994). When subjects practice the same list repeatedly, generating the same use for each word, the anterior cingulate and left lateral activations disappeared. Interestingly, these activations re-appeared when a new, unpracticed list was given to the same subjects.

Circuitry In order for a brain area to perform a supervisory function it must influence widely distributed parts of the brain where computations related to the task are performed (Posner & Raichle, 1994). Anatomical studies suggest that the anterior cingulate, like many brain regions, has close contact with many other cortical areas (Goldman-Rakic, 1988). The cingulate connections to the lateral frontal areas involved in word recognition, and the posterior parietal areas involved in orienting are particularly strong.

Recently efforts have been made to trace the dynamics of these interactions by use of ERPs (see Näätänen, 1992; Rugg & Coles, 1995 for reviews of the ERP methods). While it is difficult to determine the generator from a scalp distribution of electrical activity, if the generator is known from PET or fMRI studies it is much easier to evaluate whether the scalp distribution could come from that generator (see Heinze, Mangun, Burchert, et al., 1994, for an example of this methodology). The algorithms to relate a generator to the scalp distribution (Scherg & Berg, 1995) work best when fewer generators are involved. Thus in complex tasks, it is important to use a subtraction which isolates only a small number of brain areas.

One effort to do so is in localization of a scalp negativity that follows making an error (Dehaene, Posner, & Tucker, 1994; Gehring, Gross, Coles, et al., 1993). When subjects were aware of making an error in speeded tasks, they showed a very strong negativity following the key press in a localized area over the midfrontal scalp. Further analysis using the brain electrical source analysis (BESA) algorithm (Scherg & Berg, 1995) showed this error negativity most likely came from the anterior cingulate gyrus. Errors can be either slips, incorrect execution of a motor program, mistakes, or selection of an inappropriate intention. The Norman-Shallice model would predict supervisory system involvement in the recognition of an execution of an incorrect motor program, but not if the contention-scheduling had selected what was thought to be an appropriate response. Dehaene et al., (1994) have shown that error negativity follows a slip when the person knows the error, but not if he or she is unaware of the error (Tucker, Liotti, Potts, et al., 1994).

Studies of the generate uses minus repeat words task described above using ERPs have shown evidence of an anterior cingulate activation starting about 170 ms after the visual word (Snyder, Abdullaev, Posner, et al., 1995).

This activation was presumably related to some kind of focal attention. The cingulate activation stayed present and was joined after 50 ms by a left frontal activation.

Abdullaev and Posner (1997) took a further step in replicating the PET results. They had subjects generate uses for the same list several times. The left frontal and cingulate activations tend to go away following practice, but the activations were restored when a new list was presented or when subjects were required to generate a new use for the practiced words.

Stroop Test Another attentional task involving competitive and conflict condition is the Stroop test (Stroop, 1935). In this test, the subject is required to name the ink color of a printed word. The word can be congruent (i.e., the word *red* printed in a red color); neutral (a noncolor-related word, e.g., *top* printed in red); or incongruent (the word *blue* printed in red). In one such study (Pardo et al., 1990), imaging data were obtained by subtracting the congruent condition from the incongruent. The anterior cingulate was found to be active in three areas on the right medial portion and one area in the left inferior sulcus. In another study (Bench, Frith, Grasby, et al., 1993), an increase in right anterior cingulate activation was observed during both congruent and incongruent conditions, when compared to neutral. This finding suggests that the effort to name ink color and avoid reading the word can influence both congruent and incongruent conditions in the same way. This experiment also demonstrated that there is further enhancement of cingulate activation when the attentional demands are increased and the task is made more competitive by increasing the number of stimuli or the rate of presentation. This is to be expected if the cingulate is performing a supervisory function.

In another study of the Stroop-like effect (George, Ketter, Parekh, et al., 1994), emotional words were used instead of color words. This time there was increased activation in the left midcingulate, the left anterior cingulate, and the right midcingulate. Further, when the tasks were self-paced, there was left midcingulate activation, and the right anterior cingulate was active in externally paced tasks. These results suggest that different parts of the cingulate are involved in different computational tasks.

Thus, there is evidence suggesting involvement of the anterior cingulate in tasks that require difficult decisions. It is therefore not surprising that lesions of the frontal lobe often produce disorganized and incoherent behavior. Thus the patients having dysexecutive syndrome following closed head injury, stroke, or degenerative disorders of frontal structures have difficulty in solving problems which need prior planning (Duncan, Burgess, & Emslie, 1995; Shallice & Burgess, 1991a, b).

Cerebral strokes in the area of the cingulate gyrus cause a condition called akinetic mutism. It has been observed that these patients lack initiation for spontaneous behavior (Damasio, 1994). Work with cats and monkeys involving lesions of the cingulate (Kennard, 1955a, b) also suggests similar lack of initiation for voluntary behavior and movement. To study the supervisory function of the cingulate in a patient, the Stroop test was performed both before and after cingulotomy (Janer, & Pardo, 1991). Following cingulotomy, there was a significant deficit in performance in the congruent condition, while in the incongruent condition the performance was comparable to that in normal control subjects. Since both the congruent and incongruent conditions require a similar selective attentional mechanism, it is not clear why there was no deficit in the incongruent condition. One possibility is that the brain areas involved in executive attention may be widely distributed within the midfrontal and supporting subcortical area.

Other evidence suggesting involvement of the cingulate in supervisory attentional function comes from study of schizophrenic patients. Early positive symptoms of schizophrenia include difficulty in attention toward the right visual field and trouble in performing tasks involving Stroop-like conflict conditions (Maruff & Currie, 1995; Posner et al., 1989). These symptoms suggest dysregulation of supervisory or executive attentional functions, indicating involvement of the anterior cingulate (Early, et al, 1989a; b). Language-related problems in these patients also indicated that the deficit was in the anterior cingulate, which exercises control over both language and spatial attention. Interestingly, in a recent postmortem study, cellular abnormalities were found in the cingulate of a schizophrenic patient (Benes, 1993), suggesting possible involvement of the cingulate in the expression of schizophrenic symptoms.

Vigilance Network

The brain network responsible for maintenance of the alert state is an important component of attention because alertness is required for the execution of attentional tasks. Thus, the vigilance network should be a part of the brain's attentional system. The vigilance network comprises the noradrenergic pathways originating at the locus ceruleus of the midbrain and terminating at various locations in the cerebral cortex (Harley, 1987). This network is significantly activated when the subjects are required to maintain an alert state, particularly in the foreperiod of a reaction time task and while waiting for an infrequent target (Posner & Petersen, 1990).

During the vigilance state, heart rate and scalp electrical activities are attenuated and the blood flow in the right frontal and right parietal lobes increases. It appears that the integrity of the right frontal lobe is essential to the maintenance of attentional alertness. Patients with lesions in the right lateral frontal lobe show poor performance in tasks requiring alertness, and interestingly, these patients do not have bradycardia during the vigilance state (Wilkins, Shallice, & McCarthy, 1987). Right frontal activation has also been demonstrated in the auditory vigilance task (Cohen, Semple, Gross, et al, 1988). One of the important functions of the vigilance network is its ability to produce widespread inhibition of cortical and autonomic activities (Kahneman, 1973). When a subject is warned to attend to a target, the amplitude of background cortical activity is reduced. The reduction provides smaller background noise and helps in effective amplification of the target event.

There is evidence to suggest that at the cellular level, norepinephrine is involved in the mechanism which reduces background and enhances target activity (Jackson, Marrocco, & Posner, 1994). Thus, when a sympathomimetic drug, amphetamine, is administered, the resting blood flow of the brain decreases while the subject waits for the target and increases on arrival of the target. Similarly, administration of clonidine, an α_2-adrenerqic agonist, results in abnormal distractibility (Clark, Geffen, & Geffen, 1989). Children having attention deficit hyperactivity disorder (ADHD) have excessive distractibility, particularly if the task requires sustained attention for a long period. In fact, normal and ADHD children are the same when the target occurs within 100 ms of the cue, but, when the delay is increased to 800 ms, the performance of ADHD children is considerably poorer than normal and this is particularly true for right visual field targets (Whitehead, 1991). It has been suggested that in ADHD, there may be a failure of the vigilance mechanism, resulting in inadequate amplification for relevant signal, leading to increased distractibility (Swanson, Posner, Potkin, et al., 1991).

INTERACTION OF THE NETWORKS

The three attentional networks described above are closely interconnected. Cortical components of the orienting and executive attentional networks communicate with each other directly via cortico-cortical pathways and both of them receive input from the vigilance network through catecholaminergic projections from the locus ceruleus. In addition, prefrontal and posterior parietal cortex project to, and receive input from, the other brain regions implicated in the control of visuospatial function (Goldman-Rakic, 1988). Cortical components of these networks also communicate with the sub-cortical elements like the superior colliculus, that are involved in attentional mechanism (Jackson, Marrocco, & Posner, 1994). In addition, the executive network can modulate the activities of the orienting network indirectly through the basal ganglia. The striatum, a portion of the basal ganglia, has projections from both the prefrontal cortex, which is a part of the executive network, and the parietal cortex, which is a part of the posterior network. These connections allow the striatum to relate spatial information generated by the two networks (Jackson et al., 1994).

Alerting and Orienting

Connections between the visual orienting network and the vigilance system are strong. The locus ceruleus sends significant noradrenergic input to the parietal, pulvinar, and collicular systems (Morrison & Foote, 1986). Using these connections, the vigilance system tunes up the posterior system and, through amplification of relevant objects, enables it to interact with the information accumulating in the object recognition systems. Because of this interaction, during the highly alert state, reaction times are faster but subjects make more anticipatory reactions and have high error rates (Posner, 1978).

Basal Ganglia

A number of models have appeared suggesting specific interactions among attentional networks in the control of orienting (Jackson et al., 1994; LaBerge, 1995; LaBerge & Brown, 1989; Cohen, Romero, Servan-Schreiber, et al., 1994). These models postulate a distributed neural system the units of which interact to produce the observed functions of amplification of the attended target.

The basal ganglia have been considered to be particularly important in mediating the connection between executive and orienting networks. The structures of the basal ganglia are closely connected to the other brain areas involved in the attentional process (Jackson et al., 1994; LaBerge, 1995). The basal ganglia are united with the cortex through cortico-striatal thalamocortical circuits. It has been suggested that there are at least five such pathways through the basal ganglia, each organized in parallel and innervating different regions of the thalamus and cortex (Alexander, Crutcher, & DeLong, 1990).

The output of the basal ganglia is inhibitory and GABAergic neurons of the medial globus pallidus (GPm) and substantia nigra (SNr) are tonically active. They hold the thalamus and other structures in a state of tonic inhibition. This inhibition is modulated via two distinct pathways which are organized in opposition to one another and link the striatum to output neurons in the GPm-SNr complex. Under normal condition, these pathways are sensitively balanced by dopaminergic influence (Gerfen, 1992). Further, since the basal ganglia are the source of dopamine input to the anterior cingulate, these two structures have a close relationship.

Lesions of the basal ganglia result in spatial neglect (Villardita, Smirni, & Zappala, 1983) and it appears that the basal ganglia are important for switching attention between different sets. Thus, parkinsonian patients have reduced ability to shift between task sets (Hayes, Davidson, Keele, et al., 1998). It has been suggested that in tasks involving visual attention, the basal ganglia coordinate closely with the frontal areas to bring about suitable orientation (Posner & Dehaene, 1994). It serves the important function of uniting cortical and subcortical regions implicated in the processing of attentional information.

COGNITIVE CONTROL

In order for a brain area to perform a supervisory function it must influence widely distributed parts of the brain where computations related to the task are performed (Posner & Raichle, 1994). Anatomical studies suggest that the anterior cingulate, like many brain regions, has close contact with many other cortical areas (Goldman-Rakic, 1988). The cingulate connections to lateral frontal areas involved in word recognition and to posterior parietal areas involved in orienting are particularly strong.

What is the cingulate activation actually doing? According to our analysis the cingulate is involved in producing the local amplification in neural activity that accompanies top-down selection of items. It is easiest to understand this function in the domain of processing words. It is well-known from cognitive studies that a target word is processed more efficiently following a related prime word (Posner, 1978). A portion of this improvement occurs automatically because the prime word activates a pathway shared with the target. However, another portion of the activation is top-down because attention to the prime word leads the subject to expect a particular type of target. If the prime is masked or of low validity, the improvement in the target will be mostly automatic; however, if the prime word is of high validity or if subjects are instructed to use the prime word to think of another category, top-down effects dominate. If the target is ambiguous (e.g., the word *palm*), the prime word (e.g., *tree*) can lead to a single conscious interpretation that fits with both the prime and target words (see Simpson, 1984, for a review). We believe that the cingulate is responsible for these top-down effects by providing a boost in activation to items associated with the expectation.

Anatomically, we see the cingulate in contact with areas of the left lateral and posterior cortex that seem to be involved in understanding the meaning of a given target word. Indeed, the time course of activation of the cingulate (170 ms) and the left lateral frontal (220 ms) cortex found during the generate task support our speculation that attention interacts with the semantic activation pattern (Snyder et al., 1995).

Prime words presented to the right visual field produce rapid activation of close semantic associates, whereas prime words presented to the left visual field act more slowly and activate remote associates as well. Blocking attention to the visual word by shadowing (Nakagawa, 1991) reduces semantic priming and produces a pattern priming that resembles that found when the prime word is presented to the left visual field irrespective of the visual field to which the prime word is presented. This finding suggests a specific role of attention in producing the left hemisphere priming pattern. Similarly, prime words that are masked and those not subject to specific attentional effect based on their meaning activate a wider range of associates than those that are unmasked. These findings show evidence of the specific role of supervisory control over semantic activation patterns.

In addition, we believe that cingulate activation plays a role in the voluntary reactivation of brain areas that can also be driven automatically from input. Feature analysis of visual targets appears to involve right lateralized posterior parts of the brain. If subjects are instructed to examine a feature voluntarily, similar electrode sites are activated much later (Posner & Raichle, 1994). We believe that the cingulate is important to these activation patterns. We also believe that cingulate activation is involved when elements of a thought are reordered in time. By increasing activation of the brain area that performs a specific computation, one can change the time course of the organization of the component operations (Posner & Raichle, 1994).

The idea of attention as a network of anatomical areas makes relevant study of both the comparative anatomy of these areas and their development in infancy (Posner & Raichle, 1994). In the first few months of life, infants develop nearly adult abilities to orient to external events, but the cognitive control produced by the executive attention network requires many months or years of development. Studies of orienting and motor control are beginning to lead to an understanding of this developmental process. As more about the maturational processes of the brain and transmitter systems is understood, it could be possible to match developing attentional abilities with changing biological mechanisms. The neural mechanisms of attention must support not only common development among infants in their regulatory abilities but also the obvious differences among infants in their rates of, and success in, attentional control.

There are many disorders that are often supposed to involve attention, including neglect, closed-head injury, schizophrenia, and attention deficit hyperactivity disorder (Posner & Raichle, 1994). The specification of attention in terms of anatomy and function might be useful in clarifying the underlying bases for these disorders. The development of theories of deficits might also foster the integration of psychiatric and higher-level neurological disorders, both of which might affect the brain's attentional system.

REFERENCES

Abdullaev, Y. G., & Posner, M. I. (1997). Time course of activating brain areas in generating verbal associations. *Psychological Science, 8*, 56–59.

Alexander, G. E., Crutcher, M. D., & DeLong, M. R. (1990). Basal ganglia–thalamocortical circuits: Parallel substrates for motor, oculomotor, "prefrontal" and "limbic" functions. In H. B. M. Uylings, C. G. Van Eden, J. P. C. DeBruin, M. A. Corner, & M. G. P. Feenstra (Eds.), *Progress in brain research*, Vol. 85 (pp. 119–146). New York: Elsevier.

Bench, C. J., Frith, C. D., Grasby, P. M., Friston, K. J., Paulesu, E., Frackowiak, R. S. J., & Dolan, R. J. (1993). Investigations of the functional anatomy of attention using the Stroop test. *Neuropsychologia, 31*, 907–922.

Benes, F. M. (1993). Relationship of cingulate cortex to schizophrenia and other psychiatric disorders. In B. A. Vogt & M. Gabriel (Eds.), *Neurobiology of cingulate cortex and limbic thalamus* (pp. 581–605). Boston: Birkhäuser.

Chelazzi, L., Miller, E. K., Duncan, J., & Desimone, R. (1993). A neural basis for visual search in inferior temporal cortex. *Nature, 363,* 345–347.

Clark, C. R., Geffen, G. M, & Geffen, L. B. (1989). Catecholamines and covert orientation of attention in humans. *Neuropsychologia, 27*(2), 131–139.

Cohen, J., D., Romero, R. D., Servan-Schreiber, D., & Farah, M. J. (1994). Mechanisms of spatial attention: the relationship of marcrostructure to microstructure in parietal neglect. *Journal of Cognitive Neuroscience 6,* 377–387.

Cohen, R. M., Semple, W. E., Gross, M., Holcomb, H. J. Dowling, S. M., & Nordahl, T. E. (1988). Functional localization of sustained attention. *Neuropsychology and Behavioral Neurology, 1,* 3–20.

Corbetta, M., Miezin, F. M., Dobmeyer, S., Shulman, G. L., & Petersen, S. E. (1991). Selective and divided attention during visual discriminations of shape, color, and speed: Functional anatomy by positron emission tomography. *Journal of Neuroscience, 11,* 2383–2402.

Corbetta, M., Miezin, F. M., Shulman, G. L., & Petersen, S. E. (1993). A PET study of visuospatial attention. *Journal of Neuroscience, 13*(3), 1202–1226.

Damasio, A. R. (1994). *Descartes' error: Emotion, reason, and the human brain.* New York: Putnam.

Dehaene, S., Posner, M. I., & Tucker, D. M. (1994). Localization of a neural system for error detection and compensation. *Psychological Science, 5*(5), 303–305.

Duncan, J., Burgess, P., & Emslie, H. (1995). Fluid intelligence after frontal lobe lesion. *Neuropsychologia, 33*(3), 261–268.

Early, T. S., Posner, M. I., Reiman, E. M., & Raichle, M. E. (1989a). Hyperactivity of the left striato-pallidal projection. Part I: Lower level theory. *Psychiatric Developments, 2,* 85–108.

Early, T. S., Posner, M. I., Reiman, E. M., & Raichle, M. E. (1989b). Hyperactivity of the left striato-pallidal projection. Part II: Phenomenology and thought disorder. *Psychiatric Developments, 2,* 109–121.

Felleman, D. J., & Van Essen, D. C. (1991). Distributed hierarchical processing in the primate cerebral cortex. *Cerebral Cortex, 1*(1), 1–47.

Gehring, W. J., Gross, B., Coles, M. G. H., Meyer, D. E., & Donchin, E. (1993). A neural system for error detection and compensation. *Psychological Science, 4,* 385–390.

George, M. S., Ketter, T. A., Parekh, P. I., Rosinsky, N., Ring, H., Casey, B. J., Trimble, M. R., Horwitz, B., Herscovitch, P., & Post, R. M. (1994). Regional brain activity when selecting response despite interference: An $H_2^{15}O$ PET study of the Stroop and an emotional Stroop. *Human Brain Mapping, 1*(3), 194–209.

Gerfen, C. R. (1992). The nigrostriatal mosaic: Multiple levels of compartmental organization. *Trends in Neurosciences, 15,* 133–139.

Goldberg, M. E., & Wurtz, R. H. (1970). Effects of eye movement and stimulation on units in monkey superior colliculus. *Federation Proceedings, 29,* 453.

Goldman, P. S., & Nauta, W. J. H. (1976). Autoradiographic demonstration of a projection from prefrontal association cortex to superior colliculus in the rhesus monkey. *Brain Research, 116,* 145–149.

Goldman-Rakic, P. S. (1988). Topography of cognition: Parallel distributed networks in primate association cortex. *Annual Review of Neuroscience, 11,* 137–156.

Harley, C. W. (1987). A role for norepinephrine in arousal, emotion and learning? *Progress in Neuropsychopharmacology and Biological Psychiatry, 11,* 419–458.

Hayes, A. E., Davidson, M. C., Keele, S. W., & Rafal, R. D. (1998). Toward a functional analysis of the basal ganglia. *Journal of Cognitive Neuroscience, 10,* 178–198.

Heilman, K. M., & Van Den Abell, T. (1980). Right hemispheric dominance for attention: The mechanism underlying hemispheric asymmetries of inattention (neglect). *Neurology, 30,* 227–230.

Heinze, H. J., Mangun, G. R., Burchert, W., Hinrichs, H., Scholtz, M., Muntel, T. F., Gosel, A., Scherg, M., Johannes, S., Hundeshagen, H., Gazzaniga, M. S., & Hillyard, S. A. (1994). Combined spatial and temporal imaging of brain activity during visual selective attention in humans. *Nature, 372,* 543–546.

Hikosaka, O., & Wurtz, R. H. (1983). Visual and occulomotor functions of monkey substantia nigra pars reticulata IV: Relation of substantia nigra to superior colliculus. *Journal of Neurophysiology, 49,* 1285–1301.

Jackson, S. R., Marrocco, R., & Posner, M. I. (1994). Networks of anatomical areas controlling visual spatial attention. *Neural Networks, 7(6/7),* 925–944.

James, W. (1890). *Principles of psychology.* Vol. 1. New York: Holt.

Janer, K. W., & Pardo, J. V. (1991). Deficits in selective attention following bilateral anterior cingulotomy. *Journal of Cognitive Neuroscience, 3(3),* 231–241.

Kahneman, D. (1973). *Attention and effort.* Englewood Cliffs, NJ: Prentice-Hall.

Kennard, M. A. (1955a). The cingulate gyrus in relation to consciousness. *Journal of Nervous and Mental Diseases, 121(1),* 34–39.

Kennard, M. A. (1955b). The effect of bilateral ablation of the cingulate area on the behavior of cats. *Journal of Neurophysiology, 18(2),* 159–169.

LaBerge, D. (1995). *Attentional processing: The brain's art of mindfulness.* Cambridge, MA: Harvard University Press.

LaBerge, D., & Brown, V. (1989) Theory of attentional operations in shape identification. *Psychological Review, 96,* 101–124.

LaBerge, D., & Buchsbaum, M. S. (1990). Positron emission tomographic measurements of pulvinar activity during an attention task. *Journal of Neuroscience, 10,* 613–619.

Ladavas, E., Pesce, M. D., & Provinciali, L. (1989). Unilateral attention deficits and hemispheric asymmetries in the control of visual attention. *Neuropsychologia, 27,* 353–356.

Leichnetz, G. R., Spencer, R. F., Hardy, S. G., & Astruc, J. (1981). The prefrontal corticotectal projection in the monkey: An anterograde and retrograde horseradish paroxidase study. *Neuroscience, 6,* 1023–1041.

Lynch, J. C., Greybriel, A. M., & Lobeck, L. J. (1985). The differential projection of two cytoarchitectonic subregions of the inferior parietal lobule of macaque upon the deep layers of superior colliculus. *Journal of Comparative Neurology, 235,* 241–254.

Maruff, P., & Currie, J. (1995). An attentional grasp reflex in patients with Alzheimer's disease. *Neuropsychologia, 33(6),* 689–701.

Mesulam, M. M. (1981). A cortical network for directed attention and unilateral neglect. *Annals of Neurology, 10,* 309–325.

Moran, J., & Desimone, R. (1985). Selective attention gates visual processing in the extrastriate cortex. *Science, 229,* 782–784.

Morrison, J. H., & Foote, S. L. (1986). Adrenergic and serotonergic innervation of cortical, thalamical and tectal visual structures in Old and New World monkeys. *Journal of Comparative Neurology, 243,* 117–138.

Murtha, A., Chertkow, R., Dixon, R., Beauregard, M., & Evans, A. (1996). Anticipation causes increased blood flow to the anterior cingulate. *Human Brain Mapping, 4,* 103–112.

Näätänen, R. (1992). *Attention and brain function.* Hillsdale, NJ: Erlbaum.

Nakagawa, A. (1991). Role of anterior and posterior attention networks in hemispheric asymmetries during lexical decisions. *Journal of Cognitive Neuroscience, 3*(4), 313–321.

Norman, D. A., & Shallice, T. (1986). Attention to action. Willed and automatic control of behavior. In R. J. Davidson, G. E. Schwartz, & D. Shapiro (Eds.), *Consciousness and self-regulation* (pp. 1–17). New York: Plenum Press.

Pardo, J. V., Pardo, P. J., Janer, K. W., & Raichle, M. E. (1990). The anterior cingulate cortex mediates processing selection in the Stroop attentional conflict paradigm. *Proceedings of the National Academy of Sciences, 87,* 256–259.

Petersen, S. E., Fox, P. T., Posner, M. I., Mintun, M., & Raichle, M. E. (1988). Positron emission tomography studies of the cortical anatomy of single-word processing. *Nature, 331,* 585–588.

Petersen, S. E., Fox, P. T., Posner, M. I., Mintun, M. A., & Raichle, M. E. (1989). Positron emission tomography studies of the processing of single words. *Journal of Cognitive Neuroscience, 1,* 153–170.

Posner, M. I. (1978). *Chronometric Explorations of mind.* Hillsdale, NJ: Erlbaum.

Posner, M. I. (1988). Structure and functions of selective attention. In T. Boll & B. Bryant (Eds.), *Master Lecture in Clinical Neuropsychology and Brain Functions* (pp. 171–202). Washington, DC: American Psychological Association.

Posner, M. I., & Dehaene, S. (1994). Attentional networks. *Trends in Neuroscience, 17*(2), 75–79.

Posner, M. I., & Petersen, S. E. (1990). The attention system of the human brain. *Annual Review of Neuroscience, 13,* 25–42.

Posner, M. I., Petersen, S. E., Fox, P. T., & Raichle, M. E. (1988). Localization of cognitive functions in the human brain. *Science, 240,* 1627–1631.

Posner, M. I., & Presti, D. (1987). Selective attention and cognitive control. *Trends in Neuroscience, 10,* 12–17.

Posner, M. I., & Raichle, M. E. (1994). *Images of mind.* New York: Scientific American Library.

Posner, M. I., Sandson, J., Dhawan, M., & Shulman, G. L. (1989). Is word recognition automatic? A cognitive anatomical approach. *Journal of Cognitive Neuroscience, 1,* 50–60.

Raichle, M. E., Fiez, J. A., Videen, T. O., MacLeod, A.-M. K., Pardo, J. V., Fox, P. T., & Petersen, S. E. (1994). Practice-related changes in human brain functional anatomy during nonmotor learning. *Cerebral Cortex, 4,* 8–26.

Robertson, L. Lamb, M. R., & Knight, R. T. (1988). Effects of lesions of temporal-parietal junction on perceptual and attentional processing in humans. *Journal of Neuroscience 8,* 3757–3769.

Roland, P. E. (1984). Organization of motor control by the normal human brain. *Human Neurobiology, 2,* 205–216.

Rugg, M. D., & Coles., M. G. H. (Eds.) (1995). *Electrophysiology of mind.* Oxford: Oxford University Press.

Scherg, M., & Berg, P. (1995). *Brain electrical source analysis Handbook.* Version 2.0. NeuroScan, Inc., 10 Pidgeon Hill Drive, Suite 100, Sterling, VA 20165–6103.

Shallice, T., & Burgess, P. W. (1991a). Deficits in strategy applications following frontal lobe damage in man. *Brain, 114,* 727–741.

Shallice, T., & Burgess, P. (1991b). Higher-order cognitive impairments and frontal lobe lesions in man. In H. S. Levin, H. M. Eisenberg, & A. L. Benton (Eds.), *Frontal lobe function and dysfunction* (pp. 125–138). New York: Oxford University Press.

Simpson, G. B. (1984). Lexical ambiguity and its role in models of word recognition. *Psychological Bulletin, 96,* 316–340.

Snyder, A., Abdullaev, Y. G., Posner, M. I., & Raichle, M. E. (1995). Scalp electrical potentials reflect regional cerebral blood flow responses during processing of written words. *Proceedings of the National Academy of Sciences, 92,* 1689–1693.

Stroop, J. R. (1935). Studies of interference in serial verbal reactions. *Journal of Experimental Psychology, 18,* 643–662.

Swanson, J. M., Posner, M. I., Potkin, S., Bonforte, S., Youpa, D., Fiore, C., Cantwell, D., & Crinella, F. (1991). Activating tasks for the study of visual-spatial attention in ADHD children: A cognitive anatomic approach. *Journal of Child Neurology, 6*(Suppl.), s119–127.

Tucker, D. M., Liotti, M., Potts, G. F., Russell, G. S., & Posner, M. I. (1994). Spatiotemporal analysis of brain electrical fields. *Human Brain Mapping, 1*(2), 134–152.

Van Essen, D. C., Anderson, C. H., & Felleman, D. J. (1992). Information processing in the primate visual system: An integrated systems perspective. *Science, 255,* 419–423.

Van Essen, D. C., Anderson, C. H., & Olshausen, B. A. (1994). Dynamic routing strategies in sensory, motor, and cognitive processing. In C. Koch & J. L. Davis (Eds.), *Large-scale neuronal theories of the brain* (pp. 271–300). Cambridge, MA: MIT Press.

Villardita, C., Smirni, P., & Zappala, G. (1983). Visual neglect in Parkinson's disease. *Archives of Neurology, 40,* 737–739.

Whitehead, R. (1991). Right hemisphere processing superiority during sustained visual attention. *Journal of Cognitive Neuroscience, 3*(4), 329–334.

Wilkins, A. J., Shallice, T., & McCarthy, R. (1987). Frontal lesions and sustained attention. Neuropsychologia, 25, 359–366.

4 A Neural Network Model of Memory, Amnesia, and Cortico-Hippocampal Interactions

Jean P. Banquet, Philippe Gaussier, Jose L. Contreras-Vidal, Angelika Gissler, Yves Burnod, and Debra L. Long

Combined neuropsychological and biological evidence suggests a fundamental but selective role for the hippocampal system (Hs) in some forms of learning. Hs is necessary for rapidly (eventually, in one exposure) forming *declarative*, explicit long-term memories, whereas it appears to be unnecessary for the progressive acquisition of *procedural*, implicit memories.

Recall of previously acquired declarative memories gradually becomes independent of Hs itself. This suggests a graded process whereby traces are consolidated and stored in another structure, such as the cerebral or cerebellar cortex.

In the study of declarative explicit memory, and particularly of the role of Hs in this type of memory, human neuropsychology is historically ahead of animal neurophysiology. This unusual state of affairs raises the problem of transposing to the animal domain concepts specifically coined for human cognitive functions. Integrating in a single model concepts from neuropsychology and animal neurophysiology implicitly assumes continuity among memory processes occurring both in human and nonhuman primates or other species.

Anterograde and Retrograde Amnesia

Most authors agree that a major milestone in memory research was a result published by Scoville and Milner in 1957. They observed a dramatic but selective memory impairment following a bilateral ablation of hippocampus and related structures in the medial temporal lobe to control an otherwise intractable epilepsy. The patient H.M.'s severe memory loss can be contrasted with preserved skill learning and priming effects, including broad capacities labeled as procedural, implicit memory (Schacter, Chu, & Ochsner, 1993). Most authors draw two conclusions from these results:

1. Some (declarative) forms of memory are initially stored in Hs, and then gradually transferred to other, more permanent storage sites, such as the neocortex.

2. Other (procedural) forms of memory are directly stored in cortical areas.

These statements capture the gist of many neuropsychological results. But they do not fully explain the results. Recent results, mostly in neurophysiology, but also in neural imaging and modeling, enable more precise statements about the locus and nature of stored information. It should be noted, however, that the precise modalities of memory consolidation remain a mystery.

Hippocampus: Link-Operator Store and Multirange Buffer

Unlike some neurophysiologists (Burgess, Recce, & O'Keefe, 1994; Horel, 1994; O'Keefe & Nadel, 1978) and modelers, we suggest that Hs does not play a central role in the primitive storage and recall of the *content* of specific episodes and events. Only the *connectivities* or link operators among compressed hippocampal representations of cortical activation patterns are transiently stored in Hs. These patterns of connectivity are transferred to and developed in the cortex under Hs control. Full-fledged memory traces are initiated and finally stored at the cortical level. There is no capacity for transfer and storage of full traces in Hs. Preliminary evidence suggests that procedural memory similarly involves complex cortico-subcortical circuits but does not rely on the Hs for consolidation. The basal ganglia, in particular, appear to be involved in these cortico-subcortical circuits whenever motor responses are implicated in learned processes.

Whatever the cortico-hippocampal mechanisms involved in long-term consolidation of declarative memories, experimental results suggest that the role of the Hs extends far beyond that of a transient long-term memory (LTM) store, during the time required for cortical trace consolidation. It seems to be implicated during the very first wave of cortical processing triggered by stimulus input.

Neuropsychological evidence from amnesic patients suggests that even in the simple role of holding and buffering information, Hs is necessary in the *short-term range*, as far as information exceeds the short-term memory (STM) span. This should not be surprising since the Hs activation lag in response to an external input does not exceed a few hundred milliseconds relative to primary cortical areas. A strong conclusion is that both systems process in parallel and interactively. Similar evidence argues in favor of a crucial Hs role in the *intermediate range* as a Working Memory (WM) buffer.

A Unitary Mechanism Supporting Working and Long-Term Memory Consolidation

The Hs's multirange temporal capacity makes it a *buffer* that can reenact activation patterns of information at cortical levels. This occurs during the lengthy process of LTM consolidation and also during the moment-by-moment operation of current tasks. It functions as an intermediate register (lasting on the order of minutes) supporting WM. This last hypothetical function constitutes an *automatic working memory*. The two proposed functions are complementary; the process of LTM consolidation is engaged only when WM processing has transformed a short-lived trace to a transient LTM trace. Also, they are based on similar physiological processes, namely reenactment of cortical, electrical patterns either spontaneously or in reaction to a cortical cue. This unique process allows network activation, according to its locus of initiation, to trigger buffering and rapid learning of information in hippocampal subsystems (if the initial focus of activation is cortical) or to reactivate cortical patterns, reinstating recent memories (if the initial focus of activation is endogenous in the hippocampus).

The reactivation of cortical activity patterns derives from the capacity of the Hs to function according to two distinct, complementary modes: the *read* mode registers and processes external, cortical information; the *print* mode "endogenously" or reactively reinstates the corresponding patterns of activation locally in the hippocampal subsystems, or in both the Hs and the cortex. These two modes correspond to two clearly defined electrophysiological patterns in some animal species: theta and sharp waves (Buzsaki, 1989). In primates, only sharp waves have been consistently identified. This peculiarity may correspond: first, to a spatial localization of theta activity, which would not affect the entire hippocampal network, and second, to a functional extension of the read mode which would not be limited to the physical exploration of the enviornment but participate as a follow-up to any endogenously generated "cognitive processing." In our model, the reactivation function is related to the internal "bursting" capacity of the CA3 pyramidal neurons, and their collective capacity to synchronize under the modulation of septal inputs.

Hippocampus as a Temporal Processor

Consistent with its transient buffer function, behavioral and neurophysiological results suggest that the Hs plays a cognitive role in learning the *temporal order* of serial sequences, at least at a low level of processing. This function may be involved in the process of map formation in lower species. In addition, the conditioning literature suggests that some parts of the hippocampus play an important role in learning temporal intervals between events. Some of these functions may be based on very basic processes of differential synaptic plasticity (Granger, Whitson, Larson, et al., 1994) and on the correlational learning capacities attributed to the hippocampal subsystems, as they are applied to successive events (Banquet, Gaussier, Moga, et al., 1997a). Some other functions, such as timing, may result from population coding by cells endowed with different dynamics.

In this chapter, we review evidence for the long-term, declarative memory consolidation function attributed to long-term potentiation (LTP). In addition, we argue that the automatic WM function is supported by an intermediate transient memory (ITM) operating in parallel with the cortical WM.

We compare experimental results in both human and nonhuman primates. We contrast the WM function with the more classic LTM consolidation function attributed to Hs. We also provide physiological and behavioral evidence for Hs involvement in temporal order sequence processing and timing. This forms the basis of our neural network model implementation.

HIPPOCAMPUS IN LEARNING AND LONG-TERM MEMORY CONSOLIDATION

We propose that the Hs's memory function covers the entire temporal spectrum from STM to transient LTM, but does not include "permanent" LTM. One characteristic of Hs is the transient character of storage there. Arguments in favor of the classic LTM consolidation and WM functions will be presented successively.

We present a brief review of neuropsychology and neurophysiology of amnesia following medial temporal lobe lesion. This literature suggests that a transient LTM function of the Hs plays a causal role in LTM consolidation and learning. This role will be contrasted with a cortical function that involves mostly STM and permanent LTM registers.

• We use the term *hippocampus proper* (H) to refer specifically to the CA field (Ammon's horn).

• *Hippocampal formation* (Hf) includes the CA field, dentate gyrus (Dg), and subiculum.

• *Hippocampal system* (Hs) further includes the parahippocampal region comprising entorhinal cortex (Ec) as part of the parahippocampal gyrus, perirhinal and parahippocampal cortices.

From the vast body of experimental literature on Hs's role in memory and learning, we report only those results that are most relevant to our purpose, particularly those from neuropsychology. For a more detailed review of the experimental animal literature, see Eichenbaum, Otto, and Cohen (1994).

Our focus is the finding that a patient with an Hs lesion is unable to learn certain new information (*anterograde amnesia*) and displays graded forgetting for the most recent past preceding the lesion (*retrograde amnesia*).

Anterograde Amnesia

Hs lesions produce a profound deficit in learning new material but leave intact performance and recall based on material acquired some time before the lesion (the delay varying according to species and subjects). Scoville and Milner (1957) and Milner (1966) provided the first evidence for anterograde amnesia. They described the patient H.M., following removal of the medial temporal lobe (Hs) for the control of an otherwise intractable epilepsy. The authors proposed a relationship between the extent of the damage and the severity of the consequent amnesia.

More recent results from selective lesions in nonhuman primates and also postmortem anatomical analyses from humans have confirmed that the magnitude of the memory deficit is related to the extent of the lesion. Further, anatomically selective lesions have shown that the very nature of the functional deficit (temporal or correlational) changes with the subsystem (parahippocampal region or Hf) affected by the lesion (Eichenbaum et al., 1994).

Declarative and Procedural Memory

Whatever the extent and nature of Hs lesions, only some forms of new learning are affected. Classically, Hs is believed to be necessary for the ability to form rapid new associations for elements that one can "bring to mind," recognize as memory events, and explicitly describe. These memories can be flexibly used (in new contexts) to govern subsequent behavior. However, we argue that this close association between declarative memory and Hs function does only partial justice to the results. In particular, we argue that the declarative quality of this type of memory depends more on the cortex, the final storage site of the memory, than it does on the hippocampus itself. On the basis of experimental results, it seems likely that the Hs is involved in *correlational learning*, that is, in the formation of new associations between multiple events co-occurring in a spatiotemporal scene, where the temporal dimension is a crucial parameter taken into account by the Hs.

The temporal dimension of to-be-memorized information seems even more critical than the spatial dimension for the mandatory involvement of Hs. Here "temporal dimension" means that correlational information cannot be captured in a single snapshot, as in a simple spatial scene. Either several consecutive views of a complex scene must be taken, or the total information must be delivered in sequential parts, as in a sentence delivered word by word on a screen, or in the unfolding of a melody. This may be the reason why trace conditioning is affected by Hs lesions. Trace conditioning does not involve multidimensional stimuli, but it does involve a delay between the delivery of conditioned (CS) and unconditioned stimuli (US). Conversely, delay conditioning is not affected by Hs lesions. Delay conditioning involves a temporal dimension, but the CS and US overlap.

The declarative memory system refers specifically to LTM, and includes "episodic" memories as defined by Tulving (1983), that is, memories for the specific content of events that occur only once. Declarative memory also includes other subsystems in Tulving's taxonomy, such as *semantic* memory. In semantic memory, the factual memory aspect appears to be affected by Hs lesions, but word associations and concept or rule formation are less affected. For example, artificial grammars can be learned and used after Hs lesions. This suggests that the "declarativeness" of the memory is not as critical as whether or not information can be acquired by practice. Whenever practice is possible in the learning process, Hs becomes unnecessary. Episodic memory is just the most typical kind of declarative memory and it cannot be learned by practice. Conversely, procedural memories are characterized by the ability to learn by practice, relative inaccessibility to conscious recollection or declarative recognition, and inflexibility of use. These features are the opposite of those that characterize declarative memory. Notably, they are almost completely unaffected by Hs lesions (Schacter & Graf 1986). This suggests that much practical learning is spared in hippocampal amnesia.

Retrograde Amnesia

One characteristic of patients with Hs lesions is a temporally graded and limited retrograde amnesia. This contrasts with an ungraded and extensive amnesia following more global brain injuries involving extensive cortical damage. *Retrograde amnesia* can be defined as memory loss for events preceding the onset of amnesia. It was discovered only secondarily in hippocampal patients. Some authors question the existence of this deficit (Warrington & McCarthy, 1988; Warrington & Weiskrantz, 1978).

The first indication of retrograde amnesia in Hs lesions came from the patient H.M. who had a selective deficit for material acquired two or three years prior to surgery (Scoville & Milner, 1957). Although old material is generally spared, there is a selective deficit for prelesion memories. A forgetting gradient can be established between the two, although the specific tests used for this assessment are highly controversial.

The severity of retrograde amnesia is highly variable both between species and from one patient to the next. Its severity depends, as is the case in anterograde amnesia, on the extent of the lesion. In patients with Hs damage, retrograde amnesia spans one or two years prior to surgery (Zola-Morgan, Squire, & Amaral, 1986). With more extensive lesions, retrograde amnesia may span at least two decades (Mackinnon & Squire, 1989; Squire, Haist, & Shimamura, 1989). Thus H.M. is an exception to this rule, considering his relatively limited retrograde amnesia despite an extensive lesion.

Prospective experiments on rats and monkeys, performed at different periods before the critical Hs lesion, have confirmed the retrograde memory deficit. Different authors (Cho, Beracochea, & Jaffard, 1992; Kim & Fanselow, 1992; Winocur, 1990; Zola-Morgan & Squire, 1990) have reported severe, reliable impairments for memories acquired up to four weeks prior to surgery in monkeys, and up to a few days in rats.

Anterograde amnesia tells us that Hs is necessary in order to memorize certain new information. Graded retrograde amnesia suggests how Hs interferes with the LTM consolidation process. Together, these results provide evidence for a gradual process whereby Hs is necessary to organize and consolidate memories at the cortical (or cerebellar) level. These memories eventually become independent of the medial temporal lobe. This does not exclude the possibility that Hs is involved in their reactivation or retrieval.

INTERMEDIATE MEMORY SUPPORTING AN AUTOMATIC WORKING MEMORY COMPONENT

The existence of a graded retrograde amnesia is a strong argument in favor of a transient LTM probably based on hippocampal LTP. We now argue that WM is based on both a cortical system(s) and a hippocampal ITM. We present neuropsychological and brain imagery arguments in favor of STM and ITM functions of the hippocampus.

Psychological Arguments for an Automatic Working Memory Component

Baddeley (1986) proposed a multicomponent WM model as a substitute for Atkinson and Shiffrin's (1968) modal model. The modal model implied a unique STM store as a necessary passage to LTM. However, a single STM store could not simultaneously function as an adequate WM; therefore, it evolved into a multicomponent model (figure 4.1). Still, Baddeley viewed WM as a single common resource, with a limited capacity.

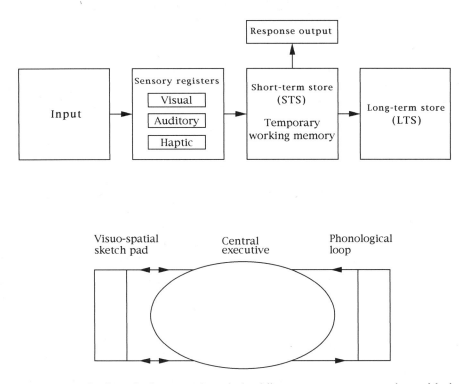

Figure 4.1 The flow of information through the different memory systems in the model of Atkinson and Shiffrin (1968) and the working memory of Baddeley (1986).

Banquet et al.: Memory, Amnesia, and Cortico-Hippocampal Interactions

Working Memory as a Cortical System

The definition of *Working Memory* as "temporary storage of information in connection with performing other, more complex tasks" is general enough to allow for many extensions and modifications of the model. Baddeley assumes a limited-capacity attentional controller, the *central executive*, that supervises two slave modality-specific systems. The *articulatory loop* rehearses speech-based information and manipulates memory for sounds. It comprises a memory store for holding phonological information for a period of 1 to 2 seconds, coupled with an articulatory control process (Baddeley, 1986). Overt or covert subvocal articulation refreshes auditory memory traces and feeds phonologically translated visual information to the phonological store. The *visuospatial sketchpad* holds and manipulates visual and spatial images. The temporary storage of visual information in a visuospatial sketchpad implies an occipital system involved in visual aspects, a parietal system involved in spatial coding, and possibly some frontal lobe participation (Goldman-Rakic, 1988). A related construct was proposed by Fuster (1995), called *active memory*. This is a state rather than a memory system and includes a widely distributed and changing representational network in the awake organism. Active memory includes WM, but does not presuppose any mental or cognitive operation.

WM function appears to be under conscious control; therefore, it is likely to have a cortical location. The same is also assumed for animal WM (Goldman-Rakic, 1988). However, the underlying brain structures that support the executive and slave systems are not fully understood. More recent versions of Baddeley's theory have incorporated results from brain imagery and animal neurophysiology (Baddeley, 1995). Unfortunately, most of the experiments to date, involving metabolic or electrical brain imaging with event-related potentials (ERPs), use paradigms that were designed to study components of Baddeley's (1986) model, the rehearsal systems in particular (Paulesu, Frith, & Frackowiak, 1993). Moreover, the ERP approach (Ruchkin, Johnson, Canoune, et al., 1991; Ruchkin, Johnson, Canoune, et al., 1992) is better suited for exploring the cortical mantle than the deep structures. Therefore, these studies confirm the involvement of cortical structures in different WM paradigms. Yet, classic recall paradigms, not formally requiring rehearsal, show joint cortical and hippocampal activation (Squire, Ojemann, Miezin, et al., 1992).

Working Memory as a Hippocampal System

Neuropsychological and imaging results suggest both an automatic component of WM supported by an intermediate register located in Hs and a controlled cortical component of the WM system, explored both in humans (Baddeley, 1986) and in animals (Fuster & Alexander, 1971). Like the cortically controlled WM, this system has both storing and processing capacity.

It is based on a complementary set of intrahippocampal and hippocampo-cortical loops. These are combined with a battery of memory registers covering a large temporal spectrum and based on transient synaptic facilitation demonstrated in different hippocampal subsystems (Buzsaki, 1988; Jones, 1993). Moreover, the operation mode of the intermediate system supporting WM is restricted to the intermediate range (minutes) of the more comprehensive LTM consolidation process generally attributed to Hs. This general process consists of maintenance or reenactment of cortical activation patterns by reverberant activity between reciprocally connected systems. A consequence of this hypothesis is that the existing dichotomy in LTM between declarative explicit memory and procedural implicit memory is extended to WM. Psychological arguments in favor of the hippocampal automatic component of WM are provided below.

Refreshing either the visuospatial sketchpad or the phonological store by rehearsal every second or so is a controlled process. This is also true of the concurrent, cognitive task, usually verbal, that is required from subjects in WM paradigms. Supposedly, the central executive responsible for planning, strategy selection, and coordination of information monitors both of these tasks. Thus, several controlled processes work in parallel. Shiffrin and Schneider (1977) demonstrated the very limited capacity for controlled processing in the human brain. Only several automatic processes, or at best, one controlled and several automatic processes, can be performed in parallel. Yet, surprisingly, the paradigms used to test WM are tractable without overwhelming difficulty, even by patients or aging subjects (Brebion, 1994). There may be several reasons for this, not necessarily mutually exclusive, and more or less implicated according to tasks and subjects. For example, a complex cognitive task used to assess WM may be largely automatized in spite of its complexity, especially when it involves verbal comprehension. Thus, attention is relatively free to focus on active rehearsal of to-be-memorized material. Alternatively, to-be-remembered information may be more or less related to the cognitive task. Therefore, competition between holding and processing functions may not be involved; rather, it may be possible to integrate the two tasks. This type of paradigm (where to-be-remembered information is related to the cognitive process in progress) is close to an actual WM involvement in natural conditions.

Certainly one cannot deny the reality of the rehearsal process. But we suggest that it is an expensive (in terms of limited, controlled processing capacity), low-level, and rote strategy that is not necessary in most everyday situations. Whenever possible, subjects use cognitive strategies to create supraordinate chunks of items to increase the limited capacity of STM. However, this is still a controlled process. We therefore propose the existence of an automatic support to WM, an ITM, that does not need rehearsal. ITM is in a functional relationship with the various cortical areas such that it readily refreshes recent memories relevant to the task in progress by simple maintenance or reenactment of the corresponding activation patterns in

Banquet et al.: Memory, Amnesia, and Cortico-Hippocampal Interactions

cortical populations. This reactivation does not preclude a state of priming or subliminal activation of the cortical areas. This function is exactly what Hs supposedly performs in the different long-term consolidation processes of declarative episodic and factual semantic memory traces. Both WM and transient LTM involve episodic, context-dependent, or factual types of to-be-memorized information. The only important distinction between the two is that one trace will have been "long-term–potentiated" and transferred to LTM, whereas the other (and eventually the activity pattern) in WM is only a candidate for LTP and must undergo a test of eligibility for permanent LTM storage.

We further hypothesize that the two proesses, LTM consolidation on the one hand, and WM refreshing on the other, are roughly similar and complementary. Only the duration during which the two types of memory traces are relevant for the brain differs. This is on the order of minutes for WMs, and weeks or months for memories that must be "permanently" consolidated in the long-term stores. They are complementary because transformation into transient LTM can only be considered when the long-term relevance of the to-be-stored information has been confirmed by processing in the intermediate hippocampal store, in the cortical WM system, or in both. The neurophysiological counterpart of information selection for long-term storage corresponds to the transition from loop-iterative and punctual activation or from short-term synaptic facilitation (based on short-term potentiation, STP) to a transient long-term synaptic facilitation (based on LTP). Both types of learning are documented at different levels of hippocampal subsystems (Buzsaki, 1988; Jones, 1993).

Neuropsychological Arguments

Neuropsychological data remain important, since brain imaging experiments performed during WM paradigms are still scarce. First, Brown (1958) and Peterson and Peterson (1959) showed that holding information in STM is dependent on rehearsal and that information is lost rapidly if active rehearsal is prevented. This fact distinguishes primary memory (James, 1890) resulting from a STM extension due to the rehearsal process from immediate STM. Second, normal subjects' responses to different recall and recognition tests show, in the absence of rehearsal, a residual memory, that is, the amount to which STM decays asymptotically. This residual memory is suppressed after a bilateral Hs lesion. Therefore, we attribute it to a hippocampal ITM component.

Classically, in amnesia following a medial temporal lobe lesion, STM is fully intact, in contrast to the complete loss of declarative LTM (Baddeley & Warrington, 1970; Cave & Squire, 1992). The picture emerging from the study of amnesic patients appears more subtle than this, particularly when one considers how the extent of the lesions influences the depth of the deficit.

The following neuropsychological arguments derive from recall and for-getting curves and visual recognition obtained by classic tests of STM and LTM, in both normals and amnesic patients. Patients show a deficit in learn-ing and recall for verbal as well as nonverbal material. In terms of our model, these tests explore both STM and ITM, according to the variable delay of recall. Since the depth and nature of a memory deficit depend on the extent and location of an Hs lesion, these parameters are taken into account in the interpretation of the results. *Bilateral* extensive lesions with complete loss of hippocampal function will be treated separately from *unilateral* lesions and partial loss of hippocampal function. But the most important parameter for separating the hippocampal from the cortical components of WM is whether or not subjects engage in controlled rehearsal, such as that performed by the articulatory loop in Baddeley's (1986) WM model.

Rehearsal Allowed

The results from subjects with complete loss of Hs function (like patient H.M.) will be emphasized since normal, or close to normal, performance on tests of STM or ITM implies normal performance when hippocampal func-tion is partially preserved. In this case, we attribute the corresponding per-formance to STM or to the controlled, cortical component of WM, since rehearsal is allowed and Hs function is lost. This complete loss of Hs func-tion results from bilateral and extensive resection of the medial temporal lobe, as in H.M.'s case, or from unilateral resection associated with severe degeneration (postmortem diagnosis) or with a severe dysfunction of the spared medial temporal hemilobe (respectively cases P.B. and H.F.).

In the first set of paradigms, rehearsal is natural, involving verbal material (consonant trigrams) well within the memory span and presented in a vari-able delay matching-to-sample task (Sidman, Stoddard, & Mohr, 1968). STM range can be extended at will in what William James (1890) called a primary memory (figure 4.2D), even for patients with total loss of hippocampal function.

In the second set of paradigms, to-be-remembered material is easily ver-balized but is at the limit of the memory span, as in the short version of the visual maze (Milner et al., 1968). This test requires memory for a sequence of turns (eight choice points). Patients cannot learn the task even after many trials. Thus, the patients have a cognitive deficit related to their inability to simultaneously maintain and organize information (type of turns to make) and implement the task (topographic translation of the turns on the maze). This is a genuine WM task in which rehearsal is not sufficient because the memory load is at the limit of the STM span. Furthermore, practice does not improve performance. There is no evidence of learning over 125 trials, as if the subject were unable to devise a learning strategy in order to split a dif-ficult task into accessible subgoals.

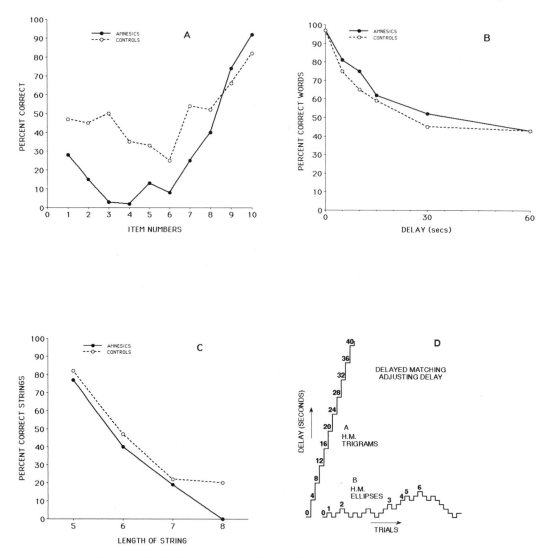

Figure 4.2 (A) Two-component free-recall task. Mean percentage correct recall (immediate recall) as a function of order of presentation for subjects presenting partial lesions of the hippocampus or Korsakoff's syndrome (amnesic) and controls. (B) Sort-term forgetting. Short-term retention of word triads for amnesic and normal controls. (C) Digit span: Immediate memory for digits in amnesic patients and normal controls. Mean percentage of sequences correct as a function of sequence length. (D) Delayed matching adjusting delay. (Adapted from Baddeley and Warrington, 1970, with permission.)

In the third set of paradigms, the to-be-memorized material is not easily verbalized (elliptic geometric forms with one variable radius to compare to a sample after various delays). In this case, extension of the STM range is not possible for patients (see figure 4.2D). Even with very sensitive measures, a limited residual control of the sample stimulus on performance is restricted to the 16 to 24-second range, the classic decremental STM range. Remarkably, this is not the case for normal subjects or even for nine to twelve year-old children. Both groups show no performance deterioration at delays up to 40 seconds. Poor performance in the case of extensive bilateral lesions has also been found in tests involving other types of geometric items (Milner et al., 1968).

Finally, evidence from classic digit span tests further extend these deficits to immediate STM. Digit sequences of various lengths are presented at a typical rate of one digit per second. Subjects name the recalled digits at their own pace. The percentage of strings correctly recalled (figure 4.2C) has an inverse linear relation to the length of the string, and is similar in amnesics and controls. But amnesics consistently perform worse on sequences exceeding the normal memory span (approximately seven items) (Baddeley & Warrington, 1970; Drachman & Arbit, 1966). These results point to another critical factor in recall performance besides the *delay of retention*, namely, *memory load*. The medial temporal lobe seems to play an important role with respect to both delay duration and memory load. Furthermore, this result shows that the medial temporal lobe helps to buffer the overflow of information out of the very-limited-capacity, attended, STM store. This suggests that rehearsal is no longer efficient as a consequence of the overflow of the immediate memory span. Still, normal subjects demonstrate residual mnemonic performance in spite of this overflow.

Taken together, these results confirm the integrity of STM for material within the immediate STM span in amnesics. They also confirm the efficiency of the articulatory loop as a rehearsal device for extending the immediate STM span into a primary memory for material that is easily verbalized. This articulatory loop is intact and efficient in Hs patients. Nevertheless, the results also suggest that rehearsal is not enough to guarantee recall or learning in patients. If the material is difficult to verbalize or exceeds the immediate memory span, as in the short version of the visual maze (Milner et al., 1968), the memory process is completely disrupted. Therefore, patients with Hs lesions find it difficult to break down a complex task into accessible subgoals. Conversely, the results do not provide strong support for a corresponding rehearsal system involved in refreshing the visual sketchpad when material is not easily verbalized. If that were the case, then patients would show normal performance in geometric tasks, which they do not.

Rehearsal Prevented

Tests in which rehearsal is prevented during the delay between learning and recall resemble experiments designed by Baddeley to test WM. Indeed, they combine holding information with an interfering task. However, they differ from genuine WM paradigms in that the to-be-remembered items are not related to the interfering task, nor are they related among themselves. Conversely, in a WM paradigm, the task is not designed to interfere with memorizing the items. The items may even be related to the task, and task performance is quantitatively evaluated. Also, in a typical WM task, STM and ITM components cannot be dissociated. These components can be dissociated in memory tests by monotonic variation of the recall delay. The results of these tests depend critically on the extent of the lesion.

Bilateral Lesions of Hs Subjects with bilateral extensive lesions of the medial temporal lobe, like the patient H.M., are in a severe, even dramatic, condition. They depend on continuous rehearsal of to-be-remembered information. Catastrophic forgetting is induced by distraction (Milner, 1966; Milner et al., 1968). The most dramatic illustration of this psychological condition was reported by Milner (1959): H.M. was able, by devising an elaborate mnemonic scheme, to remember a three-digit number for fifteen minutes, but forgot it as soon as he was distracted. Why then does a normal subject have no difficulty remembering such a number after maintaining it for fifteen minutes, even after being distracted? The hypothesis that fifteen minutes is enough exposure for a "permanent" LTM storage is not tenable. There is little chance that transient storage takes place at the cortical level; otherwise the patient H.M. should have learned this information, as he learned information in procedural memory paradigms.

Since the main difference between normals and patients in this case is the presence or absence of the Hs, it is logical to attribute the primary cause of the recall deficit to the Hs and not to the cortex. This provides no information about the actual mechanisms responsible for the storage and retrieval of information in normals. In normal subjects, continuous rehearsal cannot be directly responsible for effortless recall, since the very definition of distraction implies an interruption of the controlled rehearsal process. Recall in normals (compared to nonretrieval in patients with extensive Hs lesions) strongly suggests that continuous rehearsal somehow succeeds in rapidly laying down a trace, not at the cortical level, but at the Hs level. Our ITM hypothesis explains why normal subjects retain this information even though rehearsal is interrupted and the information is irrelevant to long-term storage (LTM consolidation was not yet involved). Fifteen minutes is well within the WM range. This is, therefore, an argument in favor of an automatic component of WM. We will see how recent findings on the multiple-range memory registers operating in the hippocampal subsystems, in conjunction with the complex closed-loop system of the hippocampus, may provide information about the actual mechanisms responsible for these transient intermediate-range remembrances (which are very useful for our moment-to-moment processing of the continuous information flow).

A more formal assessment of this type of patient was performed in a visual memory task based on face recognition. Subjects were shown twelve faces and 90 seconds later had to select these faces from an array of twenty-five. Patients' performance fell to chance level when a distracting task was interpolated between presentation of the two sets of photographs (Milner et al., 1968). We have seen previously how an excess in memory load, or difficult verbalization of to-be-remembered material, is equivalent to preventing rehearsal.

Partial Lesion of Hs   The picture is apparently different when there is *partial preservation* of hippocampal function. This is the case in patients after *unilateral temporal lobectomy*, or in alcoholic patients suffering from *Korsakoff's syndrome*. Both groups show an identical pattern of results (Baddeley & Warrington, 1970). As we have seen, delayed recall tests with interfering tasks are similar in some respects to WM paradigms. The variable delay between item presentation and recall allows a quantitative separation between deficits in STM (less than 20 to 30 seconds), and those in intermediate memory (beyond this range). This is not the case in WM paradigms, which involve a more natural situation, in the sense that the to-be-memorized material may be related to the associated processing task.

In the *short-term forgetting* task, subjects receive item sequences (three words) well within the memory span. These are presented for 3 seconds. Subjects are asked to recall the item sequences after delays varying according to trials (0, 5, 10, 15, 30, or 60 seconds). During these delays, they perform a tightly controlled intervening task designed to prevent rehearsal. The forgetting curves show an exponential decay (figure 4.2B) and reach asymptote within 30 seconds, which is the maximum range of STM. For this reason, the corresponding decay can be fully explained by STM decay. Conversely, residual information held beyond this short-term range can be attributed to an intermediate store independent of either the articulatory loop or other controlled cognitive processes, since the latter are prevented by the experimental design. Therefore, the process responsible for this memory is automatic. The two curves are similar in controls and in unilateral temporal lobectomy and Korsakoff's patients. This can be attributed to a close-to-normal cortical function sustaining the STM capacity, combined with a residual hippocampal function attributed to the spared side of the Hs. Alternatively, it may be attributed to the diffuse and partial lesions of Korsakoff's syndrome, in a situation where to-be-remembered items are well within the STM span (three items). This interpretation is strongly suggested by patients with bilateral lesions who exhibit catastrophic forgetting when faced with an interference situation. Moreover, electrical brain imaging evidence suggests that unilateral hippocampectomy causes little change in cognitive ERP patterns (in particular, P300) recorded on the scalp, with the possible exception of very limited areas of the temporal lobes where a trend toward asymmetry is seen (Johnson, 1995).

In the classic *free recall*, two-component task, lists of unrelated items exceeding the memory span (e.g., ten words) are presented to subjects at a pace similar to that of the previous experiment. Subjects recall the items after a variable delay, during which they perform an intervening task. The main difference from the previous task is that the memory load here exceeds the memory span. In the zero delay, immediate-recall condition, rehearsal is prevented by the ongoing presentation of to-be-recalled new stimuli in spite of the absence of an intervening task. The recall curves (figure 4.2A) for controls show very robust primacy and recency effects (Glanzer & Amitz, 1966). The recency effect is classically attributed to a persistence of items in STM. As such, it disappears both in patients and controls when they perform an intervening task for 30 seconds between presentation and recall. The primacy effect is also classically attributed to LTM. But in the context of our model, it is dependent on ITM. The primacy effect deteriorates at zero delay even in patients with partial preservation of medial temporal lobe functions (see figure 4.2A). It is completely abolished in the same patients after 30-second delays, whereas it persists in normal controls. Thus, partial preservation of medial temporal lobe function is no longer sufficient to prevent intermediate memory deficiency when the memory load exceeds the STM span, as is the case in the short-term forgetting task when the memory load falls within the STM span.

In summary, patients with both bilateral and unilateral lesions of the Hs show close to normal immediate STM for verbal information within the STM span (typically three items) and can extend this temporal range when rehearsal is possible. Both types of patients show catastrophic loss of information when there is overflow beyond the strict STM span. This loss of information is much less systematic and dramatic in normal subjects. There are some indications that the STM span may be reduced in patients. When information is well within the memory span, patients with unilateral temporal lesions or Korsakoff's syndrome show almost normal intermediate-range memory capacity, independent of rehearsal. This is not the case for those with bilateral temporal lesions. It must be emphasized that the side of the unilateral temporal lobectomy influences which type of performance is spared (verbal or visual). Thus, both the forgetting curves and the primacy-recency effect in partial lesions support the distinction between an immediate STM and an ITM. Further, the distinctive behavior of patients with bilateral extensive ablation or lesion of Hs corroborates ITM as a possible automatic support (non–rehearsal-based) for WM.

Brain Imaging

The development of brain imaging techniques based on electroencephalography (EEG), magnetoencephalography (MEG), positron emission tomography (PET), and functional magnetic resonance imaging (fMRI) makes it possible to investigate directly the anatomy and function of memory, both in normal subjects and in patients. The few results obtained by these techniques vary according to the experimental paradigm. They lend support to both cortical and hippocampal components of WM.

Electrical Brain Imaging

Electrical brain imaging can be used to record ERPs. ERPs are scalp potentials that reflect different cognitive processing operations performed by the brain. ERP responses are individualized on the basis of their latency and topography. Some reflect automatic identification of the stimulus, such as N200 (negativity at 200 ms) mismatch negativity; others such as processing negativity (Näätänen, 1982) reflect attended stimulus processing (Banquet, Smith, & Renault, 1990); and still others such as P300 (positivity at 300 ms) reflect context processing or updating. ERP investigations of WM confirm the involvement of various modality-specific or associative cortical regions for components later than P300, such as P600 and over (Ruchkin et al., 1991, 1992). Surprisingly, P300, which is related to context updating and probability processing (Banquet, Renault, & Lesèvre, 1981; Johnson & Donchin, 1982), does not reflect the cortical "explicit" component of WM. These results support the involvement of cortical areas in WM, but do not exclude the participation of deeper structures, such as Hs, in typical WM or other types of paradigms. Indeed, scalp electrical recordings (e.g., EEG) predominantly, if not exclusively, explore the cortical mantle. Furthermore, P300-like activity has been recorded in the hippocampus (Halgren, Squires, Wilson, et al., 1980). But the P300 hippocampal source is not the generator of cortical P300s. Further, it has little influence on cortical P300 generators, since right or left hippocampectomy does not induce any significant cortical asymmetry. There are, however, two notable exceptions. First, far-lateral temporal electrodes (T5—6) in oddball paradigms show a reduced P300 on the side of Hs removal. Second, left hippocampectomy induces a change in P300 behavior, rather than P300 asymmetry, along with a performance deficit in the number of correctly recognized items in recognition paradigms involving stimulus familiarity (Johnson, 1995).

Positron Emission Tomography and Magnetic Resonance Imaging

Neural correlates of verbal WM involving the articulatory loop have been explored by PET measures of regional cerebral blood flow in a task engaging components of the articulatory loop, the phonological store, and the subvocal rehearsal system. Performance on this task was compared to a simpler condition involving only the subvocal rehearsal system (Paulesu et al., 1993). This paradigm allowed experimenters to localize the phonological store to the left supramarginal gyrus and the subvocal rehearsal system to Broca's area. These results provide strong support for a cortical component of WM, and more specifically, the articulatory loop. Nevertheless, the absence of significant Hs involvement does not argue against the role of Hs in WM since subjects were explicitly instructed to rehearse the to-be-recognized consonants after a two-minute delay period. It must also be noted that the task involved recognition and not recall.

Squire, Ojemann, Miezin, et al. (1992) have presented one of the most salient arguments for combined cortex and hippocampus involvement in ITM. In a delayed (three-minute), cued recall paradigm involving no interfering task, subjects learned visually presented word lists (fifteen words). During cued recall, PET scans revealed significant activation of the right hippocampus and parahippocampal gyrus, plus the right (and to a lesser degree left) frontal lobes (figure 4.3) compared with baseline conditions. The left hippocampal region and amygdala did not change their activation level during cued recall. In our model, this task corresponds to a test of ITM support for WM, because recall was delayed and the memory load exceeded the STM span. The absence of any interfering task during the delay may have favored rehearsal strategies and a bias toward cortical activation. But this bias may have been limited by the length of the item list. Nevertheless, the activation of Hs along with the frontal lobes provides strong support for a WM with two components, cortical and hippocampal, combined in a closed-loop system. The selective activation of the right Hs can be explained as a bias toward processing the visual characteristics of the word forms introduced by the cued recall (visually presented stem completion).

The dual involvement of Hs in both priming and cued recall (see figure 4.3) contrasts with the selective involvement of the frontal lobes in cued recall. This suggests that the declarative aspect of memory involved in recall (in contrast to the automaticity of stem-completion priming) is a cortical, possibly frontocortical, characteristic. At the same time, it justifies the term "automatic component of WM" for ITM. Squire has interpreted these results in light of his theory of Hs's role in the declarative aspect of memory. Thus, Hs activation in the simple priming task is accounted for by a covert implication of explicit memory during priming (Squire et al., 1992). We propose a somewhat different explanation. We attribute the involvement of Hs in stem-completion priming to the automatic characteristic of this task which matches the automatic aspect of ITM support for WM. This explanation predicts a decrease in prefrontal activation to a level close to the baseline condition during the priming task. This is a reasonable prediction if we assume that the declarative character of memory is independent of the process of consolidation and that the final repository of memories is cortical.

Recent results from PET paradigms manipulating spatial WM factors in humans show the involvement of the hippocampal formation during these tasks (Owen et al., 1996; Petrides et al, 1993). More important, a PET study of prefrontal cortex (Pf)-limbic system interactions during a WM task for faces involving three delays (3.5, 12.5, and 21 seconds) shows dominant interactions between (1) extrastriate areas and anterior temporal-inferior Pf cortices at no delay, (2) hippocampal and cingulate areas at short and medium delays, and (3) Pf-cingulate and Pf-temporal/occipital cortices at long delays (McIntosh et al., 1996). Such results are consistent with our hypothesis concerning the early involvement of Hs during processing. Cortico-limbic interactions can be interpreted as a process for maintaining an iconic repre-

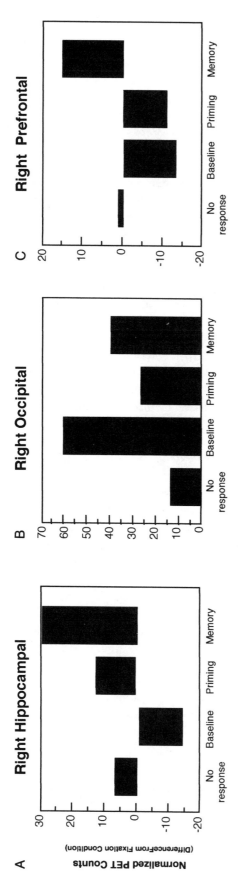

Figure 4.3 Behavior of the right hippocampal (*left*), right occipital (*middle*), and right prefrontal (*right*) regions, in comparison to the fixation-point control condition, for four task conditions: (a) no response; (b) baseline stem completion by first word to come to mind: no stem could form words presented; (c) priming: stem completion by first word to come to mind; half the stems could form words already presented; (d) stems had to be used to recall words from the list presented; half of the stems could be completed to form these words. The right hippocampal response observed in memory minus baseline subtraction (see figure 2A, table 1, in Squire et al., 1992) did not arise simply as a result of reduced hippocampal activity in the baseline condition. A right hippocampal response was observed both in the priming minus baseline subtraction and in the memory minus priming subtraction. Conversely, the right prefrontal response was more specific to the memory task. (Adapted from Squire et al., 1992, with permission.)

sentation of faces, supporting our interpretation of the function of the cortico-hippocampal loops. Decreased limbic involvement at long delays may mean the end of fast learning (with transition from active potentials to STP) and transfer of activity to previously involved cortical areas triggering the process of consolidation.

HUMAN VS. ANIMAL WORKING MEMORY

The WM construct emerged almost simultaneously in animal and human research. In parallel with human neuropsychological studies of WM (Baddeley & Hitch, 1974), the concept was developed independently by Olton et al. (1979) in animal learning to refer to the capacity to retain information across trials within a test session. These authors were among the first to propose that the Hs may be necessary for animal WM (memory for recent information that has current and specific relevance). However, the hippocampus may also be equipped for active information selection and processing, in line with human models of WM. In the radial maze of Olton et al., each arm is baited with food. On a series of trials in the same session, the animal avoids revisiting an arm from which it has already taken food, suggesting that it retains behavioral events associated with entering each arm. Thus, WM may encode specific episodes associated with specific maze arms. As such, it may represent the ITM equivalent of episodic memory. But performance may also be guided by the stronger relative familiarity of cues related to arms visited most recently.

In the 1970s, recordings performed on awake monkeys trained on delay response tasks were used to extend the concept of WM. These recordings showed that some prefrontal cortex neurons were activated during the delay period between stimulus and response (Fuster & Alexander, 1971; Niki, 1974). These activities were supposed to reflect the cellular expression of mnemonic processes. The evidence in favor of a mnemonic process rather than a motor set or any other activity was made more convincing by the discovery of some specificity in the response. In an oculomotor delayed-response paradigm, neurons alter their discharge rate for only one or a few target locations, thereby demonstrating a kind of memory field (Funahashi, Bruce, & Goldman-Rakic, 1989). This result has been extended to other brain areas, the inferotemporal cortex during delayed match-to-sample (DMS) tasks in particular (Fuster, 1997; Fuster & Jervey, 1981; Miyashita & Chang, 1988).

This form of memory has been called *active* by some authors, in contrast to *passive* (Eichenbaum et al., 1994). Passive memory is characterized by a reduced response to familiar or repeated stimuli. Some neurons in the inferior temporal cortex fired much less in response to an immediately repeated stimulus in a serial recognition task (Baylis & Rolls, 1987; Rolls, Baylis, Hasselmo, et al., 1989). Item specificity of the neuronal response was also demonstrated (Baylis & Rolls, 1987; Miller, Li, & Desimone, 1993). This paradoxical response has been interpreted as a rapid form of habituation. The decrement in stimulus-elicited firing may reflect decreased responsiveness of cortical neurons to familiar stimuli. In contrast to an active memory, this passive response may be interference-resistant and persist through the presentation of intervening mismatch choice cues within the same trial (Miller et al., 1993). Yet both active and passive memory representations disappear between trials, suggesting a system that is reset when the information is no longer relevant. Nevertheless, a gradual, cumulative decrement of response to multiple repetitions of items across testing sessions supports our hypothesis; there is a graded transition between ITM support for WM and transient LTM based on LTP support for permanent LTM consolidation. It should be noted that this decrement in response to stimulus repetition is dependent on an automatic, passive type of processing. When the sample stimulus has to be actively maintained for comparison with several test stimuli, stimulus repetition does not induce a decreased response, but an increased one (Miller and Desimone, 1994).

There are striking similarities between electrophysiological recordings in monkeys and brain imaging in humans, both electrical recording of ERPs on the scalp and metabolic PET imaging. We mentioned previously the functional significance of specific ERP components. In particular, N200 or mismatch negativity reflects automatic identification of the stimulus in an iconic or echoic memory; others such as processing negativity represent attended stimulus processing; and still others such as P300 reflect context processing or updating. When two types of stimuli are sequentially presented with different probabilities (rare and frequent), the P300 and N200 responses to rare and frequent stimuli are very similar at first and then become smaller for frequent stimuli and larger for rare stimuli. This evolution in response amplitude takes place after only a few stimuli (less than ten) for P300, but needs more stimulus presentations for N200 (Banquet & Grossberg, 1987). This kind of probability processing is fully automatic and is better reflected by P300 amplitude when the subject is not aware of it (Johnson & Donchin, 1982). The decrease in amplitude of response to frequent stimuli can be compared to the decrease in neuronal response to stimulus repetition in monkeys.

Conversely, processing negativity, corresponding to an attended, selective filtering of only some preselected stimuli, remains insensitive to event frequency and shows an increased amplitude in response to a match (i.e., repetition) condition. The same results hold for PET imaging. Decreased activation was found in the occipital cortical areas in response to items that had been recently presented (Squire et al. 1992). Squire has interpreted this as a reduction in neural computations required for processing recently presented information. The similarities between human and animal electrophysiological activities extend to a preparatory set. A contingent negative variation (CNV) paradigm in humans is a formal analog of experiments used in monkeys to explore WM (Fuster, 1997; Niki, 1974). After a warning stimulus (S1) and a delay, an imperative stimulus (S2) commands the subject to emit a (usually motor) response. Just as the delay neuron recordings in monkeys show early, late, and intermediate activity, the CNV has two distinct components in the S1–S2 interval, an early one that is related to S1 processing and a late frontocentral component with a ramplike activity preceding S2. This late component does not just correspond to a motor set, but also reflects timing and perceptual-cognitive set (Ruchkin et al., 1992).

FUNCTIONAL MODEL OF HIPPOCAMPO-CORTICAL RELATIONS

We first present the functional model of hippocampo-cortical relations, then recapitulate arguments in favor of different components of the model. In the course of this chapter, arguments from neuropsychology and brain imaging have been provided to argue that the Hs is involved in every phase of information processing, from the very short-term to the transient long-term. There are also some arguments against Hs involvement in "permanent" LTM, although opinions diverge on this issue. Thus we have chosen to contrast hippocampal function that is devoted specifically to information selection and consolidation with cortical function that supports a direct dialectic confrontation between STM and LTM during learning, recall and recognition.

The first claim concerns the complementarity between cortical and hippocampal memory systems. The cortex is primarily involved with short-term and long-term permanent memory registers, even though range variations exist from primary areas to secondary and association areas (Lü, Williamson, & Kaufman, 1992). And it has a relatively specific capacity for slow learning. The hippocampus is richly endowed with a full spectrum of temporal ranges, from the short-term to the transient long-term, possibly at the exclusion of the permanent long-term. More specifically, this combination of diverse memory registers, with diverse closed loops of different sizes, including one to at least five synaptic relays, seems unique in the brain. It is probably responsible for the one-exposure learning that is peculiar to the hippocampus. This capacity constitutes a turning point in phylogenesis, because it can be linked to the development of an actual ontological dimension in individuals, and more specifically to personality in primates. On the basis of logical arguments yet to be experimentally confirmed, we suggest that fast-transient learning should take place not only inside the hippocampus but also at the interface of the convergent cortico-hippocampal pathway (either entorhinal cortex or dentate gyrus) and at the interface of the divergent hippocampo-cortical pathway (possibly in superficial cortical layers). Conversely, experimentally confirmed slow-permanent learning in the neocortex may be restricted to the level of polysynaptic cortico-cortical connections.

The second claim concerns the complementarity of the two aspects of hippocampal transient memory: ITM, which supports WM function, and transient LTM, which supports the process of LTM consolidation. These complementary functions cooperate to fulfill the contradictory constraints of storing as much relevant information as possible in a large but limited-capacity system. The WM function thought to operate both at cortical and hippocampal levels is devoted to the segregation between information worthy to be "permanently" stored because of its relevance to survival or its human social relevance to the personal history of the subject, and information that can be forgotten without major damage. For this purpose, several hard-wired devices implement different functions in various subsystems of the hippocampus: severe filtering on the basis of stimulus intensity, duration, or repetition (mostly at the level of the entorhinal cortex); orthogonalization of noncorrelated patterns of information, with lumping correlated information or suppression of redundant patterns (possibly in the dentate gyrus), or both; and correlation of these orthogonal patterns on the basis of spatio-temporal criteria of co-occurrence (autocorrelation) or sequential ordering (heterocorrelation). The CA3 subsystem is specifically equipped for these correlational processes. There is some evidence for temporal order processing of events at the level of CA1 (Granger et al., 1994).

All of these functions argue in favor of a specific processing capacity devoted to the Hs, based on ITM. This capacity may be devoted more to temporal aspects of information (like temporal order and timing) than to spatial mapping, which is the focus of current investigation. Specifically, spatial mapping would include a strong temporal dimension (in the sequential recording of snapshots), where temporal order is no longer relevant. Correlational processing may be the hallmark of Hs and may account for many aspects of its cognitive processing, including temporal processing (Banquet et al., 1997a, b). On the basis of the CA3 associative architecture, artificial systems can be designed so that temporal order processing becomes a special case of correlational processing. The main difference is that events occur in sequence, instead of taking place simultaneously.

The other class of transient memory is transient LTM based on LTP, which supports permanent LTM consolidation. The most prominent sites of LTP in the hippocampus are at the CA1 level, but they are also in the entorhinal cortex, dentate gyrus, and CA3. LTP is not specific to the hippocampus. Different cortical areas are also prone to LTP. What seems specific to the Hs is the conjunction of systems susceptible to LTP with shorter versions of synaptic facilitation. This occurs in an architecture adapted to facilitate a smooth transition between short-term and long-term facilitation, with no need to resort to externally dependent repetitions of activation. These two functions of ITM and transient LTM are therefore complementary. Indeed, information has to proceed through the cortical or hippocampal WM in order to be certified as relevant to the history of the individual. This certification could correspond to the transition from ITM supported by short-duration synaptic facilitation (STP) to transient LTM supported by LTP.

The third claim concerns the unique mechanism that supports WM operation and LTM consolidation. This unique process takes advantage of the reciprocal, topographically organized connections between cortex and hippocampus, combined with the endogenous property of pyramidal neurons (mostly in the CA3 region) to discharge by bursts (Buzsaki, 1989), and to synchronize within populations connected by previously facilitated synapses. Sharp waves consistently recorded in rodents have also been found in primates and humans. They may form the basis for reactivation of recently facilitated neuronal populations at the hippocampal level, at the cortical level, or at both. They would correspond to what we call the print mode of the Hs. In episodic learning, the print mode would subserve the function attributed to practice during the formation of procedural memories.

Two general mechanisms cooperate in the reactivation of cortical patterns, triggered by these endogenous hippocampal bursting and synchronization capacities or by hippocampal reactions to cortical activation of cue patterns. First, there is reverberating activity between reciprocally connected networks. This has been used in neural network modeling as a mechanism for synaptic weight modification leading to class learning (Grossberg, 1976a, b). Second, neural population synchrony, a consequence of reverberant activity, has been presented as a plausible temporal coding used locally by the brain for the coalescence of features into a unified percept (Gray, König, Engel, et al., 1989; Singer, 1991). The main contention of our model is that the central location of the hippocampus as a site for both convergence from, and divergence toward, the different cortical areas allows the Hs to act as an information-selective pacemaker (Banquet, 1983; Banquet & Contreras-Vidal, 1994). As such, it can selectively synchronize distant cortical areas that have been coactivated previously. This mechanism refreshes memories during WM operation and reactivates cortical patterns during the more lengthy process of LTM consolidation. In the latter case, it creates conditions for the slow facilitation of distant polysynaptic cortico-cortical connections that eventually make recall and recognition independent of hippocampal function.

The last claim is largely but not universally accepted. Information that is processed through the hippocampus may not be permanently stored there, at least in humans. In addition to anatomical arguments like the relatively limited capacity of the system, the strongest support for this claim comes from the limited range of the retrograde amnesia in hippocampal lesions. Most memories from the distant past are spared. This suggests that information is transferred to cortical or cerebellar areas, which are among the most prominent sites of permanent storage.

We now summarize the arguments that support our model. In favor of an early Hs involvement in information processing, neurophysiological evidence suggests that the lag in Hs activation in response to an external input, compared to primary cortical areas, does not exceed one or two hundred milliseconds. In particular, the P300 ERP component can be simultaneously recorded at cortical and hippocampal sites (Halgren et al., 1980). At a behavioral level, neuropsychological evidence confirms that patients with partial Hs lesions show complete disruption of STM span performance when the memory load is at or exceeds the limit of the STM span. The prorogation by rehearsal of STM in a primary memory (James, 1890) is possible for patients in very limited conditions of memory load, absence of interference, and type of material to be memorized (easily verbalized). Thus, experimental evidence supports the existence of a period, starting as early as during immediate STM, when cortical and hippocampal activation and processing overlap. During this period, the cortex can both hold and process information, in very restrictive conditions. This interpretation explains why, at first glance, STM appears to be unaffected by hippocampal lesions. But the importance of hippocampal function, particularly in WM, may have been underestimated in previous investigations.

We will not summarize arguments in favor of a transient LTM in the hippocampus. This would amount to describing again those results that support a graded retrograde amnesia buttressing the LTM consolidation hypothesis. At the neurophysiological level, there is an extensive literature on hippocampal LTP and its potential role in learning; however, a review of this literature is beyond the scope of this chapter. Thus, we justify the distinction between STM and ITM, and also between ITM and transient LTM, on functional grounds. Both transient LTM and ITM refer to transiently stored information. The distinction between the two constructs involves the behaviorally justified dichotomy between the two functions of WM and LTM consolidation. It emphasizes two points: (1) the LTM consolidation function concerns information that has already been selected for storage; and (2) therefore it should be supported by more elaborate neurophysiological mechanisms.

Briefly stated, STM deals with the immediate STM span, and stored information there decays rapidly if it is not rehearsed. There is a floor effect to this decay, and asymptote is reached in less than 30 seconds. This constitutes the maximal range of the STM store. The spared information beyond this lapse of time can be attributed to an ITM (minutes range) store. ITM functions to retain information as an automatic support to WM. It also supports an important processing function; in cooperation with cortical processing, it allows segregation of information into storable and nonstorable parts.

At the neuropsychological level, there are several arguments in favor of ITM. First, a primacy effect in the dual-task, free-recall paradigm, and its disappearance in patients with partial Hs lesions, suggests a short-lived ITM located in Hs. The classic interpretation of the primacy effect as an LTM effect is no longer tenable, in view of evidence for a consolidation phase preceding "permanent" LTM. Further, the delay between first-item presentation and recall is on the order of a few minutes maximum. This time range has been characterized by research on amnesia as pertaining to an intermediate store. Second, the chance level performance of hippocampal patients on various delayed recognition tasks (face recognition in particular), whenever an intervening task is interpolated between performance and recall, and their failure to perform (or to learn by practice) short versions of a visual maze support a deficit in ITM. This deficit is not just a memory deficit. It is a cognitive deficit involving the inability to partition a complex goal into accessible subgoals (this is also a consequence of damage to the frontal lobes whose function relies on WM processes). ITM can be viewed as an automatic aspect of WM. Many of the delayed-response tasks in animals and humans, particularly delayed matching- or nonmatching-to-sample tasks, explore ITM. They show a dramatic perturbation with extensive Hs lesions. This perturbation in humans is conditional on the prevention of rehearsal and on the nature (geometric) of the to-be-memorized material.

Neurophysiological evidence in favor of ITM is less familiar, and therefore little emphasized in the literature. First, the architectural concatenation of Hs subsystems, and of Hs and cortex in loops with variable numbers of synaptic relays, was noted long ago, in particular the classic *trisynaptic loop*. Yet this information has had little impact on models of hippocampal function. Furthermore, the crucial importance of the trisynaptic loop as the information highway through the hippocampus has been deemphasized by the more recent discovery of the functional importance of shortcuts from the perforant path through CA3, CA1, and subiculum (Amaral & Witter, 1989; Jones, 1993). There is evidence for the actual operation of these loops, at least in experimental conditions. The same CA population of neurons first give an electrophysiological response to a single stimulation of the perforant pathway, and delayed attenuated second and eventually third iterative responses (Buzsaki 1989). The mechanism responsible for the topographic stability of the activated neuronal population during iteration is unknown. In neural network modeling, recycling information through a closed loop is a classic design for maintaining information in STM. In physiological situations, the maintenance of relevant memories in an active state does not need to be permanent for the entire duration of task performance, only punctual. It may have a twofold functionality. Cortico-hippocampal loops may maintain memory in an active state punctually during the phases of processing that actually use this information. In this way, these loops originate the activation of cortical (frontal or temporal) neurons that fire in the interval between two stimuli or between stimulus and response. Also, the intrahippocampal loops responding by a few iterative electrical responses to a single perforant path excitation may foster STP in the corresponding circuit relays and make a transition with LTP.

Relative to this last point, almost every hippocampal subsystem seems to demonstrate a capacity for LTP. In spite of this apparent uniformity in the LTP process, different phenomena seem to correspond to different mechanisms. Post-tetanic potentiation (PTP) does not exceed a few minutes; STP lasts for about one hour; LTP itself can be classified into three groups according to its rate of decrement: LTP1 lasting hours, LTP2 for a few days, and LTP3 for weeks or months. The same synapses appear able to undergo any one of these transformations, according to the intensity or duration of the activation, at least at some hippocampal sites. They may represent, under natural conditions, different steps of synaptic facilitation, generated or not according to the intensity or duration of the eliciting event. The alternative hypothesis is that different hippocampal subsystems exhibit specific types of LTP, according to the widely distinct functions they appear to perform. In this regard, entorhinal cortex has the capacity both for classic LTP and also for very short facilitation (during an input with increased frequency) that allows action potentials to overcome the hyperpolarization barrier (Jones, 1993). Dentate gyrus seems to be endowed with a wide variety of ranges, and may favor cooperativity in its mode of LTP generation because of the high convergence of perforant path fibers that it receives and its high threshold for activation. The facilitation of the mossy fiber–CA3 synapse needs postsynaptic depolarization for its generation, even though the induction of LTP there does not depend on NMDA receptors, but rather on opiate receptors which are recruited by repetitive activation. Conversely, by design, the CA3 system must be more prone to associativity. It has both ITP and LTP, according to its synaptic contact type (mossy fiber vs. associative-commissural). CA1 LTP constitutes the reference model of synaptic facilitation whose generation seems easier than at the CA3 level. Some forms may even be nondecremental in specific conditions (Staubli & Lynch, 1987).

In conclusion, a whole temporal spectrum of synaptic facilitations is available in the Hs. It is premature to claim that the hippocampus is the only system to be so richly endowed. It may also be true of cortical potentiation. The consolidation hypothesis requires a precise mapping between specific hippocampal and corresponding cortical populations, particularly at the level of the hippocampo-cortical connections. There is no anatomical support for such precise hard-wired mapping, in spite of evidence for a loose preservation of topology between cortex and hippocampus in the longitudinal dimension. A plausible implementation of such mapping may involve a transient LTP at the level of the reafferent connections taking place at the interface between hippocampus and cortical layers (Burnod, 1990). LTP is known to take place in different cortical areas. There may also be a gradient in the duration and diversity of the memory registers on the path from hippocampus to cortex through the parahippocampal system. In any case, we can state that a unique multiple-loop system resides in the Hs whose synaptic relays may be facilitated for a wide variety of durations. Topographically specific facilitations are more or less lasting according to the conditions of their induction or location, or both. The progressive elaboration of information along the transversal dimension of the hippocampus, from entry to exit, may have some heuristic value for neurobiological investigations of the connectivity inside the hippocampus. There may be some gradient along this dimension in LTP generation, in LTP duration, or in both. There is already some preliminary evidence for this hypothesis.

As already mentioned, this continuum of memory registers that share the characteristics of lasting beyond the short range and still being transient can be classified into short-lived ITM and transient LTM. These support, respectively, the functions of WM and LTM consolidation.

MATHEMATICAL MODEL

We have seen how Hs function is based on a full temporal spectrum of memory registers with different lifetimes. There are some experimental indications that Hs is involved in processing the temporal order of events at a basic level, and also in timing. The encoding of temporal order by differential synaptic facilitation, according to the order of stimulation, may take place at the level of synaptic contacts between Schaffer collaterals and CA1 pyramids (Granger et al., 1994). These experimental results confirm an algebraic model of STM and LTM for temporal sequences formulated by Grossberg (1978). The network model of temporal sequence learning we present here is based on this algebraic formulation, and involves STM and WM. As suggested above, it is possible to implement temporal order based on ITM and autocorrelation properties of the CA3 field. Temporal order can also be preserved and learned in LTM (Bapi & Levine, 1994; Grossberg, 1978; Reiss & Taylor, 1991).

The hippocampus has also been implicated in timing behavioral responses (Berger & Thompson, 1978; Solomon, 1980). Neural mechanisms underlying the hippocampal adaptive timing function during conditioning were proposed by Grossberg and Merrill (1992), among others. This basic computational competence may also be shared by the cerebellum (Bullock, Fiala, & Grossberg, 1994; Ivry & Keele, 1989). The model presented here is based on the same principles of population learning and coding of time by a limited assembly of neurons whose dynamical range of activation varies along a biologically plausible continuum. This timing system is integrated in a more complete processing system, including temporal order processing (figure 4.4). The network is designed to emulate the electrical response obtained on the scalp in humans, in a temporal conditioning paradigm. The paradigm can be viewed as a formal analog of a CNV paradigm. Once interval learning has taken place, the timing network gates the main processing trend that involves sequence and probability learning.

In our model, relations among Hs and other structures, particularly frontal cortex for temporal order processing and cerebellum for timing, are viewed as special cases of the more global function of Hs as a rehearsal system for the rapid acquisition of (temporal) information. This interpretation is supported by the fact that learning this type of information, particularly time intervals, is not really suppressed by hippocampal lesions. It just requires more trials to be learned, probably by the cerebellum, in conditioning paradigms.

TEMPORAL ORDER NETWORK

Different models of temporal order processing have been designed. The most recent ones emulate temporal processing attributed to prefrontal cortex. Guigon, Dorizzi, Burnod, et al. (1995) have designed a model directly inspired by electrophysiological studies performed in monkeys. Temporal

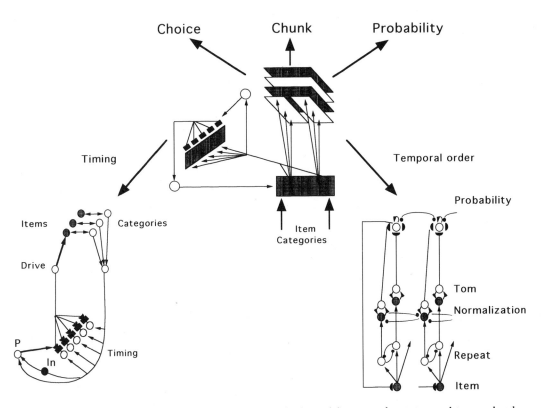

Figure 4.4 Top: Architecture of the multiple-module system for timing, and temporal order, which sends outputs to three different systems: Choice layer performs the original sequence; Probability layer integrates event local and global frequency; Chunk layer learns the repetitive prototypical sequences of a probability condition. (*Right*) Neural network components of the temporal order module (Tom). Tom is composed of three layers: Repeat, Normalization, and the Tom buffer layer. It receives inputs from the Item layer. It sends outputs to three different systems; Only probability is represented in figure 4.4. (*Left*) Timing circuit representing a population coding of the time intervals. In, inhibitory interneuron; P, now print signal; Drive, output response of expected timing.

sequences are learned, in their model, by processing units that commute between two stable states of activity (bistable units) in response to synaptic activations. After learning, the sustained activation of a given neuron represents the selective memorization of a past event, selective anticipation of a future event, or the prediction of a reinforcement. Thus, the model reproduces the functions of neurons encountered in frontal cortex. Bapi and Levine (1994), Levine and Parks (1992) and Parks and colleagues (1992) have designed network models of frontal cortex function. Sequence learning is secured by storing the transitions between the events of a sequence in LTM (synaptic weights). The different learned sequences are encoded in a compressed form and can be categorized. These models are similar in some respects to our own model of WM for temporal order and probability coding (Banquet & Contreras-Vidal, 1992a, b, 1993a, b, 1994). Levine and his

Banquet et al.: Memory, Amnesia, and Cortico-Hippocampal Interactions

colleagues' models and our model are inspired by the same design principles (Grossberg, 1978). Dehaene, Changeux, and Nadal (1987) have implemented a network that can learn temporal sequences based on biological properties of allosteric receptors.

Temporal Order as a Spatially Distributed Amplitude Gradient

Grossberg (1978) first proposed an algebraic STM model that codes temporal order by amplitude gradients of node activation (representing neural populations encoding events). Thus, spatially encoded event categories are modulated by amplitude gradients that encode temporal order. A temporal pattern is encoded as an amplitude-modulated spatial pattern with well-characterized processing and learning mechanisms.

Yet a free-recall, dual task demonstrates primacy effects, recency effects, or both according to the length of the sequence to be recalled (Atkinson & Shiffrin, 1968). In order to comply with these psychological constraints, Grossberg designed two principles:

1. An *invariance principle*, whereby amplitude-modulated spatial patterns of activation across nodes in STM are stored and reset in response to successive events in such a way as to leave unchanged STM temporal order codes of past events. The corresponding algebraic implementation involves the uniform multiplication of a previous pattern $t - 1$ by a factor omega(i) as the present i^{th} item is instated (Grossberg 1976a, 1978b).

2. A *pseudonormalization rule*, designed to implement the limited STM capacity in a more flexible way than straightforward normalization. By this rule, $S(i)$, the total activity at time i, tends asymptotically to S, a characteristic of STM limited capacity, as i increases.

Grossberg (1978) proved that the rate at which $S(i)$ tends to its asymptote S determines the form of the STM activation patterns:

- Primacy: $x(k - 1) > x(k)$ for all $k = i$
- Recency: $x(k - 1) < x(k)$
- Bowing: combines primacy for early items and recency for later ones

Bradski, Carpenter, and Grossberg (1992) designed a shunting architecture that realized invariance and pseudonormalization as emergent properties of the system dynamics. This basic architecture was adapted here in order to insert it into a system capable of coping with a continuous flow of inputs from two or more distinct categories. These inputs could be, for example, the outputs of one or several modality-specific unsupervised categorization networks like adaptive resonance theory (ART) working in parallel (Carpenter & Grossberg, 1987a, 1987b, 1990; Carpenter, Grossberg, & Reynolds, 1991).

Most of the equations for the different stages of the temporal order network (TOM) are variants of typical shunting network equations. These equations can be viewed as adaptations of the classic Hodgkin-Huxley single-neuron equation to neural populations. As such, they comprise three basic components: an excitatory term, an inhibitory term, and a passive decay term. The first two terms include a multiplication factor that represents an excitatory (or inhibitory) saturation point corresponding to excitatory (or inhibitory) equilibrium points in the Hodgkin-Huxley equations.

TOM Architecture and Simulation

The categorical (amodal or supramodal) inputs in our TOM model first go through a repeat module that sorts out repeated items belonging to the same category in a sequence the size of a STM span. Then the sorted items enter a WM module for sequence processing that has the typical STM span (approximately seven items), and corresponds to a cortical memory register. It contains a layer that remains active in the interstimulus interval (ISI) between two successive items and can be compared to cortical neurons that remain active in the interval between two stimuli, as documented in the inferior temporal cortex. The first of two layers in the WM module is a normalization layer, active during input time. It is reciprocally connected with a buffer layer, or temporal order memory proper, that tracks the activity of the normalization layer in the ISI between two stimuli. A flip-flop pattern of activation is instantiated between normalization and temporal order memory layers.

By simple variation of the passive decay coefficient in the normalization layer equation, sequences of items the size of an STM span can be encoded by the system with either a primacy gradient, a recency gradient, or a combination of the two, in accordance with experimental results. P300 amplitude variations in humans encode the temporal order of the events (Banquet, Smith & Günther, 1992; Squires et al., 1976). These results motivated our model. In our experimental paradigm (Banquet & Grossberg, 1987), sequences of about 500 stimuli were delivered to subjects in blocks of 80. Feeding such a sequence to the WM network when it was operating in a recency mode gave rise to a traveling window of waxing and waning activity in the two WM layers.

Furthermore, presenting the system with such a long sequence gave rise to emergent properties in the upper layers that receive temporal information from TOM, namely, a chunk layer for categorization of the sequences and a probability layer for learning the probability rule; patterns of probability layer activation are shown in figure 4.5. In particular, the activity in this last layer behaved as a P300 ERP component, since it tended to an equilibrium level encoding both prior probability as a baseline and temporal order of events and local probability in the fluctuations of this baseline. This combined encoding in the model is dependent on the integrity of both STM and ITM attributed to the hippocampus.

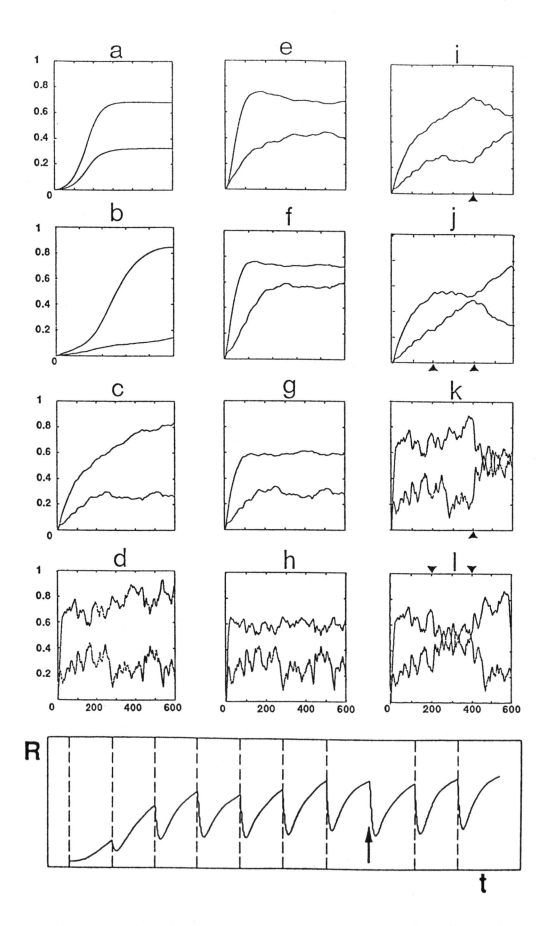

TIMING

There are several scales of biological and mental time. The scale evaluated here is relevant to coordinating integrated systemic processes as the basis of behavior. Life situations in which timing and temporal ordering of events cooperate are common, not only in perception and cognition but also in motor control. This is also true of various artificial systems devoted to sequential pattern recognition, such as speech and writing, or motion pattern generation, as in robotics. There is a strong interdependence between the different types of temporal processes. In particular, the brain's ability to learn sequences and probability is strictly dependent on the duration of the interval between events.

Timing and Classical Conditioning

Grossberg and Merrill (1992) and Bullock et al. (1994) have integrated a spectral timer (based on an array of cell populations responding at different rates) into a classical conditioning circuit. They were able to explain data concerning an animal's ability to accurately time the delay of a goal object, based on its previous experience in a given situation. This timing ability controls the right balance between exploratory and consummatory behaviors, and seems to be essential to the animal's survival.

Timing, Temporal Conditioning, and Cognitive-Motor Processes

The paradigm that we used in humans to explore cognitive-motor processes (Banquet & Grossberg, 1987) is a formal analog of temporal conditioning in animals. There is no distinct CS. The equivalent of the US is presented in Bernoulli series at regular intervals. After some practice, the time interval(s)

Figure 4.5 (*Top*) Activation of the probability layer for two categories A and B of 600 events (500 in b and f). In the left and middle columns P(A) = .2, P(B) = .8. In the right column one or two probability shifts occur at times indicated by arrows, from .2/.8 to .5/.5, or reverse.

The left column presents linear (a) or sigmoidal (b,c,d) feedback functions. Furthermore, from b to d probability node dynamics become faster. Then the system presents larger oscillations in response to sequential dependencies and local probability fluctuations. The experimental relation between local fluctuations and steady-state amplitude is better fitted by d. The middle column has the same parameters as the left one, except that LTM weights are absent, suppressing LTM learning. Oscillations and asymptotic value still exist, but amplitude probability coding is biased toward intermediate values. The right column features responses to probability changes at different points of the sequence (arrows): after 400 stimuli in i and k, and after 200 and 400 in j and l. The system adaptability to new conditions depends on previous sequence duration and on probability node dynamics, faster tracking associated with faster dynamics. (*Below*): The module for the evaluation of the interstimulus interval learns the time interval between stimuli in a sequence of events. After learning, the system becomes capable of anticipation of a response even in the case of an omission in the input sequence. The peak response corresponds to the time of presentation of the stimulus being attended to.

is learned, and a response related to priming and preparation starts prior to the onset of the stimulus. Thus, the factors that were manipulated involve learning a time interval and cognitive and motor processes. Then, it becomes possible to address the problem of timing in the context of a complex task involving perceptual, cognitive, and motor processes, embedded in a learning paradigm. We emphasize the role of timing in the planning of a perceptual, cognitive, and motor preparatory set (prior to the event-stimulus occurrence) and also in the programming, coordination, and integration of these multimodal processes after stimulus delivery. Indeed, any cognitive performance is in part irreducibly sequential, since motor and cognitive processes depend partly on perceptual evaluation of events. But we contend that a non-negligible part of learning fosters parallel rather than sequential processes among perceptual, cognitive, and motor modalities. This claim is consistent with the shift from controlled serial to automatic parallel processes during task learning.

Spectral Timing Network: Design Principles

Extra constraints must be brought to bear on a model designed to implement complex cognitive-motor behaviors. One of the most conspicuous constraints derives from the capability of the brain to process an enduring flow of information, sequentially delivered at variable speeds and loads. The brain is able to extract and learn latent regularities in the midst of noise and irrelevant variations. Then it can perform a specific adaptive response, or initiate an integrated global behavior.

Several design problems had to be solved in the network that emulates these processes: (1) the significance of each stimulus, and its bivalence as both a CS and a US suggest parallel pathways to the spectral cell population; (2) the continuous flow of inputs forbids any specific coupling by pairs, since any stimulus belongs simultaneously to two pairs, one with the preceding and one with the following stimulus; (3) the continuous flow of inputs does not allow the system to be reset after each trial, as could be done after pair presentations. The reset had to be built into the system. In spite of these constraints, the design principle of spectral timing based on population coding is robust enough to support a system that functions correctly even under severe conditions (Banquet, Gaussier, Dreher, et al., 1997b).

System's Architecture and Simulations

The spectral timer (see figure 4.4) is made of a battery of thirty nodes (empty circles). Each node is endowed with its own dynamical range. Thus, the entire population cooperates to cover the whole plausible biological range. The spectral decomposition and learning of time intervals by the node populations is made possible by a double gating of these node activations: first, by a depletable neurotransmitter gate equivalent to an ITM (filled squares), and second, by LTM weights (filled half circles) that sample and learn the activation spectrum corresponding to a particular time interval. Learning is modulated by a transiently active print (P) signal, turned on by sufficiently large and rapid increments of the input activation. The transformation of the input into a sharp phasic activity results from interaction with a feedforward activated inhibitory interneuron, In. This feature is a widespread architectural design present both in Hs and cerebellum.

The global response of the system (see figure 4.5) comes from integrating the activities of all doubly gated activation signals. This timing drive serves to gate the activation of the other structures of the architecture, such as the categorizer and the sequencing system.

DISCUSSION

There are two dimensions in our model, temporal and spatial, that correspond to the transverse and longitudinal axes of the hippocampus. In this chapter, we emphasized the temporal aspect of hippocampal processing. We compared and contrasted the neocortex and hippocampus. The neocortex is mostly endowed with dual short-term and long-term capacities relying on different functional aspects of the same neural networks. But it is also plausibly endowed with the capacity for fast-transient learning at the synaptic interface between hippocampus and cortex. The hippocampus has a full array of continuously varying memory ranges, coupled with a system of loops, both intrahippocampal and between hippocampus and cortex. The former appear to be devoted to the iteration of single-event representations. The complementary operation of the two systems, the array of registers and loops, along with the event correlation capacity of some of the hippocampal networks, may account for the capacity to register episodic and factual memories. For the sake of clarity, we have partitioned this continuum of temporal ranges into two classes, which correspond to the functional distinction between WM and transient LTM. WM includes, but is not restricted to, STM. Transient LTM is the basis of a "permanent" LTM. We emphasize how these two functions are complementary. WM, by its processing capacity, should be critical to the selection, elaboration, and organization of information flow in order to decide what should be permanently stored in LTM. Transient LTM would be the intermediary step between selected information and permanent store. Last but not least, the actual neurobiological mechanisms responsible for WM support and LTM consolidation should be similar or even identical. Both processes should be based on reactivation or reenactment of cortical patterns by endogenous and synchronous activation in the hippocampus of recently coactivated neuronal assemblies.

Along the longitudinal axis of the hippocampus, a loose topography is preserved between cortical and hippocampal connections, at the level of the anatomy. This rough topological correspondence allows for multiple possibilities with respect to the precise functional mapping between cortical networks and the hippocampus. This precise mapping would be functionally determined by previously hypothesized fast-learned transient and topologically specific synaptic facilitations at the interface between hippocampus and cortex. The mapping referred to here does not directly concern the external space (cortical areas such as parietal cortex seem more appropriate for the long-term storage of detailed spatial maps), but the cortical space. Further modeling should tell us how the hippocampus manages to mix up all cortical areas for the sake of correlation at the CA3 level, and simultaneously recover topographic information in its output for the needs of specifically targeted consolidation of cortical LTM. Direct connections from EC to CA1 may play a crucial role in this restoration of topology.

Our model integrates different elements, some of them already parts of other models. Other models relating to hippocampal function can be loosely classified according to their emphasis on explaining anterograde amnesia and hippocampal processing or retrograde amnesia, or both. Unfortunately, due to space limitations, we cannot review these models here.

CONCLUSION

Cortical processing involves two memory registers, STM and permanent LTM. The transition from the long-term to the short-term seems to be direct and normally encounters few problems. As such, it is plausible that the anatomical substrates are topographically identical (STM representing active forms of LTM) at a gross level of analysis, even if the supporting neurophysiological mechanisms are different at the fine level, involving either electrical or durable structural-chemical changes. Conversely, the transition from STM to LTM store follows a more intricate path, probably for the sake of optimizing the amount of information stored, but also for securing the storage of unique events, which constitute the unique history of each living being. Between these two extreme ranges (STM and LTM), only minor variations from primary to associative areas can be recorded, with a tendency for the temporal range of memory to increase as a function of the complexity of processing performed by these areas.

The specificity and vantage point of Hs concerns both topographic and temporal dimensions. The topographic aspect of Hs specificity as a unique compact site of input convergence and output divergence has been extensively emphasized. It has been credited with the correlational function of Hs. This anatomical characteristic is complemented by a loose topological correspondence between cortical and hippocampal systems in the longitudinal dimension. This loose correspondence may be transformed into a dynamic learning-dependent precise mapping between neuronal populations to implement the topologically specific consolidation function. This function may be implemented via the fast-transient learning capacities present within the hippocampus itself, and also at the interfaces between cortex and hippocampus. The emphasis placed on the spatial function of Hs was detrimental to the exploration of the no-less-important temporal function. This function results from the capacity of Hs to play very flexibly on a whole spectrum of registers from the short-term to the long-term, but possibly excluding permanent LTM. The unique characteristic of Hs would be the conjunction of this array of registers with a wide variety of variously sized loops. These complementary "hardware" constraints between cortex and hippocampus determine the type of cooperation established between the two structures. Further complementarity results from the direct contact of the cortex with the environment, whereas Hs is the only structure so easily prone to autoactivation. That leads, in the pathological domain, to seizure activity.

The hippocampus has the structural and biological equipment to cover the entire memory spectrum from STM to LTM. Nevertheless, at the behavioral level, this continuum can be split into two types of transient memories subserving two distinct functions. Short-lived ITM, based on STP, supports an automatic component of WM. Transient LTM, based on LTP, supports the LTM consolidation function attributed to Hs. The two functions of WM and LTM consolidation are complementary and nicely articulated. Only information previously filtered and processed in WM can aspire to permanent storage by entering the transient LTM store for consolidation. A unique mechanism sustains these two aspects of intermediate memory: namely, resonant activity in reciprocally connected networks, which can be viewed as a "nonlinear" expression of reverberating activity in closed feedback loops. This mechanism provides for synchronization, or at least fixed temporal relation, between activities in distinct neural populations, which is supposed to be necessary for the Hebbian type of synaptic learning.

The cortical controlled component of WM involves cortico-cortical loops. Some of these cortical loops, such as the articulatory loop, may be specific to the human brain. The automatic component of WM involves hippocampo-cortical loops, particularly hippocampo-frontal ones. This reverberating loop system, specifically and punctually involved in WM, is replaced for longer delays by synaptic facilitation of various durations, as documented in the Hs. These synaptic processes sustain transient LTM, which operates the consolidation of permanent LTMs at the cortical level. Thus, with the exception of cortical STM, the transience of storage at variable degrees is a hallmark of hippocampal processes and hippocampus-cortex interfaces. This transience endows the system with permanent availability for the processing and transient storage of new information.

ACKNOWLEDGMENT

We are indebted to Elaine Garibobo for useful comments on the manuscript.

REFERENCES

Alvarez, P., & Squire, L. R. (1994). Memory consolidation and the medial temporal lobe: A simple network model. *Proceedings of the National Academy of Sciences, 91*, 7041–7045.

Amaral, D. G., & Witter, M. P. (1989). The three-dimensional organization of the hippocampal formation: A review of anatomical data. *Neuroscience, 31*, 571–591.

Atkinson, R. C., & Shiffrin, R. M. (1968). Human memory: A proposed system and its control processes. In K. W. Spence & J. T. Spence (Eds.), *The psychology of learning and motivation: Advances in research and theory*, Vol. 2 (pp. 89–185). New York: Academic Press.

Baddeley, A. D. (1986). *Working memory*. Oxford, UK: Oxford University Press.

Baddeley, A. D., (1995). Working memory. In M. S. Gazzaniga (Ed.), *The cognitive neurosciences* (pp. 755–764). Cambridge, MA: MIT Press.

Baddeley, A. D., & Hitch, G. J. (1974). Working memory. In G. A. Bower (Ed.), *The psychology of learning and motivation: Advances in research and theory*, Vol. 8. (pp. 47–90). New York: Academic Press.

Baddeley, A. D., & Warrington, (1970). Amnesia and the distinction between long- and short-term memory. *Journal of Verbal Learning and Verbal Behavior, 9,* 176–189.

Banquet, J. P. (1983). Inter- and intra-hemispheric relationships of the EEG during sleep in man. *Electroencephalography and Clinical Neurophysiology, 55,* 51–59.

Banquet, J. P., & Contreras-Vidal, J. L. (1992a). An integrated neural network–event related potentials model of temporal and probability context effects on categorization. In *Proceedings of the international joint conference on neural networks* (pp. 541–546). Hillsdale, NJ: Erlbaum.

Banquet, J. P., & Contreras-Vidal, J. L. (1992b). Temporal order, timing, and probability context effects on pattern recognition and categorization. In I. Aleksander & J. Taylor (Eds.), *Artificial neural networks 2* (pp. 1885–1890). Amsterdam: North-Holland.

Banquet, J. P., & Contreras-Vidal, J. L. (1993a). Learning temporal contexts and priming preparation modes for pattern recognition. In *Proceedings of the international world conference on neural networks* (pp. 126–131). Hillsdale, NJ: Erlbaum.

Banquet, J. P., & Contreras-Vidal, J. L. (1993b). Spectral timing and integration of multimodal systemic processes. In J. Taylor (Ed.), *Artificial neural networks* (pp. 350–354). Amsterdam: Elsevier.

Banquet, J. P., & Contreras-Vidal, J. L. (1994). Medium and long-term memory in context processing: A network model of cortex-hippocampus relations. In *Proceedings of the international conference on neural networks, vol. 4,* (pp. 647–654). Hillsdale, NJ: Erlbaum.

Banquet, J. P., Gaussier, P., Dreher, J., Joulain, C., Revel, A., & Günther, W. (1997b). Space-time, order and hierarchy in fronto-hippocampal system: A neural basis of personality. In G. Matthews (Ed.), *Cognitive science perspectives on personality and emotion* (pp. 123–189). Amsterdam: Elsevier.

Banquet, J. P., Gaussier, P., Muga, S., Arnaud, R., & Joulain C. (1997a). Learning, recognition and generation of temporo-spatial sequences by a cortico-hippocampal system: A neural network model. In *Proceedings of the conference on vision, recognition, action: Neural models of mind and machine* (p. 46). Boston, MA: Center For Adaptive Systems.

Banquet, J. P., & Grossberg, S. (1987). Probing cognitive processes through the structure of event-relate potentials during learning: An experimental and theoretical analysis. *Applied Optics, 26,* 4931–4946.

Banquet, J. P., Renault, B., & Lesèvre, N. (1981). Effect of task and stimulus probability on evoked potentials. *Biological Psychology, 13,* 203–214.

Banquet, J.-P., Smith, M. J., & Günther W. (1992). Top-down processes, attention and motivation in cognitive tasks. In D. S. Levine & S. J. Leven (Eds.), *Motivation, emotion and goal direction in neural networks* (pp. 169–207). Hillsdale, NJ: Erlbaum.

Banquet, J. -P., Smith, M. J., & Renault, B. (1990). Bottom-up versus top-down: An alternative to the automatic attended dilemma? *Behavioral and Brain Sciences, 13,* 233–234.

Bapi, R. S., & Levine, D. S. (1994). Modelling the role of the frontal lobes in sequential task performance. I. Basic structure and primacy effects. *Neural Networks, 7,* 1167–1180.

Baylis, G. C., & Rolls, E. T. (1987). Responses of neurons in the inferior temporal cortex in short-term and serial recognition memory tasks. *Experimental Brain Research, 65,* 614–1622.

Berger, T. W., & Thompson, R. F. (1978). Neuronal plasticity in the limbic system during classical conditioning of the rabbit nictitatin membrane response. *Brain Research, 145,* 323–346.

Bradski, G., Carpenter, G., & Grossberg, S. (1992). Working memory network for learning temporal order with application to three-dimensional visual object recognition. *Neural Computation, 4,* 270–286.

Brebion, J. (1994). Unpublished Ph.D. dissertation, Université René Descartes, Paris.

Brown, J. (1958). Some tests of the decay theory of immediate memory. *Quarterly Journal of Experimental Psychology, 10,* 12–21.

Bullock, D., Fiala, J. C., & Grossberg, S. (1994). A neural model of timed response learning in the cerebellum. *Neural Networks, 7,* 1101–1114.

Burgess, N., Recce, M., & O'Keefe, J. (1994). A model of hippocampal function. *Neural Networks, 7,* 1065–1081.

Burnod, Y. (1990). *An adaptive neural network the cerebral cortex.* London: Prentice-Hall.

Buzsaki, G. (1988). Polysynaptic long-term potentiation: A physiological role of the perforant path–CA3/CA1 pyramidal cell synapse. *Brain Research, 455,* 192–195.

Buzsaki, G. (1989). Two-stage model of memory trace formation: A role for "noisy" brain states. *Neuroscience, 31,* 551–570.

Carpenter, G. A., & Grossberg, S. (1987a). A massively parallel architecture for a self-organizing neural pattern recognition machine. *Computer Vision, Graphics, and Image Processing, 37,* 54–115.

Carpenter, G. A., & Grossberg, S. (1987b). ART 2: Self-organization of stable category recognition codes for analog input patterns. *Applied Optics, 26,* 4919–4930.

Carpenter, G. A., & Grossberg, S. (1990). ART 3: Hierarchical search using chemical transmitters in self-organizing pattern recognition architectures. *Neural Networks, 3,* 129–152.

Carpenter, G. A., & Grossberg, S. (1993). Normal and amnesic learning, recognition, and memory by a neural model of cortico-hippocampal interactions. *Trends in Neuroscience, 16,* 131–137.

Carpenter, G. A., Grossberg, S., & Reynolds, J. H. (1991). ARTMAP: Supervised real-time learning and classification of nonstationary data by a self organizing neural network. *Neural Networks, 4,* 565–588.

Cave, C. B., & Squire, L. R. (1992). Intact and long-lasting visual object priming in amnesic patients. *Journal of Experimental Psychology, Learning, Memory, and Cognition, 18,* 509–520.

Cho, Y. H., Beracochea, D., & Jaffard, R. (1992). Differential effects of ibotenate lesions of the CA1 subfield of the hippocampus on a delayed non-matching-to-place task as a function of preoperative training in mice. *Psychobiology, 20* (4), 261–269.

Cohen, N. J., & Squire, L. R. (1980). Preserved learning and retention of pattern analysing skill in amnesia: Dissociation of knowing how and knowing that. *Science, 210,* 207–209.

Corkin, S., & Milner, B. (1968). Acquisition of motor skill after bilateral medial temporal lobe excision. *Neuropsychologia, 6,* 225–265.

Dehaene, S., Changeux, J. P., & Nadal, J. P. (1987). Neural networks that learn temporal sequences by selection. *Proceedings of the National Academy of Sciences, 84*, 2727–2731.

Drachman, D. A., & Arbit, J. A. (1966). Memory and the hippocampal complex. *Archives of Neurology, 15*, 52–61.

Eichenbaum, H., Otto, T., & Cohen, N. J. (1994). Two functional components of the hippocampal memory system. *Behavioral and Brain Science, 17*, 449–518.

Funahashi, S., Bruce, C., & Goldman-Rakic, P. W. (1989). Mnemonic coding of visual space by neurons in the monkey's dorsolateral prefrontal cortex revealed by an oculomotor delayed-response task. *Journal of Neurophysiology, 61*, 1–19.

Fuster, J. M. (1995). *Memory in the cerebral cortex.* Cambridge, MA: MIT Press.

Fuster, J. M. (1997). *The prefrontal cortex. Anatomy, physiology and neuropsychology of the frontal lobe.* 3rd ed. New York: Raven Press.

Fuster, J. M., & Alexander, G. E. (1971). Neuron activity related to short-term memory. *Science, 173*, 652–654.

Fuster, J. M., & Jervey, J. P. (1981). Inferotemporal neurons distinguish and retain behaviorally relevant features of visual stimuli. *Science, 212*, 55.

Glanzer, M., & Amitz, A. R. (1966). Two storage mechanisms in free recall. *Journal of Verbal Learning and Verbal Behavior, 5*, 351–360.

Goldman-Rakic, P. W. (1988). Topography of cognition. Parallel distributed networks in primate association cortex. *Annual Review of Neuroscience, 11*, 137–156.

Granger, R., Whitson, J., Larson, J., & Lynch, G. (1994). Non-Hebbian properties of long-term potentiation enable high-capacity encoding of temporal sequences. *Proceedings of National Academy of Sciences, 91*, 10104–10108.

Gray, C. M., König, P., Engel, A. K., & Singer, W. (1989). Oscillatory responses in cat visual cortex exhibit intercolumnar synchronizations which reflect global stimulus properties. *Nature, 338*, 334–337.

Grossberg, S. (1976a). Adaptive pattern classification and universal recording, I: Parallel development and coding of neural feature detectors. *Biological Cybernetics, 23*, 121–134.

Grossberg, S. (1976b). Adaptive pattern classification and universal recoding, II: Feedback, expectation, olfaction, and illusions. *Biological Cybernetics, 23*, 187–202.

Grossberg, S. (1978). A theory of human memory: Self-organization and performance of sensory-motor codes, maps, and plans. In R. Rosen & F. Snell, (Eds.), *Progress in theoretical biology*, Vol. 5 (pp. 233–374). New York: Academic Press. Reprinted in S. Grossberg (Ed.). *Studies of mind and brain: Neural principles of learning, perception, development, cognition, and motor control.* Boston: Reidel Press.

Grossberg, S. & Merrill, J. (1992). A neural network model of adaptively timed reinforcement learning and hippocampal dynamics. *Cognitive Brain Research, 1*, 3–38.

Guigon, E., Dorizzi, B. Burnod, Y., & Schultz, W. (1995). Neural correlates of learning in the prefrontal cortex of the monkey: A predictive model. *Cerebral Cortex, 5*, 135–147.

Halgren, E., Squires, N. K., Wilson, C. L. Rohrbaugh, J. W., Babb, T. L., & Crandall, P. H., (1980). Endogenous potentials generated in the human hippocampal formation and amygdala by infrequent events. *Science, 210*, 803–805.

Horel, J. A. (1994). The localization of general memory functions. *Behavioral and Brain Sciences, 17*, 482.

Ivry, R. B., & Keele, S. W. (1989). Timing functions of the cerebellum. *Journal of Cognitive Neuroscience, 1,* 134–150.

James, W. (1890). *The Principles of Psychology.* New York: Holt.

Johnson, R., Jr. (1995). On the neural generators of the P300: Evidence from temporal lobectomy patients. *Electroencephalography and Clinical Neurophysiology, 44* (Suppl.) 110–129.

Johnson, R., Jr., & Donchin E. (1982). Sequential expectancies and decision making in a changing environment: An electrophysiological approach. *Psychophysiology, 9,* 183–199.

Jones, R. S. G. (1993). Entorhinal-hippocampal connections: A speculative view of their function. *Trends in Neurosciences, 16,* 58–64.

Kim, J. J., & Fanselow, M. S. (1992). Modality specific retrograde amnesia of fear. *Science, 256,* 675–677.

Levine, D. S., & Parks, R. (1992). Frontal lesion effects on verbal fluency in a network model. In *Proceedings of the international joint conference on neural networks, vol. 2* (pp. 39–44).

Lü, Z. L., Williamson, S. J., & Kaufman, L. (1992). Human auditory primary and association cortex have differing lifetimes for activation traces. *Brain Research, 572,* 236–241.

MacKinnon, D. F., & Squire, L. R. (1989). Autobiographical memory and amnesia. *Psychobiology, 17,* 247–256.

McClelland, J. L., McNaughton, B. L., & O'Reilly, R. C. (1995). Why there are complementary learning systems in the hippocampus and the neocortex: Insights from the successes and failures of the connectionist models of learning and memory. *Psychological Review, 102,* 419–457.

McIntosh, A. R., Grady, C. L., Haxby, J. V., Ungerleider, L. G., & Horwitz L. G. (1996). Changes in limbic and prefrontal cortex functional interactions in a working memory test for facts. *Cerebral Cortex, 6,* 571–584.

Miller, E. K., & Desimone, R. (1994). Parallel neuronal mechanisms for short-term memory. *Science, 263,* 520–522.

Miller, E. K., Li, L., & Desimone, R. (1993). Activity of neurons in anterior inferior temporal cortex during a short-term memory task. *Journal of Neuroscience, 13,* 1460–1478.

Milner, B. (1959). The memory defect in bilateral hippocampal lesions. *Psychiatric Research Reports, 11,* 43–52.

Milner, B. (1962). Les troubles de la mémoire accompagnant les lésions hippocampiques bilatérales. In *Physiologie de l'hippocampe* (pp. 257–272). Paris: CNRS.

Milner, B. (1966). Amnesia following operation on the temporal lobes. In C. W. M. Whitty & O. L. Zangwill (Eds.), *Amnesia.* London: Butterworths.

Milner, B., Corkin, S., & Teuber, H.-L. (1968). Further analysis of the hippocampal amnesia syndrome: 14-year follow-up study of H. M. *Neuropsychologia, 6,* 215–234.

Miyashita, Y., & Chang, H. S. (1988). Neuronal correlate of pictorial short-term memory in the primate temporal cortex. *Nature, 331,* 68–70.

Näätänen, R. (1982). Processing negativity: An evoked-potential reflection of selective attention. *Psychological Bulletin, 92,* 605–640.

Niki, H. (1974). Differential activity of prefrontal units during right and left delayed response trials. *Brain Research, 70,* 346–349.

O'Keefe, J., & Nadel, L. (1978). *The hippocampus as a cognitive map.* Oxford, U.K.: Oxford University Press.

Olton, D. S., Becker, J. T., & Handelmann, G. E. (1979). Hippocampus, space and memory. *Behavioral and Brain Science, 2,* 313–365.

Owen, A. M., Morris, R. G., Sakakian, R., Polkey, C. E. & Robbins, T. W. (1996). Double dissociations of memory and executive functions in working memory tasks following frontal lobe excision, temporal lobe excision or amygdalo-hippocampectomy in man. *Brain, 119,* 1597–1615.

Parks, R. W., Levine, D. S., Long, D. L., Crockett, D. J., Dalton, I. E., Weingarther, H., Fedio, P., Coburn, K. L., Siler, G., Matthews, J. R., & Becker, R. E. (1992). Parallel distributed processing and neuropsychology: A neural network model of Wisconsin Card Sorting and verbal fluency. *Neuropsychology Review, 3,* 213–233.

Paulesu, E., Frith, C. M., & Frackowiak, R. S. J. (1993). The neural correlates of the verbal component of working memory. *Nature, 362,* 342–345.

Peterson, L. R., & Peterson, M. J. (1959). Short-term retention of individual verbal items. *Journal of Experimental Psychology, 58,* 193–198.

Petrides, M., Alivisatos, B., Evans, A., & Meyer, E. (1993). Dissociation of human mid-dorsal from postero-dorsolateral frontal cortex in memory processing. *Proceedings of the National Academy of Sciences, 90,* 873–877.

Reiss, M., & Taylor, J. (1991). Storing temporal sequences. *Neural Networks, 4,* 773–787.

Rolls, E. T. (1989). Functions of neural networks in the hippocampus and neocortex in memory. In J. H. Byrne & W. O. Berry (Eds.), *Neural models of plasticity: Theoretical and empirical approaches* (pp. 240–265). New York: Academic Press.

Rolls, E. T., Baylis, G. C., Hasselmo, M. E., & Nalwa, V. (1989). The effect of learning on the face selective responses of neurons in the cortex in the superior temporal sulcus in the monkey. *Experimental Brain Research, 76,* 153–164.

Ruchkin, D. S., Johnson, R., Jr., Canoune, H., & Ritter, W. (1991). Event-related potentials during arithmetic and mental rotation. *Electroencephalography and Clinical Neurophysiology, 79,* 473–487.

Ruchkin, D. S., Johnson, R., Jr., Grafman, J., Canoune, H., & Ritter, W. (1992). Distinctions and similarities among working memory processes: An event-related potentials study. *Cognitive Brain Research, 1,* 53–66.

Schacter, D. L., Chu, C.-Y., & Ochsner, K. N. (1993). Implicit memory: A selective review. *Annual Review of Neuroscience, 16,* 159–182.

Schacter, D. L., & Graf, P. (1986). Preserved learning in amnesic patients: Perspectives from research on direct priming. *Journal of Clinical and Experimental Neuropsychology, 6,* 727–743.

Scoville, W. B., & Milner, B. (1957). Loss of recent memory after bilateral hippocampal lesions. *Journal of Neurology, Neurosurgery, and Neuropsychiatry, 20,* 11–21.

Shiffrin, R. M., & Schneider, W. (1977). Controlled and automatic information processing. II: Perceptual learning, automatic attending and a general theory. *Psychological Review, 84,* 127–190.

Shimamura, A. P., & Squire, L. R. (1987). A neuropsychological study of fact memory and source amnesia. *Journal of Experimental Psychology: Learning, Memory and Cognition, 13,* 464–473.

Sidman, M., Stoddard, L. T., & Mohr, J. P. (1968). Some additional quantitative observations of immediate memory in a patient with bilateral hippocampal lesion. *Neuropsychologia, 6,* 245–254.

Singer, W. (1991). Neuronal activity as a shaping factor in the self-organization of neuron assemblies. In G. A. Carpenter & S. Grossberg (Eds.), *Pattern recognition by self-organizing neural networks.* Cambridge, MA: MIT Press.

Solomon, P. R. (1980). A time and a place for everything? Temporal processing views of hippocampal function with special reference to attention. *Physiological Psychology, 8,* 254–261.

Squire, L. R. (1992). Memory and the hippocampus. A synthesis from findings in rats, monkeys and humans. *Psychological Review, 99,* 195–231.

Squire, L. R., Cohen, N. J., & Nadel, L. (1984). The medial temporal lobe and memory consolidation: A new hypothesis. In H. Weingartner & E. Parker (Eds.), *Memory consolidation* (pp. 185–210). Hillsdale, NJ: Erlbaum.

Squire, L. R., Haist, F., & Shimamura, P. (1989). The neurology of memory: Quantitative assessment of retrograde amnesia in two groups of amnesic patients. *Journal of Neuroscience, 9,* 828–839.

Squire, L. R., Knowlton, B., & Musen, G. (1993). The structure and organization of memory. *Annual Review of Psychology, 44,* 453–495.

Squire, L. R., Ojemann, J. G., Miezin, F. M., Petersen, S. E., Vdeen, T. O., & Raichle, M. E. (1992). Activation of the hippocampus in normal humans: A functional anatomical study of memory. *Proceedings of the National Academy of Sciences, 89,* 1837–1841.

Squires, K. C., Wickens, C., Squires, N. C., & Donchin, E., (1976). The effect of stimulus sequence on the waveform of cortical event-related potential. *Science, 193,* 1142–1146.

Staubli, U., & Lynch, G. (1987). Stable hippocampal long-term potentiation elicited by theta pattern stimulation. *Brain Research, 435,* 227–234.

Sutherland, R. W., & Rudy, J. W. (1989). Configural association theory: The role of the hippocampal formation in learning, memory, and amnesia. *Psychobiology, 17,* 129–144.

Tulving, E. (1983). *Elements of episodic memory.* New York: Oxford University Press.

Warrington, E. K., & McCarthy, R. A. (1988). The fractionation of retrograde amnesia. *Brain and Cognition, 7,* 184–200.

Warrington, E. K., & Weiskrantz, L. (1978). Further analysis of the prior learning effect in amnesic patients. *Neuropsychologia, 16,* 169–177.

Wickelgren, W. A. (1979). Chunking and consolidation: A theoretical synthesis of semantic networks, configuring S-R versus cognitive learning, normal forgetting, the amnesic syndrome, and the hippocampal arousal system. *Psychological Review, 86,* 44–60.

Wilson, M. A., & McNaughton, B. L. (1993). Dynamics of the hippocampal ensemble code for space. *Science, 261,* 1055–1058.

Winocur, G. (1990). Anterograde amnesia in rats with dorsal hippocampal and dorsomedial thalamic lesions. *Behavioral Brain Research, 38,* 145–154.

Zola-Morgan, S., & Squire, L. (1990). The primate hippocampal formation: Evidence for a limited role in memory storage. *Science, 250,* 288–290.

Zola-Morgan, S., Squire L., & Amaral, D. G. (1986). Human amnesia and the medial temporal region: Enduring memory impairment following a bilateral lesion limited to the field CA1 of the hippocampus. *Journal of Neuroscience, 6,* 2950–2967.

II   Behavioral States

5

A Computational Model of Alcohol Dependence: Simulation of Genetic Differences in Alcohol Preference and of Therapeutic Strategies

Raymond L. Ownby

Research on alcohol use disorders during the past several years has provided important information on the possible neurobiological mechanisms of alcohol dependence. Studies have shown, for example, that chronic ethanol exposure affects the G proteins important in cellular second messenger systems (Nestler, 1992) and may also affect membrane calcium channels (Dolin & Little, 1989; Dolin, Little, Hudspith, et al., 1987; Whittington, Dolin, Patch, et al., 1991). Research shows that acute and chronic ethanol exposure affect neural transmission, especially the dopaminergic systems of the mesolimbic system (Charness, 1992; Di Chiara & Imperato, 1988a, b; Di Chiara, Acquas, & Carboni, 1992; Imperato & Di Chiara, 1986; Stinus, Cador, & Le Moal, 1992;) and serotonergic systems in other areas (George, Wozniak, & Linnoila, 1992; McBride, Murphy, Lumeng, et al., 1992; LeMarquand, Pihl, & Benkelfat, 1994; Sellers, Higgins, & Sobell, 1992). Strains of alcohol-preferring and -nonpreferring rats, for example, differ in expression and regulation of dopaminergic systems in the nucleus accumbens (NAcc) and the ventral tegmental area (VTA) and in the activity of their serotonergic systems (Murphy, McBride, Lumeng, et al., 1987). Genetic differences in the response of these rats' dopamine system to alcohol consumption have been demonstrated.

Similar differences in serotonergic function are implicated in the susceptibility to developing at least one type of alcoholism (George et al., 1992). Still other studies have suggested that brain systems that use γ-aminobutyric acid (GABA) as a neurotransmitter are important mediators of alcohol's effects. To make matters even more complex, at least part of GABA's reinforcing effects are caused by its inhibitory effects on dopaminergic pathways in the VTA (Devine, Leone, & Wise, 1993; Terenius, 1994). By inhibiting these pathways, which are in turn inhibitory to the NAcc, alcohol stimulates increased dopaminergic activity in the NAcc. Other lines of research show that glutamatergic neurotransmission, and especially the N-methyl-D-aspartate (NMDA) receptor, is involved in alcohol's reinforcing effects (Koob, Rassnick, Heinrichs, et al., 1994; Charness, 1992; Trevisan, Fitzgerald, Brose, et al., 1994). Limited data suggest that homotaurine, a GABA agonist and a glutamate antagonist, may be effective in reducing alcohol intake in rats (Koob, 1992a, b), but extensive studies have not been done in humans (Lhuintre, Daoust, Moore, et al., 1985).

Neurobiological research thus implicates a number of neurotransmitter systems in the development and maintenance of alcohol dependence. This research has led to new treatment strategies for the disorder. Studies show that opiate antagonist medications such as naltrexone reduce alcohol intake in animals and decrease subjective desire to drink and voluntary alcohol ingestion in humans (Volpicelli, Alterman, Harashida, et al., 1992; O'Malley, Jaffe, Change, et al., 1992). Similar studies with serotonergic medications such as the serotonin uptake blocker fluoxetine have shown that these medications may also reduce the subjective desire to drink and lower alcohol intake in humans (LeMarquand et al., 1994).

Koob and his associates (Koob, 1992a, b; Koob & Bloom, 1988; Koob et al., 1994) have researched the neural circuitry that probably underlies alcohol's reinforcing properties. Koob emphasizes that alcohol and other abused substances act on critical brain reinforcement systems—a neural circuit including most importantly the NAcc and VTA but other structures also (figure 5.1). Acute alcohol use results in increased dopamine release in the NAcc, an event that may be a neurophysiological correlate of behavioral reinforcement. Chronic alcohol use induces changes in this system so that when alcohol is not present it is activated. This may be the neurophysiological counterpart of the increased desire to consume alcohol that is subjectively experienced as "craving."

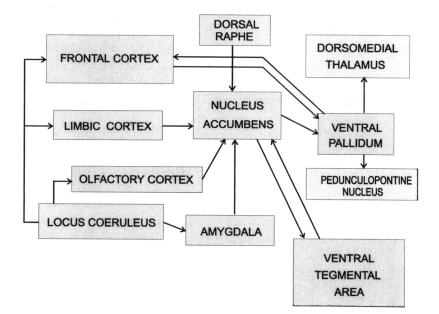

Figure 5.1 Elements of the neural circuit underlying alcohol's reinforcing effects.

Modell and his colleagues (Modell, Mountz, & Beresford, 1990) have also reviewed this circuitry. They emphasize, however, the similarity of obsessive thoughts about drinking and obsessive-compulsive disorder (OCD; Modell, Glaser, Cyr, et al., 1992a; Modell, Glaser, Mountz, et al., 1992b 1993). Modell and his colleagues argue that the same frontal cortex–dorsomedial thalamic circuit implicated in OCD symptoms may also mediate obsessive thoughts about alcohol in alcohol-dependent persons. They suggest that activity in this corticothalamic loop is regulated by an inhibitory circuit that includes the NAcc and ventral pallidum. Inhibitory serotonergic inputs from the dorsal raphe nuclei also modulate activity in these loops via input to the NAcc. Ethanol intake acutely increases dopaminergic activity in the NAcc, reducing inhibition in the NAcc–ventral pallidum circuit. The result of this combination of excitation and inhibition is increased activity in the frontothalamic circuit implicated in obsessions. Increased activity in this frontothalamic circuit results in subjectively experienced obsessive thoughts about alcohol. The behavioral outcome of activation in this circuit is alcohol consumption.

These analyses have considerable heuristic value and are solidly based in neuroanatomical and neurophysiological research. They are the most comprehensive current formulations of the neural mechanisms involved in alcohol dependence, and integrate much current knowledge about the neurobiology of alcoholism. As proposed theories, though, they are static and conceptual; although interesting, they are not amenable to dynamic testing. A suitable in vitro model of the neural elements involved in alcohol dependence would allow dynamic testing of hypotheses about etiology and treatment, but at present is technically unfeasible. Computational modeling of anatomical neural networks, however, provides a way to examine relations among neural structures implicated in symptoms of alcohol dependence, such as changes in the desire to drink or thoughts about drinking. Such models can represent underlying physical systems in ways that allow experiments that are otherwise difficult or impossible (such as assessing the effects of new medications on neurotransmitter systems). For further discussion of applications of computational modeling and their usefulness, see chapter 1 in this book.

METHOD

Model Development

The anatomical models developed by Koob et al. (Koob, 1992a, b; Koob & Bloom, 1988; Koob et al., 1994) and Modell et al. (Modell et al., 1990) were the basis for the network created in this study (see figures 5.1 and 5.2). The central characteristics of the biological circuitry simulated are (a) the changes in dopaminergic responsivity in the NAcc and VTA system accompanying alcohol intake that are under genetic control in certain strains of rats; and (b) the dorsomedial thalamus and orbitofrontal cortex system, believed to be overactive in both OCD (Modell, Mountz, Curtis, et al., 1989) and alcohol

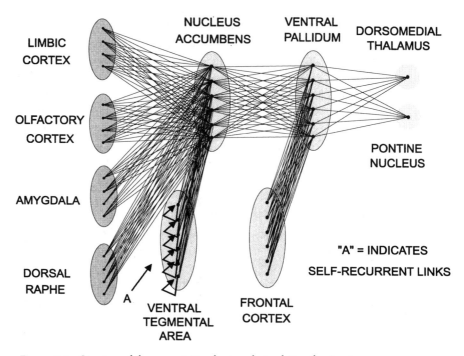

Figure 5.2 Structure of the computational network simulating the circuit.

dependence. This second circuit is believed to underlie the subjectively experienced intense desire to consume alcohol, similar to the intense obsessions and irresistible compulsions experienced by patients with OCD (Modell et al., 1990).

A target symptom of alcohol dependence was chosen to simulate the desire to drink an alcoholic beverage. It was chosen for several reasons. First, it can be argued that the desire to drink alcohol can be experienced at high intensities by persons who are not dependent on or abusers of alcohol (e.g., in the context of significant thirst after working outside on a hot day, when someone might anticipate that a cold beer would be very refreshing). It is assumed that a person not dependent on alcohol would have a desire to drink that is qualitatively similar to that of persons who are. When this desire becomes abnormally intense in relation to environmental cues and the likely social and medical consequences of drinking, it is pathological. The same network may thus be trained to simulate both a normal and an abnormal desire to drink alcohol. Second, although the relation between experienced desire to drink and actual drinking behavior is inexact, it can be argued that it exists (Bauer, 1992). Simulation of level of desire for alcohol is thus a meaningful goal. Third, at a more integrative level, the numerical value arbitrarily assigned to represent levels of desire can be understood to reflect the level of activation in the network produced by inputs and other experimental manipulations. Although it is not certain that the network's output to the dorsomedial thalamus or pedunculopontine nuclei corresponds

Table 5.1 Training set illustrating inputs and outputs

Bias Units	Limbic Cortex	Olfactory Cortex	Amygdala	Dorsal Raphe	Outputs
.1.1.1.1	0 0 0 1	0 0 0 1	0 0 0 1	−.1−.1−.1−.1	0.1 0.1
.2.2.2.2	0 0 1 0	0 0 1 0	0 0 1 0	−.2−.2−.2−.2	0.2 0.2
.3.3.3.3	0 0 1 1	0 0 1 1	0 0 1 1	−.3−.3−.3−.3	0.3 0.3
.4.4.4.4	0 1 0 0	0 1 0 0	0 1 0 0	−.4−.4−.4−.4	0.4 0.4
.5.5.5.5	0 1 0 1	0 1 0 1	0 1 0 1	−.5−.5−.5−.5	0.5 0.5
.6.6.6.6	0 1 1 0	0 1 1 0	0 1 1 0	−.6−.6−.6−.6	0.6 0.6
.7.7.7.7	0 1 1 1	0 1 1 1	0 1 1 1	−.7−.7−.7−.7	0.7 0.7
.8.8.8.8	1 0 0 0	1 0 0 0	1 0 0 0	−.8−.8−.8−.8	0.8 0.8
.9.9.9.9	1 0 0 1	1 0 0 1	1 0 0 1	−.9−.9−.9−.9	0.9 0.9
1 1 1 1	1 0 1 0	1 0 1 0	1 0 1 0	−1 − 1 − 1 − 1	1.0 1.0

to a subjective desire to drink, it is likely that it is related to the behavioral activation resulting from presentation of alcohol-related cues (Dolinsky, Morse, Kaplan, et al., 1987; Turkkan, McCaul, & Stitzer, 1989). Reported desire to drink alcohol can thus be understood to be the experienced counterpart of activation in the frontothalamic circuit. Activation can be read out at the dorsomedial thalamus and the pedunculopontine nucleus. A person's report of this readout, however, is affected by many other variables, including memory, environmental cues, and attentional focus. The network can thus be broadly conceived as processing sensory and motivational inputs from the olfactory and limbic cortices and the amygdala, under the influence of serotonergic and dopaminergic inputs. The output of the network represents different levels of activation of the circuit, corresponding to subjectively experienced obsessive thoughts about drinking alcohol, often referred to as "craving."

Overall Strategy for the Model To develop a model of the pathological need to drink alcohol, it was first necessary to develop a neural network that could simulate normal desire. The network would associate low levels of sensory and motivational cues with low levels of desire to drink, and higher levels of cues with higher levels of desire. The data used initially to train the network were arranged so that inputs from limbic and olfactory cortices and the amygdala conveyed gradual increases in value, conceptually associated with increased intensity of cues. Inputs from the dorsal raphe were increasingly negative, consistent with the inhibitory function of serotonergic projections from it to the NAcc. Inputs from bias units to the NAcc were increasingly positive, consistent with increases in dopaminergic activation associated with more intense sensory and motivational cues (table 5.1).

Inputs from these four systems to the NAcc are modeled. These systems were chosen because of their importance in alcohol-reinforcing mechanisms, as discussed by Koob and colleagues (Koob, 1992a, b; Koob & Bloom, 1988;

Koob et al., 1994) and Modell et al. (1990). The actual network was constructed with four input units for each system, for a total of sixteen input units, with an additional four bias units. The next layer of this four-layer network comprised six units, corresponding to the anatomical NAcc. These six units are connected to six context units; this interactive system simulates the reciprocal anatomical interconnections of the VTA and the NAcc. The next layer of six units represents the ventral pallidum, again according to the anatomical hypotheses of Koob and Bloom (1988). It in turn has six context units connected to it, simulating the reciprocal anatomical connections to the frontal cortex area thought to be important in alcohol's reinforcing properties. Note that this frontal cortex area is not believed to be the same orbitofrontal area that combines with the dorsomedial thalamus in the overactive circuit underlying obsessions in OCD or obsessive thoughts about alcohol in alcohol dependence (Modell et al., 1990; Modell et al., 1989). The output systems are modeled with one unit (each unit is represented by a black dot in figure 5.2). These represent the dorsomedial thalamus and the pedunculopontine nucleus, both important targets because of their relevance to behavioral activation.

The network thus has a partially recurrent, or Elman architecture (Hertz, Krogh, & Palmer, 1991). Although this architecture is typically used to learn tasks that require learning over time, it is used to here to create a network structure that is the analog of the underlying anatomical network.

A sequence of inputs was developed to train the network and is illustrated in table 5.1. Low levels of cue intensity are represented initially by "0 0 0 1" (binary one) with increasing levels of cue intensity ranging through "0101" (binary 5) to "1 0 1 1" (binary ten). Dorsal raphe inputs decrease in smaller increments (becoming more negative) while bias unit inputs increase in the same increments (becoming more positive). These ten inputs reflect a sequence of states of activation of the neural system important in mediating desire for alcohol. The first several lines of table 5.1 show what occurs when motivational and sensory cues are weak—the level of desire to drink is correspondingly low. The next several lines illustrate changes in these parameters associated with increasing intensity of cues, and the desire to drink increases. The last lines show what might happen when cues are more intense. The person may experience a desire to drink that overwhelms inhibitory influences.

Training Procedure and Post-Training Assessment A network with twenty input units was created, with four units each for the four systems and four bias units (see figure 5.2). Six units with six corresponding and reciprocally interconnected context units were created in the two middle, or hidden, layers; these were analogous to the processing elements in the NAcc and VTA and the ventral pallidum and frontal cortex circuits. One output unit was created for each output of the system. The network was trained using a backpropagation algorithm (see Hertz et al., 1991, and Parks, Levine,

& Long, chapter 1 in this book). The model was then trained to simulate various levels of desire to drink, using the backpropagation algorithm described in detail elsewhere (Rumelhart, Hinton, & Williams, 1986; see chapter 1).

Briefly, in a backpropagation network, the model is presented with a set of matched pairs of inputs and their corresponding desired outputs. Training of the model begins when inputs are propagated forward through the several levels of neural elements. Firing of individual units is determined by the synaptic weights between the elements and the unit's firing threshold. In this case, weights are analogs of the strength of the connection between two neurons, and thresholds are analogs of the critical voltage required for a neuron to generate an action potential. Weights are initially assigned randomly.

Inputs are then propagated forward to the output where some value results. This actual output of the network is compared with desired output (already specified), and the error is calculated as the difference between actual and desired outputs. This error is then propagated back through the network, resulting in adjustments to the synaptic weights. The cycle is repeated for each pair of inputs and outputs until the network performs at a desired level of accuracy, usually at less than 1 percent mean squared error, or MSE (see Rumelhart et al., 1986, for a more detailed explanation).

As initial seedings of synaptic weights are random and backpropagation learning employs a minimization of error algorithm, it is possible that any one network could arrive at a solution based on a spurious local minimum. To control for this problem, five networks were constructed and tested in each experimental condition described below. With the small number of outputs in experimental conditions (ten for each), it was possible that the assumptions underlying the use of parametric statistics would be violated in tests of differences between network outputs. In these cases nonparametric tests were used to assess differences in network outputs, with a nominal alpha value of 0.05 (Siegel & Castellan, 1987). In these cases, two-tailed tests were employed throughout. In one experimental condition in which the rate of learning in two types of networks was compared over multiple trials, parametric repeated measures analysis of variance (ANOVA) was used. This appeared justified because of the large number of data points used (four per network times fifty networks) and statistical evidence that parametric assumptions were met (Winer, 1971; discussed further below). In order to assess whether results were caused by local minima or other factors associated with one network, a total of five networks was constructed and trained.

Each of the five networks was easily trained to an MSE level of less than 1 percent. After training to assess the network's learning, each was tested by presenting it with the same training inputs but without the desired outputs. Trained outputs were examined to determine whether the network operated as intended.

Outputs of the five networks after training were not significantly different (Wilcoxon Matched-Pairs Signed Ranks tests; all probabilities >0.10). To

Table 5.2 Outputs after training from each of five networks

Network A		Network B		Network C		Network D		Network E	
.112	.099	.108	.103	.103	.108	.113	.114	.106	.108
.198	.201	.200	.200	.198	.208	.196	.203	.203	.098
.305	.297	.300	.297	.307	.292	.298	.294	.298	.303
.392	.400	.400	.399	.398	.401	.398	.397	.402	.396
.497	.504	.495	.498	.486	.487	.492	.496	.495	.496
.603	.607	.599	.604	.598	.595	.605	.599	.601	.603
.702	.696	.700	.707	.721	.716	.709	.708	.703	.702
0912	.807	.813	.802	.824	.838	.806	.808	.810	.809
.897	.895	.908	.905	.890	.896	.903	.905	.900	.902
.952	.953	.948	.947	.927	.924	.947	.947	.951	.951

Note: This table presents outputs from each network after training. Each net was presented with the same set of inputs (the training set in table 5.1, but without the output) and its output was recorded to assess whether each network's output was substantially the same.

further assess the extent to which all five networks behaved the same, new test inputs were constructed and presented to the networks. These were constructed on the rationale of holding the input of four of the systems constant and varying the fifth. This was an important test, since several of the planned experimental manipulations of the networks would assess the changes in the networks' outputs caused by changes in inputs. The outputs of each of the five networks for each of five conditions were compared using Wilcoxon Matched-Pairs Rank-Sum tests. They did not differ significantly ($P > .10$) (table 5.2). All five networks were then tested in all subsequent conditions. Unless otherwise noted, the outputs did not significantly differ among the networks across conditions.

The study presented in this chapter used neural network software developed at the University of Stuttgart Institute for Parallel and Distributed High Performance Systems (Zell, Mamier, & Vogt, 1996). It was run on a Pentium computer using the Linux operating system (Volkerding, Richard, & Johnson, 1996).

Test Conditions

Experimental manipulations to simulate alcohol-related desire to drink were of three kinds: (1) changes in inputs to the bias units to the NAcc to simulate changes in dopaminergic activity in it to simulate normal and abnormal levels of desire for alcohol—normal and abnormal levels of desire to drink; (2) changes in the self-recurrent weights in the context units to simulate inherently higher levels of dopaminergic activity in those systems to simulate increased genetic vulnerability to developing alcohol dependence; and (3) changes in inputs to the networks to simulate changes in the state of the system each input represents to simulate the effects of therapeutic interventions on the network.

Changes in Bias Units   During training, the four bias units were each set to increase by 0.1 unit to simulate the increase in dopaminergic activation of the NAcc with changes in cue intensity. To investigate whether increased dopaminergic activity in the NAcc would affect the level of desire to drink, inputs were changed to 1.0 for all cue levels. To simulate decreased dopaminergic activity resulting from blocking dopaminergic inputs by opiate antagonist medications, in another condition inputs were changed to −1.0.

Changes in Self-Recurrent Weights   In the architecture of the network as constructed, each of the six context units was reciprocally interconnected to simulate the NAcc-VTA circuit. Each context unit in turn has a self-recurrent connection, so that during training part of its own output is fed back to it. These self-recurrent weights are usually set to zero (Zell et al., 1995). To simulate increased dopaminergic activity in this circuit, these weights were increased to 0.8—in this way, making the circuit inherently more active. In the normal condition, the network simulated alcohol-nonpreferring rat strains, while with increased dopaminergic activity it simulated alcohol-preferring rats. The rates of learning in two groups of twenty-five networks, one with normal dopaminergic activation and one with increased activation, were compared at four points via repeated measures ANOVA and post hoc t-tests.

Therapeutic Conditions   The network was assessed as well under conditions simulating therapeutic interventions in alcohol dependence. Opioid antagonist medications have been effective in treatment of alcohol dependence, presumably by antagonizing μ and κ opiate receptors in the NAcc (Di Chiara & Imperato, 1988b). This antagonism results in decreased dopaminergic activity in the NAcc. Although simulating changes in the inherent activity of the network via changes in the self-recurrent weights as described above was possible, it was not possible nor would it be realistic to manipulate these weights after learning had occurred in the network. The effect of decreased dopaminergic activity in the NAcc was therefore simulated by decreased inputs to the NAcc from the bias units. Serotonin reuptake inhibitors have also been used to treat alcohol dependence. The possible effect on the serotonergic system of the use of these medications was simulated by changing the serotonergic input to the system from the dorsal raphe.

Finally, psychosocial treatments are effective in treating alcohol dependence (Marlatt & Gordon, 1985; Monti, Abrams, Kadden, et al., 1989). The neurophysiological mechanism by which psychosocial therapies work is not readily apparent, and different psychosocial therapies may operate on different neurophysiological substrates. Coping skills therapy might increase frontal cortex control over drinking behavior, for example, while the understanding of the determinants of drinking behavior resulting from participation in Alcoholics Anonymous might decrease the intensity of motivational inputs to the system. In this study, the impact of psychosocial therapy was simulated by decreasing limbic system inputs to the system, consistent with the hypothesis that psychosocial therapy decreases the intensity of motivational inputs to the NAcc. Although this approach to simulating psychotherapy's effects is speculative, it should be noted that Baxter and his colleagues (Baxter, Schwartz, Bergman, et al., 1992) showed that both pharmacological and behavior therapy for OCD changed metabolic rates in anatomical structures that are parts of the circuit hypothesized here to be central to alcohol dependence.

Experiment One: "Normal" Desire to Drink

Networks were constructed and trained as described. To assess whether each of the five networks behaved similarly after being trained, the outputs of each network at the end of training were statistically compared. The behavior of each network in other conditions was then tested with new input patterns. These new inputs consisted of a set of five inputs from each system (limbic and olfactory cortices, amygdala, dorsal raphe, and dopaminergic bias units). In each group, one input was set at the level corresponding to the highest level of desire to drink, with all others at the minimum. In this way, the effects of inputs from individual anatomical systems on each network could be assessed. This was done because later experimental conditions would manipulate these inputs and it was therefore essential to determine whether the experimental interventions affected each network in the same way. Each of the resulting outputs was tested for equivalence. If outputs from each of five networks were not significantly different across multiple conditions, solutions were probably not based on local minima.

Experiment Two: "Abnormal" Desire to Drink

The ability of the network to simulate very high levels of desire to drink in response to minimal alcohol-related stimuli (as occurs in alcohol-dependent persons; Rohsenow, Niaura, Childress, et al., 1990–1991) was then assessed. It has been hypothesized that alcohol-related stimuli cause an increase in dopaminergic activity in the NAcc with a resultant loss of inhibition to the frontocortical-thalamic circuit involved in the subjective desire to drink (Modell et al., 1990). Inputs to the bias units, used to simulate levels of dopaminergic activity in the NAcc, were increased to simulate this experimental condition. At the same time, the same inputs (simulating "normal" environmental stimuli) were presented at other network inputs.

Experiment Three: Genetic Vulnerability

Several neurochemical differences have been demonstrated in strains of alcohol-preferring and -nonpreferring rats. The most salient of these is the increased response of their NAcc-VTA dopaminergic system to the administration of alcohol (Charness, 1992; Weiss, Lorang, Bloom, et al., 1993). The architecture of the current network, with several layers of hidden units and corresponding groups of context units (see figure 5.2), allowed for simulation of this increased pattern of reactivity. Each of the context units (see A in figure 5.2) has a self-recurrent link that is usually constrained to be zero. By increasing this value to a positive nonzero value, the inherent activity of the circuit is increased, similar to the activity in this circuit in alcohol-preferring strains of rats. It was hypothesized that with increased activity in this circuit, the network would more rapidly and completely acquire multiple levels of desire to drink. To assess rate and completeness of learning, the networks' level of error (MSE) was assessed at four learning points: after 500, 1000, 1500, and 2000 learning trials. To assess adequately whether differences were not due to random differences and to allow a larger data set for parametric analysis, twenty-five networks were trained and assessed in each of the two conditions (low and high dopaminergic reactivity).

Experiment Four: Therapeutic Modalities

Animal and human studies have shown that serotonin reuptake blocking and opiate antagonist medications can reduce alcohol intake, and in humans, reduce reported desire to drink (Anton, 1995). Psychosocial therapies, such as Alcoholics Anonymous, relapse prevention (Marlatt & Gordon, 1985), and coping skills therapy (Monti et al., 1989) are effective in treating alcohol dependence. The effects of simulations of these treatments on levels of desire to drink were therefore studied.

In all cases, "alcohol-preferring" networks were used for tests of therapeutic modalities. Abnormal desire to drink was simulated as outlined in experiment two (above), and inputs were varied to simulate the impact of therapeutic interventions. To simulate the use of serotonin reuptake blockers, dorsal raphe inputs were increased by a factor of 10. The effects of opiate antagonist medications (decreases in dopaminergic activity in NAcc in response to stimuli) were simulated by decreasing inputs from the dopaminergic bias units. Psychosocial therapies were hypothesized to reduce motivation to drink; this decrease in motivation was simulated by reductions in limbic system inputs to the system.

RESULTS

Experiment One: "Normal" Levels of Desire to Drink

The hypothesis that the network could learn to simulate "normal" desire to drink alcohol, and even high levels of desire associated with multiple internal and external cues and motivational states, was tested first. The output of the network in its untrained state was compared with its output after 2000 training trials with a resulting MSE less than 1 percent. The network simulated "normal" levels of desire for alcohol: the two sets of output differed significantly ($z = -2.80$, $P < .01$).

Experiment Two: "Abnormal" Levels of Desire to Drink

The hypothesis was also tested that abnormally high levels of desire to drink, in response to minimal cues, could be simulated by the network. With dopaminergic input from bias units to the NAcc increased, the same stimuli representing internal and external cues and motivational states were again presented to the network. The network's output was significantly increased (i.e., indicated higher levels of desire to drink) in this condition ($z = 2.70$; $P < .01$).

Experiment Three: Genetic Vulnerability

As outlined above, increased dopaminergic activity in the NAcc-VTA circuit was simulated by changes in self-recurrent weights (see figure 5.2), and rates of learning of "nonpreferring" and "preferring" networks were compared. Twenty-five networks in each condition were assessed at four time points. Repeated measures ANOVA showed a main effect of time (Hotelling's $T^2 = 20.21$; $F = 227.41$; $df = 4.45$; $P < .001$), as expected with effective training of both networks (figure 5.3). There was a significant interaction of group with time (Hotelling's $T^2 = 1.80$; $F = 20.23$; $df = 4$, 45; $P < .001$), suggesting that each group had a different learning rate. The graph of the MSE for each condition (see figure 5.3) illustrates the slower learning rate for the nonpreferring network. Post hoc tests of these mean differences show that although each group of networks started at approximately the same level of error (comparison of baseline MSEs before training each network; $t = -0.25$, $df = 48$; $P > .10$), their MSEs differed at each subsequent point (t-value at 500 trials $= 9.19$, $df = 48$; $P < .001$; t-value at 1000 trials $= 7.01$, $df = 48$; $P < .001$; t-value at 1500 trials $= 4.69$, $df = 48$; $P < .001$; t-value at 2000 trials $= 3.61$, $df = 48$; $P < .001$; all values significant after Bonferroni correction for multiple comparisons). The significant difference obtained after 2000 learning trials suggests that the preferring networks not only learned to desire alcohol more readily but also more completely, as might occur in a person genetically vulnerable to the development of alcohol dependence.

Experiment Four: Therapeutic Modalities

In each case, simulation of therapeutic modalities resulted in significant decreases in level of desire to drink. Opiate antagonist treatment reduced simulated desire to drink (all tests were Wilcoxon Matched-Pairs Signed Ranks tests; here, $z = -2.80$; $P < .01$), as did treatment with serotonin reuptake blockers ($z = -2.80$; $P < .01$). Psychosocial treatment alone reduced the desire to drink significantly ($z = -2.70$; $P < .01$), but this decrease was

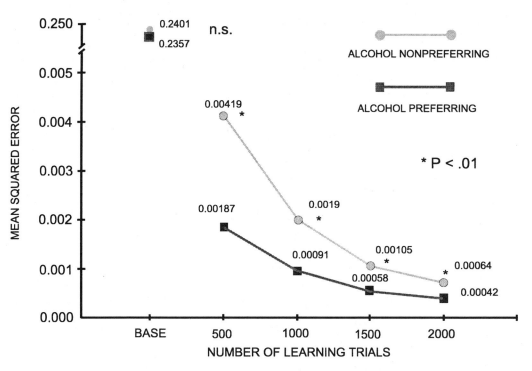

Figure 5.3 Comparison of learning in alcohol-preferring and -nonpreferring networks.

smaller than that caused by opiate antagonist treatment alone ($z = -2.80$; $P < .01$). Combined treatment with opiate antagonist and serotonin reuptake blockers was significantly better than either treatment alone (opiate antagonist alone vs. opiate antagonist with serotonin reuptake blocker: $z = -2.24$, $P < .05$; serotonin reuptake blocker vs. combination: $z = -2.80$, $P < .01$).

DISCUSSION

The results of this study show that a computational model can simulate symptoms of alcohol dependence. Differences in desire to drink alcohol were produced under both normal and abnormal conditions. Normal levels of desire to drink alcohol were consistently associated with inputs to the networks. Mild desire to drink was associated with weak stimuli, and strong desire was only associated with strong stimuli. In contrast, when the network changed to simulate the increased levels of dopaminergic function in the NAcc found in alcohol dependence, even weak stimuli elicited strong desire to drink. This finding is similar to the experience of persons who are dependent on alcohol. Minimal environmental stimuli, such as seeing others drinking, and even internal stimuli, such as thinking about alcohol, can elicit strong desires to drink. This condition replicates the situation hypothesized by Modell et al. (1990), when an alcohol-dependent individual takes his or her first drink.

Modell and colleagues argue that the acute effects of alcohol intake increase dopaminergic activity in the NAcc. This increased activity in turn results in higher levels of desire to drink via activity in the frontothalamic loop. In this simulation, the excitatory feedback to the system from the frontothalamic circuit is represented by increased activation of dopaminergic bias units. The ability of the network to portray both normal and abnormal levels of desire to drink is a necessary first step toward validating the model for other uses. Its ability to perform this simulation is not surprising in light of the capacity of computational models to simulate other psychiatric syndromes, such as schizophrenia (Cohen & Servan-Schreiber, 1992; Hoffman, 1987;) or anxiety disorders (Ownby & Carmin, 1995).

The model was next modified to simulate a more dynamic process involved in the development of alcohol dependence: the acquisition of increased network activation in response to environmental and internal cues. By increasing the inherent dopaminergic activity of the loop, including the NAcc and VTA, it was possible to simulate genetically based differences in strains of rats. Alcohol-preferring and -nonpreferring rats have been shown to have different dopaminergic responses in the NAcc and VTA to alcohol administration (Weiss et al., 1993), with alcohol-preferring rats having larger increases in dopaminergic activity after alcohol intake. The ability of the model to simulate this effect suggests that it could test any strategy that might be developed for reducing this inherent activity. For example, if a dopamine blocking agent selective for receptors in this circuit were to be developed, its effects on the development of alcohol dependence could be assessed with this model.

The network also was able to simulate the effects of both psychosocial and pharmacological treatments of alcohol dependence. As modeled, both categories of treatment reduced abnormal levels of desire to drink, although psychosocial treatment was less effective than were serotonergic or opioidergic treatments. The model predicts that combinations of treatments, especially combinations of pharmacological and psychosocial treatment, are likely to be more effective than either treatment alone. Research has provided limited support for this prediction (Mason, 1994). The model also shows that augmentation of opioidergic treatment with serotonergic treatment should also be significantly better than either treatment alone. Preliminary data from an ongoing trial of the opioid antagonist nalmefene augmented with the serotonin reuptake blocker sertraline suggest that this is also true (B. J. Mason, personal communication, May 8, 1997).

The demonstration that psychosocial and pharmacological treatments result in similar effects provides an integrative rationale for both types of treatments' effects on the brain. This is reminiscent of brain imaging findings in the treatment of OCD. Those studies have shown that successful symptomatic relief of OCD symptoms by either pharmacological and behavioral treatment reduced metabolic activity in a part of the basal ganglia (Baxter et al., 1992). These basal ganglia structures are believed by Modell et al. (1990)

to be part of the same circuit involved in obsessions and in the obsession-like quality of alcoholics' intense desires to consume alcohol. Behavioral and pharmacological treatments may have impacts on different parts of the network, but have similar results on the same symptom-related structures.

The model used a partially recurrent architecture normally used for problem solving in situations in which changes across time must be learned. In this simulation, however, the network architecture is used to simulate neural loops that regulate the flow of information from input to output units.

The usefulness of this model in simulating observed clinical phenomena is intriguing, but its eventual usefulness will lie in its ability to test strategies for changing the activity of this neural system and to generate testable hypotheses about modes of treatment. The prediction that augmentation of opioidergic treatment with serotonergic treatment was made independent of knowledge about the usefulness of sertraline augmentation of nalmefene treatment for alcohol dependence and was a minor test of the model. Since the idea that addressing intense desire to drink via two neurotransmitter systems would be better than via one is intuitive, however, this finding cannot be considered a strong test of the model.

In the future, it is hoped that other tests of the model can be devised which are stronger. For example, it might be possible to compare the network's predictions on the relative efficacies of several psychosocial treatments with actual treatment data. Would treatment focused on reducing the salience of alcohol-related cues be superior to that focused on coping skills or relapse prevention? It could be hypothesized that cue-related treatment would reduce sensory and motivational inputs to the network, while coping skills might increase inhibition of the circuit through parts of the frontal cortex. Although the net effect of these interventions should be to reduce abnormally intense desire to drink, it is not clear which strategy might produce larger effects. Such a simulation is complicated by difficulties in quantifying the changes in different neurotransmitter systems caused by interventions. At present, only qualitative changes can be reliably shown, but it is hoped that further research about receptor binding affinities will allow at least rough estimates of the relative effects on neurotransmission of various opioid antagonists compared, for example, to serotonin reuptake blockers. Further development of neural modeling software and computational algorithms may solve this and other technical problems, and additional neuroscience research on the phenomenon of alcohol dependence may provide additional data with which to refine the simulation. Continuing work on the model thus appears warranted.

ACKNOWLEDGMENT

This chapter received the 1996 Resident Research Award sponsored by the American Psychiatric Association and Lilly Pharmaceuticals.

REFERENCES

Anton, R. F. (1995). New directions in the pharmacotherapy of alcoholism. *Psychiatric Annals, 25,* 353–362.

Bauer, L. O. (1992). Psychobiology of craving. In J. H. Lowinson, P. Ruiz, & R. B. Millman (Eds.), *Substance abuse: A comprehensive textbook* (pp. 51–55). Baltimore: Williams & Wilkins.

Baxter, L. R., Schwartz, J. M., Bergman, K. S., Szuba M. P., Guze, B. H., Mazziotta, J. C., Alazraki, A., Selin, C. E., Fernig, H., Munford, P., & Phelps, M. E. (1992). Caudate glucose metabolic rate changes with both drug and behavior therapy for obsessive-compulsive disorder. *Archives of General Psychiatry, 49,* 681–689.

Charness, M. E. (1992). Molecular mechanisms of ethanol intoxication, tolerance, and physical dependence. In J. H. Mendelson & N. K. Mello (Eds.), *Diagnosis and treatment of alcoholism* (pp. 155–199). New York: McGraw-Hill.

Cohen, J. D. & Servan-Schreiber, D. (1992). Context, cortex, and dopamine: A connectionist approach to behavior and biology in schizophrenia. *Psychological Review, 99,* 45–77.

Devine, D. P., Leone, P., & Wise, R. A. (1993). Mesolimbic dopamine neurotransmission is increased by administration of μ-opioid receptor antagonists. *European Journal of Pharmacology, 243,* 55–64.

Di Chiara, G., Acquas E., & Carboni, E. (1992). Drug motivation and abuse: A neurobiological perspective. *Annals of the New York Academy of Sciences, 654,* 207–219.

Di Chiara, G., & Imperato, A. (1988a). Drugs abused by humans preferentially increase synaptic dopamine concentrations in the mesolimbic system of freely moving rats. *Proceedings of the National Academy of Sciences, 85,* 5274–5278.

Di Chiara, G., & Imperato, A. (1988b). Opposite effects of *mu* and *kappa* opiate agonists on dopamine release in the nucleus accumbens and in the dorsal caudate of freely moving rats. *Journal of Pharmacology and Experimental Therapeutics, 244,* 1067–1080.

Dolin, S. J., & Little, H. J. (1989). Are changes in neuronal calcium channels involved in ethanol tolerance? *Journal of Pharmacology and Experimental Therapeutics, 250,* 985–989.

Dolin, S., Little, H., Hudspith, M., Pagonis, C., & Littleton, J. (1987). Increased dihydropyridine-sensitive calcium channels in rat brain may underlie ethanol physical dependence. *Neuropharmacology, 26,* 275–279.

Dolinsky, Z. S., Morse, D. E., Kaplan, R. F., Meyer, R. E. Corry, P., & Pomerleau, O. F. (1987) Neuroendocrine, psychophysiological, and subjective reactivity to an alcohol placebo in male alcoholic patients. *Alcoholism: Clinical and Experimental Research, 11,* 296–300.

George, D. T., Wozniak, K., & Linnolia, M. (1992). Basic and clinical studies on serotonin, alcohol and alcoholics. In C. A. Naranjo & E. M. Sellers (Eds.), *Novel pharmacologic interventions for alcoholism* (pp. 92–104). New York: Springer-Verlag.

Hertz, J., Krogh, A., & Palmer, R. G. (1991). *Introduction to the theory of neural computation.* Reading, MA: Addison-Wesley.

Hoffman, R. E. (1987). Computer simulations of neural information processing and the schizophrenia-mania dichotomy. *Archives of General Psychiatry, 44,* 178–188.

Imperato, A., & Di Chiara, G. (1986). Preferential stimulation of dopamine release in the nucleus accumbens of freely moving rats by ethanol. *Journal of Pharmacology and Experimental Therapeutics, 239,* 219–228.

Koob, G. F. (1992a). Neural mechanisms of drug reinforcement. *Annals of the New York Academy of Sciences, 654,* 171–191.

Koob, G. F. (1992b). Drugs of abuse: Anatomy, pharmacology and function of reward pathways. *Trends in Pharmacological Sciences, 13*, 177–184.

Koob, G. F., & Bloom, F. E. (1988). Cellular and molecular mechanisms of drug dependence. *Science, 242*, 715–723.

Koob, G. F., Rassnick, S., Heinrichs, S., & Weiss, F. (1994). Alcohol, the reward system and dependence. *EXS, 71*, 103–114.

LeMarquand, D., Pihl R. O., & Benkelfat, C. (1994). Serotonin and alcohol intake, abuse, and dependence: Clinical evidence. *Biological Psychiatry, 36*, 326–337.

Lhuintre, J. P., Daoust, M., Moore, N. E., Chretien, D., Saligaut, C., Tran, G., Bosimare, F., & Hillemand, B. (1985). Ability of calcium bis acetyl homotaurine, a GABA agonist, to prevent relapse in weaned alcoholics. *Lancet, 1*, 1014–1016.

Ludwig, A. M. (1986). The mystery of craving. *Alcohol Health and Research World, 10*, 12–17, 69.

Marlatt, G. A., & Gordon, J. R. (Eds.) (1985). *Relapse prevention: Maintenance strategies in the treatment of addictive behavior.* New York: Guilford..

Mason, B. J. (1994). Effects of psychosocial and pharmacologic treatments individually and combined on alcohol dependence. Presented at the annual meeting of the Society for Biomedical Research in Alcoholism, Brisbane, Australia, June 1994.

McBride, W. J., Murphy, J. M., Lumeng, L., & Li, T.-K. (1992). Serotonin and alcohol consumption. In C. A. Naranjo & E. M. Sellers (Eds.), *Novel pharmacologic interventions for alcoholism* (pp. 59–67). New York: Springer-Verlag.

Modell, J. G., Glaser, F. B., Cyr, L., & Mountz, J. M. (1992a). Obsessive and compulsive characteristics of craving for alcohol in alcohol abuse and dependence. *Alcoholism: Clinical and Experimental Research, 16*, 272–274.

Modell, J. G., Glaser, F. B., Mountz, J. M., & Lee, J. Y. (1993). Effect of haloperidol on measures of craving and impaired control in alcoholic subjects. *Alcoholism: Clinical and Experimental Research, 17*, 234–240.

Modell, J. G., Glaser, F. B., Mountz, J. M., Schmaltz, S., & Cyr L. (1992b). Obsessive and compulsive characteristics of alcohol abuse and dependence: Quantification by a newly developed questionnaire. *Alcoholism: Clinical and Experimental Research, 16*, 266–271.

Modell, J. G., Mountz, J. M., & Beresford, T. P. (1990). Basal ganglia/limbic striatal and thalamocortical involvement in craving and loss of control in alcoholism. *Journal of Neuropsychiatry and Clinical Neuroscience, 2*, 123–144.

Modell, J. G., Mountz, J. M., Curtis, G. C., & Greden, J. F. (1989). Neurophysiologic dysfunction in basal ganglia/limbic striatal and thalamocortical circuits as a pathogenetic mechanism of obsessive-compulsive disorder. *Journal of Neuropsychiatry, 1*, 27–36.

Monti, P. M., Abrams, D. B., Kadden, R. M., & Cooney, N. L. (1989). Treating alcohol dependence: A coping skills training guide. New York: Guilford.

Murphy, J. M., McBride, W. J., Lumeng, L., Li, T.-K. (1987). Contents of monoamines in forebrain regions of alcohol-preferring (P) and -nonpreferring (NP) lines of rats. *Pharmacology, Biochemistry, and Behavior, 26*, 389–392.

Nestler, E. J. (1992). Molecular mechanisms of drug addiction. *Journal of Neuroscience, 12*, 2439–2450.

O'Malley, S. S., Jaffe, A. J., Change, G., Schottenfeld, R. S., Meyer, R. E., & Rounsaville, B. (1992). Naltrexone and coping skills therapy for alcohol dependence. *Archives of General Psychiatry, 49*, 881–887.

Ownby, R. L., & Carmin, C. N. (1995). A neural network model of panic disorder (abstract). *Biological Psychiatry, 37,* 616.

Rohsenow, D. J., Niaura, R. S., Childress, A. R., Abrams, P. M., & Monti, P. M. (1990–1991). Cue reactivity in addictive behaviors: Theoretical and treatment implications. *International Journal of the Addictions, 25,* 957–993.

Rumelhart, D. E., Hinton, G. E., & Williams, R. J. (1986). Learning internal representations by error propagation. In D. Rumelhart, J. L. McClelland, & the PDP Research Group (Eds.) *Parallel distributed processing: Explorations in the microstructure of cognition,* Vol. 1 (pp. 318–362). Cambridge, MA: MIT Press.

Sellers, E. M., Higgins, G. A., & Sobell, M. B. (1992). 5-HT and alcohol abuse. *Trends in Pharmacological Sciences, 13,* 69–75.

Siegel, S., & Castellan, N. J. (1987). *Nonparametric statistics,* 2nd ed.. New York: McGraw-Hill.

Stinus, L., Cador, M., & Le Moal, M. (1992). Interaction between endogenous opioids and dopamine within the nucleus accumbens. *Annals of the New York Academy of Sciences, 654,* 254–273.

Terenius, L. (1994). Reward and its control by dynorphin peptides. *EXS, 71,* 9–17.

Trevisan, L., Fitzgerald, L. W., Brose, N., Gasic, G. P., Heinemann, S. F., Duman, R. S., & Nestler, R. J. (1994). Chronic ethanol upregulates NMDAR1 receptor subunit immunoreactivity in rat hippocampus. *Journal of Neurochemistry, 62,* 1635–1638.

Turkkan, J. S., McCaul, M. E., & Stitzer, M. L. (1989). Psychophysiological effects of alcohol related stimuli. II. Enhancement with alcohol availability. *Alcoholism: Clinical and Experimental Research, 13,* 392–398.

Volkerding, P., Richard, K., & Johnson, E. F. (1996). *Linux, configuration and installation,* 2nd ed.. New York: MIS Press.

Volpicelli, J. R., Alterman, A. I., Harashida, M., & O'Brien, C. P. (1992). Naltrexone in the treatment of alcohol dependence. *Archives of General Psychiatry, 49,* 876–880.

Weiss, F., Lorang, M. T., Bloom, F. E., & Koob, G. F. (1993). Oral alcohol self-administration stimulates dopamine release in the rat nucleus accumbens: Genetic and motivational determinants. *Journal of Pharmacology and Experimental Therapeutics, 267,* 250–258.

Whittington, M. A., Dolin, S. J., Patch, T. L., Siarey, R. J., et al. (1991). Chronic dihydropyridine treatment can reverse the behavioural consequences of and prevent adaptations to chronic ethanol treatment. *British Journal of Pharmacology, 103,* 1669–1676.

Winer, B. J. (1971). *Statistical principles in experimental design,* 2nd ed.. New York: McGraw-Hill.

Zell, A., Mamier, G., & Vogt, M. (1996). Stuttgart Neural Network Simulator user's manual, version 4.1. Stuttgart: University of Stuttgart Institute for Parallel and Distributed High Performance Systems. [The World Wide Web page on the simulator is at http://www.informatik.uni-stuttgart.de/ipvr/bv/projekte/snns/snns.html. The software is available for download at: ftp://ftp.informatik.uni-stuttgart.de/pub/SNNS.]

6 A Computational Perspective on Learned Helplessness and Depression

Sam Leven

One of the most persistent syndromes in human behavior is depression. It yields partly to drug treatment (Richelson, 1997) and partly to psychotherapy (Beck, 1997; Padesky & Greenberger, 1995). More intractable is atypical depression, which is characterized by a mixture of problematic behaviors associated with the underlying dysphoric state. Tyrer and Steinberg (1993) have suggested five mutually exclusive models of behavior dysfunction: disease, psychodynamic, behavioral, cognitive, and psychosocial (table 6.1). Each approach has its own internally consistent theoretical basis, treatment options, and evaluations. However, each alone provides an inadequate explanation of depression.

In this chapter, we present an integrated view of the processes that produce depression based on a neural network architecture. Neural networks appear to be eminently suitable for modeling complex phenomena involving neurochemical and neuroelectrical phenomena, such as depression. There is no other environment for asking such complex questions as, What role does inhibition of one sensory process play in some apparently unrelated behavior? What effects do changes in expectancies and preparatory set have in speeding this behavior or magnifying its importance? And, what is the impact of the chemical "signature" (Black, Adler, Dreyfuss, et al., 1988) on the representational process? Investigating such questions requires a branch of neural networks that comprehends higher-order processes (Grossberg, 1980). While neural network models of such processes must be reductionist, they remain a useful way to query the system, to pose testable theories in a rigorous manner, and to compare explanations of what may not seem fully comparable data (Leven, 1988).

In the following section, we describe a model of "learned helplessness" (Seligman, 1975), a dysfunction frequently considered an animal model for human depression and anxiety. Despite ongoing controversy about the causes, course, and treatment of learned helplessness (Leven, 1992; Peterson, Maier, & Seligman, 1993), a consensus seems to be forming that allows for the formalizing function and modeling clarity neural networks can provide (Levine, 1991, chapter 7). The next section addresses some of the controversial issues. In addition, the important assumptions of Samson's research

Table 6.1 Standard models: assumed problems and treatment

Model	Problem	Treatment
Disease	Chemical imbalance	Drug treatment
Psychodynamic	Trauma expression	Deep analysis
Behavioral	Action failure	Retraining
Cognitive	Categorizing error	Restructure planning
Psychosocial	External influences	Self-efficacy training

provide the emerging foundational consensus (Samson, Mirin, Hauser, et al., 1992).

TYPES OF HELPLESSNESS

Theories of the cause and treatment of depression are numerous and some-times inadequate. Psychoanalytic therapies (Arieti & Bemporad, 1982) focus on previous infliction of injuries to the self; cognitive therapies (Alford & Beck, 1997; Beck, A., 1976, 1997; Beck, J., 1995; Beck, Rush, Shaw, et al., 1987) find failures in explanatory styles; somatic therapies (Lowen, 1971) treat sensorimotor conflicts with the current environment. Among psycho-pharmacologists, the conflict is not over therapies as much as theories (Cooper, Bloom, & Roth, 1991): which brain structures and functions account for the development of depression? The animal models upon which human treatments usually rely have produced many theories. Leven (1992) has sug-gested some potential limitations in these models. We briefly summarize recent work by leading scholars who bring together the experimental tradi-tions of Weiss, Seligman, Petty, and collaborators, and then review ours.

Figure 6.1 represents work from two separate experimental traditions which converge toward a single solution. Minor, Dess, and Overmier (1991) have described three sets of experiments which induce three similar but dif-ferentiable subtypes of learned helplessness. They describe these as motoric, vegetative, and cognitive. Gray (1987) advanced a related model. His three systems have biological components, but do not explain the broad systems of neuromodulators which underlie psychopathology (van der Kolk, 1987). In the human post-traumatic stress disorder literature, a closely matching set of categories is introduced (for reviews, see Herman, 1992): hyperarousal, constriction, and intrusion. These models derive from different sources. Lab-oratory work in animal models has emulated human behavior through shock, variable schedules designed to discourage, and isolation. Lesions and other intrusive methods have allowed development of schematic models. Drug therapies have suggested underlying chemical systems (Richelson, 1997). And human subjects (both depressive and anxiety disorder and traumatic stress sufferers) have confirmed the outlines of the experimental observa-tions. What remains is to create a synthesis of these efforts, design testable

Herman (1992)	Minor, Dess, and Overmier (1991)	Gray (1987)
HYPERAROUSAL	MOTORIC	APPROACH
chronic stress; elevated baseline of arousal	stress-induced; motor programs	Substantia nigra --> Ventral tegmentum --> Nucleus accumbens; Dopamine; Nucleus accumbens --> Cingulate cortex
CONSTRICTION	VEGETATIVE	FIGHT/FLIGHT
altered numbness; analgesia; withdrawal	H-P-A axis	Amygdala/Septum-Hippocampus --> Hypothalamus 5-HT; GABA; Opiate
INTRUSION	COGNITIVE	BEHAVIORAL INHIBITION
"active memory'; need to complete tasks; effort at mastery	unlisted; assume neocortex	Neocortex --> Entorhinal cortex --> Hippocampus; GABA (Opiate, Dopamine)

Figure 6.1 Theoretical models of depression and post-traumatic stress disorder.

network architectures to emulate them, and then redesign them as new data arise.

The physiological circuitries of the three subtypes are described by all these researchers in varying detail, but with some agreement. Their chemical substrates are described in the experimental traditions we have surveyed above and elsewhere (Leven, 1993). The evidence suggests three ways of becoming, acting, and perhaps stopping being helpless. Motoric (using Minor, Dess, & Overmier's terms) depression is a "stuckness," an inability to avoid repeated and ineffective behaviors, or simply giving up because those are the only choices available. Its main chemical message, norepinephrine (NE) shortage, and main behavioral cause, intermittent frustration of simple behavior, have been "resolved" in laboratory experiment by radical increases in NE supply and high physical arousal leading to consistent success (Weiss, 1991).[1] In human subjects, Herman (1992) finds chronic stress and an elevated baseline of arousal which lead to either form of "stuckness" observed in the animal literature: perseveration without recognition of novelty, or freezing.

Vegetative depression is "aloneness," lack of good feeling. Being separated from loved ones under arbitrary conditions and being deprived of endogenous opiates have produced this sense of "personal loss." Eventually, voluntary isolation tends to result. Induced, consistent belonging with loved ones and induction of supply of endogenous opiate resources tend to restore effective behavior in laboratory animals. In humans, Herman (1992) describes

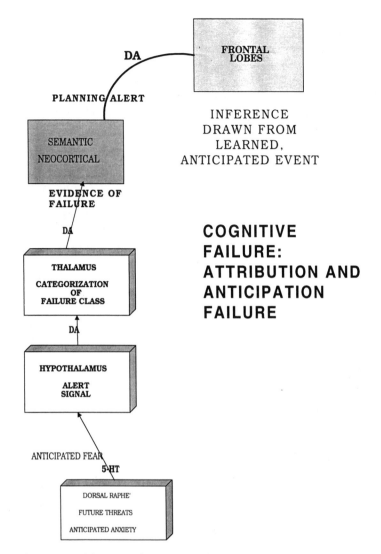

Figure 6.2 Seligman-Beck "cognitive" depression.

alterations in pain tolerance, fear of painful social encounters, and withdrawal—patients tend to "self-medicate" with externally induced opiates and alcohol. Cognitive depression, described by Beck (1976, 1997) and Peterson et al. (1993), involves misuse of available information about the possibility of effective behavior (figure 6.2). The confusion can lead to fear and immobility. Dias, Robbins, and Roberts (1996) have confirmed the model presented by Pribram and McGuinness (1975), that the same system which provides the basis for semantic categorization also facilitates attentional focus in frontal regions.

Petty, Kramer, and Hendrickse (1993) have eliminated a similar deficit in laboratory animals by inducing greater γ-aminobutyric (GABA) availability in cortical regions; Beck's cognitive therapy enables efficient analysis and accurate explanations of events that have led to depression (Beck, 1976, 1997; Beck, Rush, Shaw, et al., 1987). Like Beck, Herman (1992) finds that false or inadequate explanations tend to induce reasoning from distorted grounds, and the need for a "superior explanation" to the one currently employed.

While these types may be separately characterized and detected, they are unlikely to be totally unrelated. Instead, as in most complex behaviors, multiple "feedback loops" (Miller, Galanter, & Pribram, 1960) lead to the very atypical, mixed problems which characterize the clients practitioners encounter today (Leven, 1987)

These same systems emerge in autistic disorder and pervasive developmental disorder (PDD) (Baron-Cohen, 1995). Baron-Cohen suggests that a sense of self required to develop intentionality and the ability to recognize others' intentional states can be interrupted at three preliminary stages (eye direction detection, intentionality detection, and development of a "shared attention mechanism"). Failure at these earlier stages prevents induction of a "theory of mind mechanism," which facilitates the recognition of one's own and others' meaningful behaviors.

Baron-Cohen specifies neurological centers which permit development of these facilities. Eye direction detection takes place in the superior temporal sulcus, intentionality detection in the temporal lobes, and shared attention awareness in the hippocampal complex. The ultimate development of one's own "theory of mind," Baron-Cohen asserts, takes place orbitofrontally. These general functional mappings, drawn on research on dysfunction, are also reflected in theoretical analyses by Pribram (1991) and MacLean (1990). Psycholinguistic analyses continue to support these views (Fauconnier, 1994). Specific emotional mappings which are similar include work by Gray (1987), Gilbert (1984), and Leven (1992).

Samson: Mastery vs. Control

Our target problem is a finding of Samson et al. (1992):

There is a link between cognitive processes associated with coping responses and noradrenergic neuronal activity.... [We] suggest the possibility that noradrenergic neuronal activity is related to the cognitive interpretation constructed by the individual to explain environmental events—higher norepinephrine output is associated with perceptions of powerlessness, and lower norepinephrine output is associated with perceptions of mastery. (p. 808)

Samson's work identified two statistically distinguishable groups of helpless (depressed) people, distinguishing them by their neurochemical structure and the way they described their sense of helplessness (explanatory style).

The distinction in subjects' discussions was based on a pair of standard instruments for measuring whether people feel that (1) they control the essential decisions and actions they take; (2) they act at random—there is no control they can detect over their own behavior; or, (3) other forces control their behavior. The three groups are plainly separable and their views are essential to the therapeutic approach. The cognitive therapy of depression (Beck, 1976, 1997, Beck, Rush, Shaw, et al., 1987; Peterson et al., 1993) suggests that depressives fall into two groups: those with purely organic difficulties (such as brain injury) and those who have faulty explanatory style. The group that lacks physical impairment is held to mistake unfortunate outcomes with failures they have caused. Treatment consists of providing accurate information to eliminate the inferential failures (while curing problems that have resulted from the inappropriate thinking).

Samson et al. (1992) produced a finding that presents a problem for traditional models of depression and its animal analog, learned helplessness. The group, following the leading work of Schildkraut (1965) on the catecholamine theory of depression, has established the unique role of NE in a subtype of depressive behavior (Shatzberg, et al., 1989). The most recent findings of Samson and colleagues established that human subjects testing low on a marker for NE level (the metabolite methoxyhydroxyphenylglycol) also experienced an increased sense that outside influences controlled outcomes in their lives.

NE provides the "focusing" process in brain function (Willner, 1985)[2] and it is generally consistent with Grossberg's gain control function. Further, it inhibits serotonin (5-HT) release from the amygdala, interrupting data on "values" (Pribram, 1991)—in some cases, the release of high amounts of NE can block release of effective quantities of 5-HT, resulting in deletion from the system of critical information about rates of success, identification of relevant positive information (through interruption of its feedback to cortical areas), and preventing the blocking ("forgetting") of traumatic information (Deakin, 1994). NE enervation also facilitates effectiveness of acetylcholine (ACh) release and reception; this allows motivational features to be delivered throughout the brain.

The main sources of NE are the basal ganglia and hypothalamus; these regions feed the locus ceruleus (LC), the central source for the "LC system" (Nieuwenhuys, 1985). Deakin (1994) reports that the median raphe nucleus, a serotonergic body placed in the center of the information flow, plays the unique informational role of identifying learned stress stimuli, sources of chronic fear, and environments in which control is absent. A signal to the amygdala allows that organ to interrupt stressful recollections (preventing phenomena like post-traumatic stress and "freezing," as argued in Herman's, 1992, review). The dorsal raphe nucleus is the source of information on future threats and anticipations of anxiety-producing circumstances in cortical regions (Deakin, 1994). In addition, a recent "learned helplessness" positron emission tomography study suggested reciprocal diencephalic and limbic activation with neuropsychological tests of solvable and unsolvable anagrams (Schneider, Gur, Alavi, et al., 1996).

We interpret Samson to suggest, as Weiss (1991) does, that in the presence of sufficient NE, motor and self-control–related helplessness would not emerge, even if experimental subjects were placed in variable-schedule, pain-producing tasks. Rat subjects, Weiss and Simson (1989) have reported, have proved resilient to such discouragement. These subjects would be consistent with traditional "cognitive" explanations of inference-produced depression.[3] Yet the NE-reduced helplessness Samson observed could only happen in the Weiss-style situation (uncontrollable stress accompanied by exhaustion of NE production at the locus ceruleus). This animal experiment result would tend to confirm Samson's finding that those with chronically exhausted NE resources would act like Weiss's NE-reduced rats. In other words, they would show some evidence that their own actions would have no effect and that others would control their worlds.

Norepinephrine and the Loss of Internal Control Without Explanation: Dopamine

Samson et al. (1992) established a clear marker of a specifically detectable depressive symptom. It was the stable coincidence of a specific chemical state (low NE utilization) with a specific dispositional state (loss of sense of personal control). This detected symptom was the way subjects explained their beliefs about their own condition. Hence this was a higher-order marker.

Other symptoms, when related through the same discriminant analysis, showed no similar statistical significance. Among these unrelated symptoms were other explanations. These other nonsignificant explanations have been related, in the experimental literature, to other neurotransmitters. This result alters the "single-bullet" approach to theories of depressive mentation involving chemical and dispositional state. Samson and associates showed that a separate symptom was tied to a subtype of behavior. We expand on their foundation and suggest the symptom could be causally linked to the behavior by existing theory and observation.

The contrast in the two groups would have been clarified had Samson et al. (1992) established whether homovanillic acid (HVA) levels were low in their other group. HVA is a metabolite of dopamine (DA); a diminished level might suggest that the raphe-potentiating signal to cortical GABA was the source of the alternative behavior.[4] This would have further emphasized the qualitative distinction between two architectures, motivated by different chemical message systems, determining different types of depressive behaviors. Had the two groups been differentiated on that basis, two types could have been understood on the basis of an existing typology of both learned helplessness and depression (Leven, 1992, 1993). The chemistry of Weiss's and the Samson group's helplessness, NE and 5-HT, could have been distinguished from the "cognitive" type suggested by work by Deakin (1994) that we and others have discussed, produced by a different physiological route and different neurochemistry.

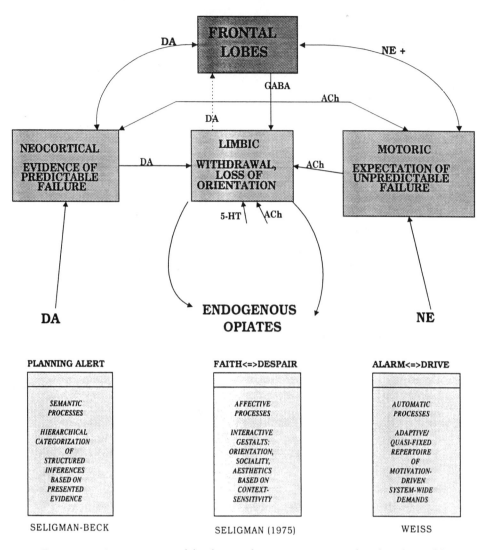

Figure 6.3 A systems view of dysphoria and post-traumatic stress disorder. The model as initially conceived.

A Model of Samson's "Mastery" Type

How can the same stressful, discouraging event produce two qualitatively different types of helpless behavior? First, we describe our hypothesis in some detail. Then, we report an experimental result which clarifies further the distinction we have drawn and raises higher-order questions.

In order to understand our hypothesis, it is helpful to examine in more detail the network diagrams of figures 6.3 and 6.4. Note that, in both figures, the dorsal raphe recognizes the incoming stress and, eventually, produces a DA output to cortex. In figure 6.3, this output (because it does not suggest impending failure) does not reach threshold quantities at cortex and is

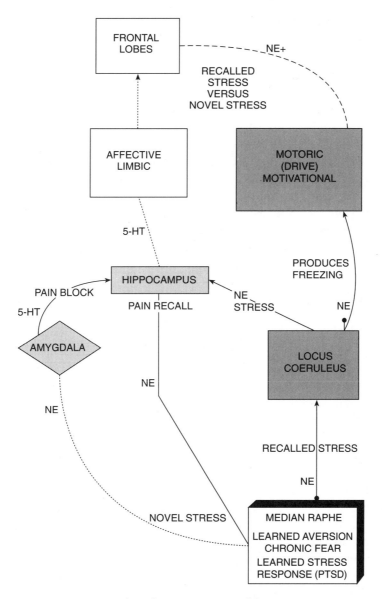

Figure 6.4 Stress produces freezing (Weiss's model).

ignored. Meanwhile, the median raphe and LC observe the stressful situation and fire an identifying "signature" signal electrically (from the dorsal raphe) and a stressful NE signal from the both median raphe and LC to the hippocampus. The stress signal induces heightened plasticity at the hippocampus for the raphe signal and excites α_2-adrenergic receptors, Weiss (1991) asserts, which mediate NE activity here. However, the plasticity is insufficient to induce storage of the signal. The signal then falls below normal and the α_2-receptors, sensing the shortfall, upregulate (increase their population density) at the reception site as a normal part of homeostasis. Eventually, NE stocks are replenished, although at a lower level than normal. Ordinarily, the receptor population would diminish. Instead, in the Weiss training, helplessness-inducing stress is reintroduced before the drop in receptor population. The rush of NE again reaches the hippocampus with the raphe signal, then again falls to below normal levels. Upregulation of α_2-receptors takes place, further increasing the receptor population. Finally, after return to somewhat subnormal NE levels, a third Weiss training occurs. The rush of NE sensitizes an even larger number of α_2-receptors to the signal, finally bringing the signal above the threshold required for memory impression.

Now that the signal is "imprinted" (Bateson, 1972); an automatic response is engendered to the stimulus. The state of helplessness is recalled, and the shortage of NE is experienced. The receptor population, now returned to a near-normal state, experiences none of the "driving" influence of NE and yields an indication to cortical levels that failure has occurred.

Affect-Driven Helplessness: GABA

Let us turn now to figure 6.1, which presents the contrary case. The dorsal raphe identifies a potential future threat and releases sufficient DA to impress the cortex that something significantly stressful is about to occur. Information presented to the cortex confirms that failure has occurred (Levine, Leven, & Prueitt, 1992). The chemical and informational signal suggests the predictive capacity of this event for failure. As a series of conditioning models demonstrates, repeated presentation of co-occurring signals will produce "cognitive" learning (for review, see Grossberg, 1980). Our model represents this mechanism by sending a dual signal from the dorsal raphe to the neocortex. The informational (electrical) pattern denotes the actual anticipated circumstance and the DA records the urgency.

Petty et al. (1993) and Suomi (1991) have suggested that the DA signal is mediated by GABA in neocortical regions (figure 6.5). GABA inhibits frontal "noise" (Cooper et al., 1991) and enables focus on relevant information which would distinguish most situations from the recalled or "trained" case. This work suggests (Leven, 1992, 1993) that reduced GABA, produced as a result of the DA signal, could lessen the ability of the cortex to distinguish between helplessness-producing and non–helplessness-producing behaviors (reduce Grossberg's "gain control"). The resulting confusion could lead to overgeneralization of failing cures and more directly produce Samson's "cognitive helpless" group.

Perseveration, Automaticity, and Norepinephrine-Mediated Depression

Experimental results from Fieve's group (Corwin, Peselow, Fennan, et al., 1990) support the notion that NE mediation of "decision" processes among

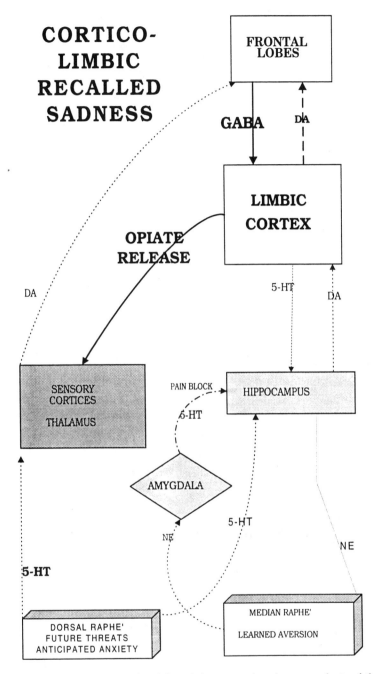

Figure 6.5 Schematic of withdrawal depression, based on a synthesis of the ideas of Suomi (1991) and Petty et al. (1993).

depressives differs from other chemical signaling effects. The experimenters presented exemplars and possible matches to a group of depressives and varied the reward schedule for successful categorization. Fieve's group tested them, then treated one group with propranolol (a blocker of NE). While all groups of depressives tend to be cautious about category identification and switching, the NE-deprived depressives showed "decision rule deficits." In other words, they employed conservative, less risky strategies for categorizing items about which they were uncertain. The NE-depressed group made no more errors in discriminating between "right" and "wrong" answers than the others. NE-deprived subjects were less flexible, more automatic in deciding in an uncertain situation. The chemical impairment led them to greater consistency of choice, despite adverse consequences (Levine et al., 1992). These choice biases are unrelated to the better-known "heuristics" (Kahneman & Tversky, 1982), which involves systematic adjustments to information.

This pattern of systematic error, normally attributed to cognitive deficit (Beck, 1976, 1997), may be differentiated from other errors which require complex categorization and analysis. The subjects are more averse to risk because of traumatic experience (as in the post-traumatic studies summarized in Herman, 1992, chapter 2). The stable failure is predicted by stress of the Weiss-Samson type, not by attributional and expectancy effects. This result mimics frontal lesions which lead to perseveration in formerly rewarding behavior (Eslinger, Grattan, & Geder, 1996; Levin, Eisenberg, & Benton, 1991; Levine, Parks, & Prueitt, 1993). Both the perseveration in failed efforts and the delays in responding to change are present in the Fieve group results.

Hence, NE deficits, which are often induced by a depressive state, can produce failures that have been categorized as cognitive. These results underline the complexity of the depressive state and the profundity of the "catecholamine balance" hypothesis. This state will be compared with its counterpart in the appendix. There, we illustrate the differing anatomies and chemistries of these two conditions and describe simulations which qualitatively capture their unique qualities.

A COGNITIVE SYSTEMS INTERPRETATION OF DEPRESSION

This preliminary model follows the models laid down by Levine and Leven (1992) and Grossberg (1980). We have emulated available descriptions of neural systems, including neurochemical signaling (Black et al., 1988). This model allows for chemical, physiological (lesion), and behavioral inductions and eliminations of distinct subtypes of helpless behavior in animals. As Samson (personal communication, September 25, 1995) and Herman (1992) emphasize, these stress-and-fear systems are reentrant. That is, a cognitive form of induced depression ("I am logically bound to fail") and the resulting unsatisfactory outcome leads to learned motor and automatic system responses (a stimulus response, Weiss depression). Such a set of discouraging outcomes can produce low enough self-esteem to produce isolation and concomitant affective depression (Suomi, 1991).

We adapt aspects of Grossberg's (1980) notion of intuitive mismatch, where largely insulated distributed systems require understanding of other such systems, because their significance often comes at their interaction. Our model places importance on cognition, conation, and affect. We have made significant progress by applying neural network principles to successive approximations of human behavior as convergent themes across neuropsychology and modeling emerge (Hestenes, 1992; Leven, 1992, 1993; Levine 1991). Pribram and Gill (1976) remind us of the task, saying that "there is a place in the scientific scheme for investigators and practitioners working at the interface between disciplines [and] often, though not always, the most significant advances in understanding and in practice arise at such interfaces" (p. 168). Experimentalists like Samson and Schildkraut advance models and perform experiments to establish connections between behavior, symptoms, and therapeutic success. As theorists, we hope to build upon and advance their efforts.

APPENDIX: BUILDING A MODEL OF LEARNED HELPLESSNESS—IN STEPS

Step 1: The American Psychological Society "Model in Principle"

Beginning with the models presented above, we specify the central biological units involved. We recognize that three parallel systems are required to emulate the three subtypes of helplessness. This insight (first discussed in Leven, 1992), became much clearer after the appearance of the article by Minor and associates (1991). A formal model that could capture the qualities described in the two approaches seemed to promise a way of designing computational and biological experiments.

For presentation at the American Psychological Society (Leven, 1993), our simulation simply consisted of four interacting networks. These were characterized by their apparent similarity in processing output to the three biological networks and a trivial model of frontal function. Little effort was made to emulate critical upstream functions. The goal was to demonstrate the feasibility of producing three characteristic "disabilities," using a set of networks with different topologies and underlying theories.

This system, broadly described in figures 6.4 and 6.6 (the latter to be described below under Step 4), is very similar to the dialogic neural networks described in Leven (1988) and Leven and Elsberry (1990). As in those sources, the networks were classic backpropagation (of the Werbos, 1974, type) representing semantic failure; the standard Hopfield-Tank (1986) model representing motoric failure; and standard adaptive resonance (of the Carpenter and Grossberg, 1987, type) representing affective failure. The frontal lobes emulation was a summation operator, allowing failures to be represented as outputs of the system.

While it was possible to demonstrate the qualitative behavior of the described systems, it was impossible to demonstrate interactive effects. Such a model was adequate only as a demonstration in principle.

Step 2: The World Congress on Neural Networks '95 Model

The next step was to study the computational possibilities of a model which processed semantic information in three qualitatively different ways and to relate those to a model of depression. We recognized limitations inherent in the original Leven (1988) choices: standard backpropagation lacked the capacity to build extensive categories or "dynamic schemas" (Rumelhart, Smolensky, McClelland, & Hinton, 1986) and the Hopfield-Tank model lacked learning ability and a reasonable means of modeling chemical signaling.

We modified backpropagation (as discussed in Leven, 1995) by training simple systems to recognize three classes of logic: default (if-then), modal (when or how-then), and nonmonotonic (if pattern-then). These networks proved capable of parsing classifications and categories (figures 6.7 and 6.8).

Similarly, we trained basic backpropagation networks to recognize basic set relations: into (included in), onto (equivalent to), and subsumes (includes these). These networks recognized hierarchical classes (figure 6.9).

Combining these, we were able to design semantic networks capable of basic classification and logic-tree construction. We devised a simple mismatch control structure which was designed to allow the system to "reset" when it received error feedback from other subsystems (affective, motoric, or frontal lobes), as shown in figure 6.9. The combination of capabilities allowed us to claim that we had developed a continuously learning semantic system (figure 6.10).

The other focus was to revise the motoric system, to allow it to employ the limited flexibility that human procedural systems allow. The vector Preisach model (Mayergoyz, 1989) had the capacity to accommodate many inputs, store associated patterns within clusters, and modify learning in the face of failure of its "base structures" (minima). We suggested a means of modeling the NE system using this approach.

Step 3: Washington Evolutionary Systems Society '95

By now, we had reviewed the literature more carefully and had begun to describe individual structures. This was the beginning of developing the capacity to test experimental data against the model structure. As Levine (personal communication, January 23, 1993) has suggested, the hippocampus seems well analogized by adaptive resonance–like architectures. Dipole fields seem best suited to the sensory-filtering and merging functions that

PRIBRAM-FAUCONNIER MODEL:
BLENDED SPACES AND CONTEXT-SENSITIVITY

Expectancy cues mental spaces and creates frame:
Each Modality (Habit, Affect, Semantic) responds to stimuli;
Modalities are blended and the blend is attached to a cued frame. Consonant
with Pribram's view of "deep" and "emergent" structures.

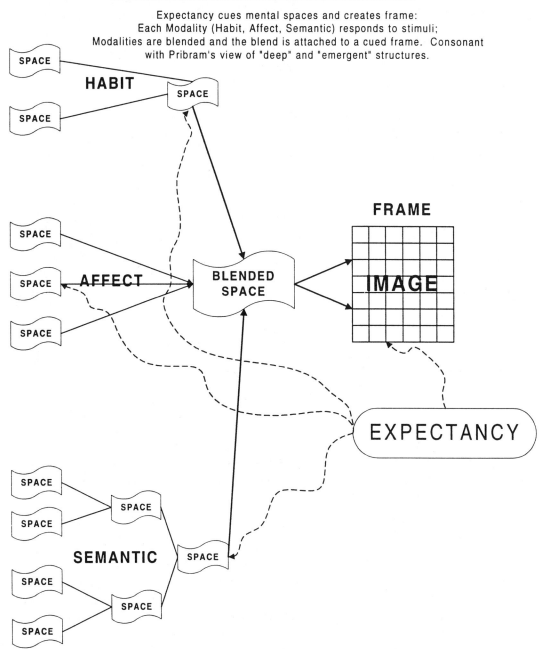

Figure 6.6 Overview of the "work in progress" model: see appendix for details.

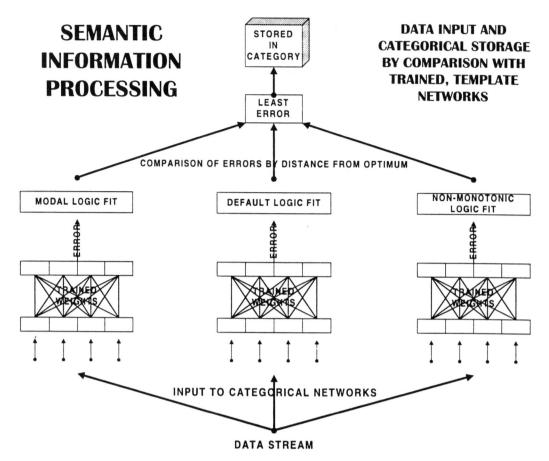

SEMANTIC INFORMATION PROCESSING

STORED IN CATEGORY

DATA INPUT AND CATEGORICAL STORAGE BY COMPARISON WITH TRAINED, TEMPLATE NETWORKS

LEAST ERROR

COMPARISON OF ERRORS BY DISTANCE FROM OPTIMUM

MODAL LOGIC FIT

DEFAULT LOGIC FIT

NON-MONOTONIC LOGIC FIT

ERROR

TRAINED WEIGHTS

INPUT TO CATEGORICAL NETWORKS

DATA STREAM

Figure 6.7   Inference based on ideal data types.

underlie it and to represent interactions between limbic and output areas. These dipole fields were introduced and seemed to replicate the reported functions (figure 6.11).

Step 4: Ongoing Work

Recent work by Self, Barnhart, Lehman, et al. (1996) points to increasing complexity in describing these systems. D1 receptors in corticolimbic systems induce different responses from D2 receptors in the presence of stimulants. D1 agonists couple attention to, and excitement about, novel events with pleasure; D2 agonists induce craving for excitation. Self is concerned with addictive responses to D2 stimulation; we may generalize that D2 sensitization produces craving for excitation, even in normals. The simpler role of D1, producing focus and pleasure, suggests the basic deprivation model we produced earlier, but combined with D2 responses. We are attempting to produce a model which has rebound effects. Rebound may be mediated by opiate production in some normals and may be minimized in others (see figures 6.6 and 6.12). This is also reflected in a preliminary model being

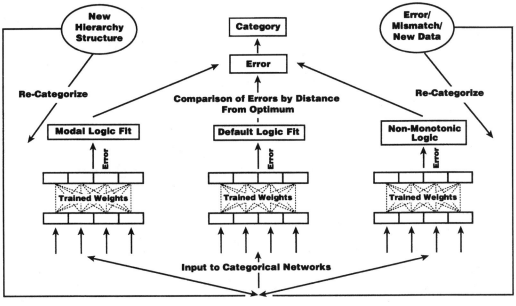

Figure 6.8   Recategorizing by errors in data and structure.

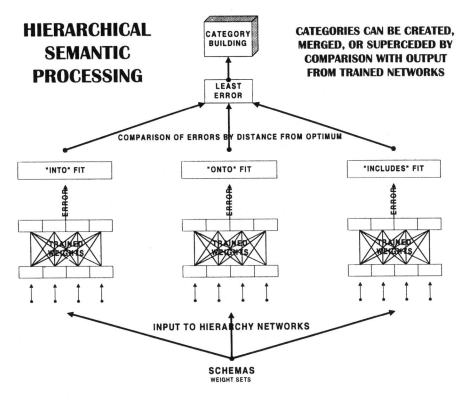

Figure 6.9   Hierarchical processes, derived from ideal types.

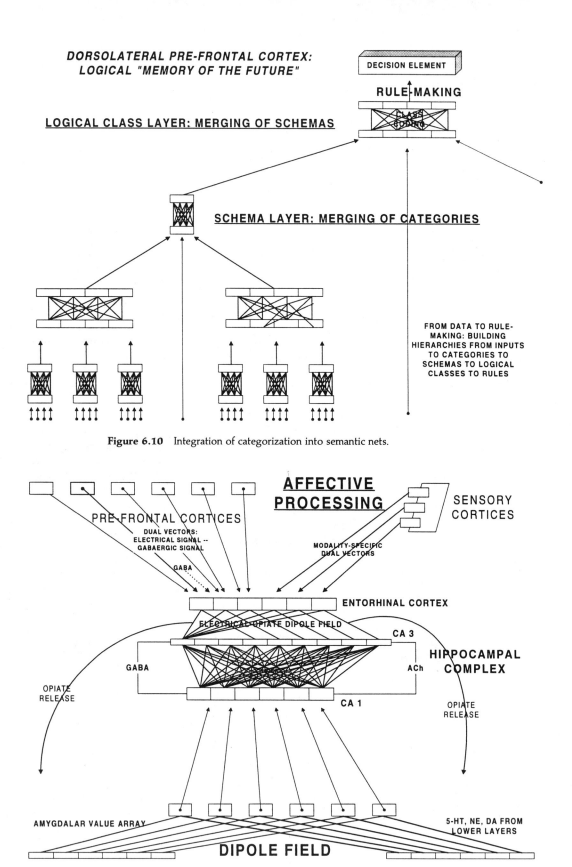

Figure 6.10 Integration of categorization into semantic nets.

Figure 6.11 The modern model of affective processing.

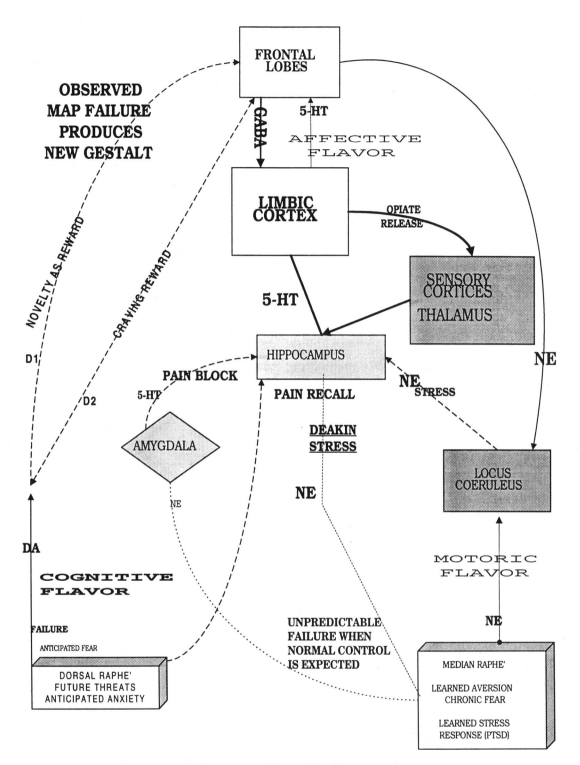

Figure 6.12 Work in progress: theoretical model.

developed by Pribram. In addition, testable models concerning receptor-specificity issues are currently being addressed.

NOTES

1. Among the many abnormalities induced by Weiss and in related work are disturbances in sleep, appetite, weight, and arousability by changes in environment or novelty.

2. NE is generally inhibitory (Cooper et al., 1991, chapter 6). As do all central neurotransmitters, NE performs a variety of critical functions at different locations in the brain; these are beyond the scope of this discussion.

3. Samson (personal communication, September 25, 1993) points out that multiple devices may result in an NE-mediated depression; heightened NE turnover and functional deficits in the system are both indicated.

4. There might be three possible behaviors in the Samson group, not two (see Leven, 1992; Minor et al., 1991). If the other group were at least partly homogeneous, HVA levels might prove ambiguous. In that case, on might also study endogenous opiate levels, as suggested by Maier (in Peterson et al., 1993) and draw finer distinctions among the companion group.

REFERENCES

Alford, B. A., & Beck, A. T. (1997). *The integrative power of cognitive therapy.* New York: Guilford Press.

Arieti, S., & Bemporad, J. (1982). *Severe and mild depression.* New York: Basic Books.

Baron-Cohen, S. (1995). *Mindblindness: An essay on autism and theory of mind.* Cambridge, MA: MIT Press.

Bateson, G. (1972). *Steps toward an ecology of mind.* New York: Ballantine Books.

Beck, A. T. (1976). *Cognitive therapy and the emotional disorders.* New York: Meridian.

Beck, A. T. (1997). The past and future of cognitive therapy. *Journal of Psychotherapy Practice and Research, 6,* 276–284.

Beck, A. T., Rush, J. A., Shaw, B. F., & Emery, G. (1987). *Cognitive therapy of depression.* New York: Guilford Press.

Beck, J. S. (1995). *Cognitive therapy: Basics and beyond.* New York: Guilford Press.

Black, I., Adler, J., Dreyfuss, C., Friedman, W., LaGamma, E., & Roach, A. (1988). Experience and the biochemistry of information storage in the nervous system. In M. Gazzaniga (Ed.), *Perspectives in memory research* (pp. 3–22). Cambridge, MA: MIT Press.

Carpenter, G. A., & Grossberg, S. (1987). A massively parallel architecture for a self-organizing neural pattern recognition machine. *Computer Vision, Graphics, and Image Processing, 37,* 54–115.

Cooper, J., Bloom, F., & Roth, R. (1991). *The biochemical basis of neuropharmacology,* 6th ed. New York: Cambridge University Press.

Corwin, J., Peselow, E., Fennan, K., Rotrosen, J., & Fieve, R. (1990). Disorders of decision in affective disease: An effect of β-adrenergic dysfunction? *Biological Psychiatry, 27,* 813–833.

Deakin, J. F. W. (1994). The clinical anxiolytic and antidepressant efficacy of drugs with actions on serotonin systems. In J. Den Boer & J. M. AdSitsen (Eds.), *Handbook of depression and anxiety* (pp. 447–472). New York: Marcel Dekker.

Dias, R., Robbins, T. W., & Roberts, A. C. (1996). Dissociation in prefrontal cortex of affective and attentional shifts. *Nature, 380,* 69–72.

Eslinger, P. J., Grattan, L. M., & Geder, L. (1996). Neurologic and neuropsychologic aspects of frontal lobe impairments in postconcussive syndrome. In M. Rizzo & D. Tranel (Eds.), *Head injury and postconcussive syndrome* (pp. 415–440). New York: Churchill Livingstone.

Fauconnier, G. (1994). *Mental spaces.* New York: Cambridge University Press.

Fillenz, M. (1990). *Noradrenergic neurons.* Cambridge: Cambridge University Press.

Gilbert, P. (1984). *Depression: From psychology to brain state.* Hillsdale, NJ: Erlbaum.

Gray, J. A. (1987). *The psychology of fear and stress.* New York: Cambridge University Press.

Grossberg, S. (1980). How does a brain build a cognitive code? *Psychological Review, 87,* 1–51.

Harre, R., & Gillett, G. (1994). *The discursive mind.* London: Sage.

Herman, J. L. (1992). *Trauma and recovery.* New York: Basic Books.

Hestenes, D. (1992). A neural network theory of manic-depressive illness. In D. S. Levine & S. J. Leven (Eds.), *Motivation, emotion, and goal direction in neural networks* (pp. 209–257). Hillsdale, NJ: Erlbaum.

Hopfield, J. J., & Tank, D. W. (1986). Computing with neural circuits: A model. *Science, 233,* 625–633.

Kahneman, D., & Tversky, A. (1982). The framing of decisions. *Science, 250,* 181–183.

Leven, S. J. (1987). *S.A.M.: A triune extension to the ART model.* Presented at the Conference on Networks in Brain and Computer Architecture, Denton, TX, October 9, 1987.

Leven, S. J. (1988). *Memory and learned helplessness: A triune approach.* Presented at the M.I.N.D. Conference on Motivation, Emotion, and Goal Direction in Neural Networks. Dallas, May 23, 1988.

Leven, S. J. (1992). Learned helplessness, memory, and the dynamics of hope. In D. S. Levine & J. S. Leven (Eds.), *Motivation, emotion, and goal direction in neural networks* (pp. 259–300). Hillsdale, NJ: Erlbaum.

Leven, S. J. (1993). *Depression as a dynamical system.* Presented at the American Psychological Society Annual Meeting, Chicago, June 10, 1993.

Leven, S. J. (1995). Intelligent, creative, and neurotic agents: Tools for effective neural net user support. In *World Congress on Neural Networks,* Vol. 2, (pp. 293–304). Mahwah, NJ: Erlbaum.

Leven, S. J., & Elsberry, W. R. (1990). Interactions among embedded networks under uncertainty. In *IJCNN International Joint Conference on Neural Networks,* Vol. 3, (pp. 739–742). San Diego: IEEE.

Levin, H. S., Eisenberg, H. M., & Benton, A. L. (Eds.). (1991). *Frontal lobe function and dysfunction.* New York: Oxford University Press.

Levine, D. S. (1991). *Introduction to neural and cognitive modeling.* Hillsdale, NJ: Erlbaum.

Levine, D. S., & Leven, S. J. (Eds.). (1992). Preface. In *Motivation, emotion, and goal direction in neural networks.* Hillsdale, NJ: Erlbaum.

Levine, D. S., Leven, S. J., & Prueitt, P. S. (1992). Integration, disintegration, and the frontal lobes. In D. S. Levine & S. J. Leven (Eds.), *Motivation, emotion, and goal direction in neural networks* (pp. 301–335). Hillsdale, NJ: Erlbaum.

Levine, D. S., Parks, R. W., & Prueitt, P. S. (1993). Methodological and theoretical issues in neural network models of frontal cognitive functions. *International Journal of Neuroscience, 72,* 209–233.

Lowen, A. (1971). *The language of the body*. New York: Collier Books.

Mayergoyz, I. D. (1989). Dynamic Preisach models of hysteresis. *IEEE Transactions on Magnetics, 24,* 2925–2927.

MacLean, P. D. (1990). *The triune brain in evolution: Role in paleocerebral functions.* New York: Plenum Press.

Miller, G., Galanter, E., & Pribram, K. (1960). *Plans and the structure of behavior.* New York: Random House.

Minor, T. R., Dess, N. K., & Overmier, J. B. (1991). Inverting the traditional view of "learned helplessness." In M. R. Denny (Ed.), *Fear, avoidance, and phobias* (pp. 87–133). Hillsdale, NJ: Erlbaum.

Nieuwenhuys, R. (1985). *Chemoarchitecture of the brain.* New York: Springer-Verlag.

Padesky, C. A., & Greenberger, D. (1995). *Clinician's guide to mind over mood.* New York: Guilford Publications, Inc.

Peterson, C., Maier, S., & Seligman, M. (1993). *Learned helplessness.* New York: Oxford University Press.

Petty, F., Kramer, G., & Hendrickse, W. (1993). GABA and depression. In J. Mann & D. Kupfer (Eds.), *Biology of depressive disorders,* Part A (pp. 79–108). New York: Plenum Press.

Pribram, K. (1991). *Brain and perception.* Hillsdale, NJ: Erlbaum.

Pribram, K., & Gill, M. (1976). *Freud's project reassessed.* New York: Basic Books.

Pribram, K., & McGuinness, D. (1975). Arousal, activation, and effort in the control of attention. *Psychological Review, 82,* 116–149.

Richelson, E. (1997). Pharmacokinetic drug interactions of new antidepressants: A review of the effects on the metabolism of other drugs. *Mayo Clinical Proceedings, 72,* 835–847.

Rumelhart, D. E., Smolensky, P., McClelland, J. L., & Hinton, G.E. (1986). Schemata and sequential thought processes in PDP models. In J. L. McClelland & D. Rumelhart (Eds.), *Parallel distributed processing,* Vol. 2 (pp. 7–57). Cambridge, MA: MIT Press.

Samson, J. A., Mirin, S. M., Hauser, S. T., Fenton, B. T., & Schildkraut, J.J. (1992). Learned helplessness and urinary MHPG levels in unipolar depression. *American Journal of Psychiatry, 149,* 806–809.

Schatzberg, A., Samson, J., Bloomingdale, K., Orsulak, P., Gerson, B., Kizuka, P., Cole, J., & Schildkraut, J. (1989). Toward a biochemical classification of depressive disorders, X: Urinary catecholamines, their metabolites, and D-type scores in subgroups of depressive disorders. *Archives of General Psychiatry, 46,* 260–268.

Schildkraut, J. (1965). The catecholamine hypothesis of affective disorders: a review of supporting evidence. *American Journal of Psychiatry, 122,* 509–522.

Schneider, F., Gur, R. E., Alavi, A., Seligman, M. E., Mozley, L. H., Smith, R. J. Mozley, P. D., & Gur, R. C. (1996). Cerebral blood flow changes in limbic regions induced by unsolvable anagram tasks. *American Journal of Psychiatry, 153,* 206–212.

Self, D. W., Barnhart, W. J., Lehman, D. A., & Nestler, D. (1996). Opposite modulation of cocaine-seeking behavior by D1- and D2-like dopamine receptor agonists. *Science, 271,* 1586–1589.

Seligman, M. E. (1975). *Helplessness.* New York: W. H. Freeman.

Suomi, S. J. (1991). Primate separation models of affective disorders. In J. Madden, IV (Ed.), *Neurobiology of learning, emotion, and affect* (pp. 195–214). New York: Raven Press.

Tyrer, P., & Steinberg, D. (1993). *Models for mental disorder*. New York: Wiley.

Van der Kolk, B. A. (Ed.). (1987). *Psychological trauma*. Washington, DC: American Psychiatric Press.

Weiss, J. M. (1991). Stress-induced depression: Critical neurochemical and electrophysiological changes. In J. Madden, IV (Ed.), *Neurobiology of learning, motion, and affect* (pp. 123–154). New York: Raven.

Weiss, J., & Simson, P. (1989). Electrophysiology of the locus coeruleus: Implications for stress-induced depression. In G. Koob, C. Ehlers, & D. Kupfer (Eds.), *Animal models of depression* (pp. 111–134). Boston: Birkhäuser.

Werbos, P. J. (1974). Beyond regression: New tools for prediction and analysis in the behavioral sciences. Unpublished Ph.D. dissertation, Harvard University, Cambridge, MA. Reprinted in Werbos, P. J. (1993). *The roots of backpropagation: From ordered derivatives to neural networks and political forecasting*. New York: Wiley.

Willner, P. (1985). *Depression: A psychobiological synthesis*. New York: Wiley-Interscience.

7 Waking and Sleeping States

Jeffrey P. Sutton and J. Allan Hobson

Waking and sleep are behavioral states present in all mammals and the rhythmicity between these states is essential to survival (Rechtschaffen, Bergmann, Everson, et al., 1989). Sleep changes during development and aging (Roffwarg, Muzio, and Dement, 1966), and it subserves important functions related to energy conservation, neuroimmunoendocrine control, appetite, and thermoregulation (Moore, 1979). In addition, sleep is linked to memory, learning, and other cognitive functions (Hobson, 1988b), and there is a long-standing, although largely inferential, notion that sleep is important for affective regulation (Kramer & Roth, 1972). There are also well-established correlations between disturbances in sleep and disorders of brain and mind.

From the perspective of modeling, studies of sleep fall into three main categories. The first category concerns circadian and other biological rhythms (e.g., ultradian and infradian rhythms). Several mathematical models have been proposed that capture features of these rhythms, as well as the coupled oscillations among endocrine, sleep-wake and seasonal cycles (Kronauer, Czeisler, Pilato, et al., 1982, Strogatz, 1986, Moore-Ede & Czeisler, 1984). These chronobiological models do not necessarily incorporate anatomical or neurophysiological details of sleep.

A second category of models deals with circadian control and modulation on detailed neurobiological systems. While some integrative work regarding the molecular biology and genetics of circadian rhythms has been performed (Takahashi, 1995), most investigations in this category have focused on individual neurons and small networks. Models of cellular networks have been helpful in synthesizing information about brainstem circuitry and thalamo-cortical interactions (Steriade, Pare, Parent, et al., 1993; McCarley & Hobson, 1975). Furthermore, many predictions have been confirmed by induced behavioral or pharmacological alterations in sleep-wake physiology (Steriade & McCarley, 1990).

The third category of models uses large-scale neural network models to examine the effects of sleep on cognitive processes. Models in this category have less anatomical detail than the models in the second category, but they emphasize the cooperative effects among many neuron-like units. They are useful for exploring some of the computational principles that may underlie information storage, transfer, sequencing, and learning during sleep (Sutton, Mamelak, & Hobson, et al., 1992a). Generally, this is accomplished by studying network properties during simulated states of neuromodulation that characterize wake and sleep.

In this chapter, we present an overview of neural network models of sleep. We briefly review some of the relevant behavioral, cognitive, and physiological data, and then describe different models that attempt to integrate these data. Our emphasis is on how shifts in the relative balances of aminergic and cholinergic modulation, occurring during waking and sleep, influence information sequencing and learning in large-scale networks, including the cerebral cortex. We suggest that modeling the effects of neuromodulation on network dynamics is a useful way to study some aspects of sleep. Moreover, we claim that similar approaches are relevant to modeling a variety of behavioral states and disorders affecting the brain and cognition.

EXPERIMENTAL CONSIDERATIONS

General Features

The sleep-wake cycle consists of three main behavioral states: the waking state, nonrapid eye movement (NREM) sleep, and rapid eye movement (REM) sleep. Each state has distinctive behavioral and electrophysiological properties, as well as characteristic neurophysiological features. In humans, different cognitive attributes have been ascribed to each of the three states (figure 7.1).

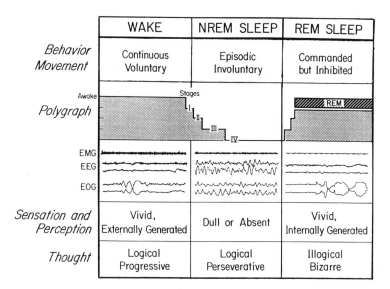

Figure 7.1 Chart summarizing behavioral, electrophysiological, and psychological manifestations of the waking state and NREM and REM sleep in humans. EMG, electromyelogram; EEG, electroencephalogram; EOG, electro-oculogram. (Modified from Hobson & Steriade, 1986.)

During the waking state, skeletal and eye movements are abundant. These diminish significantly during NREM sleep, which accounts for 80 percent of all sleep in adult humans. Approximately six episodes of REM sleep, each lasting eight to fifteen minutes, are interspersed among the NREM sleep periods. REM sleep is partially distinguished by skeletal muscle atonia, along with phasic bursting eye movements (Hobson & Steriade, 1986).

The waking state and REM sleep are correlated with low-amplitude, high-frequency electroencephalogram (EEG) recordings (Aserinsky & Kleitman, 1953). In contrast, NREM sleep is manifest by high-amplitude, low-frequency waveforms. To completely specify state, sleep laboratory paradigms typically involve recordings of behavioral information, the EEG, and other physiological recordings, including the electro-oculogram (EOG), electromyelogram (EMG), core temperature, and heart rate (Hobson, 1988a; Somers, Dyken; Mark, et al., 1993).

Cognitive Properties

Throughout the sleep-wake cycle, there are changes in mental processes that alter perception, thought form and content, orientation, and mood (Bootzin, Kihlstrom, & Schacter, 1990). Dreaming is the hallmark psychological experience characterizing sleep. It is known to be predominantly a REM sleep phenomenon (Aserinsky & Kleitman, 1953; Dement & Kleitman, 1957). Dreams have been described since biblical times, and despite voluminous anecdotal reports and intuitions about dreaming (Brook, 1987), relatively few rigorous scientific studies have been made of this fascinating state of mind (Hobson, 1988a). A fundamental obstacle, of course, is that it is difficult to elucidate exact relationships between sleep and cognition, since observations are limited to psychophysical data collected during behavioral states that border on sleep (i.e., the waking state, falling asleep, waking up).

Nevertheless, there is growing scientific evidence that cognition is state-dependent, in the sense that different types of cognitive processes are associated with different neurophysiological states. These states include, but are not limited to sleep, and encompass states of anxiety, meditation, and drug-induced psychosis. In the waking state, thoughts are generally logical, consistent, and continuous. In NREM sleep, thought processing typically consists of ruminative sequences (Antrobus, 1983), not unlike the perseveration or rumination that occurs in obsessive-compulsive disorder. In contrast to the waking state and NREM sleep, REM sleep is associated with graphic and formally bizarre images containing discontinuities, incongruities, and uncertainties (McCarley & Hoffman, 1981; Foulkes, 1985). The predominantly external perceptual cues of the waking state shift to internal sources during sleep and dreaming.

In addition to changes in thinking associated with different states, there are alterations in other aspects of the mental status. These are usually described qualitatively, with considerable focus on the content and inferred meaning of dreams (Freud, 1900). However, some excellent quantitative work has also been conducted on the formal properties of cognition during sleep (Baars & Banks, 1994). For example, Hobson and co-workers have quantified how sensory perception differs in waking and sleep (Williams, Merritt, Ritlenhouse, et al., 1992).

One impressive way in which cognition appears to be state-dependent is with respect to discontinuities in visual attention and orientation (Hobson, Hoffman, Helford, et al., 1987). In sleep, and specifically REM sleep, shifts in attention during dreams are reported to occur more frequently relative to waking. The shifts are often sudden and unexpected. They are also experienced in association with intense emotion, especially anxiety (Merritt, Stickgold, Pace-Schott, et al., 1994; Sutton, Ritlenhouse, Pace-schott, et al., 1994b).

The magnitude of discontinuities in attention can be determined from narrative reports describing experiences during the waking state and sleep. Narrative graphing is a reliable technique developed for mapping language-based reports onto geometric graphs (Sutton, Ritlenhouse, Pace-Schott, et al., 1994a). The method is not specific for state, and the graphs are helpful in determining the magnitude of discontinuities in visual scenes, which are reflective of changes in attention (figure 7.2a). They are also useful for representing temporal sequences of information and thought (figure 7.2b). Narrative graphing has been used to map, in detail, discontinuities and bifurcations in information sequencing in dream reports (Sutton et al., 1994a).

In addition to changes in thought sequencing, memory and learning have state-dependent features. Memory and learning are intermingled processes. They vary with development as well as with state, with maximal learning occurring early in ontogeny and decreasing with age. This pattern is loosely correlated with the amount of REM sleep, which can reach levels of 50 to 80 percent early in life (Roffwarg et al., 1966). There is also an interesting relationship between the integrity of REM sleep and the ability to learn visual attention tasks (Karni, Tanne, Rubeastein, et al., 1994). It is known that learning is impaired by REM sleep deprivation (Fishbein, Kactaniotis, & Chattman, 1974), and that increases in REM sleep follow periods of learning in adult humans (Smith, Kitahama, Valatx, et al., 1980). With new techniques of multiunit recordings and noninvasive neuroimaging, such as functional magnetic resonance imaging (MRI), it is becoming possible to examine real-time brain changes associated with learning (e.g., Recanzone, Merzenich, Jenkins, et al., 1992; Karni Meyer, Vezzard, et al., 1995). It will be very interesting to examine the state-dependent aspects of learning with these new technologies. Some progress has already been made in this direction (Wilson & McNaughton, 1994).

Neurophysiological Data

At the cellular level, the biogenic amines are chemical substances known to be important for memory, attention, and learning (Flicker, McCarley, &

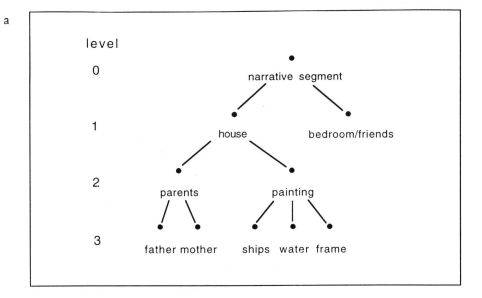

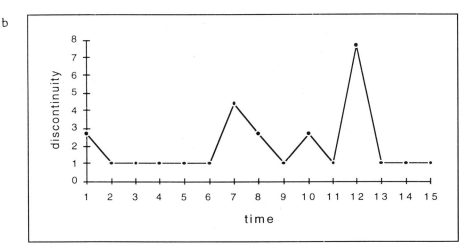

Figure 7.2 a, Hierarchy graph representing a narrative report. Starting with a written account of visual imagery (not shown), objects are identified in the report and mapped onto a graph following a set of reliable rules (Sutton et al., 1994a). Different levels of the hierarchy are determined based on part-whole relationships. The narrative segment itself is the zeroth level, or root node, of the hierarchy. Two principal scenes are identified in the example graph. One scene is a house and the second scene is a bedroom (in a different house with some friends). These scenes form first-level objects. Parents and a painting are contained within the house and make up second-level objects. At the third level, two parents are identified along with three objects named in the painting. b, Once the hierarchy graph is obtained, the time course of attention among the visual objects can be plotted. Each transition between two objects is assigned a measure of discontinuity based on how far the transition moves within the hierarchy graph (Sutton et al., 1994a). The extent of discontinuity is plotted as a function of time, as shown in (b). It has been reported that large discontinuities (e.g., at time step 12) are correlated with subjective experiences of intense emotion (Sutton et al., 1994b). (Modified from Sutton et al., 1994a.)

Hobson, 1981; Schmajuk & Moore, 1985; Jarbe, Callenholm, Mahammed, et al., 1981; Kandel, Klein, Hochner, et al., 1987; Hopkins & Johnston, 1988). It is therefore not surprising to discover that changes in the relative balances of some of these chemicals are associated with different waking and sleep states. The details of the changes help to explain some well-known phenomena, such as the amnesia occurring with sleep (Hobson, 1988a). During sleep, the main chemical changes involve norepinephrine (NE), serotonin (5-HT), and acetylcholine (ACh).

Much of the knowledge about brain chemistry during sleep has been gleaned from studies of behavioral state control at the brainstem level (Steriade & McCarley, 1990; Datta, 1995). There has also been excellent work done to elucidate the activity of forebrain neural populations during the waking state and sleep (Wilson & McNaughton, 1993; Poe, Rector, & Harper, 1994). Within the brain stem, pontine cells which are most active during the waking state and silent during REM sleep, release the monoamines NE and 5-HT from the locus ceruleus and dorsal raphe nucleus, respectively (Hobson, McCarley, & Wyzirki, 1975). Among the many cell populations that become active during REM sleep are cells associated with ACh release. These cells, located in the peribrachial pons, are generally quiescent, except during the startle response when they fire briefly but dramatically (Bowker & Morrison, 1976). In NREM and REM sleep, the cessation of NE and 5-HT neural activation is coupled with relative increases in cholinergic activity. Some of the principal pathways are summarized in figure 7.3.

While the aminergic and cholinergic systems account for less than approximately 5 percent of all neurons, they are strategically positioned to induce widespread neuromodulatory effects on cortical circuits. Both NE and 5-HT inhibit the spontaneous firing rate of certain forebrain neurons (Aghajanian & Van der Maelen, 1986), and they increase the signal-to-noise ratio in neural networks (Segal, 1985; Servan-Schreiber, Printz, & Cohen, 1990). In NREM sleep, the forebrain receives approximately 50 percent less aminergic modulation compared to the waking state. In REM sleep, the forebrain is relatively free of aminergic modulation (Hobson & Steriade, 1986). These changes result in widespread circuits with increased spontaneous neural activation.

Cholinoceptive neurons exist throughout the cortex, hippocampus, and thalamus (Olivier, Parent, & Poirer, 1970; Bear & Singer, 1986). Primary sources of ACh to the cortex are from neurons in the basal forebrain, while the thalamus receives its supply from peribrachial neuron projections (Steriade et al., 1988). The principle action of ACh release is thought to facilitate neural firing (Steriade & Llinás, 1988). Global cholinergic activity in NREM sleep declines to approximately 50 percent of its value found in the waking state; but it increases to a level comparable to that present in the waking state during REM sleep. This is due to the effect of phasic bursting from brainstem neurons which generate characteristic EEG tracings termed *ponto-*

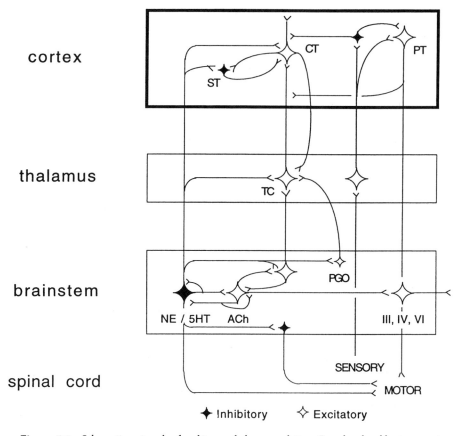

cortex

thalamus

brainstem

spinal cord

✦ Inhibitory   ✧ Excitatory

Figure 7.3 Schematic network of waking and sleep regulation. Four levels of brain organization are shown with representative excitatory (open neurons) and inhibitory (solid neurons) pathways. Reciprocally connected aminergic and cholinergic systems within the brain stem induce widespread modulatory effects. Aminergic disinhibition and cholinergic excitation in REM sleep are associated with rapid eye movements, EEG desynchronization, and ponto-geniculo-occipital burst cell (PGO) waves. Muscle twitches occur when phasic excitation overcomes tonic inhibition within the spinal cord. Sutton, Mamelak, and Hobson (1992b) have simulated the simplified cortical architecture (heavy outline) on a Sun workstation. CT, cortical cell; ST, stellate cell; PT, pyramidal cell; TC, thalamocortical cell; NE, norepinephrine; 5HT, serotonin; Ach, acetylcholine; III, oculomotor, IV, trochlear, and V, trigeminal motor nuclei. (Adapted from Hobson, 1990b, and Sutton and Hobson, 1994.)

geniculo-occipital (PGO) waves (Brooks & Bizzi, 1963; Steriade & Llinás, 1988). This cholinergically mediated stimulation conveys information about the direction of eye movements which become, in REM sleep, completely decoupled from external stimulus control (Callaway, Lydic, Baghdoyan, et al., 1987).

In humans, evidence for PGO activity has been demonstrated by McCarley, Winkelman, and Duffy (1983), using EEG mapping techniques. Functional neuroimaging using positron emission tomography (PET) has demonstrated decreased glucose utilization in the hippocampus during

NREM sleep relative to waking and REM sleep (Ramm & Frost, 1986; Maquet, Dive, Salmon, et al., 1990). Decreased metabolism in the thalamus and midbrain has also been observed during sleep deprivation (Wu, Gillin, Buchsbaum, et al., 1991). These findings support the notion that human sleep, like sleep in other mammals, is a hypoadrenergic, hypercholinergic state relative to the waking state.

Sleep and Neuropsychiatric Illness

There are several brain and sleep disorders that are characterized by abnormalities of the aminergic and cholinergic systems (Hobson & Steriade, 1986). Clinical depression, for instance, is a disorder associated with altered catecholamine balance. An excellent biological marker for depression is a sleep disturbance, which is partially manifest by shortening of the latency to the first REM sleep period (Gillin & Borbely, 1985). The cognitive impairments and pharmacological treatments of this common mood disorder are consistent with it being a hypoadrenergic, hypercholinergic state. The reader is referred to Hobson and Steriade (1986) and Montplaisir and Godbout (1990) for further discussion of the relationships between sleep and disorders in psychiatry and medicine.

COMPUTATIONAL MODELS

Overview

There is a long history of using neural network models to study states of brain and mind related to waking and sleep. Freud, for example, developed a model of neurons linked by artificial synapses into a network driven by non-physiological energy forces that altered conscious processes (Freud, 1895). McCulloch, the psychiatrist and modeler known, in part, for his seminal work with Pitts on networks of binary valued neurons, examined network models of altered state processes, including delusions (McCulloch & Pitts, 1943; McCulloch, 1965).

These and other models laid the groundwork for more recent theoretical work that specifically addresses neurophysiologically based correlates of sleep and waking states. As outlined earlier, there are two broad, yet partially overlapping, categories of models. One category deals with state control, and focuses primarily on brainstem and thalamic systems, while the second category examines forebrain networks and the effects of modulation on large-scale neural populations. In common with all brain models, simplifications of anatomy and physiology are required to make investigations tractable. One of the great challenges in neural modeling is determining how to reduce the complexity of biological systems to foster rigorous study while maintaining pertinent details. Examples of such simplifications are discussed in this section with regard to computational modeling.

Brainstem and Thalamic Models

The phenomenology of REM sleep as a rhythm mediated by neural networks has been investigated in several complementary ways. In 1975, McCarley and Hobson proposed a mathematical model of reciprocally interacting populations of brainstem neurons (McCarley & Hobson, 1975). As illustrated in figure 7.4a, one population corresponded to aminergic cells that inhibited a second population of neurons, as well as itself. The second population was cholinergically mediated, with excitatory projections to the aminergic cells and back to the cholinergically mediated population. Using Volterra-Lotka equations employed in simple field biology models of predators and prey (Volterra, 1931; Lotka, 1956), the reciprocal interaction model displayed oscillatory behavior consistent with physiological behavior regulating sleep-wake cycles (McCarley & Hobson, 1975). The model also made several predictions regarding aminergic and cholinergic interactions, and many of these have been subsequently confirmed (Hobson & Steriade, 1986).

One of the limitations of the reciprocal interaction model was that it was exquisitely sensitive to initial conditions. It would have to be reset each night. To combat this and other shortcomings, a limit-cycle model was introduced that took into consideration more physiological details, including constraints on neuron firing rates (McCarley & Massaquoi, 1986). Other investigators used models of brainstem and thalamic circuitry to demonstrate how transitions in physiological state may be associated with changes in the dynamics of individual neurons and neural populations (Steriade, McCormick, & Sejnowski, 1993). In particular, thalamocortical oscillations and resonance among neural populations have been a topic of considerable recent interest. In one approach, oscillations critical to binding neural populations are modulated in sleep and waking by different sensory inputs (Llinás & Ribary, 1994).

Distributed and Cortical Network Models

In contrast to the models discussed in the previous subsection, large-scale models sacrifice relatively greater anatomical and physiological detail in exchange for a better understanding of computational principles involving parallel distributed networks. Large-scale models typically address the following question: What are the functions associated with different states of correlated physiological and mental activity? From a computational, as well as a biological perspective, different states of operation presumably have specialized tasks that allow the system as a whole to perform in an adaptive, diverse, and efficient manner. A common theme of large-scale models is that changes in modulation specify state and provide clues to the types of information processing that occur. Surprisingly, very little computational work has actually been done on sleep and waking using such networks.

Behavioral States

a

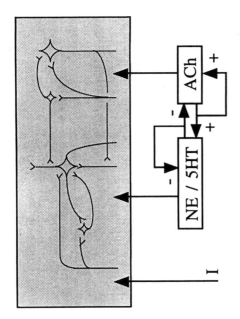

I

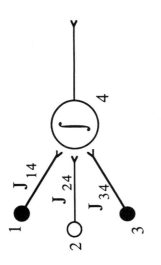

b

c

Probability of Firing

$\beta = 3.0 \quad 1.5 \quad 1.0$

0.5

0.5

$h - \theta$

Membrane Potential Relative to Threshold

d

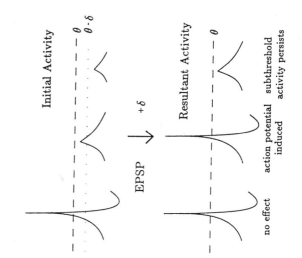

Initial Activity

θ
$\theta - \delta$

EPSP $\longrightarrow$ $+\delta$

Resultant Activity

θ

no effect   action potential   subthreshold
             induced   activity persists

Figure 7.4 Construction of a temporal sequencing network with modulation. a, Model neurons are connected together and are capable of collectively storing and recalling sequences of information (shaded region). The network is subject to inputs from an aminergic source (NE/5HT), a cholinergically mediated source (ACh), and other external sources (I). The aminergic and cholinergic sources emanate from systems that are reciprocally interconnected. b, Within the shaded network, neurons are linked by weights J_{ij}. These weights are determined by the firing correlations between neurons and allow the memory patterns and temporal sequences to be stored in a parallel distributed manner (see appendix for details). In (b), some of the connections between four neurons are shown. Neuron 4 integrates the inputs from neurons 1, 2, and 3, and then determines whether or not it fires an action potential. c, The probability that an individual neuron fires is determined, in part, by the fidelity of synaptic transmission. This is aminergically modulated. More aminergic modulation corresponds to a sharp response curve (e.g., $b = 3.0$); whereas during aminergic withdrawal the response curve is flattened (e.g., $b = 0.5$). d, The action of the cholinergically mediated ponto-geniculo-occipital (PGO) system on the network is shown. PGO bursting does not affect neural activity unless the initial activity of a neuron is just subthreshold (i.e., within d of threshold q). In that case, a quiescent neuron generates an action potential (i.e., it fires). (Adapted from Mamelak & Hobson, 1989, and Sutton et al., 1992b.)

The first model to detail state-dependent processing based on neuro-physiological changes occurring during waking and sleep was the activation-synthesis hypothesis of Hobson and McCarley (1977). In their model, activation was due to PGO bursting. This originated in the pontine brain stem and drove the cortex in REM sleep to generate, or at least facilitate, the cognitive process of dreaming. The model posited a brain-based notion of dreaming that departed from previous psychological theories of dreaming (e.g., Freud, 1900).

The importance of phasic PGO bursting during REM sleep has also be recognized by other researchers. PGO activity is related to theta rhythms, which have been proposed to mediate memory encoding during REM sleep (Winson, 1990). This is an interesting suggestion given the role of phasic ACh in some models of memory. One mechanism of action may be that ACh excites inhibitory neurons, which in turn hyperpolarize or clamp other neurons during the encoding of novel inputs (Hasslemo, 1993). The PGO system may also be relevant to memory consolidation according to a two-stage hippocampal learning model proposed by Buzsaki (1989). Off-line consolidation during NREM sleep is also a central feature of interleaved learning in a hippocampal-cortical model recently proposed by McClelland, McNavghton, and O'Reilly (1994).

In general, neuromodulatory changes in sleep have been used metaphorically in a variety of neural network models of associative memory (Geszti & Pazmandi, 1987). Phase transitions in the dynamics of distributed neural networks have also been attributed to inhibition associated with 5-HT levels in simulated waking and sleep states (Nakao, Takahashi, Mizutani, et al., 1990). Sometimes, striking changes in the phase or state of an artificial neural network are referenced in the context of sleep and waking states, to emphasize shifts in processing rather than to make a connection with sleep-wake physiology (Hinton, Dayan, Frey, et al., 1995).

A provocative hypothesis postulated by Crick and Mitchison (1983) suggested that PGO activation during REM sleep may have an unlearning effect to help prevent memory overload. Their argument, which was independently proposed by Hopfield, Feinstein, and Palmer (1983) and Clark, Rafelski, and Winston (1985) in different contexts, was based on the utility of random PGO-like inputs for unlearning within nonsequencing neural networks operating near maximal capacity. The universality of unlearning as a computational principle has gained increased attention in recent years (Wimbauer, Klemmer, & van Hemmen, 1994). However, it is not known how PGO-like inputs might affect networks with temporal sequencing features or what roles aminergic withdrawal may play in unlearning.

Mamelak and Hobson (1989) incorporated PGO phasic activation with aminergic withdrawal in a model of forebrain demodulation during sleep (see figure 7.4). Their model built on the activation-synthesis model (Hobson & McCarley, 1977). It suggested that bifurcations and bizarreness in dreams may be due to combined aminergic and cholinergic interactions. The aminergic system in the model served as a random noise filter or gain function (Segal, 1985; Keeler, Pichler, & Ross, 1989). Aminergic withdrawal was tonic or steady, and it resulted in a flattening of the sigmoid response curve that relates the probability of a neuron firing to its firing threshold (Little, 1974; Freeman, 1975). This relationship, which is one of several effects attributed to the biogenic amines, is shown in figure 7.4c. The facilitation induced by phasic cholinergic excitation is illustrated in figure 7.4d. The combined effects of these modulatory changes on sleep and other states has also been discussed in depth by Hobson (1990).

Sutton et al. (1992b) tested the model of Mamelak and co-worker through computer simulations on a temporal sequencing network. They confirmed that bifurcations between embedded sequences were indeed possible with changes in simulated aminergic and cholinergic modulation. Perhaps more impressive was the rich repertoire of sequencing and learning possibilities associated with changes in modulation in a state of simulated REM sleep. Apparently random alterations, such as increased synaptic noise due to aminergic withdrawal and intermittent global excitation due to PGO bursting, did not yield random outputs. Rather, the network remained highly constrained in its information capabilities. Seemingly bizarre outputs had a deep structure linked to the embedded sequencing and learning rules. While the exact relationships between the simulation results and neurobiology remain unclear, the emergence of deep order in the context of demodulation, or noise, is now a well-recognized phenomenon (Collins, Chow, & lmhoff, 1995; Moss & Wiesenfeld, 1995). This is discussed further in the next two sections.

STATE-DEPENDENT SEQUENCING AND MODULATION

General Considerations

Distributed network models that attempt to link psychological events with underlying neural dynamics in waking and sleep rely primarily on the idea that physiological state changes are regulated by changes in neuromodulation. While this concept applies to sleep-wake physiology, there is an impressive literature demonstrating a spectrum of behaviors in neural networks subjected to changes in neuromodulation (Selverston, 1985; Davis, Jacobs, & Schoenfield, 1989; Harris-Warrick & Marder, 1991; Silberstein, 1995). Furthermore, the notion of critically altering the dynamic behavior of a system by varying a quantity, such as a neuromodulatory chemical, applies not only to neural systems but to many systems in biology and physics. Indeed, there is an analogy between transitions in physiological states and transitions in physical states (Sutton, 1995).

Assumptions in Modeling

There are many different ways to study distributed networks and to investigate the effects of modulation and state transitions (Anderson and Rosenfeld, 1988; Hobson, Mamelak, & Sutton, 1992). In bridging aspects of neuromodulation with changes in state-dependent cognition, and discontinuities in visual imagery and memory in particular, a reasonable approach has been to examine networks with two essential features. The networks should generate temporal sequences of cognitive information and the networks should simulate the effects of aminergic and cholinergic modulation. We have incorporated these criteria into an impressionistic model that is outlined here (Sutton et al, 1992b; see figure 7.3). We maintain that the rich behaviors associated with our simplistic model underscore the enormous complexities of state-dependent behaviors present in mammalian systems during waking and sleep. The simplicity attempts to extract key concepts at the expense of details, and we emphasize that the modeling should not be construed as an effort to replicate the behavior of the cerebral cortex and deeper structures in waking and sleep.

To make explicit what we have attempted to do, we list the pertinent assumptions and limitations below:

1. The network consists of model neurons, and the collective activity of the neurons at a given instant in time generates a pattern of neuron firing throughout the network.

2. A small fraction of the firing patterns are quasi-stable. Once the network enters a quasi-stable pattern, it remains in that pattern for a period of time before moving to another pattern. The quasi-stable patterns serve as the network's memory.

3. The ability to store information about the memory, or quasi-stable, patterns is encoded distributively among the connections linking individual neurons within the network.

4. Information about how particular memory patterns are temporally linked to each other is also distributively stored among the connections. When the network enters one memory pattern, it sequentially makes a transition to the next stored pattern in the sequence.

5. The dynamics of the network are governed by a computational rule that updates all of the neurons in a synchronous, parallel manner. Each neuron determines its inputs at a given instant in time, and after comparing the sum of the inputs with its threshold value, each neuron determines whether or not it fires. Once a neuron is firing, it requires continued input to remain firing; otherwise, it becomes quiescent. The updating rules on firing and the temporal evolution of the network are partially based on physiology and partially based on computational convenience (Abeles, Bergman, Gat, et al., 1995).

6. Inputs from the aminergic and cholinergic systems are incorporated at each time step in the evolution of the network.

7. The instantaneous output of the network is given by the global pattern of activity among the neurons. This can be expressed as an overlap between the instantaneous pattern and each of the embedded memory patterns. Complete overlap with a single memory pattern signifies that the network is in that memory. The network may partially overlap with a combination of memory patterns, or it may be in a random pattern with no obvious overlap with any memory pattern.

Neural Network Model

Many attractor neural networks can be modified to have the required sequencing properties (Amit, 1989; Reiss & Taylor, 1991). We chose to adapt a model which had well-characterized temporal sequencing properties and which was amenable to adding neuromodulatory features (Kleinfeld, 1986; Sompolinsky & Kanter, 1986; Gutfreund & Mezard, 1988). In our network, memory patterns encoded visual memories, and sequences of memories represented temporal orderings or flows among visual images (Sutton et al., 1992b). For illustrative purposes, we considered the case where two sequences of memory patterns were stored in the network. Both sequences contained three memory patterns each, and these were arranged into two loops. Loop A consisted of memory patterns A1, A2, and A3, which made transitions sequentially as A1 → A2 → A3 → A1.... Similarly, loop B comprised the sequence of memory patterns B1 → B2 → B3 → B1.... Continuities and discontinuities of visual information were represented by the degree to which transitions among memory patterns in the model remained within or jumped between loops A and B.

Aminergic regulation was modeled by intrinsic noise at the level of the synapses (see figure 7.4c). We consolidated NE and 5-HT together, although it was recognized that these modulators have subtypes and heterogeneity of function. Cholinergic facilitation was an extrinsically generated input which nonselectively excited all the neurons in the network (see figure 7.4d). The connection weights among the neurons and the membrane thresholds were held constant during the simulations, although the effects of learning were subsequently examined. A mathematical outline of the model is provided in the appendix, and the interested reader is referred to Sutton et al. (1992b) for details.

SIMULATION RESULTS AND LEARNING

Simulation Results

The model's parameters were selected to allow the network to generate, in the simulated waking state, repetitive and stable sequences of memories. A typical output pattern is illustrated in figure 7.5a. Not surprisingly, the principal mechanism for making transitions from one loop to the other was to provide an external input closely resembling a memory pattern in the second loop.

As the amount of aminergic modulation was decreased, partially characterizing the model NREM state, sequencing within a loop persisted, but with decreased stability. Relatively small perturbations disrupted the preset transitions. The instability of sequences at the level of the entire network was correlated with fluctuations at the synaptic and membrane levels. As the aminergic system turned off, there was increased noise in synaptic transmission, with corresponding increases in membrane potential fluctuations. On average, a larger proportion of neurons remained closer to their firing thresholds when there was aminergic withdrawal.

With further aminergic decreases and the disinhibition of phasic cholinergic effects on the network, a spectrum of interrelated phenomena was observed. This included (a) sequences that bifurcated between loops; (b) a change from orderly intraloop sequencing to apparent disorder,[1] (c) a change from apparent disorder to orderly progression within a single loop ("defibrillation" effect); (d) a change from a disorderly pattern to another disorderly pattern; and (e) no or little effect on identifiable intraloop sequencing. An example of transition types (b) and (c), with the overall effect of inducing a bifurcation between the two loops, is shown in figure 7.5b.

In general, lower-intensity, longer-duration PGO bursts were more effective in inducing bifurcations than higher-intensity, shorter-duration bursts. The networks also appeared to be surprisingly sensitive to the timing of the PGO-type bursts in determining the form of the transitions. PGO-induced bifurcations were possible in all states, including the simulated waking state, if the bursting was intense, of long duration, and occurred at selective times with respect to the microscopic dynamics. This finding had an analogy with the shifts in attention correlated with PGO bursting during the startle response in wakefulness. Finally, the mechanism of phasic excitatory facilitation, via PGO bursts, was not unique in inducing a plethora of network responses. For example, superimposing phasic aminergic withdrawal on a state of tonic aminergic decrease led to results similar to those just described.

In summary, the findings suggested ways whereby networks dramatically alter their sequencing properties through changes in modulation. The results do not prove that combined aminergic and cholinergic changes mediate bifurcations in visual imagery, but they are certainly consistent with the notion that neurophysiological state changes alter global processes in large-scale networks. Different processing states not only exist within the same network but relatively small changes in neuromodulation can induce significant state transitions over widespread regions. In biological networks, widespread regions are linked to cognitive processes.

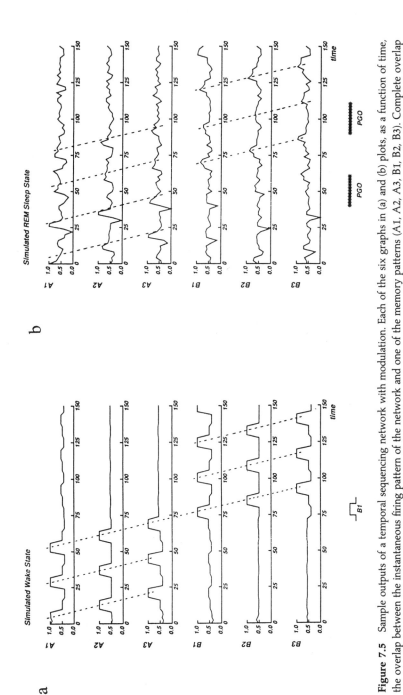

Figure 7.5 Sample outputs of a temporal sequencing network with modulation. Each of the six graphs in (a) and (b) plots, as a function of time, the overlap between the instantaneous firing pattern of the network and one of the memory patterns (A1, A2, A3, B1, B2, B3). Complete overlap with a memory pattern has the value 1.0; a random overlap has the value 0.5. *a*, Simulated waking state. The network begins sequencing in loop A. There is complete overlap, which lasts for eight time steps, with each of the sequential memory patterns A1, A2, and A3. At time *t* = 75, pattern B1 is externally inputted into the network. The network subsequently begins transitioning within loop B. *b*, Simulated REM sleep state. The amount of aminergic-like modulation is reduced resulting in increased noise in the overlap plots. Two bursts of ponto-geniculo-occipital (PGO)–like excitation are shown (asterisks). One burst occurs between *t* = 40 and *t* = 60, and a second burst occurs between *t* = 90 and *t* = 110. The simulated coupling of phasic PGO activity and tonic aminergic disinhibition results in a bifurcation between loops A and B. In contrast to (a), the bifurcation occurs in the absence of a specific external switching mechanism (i.e., the network is not reset by external input from B1, B2, or B3). (Modified from Sutton et al., 1992b.)

Learning

It is generally accepted that memory and learning are interrelated processes, and that sleep is critical homeostatic mechanism in normal cognition. We have extended our theoretical approach to include state-dependent learning by including modifiable synapses in the sequencing network. A central assumption in doing this was that basic synaptic mechanisms underlying plasticity were essentially the same across different states. However, their local efficiencies may be decreased due to the withdrawal of the biogenic amines, especially NE, in sleep relative to waking.

Our results are preliminary. We implemented standard biophysical mechanisms to incorporate features of use-dependent synaptic changes, including long-term enhancement and depression, or forgetting (Brown, Kairiss, & Keenan, 1990). The general mathematical formulation is included in the appendix. While more simulations are required, we have found that the REM sleep state is particularly well suited for certain types of computation, such as rapid scanning and course learning. In the sequencing model, the system had the capacity to move readily between apparently uncorrelated patterns, whereas, in the waking and NREM sleep states, it did not spontaneously do this.

When coupled with a relatively withdrawn, but nevertheless present, source of local plasticity, the possibility of novel memory formation, via unsupervised learning, was abundantly clear in the REM sleep state. The network appeared to be computing by superimposing phasic and tonic noise upon an otherwise highly constrained system. In making transitions out of the REM sleep state back into the NREM sleep and waking states, the learning became more supervised and efficacious in response to external inputs.

DISCUSSION

In this chapter, we have outlined an approach to investigating sleep and cognition using artificial neural networks. While the models are impressionistic, they nevertheless allow computational studies of the intricate relationships between neuromodulation, state-dependent cognition, and plasticity. Our studies support the hypothesis that different neurophysiological states mediate different types of sequencing and learning operations, and they suggest that an evolution of state changes may enhance the overall learning capability and efficiency of biological neural networks.

Our work complements the research of other investigators exploring the seemingly hidden domain of the sleeping brain. We are optimistic that newer techniques, such as functional MRI, combined with neural network methods, electrophysiology, and subjective reports, will begin to weave an integrated story of neural computation in human waking and sleep.

ACKNOWLEDGMENTS

We acknowledge support from the McDonnell-Pew Program in Cognitive Neuroscience, the MacArthur Foundation and the National Institutes of Health, MH grants R01 13923 and K21 01080.

NOTE

1. The apparent disorder revealed several sequences in loops A and B running out of phase with relative delays. These delays were generally less than the time constant for intermemory transitions within a single loop.

REFERENCES

Abeles, M., Bergman, H., Gat, I., Meilijson, I., Seidemann, E., Tishby, N., & Vaadia, E. (1995). Cortical activity flips among quasi-stationary states. *Proceedings of the National Academy of Sciences, 92,* 8616–8620.

Aghajanian, G., & Van der Maelen, C. (1986). Specific systems of the reticular core: Serotonin. In V. Mountcastle (Ed.), *Handbook of physiology—The nervous system,* Vol. 4 (pp. 237–256). Bethesda, MD: American Physiological Society.

Amit, D. J. (1989). *Modeling brain function.* Cambridge, U.K.: Cambridge University Press.

Anderson, J. A., & Rosenfeld, E. (Eds.). (1988). *Neurocomputing.* Cambridge, MA: MIT Press.

Antrobus, J. S. (1983). REM and NREM sleep reports: Comparison of word frequencies by cognitive classes. *Psychophysiology, 20,* 562–568.

Aserinsky, E., & Kleitman, N. (1953). Regularly occurring periods of ocular motility and concomitant phenomena during sleep. *Science, 118,* 361–375.

Baars, B. J., & Banks, W. P. (Eds.). (1994). *Consciousness and cognition.* New York: Academic Press.

Bear, M. F., & Singer, W. (1986). Modulation of visual cortical plasticity by acetylcholine and noradrenaline. *Nature, 320,* 172–176.

Bootzin, R. R., Kihlstrom, J., F, & Schacter, D. L. (1990). *Sleep and cognition.* Washington, DC: American Psychological Association.

Bowker, R. M., & Morrison, A. R. (1976). The startle reflex and PGO spikes. *Brain Research, 102,* 185–190.

Brook, S. (Ed.). (1987). *The Oxford book of dreams.* Oxford, U.K.: Oxford University Press.

Brooks, D. C., & Bizzi, E. (1963). Brain stem electrical activity during deep sleep. *Archives Italiennes de Biologie, 101,* 648–665.

Brown, T. H., Kairiss, E. W., & Keenan, C. L. (1990). Hebbian synapses: Biophysical mechanisms and algorithms. *Annual Review of Neuroscience, 13,* 475–511.

Buzsaki, G. (1989). Two-stage model of memory trace formation: a role for noisy brain states. *Neuroscience, 31,* 551–570.

Callaway, C. W., Lydic, R., Baghdoyan, H. A., & Hobson, J. A. (1987). Ponto-geniculo-occipital waves: Spontaneous visual system activation occurring in REM sleep. *Cellular and Molecular Neurobiology, 7,* 105–149.

Clark, J. W., Rafelski, J., & Winston, J. V. (1985). Brain without mind: Computer simulation of neural networks with modifiable neuronal interactions. *Physical Reports, 123*(4), 215–273.

Collins, J. J., Chow, C. C., & Imhoff, T. T. (1995). Stochastic resonance without tuning. *Nature, 376*, 236–238.

Crick, F., & Mitchison, G. (1983). The function of dream sleep. *Nature, 304*, 111–114.

Datta, S. (1995). Neuronal activity in the peribrachial area: Relationship to behavioral state control. *Neuroscience and Biobehavioral Reviews, 19*(1), 67–84.

Davis, M., Jacobs, B. L., & Schoenfeld, R. I. (Eds.). (1989). *Modulation of defined vertebrate neural circuits.* New York: New York Academy of Sciences.

Dement, W., & Kleitman, N. (1957). Cyclic variations in EEG during sleep and their relation to eye movements, body mobility and dreaming. *Electroencephalography and Clinical Neurophysiology, 9*, 673–690.

Fishbein, W., Kastaniotis, C., & Chattman, D. (1974). Paradoxical sleep: Prolonged augmentation following learning. *Brain Research, 79*, 61–77.

Flicker, C., McCarley, R. W., & Hobson, J. A. (1981). Aminergic neurons: State control and plasticity in three model systems. *Cellular and Molecular Neurobiology, 1*(2), 123–166.

Foulkes, D. (1985). *Dreaming: A cognitive-psychological analysis.* Hillsdale, NJ: Erlbaum.

Freeman, W. J. (1975). *Mass action in the nervous system.* New York: Academic Press.

Freud, S. (1895). Project for a scientific psychology. In *Standard edition of the complete psychological works of Sigmund Freud* (J. Strachey, trans.), Vol. 1 (pp. 281–397). London: Hogarth, 1953–1974.

Freud, S. (1900). *The interpretation of dreams* (J., Strachey, trans.). New York: Avon 1965.

Geszti, T., & Pazmandi, F. (1987). Learning within bounds and dream sleep. *Journal of Physics A: Mathematical and General, 20*, L1299–L1303.

Gillin, J. C., & Borbely, A. A. (1985). Sleep: A neurobiological window on affective disorders. *Trends in Neuroscience, 8*, 537–542.

Gutfreund, H., & Mezard, M. (1988). Processing of temporal sequences in neural networks. *Physical Review Letters, 61*, 235–238.

Harris-Warrick, R. M., & Marder, E. (1991). Modulation of neural networks for behavior. *Annual Review of Neuroscience, 14*, 39–57.

Hasselmo, M. E. (1993). Acetylcholine and learning in a cortical associative memory. *Neural Computation, 5*, 32–44.

Hinton, G. E., Dayan, P., Frey, B. J., & Neal, R. M. (1995). The "wake-sleep" algorithm for unsupervised neural networks. *Science, 268*, 1158–1161.

Hobson, J. A. (1988a). *The dreaming brain.* New York: Basic Books.

Hobson, J. A. (1988b). Homeostasis and heteroplasticity: Functional significance of behavioral state sequences. In R. Lydic & J. F. Biebuyck (Eds.), *Clinical physiology of sleep* (pp. 199–220). Bethesda, MD: American Physiological Society.

Hobson, J. A. (1990). Activation, input source, and modulation. In R. R. Bootzin, J. F. Kihlstrom, & D. L. Schacter (Eds.), *Sleep and cognition* (pp. 25–40). Washington, DC: American Psychological Association.

Hobson, J. A., Hoffman, S. A., Helfand, R., & Kosner, D. (1987). Dream bizarreness and the activation-synthesis hypothesis. *Human Neurobiology, 6*, 157–164.

Hobson, J. A., Mamelak, A. N., & Sutton, J. P. (1992). Models wanted: Must fit dimensions of sleep and dreaming. In J. E. Moody, S. J. Hanson, & R. Lippmann (Eds.), *Advances in neural information processing systems 4* (pp. 3–10). San Mateo, CA: Morgan Kaufmann.

Hobson, J. A., & McCarley, R. W. (1977). The brain as a dream-state generator: An activation-synthesis hypothesis of the dream process. *American Journal of Psychiatry, 134,* 1335–1368.

Hobson, J. A., McCarley, R. W., & Wyzinki, P. W. (1975). Sleep cycle oscillation: reciprocal discharge by two brainstem neuronal groups. *Science, 189,* 55–58.

Hobson, J. A., & Steriade, M. (1986). Neuronal basis of behavioral state control. In V. B. Mountcastle (Ed.), *Handbook of physiology—The nervous system,* Vol 4 (pp. 701–823). Bethesda, MD: American Physiological Society.

Hopfield, J. J., Feinstein, D. I., & Palmer, R. G. (1983). Unlearning has a stabilizing effect in collective memories. *Nature, 304,* 158–159.

Hopkins, W. F., & Johnston, D. J. (1988). Noradrenergic enhancement of long-term potentiation at mossy fiber synapses in the hippocampus. *Journal of Neurophysiology, 59(2),* 667–687.

Jarbe, T. U. C., Callenholm, N. E. B., Mahammed, A. D., & Archer, T. (1981). Noradrenaline and the context-dependent extinction effect. *Physiology and Behavior, 38,* 495–501.

Kandel, E. R., Klein, M., Hochner, B., Shuster, M., Siegelbaum, S., Hawkins, R., Glanzman D. L., Castellucci, V. F., & Abrams, T. W. (1987). Synaptic modulation and learning: New insights into synaptic transmission from the study of behavior. In G. M. Edelman, W. E. Gall, & W. M. Cowan (Eds.), *Synaptic Function.* New York: Wiley.

Karni, A., Meyer, G., Jezzard, P., Adams, M. M., Turner, R., & Ungerleider, L. G. (1995). Functional MRI evidence for adult motor cortex plasticity during motor skill learing. *Nature, 377,* 155–158.

Karni, A., Tanne, D., Rubenstein, B. S., Askenasy, J. J. M., & Sagi, D. (1994). Dependence on REM sleep of overnight improvement of a perceptual skill. *Science, 265,* 679–682.

Keeler, J. D., Pichler, E. E., & Ross, J. (1989). Noise in neural networks: Thresholds, hysteresis, and neuromodulation of signal-to-noise. *Proceedings of the National Academy of Sciences, 86,* 1712–1716.

Kleinfeld, D. (1986). Sequential state generation by model neural networks. *Proceedings of the National Academy of Sciences, 83,* 9469–9473.

Kramer, M., & Roth, T. (1972). The mood-regulatory function of sleep. In W. P. Koella & P. Levin (Eds.), *Sleep* (pp. 563–570). Basel: Karger.

Kronauer, R. E., Czeisler, C. A., Pilato, S. F., Moore-Ede, M. C., & Weitzman, E. D. (1982). Mathematical model of the human circadian system with two interacting oscillators. *American Journal of Physiology, 242(11),* R3–R17.

Little, W. A. (1974). The existence of persistent states in the brain. *Mathematical Biosciences, 19,* 101–120.

Llinás, R. R., & Ribary, U. (1994). Perception as an oneiric-like state modulated by the senses. In C. Koch & J. L. Davis (Eds.), *Large-scale neuronal theories of the brain* Cambridge, MA: MIT Press.

Lotka, A. (1956). *Elements of physical biology.* New York: Dover Press.

Mamelak, A. N., & Hobson, J. A. (1989). Dream bizarrenes as the cognitive correlate of altered neuronal behavior in REM sleep. *Journal of Cognitive Neuroscience, 1(3),* 201–222.

Maquet, P., Dive, D., Salmon, E., Sadzot, B., Franco, G., Poirrier, R., von Frenkell, R., & Frank, G. (1990). Cerebral glucose utilization during sleep-wake cycle in man determined by positron emission tomography and [18F]2-fluoro-2-deoxy-D-glucose method. *Brain Research, 513,* 136–143.

McCarley, R. W., & Hobson, J. A. (1975). Neuronal excitability over the sleep cycle: A structural and mathematical model. *Science, 189,* 58–60.

McCarley, R. W., & Hoffman, E. (1981). REM sleep dreams and the activation-synthesis hypothesis. *American Journal of Psychiatry, 138,* 904–912.

McCarley, R. W., & Massaquoi, S. G. (1986). A limit cycle mathematical model of the REM sleep oscillator system. *American Journal of Physiology, 251,* R1011–R1029.

McCarley, R. W., Winkelman, J. W., & Duffy, F. H. (1983). Human cerebral potential associated with REM sleep rapid eye movements: Links to PGO waves and waking potentials. *Brain Research, 274,* 359–364.

McClelland, J. L., McNaughton, B. L., & O'Reilly, R. C. (1994). *Why there are complementary learning systems in the hippocampus and neocortex: Insights from the success and failures of connectionist models of learning and memory.* CMU Technical Report No. PDP.CNS.94.1.

McCulloch, W. S. (1965). *Embodiments of mind.* Cambridge, MA: MIT Press.

McCulloch, W. S., & Pitts, W. (1943). A logical calculus of the ideas immanent in nervous activity. *Bulletin of Mathematical Biophysics, 9,* 115–133.

Merritt, J. M., Stickgold, R., Pace-Schott, E., Williams, J., & Hobson, J. A. (1994). Emotion profiles in the dreams of men and women. *Consciousness and Cognition, 3*(1), 46–60.

Montplaisir, J., & Godbout, R. (Eds.). (1990). *Sleep and biological rhythms: Basic mechanisms and applications to psychiatry.* Oxford, U.K.: Oxford University Press.

Moore, R. Y. (1979). The anatomy of central neural mechanisms regulating endocrine rhythms. In D. T. Krieger (Ed.), *Endocrine rhythms* (pp. 63–87). New York: Raven Press.

Moore-Ede, M. C., & Czeisler, C. A. (Eds.). (1984). *Mathematical models of the circadian sleep-wake cycle.* New York: Raven Press.

Moss, F., & Wiesenfeld, K. (1995). The benefits of background noise. *Scientific American, 273*(2), 66–69.

Nakao, M., Takahashi, T., Mizutani, Y., & Yamamoto, M. (1990). Simulation study on dynamics transition in neuronal activity during sleep cycle by using asynchronous and symmetry neural network model. *Biological Cybernetics, 63,* 243–250.

Olivier, A., Parent, A., & Poirer, L. J. (1970). Identification of the thalamic nuclei on the basis of their cholinesterase content in the monkey. *Journal of Anatomy, 106,* 37–50.

Poe, G. R., Rector, D. M., & Harper, R. M. (1994). Hippocampal reflected optical patterns during sleep and waking states in the freely behaving cat. *Journal of Neuroscience, 14*(5), 2933–2942.

Ramm, P., & Frost, B. J. (1986). Cerebral and local cerebral metabolism in the cat during slow wave and REM sleep. *Brain Research, 365,* 112–124.

Recanzone, G. H., Merzenich, M. M., Jenkins, W. M., Grajski, K. A., & Dinse, H. R. (1992). *Journal of Neurophysiology, 67,* 1031–1056.

Rechtschaffen, A., Bergmann, B. M., Everson, C., Kushida, C. A., & Gilliland, M. A. (1989). Sleep deprivation in the rat: X. Integration and discussion of the findings. *Sleep, 12,* 68–87.

Reiss, M., & Taylor, J. G. (1991). Storing temporal sequences. *Neural Networks, 4,* 773–787.

Roffwarg, H. P., Muzio, J. N., & Dement, W. C. (1966). Ontogenetic development of the human sleep-dream cycle. *Science, 152,* 604–619.

Schmajuk, N. A., & Moore, J. W. (1985). Real-time attentional models for classical conditioning in the hippocampus. *Physiological Psychology, 13,* 278–290.

Segal, M. (1985). Mechanisms of action of noradrenaline in the brain. In B. Will, P. Schmitt, & R. Dalrymple-Alford (Eds.), *Brain plasticity, learning and memory* (pp. 235–239). New York: Plenum Press.

Selverston, A. I. (Ed.). (1985). *Model neural networks and behavior*. New York: Plenum Press.

Servan-Schreiber, Printz, H., & Cohen, J. D. (1990). A network model of catecholamine effects: Gain, signal-to-noise ratio, and behavior. *Science, 249,* 892–895.

Silberstein, R. B. (1995). Neuromodulation of neocortical dynamics. In P. L. Nunez (Ed.), *Neocortical dynamics and human EEG rhythms* (pp. 591–627). Oxford, U.K.: Oxford University Press.

Smith, C., Kitahama, K., Valatx, J. L., & Jouvet, M. (1980). Prolonged increases in paradoxical sleep during and after avoidance-task acquisition. *Sleep, 3*(1), 67–81.

Somers, V. K., Dyken, M. E., Mark, A. L., & Abboud, F. M. (1993). Sympathetic-nerve activity during sleep in normal subjects. *New England Journal of Medicine, 328,* 303–307.

Sompolinsky, H., & Kanter, I. (1986). Temporal association in asymmetric neural networks. *Physical Reviews Letters, 57,* 2861–2864.

Steriade, M., & Llinás, R. R. (1988). The functional states of the thalamus and associated neuronal interplay. *Physiological Reviews, 68*(3), 649–742.

Steriade, M., & McCarley, R. W. (1990). *Brainstem control of wakefulness and sleep*. New York: Plenum Press.

Steriade, M., McCormick, D. A., & Sejnowski, T. J. (1993). Thalamocortical oscillations in the sleeping and aroused brain. *Science, 262,* 679–685.

Sutton, J. P., & Hobson, J. A. (1994). State-dependent sequencing and learning. In F. H. Eeckman (Ed.), *Computation in neurons and neural systems* (pp. 275–280). Boston: Kluwer Academic Publisher.

Steriade, M., Pare, D., Parent, A., & Smith, Y. (1988). Projections of cholinergic and non-cholinergic neurons of the brainstem core to relay and associational thalamic nuclei in the cat and macaque monkey. *Neuroscience, 25,* 47–67.

Strogatz, S. H. (1986). *The mathematical structure of the human sleep-wake cycle*. New York: Springer-Verlag.

Sutton, J. P. (1995). Neuroscience and computing algorithms. *Information Sciences, 84,* 199–208.

Sutton, J. P., Mamelak, A. N., & Hobson, J. A. (1992a). Modeling states of waking and sleeping. *Psychiatric Annals, 22*(3), 137–143.

Sutton, J. P., Mamelak, A. N., & Hobson, J. A. (1992b). Network model of state-dependent sequencing. In J. E. Moody, S. J. Hanson, & R. P. Lippmann (Eds.), *Advances in neural information processing systems 4* (pp. 283–290). San Mateo, CA: Morgan Kaufmann.

Sutton, J. P., Rittenhouse, C. D., Pace-Schott, E., Merritt, J. M., Stickgold, R., & Hobson, J. A. (1994a). Emotion and visual imagery in dream reports: A narrative graphing approach. *Consciousness and Cognition, 3*(1), 89–99.

Sutton, J. P., Rittenhouse, C. D., Pace-Schott, E., Stickgold, R., & Hobson, J. A. (1994b). A new approach to dream bizarreness: Graphing continuity and discontinuity of visual attention in narrative reports. *Consciousness and Cognition, 3*(1), 61–88.

Takahashi, J. S. (1995). Molecular neurobiology and genetics of circadian rhythms in mammals. *Annual Review of Neuroscience, 18,* 531–553.

Volterra, V. (1931). *Leçons sur la théorie mathématique de la lutte pour la vie*. Paris: Gauthier-Villars.

Williams, J., Merritt, J., Rittenhouse, C., & Hobson, J. A. (1992). Bizarreness in dreams and fantasies: The activation-synthesis hypothesis. *Consciousness and Cognition, 1,* 172–185.

Wilson, M. A., & McNaughton, B. L. (1993). Dynamics of the hippocampal ensemble code for space. *Science, 261,* 1055–1058.

Wilson, M. A., & McNaughton, B. L. (1994). Reactivation of hippocampal ensemble memories during sleep. *Science, 265,* 676–679.

Wimbauer, S., Klemmer, N., & van Hemmen, J. L. (1994). Universality of unlearning. *Neural Networks, 7*(2), 261–270.

Winson, J. (1990). The meaning of dreams. *Scientific American, 263*(5), 86–96.

Wu, J. C., Gillin, J. C., Buchsbaum, M. S., Hershey, Wu, Gillin, Bu, Hesshey T, Hazlett, E., Sicotle, N., & Bunney, W. E. Jr. T., (1991). The effect of sleep deprivation on cerebral glucose metabolic rate in normal humans assessed with positron emission tomography. *Sleep, 14,* 155–162.

APPENDIX

Mathematically, the temporal sequencing network consists of N model neurons. Each neuron is assigned a value $S_i(t) = \pm 1$, $i = 1, \ldots, N$, corresponding to whether or not it is firing at time t. The neurons are linked together by two kinds of synapses, $J_{ij}^{(1)}$ and $J_{ij}^{(2)}$.

$$J_{ij}^{(1)} = \frac{1}{N} \sum_{\mu=1}^{p} \xi_i^{\mu} \xi_j^{\mu}, \quad i \neq j, \tag{1}$$

encodes a set of p uncorrelated patterns $\{\xi_i^{\mu}\}_{i=1}^{N}$, $\mu = 1, \ldots, p$, where each ξ_i^{μ} has the value ± 1 with equal probability. These patterns are the quasi-stable memories. Sequential transitions among memories $\mu = 1 \to 2 \to \cdots \to q < p$ are induced by

$$J_{ij}^{(2)} = \frac{\lambda}{N} \sum_{\mu=1}^{q-1} \xi_i^{\mu+1} \xi_j^{\mu}, \tag{2}$$

where λ is a relative weight term. The average time spent in a memory pattern is τ. The membrane potential is given by

$$h_i(t) = \sum_{j=1}^{N} [J_{ij}^{(1)} S_j(t) + J_{ij}^{(2)} S_j(t - \tau)] + \delta_i(t) + I_i(t). \tag{3}$$

The two terms contained in the brackets reflect intrinsic network interactions, while phasic PGO effects are given by $\delta_i(t)$. External, non-PGO, inputs are denoted by $I_i(t)$. Dynamic evolution follows the synchronous updating rule

$$S_i(t + 1) = \pm 1, \quad \text{with probability} \quad \{1 + e^{\mp 2\beta[h_i(t) - \theta_i(t)]}\}^{-1}. \tag{4}$$

$\theta_i(t)$ is the membrane threshold and β parameterizes the amount of aminergic-like modulation. Synaptic learning in equations (1) and (2) has the form

$$J_{ij}^{(k)}(t + 1) = J_{ij}^{(k)}(t) + \varepsilon F[S_i(t), S_j(t)], \quad k = 1, 2. \tag{5}$$

F is a function of presynaptic and postsynaptic firing, and ε gives the learning rate, which is maximal in the simulated waking state and minimal during the model REM sleep state.

III Neuropsychological Tests and Clinical Syndromes

8 Stroop Task, Language, and Neuromodulation: Models of Cognitive Deficits in Schizophrenia

David Servan-Schreiber and Jonathan D. Cohen

Ultimately, a complete understanding of human behavior must derive from an understanding of the biological mechanisms upon which it relies. Despite this obvious, and intimate link between behavior and biology, research in each of these domains has remained relatively autonomous—particularly when it concerns psychopathology. For example, schizophrenia is marked by a wide variety of behavioral deficits, including disturbances of attention, language processing, and problem solving. At the same time, schizophrenia is characterized by biological abnormalities, including disturbances in specific neurotransmitter systems (e.g., dopamine and norepinephrine) and anatomical structures (e.g., the prefrontal cortex, or PFC, and the hippocampus). However, the behavior and biology of schizophrenia have remained separate fields of inquiry. Despite a modern consensus that information-processing deficits in schizophrenia are the result of underlying biological abnormalities, few efforts have been made to specify exactly how these phenomena relate to one another.

In this chapter we draw upon the framework of connectionist models to address this gap between behavior and biology. The modeling framework provides theoretical concepts that are intermediate between the details of neuroscientific observations and the box-and-arrow diagrams of traditional information processing or neuropsychological theories. In particular, we explore the ability of connectionist models to explain aspects of schizophrenic behavior in terms of specific underlying biological disturbances. At the behavioral level, the models address both normal and schizophrenic performance in three experimental tasks: two that tap attentional performance (the Stroop task and the continuous performance test), and one that measures language-processing abilities (a lexical disambiguation task). The models use a common set of information-processing mechanisms, and show how a number of seemingly disparate observations about schizophrenic behavior can all be related to a single functional deficit: a disturbance in the processing of context.

The models also suggest that this functional deficit may be explained by a specific biological disturbance: a reduction in the effects of the neurotransmitter dopamine in the PFC. First, we show how a particular parameter of the models can be used to simulate the neuromodulatory effects of dopamine at the neuronal level. We then present the results of simulations in which this parameter is disturbed within a module corresponding to the function of the PFC. In each of the three behavioral simulations, this disturbance leads to changes in performance that quantitatively match those observed for patients with schizophrenia in the corresponding tasks. These findings suggest that a number of the disturbances of attention and language found in schizophrenia may all result from a disturbance in the processing of context which, in turn, may be explained by a single biological abnormality, a reduction of dopaminergic activity in the PFC.

The background of the models presented in this chapter spans a large and diverse literature concerning cognitive deficits in schizophrenia, the anatomy and physiology of dopamine systems, the neurophysiology and neuropsychology of frontal cortex, and the role of these biological systems in schizophrenia. A full review of these data is beyond the scope of this communication (see J. D. Cohen & Servan-Schreiber, 1992, for a more comprehensive review). Here, we highlight five empirical observations concerning information processing and biological deficits in schizophrenia. The purpose of our simulations is to show how these observations—which range from the biological to the cognitive level—can be articulated within the same model and account for specific aspects of behavior. These observations are: (1) The performance of patients in a variety of cognitive tasks indicates a decreased ability to use context information for selecting appropriate behavior. By *context*, we mean information that is relevant to, but is not part of, the content of a behavioral response. This can be task instructions or specific previous stimuli that determine correct behavior. (2) The PFC is directly involved in, and necessary for, the representation and maintenance of context information. (3) The normal function of the PFC relies on the activity of the mesocortical dopamine system. (4) Dopamine has a modulatory effect on the activity of the PFC by influencing the responsivity, or *gain*, of cells in this brain region. (5) Schizophrenia is associated with abnormalities of both frontal cortex and dopamine activity.

DISTURBANCES IN THE PROCESSING OF CONTEXT

The Stroop Task

This task taps a fundamental attentional phenomenon: the ability to respond to one set of stimuli, even when other, more compelling stimuli are available. The paradigm consists of two subtasks. In one, subjects name the color of the ink in which a word is printed. In the other, subjects read the word aloud while ignoring ink color. Normal subjects are less able to attend selectively to colors (i.e., ignore words) than the reverse. If patients with schizophrenia suffer from an attentional deficit, then this effect should be exacerbated; that is, they should be less able to ignore word information, and should show a greater interference effect. This prediction is supported by studies of performance by patients with schizophrenia in the Stroop task (Abramczyk, Jordan, & Hegel, 1983; Wapner & Krus, 1960). However, because an overall slowing of reaction time is also observed, the significance of an increase in interference has been called into question: This may simply reflect an unanticipated effect of general slowing of performance, rather than of a specific attentional deficit. This issue has not been resolved in the literature. Below, we show how a simulation model of this task can help distinguish the effects of a general slowing from those of a specific attentional deficit.

Considerations of the Stroop effect typically focus on the role of selective attention. However, the processing of context is also central to this task. In order to respond to the appropriate dimension of the stimulus, the subject must hold in mind the task instructions for that trial. These provide the necessary context for interpreting the stimulus and generating the correct response. In Stroop experiments, trials are typically blocked by task (e.g., all color naming, or all word reading), so that the proper context is consistent, and regularly reinforced. However, in other attentional tasks—such as the continuous performance test (CPT)—this is not the case.

The Continuous Performance Test

In the CPT, subjects are asked to detect a target event among a sequence of briefly presented stimuli, and to avoid responding to distractor stimuli. The target event may be the appearance of a single stimulus (e.g., detect the letter X appearing in a stream of other letters), or a stimulus appearing in a particular context (e.g., respond to X preceded by A). Patients with schizophrenia (and often their biological relatives) are typically impaired in their ability to discriminate between target and distractors on this task, compared with normal and patient controls (e.g., Kornetsky, 1972; Nuechterlein, 1984). This deficit is most apparent in versions of the task that make high processing demands. For example, in the "CPT-double" a target event consists of two consecutive identical letters. Memory for the previous letter provides the context necessary to evaluate the significance of the current letter; inability to use this context would impair performance. Patients with schizophrenia perform especially poorly in this and similar versions of the task.

Schizophrenic Language Deficits

Patients with schizophrenia also show poor use of context in language processing. Chapman, Chapman, and Miller (1964) first demonstrated this in a study of these patients' interpretation of lexical ambiguities. They found that the patients tended to interpret the strong (dominant) meaning of a homonym used in a sentence, even when context suggested the weaker (subordinate) meaning. For example, given the sentence "The farmer needed a new *pen* for his cattle," the patients interpreted the word "pen" to mean writing implement more frequently than did control subjects. They did not differ from control subjects in the number of unrelated meaning responses that were made (e.g., interpreting "pen" to mean "fire truck"), nor did they differ in the number of errors made when the strong meaning was correct. Recently, we tested the idea that patients with schizophrenia are restricted in the *temporal range* over which they can process linguistic context (Cohen, Servan-Schreiber, Targ, et al., 1992). We designed a lexical ambiguity task, similar to the one used by Chapman and his colleagues, in which we could manipulate the temporal parameters involved.

Subjects were presented with sentences made up of two clauses; each clause appeared one at a time on a computer screen. One clause contained an ambiguous word in a neutral context (e.g., "you need a PEN"), while the other clause provided disambiguating context (e.g., "in order to keep chickens" or "in order to sign a check"). Clauses were designed so that they could be presented in either order: context first or context last. The ambiguity in each sentence always appeared in capital letters, so that it could be identified by the subject. Subjects were presented with the sentences and, following each, were asked to interpret the meaning of the ambiguity as it was used in the sentence. Sentences were distributed across three conditions: (a) *weak* meaning correct, context *last*; (b) weak meaning correct, context *first*; (c) *strong* meaning correct, context first. For example, a given subject would have seen the ambiguity "pen" in one of the three following conditions, and then have chosen his or her response from the list of possible meanings:

(a) you can't keep chickens (*weak meaning, context first*)
     [*clear screen/pause*]
     without a PEN

     or

(b) without a PEN (*weak meaning, context last*)
     [*clear screen/pause*]
     you can't keep chickens

     or

(c) you can't sign a check (*strong meaning, context first*)
     [*clear screen/pause*]
     without a PEN
     [*clear screen/pause*]

The meaning of the word in capital letters is:

a writing implement (*strong meaning*)
a fenced enclosure (*weak meaning*)
a kind of truck (*unrelated meaning*)

The results of this study (shown in figure 8.7A) corroborated both the original findings of Chapman et al., and the explanation of their findings in terms of an inability to maintain context. Thus, as the authors found, patients with schizophrenia made significantly more dominant meaning errors than did controls when the weak meaning was correct. However, this only occurred when the context came *first* (i.e., less recently—condition [b] above) and therefore had to be maintained until the time when the ambiguous ("pen") is processed. When context came last (i.e., more recently), patients with schizophrenia correctly chose the weak meaning. This was the only type of error that reliably distinguished these patients from controls.

These findings suggest that the impairment observed in language tasks may be similar in nature to the impairments observed in attentional tasks: a difficulty in representing and maintaining context over time.

PREFRONTAL CORTEX, CONTEXT, AND DOPAMINE

Several studies suggest that frontal areas are specifically involved in maintaining context information for the control of action. For example, at the neurophysiological level, Fuster (1997) and Goldman-Rakic (1987) have observed cells in the PFC that are specific to a particular stimulus and response, and that remain active during a delay between these. They have argued that neural patterns of activity are maintained in the PFC which encode the temporary information needed to guide a response. At the behavioral level, these authors and Diamond (e.g., 1989) have also reported data showing that the PFC is needed to perform tasks involving delayed responses to ambiguous stimuli. Diamond has emphasized that prefrontal memory is required, in particular, to overcome reflexive or previously reinforced response tendencies to mediate a contextually relevant—but otherwise weaker—response.

Furthermore, it has been shown that dopaminergic innervation of the PFC is necessary for this brain region to maintain contextual information. Experimental lesions in animals, or clinical lesions in humans, to this dopaminergic supply can mimic the effect of lesions to the PFC itself on behavioral tasks requiring memory for context (e.g., Brozoski, Brown, Rosvold, et al., 1979).

NEUROMODULATORY EFFECTS OF DOPAMINE

Several anatomical and physiological observations support the idea that catecholamines such as dopamine and norepinephrine modulate information processing in the brain. Dopamine and norepinephrine neurons originate in discrete nuclei localized in the brain stem and their fibers project radially to several functionally different areas of the central nervous system (CNS). The baseline firing rate of these neurons is low and stable, and the conduction velocity along their fibers is slow. These characteristics result in a steady state of transmitter release and relatively long-lasting postsynaptic effects that are consistent with a modulatory role. Most important, recent evidence suggests that the effect of dopamine release is not to directly increase or reduce the firing frequency of target cells (e.g., Chiodo & Berger, 1986). Rather, like norepinephrine, dopamine seems to modulate the response properties of postsynaptic cells such that both inhibitory and excitatory responses to other afferent inputs are *potentiated*. This effect has been described as an increase in the "signal-to-noise ratio" of the cells' behavior or an "enabling" of its response (e.g., Foote, Freedman, & Oliver 1975).

PREFRONTAL CORTEX AND DOPAMINE IN SCHIZOPHRENIA

The behavioral data reviewed earlier concerning schizophrenic performance deficits indicate an insensitivity to context, and a dominant response tendency. This is consistent with evidence that schizophrenia is associated with frontal lobe impairment. Patients with schizophrenia show typical frontal lobe deficits on standard neuropsychological tests, including the Wisconsin Card Sorting test (WCST) (e.g., Malmo, 1974) and the Stroop task (as described above). In addition, imaging and electrophysiological studies suggest an atrophy and abnormal metabolism in the frontal lobes of schizophrenic patients (e.g., Ingvar & Franzen, 1974). Recent studies have even demonstrated abnormal metabolism in the PFC of schizophrenic patients, specifically during performance on tasks requiring memory for context such as the WCST and a variant of the CPT (Weinberger, Berman, & Zec, 1986; R.M. Cohen, Semple, Gross, et al., 1987). This work confirms that anatomical and physiological deficits of frontal cortex may indeed be associated with some behavioral deficits observed in schizophrenic patients.

Frontal lobe dysfunction in schizophrenia fits well with the prevailing neurochemical and psychopharmacological data concerning this illness. The PFC is a primary projection area for the mesocortical dopamine system, a disturbance of which has consistently been implicated in schizophrenia (e.g., Meltzer & Stahl, 1976). In view of these findings, several authors have proposed that reduced dopaminergic tone in PFC may be associated with hypofrontality in schizophrenia, and may be responsible for several of the cognitive deficits that have been observed (e.g., Weinberger & Berman, 1988).

SUMMARY

We referred to evidence that patients with schizophrenia inadequately maintain context for the control of action; that the PFC plays a role in maintaining context; that an intact mesocortical dopamine system is necessary for normal PFC function; and finally, that the mesocortical dopamine system is affected in schizophrenia. Despite a growing recognition that these observations are related, no theory has yet been proposed which explains—in terms of causal mechanisms—the relationship between disturbances in the PFC and dopamine on the one hand, and behavioral deficits on the other. In the remainder of this chapter, we present a set of connectionist models that simulate the performance of patients with schizophrenia in the tasks described above.

SIMULATION OF THE PHYSIOLOGICAL EFFECTS OF DOPAMINE

In the models, the action of dopamine is simulated as a change in a parameter of the function relating a unit's input to its activation value. To do so, we first assume that the relationship between the input to a neuron and the neuron's frequency of firing can be simulated as a nonlinear function relating the net input of a model unit to its activation value. Physiological experiments suggest that in biological systems the shape of this function is sigmoid, with its steepest slope around the baseline firing rate (e.g., Freeman, 1979). The same experiments also indicate that small increments in excitatory drive result in greater changes in firing frequency than equivalent increments in inhibitory input. These properties can be captured by the logistic function with a constant negative bias:

$$\text{Activation} = \frac{1}{1 + e^{-(\text{gain} * \text{net}) + \text{bias}}}$$

(See figure 8.1, gain = 1.0.)

The potentiating effects of dopamine can be simulated by increasing the gain parameter of the logistic function. As figure 8.1 (gain = 2.0) illustrates, with a higher gain the unit is more sensitive to afferent signals, while its baseline firing rate (net input = 0) remains the same. Elsewhere, we have

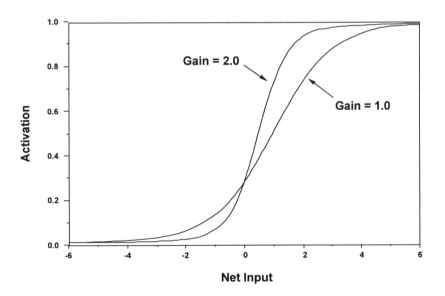

Figure 8.1 The influence of the gain parameter on the logistic activation function of an individual unit. Note that, with an increase in gain, the effect of the net input on the unit's activation is increased, while the reverse is true with a decrease in gain. These effects simulate the consequences of dopamine release on target neurons in the CNS.

shown that such a change in gain can simulate a number of different catecholaminergic effects at both the biological and behavioral levels (e.g., Servan-Schreiber, Printz, & Cohen, 1990).

In order to simulate the effect of a neuromodulator, we change gain equally for all units in the model that are assumed to be influenced by that neuromodulator. For example, the mesocortical dopamine system has extensive projections to the PFC. To model the action of dopamine in this brain area, we change the gain of all units in the module corresponding to this area. In the models described below, decreased dopamine activity in prefrontal cortex was simulated by reducing the gain of units in the module used to represent and maintain context. In all three models, simulation of performance of patients with schizophrenia was conducted by reducing gain from a normal value of 1.0 to a lower value in the range 0.6 to 0.7.

SIMULATION OF THE STROOP EFFECT

Elsewhere, we have described a connectionist model of selective attention that simulates human performance in the Stroop task (Cohen, Dunbar, & McClelland, 1990). In brief, this model consists of two processing pathways, one for color naming and one for word reading, and a task demand module that can selectively facilitate processing in either pathway (figure 8.2) Simulations are conducted by activating input units corresponding to stimuli used in an actual experiment (e.g., the input unit in the color-naming pathway representing the color red) and the appropriate task demand unit. Activation is then allowed to spread through the network. After training with backpropagation, this leads to activation of the output unit corresponding to the appropriate response (e.g., "red"). During backpropagation learning, the network is trained on "reading words" (i.e., associating inputs in the word-processing pathway with the corresponding output unit while the "word-reading" task demand unit is active) ten times more frequently than it is trained on "naming colors." The asymmetry in the training regimen produces larger weights in the word-reading pathway than in the color-naming pathway, which underlies the basic Stroop effect.

This simple model is able to simulate an impressive number of empirical phenomena associated with the Stroop task. It captures the three basic effects: (1) the asymmetry in speed of processing between word reading and color naming, (2) the immunity of word reading to the effects of color, and (3) the susceptibility of color naming to interference and facilitation from words—including the fact that the interference effect is larger than facilitation. The model also captures the influence of practice on interference and facilitation effects, the relative nature of these effects (i.e., their susceptibility to training), response set effects, and stimulus onset asynchrony effects (see Cohen et al., 1990).

This model also exhibits behaviors that make it relevant to understanding schizophrenic disturbances of attention, and their relationship to the pro-

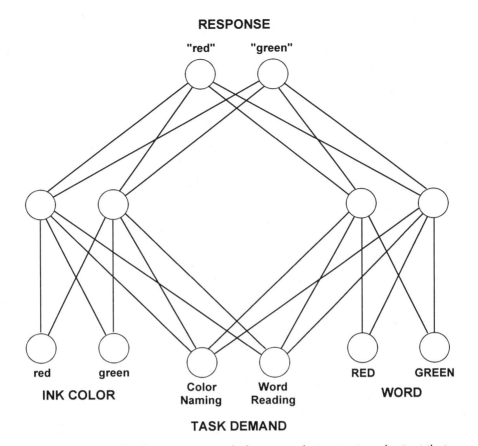

RESPONSE

"red"   "green"

red   green   RED   GREEN
INK COLOR   Color   Word   **WORD**
Naming   Reading

TASK DEMAND

Figure 8.2   Network architecture. Units at the bottom are the input units, and units at the top are the output (response) units.

cessing of context. The model shows how attention can be viewed as the effect that context has on selecting the appropriate pathway for responding. Here, context is provided by the task instructions. Thus, when subjects are presented with conflicting input in two dimensions (e.g., the word GREEN in red ink), they respond to one dimension and not the other, depending upon the *context* in which it appears (i.e., the task: color naming or word reading). If the frontal cortex is responsible for maintaining this context, and if schizophrenia involves a disturbance of frontal lobe function, then we should be able to simulate the performance of schizophrenic patients in the Stroop task by disturbing processing in the task demand module. More specifically, if frontal lobe dysfunction in schizophrenia is due to a reduction in the activity of its dopaminergic input, then we should be able to simulate this by reducing the gain of units in the task demand module.

Figure 8.3B shows the results of such a simulation, in which the gain of only the task units was reduced; all other units were unperturbed. This change in the context (task demand) module produced effects similar

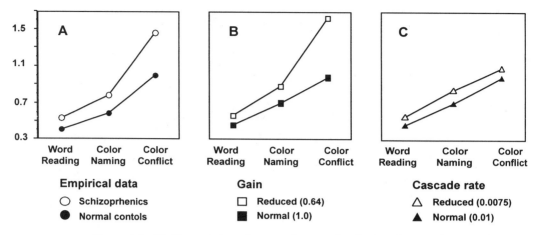

Figure 8.3 (A) Stroop task performance for normal and schizophrenic subjects, and results from simulations manipulating (B) the gain parameter (task demand units only) and (C) the cascade rate (all units) in the network. Empirical data are the response times (in seconds) for stimuli in each condition of the Stroop task, averaged over three empirical studies (Wapner & Krus, 1960; Abramczyk et al., 1983; Wysocki & Sweet, 1985); Simulation data are the number of cycles required for processing stimuli of each type, scaled by a constant (0.2) to facilitate comparison between these and the empirical data.

to those observed in patients with schizophrenia: an increase in overall response time, with a disproportionate increase for color-naming interference trials. Thus, the model shows that a lesion restricted to the mechanism for processing context can produce both an overall degradation in performance as well as the expected attentional deficit.

The model also allows us to compare the effects of this specific disturbance to those of a more general disturbance, addressing a common difficulty in schizophrenia research. It is often argued that, in the presence of a general degradation of performance in patients with schizophrenia (e.g., overall slowing of response), it is difficult to know whether degradation in a particular experimental condition is due to a specific deficit or a more generalized one. However, this difficulty arises primarily when the mechanisms for the deficits involved have not been specified. The model provides us with a tool for doing this. Above, we described the mechanism for a specific attentional deficit related to disturbances of dopamine activity in the PFC. To compare this to a more generalized deficit, we induced overall slowing in the model by decreasing the rate at which information accumulates for each unit (cascade rate); this was done for *all* units in the model (figure 8.3C). A lower cascade rate induced an overall slowing of response, but no disproportionate slowing in the interference condition. In contrast, the specific disturbance in context representation produced both effects. Thus, the context hypothesis provides a better account for the data than at least one type of generalized deficit. We have explored others (e.g., an increase in the response threshold), with similar results.

SIMULATION OF THE CONTINUOUS PERFORMANCE TEST

The Stroop model shows how contextual information and its attentional effects can be represented in a connectionist model, and how a specific biologically relevant disturbance in this mechanism can explain aspects of schizophrenic performance. One question we might ask is: How general are these findings? Here, we extend the principles applied in the Stroop model to account for performance in the CPT.

As we discussed earlier, patients with schizophrenia show consistent deficits in the CPT. This is particularly true for variants in which a demand is placed on memory for context. For example, in the CPT-double, a target consists of any consecutive reoccurrence of a letter (e.g., a *B* immediately following a *B*). Thus, subjects must remember the previous letter, which provides the necessary context for responding to the subsequent one. Patients with schizophrenia perform poorly in this task. This may be due to an impairment in the processing of context that, like deficits in the Stroop task, might be explained by a reduction of dopaminergic tone in the PFC. If this is so, then we should be able to simulate schizophrenic deficits in the CPT-double using the same manipulation used to produce deficits in the Stroop task: a reduction of gain in the module responsible for representing and, in this case, maintaining, context. To test this, we constructed a network to perform the CPT-double.

The network consisted of four modules: (1) an input module, (2) an intermediate (associative) module, (3) a letter identification module, and (4) a response module (figure 8.4). The input module was used to represent the visual features of individual letters. Stimulus presentation was simulated by activating the input units corresponding to the features of the stimulus letter. The network was trained to associate these input patterns with the corresponding letter units in the letter identification module. In addition, the network was trained to activate the unit in the response module whenever a stimulus letter appeared twice or more in a row. This was made possible by introducing a set of connections from the letter units back to the intermediate units. This allowed the network to store and use information about the previous as well as the current stimulus (see J. D. Cohen & Servan-Schreiber, 1992, for a more complete account of training and processing in this model). Note that there is a direct analogy between the role played by the letter units in this model, and the role played by the task demand units in the Stroop model. The representation over the letter units in the CPT model provided the context for disambiguating the response to a particular pattern of input, just as the task demand units did in the Stroop model. In the CPT model, however, context was determined by the previous input, and therefore changed from trial to trial.

Following training, the network was able to perform the CPT-double task perfectly for a set of twenty-six different stimuli. To simulate the performance of normal subjects—who typically miss on 17 percent of trials and set off false alarms on 5 percent of trials (figure 8.5)—noise was added to the

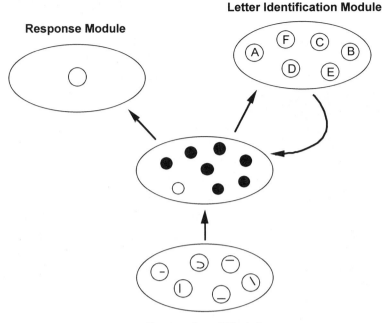

Figure 8.4 Network used to simulate the continuous performance test–double. Note the bidirectional connections between units in the intermediate and letter identification modules.

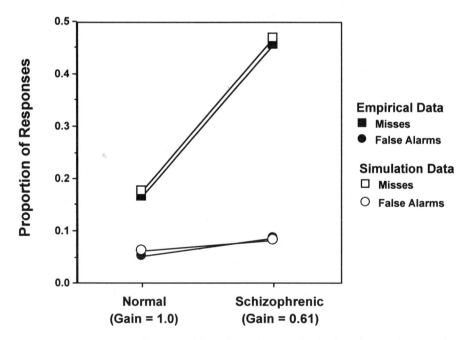

Figure 8.5 Percentage of misses and false alarms for normal and schizophrenic subjects in the continuous performance test (filled squares and circles), and for the simulation (open squares and circles) run with normal and low gain on units in the letter identification module. Empirical data are taken from Cornblatt, Lenzenweger, & Erlenmenger-Kimling, (1989).

net input, with the amount adjusted to match the performance of the network with that of human subjects. The results of this simulation appear in figure 8.5 (gain = 1.0). Then, to simulate the performance of schizophrenic patients, we disturbed processing in the letter module—which was responsible for representing and maintaining context—by decreasing the gain of these units by an amount comparable to the amount used in the Stroop simulation (0.66). The percentage of misses increased to 46 percent, while false alarms increased slightly to 8 percent. These numbers closely match the results of empirical observations of schizophrenic subjects.

Although some authors have interpreted the performance of patients with schizophrenia in the CPT in terms of a deficit in sensory processing, our model suggests an alternative hypothesis: performance deficits are due to a degradation in the memory trace required—as context—for processing the current stimulus. We assume that this memory trace is maintained in the PFC, and is directly influenced by changes in the dopaminergic supply to this area. This hypothesis is consistent with our account of Stroop performance, and with disturbances of language processing, which we turn to next.

SIMULATION OF CONTEXT-DEPENDENT LEXICAL DISAMBIGUATION

The language model (figure 8.6) incorporates elements of the two previous simulations. The network was similar to the CPT model. It was trained to associate input patterns representing lexical stimuli (e.g., the word PEN) to patterns in two output modules: a response module and a discourse module. Patterns in the response module specified the meaning of the input words (e.g., "writing implement"), while the discourse module represented the topic of the current sequence of inputs (i.e., the meaning of the sentence, rather than the meaning of individual words). As in the CPT model, there were two-way connections between the intermediate module and the context (discourse) module. Thus, once a discourse representation had been activated by an input pattern, it could be used to influence the processing of subsequent stimuli in the semantic module. This provided the mechanism by which context could be used to resolve lexical ambiguity.

Using backpropagation, the model was trained to produce local output and discourse representations for thirty different input words, some of which were ambiguous. In the case of ambiguous words, the model was trained to produce the response and discourse patterns related to one meaning (e.g., PEN → "writing implement" and WRITING) more than the other (e.g., PEN →, "fenced enclosure" and FARMING). This asymmetry of training was similar to that of the Stroop model (trained on words more than colors), with a comparable result: when presented with an ambiguous input word, the network preferentially activated the strong (more frequently trained) response and discourse representations. To permit access to the weaker meaning, the network was sometimes presented with an ambiguous word as input along with

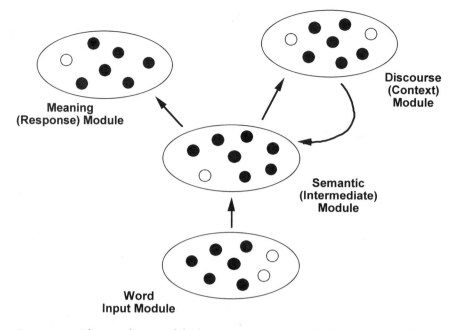

Figure 8.6 Schematic diagram of the language-processing model. Patterns of activation over the units in the input module are assumed to represent the current sensory stimulus (e.g., the orthographic code for a written word), while the output module is assumed to represent the information necessary to generate an overt response (e.g., the phonological code needed to pronounce the meaning of the word). Note that the connections between the semantic and discourse modules are bidirectional.

one of its associated discourse representations (e.g., PEN and FARMING), and trained to generate the appropriate response (i.e., "fenced enclosure"). Finally, the network was trained on a set of context words, each of which was related to one meaning of an ambiguity; these words (e.g., CHICKEN) were trained to produce their own meaning as the response ("fowl") as well as a discourse representation that was identical to the one for the corresponding meaning of the related ambiguity (FARMING). The combined effects of these training procedures was that when an ambiguous word was presented and there was no representation active over the discourse units, the output was a blend of the two meanings of the word, with elements of the more frequently trained (dominant) meaning being more active than the other (subordinate) meaning. However, when a discourse representation was active, the model successfully disambiguated the input and activated only the relevant meaning response.

In this model, patterns of activation in the semantic module are derived from the learning algorithm rather than being determined by the experimenter. Each pattern of activation produced by the activation of a particular input unit ("word") and of a discourse module unit is a distributed conjunctive representation of the word-within-discourse (e.g., PEN-within-FARMING). Such representations contain all the information necessary to activate a single output unit corresponding to a given interpretation of the input (e.g., "fenced enclosure") on the response module.

We tested the model's ability to simulate—in very simple form—the use of context in natural language processing. Most words in English have more than one meaning; language processing relies on context provided by prior stimuli to disambiguate current ones. In the model, this occurred through activation of a discourse representation in response to each lexical input, which then provided context for processing subsequent stimuli. We tested the model for this ability by first presenting it with a word related to one of the meanings of an ambiguity (e.g., CHICKEN), allowing activation to spread through the network, then presenting the ambiguity (e.g., PEN) and observing the output. Note that, in this case, the model was not directly provided with a discourse representation. Rather, it had to construct this from the first input, and then use it to disambiguate the second. Tested in this way with all context-word–ambiguous-word pairs (e.g., either CHICKEN or PAPER followed by PEN), the model was consistently able to generate the meaning response appropriate for the context.

To simulate performance in our experiment (see earlier discussion), the model was presented with pairs of context and ambiguous words (representing the clauses used in the experiment) in either order. Following each pair, the network was probed with the ambiguous word, simulating the subjects' process of reminding themselves of the ambiguity, and choosing its meaning. At each time step of processing, a small amount of noise was added to the activation of every unit. The amount of noise was adjusted so that the simulation produced an overall error rate comparable to that of control subjects. The model's response on each trial was considered to be the meaning that was most active over the output units after the probe was presented. To simulate the performance of patients with schizophrenia, we introduced a disturbance analogous to the one in the CPT model: a reduction in gain of units in the context module.

The results of this simulation (shown in figure 8.7B) show a strong resemblance to the empirical data (figure 8.7A). They demonstrate both significant effects: (a) in the low gain mode, the simulation makes about as many more dominant response errors as do the subjects with schizophrenia; however, (b) as with the human subjects, this only occurred when context came first. The model provides a clear view of this relationship between dominant response bias and memory. When gain is reduced in the context module, the representation of context is degraded; as a consequence, it is more susceptible to the cumulative effects of noise. If a contextual representation is used quickly, these effects are less, and the representation is sufficient to overcome a dominant response bias. However, if time passes (as when context is presented first), the effects of noise accumulate, and the context representation is no longer strong enough to mediate the weaker of the two competing responses.

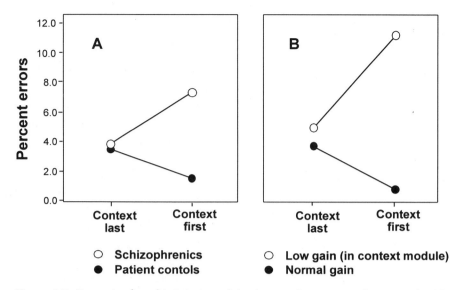

○ Schizophrenics   ○ Low gain (in context module)
● Patient contols   ● Normal gain

Figure 8.7 Error rates for subjects in two of the three conditions run in the empirical study and for the language model simulation. The rate of unrelated errors in all conditions (not shown), and of weak meaning responses when the strong meaning was correct (also not shown) were approximately the same in the normal and low-gain conditions of the simulation, and of the same magnitude as that observed in human subjects (about 1 to 2 percent).

CONCLUSION

The three models we have presented showed how the connectionist framework can be used to link biological and behavioral observations. This was achieved by bringing a common set of mechanisms to bear simultaneously on physiological and psychological phenomena. Specifically, the models served several purposes: (a) they simulated quantitative aspects of performance in three previously unrelated behavioral tasks; (b) they elucidated the role of processing of context in both the attentional and linguistic tasks; (c) they related processing of context to biological processes; and (d) they showed how a specific disturbance at the biological level could account for schizophrenic patterns of performance. The models, and the simulations based on them, relied on many simplifying assumptions and provided, at best, a coarse approximation of the mechanisms underlying both normal and schizophrenic behavior. While accounting for empirical data is a primary goal in the development of computer simulation models, McClelland (1988) has argued that this may not be the only basis for their evaluation. Models are useful if, among other things, they offer new interpretations of empirical phenomena and unify previously unrelated observations. We have indicated how our models—simple as they are—may fulfill these different functions. Finally, models can be used to derive predictions that can be tested in empirical studies. We have recently found confirmation for predictions made by our models using a variant of the CPT task described here (Servan-Schreiber, Cohen, & Steingard, 1996).

Although our models may have met these specific criteria, our overarching hope is that they will have helped provide a more refined and integrated approach to the riddle of behavioral and biological disturbances in schizophrenia and to the study of brain-behavior relationships in general.

ACKNOWLEDGMENT

This work was supported by an NIMH Physician Scientist Award (MH00673) to Johathan D. Cohen and an NIMH Individual Fellow Award (MH09696) to David Servan-Schreiber.

REFERENCES

Abramczyk, R. R., Jordan, D. E., & Hegel, M. (1983). "Reverse" Stroop effect in the performance of schizophrenics. *Perceptual and Motor Skills, 56*, 99–106.

Brozoski, T. J., Brown, R. M., Rosvold, H. E., & Goldman, P. S. (1979). Cognitive deficit caused by regional depletion of dopamine in prefrontal cortex of Rhesus monkey. *Science, 205*, 929–931.

Chapman, L. J., Chapman, J. P., & Miller, G. A. (1964). A theory of verbal behavior in schizophrenia. In B. A. Maher, (Ed.), *Progress in experimental personality research*, Vol 1. New York: Academic Press.

Chiodo, L. A., & Berger, T. W. (1986). Interactions between dopamine and amino acid–induced excitation and inhibition in the striatum. *Brain Research, 375*, 198–203.

Cohen, J. D., Dunbar, K., & McClelland, J. L. (1990). On the control of automatic processes: A parallel distributed processing model of the Stroop effect. *Psychological Review, 97*(3), 332–361.

Cohen, J. D., & Servan-Schreiber, D. (1992). Context, cortex and dopamine: A connectionist approach to behavior and biology in schizophrenia. *Psychological Review, 99*(1), 45–77.

Cohen, J. D., Servan-Schreiber, D., Targ, E., & Spiegel, D. (1992). The fabric of thought disorder: A cognitive neuroscience approach to disturbances in the processing of context in schizophrenia. In D. Stein, & J. Young (Eds.), *Cognitive science and clinical disorders* (pp. 99–126). New York: Academic Press.

Cohen, R. M., Semple, W. E., Gross, M., Nordahl, T. E., DeLisi, L. E., Holcomb, H. H., King, A. C., Morihisa, J. M., & Pickar, D. (1987). Dysfunction in a prefrontal substrate of sustained attention in schizophrenia. *Life Sciences, 40*, 2031–2039.

Cornblatt, B., Lenzenweger, M. F., & Erlenmeyer-Kimling, L. (1989). A continuous performance test, identical pairs version: II. Contrasting attentional profiles in schizophrenic and depressed patients. *Psychiatry Research, 29*, 65–85.

Diamond, A. (1989). *The development and neural bases of higher cognitive functions*. New York: New York Academy of Science.

Foote, S. L., Freedman, R., & Oliver, A. P. (1975). Effects of putative neurotransmitters on neuronal activity in monkey auditory cortex. *Brain Research, 86*, 229–242.

Freeman, W. J. (1979). Nonlinear gain mediating cortical stimulus-response relations. *Biological Cybernetics, 33*, 243–247.

Fuster, J. M. (1997). *The prefrontal cortex: Anatomy, physiology and neuropsychology of the frontal lobe,* 3rd ed. New York: Raven Press.

Goldman-Rakic, P. S. (1987). Circuitry of primate prefrontal cortex and regulation of behavior by representational memory. In F. Plum (Ed.), *Handbook of physiology: The nervous system,* Vol. 5 (pp. 373–417). Bethesda, MD: American Psysiological Society.

Ingvar, D. H., & Franzen, G. (1974). Abnormalities of cerebral flow distribution in patients with chronic schizophrenia. *Acta Psychiatrica Scandinavia, 50,* 425–462.

Kornetsky, C. (1972). The use of a simple test of attention as a measure of drug effects in schizophrenic patients. *Psychopharmacology, (Berlin), 8,* 99–106.

Malmo, H. P. (1974). On frontal lobe functions: Psychiatric patient controls. *Cortex, 10,* 231–237.

McClelland, J. L. (1988). Connectionist models and psychological evidence. *Journal of Memory and Language, 27,* 107–123.

Meltzer, H. Y., & Stahl, S. M. (1976). The dopamine hypothesis of schizophrenia: A review. *Schizophrenia Bulletin, 2,* 19–76.

Nuechterlein, K. H. (1984). Information processing and attentional functioning in the developmental course of schizophrenic disorders. *Schizophrenia Bulletin, 10,* 160–203.

Servan-Schreiber, D., Cohen, J. D., & Steingard, S. (1996). Schizophrenic deficits in the processing of context: A test of neural network simulations of cognitive functioning in schizophrenia. *Archives of General Psychiatry, 53,* 1105–1112.

Servan-Schreiber, D., Printz, H., & Cohen, J. D. (1990). A network model of catecholamine effects: Gain, signal-to-noise ratio and behavior. *Science, 249,* 892–895.

Wapner, S., & Krus, D. M. (1960). Effects of lysergic acid diethylamide, and differences between normals and schizophrenics on the Stroop color-word test. *Journal of Neuropsychiatry, 2,* 76–81.

Weinberger, D. R., & Berman, K. F. (1988). Speculation on the meaning of metabolic hypofrontality in schizophrenia. *Schizophrenia Bulletin, 14,* 157–168.

Weinberger, D. R., Berman, K. F., & Zec, R. F. (1986). Physiological dysfunction of dorsolateral prefrontal cortex in schizophrenia: I. Regional cerebral blood flow evidence. *Archives of General Psychiatry, 43,* 114–125.

Wysocki, J. J., & Sweet, J. J. (1985). Identification of brain-damaged, schizophrenic, and normal medical patients using a brief neuropsychological screening battery. *International Journal of Clinical Neuropsychology, 7(1),* 40–49.

9 Neural Network Modeling of Executive Functioning with the Tower of Hanoi Test in Frontal Lobe–Lesioned Patients

John Cardoso and Randolph W. Parks

Some of the common elements of executive functioning in humans include abstract reasoning, problem solving, mental flexibility, response inhibition, self-monitoring, and maintenance of mental sets (Fletcher, 1996; Walsh, 1978). Lezak (1995) suggested that a key element in executive functioning is planning: "The identification and organization of the steps and elements needed to carry out an intention or achieve a goal constitute planning ..." (pp. 653–654). These definitions, while not exhaustive, constitute the critical elements in successful completion of the Tower of Hanoi (TOH) neuropsychological test. In contrast, brain-damaged persons with anterior brain lesions often perseverate responses and exhibit failure to maintain set on tests such as verbal fluency and the Stroop (Benton, 1968; Crockett, Bilsker, Hurwitz, et al., 1986; Holst & Vilkki, 1988; Perret, 1974), and Wisconsin Card Sorting tests (Arnett, Rao, Bernardin, et al., 1994; Robinson, Heaton, Lehman, et al., 1980). Other research has not supported the emphasis of these tests to anterior brain regions, noting that size, shape, depth, and critical impact of damaged neural circuitry are also very important (S. W. Anderson, Damasio, Jones, et al., 1991; Dodrill, 1997; Newcombe, 1969).

Since its introduction, apparently by de Parville in *La Nature* (Paris, 1883), the TOH puzzle has challenged the problem-solving and planning abilities of many researchers. Mathematicians, computer scientists, and artificial intelligence researchers view the TOH test as an important example of recursion, one of the fundamental techniques used in the design of computer algorithms. Many computer science textbooks use the TOH to teach recursion. While the TOH can easily be solved by a computer, using either recursive or iterative algorithms and traditional procedural programming methods, we utilized artificial neural networks to solve the task.

CLINICAL NEUROPSYCHOLOGICAL DATA

For many years the TOH and related versions have been used in clinical assessment of various frontal populations (Owen, Downes, Sahakian, et al., 1990). Shallice (1982), for example, conducted a study of brain-lesioned groups (left frontal, left anterior, and homologous right-lesioned patients) to control subjects on a related test (Tower of London). He found the left anterior group was most impaired in a timed version of the test compared with the other groups. Glosser and Goodglass (1990), in a similar experiment with the TOH (using moves and violations as variables), found only the left frontal group was impaired compared with the other lesion groups and controls. In our study, we focused on those neural network attributes concerned primarily with the left frontal lobe. This was done because of frontal lobe heterogeneity and because most of the above-named studies that supported a frontal hypothesis emphasized a left frontal primacy. To a lesser extent, we added neural network parameters concerned with attentional factors and visuospatial components, since a brain imaging study had also implicated these latter regions (Andreasen, Rezai, Alliget, et al., 1992). In this chapter, using backpropagation networks, we shall demonstrate how the computer learned to solve the TOH test. In addition, we examined the effects of deliberately "harming" (computer programmers use the terms "mutilation" or "degraded" to refer to these large changes in synaptic connections) the neural network by massively altering the values of large sections of the net's weights with data reflecting left frontal lobe lesions.

The neuropsychological data were acquired from Glosser and Goodglass (1990). Briefly, those authors used several test measures of frontal executive functioning in various left hemisphere aphasic and right hemisphere non-aphasic damaged patients and compared them with normal controls. The part of the experiment relevant to ours was the finding that the left frontal group's performance was significantly impaired compared (MANOVA [multiple variate analysis of variance] calculations: combined moves and violations) with normal controls on the TOH. The mean number of TOH moves (total number of moves) was $M = 14.00$, SD $= 4.44$ in the left frontal group and $M = 10.13$, SD $= 3.62$ in the normal control group.

STRATEGIES TO SOLVE THE TOWER OF HANOI PUZZLE

Solving the TOH (see figure 1.2 in chapter 1) consists in moving the rings from their original peg (the source peg) to one of the other pegs (the target peg), and stacking them in the same initial order by using two simple rules: (1) move only one ring at a time and (2) never stack a ring on top of a smaller one. For n number of rings, the minimum number of moves capable of solving the puzzle is $2^n - 1$. For instance, for a three-ring tower it will take at least seven moves to solve the puzzle. The apparent simplicity of the TOH puzzle can be misleading. Although a three-ring puzzle is relatively easy to solve in the least number of steps, once the number of rings is increased, the optimal solution to the puzzle becomes harder to find. Careful testing and observation of people engaged in solving the TOH show that there are different strategies that can be used.

In his paper "The Functional Equivalence of Problem Solving Skills," H. A. Simon (1975) examined four of those types of strategies, respectively: (1)

rote, (2) goal-recursion, (3) perceptual, and (4) move-pattern strategies. Each of these was considered to have its psychological consequences; for instance, different strategies place different loads on short-term memory.

Simon attempted to address what was involved in learning to solve the TOH puzzle. A computer program was created with the purpose of clearly identifying the steps and strategies that must be learned to solve the TOH problem. The General Problem Solver (GPS), a program that uses means-ends analysis as its primary method, and which appeared, in the opinion of the authors (Newell & Simon, 1972), to describe well the organization of human problem-solving processes, was also used. The GPS program has been successfully used to solve problems in which each situation, or step, can be compared with a goal situation, to discover one or more differences between them. The program uses a set of operators that can be used to eliminate the differences between the current and goal situations. If an operator cannot be applied, the current situation is compared with the conditions for applying the operator, and if some difference is discovered between them, the GPS is then applied recursively to eliminate this difference. Simon's conclusion was that, except for the rote programs, the programs used to solve the puzzle all used the same type of means-ends analysis used by the GPS program.

How would one solve the TOH puzzle in the early 1970s? Starting with the simplest possible case, a tower of one ring ($n = 1$), we simply transfer the ring from the source peg to the target peg and complete the puzzle in the minimum possible number of moves, that is, $2^n - 1$ or one single move. The degree of difficulty increases with a two-ring tower ($n = 2$). To solve a two-ring tower we move the small ring to the spare peg and move the large ring to the target peg. Then we move the small ring from the spare peg to the target peg, and stack it on the top of the large ring, thus completing the puzzle in the minimum possible number of moves, that is, $2^n - 1$, or three moves. What we need to do is to store the small ring momentarily on the spare peg to allow for the move of the larger ring from the source peg to the target peg.

Finally, for a three-ring tower ($n = 3$): according to our formula ($2^n - 1$), we should be able to solve the puzzle in seven moves. The following lists the moves:

1. Move the small ring to the empty target peg.
2. Move the middle ring to the empty spare peg.
3. Move the small ring to the spare peg.
4. Move the large ring to the empty target peg.
5. Move the small ring to the empty source peg.
6. Move the middle ring to the target peg.
7. Move the small ring to the target peg.

Note that we had to make room to move the large ring to the target peg. Once the large ring was moved from the source peg to the target peg, the problem became simpler, and one that we have already solved, the problem of moving a two-ring tower. In summary, moving a tower of n rings from the source peg to the target peg is equivalent to moving a tower of $n-1$ rings to the spare peg, the largest ring from the source to the target, and the $n-1$ ring tower from the spare to the target. We can use a recursive procedure to solve the puzzle, because the problem is recurrent in character. A Tower recursive procedure to solve the TOH puzzle can be expressed in pseudocode as follows:

```
Tower (n, source, target):
  IF n=1
THEN
  Move (n, source, target);
ELSE
  Tower (n-1, source, spare),
  Move (n, source, target),
  Tower (n-1, spare, source).
```

This recursive procedure will succeed in solving the TOH puzzle for three pegs and for n rings. Although recursive procedures are very powerful mechanisms that provide simple and elegant ways of thinking about these types of problems, they do not always use computer resources, such as time and working memory, in the most efficient manner. Problems of a recurrent nature can also be solved using iterative procedures. Iterative procedures use very little memory in comparison with their recursive counterparts. There is, however, a price to be paid: the program has to keep track of the position of the rings at all times.

Whether a computer program uses recursion or iteration to solve the TOH puzzle, the programmer will have to provide the computer with a set of commands that must be followed in a predetermined sequence to reach the correct solution. Computer programs are usually rigid and inflexible. Since it is doubtful that the human brain uses these types of operations to solve everyday problems, researchers have looked into other problem-solving techniques, such as artificial neural networks, that could be potentially closer to the brain's methods and help to understand how neurons may learn and operate.

ENCODING THE MOVES

The TOH, like its counterparts Tower of London (hierarchically arranged training sets) and Tower of Toronto (adding a fourth ring), requires the ability to anticipate subroutine steps to achieve the desired final position of the rings. To construct our current network we had to conduct some theoretical mathematical tests to assist with the development of the details of the computer architecture, such as learning rule, placement of rings, and efficient sequencing parameters (Cardoso, 1991). There are many different types of neural nets and different types of training algorithms to choose from (Lippmann, 1987). The choice of a feedforward, multilayer architecture using the backpropagation training algorithm to solve the TOH was made because of versatility, learning capabilities, and reliability (Chauvin & Rumelhart, 1995). The results are described below, after considering some general information about the computational ability and the functionality of neural nets.

How can we represent, or encode, the TOH puzzle so that the net learns and later remembers how to solve the puzzle? The graphical display of figure 9.1 helps in understanding the encoding method that was selected. The "Initial Position" diagram depicts the three disks, stacked on the leftmost peg by order of size with the largest disk on the bottom of the pile (denoted by the three horizontally adjacent black squares) and the smallest

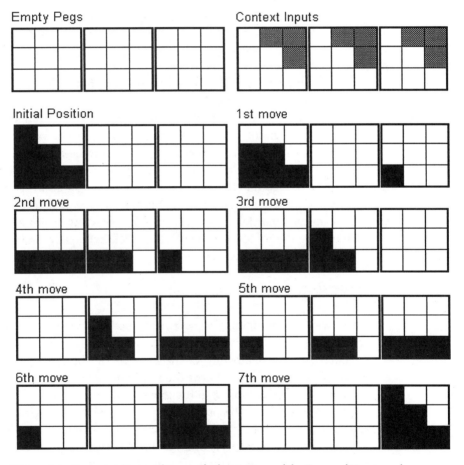

Figure 9.1 Representation used to encode the positions of the Tower of Hanoi puzzle.

disk on top (denoted by the single black square on the topmost row). The following sections of the picture (1st to 7th moves) show the shortest sequence of moves necessary to solve the three-disk TOH puzzle. Note that we need nine small squares to represent the condition of each peg at any given time. We need twenty-seven small squares to represent the state of the puzzle. Each one of the small squares will be encoded as a separate input to the net. We proceed from this intermediate graphical representation to the final mathematical vector representation by encoding a vacant (white) square as a 0 (zero) and an occupied (black) square as a 1 (one), while moving from left to right on each row, and from the top to the bottom row. With this method, the initial position of the puzzle is represented by the vector (1 0 0 0 0 0 0 1 1 0 0 0 0 0 0 1 1 1 0 0 0 0 0 0 0), and the final position by the vector (0 0 0 0 0 1 0 0 0 0 0 0 0 1 1 0 0 0 0 0 0 0 1 1 1). Both vectors have a length of twenty-seven.

In addition, the network will need some sort of "context inputs." Three of every nine squares of each peg, depicted in figure 9.1 as shaded squares, are reserved to be used as context inputs. These context inputs are necessary because, in most cases, for every position in the puzzle there are usually three legal moves. During the training phase, we have to provide a mechanism to help the neural net to differentiate these moves. For this reason, associated with each move there is a "move-quality descriptor" (M-Q). There are three types of M-Q descriptors, one for each move type, respectively: "best," "regressive," and "long."

The number of M-Q descriptors is unrelated to the number of context squares per peg; the number of context squares per peg was arbitrarily chosen. Best moves (moves that lead to the shortest route) are indicated by the presence of one or more (one, two, or three) context squares in the *left* peg. Long moves (moves that lead to a longer route) are encoded by the presence of one or more context squares in the *middle* peg. Regressive moves (moves that take you back to some previously visited position) are indicated by the presence of one or more context squares in the *right* peg. In this experiment, the M-Q descriptors use all three context inputs.

SELECTING THE TRAINING SET

There were thirty-nine input patterns in the training set, each pattern representing a given position in the progression to solve the tower puzzle. The selection and the numbering of the patterns can be described as a directed graph (figure 9.2). The patterns used are only a small subset of all possible patterns. The nodes (boxes) in the graph of figure 9.2 stand for a given state (or position) of the TOH puzzle. The number(s) inside each box serve only to identify a particular state. The directed arrows leaving a node (marked "l" for long, "r" for regressive, and "b" for best) represent moves, and clearly show what states are possible to reach from that node. The node numbers are only an identification (ID) tag; they do not have any other special mean-

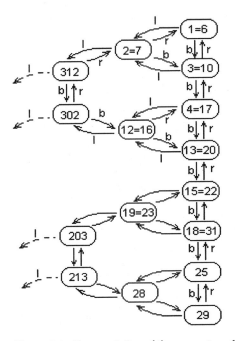

Figure 9.2 Representation of the succession of moves selected to train the neural net to solve the Tower of Hanoi puzzle.

ing nor are they used by the net at any time. They are used only to facilitate our identification of the states or positions of the puzzle. The large ID numbers that appear in the leftmost column of nodes (312, 302, 203, and 213), unlike the others, are not a result of any numerical sequence; they were arbitrarily chosen to represent the position and size of the rings that sit at the bottom of each peg. See figure 9.3 to understand how these numbers were chosen.

Figure 9.3 is another way of representing what positions can be reached during the first two moves of a three-ring puzzle. Each large square has three columns and represents the state of the puzzle at any given time. Each column, of three small squares, represents a different peg. The digits within the squares represent the rings, with the largest digit representing the largest ring. A zero stands for "empty." The digits preceded by "#," and located outside the large squares, are the ID tags of the states, or positions, of the puzzle.

The first move from a three-ring puzzle can take us to two different states or positions, respectively: states #2 and #3. In this example we will not consider the sequence of moves derived from state #2; we will use only the sequence of moves originated from state #3. From state #3 there are a total of four possible reachable states, respectively: #4, #5, #6, and #7. We will discard state #5 because it is an illegal state (no ring can be placed on top of a smaller one). The second move can thus take us to one of three valid positions: #4 (the best move), #6 (a regressive move), and #7 (a long move).

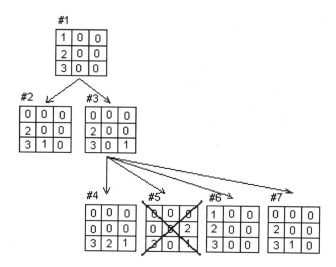

Figure 9.3 Representation of various Tower of Hanoi moves and illegal state (crossed out).

This brief explanation should elucidate how the positions were identified and the moves. Some of the boxes in figure 9.2 do contain more than one number because some states appear to repeat. For instance, in figure 9.3 we can see that state #2 is identical to state #7, and state #1 is identical to state #6. The shortest sequence of moves to solve the three-ring TOH puzzle is shown, in figure 9.2, in the rightmost column of nodes. As we move to the columns on the left we find ourselves taking longer routes to the solution.

One can think of each line of the training set as representing the arrows between nodes of the graph in figure 9.3. There are thirty-nine lines in the training-set table. The reader is cautioned that while each of the thirty-nine lines might be interpreted as "moving a ring in the TOH," this is not necessarily the case. One of the functions of the thirty-nine lines of input/output vectors is their use as placeholders in a computer matrix. In their function as placeholders, the network is allowed to choose from a range of responses during training. The more a neural network is degraded, or, to use a human metaphor, lesioned, the number of input/output vectors being utilized is likely to increase. Each line has two vectors: the first vector (on the left) is the *input* pattern, the second vector is the *target* pattern (the expected output from the net for its corresponding input pattern). In supervised learning during each training step we need to provide the net with both vectors simultaneously. Here the network must learn to associate the input vector with the target vector. There are thirty-nine input-target vector pairs (see figure 9.4). As mentioned before, the move from state #1 to state #2 was arbitrarily disregarded because it leads to a different sequence of moves (one that ends with the rings stacked on a different peg, i.e., the center peg).

The net was trained to generate the target patterns when it was presented with the input patterns. For example, in the first sample of the training, the

Input vector	Target vector
1 1 1 0 0 0 0 0 0 1 1 1 0 0 0 0 0 0 1 1 1 0 0 0 0 0 0	0 0 0 0 0 0 0 0 1 1 0 0 0 0 0 0 0 1 1 1 0 0 0 1 0 0
0 1 1 0 0 0 0 0 0 1 1 1 0 0 0 0 0 0 1 1 1 0 0 0 1 0 0	0 0 0 0 0 0 0 0 0 0 0 0 0 0 0 0 0 1 1 1 1 1 0 1 0 0
0 0 0 0 0 0 0 1 1 1 1 0 0 0 0 0 0 1 1 1 1 0 0 0 1 0 0	1 0 0 0 0 0 0 0 0 1 1 0 0 0 0 0 0 0 1 1 1 0 0 0 0 0 0
0 0 0 0 1 1 0 0 0 1 1 0 0 0 1 0 0 0 1 1 1 0 0 0 1 0 0	0 0 0 0 0 0 0 0 1 1 0 0 0 0 0 0 0 1 1 1 1 0 0 0 0 0
0 0 0 0 0 0 0 1 1 0 0 0 0 0 0 0 0 1 1 1 1 1 1 0 1 0 0	0 0 0 0 0 0 0 0 1 1 0 0 0 0 0 0 0 1 1 1 0 0 0 1 0 0
0 0 0 0 1 1 0 0 0 0 0 0 0 0 1 0 0 0 1 1 1 1 1 0 1 0 0	0 0 0 0 0 0 0 0 1 0 0 0 0 0 1 0 0 0 0 0 1 1 1 1 1 0 0 0 0
0 1 1 0 0 0 0 0 0 0 0 1 0 0 0 0 0 0 1 1 1 1 1 0 1 0 0	0 0 0 0 0 0 0 0 0 0 0 1 0 0 0 0 0 1 1 1 1 0 0 0 0
0 0 0 0 0 0 0 1 1 1 1 0 0 0 0 0 0 1 1 1 1 1 0 0 0 0 0	1 0 0 0 0 0 0 0 0 1 1 0 0 0 0 0 0 0 1 1 1 0 0 0 0 0 0
0 1 1 0 0 0 0 0 0 1 1 1 0 0 0 0 0 0 1 1 1 1 0 0 0 0 0	0 0 0 0 0 0 0 0 1 1 0 0 0 0 0 0 0 1 1 1 0 0 0 1 0 0
0 0 0 0 1 1 0 0 0 1 1 0 0 0 1 0 0 0 1 1 1 1 0 0 0 0 0	0 0 0 0 0 0 0 0 0 0 0 0 0 0 0 0 0 1 1 1 1 0 0 1 1 0
0 0 0 0 0 0 0 1 1 0 0 0 0 0 0 0 0 1 1 1 1 1 0 0 1 1 0	0 0 0 0 0 0 0 0 1 1 0 0 0 0 0 0 0 1 1 1 1 0 0 0 0 0
0 1 1 0 0 0 0 0 0 0 1 0 0 0 0 0 0 1 1 1 1 0 0 1 1 0	0 0 0 0 0 0 0 0 1 0 0 0 0 0 0 0 0 1 1 1 0 0 0 1 1 0
0 1 1 0 0 0 0 0 1 0 1 0 0 0 0 0 0 1 1 1 0 0 0 1 1 0	0 0 0 0 0 0 0 0 1 0 0 0 0 0 0 0 0 1 1 1 1 1 0 0 0 0
0 0 0 0 0 0 0 1 1 0 0 0 0 0 0 0 0 1 1 1 1 0 0 0 1 1 0	0 0 0 0 0 0 0 0 0 0 0 0 0 0 0 0 0 1 1 1 1 0 0 1 1 0
0 1 1 0 0 0 0 0 1 0 1 0 0 0 0 0 0 1 1 1 1 1 0 0 0 0	0 0 0 0 0 0 0 0 0 0 0 1 0 0 0 0 0 1 1 1 1 0 0 0 0
0 0 0 0 0 0 0 1 1 0 0 0 0 0 0 0 0 1 1 1 1 1 0 0 0 0	0 0 0 0 0 0 0 0 0 0 0 0 0 0 0 0 0 1 1 1 1 1 0 1 0 0
0 0 0 0 1 1 0 0 0 1 0 0 0 0 1 0 0 0 1 1 1 1 1 0 0 0 0	0 0 0 0 0 0 0 0 1 0 0 0 0 0 0 0 0 1 1 1 0 0 0 1 1 0
0 1 1 0 0 0 0 0 0 0 1 1 0 0 0 0 0 1 1 1 1 0 0 0 0	0 0 0 0 0 0 0 0 0 0 0 1 0 0 0 0 0 0 1 1 0 1 1 1
0 0 0 0 1 1 0 0 0 0 0 0 1 0 1 0 0 0 1 1 1 1 0 0 0 0	0 0 0 0 0 0 0 0 1 0 0 0 0 0 0 0 0 1 1 1 1 1 0 0 0 0
0 0 0 0 0 0 0 1 1 0 0 0 1 0 0 0 0 1 1 1 1 1 0 0 0 0	0 0 0 0 0 0 0 0 0 0 0 0 0 0 0 0 0 1 1 1 1 1 0 1 0 0
0 1 1 0 0 0 0 0 0 0 1 1 0 0 0 0 0 0 0 1 1 0 1 1 1	0 0 0 0 0 0 0 0 0 0 0 0 0 0 0 0 0 1 0 0 1 1 0 1 1 1
0 0 0 0 1 1 0 0 0 0 0 1 0 1 0 0 0 0 0 1 1 0 1 1 1	0 0 0 0 0 0 0 0 0 0 0 0 0 0 0 1 0 0 0 0 0 1 1 0 1 1 1
0 0 0 0 0 0 0 1 1 0 0 0 1 0 0 0 0 1 0 0 0 1 1 0 1 1 1	0 0 0 0 0 0 0 0 0 0 0 1 0 0 0 0 0 1 1 1 1 1 0 0 0 0
0 0 0 0 0 0 0 1 1 0 0 0 0 0 0 0 0 1 1 0 0 1 1 0 1 1 1	0 0 0 0 0 0 0 0 0 0 0 1 0 0 0 0 0 0 0 1 1 0 1 1 1
0 0 0 0 1 1 0 0 0 0 0 0 0 1 0 0 0 1 0 0 1 1 0 1 1 1	0 0 0 0 0 0 0 0 0 0 0 0 0 0 0 0 1 0 0 0 0 1 1 0 1 1 1
0 1 1 0 0 0 0 0 0 0 1 0 0 0 0 0 0 1 0 0 1 1 0 1 1 1	0 0 0 0 0 0 0 0 0 0 0 0 0 0 1 1 0 1 0 0 0 0 0 1 1 1
0 1 1 0 0 0 0 0 0 0 1 0 0 0 1 0 0 0 0 0 1 1 0 1 1 1	0 0 0 0 0 0 0 0 0 0 0 0 0 0 0 0 0 1 0 0 1 1 0 1 1 1
0 0 0 0 0 0 0 1 1 0 0 0 0 0 1 0 1 0 0 0 1 1 0 1 1 1	0 0 0 0 0 0 0 0 0 0 0 1 0 0 0 0 0 0 0 1 1 0 1 1 1
0 0 0 0 1 1 0 0 0 0 0 0 0 0 1 1 0 0 0 0 1 1 0 1 1 1	0 0 0 0 0 0 0 0 0 0 0 0 0 0 0 0 1 0 0 0 0 1 1 0 1 1 1
0 0 0 0 0 0 0 1 1 0 0 0 0 0 1 0 1 1 0 0 0 0 1 1 1	0 0 0 0 0 0 0 0 0 0 0 0 0 0 0 0 1 1 0 1 0 0 0 0 0 1 1 1
0 1 1 0 0 0 0 0 0 0 1 0 0 0 1 0 0 1 1 0 0 0 0 1 1 1	0 0 0 0 0 0 0 0 0 0 0 0 0 0 0 0 0 1 0 0 1 1 0 0 0 0 1 1 1
0 0 0 0 0 0 0 1 1 0 0 0 0 0 0 0 1 1 1 0 1 0 0 1 1 1	0 0 0 0 0 0 0 0 0 0 0 1 0 0 0 0 0 0 0 1 1 0 1 1 1
0 1 1 0 0 0 0 0 0 0 1 0 0 0 0 0 0 1 1 0 1 0 0 1 1 1	0 0 0 0 0 0 0 0 0 0 0 0 0 0 0 0 1 1 0 0 0 0 1 0 0 1 1 1
0 0 0 0 1 1 0 0 0 0 0 0 0 0 1 1 1 0 1 0 0 0 0 1 1 1	0 0 0 0 0 0 0 0 0 0 0 0 0 0 0 0 1 1 0 0 0 0 1 0 0 1 1 1
0 1 1 0 0 0 0 0 0 0 1 0 0 0 1 1 0 1 0 0 0 0 0 1 1 1	0 0 0 0 0 1 0 0 0 0 0 0 0 0 1 1 0 0 0 0 0 0 0 1 1 1
0 0 0 0 0 0 0 1 1 0 0 0 0 0 0 1 1 1 1 0 0 0 0 0 1 1 1	0 0 0 0 0 0 0 0 0 0 0 0 0 0 0 0 0 1 0 0 1 1 0 1 1 1
0 1 1 0 0 0 0 0 0 0 1 0 0 0 1 1 0 0 0 0 1 0 0 1 1 1	0 0 0 0 0 1 0 0 0 0 0 0 0 0 1 1 0 0 0 0 0 0 0 1 1 1
0 0 0 0 0 0 0 1 1 0 0 0 0 0 0 1 1 1 0 0 0 1 0 0 1 1 1	0 0 0 0 0 0 0 0 0 0 0 0 0 0 0 0 1 1 0 1 0 0 0 0 0 1 1 1
0 0 0 0 1 1 0 0 0 0 0 0 0 1 1 1 0 0 0 0 1 0 0 1 1 1	0 0 0 0 0 0 0 0 0 0 0 0 0 0 0 0 0 1 1 0 1 0 0 0 0 0 1 1 1

Figure 9.4 Representations of input and target pairs.

input-pattern vector is: (1 **1 1** 0 0 0 0 0 0 1 1 **1** 0 0 0 0 0 0 1 1 1 0 0 0 0 0 0 0). When presented with this pattern, the net was trained to generate the target-pattern vector: (0 0 0 0 0 0 0 0 1 1 0 0 0 0 0 0 0 1 1 1 0 0 0 1 0 0). Note that included in each *input-pattern* there are also the bits that encode the M-Q descriptor for that move. In the example above, for easy identification, these are indicated in bold type. In this case, moving from position #1 to position #3 is encoded as the "best" move.

TRAINING THE NEURAL NETWORK

The backpropagation algorithm, based upon the generalized delta rule, was selected to train the feedforward multilayer network. This learning algorithm has been discussed by other authors (Chauvin & Rumelhart, 1995; Pao, 1989) and the mathematics of the process will not be reviewed here. As mentioned in chapter 1, the input is propagated forward, from the input layer through the middle layer to the output layer, and then the resulting output is propagated backward, from the output layer through the middle to the input layer, to compute the error δ. Subsequently, the weight error derivatives and the weight changes are computed. The network was trained using the parameters shown in table 9.1. Training the network consisted of repeatedly presenting the patterns in the training set to the net until the generated error was acceptable. The patterns were randomly selected for presentation, and a random value between ± 9.9 percent of noise was added to each input. The graph of figure 9.5 shows the learning curve of the network. The sharp initial slope of the curve and its slow settling indicates that the net had no difficulty in learning the thirty-nine input patterns in the training. Learning was completed in 431 iterations. That is, the patterns in the training set were pre-

Table 9.1 Parameters used during Tower of Hanoi learning

Parameter Type	Value
Momentum	0.9
Learning rate	0.7
Maximum total error	0.01
Maximum individual-unit error	0.001

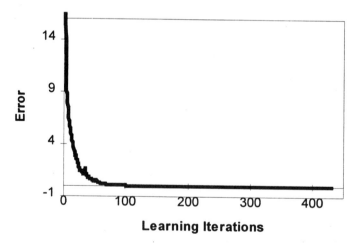

Figure 9.5 Learning curve for the 27-15-25 neural network during the Tower of Hanoi training session.

sented to the net 431 times before the net could learn to associate each input pattern with its corresponding output pattern. Clearly this number could have been reduced if larger error values had been selected; in our case, this was not a concern.

THE EFFECTS OF LEARNING

The purpose of the learning phase is to compute a set of weights that will allow the network to execute its job adequately. In our experiment, this refers to one of the TOH's positions and the ability of the network to produce one of the next allowable positions. In a three-layer network there are two distinct weight sets, respectively: the *hidden-layer weights* (the weights of the connections between the input and the hidden layers) and the *output-layer weights* (the weights of the connections between the hidden and output layers). The hidden-layer weights are understood to be responsible for allowing the hidden-layer neurons to extract relevant features from the input patterns. These features are then passed to the output neurons, through the output-layer connections, and the net will then generate its final output. It is generally understood that for a successful knowledge distribution over all weights, most weights will have near-zero values. These weights will have a near-normal distribution around zero. Other weight distributions are generally a sign of local representation, rather than distributed. A distributed representation is generally the most desirable. As in the brain, a distributed representation will protect the system from forgetting all it has learned in case of injury or malfunctioning. In such cases, whether by accidental or deliberate damage, the system's performance will suffer little or no degradation, and the system will not be rendered totally useless.

Figure 9.6 shows the histogram of the frequency distribution of the hidden-layer weights; most of these weights have near-zero values. The kurtosis (curvedness) of the distribution is 3.638, indicating that the distribution is fairly sharp. The skewness (symmetry measure) of the distribution is

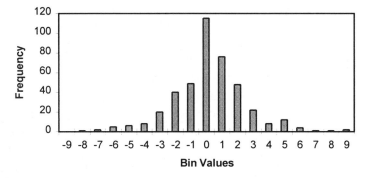

Figure 9.6 Frequency distribution of hidden-layer weights.

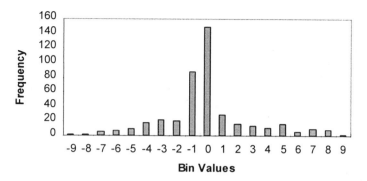

Figure 9.7 Frequency distribution of output-layer weights.

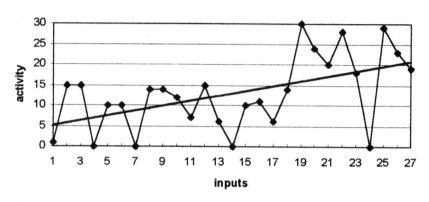

Figure 9.8 Activity generated in the input layer by the patterns in the training set and its linear trend line.

1.930, indicating that the scores trail off to the right (positively skewed). The histogram in figure 9.7 shows the frequency distribution of the output-layer weights. The curve is much sharper, with a kurtosis value of 9.139, and the skewness, 2.985, is still positive (trailing to the right) but larger.

Let us look now at the distribution of the input activity during training. "Activity," in our case, is the total number of active signals that reach a given input. An input is said to be active when the incoming signal is a 1 (one). Figure 9.8 graphs the activity distribution over the input lines. Over the thirty-nine input patterns in the training set there is a total of 1053 (27 × 39) input signals, that is, 351 ones and 702 zeros. This disparity may explain the inhibitory trend of the network weights. The graph of figure 9.8 shows most of the activity located over the last third of the inputs (between 19 and 27). This is a direct consequence of the type of encoding that was chosen (see figure 9.1). This active area corresponds to the inputs that "see" the bottom layer of the pegs, which is always the busiest of the three layers. The line across the graph plots the linear trend of the data.

Table 9.2 Results of testing the unmutilated network with the set of 3584 patterns

Best Moves	Long Moves	Regressive Moves	Other Moves
931 (0.26)	666 (0.19)	292 (0.08)	1695 (0.47)

Note: Numbers in parentheses represent percentage ratios.

TESTING THE NEURAL NETWORK

After learning, the neural net was tested with a set of all 3584 (512×7) possible pattern variations derived from positions 1, 3, 4, 13, 15, 18, and 25. These positions are those that solve the puzzle in the minimum number of moves (see rightmost column of figure 9.2). Pattern variations, for a given position, are obtained by OR-ing the position's true pattern (the bits that represent possible ring positions) with all possible binary combinations of the nine M-Q descriptor bits. For instance, the true pattern for position 1 is (1x0x0x11x00x00x111000000), where the symbols "x" are placeholders for the M-Q descriptors. There are nine M-Q descriptor bits in each pattern. Since each of these bits can have one of two values (0 or 1), we can create 2^9 (512) variations of a given pattern for a total of 3584 for all seven chosen patterns. These 3584 patterns constituted the testing set that was used in our tests. The first tests that modeled the normal controls used the network with all its connections intact (nondegraded). The results are summarized in table 9.2. Correct responses include "best," "long," and "regressive" moves. Incorrect responses, the figure in the "Other Moves" column, include all other network responses ($1695 = 3584 - 931 - 666 - 292$); these responses may include false moves, nonexistent pattern codes, or existent but unreachable or invalid moves. In this test, the *best*/(*best* + *long* + *regressive*) move ratio is approximately 0.5 ($931/(931 + 666 + 292)$). Let us call this ratio the performance index value (PIV) of the net. Assuming that we take the PIV of 0.5 as the measure of the performance of our "normal" (unmutilated) net in solving the puzzle, we can then contrast this value with a "normal" person's PIV.

An experimental study (Glosser & Goodglass, 1990) has shown that a "normal" person takes, on average, ten moves to solve the TOH puzzle, while a left frontal lobe–damaged person takes fourteen moves. Since the minimum possible number of moves is seven, we can assume that a normal person's PIV is approximately 0.7. Although, by simply looking at those figures, we do not know the types of the moves each person makes, this value arises from the fact that if one takes more than seven moves to solve the puzzle, then some of these moves must be from the "long" and/or "regressive" type.

DEGRADATION OF THE NEURAL NETWORK

Recall that there are twenty-seven output neurons. Each output neuron has sixteen input connections, each one of these connections linking the neuron

Table 9.3 Results of weight-degradation tests for Tower of Hanoi position 1, 3, 4, 13, 15, 18, and 25 patterns

Degradation to Weight matrix's	Best Moves	Long Moves	Regressive Moves	Other Moves
Top half	931 (0.26)	664 (0.18)	292 (0.08)	1697 (0.47)
Bottom half	931 (0.26)	666 (0.18)	292 (0.08)	1695 (0.47)
Left half	852 (0.24)	251 (0.07)	0 (0.0)	2481 (0.69)
Right half	0 (0.0)	116 (0.03)	223 (0.06)	3245 (0.91)
Top-left quarter	963 (0.27)	84 (0.02)	594 (0.17)	1943 (0.54)
Top-right quarter	10 (0.003)	425 (0.12)	80 (0.02)	3069 (0.86)
Bottom-left quarter	576 (0.16)	293 (0.08)	0 (0.0)	2715 (0.76)
Bottom-right quarter	237 (0.06)	158 (0.04)	318 (0.09)	2871 (0.80)

Note: The figures in parentheses represent the corresponding percentage ratio to the total number of patterns (3584).

to each neuron in the hidden layer; there is one additional connection from a bias neuron. We can store the weights of these connections in a 27 row × 16 column weight matrix (W). The rows correspond to the output neurons and the columns correspond to the hidden neurons (i.e., the value in W[23,10] stands for the weight of the connection between hidden neuron 10 and output neuron 23). To investigate the results of degradation of different sectors of the output-layer connections on the performance of the network, this weight matrix was subdivided into eight submatrices, corresponding to the top (W[1–13,1–16]), bottom (W[14–27, 1–16], left ([W1–27, 1–8]), and right (W[1–27, 9–16]) halves and to the top-left (W[1–13, 1–8]), top-right (W[1–13, 9–16]), bottom-left (W[13–27, 1–8]), and bottom-right (W[13–27, 9–16]) quarters of the output-layer connections. Degradation of a weight submatrix consisted in reducing its values to 1 percent of its initial value. This drastic change forced the values of these weights to near zero, practically turning these connections off. The network, with its degraded connections, was then tested using the same 3584 patterns previously used. Eight separate tests were performed, one for each degraded submatrix. The results of these tests are displayed in table 9.3.

A left frontal lobe–damaged patient takes, on average, fourteen moves to solve the puzzle. Using the same criteria that we used before, we can also compute the PIV for the average frontal lobe–damaged person as the ratio *best/(best + long + regressive)* moves, which would be approximately 0.5 (7/14). Assuming a linear relationship, if a nongraded network, with a PIV of approximately 0.5, corresponds to a normal person, with a PIV of 0.7, then a degraded net, with a PIV around 0.35, would correspond to a left frontal lobe–damaged patient with a PIV of 0.5. The network with a degraded bottom-right quarter, similarly to a frontal lobe–damaged patient, has a PIV of approximately 0.35 (table 9.4).

To investigate the mutilation effects on the responses to a single move, one pattern (pattern for position #3) was randomly chosen and tested first

Table 9.4 Performance index values (PIVs) for the various degraded networks

Degraded	PIV (approx.)
Top half	0.50
Bottom half	0.50
Left half	0.70
Right half	0.00
Top-left quarter	0.58
Top-right quarter	0.02
Bottom-left quarter	0.66
Bottom-right quarter	0.36

Table 9.5 Results of testing an nondegraded network using position #3 patterns

Best Moves	Long Moves	Regressive Moves	Other Moves
35 (0.07)	273 (0.53)	44 (0.09)	160 (0.31)

Note: The figures in parentheses represent the corresponding percentage ratio to the total number of patterns (512).

Table 9.6 Results of weight-degradation tests using Tower of Hanoi position #3 patterns

Degradation to Weight-Matrix's	Best Moves	Long Moves	Regressive Moves	Other Moves
Top half	35 (0.07)	270 (0.53)	44 (0.09)	163 (0.31)
Bottom half	35 (0.07)	272 (0.53)	44 (0.09)	161 (0.31)
Left half	0 (0.0)	0 (0.0)	0 (0.0)	512 (1.0)
Right half	0 (0.0)	116 (0.23)	165 (0.32)	231 (0.45)
Top-left quarter	5 (0.01)	0 (0.0)	0 (0.0)	507 (0.99)
Top-right quarter	0 (0.0)	192 (0.38)	56 (0.11)	264 (0.51)
Bottom-left quarter	0 (0.0)	0 (0.0)	0 (0.0)	512 (1.0)
Bottom-right quarter	0 (0.0)	158 (0.30)	52 (0.10)	302 (0.60)

Note: The figures in parentheses represent the corresponding percentage ratio to the total number of patterns (512).

using a nondegraded network, and then with the different degraded networks. Tables 9.5 and 9.6 show the results of these tests using the 512 pattern variations for position #3. The results obtained from the eight degradation tests indicate that degradation to different areas of the output weight matrix affects the network in different degrees. Moreover, the network suffers little or no performance loss when damage is done to the top (W[1–13, 1–16]) or bottom (W[13–27, 1–16]) halves of its weight matrix, but suffers a large performance loss in all other cases. For the tests with pattern #3, the network seems to suffer nearly the same loss in performance whether the damage is done to the left half or to the bottom-left or top-left quarters of the output weight matrix. This seems to indicate that most of the information necessary to do the third move of the TOH resides in the connections between the output neurons and hidden neurons 1 to 8.

SUMMARY

Under ideal learning and testing conditions, the neural network solved the TOH puzzle in seven moves. Our neural network underestimated normal controls' performance by approximately three moves. This was not unexpected, since a neural network can be very efficient in solving tasks when degradation is not present.

Our PIV was used to give us an approximate measure of performance in solving the TOH, both for humans and for the neural net. The total number of errors was inexorably tied to the degradation of the neural network. This was not just a superficial reproduction of the input/output of the data. While it is true that certain aspects of the mathematical algorithms and computer architecture set rigid boundaries of experimentation, there are wide amounts of variability in potential outcomes. The dynamic qualities included varying degrees of flexibility in "solving" the puzzle. This was sometimes represented in the apparent perseveration, as reflected in regressive TOH moves in the neural network. More specifically, the PIV index is a quantitative measure that also indicates that the ratio between the "best moves" and the total number of moves was larger for the normal controls. In addition, we were very surprised that with near-catastrophic degradation of the computer neural network, that is, running the computer program with only a small number of connections intact, the left frontal–damaged group could still solve the TOH in approximately fourteen moves, albeit with more error violations.

These experiments were our first attempts aimed at investigating the effects of degradation (radical changes) of the connections of feedforward multilayer neural nets. In our main test, the modified weights were those of the connections between the output and hidden layers. The simplicity of our statement above—"degradation of different areas of the output weight matrix affects the network in different degrees"—might be interpreted as misleading. What did the network learn? What was it trained to do? A simple backpropagation network, like the one used in this work, can learn how to generate a particular output in response to a given input. Perhaps it might be argued that presenting the network with a pattern representing one of the TOH positions, and training it to produce one of the next possible puzzle positions, is not the same as teaching the net how to solve the TOH puzzle. The "sequence" or succession of moves is introduced in the process when the researcher intentionally takes one output pattern generated by the net and feeds it back to its input to obtain yet another response. Nevertheless, it is reasonable to say that the net has learned to generate correct responses, and may be capable of making some generalizations based on what it has learned.

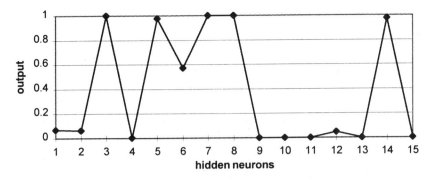

Figure 9.9 Plot of the output activity generated in the hidden-layer neurons by the pattern representative of position 3.

Careful investigation shows why the performance of the network was seriously affected when mutilating the left side of the output weight matrix: it was mostly because the affected connections were coming from the *active neurons* in the hidden layer. Further analysis of the response of the hidden-layer neurons to the pattern of position #3 (pp3) (see figure 9.3), shows that the neurons that become most active are neurons 3, 5, 6, 7, 8, and 14 (figure 9.9). Because the majority of the active neurons (neurons 3,5,6,7,8) are located on the left side of the matrix, changing the weights of these connections would have the largest effect on the performance of the neural network. Therefore, a combination of factors is responsible for the degradation of the network's performance.

These observations seem to support the view that, at least in our case, training a feedforward multilayer neural net will shape a network in which the acquired "knowledge" is stored both locally and in a distributed manner. In the case of pp3, which can also be interpreted as an individual pattern, thing, or event, only six of the fifteen hidden neurons respond to the pattern. This means that the net uses both a local (not every neuron will fire), and a distributed internal (more than one neuron will fire) representation of its "world." Top-down interpretation of the network's learning process will confirm that degradation of connections, by itself, will not necessarily affect the network's performance. Loss of performance for a given task is most noticeable when degradation is done to the "relevant" connections. These connections come from the active areas of the network. Neural networks are capable under most conditions of creating internal representations of their "outside world" that enable them to perform reasonably well in the tasks for which they are trained.

Further evidence of the TOH relationship, using the related Tower of London test, to the left frontal region is found in a brain imaging (single photon emission computed tomography, SPECT) study by Andreasen et al. (1992). It was shown that normal controls activated the left frontal lobe, but two groups of schizophrenic patients (neuroleptic-naive and non-naive

Cardoso & Parks: Executive Functioning

patients with a three-week medication washout) did not activate this area. Andreasen et al. pointed out, "The task involves planning (often considered a dorsolateral frontal function), attention (often considered a mesial frontal and cingulate function), and manipulation of shapes (a right parietal function) ... These results emphasize the importance of conceptualizing cognitive challenges in terms of the multiple circuits that are likely to be activated" (p. 955). Another SPECT study with the Tower of London test found activation primarily in the left frontal lobe (Morris, Ahmed, Syed, et al., 1993). This executive function of the ability to plan or anticipate was modeled well in the components of the neural network architecture and during learning trials. In other words, one could say that the input vector is the "where the TOH ring is" and the target vector is the "where I want to move the ring." The simultaneous integration of the input and target vectors represent a human-type anticipatory or executive function.

Our network also contains attentional elements. In a well-developed neural network model of Stroop test performance, Cohen, Dunbar, and McClelland (1990) viewed attention as a modulation of processing in which additional sources of information provide a sustained context for the processing of signals within a particular pathway. In our present model the attentional parameters are served by modification of the delta rule with a "momentum" factor. The gradient-descent algorithms are subject to incompletion of a task because of lowered inertia as a function of the learning trials. By analogy, Caudill and Butler (1990) have indicated that "a sled can overcome small bumps or even short rises in its path if it has generated enough physical momentum to carry it over such perturbations and to allow it to continue its original direction ..." (p. 190). The modulation ability to sustain the neural network appears more prominent in the early learning trials. With major degradation of our neural network, there was a negligible decrease in the overall ability to keep focused on solving the TOH. With our current limitations it is not easy to separate executive functions from the attentional functions with the backpropagation rule. Indeed, one of the major tasks for neural network modelers will be to work with the limitations of targeted neuropsychological tests, many of which are multifactorial in cognitive processing. These limitations do not negate the utility of the TOH's ability to delineate differences in clinical populations. For example, Butters, Wolfe, Martone, et al. (1985) used TOH procedures as an index of procedural learning and demonstrated that early Huntington's disease patients and controls were able to acquire the solution of the puzzle, but advanced Huntington's disease patients and amnesics showed little improvement after repeated trials. These researchers concluded that the TOH was of limited value for investigation of procedural learning because of dependence on problem-solving abilities.

Shallice (1982) based some of his findings on an earlier computer model of the TOH. That artificial intelligence (AI) model had its origins in a hypothetical serial processing paradigm (Newell & Simon, 1972; Simon, 1975).

This AI computer model, by today's standards, was limited by its slow speed, simple architecture, and small storage capacity. It could not adequately solve multiple tasks simultaneously. The reason for most of these limitations was the program's use of traditional procedural programming languages and methods, where one step follows another in a sequential recipe style. In this type of program a minor perturbation in the hardware, in the program code, or in its data, usually causes the entire program to fail or to stop. In our current model, a connectionist model, the computer processes its tasks in a distributed way. Connectionist architectures can process multiple tasks simultaneously and function reasonably well even after suffering significant damage to the network, or to its data. Nevertheless, Simon made a significant contribution to our understanding of executive functioning. In a rigorous task analysis of how to solve the TOH, Simon suggested four main approaches: (1) rote strategy, (2) perceptual strategies, (3) move-pattern strategies, and (4) goal-recursion strategies. The last, the goal-recursion strategy, was determined to be the most efficient method of solving the puzzle because it used "goal and subgoal structures to determine what to do next" (p. 273). J. R. Anderson (1993) and colleagues (J. R. Anderson, Kushmerick, & Lebiere, 1993) have provided empirical evidence to show that the time to make a move in the TOH is strongly correlated with the number of subgoals that must be set before that move. Maximum subgoaling behavior was a characteristic of our neural network of human TOH behavior, whereas the left brain–damaged computer program group had more difficulty in modifying behavior and made more regressive moves. A characteristic of executive functioning is that frontally damaged patients have difficulty with cognitive flexibility, considering response alternatives, and modifying plans (Eslinger & Grattan, 1993; Morris, Miotto, Feigenbaum, et al. 1997). This finding of impaired executive subgoaling holds true for patients with schizophrenia, Parkinson's disease, and Huntington's disease (Hanes, Andrews, Smith, et al., 1996). Moreover, when the problem solving complexity of the TOH is increased by adding another disk, performance declines with normal aging (Brennan, Welsh, & Fisher, 1997).

From a developmental perspective, using a modified Tower of London procedure in head-injured children and adolescents, Levin, Fletcher, Kufera, et al. (1996) were able to demonstrate that this task involves several components. For example, the number of rules that were broken and the quantity of problems solved loaded on a mental construct of "planning." "Schema" was related to number of problems solved during the first trial and "inhibition" was associated with initial planning time. Some difficulties remain in comparing the TOH and Tower of London tasks owing to validity and standardization issues (P. Anderson, Anderson, & Lajoie, 1996; Kafer & Hunter, 1997). In addition, some evidence suggests only moderate correlations between the two tests (Welsh, Petterson, Cartmell, et al., 1997).

The current program does have parameters to account for the visuospatial functions of the TOH task. One of the uses of the "context inputs" depicted in figure 9.1 was to help the neural net during training to distinguish between the different types of legal moves. The network for both the normals and the left frontal group would have made numerous visuospatial errors in stacking the rings without this function (illegal state #5 in figure 9.3 of stacking a larger ring on a smaller ring). One type of error that the left frontal lobe–damaged group made in our neural network was a regressive move (#6 in figure 9.3). This could also be called a perseverative error. This is the same as the inefficient "perceptual strategy" from Simon (1974) in which individuals sometimes find themselves repeating the same task.

In spite of the limitations of our current ability to program complex neuropsychological test performance, we were able to show some of the more salient elements of executive functioning in the network and approximations in a clinical population. In our laboratories we are programming features to articulate more fully the role of working memory and inhibition. A recent theoretical model has implicated working memory in an interactive framework of executive functioning and the frontal lobes (Levine & Prueitt, 1989; Roberts & Pennington, 1996). In agreement with Cohen and Servan-Schreiber (1992), we have designed a rudimentary system using statistical and clinical data to capture those features which are most relevant at a cognitive level analysis "without having to reproduce the entire brain to do so" (p. 117). Future testing of neural network programs that are interfaced by clinical neuropsychological data and in vivo brain imaging, for example, positron emission tomography (PET), SPECT, functional magnetic resonance imaging, and high-resolution electroencephalography would help to establish a more solid understanding of the learning and internal representation processes and the mechanisms involved when dealing with feedforward multilayer nets. For example, recent PET studies with the Tower of London task found distributed networks of cortical areas incorporating prefrontal and parietal areas (Owen, Evans, & Petrides, 1996) in addition to cingulate, premotor, parietal, and occipital cortices (Baker, Rogers, Owen, et al., 1996). Baker and co-workers concluded that a supervisory attentional system model, "provided a firm theoretical perspective from which to regard complex problem solving by man and machine" (p. 524). Currently, brain imaging has far exceeded current modelers' expectations of demonstrating distributed neuropsychological systems (Baker et al., 1996; Crammond, 1997; Frackowiak, 1994; Gevins, Leong, Smith, et al., 1995; Grady, Maisog, Horwitz, et al., 1994; Grady, McIntosh, Horwitz, et al., 1995; Parks, Loewenstein, Dodrill, et al., 1988); and executive functions in neuropathological populations (Levine, Parks, & Prueitt, 1993; Weinberger, 1993).

ACKNOWLEDGMENTS

Significant portions of this chapter were adapted and reproduced from "Parallel Distributed Processing and Executive Functioning: Tower of Hanoi Neural Network Model in Healthy Controls and Left Frontal Lobe Patients" by R. W. Parks and J. Cardoso (1997), *International Journal of Neuroscience*, NeuroCommunication Research, used with permission. The Tower test, a standardized variation of the TOH for children, may be found in a subtest of the NEPSY neuropsychological battery (Korkman, Kirk, & Kemp, 1997). Computerized versions of the TOH, Tower of Toronto, and Tower of London tests may be obtained from Colorado Assessment Tests, 102 E. Jefferson, Colorado Springs, CO 80907, and Psychological Software Services, Inc, 6555 Carrollton Avenue, Indianapolis, IN 46220.

REFERENCES

Anderson, J. R. (1993). Problem solving and learning. *American Psychologist, 48*, 35–44.

Anderson, J. R., Kushmerick, N. & Lebiere, C. (1993). Tower of Hanoi and goal structures. In J. R. Anderson (Ed.), *Rules of the mind* (pp. 121–142). Hillsdale, NJ: Erlbaum.

Anderson, P., Anderson, V., & Lajoie, G. (1996). The Tower of London test: Validation and standardization for pediatric populations. *The Clinical Neuropsychologist, 10*, 55–65.

Anderson, S. W., Damasio, H., Jones, R. D., & Tranel, D. (1991). Wisconsin Card Sorting test performance as a measure of frontal lobe damage. *Journal of Clinical and Experimental Neuropsychology, 13*, 909–922.

Andreasen, N. C., Rezai, K, Alliger, R., Swayze, V. W., Flaum, M., Kirchner, P., Cohen, G., & O'Leary, D. S. (1992). Hypofrontality in neuroleptic-naive patients and in patients with chronic schizophrenia: Assessment with xenon 133 single-photon emission computed tomography and the Tower of London. *Archives of General Psychiatry, 49*, 943–958.

Arnett, P. A., Rao, S. M., Bernardin, L, Grafman, J., Yetkin, F. Z., & Lobeck, L. (1994). Relationship between frontal lobe lesions and Wisconsin Card Sorting test performance in patients with multiple sclerosis. *Neurology, 44*, 420–425.

Baker, S. C., Rogers, R. D., Owen, A. M. Frith, C. D., Dolan, R. J., Frackowiak, R. S. J., & Robbins, T. W. (1996). Neural systems engaged by planning: a PET study of the Tower of London task. *Neuropsychologia, 34*, 515–526.

Benton, A. (1968). Differential behavioral effects in frontal lobe disease. *Neuropsychologia, 6*, 53–60.

Brennan, M, Welsh, M. C., & Fisher, C. B. (1997). Aging and executive function skills: An examination of a community-dwelling older adult population. *Perceptual and Motor Skills, 84*, 1187–1197.

Butters, N., Wolfe, J., Martone, M., Granholm, E., & Cermak, L. S. (1985). Memory disorders associated with Huntington's disease: Verbal recall, verbal recognition and procedural memory. *Neuropsychologia, 23*, 729–743.

Cardoso, J. (1991). *Revisiting the Towers of Hanoi.* AI Expert, October, 49–53.

Caudill, M., & Butler, C. (1990). *Naturally intelligent systems.* Cambridge, MA: MIT Press.

Chauvin, Y., & Rumelhart, D. E. (1995). *Backpropagation: Theory, architectures, and applications.* Hillsdale, NJ: Erlbaum.

Cohen, J. D., Dunbar, K., & McClelland, J. L. (1990). On the control of automatic processes: A parallel distributed processing account of the stroop effect. *Psychological Review, 97*, 332–361.

Cohen, J. D., & Servan-Schreiber, D. (1992). Introduction to neural network models in psychiatry. *Psychiatric Annals, 22*, 113–118.

Crammond, D. J. (1997). Motor imagery: Never in your wildest dream. *Trends in Neurosciences, 20,* 54–57.

Crockett, D. J., Bilsker, D., Hurwitz, T., & Kozak, J. (1986). Clinical utility of three measures of frontal lobe dysfunction in neuropsychiatric samples. *International Journal of Neuroscience, 30,* 241–248.

Dodrill, C. B. (1997). Myths of neuropsychology. *The Clinical Neuropsychologist, 11,* 1–17.

Eslinger, P. A., & Grattan, L. M. (1993). Frontal lobe and frontal-striatal substrates for different forms of human cognitive flexibility. *Neuropsychologia, 31,* 17–28.

Fletcher, J. M. (1996). Executive functions in children: Introduction to special series. *Developmental Neuropsychology, 12,* 1–3.

Frackowiak, R. S. J. (1994). Functional mapping of verbal memory and language. *Trends in Neurosciences, 17,* 109–115.

Gevins, A., Leong, H., Smith, M. E., Le, J., & Du, R. (1995). Mapping cognitive brain function with modern high-resolution electroencephalography. *Trends in Neurosciences, 18,* 429–436.

Glosser, G., & Goodglass, H. (1990). Disorders in executive control among aphasic and other brain damaged patients. *Journal of Clinical and Experimental Neuropsychology, 12,* 485–501.

Grady, C. L., Maisog, J. M., Horwitz, B., Ungerleider, L. G., Mentis, M. J., Salerno, J. A., Pietrini, P., Wagner, E., & Haxby, J. V. (1994). Age-related changes in cortical blood flow activation during visual processing of faces and location. *The Journal of Neuroscience, 14,* 1450–1462.

Grady, C. L., McIntosh, A. R., Horwitz, B., Maisog, J. M., Ungerleider, L. G., Mentis, M. J., Pietrini, P., Schapiro, M. B., & Haxby, J. V. (1995). Age-related reductions in human recognition memory due to impaired encoding. *Science, 269,* 218–221.

Hanes, K. R., Andrews, D. G., Smith, D. J., & Pantelis, C. (1996). A brief assessment of executive control dysfunction: Discriminant validity and homogeneity of planning, set shift, and fluency measures. *Archives of Clinical Neuropsychology, 11,* 185–191.

Holst, P., & Vilkki, J. (1988). Effect of frontomedial lesions on performance on the Stroop test and word fluency tasks. *Journal of Clinical and Experimental Neuropsychology, 10,* 79.

Kafer, K. L., & Hunter, M. (1997). On testing the face validity of planning/problem-solving tasks in a normal population. *Journal of the International Neuropsychological Society, 3,* 108–119.

Korkman, M., Kirk, U., & Kemp, S. (1997). *NEPSY manual.* San Antonio, TX: Psychological Corporation.

Levin, H. S., Fletcher, J. M., Kufera, J. A., Harward, H., Lilly, M. A., Mendelsohn, D., Bruce, D., & Eisenberg, H. M. (1996). Dimensions of cognition measured by the Tower of London and other cognitive tasks in head-injured children and adolescents. *Developmental Neuropsychology, 12,* 17–34.

Levine, D. S., Parks, R. W., & Prueitt, P. S. (1993). Methodological and theoretical issues in neural network models of frontal cognitive functions. *International Journal of Neuroscience, 72,* 209–233.

Levine, D. S., & Prueitt, P. S. (1989). Modeling some effects of frontal lobe damage: Novelty and perseveration. *Neural Networks, 2,* 103–116.

Lezak, M. D. (1995), *Neuropsychological assessment* (3rd ed.). New York: Oxford University Press.

Lippmann, R. P. (1987). *An introduction to computing with neural nets.* IEEE ASSP Magazine, April, 4–22. Reprinted in *Artificial Neural Networks: Theoretical Concepts.* Washington, D.C.: IEEE, Computer Society Press, 36:54

Morris, R. G., Ahmed, S., Syed, G. M. S., & Toone, B. K. (1993). Neural correlates of planning ability: Frontal lobe activation during the Tower of London test. *Neuropsychologia, 31*, 1367–1378.

Morris, R. G., Miotto, E. C., Feigenbaum, J. D., Bullock, P., & Polkey, C. E. (1997). The effect of goal-subgoal conflict on planning ability after frontal and temporal-lobe lesions in humans. *Neuropsychologia, 35*, 1147–1157.

Newcombe, F. (1969). *Missile wounds of the brain*. London: Oxford University Press.

Newell, A., & Simon, H. A. (1972). *Human problem solving*. Englewood Cliffs, NJ: Prentice-Hall.

Owen, A. M., Downes, J. J., Sahakian, B. J., Polkey, C. E., & Robbins, T. W. (1990). Planning and spatial working memory following frontal lobe lesions in man. *Neuropsychologia, 28*, 1021–1034.

Owen, A. M., Evans, A. C., & Petrides, M. (1996). Evidence for a two-stage model of spatial memory processing within the lateral frontal cortex: A positron emission tomography study. *Cerebral Cortex, 6*, 31–38.

Pao, Y-H. (1989). *Adaptive pattern recognition and neural networks*. New York: Addison-Wesley.

Parks, R. W., & Cardoso, J. (1997). Parallel distributed processing and executive functioning: Tower of Hanoi neural network model in healthy controls and left frontal lobe patients. *International Journal of Neuroscience, 89*, 217–240.

Parks, R., Loewenstein, D., Dodrill, K., Barker, W., Yoshii, F., Chang, J., Emran, A., Apicella, A., Sheramata, W., & Duara, R. (1988). Cerebral metabolic effects of a verbal fluency test: A PET scan study. *Journal of Clinical and Experimental Neuropsychology, 10*, 565–575.

Perret, E. (1974). The left frontal lobe of man and the suppression of habitual responses in verbal categorical behavior. *Neuropsychologia, 12*, 323–330.

Roberts, R. J., & Pennington, B. F. (1996). An interactive framework for examining prefrontal cognitive processes. *Developmental Neuropsychology, 12*, 105–126.

Robinson, A. L., Heaton, R. K., Lehman, R. A. W., & Stilson, D. W. (1980). The utility of the Wisconsin Card Sorting test in detecting and localizing frontal lobe lesions. *Journal of Consulting and Clinical Psychology, 48*, 605–614.

Shallice, T. (1982). Specific impairments in planning. *Philosophical Transactions of the Royal Society of London, 298*, 199–209.

Simon, H. A. (1975). The functional equivalence of problem solving skills. *Cognitive Psychology, 7*, 268–288.

Walsh, K. W. (1978). *Neuropsychology: A clinical approach*. New York: Churchill Livingston.

Weinberger, D. R. (1993). A connectionist approach to the prefrontal cortex. *Journal of Neuropsychiatry, 5*, 241–253.

Welsh, M., Petterson, N., Cartmell, T., & Stein, M. (1997). What cognitive processes are tapped by the Towers of Hanoi and London? *Journal of the International Neuropsychological Society, 3*, 29.

10 Neuronal Network Models of Acalculia and Prefrontal Deficits

Stanislas Dehaene, Laurent Cohen, and Jean-Pierre Changeux

How do we recognize that $20 + 21 = 91$ is an "obviously" false operation? What are the cerebral circuits involved in mathematical reasoning? What sequences of cell firing encode the complex steps of calculations involved in computing, say, 13×20? And how do localized brain lesions disrupt these operations? This chapter focuses on neuropsychological studies and neuronal network models of some of the most evolved functions of the human brain: arithmetic, mathematics, reasoning, and abstract rule formation. The neurobiological database that would support accurate modeling of these functions at the neuronal level is still lacking. Nevertheless, there is a growing body of evidence on the large-scale networks underlying arithmetic, both from single-case studies of brain-lesioned patients and from brain imaging studies in normals. The development of adequate models of the large networks of brain areas involved in calculation and reasoning, together with more speculative modeling at the neuronal level, may ultimately set the stage for finer neurobiological experiments.

NEURONAL MODELS OF COGNITIVE FUNCTIONS

Before building neuronal models of cognitive functions as complex as the production of mathematics, the theoretical bases of such an enterprise must be set. With its billions of cells and connections, woven by evolution over hundreds of millions of years, the brain is the most complex organ we know of. Relating cognitive functions to their neuronal substrates is fraught with epistemological difficulties. In an article that appeared in 1989 in the journal *Cognition*, two of us presented what we believe are the minimal preconditions for neuronal modeling of cognitive functions (Changeux & Dehaene, 1989). Two conditions are crucial: the distinction of levels of cerebral organization, and the modeling of modes of transition between these levels.

The first theoretical enterprise, which is essentially qualitative, consists in cleaving a complex architecture into hierarchical levels of organization, the appearance of which coincided, in the course of evolution, with the emergence of new functions. The first level, that of molecules, includes genes and proteins. Intuition notwithstanding, the molecular level is often directly relevant to some cognitive functions, as attested, for instance, by the key role of pharmacological agents in psychiatric diseases. Immediately above the molecular level stands the cellular level, which is characterized by an anatomical disposition unique in the organism: the ability of nerve cells to form topological networks defined by their multiple axonal and dendritic projections. At this level, the elementary functions of some cells may have a measurable influence on an organism's behavior. This is especially true in the case of identifiable neurons such as the Mauthner cell, which governs the fleeing behavior of fish.

The level of organization immediately above the cellular level is that of small ensembles of cells, or the circuit level. Each circuit is composed of several hundred of thousands of neurons interconnected for performing a defined function. One of the simplest examples is the network of motor cells in the spinal cord of a primitive vertebrate, the lamprey. The circuits that govern the lamprey's different swimming modes are known in great detail, to the point that it is possible to simulate on computer the oscillatory behavior of identified neurons and to predict the effect of lesions or of pharmacological agents on behavior.

At a higher level, the circuits connect in complex assemblies whose functions, in the human brain are only beginning to be delineated. It is well known, for instance, that visual functions are represented in a posterior network which may be subdivided in further assemblies coding mainly for the position and identity of visual objects. At a yet more integrated level, a set of prefrontal cortical areas is crucial to the planning of actions in time and space, and contributes to the construction of motor programs and of novel hypotheses. The surface of the prefrontal cortex sharply increased in evolution, reaching its maximum in man where it occupies almost a third of all cortex. It therefore seems legitimate to propose that the prefrontal cortex participates in the "architecture of reason," which characterizes the brain of *Homo sapiens*. Here, the cleavage into levels of organization clearly remains approximate and will have to be progressively refined as new techniques allow for more precise analyses of cortical activity in humans.

Neuronal modeling of any cognitive function therefore starts with the choice of the levels of organization relevant to this function. In the case of number processing and prefrontal functions, we will not address the molecular or cellular levels. However, the models that we examine do lead to specific predictions concerning the cellular and molecular learning mechanisms that underlie cognitive development. The levels that we consider here concern the neuronal circuits and the "circuits of circuits" (assemblies). We will see that it is possible to outline a plausible diagram of the main areas for number processing in the human brain, to set out a neuronal model for the development of a crucial component of this diagram (the quantity representation), and finally, to speculate on the role of prefrontal areas in more advanced calculation and reasoning abilities.

The second precondition for building neuronal models of cognitive functions consists in defining the transitions from one level of organization to the next. In the context of the application of evolutionary theory to the development of the nervous system (Changeux, Courrège, & Danchin, 1973; Changeux, 1983; Changeux & Danchin 1976; Changeux, Heidman, & Patte, 1984; Changeux & Dehaene, 1989), we have proposed an acccount of the transitions between levels with a variation-selection scheme, also called a generalized Darwinian scheme (see also Edelman, 1978, 1987). At each level, a "generator of diversity" introduces variations in functional organization which are selected and propagated or eliminated depending on their relevance to higher levels.

At the circuit level and beyond, this internal evolution is epigenetic and does not require genomic modifications. In the course of development, the variable elements are the neurons themselves and the topology of their connections. The selective stabilization of synapses, together with the elimination of connections, establishes a circuit adapted to a given function. At higher cognitive levels, the extension of the evolutionary paradigm suggests that the brain functions on a projective mode by permanently producing tentative representations or "prerepresentations" variable in time and space that are adopted or rejected by the organism based on their adequation to the external world. In this "mental Darwinism" framework, development and learning can be described as a progressive reduction of a vast initial repertoire of prerepresentations. We shall see below several examples of how this conception of development applies to the acquisition of elementary numerical knowledge and to simple reasoning.

A NETWORK OF AREAS FOR NUMBER PROCESSING

According to the above principles, the first step in achieving a neuronal model of number processing and calculation consists in identifying the gross network of cortical areas involved and their individual functional contributions. Drawing from studies of mental chronometry, neuropsychology, and brain imaging, we have recently outlined a tentative model of the cerebral circuitry for number processing (Dehaene, 1992; Dehaene & Cohen 1995).

Our "triple-code model" acknowledges that there are three main ways in which numbers can be manipulated mentally: (1) a visual arabic code, (2) a verbal code, and (3) an analogical magnitude code. In the visual arabic code, numbers are encoded as strings of digits on an internal visuospatial scratchpad which, by analogy with word processing, is called the visual number form. In the verbal code, they are encoded as sequences of number words. Finally, in the magnitude code, numerical quantities are represented by local distributions of activation on an oriented number line. Numerical relations, such as the fact that 9 is larger that 5, are then implicitly represented by proximity relations on the number line.

The model assumes that the three cardinal representations are linked by direct transcoding routes that enable numbers to be rapidly re-encoded in a different format. For instance, a printed arabic numeral is initially identified and encoded in the visual arabic numeral form. If the task requires assessing its magnitude, then its identity will be transmitted and re-encoded on the quantity representation. If, on the contrary, the task requires reading the numeral aloud, then its identity will be transmitted to the verbal system where an appropriate sequence of words will be composed. In the course of more complex tasks, such as a multidigit multiplication, several such transcodings may take place back and forth between the three cardinal representations.

A crucial hypothesis of the model is that each of the internal numerical representations is well suited for a different set of functions. The visual number form, holding a representation of the spatial layout of digits, is well suited for performing spatially organized mental calculations with multidigit arabic numerals. The verbal format, on the other hand, is well suited for accessing a stored table of rote arithmetic facts, which we suppose to be encoded in the form of short sentences in verbal memory (e.g., "two times three, six"). Finally, the analogical quantity representation is ideal for representing approximate relations between numerical magnitudes, such as knowing that 11 is about 10, or that 7 is slightly larger than 5.

Thanks to several single-case and brain imaging studies, reviewed in Dehaene and Cohen (1995), a schematic model of the anatomical network of areas underlying the triple-code model may be proposed (figure 10.1). The visual number form corresponds to the endpoint of a cascade of areas culminating in the medial occipitotemporal region of both hemispheres. The analogical quantity representation is computed by areas in the vicinity of the parieto-occipitotemporal junction of both hemispheres. Finally, the verbal word frame is computed by the perisylvian language areas of the left hemisphere. We postulate that homologous left and right hemisphere regions—

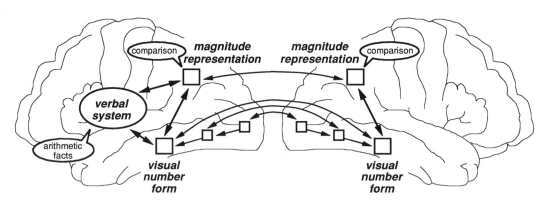

Figure 10.1 Schematic diagram of the anatomical and functional circuits postulated by the triple-code model to underlie simple number processing (Dehaene & Cohen, 1995).

the two visual number forms and the two quantity representations—are connected into a single functional unit by transcallosal fibers. Within the left hemisphere, we also suppose the visual, verbal, and quantity representations to be fully interconnected by dedicated neural transcoding pathways.

Support in favor of this network organization of numerical representations has come from the observation of highly selective deficits of number processing in cases of focal brain lesions. For the sake of brevity, only a few such observations are discussed here (see Dehaene & Cohen, 1995). First, studies of split-brain patients in whom the corpus callosum has been cut (Gazzaniga & Hillyard, 1971, Gazzaniga & Smylie, 1984; Seymour, Reuter-Lorenz, and Gazzaniga, 1994) or lesioned (Cohen & Dehaene, 1996) conform in great detail to the predictions expected from the model. When digits are flashed in their right hemifield, therefore contacting the patients' left hemisphere visual system, split-brain patients can name them, judge their numerical size, and calculate with them. This is consistent with the presence of a full network comprising visual, verbal, and quantity representations within the left hemisphere. The situation is different when digits are flashed within the left hemifield and therefore contact the right hemisphere. Split-brain patients may still judge whether two digits are the same or different, point to the appropriate digits in an array, and find the larger of the two digits. This confirms that the right hemisphere can both identify digits and associate them with the corresponding numerical quantity. However, the patients cannot read the very same stimuli aloud, nor can they calculate with them, a deficit which is predicted in our model by the lack of a verbal representation of numbers in the right hemisphere. A similar dissociation between preserved comprehension of numerical quantities and impaired reading and calculation has also been observed in several patients with extensive left hemisphere lesions (e.g. Cohen, Dehaene, &, Verstichel, 1994; Dehaene & Cohen, 1991; Grafman, Kampen, Rosenberg, et al., 1989).

A second type of patient that yielded valuable data suffered from a left medial occipitotemporal lesion, resulting in a severe deficit of reading called pure alexia (Cohen & Dehaene, 1995; Dejerine, 1891, 1892). In our model, such a lesion is predicted to disrupt the formation of the left visual number form, while sparing completely the right visual number form. As can be seen in figure 10.1, this should have the effect of disconnecting the verbal system from direct visual inputs, while leaving the quantity representation appropriately connected to visual inputs via the right hemisphere visual system. The observed impairments conform to this pattern. Patients with pure alexia are largely unable to read arabic digits aloud, but they can make very accurate larger/smaller comparisons with the same stimuli, indicating a well-preserved comprehension of quantities. Likewise, they are unable to perform even simple calculations with written arabic stimuli (e.g., 2 + 2), because their left hemisphere verbal system cannot be directly informed of the identity of the visual operands. Yet they perform the very same calculations with perfect accuracy when the problems are presented orally, thus proving that the verbal representation and calculation modules themselves are intact and can still be accessed from the auditory modality. Overall, these patients provide a striking illustration of the specific deficits that can occur when a single circuit or connection is disrupted within the large-scale network of areas for number processing.

A NEURONAL MODEL FOR THE DETECTION AND INTERNAL REPRESENTATION OF NUMERICAL QUANTITIES

The triple-code model accounts for aspects of mental arithmetic and acalculia at an abstract level of organization that correspond roughly to that of "circuits of circuits." The internal representations in the model are currently described verbally and without explicit simulation. Ultimately, it would be desirable to understand their implementation within local neuronal networks. As a step in this direction, we have proposed a detailed neuronal model for a crucial part of the triple-code model, namely, the quantity representation (Dehaene & Changeux, 1993).

In many nonverbal organisms such as rats and pigeons, and even in human babies in their first year of life, the quantity representation seems to be functional in the absence of any symbolic visual or verbal representation of numbers. Young infants can discriminate small numbers of objects, such as two vs. three, regardless of the modality of input (e.g. Starkey & Cooper, 1980; Bijeljac-Babic, Bertoncini, & Mehler, 1991; Starkey, Spekle, & Gelman, 1983, 1990). Several animal species can determine the numerosity of collections of objects and learn to associate specific behaviors with specific numerical quantities. For instance, Meck and Church (1983) taught rats to press one lever when they heard two sounds and another level when they heard eight sounds, regardless of their duration. Importantly, animals can use this representation to perform larger/smaller comparisons (e.g., Mitchell, Yao, Sherman, et al., 1985; Rumbaugh, Savage-Rumbaugh, & Hegel, 1987), and in doing so they seem to be using the same kind of analogical representation that adult humans use. In number comparisons, both animals and adult humans are affected by a distance effect (comparison speed and accuracy drop for increasing numerical distance between the two compared numbers) and by a magnitude effect (for equal distances, speed and accuracy drop for increasingly larger numbers). These parallels have led to the hypothesis that humans and animals are endowed from birth with a preverbal representation of numerical quantities which, only in humans, later connects to visual and verbal symbolic codes to form the complete triple-code model (Dehaene, 1992; Gallistel & Gelman, 1992).

Given such data, our goal was to provide a plausible neuronal network that would reproduce the functions of the preverbal quantity representation found in animals and in young infants. Such a network, when presented with a set of visual or auditory objects, should detect approximately how many

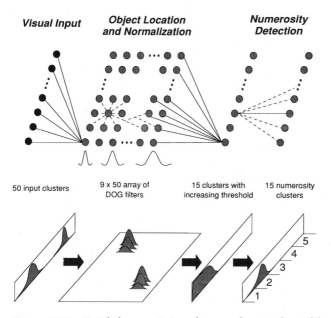

Figure 10.2 Detailed connectivity of a neural network model capable of extracting the numerosity of a set of objects (Dehaene & Changeux, 1993).

objects are present and encode that approximate number on a representation compatible with the experimentally observed distance and magnitude effects.

The first crucial component in our model is a numerosity detection system (Dehaene & Changeux, 1993; see figure 10.2; see also figure 10.4 A). This prewired network comprises three distinct modules: (1) an input "retina" on which visual objects of different sizes can be presented; (2) an intermediate topographic map of object locations, on which each object, independently of its original size, is represented by an approximately constant pool of active neurons, and (3) an array of numerosity detectors that compute the total activation over the location map, thus producing a quantity highly correlated with the number of objects on the retina. This architecture defines a parallel algorithm for enumerating objects of different sizes. A sequential auditory input was also defined and connected to numerosity detectors with weights matched to the weights from the location map. As a result, the numerical output of the system was amodal. Thanks to the size normalization operation, all visual and auditory objects were counted as "one."

Figure 10.2 shows in greater detail our computer implementation of this neuronal network model. Each neuronal circuit is composed of many units called "neuronal clusters," each representing a small ensemble of about 100 or 1000 highly interconnected neurons with similar response characteristics. This reproduces to some extent the columnar organization of the cortex (Mountcastle, 1978; Goldman-Rakic, 1984). Clusters are connected by bundles of synapses (see Dehaene & Changeux, 1993, for a precise description of the connectivity used).

Dehaene, Cohen, & Changeux: Acalculia and Prefrontal Deficits

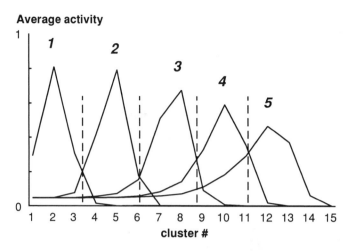

Figure 10.3 Simulated responses of fifteen output units ("numerosity detectors") to different numbers of input objects (Dehaene & Changeux, 1993).

In one simulation, we presented 2500 sets of one to five blobs of different sizes on the input retina. As shown in figure 10.3, each output cluster of the network activates reproducibly when a certain given number of objects is present at input. We therefore termed these units "numerosity detectors." Similar results were obtained with objects presented in the auditory modality, or with simultaneous auditory and visual inputs. Each numerosity detector responds to a fixed total number of objects, regardless of their input modality.

Figure 10.3 makes it clear that the coding of numbers in this network is quite different from the symbolic and discrete representations used in computers. Owing to an intrinsic variability in the normalization operation, the activations evoked by different numbers of input objects overlap in part. For instance, some numerosity detectors react when either four or five objects are present, indicating that number coding is approximate and analogical rather than digital. Note that the activation overlap decreases with numerical distance (distance effect). Furthermore, for equal numerical distances, the activation overlap increases with numerosity: the activation peaks evoked by 4 and 5 overlap more than those evoked by 1 and 2 (magnitude effect). In fact, the network codes numerosity with fairly discrete peaks only up to three objects, thus providing a natural account of the so-called subitizing range of one to three items, over which humans are very accurate in assessing numbers of objects without counting (Mandler & Shebo, 1982; Dehaene & Cohen, 1994). The decreasing precision of numerosity coding in the network derives directly from the manner in which numerosity is estimated as a sum of approximately constant activations associated with each counted object: the more terms in this sum, the higher the variance in the final estimate.

CONDITIONING TO NUMEROSITY

In order to directly simulate animal conditioning experiments, we have connected the numerosity detectors to a number of output clusters (figure 10.4B). The numerosity-to-output connections are variable and their efficacy is determined by a Hebb rule modulated by a reward signal (Dehaene & Changeux, 1989, 1991, 1993). Initially, these connections have a random efficacy and the simulated organism therefore responds randomly. When the response happens to be adequate for the desired behavior, it is selected by giving the network a positive reward which has the effect, thanks to the Hebb rule, of stabilizing recent neuronal activity and therefore of increasing the chances that this correct behavior will be reproduced later on. When the response is inadequate, a negative reinforcement signal is sent which has the effect of destabilizing recent activity and therefore favoring the selection of a different response on later trials.

We trained the simulated network on a numerosity discrimination task similar to a task used with rats. For 2 vs. 4 discrimination, for instance, when two objects were presented at input, the correct response was to activate output cluster A, and when four objects were presented, to activate output cluster B. The network was trained three times with each pair of numerosities between 1 and 5 (1 vs. 2, 1 vs. 3, 2 vs. 3, etc.). In all cases, fewer than 300 trials were necessary to reach a stringent criterion of twenty successes in a row, and asymptotic performance varied between 78.5 and 97.8 percent correct. Two fundamental characteristics of animal numerical conditioning were reproduced by the model. First, the learning time was longer, and the final performance was worse, when the numerical distance between the two discriminated numbers decreased (distance effect). Thus, it took 285 trials to learn to discriminate 4 vs. 5 with 78.5 percent final accuracy, but only 81 trials to learn to discriminate 1 vs. 4 with 96.8 percent final accuracy. Second, the magnitude effect was also found: it was easier for the network to learn to discriminate, say, 1 vs. 2 than 4 vs. 5.

Figure 10.5 shows the connection strengths developed when learning various numerical discrimination tasks. For the discrimination of 2 vs. 4, for instance, the numerosity detectors that were regularly activated by the presentation of two objects developed excitatory connections toward the output cluster associated with the response "2." Similar connections were found for the response "4." These connections were not strictly limited to the numerosities 2 and 4, but spread to neighboring numerosity detectors, thus providing the network with properties of robustness and generalization.

Why are these simulations relevant to the neuropsychology of number processing? A frequent finding in patients with acalculia is that the ability to approximate numbers can be preserved even in the face of a complete disruption of exact calculation abilities. For example, patient N.A.U., who could not calculate $2 + 2$, nevertheless knew that it could not make 9 (Dehaene & Cohen, 1991). He also had excellent knowledge of proximity relations

A. Numerosity Detection System

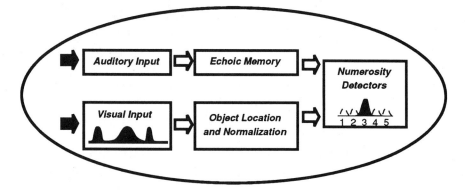

C. Comparison of two numerosities

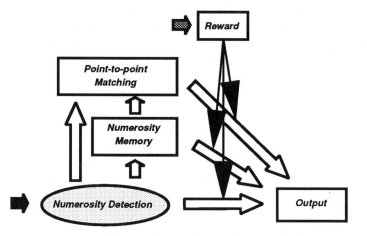

Figure 10.4 Schematic diagrams of successive levels of development of a network simulating numerosity processing in animals and preverbal children (Dehaene & Changeux, 1993).

between quantities, such as knowing that 12 is not very different from 8 or 10. Other patients have shown a proximity effect on naming errors, for instance, frequently naming digit 2 as "three" or "four", but never as "nine" (e.g., Macaruso, McCloskey, & Aliminosa, 1993; Campbell & Clark, 1988). This evidence suggests that an analogical representation of numerical quantities, such as the one provided by the numerosity detectors in our model, underlies the patients' judgments. It also supports a postulate of the triple-code model that symbolic verbal and digital representations of number are dissociable for core knowledge about approximate numerical quantities.

In the animal and human brain, the size normalization and numerosity detection operations postulated in the model may be performed by the dorsal stream of occipital and parietal areas, which are known to participate

B. Output and Conditioning by Reward

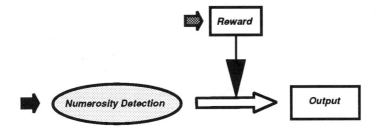

D. Self-organisation

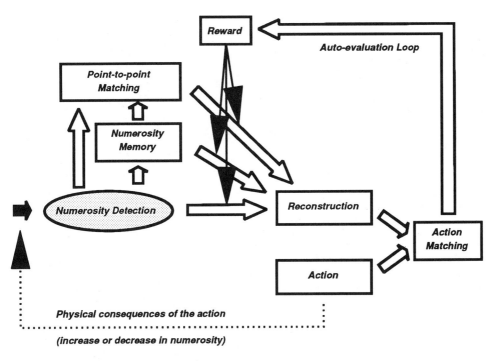

Figure 10.4 (continued)

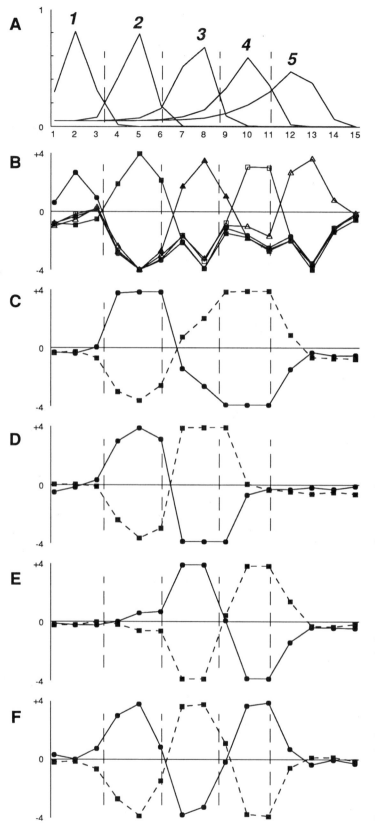

Figure 10.5 A, Connection strengths between numerosity detectors and output units, developed through learning by reinforcement in various tasks. B, Numerosity labeling task. Five output units were trained to respond selectively to the number of input objects. C–F, Numerosity discrimination tasks. Two output units were trained to discriminate numerosities 2 vs. 4 (C), 2 vs. 3 (D), 3 vs. 4 (E), and 2 or 4 vs. 3 (F).

in the coding of object location and size. In the course of evolution, the location map may have originally evolved for the parallel computation of object location and size for the purpose of guiding motor gestures. The numerosity detection network may later have preempted part of this spatiomotor guiding system. The close links between numerosity extraction and location coding may explain why bilateral inferior parietal or parieto-occipito-temporal areas activate during various number-processing tasks (e.g. Roland & Friberg, 1985; Dehaene, Tzourio, Frak, et al., 1996; Dehaene, 1996), and why these areas, in the left hemisphere, are a critical site for acalculia (e.g., Gerstmann, 1940). At a somewhat homologous location in the associative cortex of the cat, Thompson, Mayers, Robertson, et al. (1970) have recorded single neurons that fired only after a fixed number of auditory or visual stimuli were presented. These neurons thus appeared quite similar to the numerosity detectors postulated in our model. The authors' findings, however, have not yet been pursued with modern neurophysiological techniques.

LEARNING TO ORDER NUMEROSITY DETECTORS

The numerosity detection network mimics an initial stage of human or animal numerical cognition. However, animals and young children are also able to choose the larger of two sets, an ability that the above network cannot simulate merely because only one numerosity is processed at any given time. To simulate the development of number comparison abilities, we therefore introduced an additional memory circuit that could maintain, in short-term memory, a representation of the preceding numerosity while a new one was being processed. Two novel neuronal networks were introduced (figure 10.4C). First, a short-term memory network was connected to the numerosity detectors. It comprised an array of clusters with strong recurrent excitatory connections, capable of maintaining a sustained activity after the stimulus that activated them had disappeared (Dehaene & Changeux, 1989, 1991, 1993). Each memory cluster therefore kept in its "remanent activity" a trace of the preceding activity level of the corresponding numerosity detector. Second, we also introduced a point-to-point matching network, the clusters of which activated only when the two numerosity and memory clusters that were topographically connected to them became active.

The memory and matching networks, just like the numerosity detectors, were connected to output clusters with connections of variable strength modifiable by the Hebb rule. In order to teach the network a larger/smaller comparison task, we successively presented on the input retina a set of n_1 objects for thirty-two simulation cycles, and then another set of n_2 objects for sixteen cycles. The simulated organism had to activate an output cluster A when n_1 was larger than n_2, and another output cluster B when n_1 was smaller than n_2. On each trial, the network received a positive or negative reward depending on the correctness of its response, and connections were

Dehaene, Cohen, & Changeux: Acalculia and Prefrontal Deficits modified accordingly. After about 300 trials, the network reached an asymptotic performance of 88.9 percent correct. Once again, the distance and magnitude effects were found. Without entering further into details, we were able to simulate a large number of experimental results on sequential order learning in animals and children, including the so-called transitive inference tasks (Bryant & Trabasso, 1971; McGonigle & Chalmers, 1977; von Fersen, Wynne, Delius, et al., 1991).

The type of learning by reinforcement that we have used in our simulations provides a natural account of animal conditioning experiments. However, young children do not require any explicit conditioning to acquire concepts of larger vs. smaller numbers. At fourteen months of age, they spontaneously choose the larger of two sets (Sophian & Adams, 1987; see also Cooper, 1984). As a first step toward simulating such auto-organization, in the most elaborated version of our model we have introduced an architecture in which reward signals are not provided by an external teacher, but are generated internally by an autoevaluation loop (figure 10.4D). The idea is that the simulated organism plays with a set of objects by randomly choosing one of two actions: adding one object, or removing one object. The concomitant variations in numerosity are noticed by the numerosity detection network. By comparing the previously memorized numerosity with the new one, the organism attempts to reconstruct, a posteriori, the action that was performed. An internal comparison module evaluates the similarity of the reconstructed and actual actions. When they match, an internal positive reward is generated by this autoevaluation loop. On this basis, the system progressively discovers that an increase in numerosity implies that an addition was performed, and that a decrease in numerosity implies a subtraction.

We have simulated this architecture and shown that indeed, based solely on a correlation between actions and the corresponding changes in numerosity, the system can discover ordinality relations, first between consecutive numerosities and, by later generalization, between any pair of numerosities. Thus, our network implements in a working simulation Cooper's suggestion that "it is the relationship between the numerosity detector states and the effects of addition and subtraction that give rise to the notions of more and less. From the child's point of view 'more' is invented in this process." (Cooper, 1984, p. 166). Our simulation can be viewed as an existence proof that such a learning mechanism is feasible. Whether children and animals actually use such a mechanism to learn ordinality, or whether they have more innate knowledge about the ordering of numerosity detectors, however, remains to be conclusively studied.

A HIERARCHY OF NETWORKS FOR EXACT CALCULATION

Having described network implementations for the most elementary of numerical abilities—numerosity detection, encoding, and comparison—we

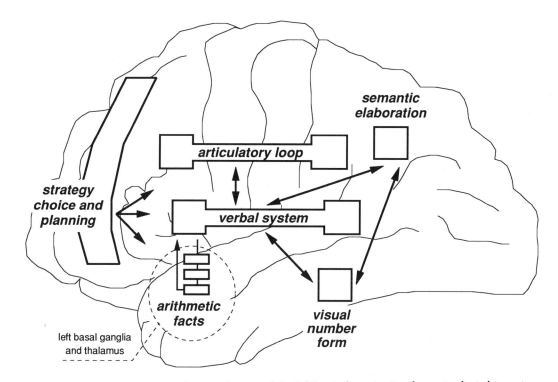

Figure 10.6 Schematic diagram of the left hemisphere circuits of areas implicated in various levels of number processing according to the triple-code model (Dehaene & Cohen, 1995).

now turn to the more complex case of the specifically human ability to perform exact calculations such as $2 + 3 = 5$ or $12345679 \times 9 = 111111111$. Here again, we believe that the distinction of levels of organization is crucial to an understanding of the large network of areas, including subcortical, inferior parietal, and prefrontal components, that may yield different forms of acalculia if they are lesioned (Dehaene & Cohen, 1995). A coarse diagram of multiple circuits involved is shown in figure 10.6.

At the simplest level, studies of normal adults have repeatedly suggested that most simple arithmetic problems, such as $2 \times 3 = 6$, are stored and retrieved from rote memory (for review, see Ashcraft, 1992). Anatomically, we believe that arithmetical fact retrieval rests on (a) left hemisphere perisylvian language areas for encoding the arithmetic problem into a verbal form such as "two times three," and (b) a left corticostriatal loop for automatically retrieving the associated verbal response ("six"). This anatomical organization, while clearly speculative, may explain why fact retrieval deficits occur (a) in patients that are unable to encode digits into verbal form, such as in persons with pure alexia (e.g., Cohen & Dehaene, 1995), or (b) in patients with lesions of the left basal ganglia (Corbett, McCusker, & Davidson, 1988; Hittmair-Delazer, Semenza, & Denes, 1994; Whitaker, Habiger, & Ivers, 1985).

At a second level, some arithmetic problems do not have a memorized answer and must be recoded in a different form before retrieval, a process that we call "semantic elaboration" (Dehaene & Cohen, 1995). For instance, evidence from normal subjects suggests that additions such as $9 + 6$ are often recoded as $10 + 5$ and that operands may have to be reordered before retrieval, $2 + 7$ being recoded as $7 + 2$. Because such recoding requires an understanding of quantitative properties (e.g., that 9 is close to 10 or that 2 is smaller than 7), we think that it involves activation of the quantity representation in inferior parietal cortex. Indeed, left inferior parietal or parieto-occipitotemporal lesions yield a classic acalculia of the Gerstmann type, which we claim is due to an inability to guide rote verbal memory retrieval by quantitative knowledge of numbers. Such patients often show dramatic impairments with large addition and multiplication facts that are least known and which therefore require semantic elaboration (e.g., 8×7, $9 + 8$). Subtraction and division problems, which are presumably not stored in rote verbal memory, may also be disproportionately impaired. However, simple rote facts such as $2 + 2$ or 3×3 are almost invariably spared (e.g. McCloskey, Harley, & Sokol, 1991), as predicted by their storing at a lower level.

A third level is reached for operations that require holding intermediate results in working memory, for instance, when multiple digits or carry operations are involved. Research with normal subjects has demonstrated the involvement of visuospatial and auditory verbal working memory in complex calculation (e.g. Hitch, 1978; Logie, Gilhooly, & Wynn, 1994). Anatomically, verbal working memory results from the collective function of a network of areas constituting the left supramarginal gyrus, the left inferior frontal region, the insula, and the left superior temporal gyrus (Paulesu, Frith, & Frackowiak, 1993). Visuospatial working memory may rely on a right-lateralized prefrontal parieto-occipital network (Jonides, Smith, Koeppe, et al., 1993; McCarthy, Blamire, Puce, et al., 1994).

Finally, at a fourth level, the most complex arithmetic problems require sequential planning and control processes. Multidigit operations, for instance, involve the resolution, in a strict order, of many single-digit problems. The selection and execution of each elementary operation must be controlled and possibly corrected. Such higher-level supervisory functions are likely to involve an anterior neuronal network including the dorsolateral prefrontal cortex and the anterior cingulate Cortex (Shallice, 1988; Posner & Raichle, 1994). Some acalculic patients show selective impairments in these procedural aspects of calculation, for instance, misapplying the addition procedure to a multidigit multiplication problem or failing to carry properly (Caramazza & McCloskey, 1987). Patients with prefrontal lesions show deficits in nonroutine arithmetic word problems in which a novel sequence of calculations must be planned to fit verbal instructions (e.g. Fasotti, Eling, & Bremer, 1992; Fasotti, Eling, & van Houtem, 1994; Luria, 1980). Frontal-lesioned patients are also impaired in a cognitive estimation test in which simple but unusual numerical questions must be solved (e.g., what is the height of the highest building in London?, to which one patient responded, "6000 meters"). According to Shallice and Evans (1978), this test requires planning a search for relevant facts in memory and verifying the plausibility of a result. Both components might be perturbed by frontal lesions.

THE WISCONSIN CARD SORTING TEST, PREFRONTAL CORTEX, AND FAST RULE SWITCHING

While the large-scale network of perisylvian, subcortical, parietal, and prefrontal areas that collectively mediate the execution of complex arithmetical operations begins to be characterized, it would clearly be premature to undertake a detailed simulation of this entire network at the smaller scale of individual neuronal circuits. Instead, we have again adopted the strategy of attempting to model only a component of this network, namely, the role of prefrontal cortex in working memory and task control. Two types of tasks were simulated: the delayed-response tasks, in which an animal must memorize a response cue throughout a time delay (Dehaene & Changeux, 1991), and the Wisconsin Card Sorting test (WCST), in which subjects have to discover, by trial and error, rules for sorting a deck of cards (Dehaene & Changeux, 1993). We focus here on the latter test, which is a classic neuropsychological test of prefrontal damage (e.g., Milner, 1963).

The problem facing our simulated network is the same that confronts subjects taking the WCST. A card bearing some colored geometric symbols is presented at input, and there is a choice of four output stacks on which to sort it. There are multiple available mappings between inputs and outputs, which correspond to the different ways of sorting the cards by color, by shape, and by number. Each time a card is sorted, the system is informed whether its response is correct or not. The issue is, how can such a system find the correct sorting rule, and how can it switch rapidly to a new rule in case the current one is found to be incorrect?

In our simulation, we again solved the problem by introducing a layered hierarchical architecture. At the lowest level were input units coding for the features of the input card, with separate networks for shape, color, and number, and four output units coding for the four available sorting responses. Above this level were layers of memory and intention units, isomorphic to the sensory and motor layers, but capable of maintaining a sustained activity, in the absence of overt inputs and output, using recurrent excitatory connections. These units therefore provided the network with a "working memory space" in which to test anticipatory hypotheses about the coming response.

At a higher level, above and beyond the basic mapping between memory and intention units, our simulation included a network of abstract rule-coding clusters (figure 10.7). These units were able to modulate an entire set of connections of the lower level. Their state of activity therefore drastically affected information processing. When the cluster coding for the "color rule"

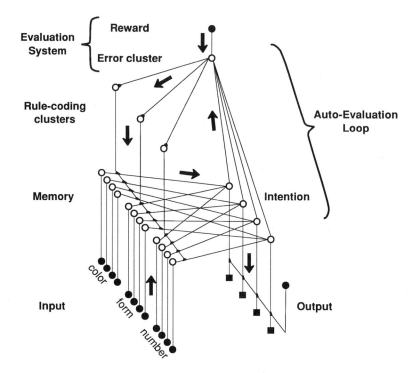

Figure 10.7 Neural network capable of passing the Wisconsin Card Sorting test (Dehaene & Changeux, 1991).

was active, for instance, color, rather than number or shape information, was paid attention to and stored in the memory-intention circuit. The network then sorted the input cards by color.

Changing the sorting rule simply consisted in changing the state of activity of rule-coding clusters. Because rules were encoded as patterns of activity rather than as fixed sets of connections, they could be changed rapidly under the control of a specialized evaluation system (see figure 10.7). Whenever negative reward was received, signaling an erroneous response, an error-coding unit fired. This had the effect of desensitizing recently active connections among the rule-coding units, and therefore of destabilizing their current activity. As a result, the rule-coding cluster that was active when the error was made was deactivated, allowing the other sorting rules to enter a competition for the control of behavior. This process continued from trial to trial until a satisfactory rule was found, one that did not lead to a negative reward.

An important property of this model is its ability to implement, in elementary form, a purely internal process of reasoning. When a negative reward is received, thus activating the error cluster, connections from intention to error clusters can learn the relation between the previous intention and the error. Hence, the previous intention is labeled as incorrect. Later, when a new rule is selected, it is applied to the memorized features of the preceeding input, creating a new pattern of activity of intention units. If, in fact, this pattern is identical to the previous one, this means that the network is about to make the same error a second time. The intention-to-error connections can recognize this and avoid a second failure by automatically activating the error cluster, without waiting for an external reward input. This internal testing of rules, which we call "autoevaluation," continues until a potentially valid rule is found, one for which it cannot be known a priori whether positive or negative reward will ensue.

Several aspects of this model are relevant to the neuropsychology of planning, reasoning, and intentional decision making. First, lesioning the model leads to functional deficits similar to those seen in frontal-lesioned patients. Notably, damage to the rule-coding clusters or to the evaluation network yields perseverations similar to those seen in actual WCST performance (e.g., Milner, 1963). Second, several aspects of the model are in rough correspondence to actual anatomical and neurobiological structures. The memory and intention clusters may correspond to dorsolateral prefrontal cortex, where neurons maintaining a sustained activity during the delay period of delayed-response tasks and coding either for retrospective aspects of past stimuli or for prospective aspects of future actions have been recorded (e.g. Fuster, 1997). The rule-coding network, with its ability to rapidly switch rules, may correspond to the "central executive" (Baddeley, 1986), "supervisory attentional system" (Shallice, 1988), or the "attention for action" system (Posner & Dehaene, 1994) postulated by psychologists to underlie flexible task control, and anatomically related to the prefrontal and anterior cingulate cortex. Finally, the evaluation system may correspond to prefrontal-limbic loops (Goldman-Rakic, 1988). Diffuse ascending neuromodulatory systems may mediate the postulated effect of negative reward on prefrontal activity, perhaps via allosteric transitions of postsynaptic receptor molecules (Dehaene & Changeux, 1991). Hence, speculative links can begin to be drawn between high-level functions such as reasoning and the underlying anatomical and even molecular structures.

CONCLUSION

Several types of network models have been described in this chapter. Some were framed at the global level of "circuits of circuits" and addressed the large-scale interactions between brain regions involved in number processing and calculation, using the classic box-and-arrow diagrams of neuropsychology. Others aimed at providing a more detailed and necessarily more tentative simulation of the neuronal circuits underlying high-level behaviors such as the delayed-response tasks or the Wisconsin Card Sorting test. Finally, a specific model of a single crucial circuit of the global model, the quantity representation, was simulated in detail using more plausible biological assumptions about neuronal architecture. We would like to conclude that a whole range of approaches to modeling may be useful in neuropsychology. Much of cognitive neuropsychology is still dominated by functional box-and-arrow models, the usefulness of which is unquestionable for the initial charting of the main dissociations within a given cognitive domain. Nevertheless, detailed neuronal network simulations are also important, both for specifying the inner workings of the boxes in classic neuropsychological diagrams, and for drawing relations between behavioral and neurobiological data.

REFERENCES

Ashcraft, M. H. (1992). Cognitive arithmetic: A review of data and theory. *Cognition, 44,* 75–106.

Baddeley, A. (1986). *Working memory.* Oxford, U.K.: Oxford University Press.

Bijeljac-Babic, R., Bertoncini, J., & Mehler, J. (1991). How do four-day-old infants categorize multisyllabic utterances? *Developmental Psychology, 29,* 711–721.

Bryant, P. E., & Trabasso, T. (1971). Transitive inferences and memory in young children. *Nature, 232,* 456–458.

Campbell, J. I. D., & Clark, J. M. (1988). An encoding complex view of cognitive number processing: Comment on McCloskey, Sokol, & Goodman (1986). *Journal of Experimental Psychology: General, 117,* 204–214.

Caramazza, A., & McCloskey, M. (1987). Dissociations of calculation processes. In G. Deloche & X. Seron (Eds.), *Mathematical Disabilities: A cognitive neuropsychological perspective* (pp. 221–234). Hillsdale, N.J.: Erlbaum.

Changeux, J. P. (1983). *L'homme neuronal.* Paris: Fayard.

Changeux, J. P., & Danchin, A. (1976). Selective stabilization of developing synapses as a mechanism for the specification of neuronal networks. *Nature, 264,* 705–712.

Changeux, J. P., & Dehaene, S. (1989). Neuronal models of cognitive functions. *Cognition, 33,* 63–109.

Changeux, J. P., Courrège, P., & Danchin, A. (1973). A theory of the epigenesis of neural networks by selective stabilization of synapses. *Proceedings of the National Academy of Sciences, 70,* 2974–2978.

Changeux, J. P., Heidmann, T., & Patte, P. (1984). Learning by selection. In P. Marler & H. Terrace (Eds.), *The biology of learning* (pp. 115–139). Berlin: Springer-Verlag.

Cohen, L., & Dehaene, S. (1995). Number processing in pure alexia: The effect of hemispheric asymmetries and task demands. *NeuroCase, 1,* 121–137.

Cohen, L., & Dehaene, S. (1996). Cerebral networks for number processing: Evidence from a case of posterior callosal lesion. *NeuroCase, 2,* 155–174.

Cohen, L., Dehaene, S., & Verstichel, P. (1994). Number words and number non-words: A case of deep dyslexia extending to arabic numerals. *Brain, 117,* 267–279.

Cooper, R. G. (1984). Early number development: Discovering number space with addition and subtraction. In C. Sophian (Ed.), *Origins of cognitive skills* (pp. 157–192). Hillsdale, NJ: Erlbaum.

Corbett, A. J., McCusker, E. A., & Davidson, O. R. (1988). Acalculia following a dominant-hemisphere subcortical infarct. *Archives of Neurology, 43,* 964–966.

Dehaene, S. (1992). Varieties of numerical abilities. *Cognition, 44,* 1–42.

Dehaene, S. (1996). The organization of brain activations in number comparison: Event-related potentials and the additive-factors methods. *Journal of Cognitive Neuroscience, 8,* 47–68.

Dehaene, S., & Changeux, J. P. (1989). A simple model of prefrontal cortex function in delayed-response tasks. *Journal of Cognitive Neuroscience, 1*: 244–261.

Dehaene, S., & Changeux, J. P. (1991). The Wisconsin Card Sorting test: Theoretical analysis and modelling in a neuronal network. *Cerebral Cortex, 1,* 62–79.

Dehaene, S., & Changeux, J. P. (1993). Development of elementary numerical abilities: A neuronal model. *Journal of Cognitive Neuroscience, 5,* 390–407.

Dehaene, S., & Cohen, L. (1991). Two mental calculation systems: A case study of severe acalculia with preserved approximation. *Neuropsychologia, 29,* 1045–1074.

Dehaene, S., & Cohen, L. (1994). Dissociable mechanisms of subitizing and counting—Neuropsychological evidence from simultanagnosic patients. *Journal of Experimental Psychology: Human Perception and Performance, 20,* 958–975.

Dehaene, S., & Cohen, L. (1995). Towards an anatomical and functional model of number processing. *Mathematical Cognition, 1,* 83–120.

Dehaene, S., Tzourio, N., Frak, V., Raynaud, L., Cohen, L., Mehler, J., & Mazoyer, B. (1996). Cerebral activations during number multiplication and comparison: A PET study. *Neuropsychologia, 34,* 1097–1106.

Dejerine, J. (1891). Sur un cas de cécité verbale avec agraphie, suivi d'autopsie. *Mémoires de la Société de Biologie, 3,* 197–201.

Dejerine, J. (1892). Contribution à l'étude anatomo-pathologique et clinique des différentes variétés de cécité verbale. *Mémoires de la Société de Biologie, 4,* 61–90.

Edelman, G. (1978). *The mindful brain. Cortical organization and the group-selective theory of higher brain function.* Cambridge, MA: MIT Press

Edelman, G. (1987). *Neural Darwinism.* New York: Basic Books.

Fasotti, L., Eling, P. A. T. M., & Bremer, J. J. C. B. (1992). The internal representation of arithmetical word problem sentences: Frontal and posterior patients compared. *Brain and Cognition, 20,* 245–263.

Fasotti, L., Eling, P. A. T. M., & van Houtem, J. (1994). Categorization of arithmetic word problems by normals, frontal and posterior-injured patients. *Journal of Clinical and Experimental Neuropsychology, 16,* 723–733.

Fuster, J. M. (1997). *The prefrontal cortex,* 3rd ed. New York: Raven Press.

Gallistel, C. R., & Gelman, R. (1992). Preverbal and verbal counting and computation. *Cognition, 44,* 43–74.

Gazzaniga, M. S., & Hillyard, S. A. (1971). Language and speech capacity of the right hemisphere. *Neuropsychologia, 9,* 273–280.

Gazzaniga, M. S., & Smylie, C. E. (1984). Dissociation of language and cognition: A psychological profile of two disconnected right hemispheres. *Brain, 107,* 145–153.

Gerstmann, J. (1940). Syndrome of finger agnosia, disorientation for right and left, agraphia and acalculia. *Archives of Neurology and Psychiatry, 44,* 398–408.

Goldman-Rakic, P. S. (1984). Modular organization of prefrontal cortex. *Trends in Neuroscience, 7,* 419–424.

Goldman-Rakic, P. S. (1988). Topography of cognition: Parallel distributed networks in primate association cortex. *Annual Review of Neuroscience, 11,* 137–156.

Grafman, J., Kampen, D., Rosenberg, J., Salazar, A., & Boller, F. (1989). Calculation abilities in a patient with a virtual left hemispherectomy. *Behavioural Neurology, 2,* 183–194.

Hitch, G. J. (1978). The role of short-term working memory in mental arithmetic. *Cognitive Psychology, 10,* 302–322.

Hittmair-Delazer, M., Semenza, C., & Denes, G. (1994). Concepts and facts in calculation. *Brain, 117,* 715–728.

Jonides, J., Smith, E. E., Koeppe, R. A., Awh, E., Minoshima, S., & Mintun, M. A. (1993). Spatial working memory in humans as revealed by PET. *Nature, 363,* 623–625.

Logie, R. H., Gilhooly, K. J., & Wynn, V. (1994). Counting on working memory in arithmetic problem solving. *Memory and Cognition, 22,* 395–410.

Luria, A. R. (1980). *The higher cortical functions in man,* 2nd ed. New York: Basic Books.

Macaruso, P., McCloskey, M., & Aliminosa, D. (1993). The functional architecture of the cognitive numerical-processing system: Evidence from a patient with multiple impairments. *Cognitive Neuropsychology, 10,* 341–376.

Mandler, G., & Shebo, B. J. (1982). Subitizing: An analysis of its component processes. *Journal of Experimental Psychology: General, 111,* 1–21.

McCarthy, G., Blamire, A. M., Puce, A., Nobre, A. C., Bloch, G., Hyder, F., Goldman-Rakic, P., & Shulman, R. G. (1994). Functional magnetic resonance imaging of human prefrontal cortex activation during a spatial working memory task. *Proceedings of the National Academy of Sciences, 91,* 8690–8694.

McCloskey, M., Caramazza, A., & Basili, A. (1985). Cognitive mechanisms in number processing and calculation: Evidence from dyscalculia. *Brain and Cognition, 4,* 171–196.

McCloskey, M., Harley, W., & Sokol, S. M. (1991). Models of arithmetic fact retrieval: An evaluation in light of findings from normal and brain-damaged subjects. *Journal of Experimental Psychology: Learning, Memory and Cognition, 17,* 377–397.

McGonigle, B. O., Chalmers, M. (1977). Are monkeys logical? *Nature, 267* (June), 694–695.

Meck, W. H., & Church, R. M. (1983). A mode control model of counting and timing processes. *Journal of Experimental Psychology: Animal Behavior Processes, 9,* 320–334.

Milner, B. (1963). Effects of brain lesions on card sorting. *Archives of Neurology, 9,* 90–100.

Mitchell, R. W., Yao, P., Sherman, P. T., & O'Regan, M. (1985). Discriminative responding of a dolphin (*Tursiops truncatus*) to differentially rewarded stimuli. *Journal of Comparative Psychology, 99,* 218–225.

Mountcastle, V. B. (1978). An organizing principle for cerebral function: The unit module and the distributed system. In G. M. Edelman, & V. B. Mountcastle, (Eds.), *The mindful brain,* Cambridge, MA: MIT Press.

Paulesu, E., Frith, C. D., & Frackowiak, R. S. J. (1993). The neural correlates of the verbal component of working memory. *Nature, 362,* 342–345.

Posner, M. I., & Dehaene, S. (1994). Attentional networks. *Trends in Neurosciences, 17,* 75–79.

Posner, M. I., & Raichle, M. E. (1994). *Images of mind.* New York: Scientific American Library.

Roland, P. E., & Friberg, L. (1985). Localization of cortical areas activated by thinking. *Journal of Neurophysiology, 53,* 1219–1243.

Rumbaugh, D. M., Savage-Rumbaugh, S., & Hegel, M. T. (1987). Summation in the chimpanzee (*Pan troglodytes*). *Journal of Experimental Psychology: Animal Behavior Processes, 13,* 107–115.

Seymour, S. E., Reuter-Lorenz, P. A., & Gazzaniga, M. S. (1994). The disconnection syndrome: basic findings reaffirmed. *Brain, 117,* 105–115.

Shallice, T. (1988). *From neuropsychology to mental structure.* Cambridge, U.K.: Cambridge University Press.

Shallice, T., & Evans, M. E. (1978). The involvement of the frontal lobes in cognitive estimation. *Cortex, 14,* 294–303.

Sophian, C., & Adams, N. (1987). Infants' understanding of numerical transformations. *British Journal of Developmental Psychology, 5,* 257–264.

Starkey, P., & Cooper, R. G., Jr. (1980). Perception of numbers by human infants. *Science, 210,* 1033–1035.

Starkey, P., Spelke, E. S., & Gelman, R. (1983). Detection of intermodal numerical correspondences by human infants. *Science, 222,* 179–181.

Starkey, P., Spelke, E. S., & Gelman, R. (1990). Numerical abstraction by human infants. *Cognition, 36,* 97–127.

Thompson, R. F., Mayers, K. S., Robertson, R. T., & Patterson, C. J. (1970). Number coding in association cortex of the cat. *Science, 168,* 271–273.

von Fersen, L., Wynne, C. D. L., Delius, J. D., & Staddon, J. E. R. (1991). Transitive inference formation in pigeons. *Journal of Experimental Psychology: Animal Behavior Processes, 17,* 334–1341.

Whitaker, H., Habiger, J., & Ivers, R. (1985). Acalculia from a lenticular-caudate lesion. *Neurology, 35* (Suppl. 1), 161.

11 Neuropsychological Assessment of Attention and Its Disorders: Computational Models for Neglect, Extinction, and Sustained Attention

Raymond L. Ownby and Dylan G. Harwood

Patients who have undergone some form of neurological injury, most commonly that due to a cerebrovascular accident, may display a range of cognitive phenomena that suggest that they do not perceive parts of space around them. These phenomena may include such bizarre behavior as an inability to recognize the contralesional arm as the patient's own, failing to dress or shave the part of the body opposite the lesion, or an inability to attend to events occurring in the contralesional hemispace. Hemineglect may be manifest in more subtle forms, however, such as deficient performance in recognizing target letters in an array of letters placed in the contralesional hemispace, in correctly dividing a line into two equal parts, or in recognizing stimuli in the contralesional hemispace when another stimulus is simultaneously presented in the ipsilesional space.

Hemineglect and related phenomena are often associated with damage to the parietal lobe, most often with dominant parietal damage and perhaps especially that occurring in the temporoparietal junction. Patients with this sort of damage seem to behave as though the half of space contralateral to the injury does not exist. This is true even though their sensory abilities are intact—these patients do not have, for example, hemianopia for the unattended hemispace. Such patients, when their attention is directed, can often correctly identify objects in the hemispace opposite the injury. When their performance depends on their own initiative in visually exploring space around them or on acting upon objects represented bilaterally, however, their performance suggests inattention to the area opposite their neurological lesion (see Rafal, 1997, for a more complete review of the cognitive manifestations of neglect). The presence of neglect is usually most dramatic after acute focal injuries, but may persist after a considerable period of recovery.

Neuropsychologists have devised a number of measures to assess neglect-related phenomena. Two tasks that have been used to assess neglect are the *line bisection* and *letter cancellation*. In the line bisection task, the patient is asked to draw a line dividing a previously printed line in two. Patients who display neglect place the lines they draw to one side or another, away from the part of space they neglect. Rather than neatly cutting the line in two, for

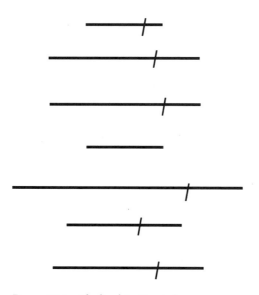

Figure 11.1 The line bisection task.

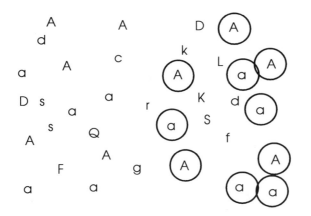

Figure 11.2 The letter cancellation task.

example, a patient with right parietal damage is likely to place the line far to the right of the line's true midline. This suggests that the patient does not notice, or experience, the left half of space. A similar phenomenon occurs with left (more properly, dominant) parietal damage, although less frequently. (See figure 11.1 for examples.) The reason for this difference is discussed below.

In the letter cancellation task (figure 11.2), the patient is presented with an array of various letters, often of various sizes and in various orientations. The patient's task is to detect all instances of a target letter and to mark them. Patients who exhibit neglect will not notice the target letter in the neglected hemispace.

Various other sensory phenomena are associated with hemineglect, among them *sensory extinction*. Some patients who do not exhibit obvious sensory neglect may not recognize one of two stimuli presented to them simultaneously and bilaterally. For example, a patient touched lightly on either the right or left arm may readily recognize unilateral stimulation, but will recognize only one stimulus when touched bilaterally. The patient will fail to recognize the stimulus presented contralateral to the parietal injury. The most commonly accepted interpretation of this phenomenon is that sensory extinction is a subtle form of neglect.

Several mechanisms have been described to account for neglect and extinction, encompassing both cognitive and anatomical explanations (see Heilman, Watson, & Valenstein, 1993, for a more complete review). Some have argued, for example, that deficits in line bisection or letter cancellation tasks result from lack of attention to the hemispace contralateral to the injury, and perhaps may be due to dysfunction of a mechanism by which the patient disengages his or her attention from the ipsilateral hemispace. Evidence for and against this type of *attentional* neglect has been presented (Coslett, Bowers, Fitzpatrick, et al., 1990). Others have argued that deficient performances on these tasks stem from a directional hypokinesia that becomes evident when the examiner demands a motor performance from the patient. Similarly, evidence for and against this type of *intentional* neglect also exists (Coslett et al., 1990).

An explanation for extinction in the context of preserved sensation for unilateral stimuli is less obvious. One explanation that is intuitively appealing is that cortical or subcortical damage may result in weakened representations of stimuli appearing in the hemispace contralateral to the damaged hemisphere. Even though the patient may be aware of such weakened representations of stimuli when they are presented unilaterally, they may be below the threshold of awareness when they compete with intact representations in the ipsilateral hemispace. These accounts of neglect are cognitive in that they rely on mental constructs such as perceptual representations for their explanation of neglect. Others have focused on the anatomy of attention and its disorders.

Mesulam and his colleagues (Mesulam, 1981, 1990; Morecraft, Geula, & Mesulam, 1993), for example, present a coherent anatomical account of a neural system for the control of directed attention. Many neglect-associated phenomena can be understood as resulting from damage to various parts of this system. Mesulam argues that an anatomical neural network comprising portions of frontal, parietal, and cingulate cortices in addition to parts of the basal ganglia and thalamus is responsible for the direction of attention in primates (figure 11.3). Each anatomical component makes a specific contribution to the diverse cognitive components underlying attention. The parietal component helps develop a representation of space, and the frontal component, Mesulam (1990) suggests, "provides a map for the distribution of

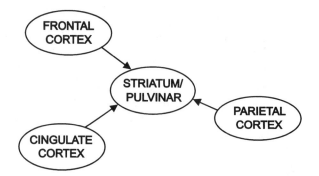

Figure 11.3 Schematic of the anatomical network.

orienting and exploratory movements ... " (p. 598). The portion of cingulate cortex involved in the network "provides a map for assigning value to spatial coordinates" (p. 598). Importantly, anatomical studies have shown that the organization of this network is consistent with a parallel distributed processing model (Mesulam, 1990; Morecraft et al., 1993). Subcomponents of the network are internally cross-connected in such a way that they function as independent but interconnected processing modules.

Its modular architecture makes this anatomical network especially suitable for computational simulation—the anatomical network can be represented by a computational architecture that is similar in its structure and function. Other investigators (e.g., Cohen, Romero, Servan-Schreiber, et al., 1994) have used computational modeling to investigate attention-related phenomena. Cohen et al. (1994), for example, showed that a neural network for attention could show evidence of hemineglect without requiring a specific "disengage" mechanism. These authors argued that the apparent disengage mechanism was an emergent property of the neural network. In this way, Cohen et al. showed that computational modeling can help in understanding attention-related phenomena.

The anatomical network proposed by Mesulam and others also probably utilizes parallel distributed processing (Morecraft et al., 1993). It is thus reasonable to create an artificial network that could simulate the anatomical network's activity using a similar computational architecture. Such a simulation would also allow study of the effects of various types of perceptual stimuli and lesions on the behavior of the network as well. In this manner, the effects of lesioning could be observed to determine whether a network that simulates normal attentional processes would also simulate cognitive phenomena associated with lesions, such as deficits in line bisection or letter cancellation or perceptual extinction in the context of bilateral simultaneous stimulation. The purpose of these studies was thus to determine whether an artificial neural network could accurately simulate normal and disordered attentional processes in neglect-associated processes.

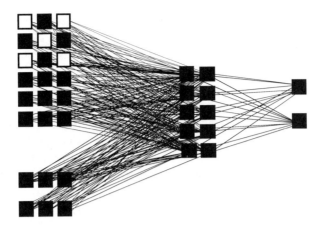

Figure 11.4 Implementation of the network.

A secondary goal was to show that the same network architecture could simulate disordered attentional processes seen in another disorder, attention-deficit hyperactivity disorder. The purpose of this simulation was to determine whether the network model created to simulate one disorder could accurately simulate an unrelated disorder that presumably also depends on dysfunction of the same anatomical structures.

These studies should be regarded as preliminary since they involve a simulation of the anatomical network that is improbably simple. These preliminary studies are presented here to illustrate the ways in which computational modeling can facilitate understanding of neuropsychological phenomena.

COMPUTATIONAL MODELS

Study 1: Normal Attentional Processes

Method The essential components of the network include portions of the parietal, cingulate, and frontal cortices, as well as portions of the striatum. Figure 11.4 illustrates the organization of the anatomical network as implemented in the artificial network. An input array of two sets of nine units with dimensions three units three units simulates parietal cortex. The first three columns represent the left cortex, and the next three represent the right. The nine elements in each half of this array allow digital presentation of either an X or an O to either the right or left hemispace (see figure 11.4). An X can thus be encoded as 1's representing a dark pixel and 0's representing a light (imagine drawing two lines that connect the 1's):

1 0 1
0 1 0
1 0 1

The letter O can similarly be represented as illustrated in figure 11.4.

The next two groups of input units represent frontal and cingulate cortices (the two lower arrays of input units at the left of figure 11.4). Various patterns in the frontal units simulate different levels of exploratory activity—these change to represent different intensities of attention to the right or left hemispace. Cingulate units simulate increasing motivational levels demanded by increased exploratory behavior. A set of ten hidden units represents the integrative function of the striatum and pulvinar; two output units allow a readout of whether the input pattern is an X or an O, whether it was presented in the right or left hemispace, and its distance from the midline. Outputs of 0.7, 0.8, and 0.9 represented an X at different distances from the midline, with larger values correlated with increased inputs to the frontal units, while outputs of 0.3, 0.2, 0.1 in the same way represented O's. An output of 0.5 represented neutral attention, or a midline position in space. The network was constructed and trained using a backpropagation algorithm using available network simulation software (the Stuttgart Neural Network Simulator; Zell, Mamier, & Vogt, 1996). As learning in a backpropagation network is susceptible to the effects of local minima, a total of five networks was constructed and trained.

Results

A mean squared error value of less than 0.001 was readily obtained over 4000 learning trials for each network. Comparison of network outputs showed that none differed significantly (all P's > .10). Results for one network are thus presented here. Comparison of network outputs before and after training showed that training changed outputs so that they were correct (table 11.1; compare columns under "Correct," "Untrained," and

Table 11.1 Training set and results of lesioning

Correct		Untrained		Trained		10% Lesion		20% Lesion		30% Lesion	
Left	Right	Left	Right	Left	Right	Left	Right	Left	Right	Left	Right
.700	.500	.702	.578	.699	.500	.633	.642	.567	.610	.495	.443
.800	.500	.745	.531	.802	.499	.741	.670	.669	.651	.479	.503
.900	.500	.664	.568	.898	.501	.861	.699	.769	.729	.514	.638
.300	.500	.654	.558	.300	.500	.284	.679	.276	.719	.383	.776
.200	.500	.688	.556	.199	.501	.210	.722	.208	.788	.302	.843
.100	.500	.648	.601	.103	.499	.118	.714	.123	.790	.171	.834
.500	.700	.596	.425	.500	.700	.500	.700	.500	.700	.500	.700
.500	.800	.600	.473	.500	.802	.500	.802	.500	.802	.500	.802
.500	.900	.675	.405	.500	.897	.500	.897	.500	.897	.500	.897
.500	.300	.452	.693	.500	.299	.500	.299	.500	.299	.500	.299
.500	.200	.611	.666	.500	.199	.500	.199	.500	.199	.500	.199
.500	.100	.238	.674	.500	.103	.500	.103	.500	.103	.500	.103

"Trained"). Inspection of the network's trained outputs indicates that the network readily learned to discriminate whether an X or an O was presented to it in either the right or left hemispace, and the distance from the midline at which it was presented. This first study thus confirmed that the general strategy of creating a backpropagation network that would simulate normal attentional processes could be successful. It thus was warranted to proceed to the next phase of developing the model, simulating neglect.

Study 2: Simulation of Hemineglect

Method Experimental lesions of artificial neural networks have been used to study the effects of neurological injuries in clinically studied disorders such as dyslexia (Hinton & Shallice, 1991) and Alzheimer's disease (Tippett & Farah, 1994). Units, or connections between units, may be removed from the network to simulate the effects of damage to the simulated underlying neural structures. These lesions thus presumably represent damage to specific areas of cortex or to the fiber tracts connecting these structures. In this study, different numbers of connections between input and hidden units were deleted to create different levels of injury severity. Connections were deleted from primarily the right- or left-sided input units to simulate lateralized neurological injury. Connections were randomly deleted from the entire network to simulate the effects of diffuse injury, to assess the effects of this type of injury on network performance. It was hypothesized that unilateral injuries would simulate hemineglect, while diffuse injury would reduce network accuracy without affecting in which hemispace stimuli were perceived. As before, a total of five networks were constructed, trained, and tested in each condition to assure that findings from any single network were not due to local minima achieved in the learning process (Ownby, 1995; 1996a).

Results Results did not differ significantly across networks, and results for one representative network are thus presented in table 11.1. Results of right, left, and diffuse experimental lesions were consistent with the hypothesized relations; Table 11.1 illustrates simulated right hemisphere injury. Correct network responses are listed in the first column for comparison. With experimental lesions generally, the performance of the network slowly became less accurate with lesions of increasing severity. At more severe levels of unilateral injury, the network's performance suggested a tendency to report that stimuli were present in the hemispace contralateral to the injury, consistent with clinically observed hemineglect. Inspection of the "Left" column, for example, under "20% Lesion" shows that the accuracy of the leftward response was reduced, while the magnitude of the response in the right output was significantly increased (Wilcoxon Matched-Paris Signed-Ranks test; $z = -2.20$; $P = .03$). Decreased magnitude of leftward response and increased magnitude of rightward response in a right hemisphere–lesioned network is thus consistent with neglect. It may be recalled that patients with right hemisphere lesions are expected to neglect the left side of space and to demonstrate increased attention to the right hemispace. Left hemisphere lesions produced similar results. Diffuse lesions, as hypothesized, reduced the network's accuracy, but did not produce lateralization. The network based on Mesulam's anatomical model thus, at least at this rudimentary level, simulated both normal and disordered attentional processes.

Study 3: Simulation of Attention-Deficit Hyperactivity Disorder

Attention-deficit hyperactivity disorder (ADHD) is a psychiatric condition most often diagnosed among children, who may present evidence of disordered attention, motivation, and behavioral or emotional regulation. A hallmark of the disorder, however, is the patient's difficulties in sustaining attention so that he or she is described as unable to pay attention in the classroom or to complete other activities that require sustained attention.

Patients with this disorder often also have difficulties in sustaining attention on the continuous performance test (CPT). This measure requires that a patient monitor some form of display on which test stimuli are presented, and make a response when a target stimulus appears. Most often, the patient is required to differentiate relevant from irrelevant stimuli, for example, by detecting instances of the letter *r* in a serial presentation of other letters.

Difficulties in sustaining attention are also observed in patients who have sustained neurological insults. Although attentional problems may be seen in patients with focal injuries, they are also seen in patients who have undergone relatively mild but diffuse trauma, as may occur in patients with closed head injuries (Gronwall, 1989). It thus seems likely that a disorder of the network for directed attention might underlie the sorts of attentional deficits observed in clinical populations. This problem thus could be investigated by simulation of normal and disordered performance on a measure of sustained attention, the CPT. Different types of lesions might be investigated with the purpose of assessing what types and foci of lesions might cause deficits in performance on a simulation of the CPT.

Method The network described above was trained and then subjected to random lesions of varying degrees of severity. In this instance, however, the network was trained to respond with 0.1 for all letters other than *X*, for which it gave an output of 0.9. Lesions were not lateralized and stimuli were presented bilaterally (Ownby, 1996b). The network's performance was assessed before and after training and after each stage of lesioning.

Results Results show that minor degrees of lesioning did not substantially affect the network's performance. Lesions of greater extent, however, resulted in substantial decrements in performance. Inspection of the network's outputs showed that although accuracy declined with increasing severity of lesion, outputs did not suggest increased or decreased attention to either hemispace. The network thus accurately simulated one aspect of patients' performance on the CPT—decreased accuracy in detecting a target stimulus.

Study 4: Simulation of Line Bisection and Letter Cancellation

As reviewed above, several authors have suggested that distinct behavioral types of neglect behavior may occur and that these subtypes are related to the locus of the underlying neurological injury. For example, frontal injury is said to impair letter cancellation performance more than line bisection, since the patient with this type of lesion may have a deficit in the exploratory behavior required for performance of this task. Conversely, patients with parietal injury may perform worse on line bisection tasks, perhaps because they are relatively more impaired in the visuospatial abilities required for performance on this task. The purpose of this study was to investigate whether an artificial neural network constructed to simulate the different contributions of parietal and frontal cortex to performance on these tasks could do so (Ownby, 1996a).

Method A three-layer backpropagation network was again constructed, with the input layer representing the three cortical elements of the corresponding anatomical network as before. The middle, or hidden, layer, represented the intersection of inputs and outputs of the cortical units in the striatum and pulvinar. Two output units represented either line bisection or letter cancellation outputs. The network was trained to an acceptable level of accuracy (less than a mean squared error of 0.001); one output unit was trained to make judgments about the position of letters at three positions either to the right or left of midline, while the other output unit made similar judgments in a line bisection task. The organization of training data made the letter cancellation task more dependent on frontal inputs, while the line bisection task was more dependent on parietal inputs. The network was then experimentally lesioned in several ways, including presenting it with degraded information and by removing connections between layers. These methods represent damage to cortical areas or to fiber tracts.

Results After training, the network was able to perform both letter cancellation and line bisection tasks at a 100 percent correct level of accuracy. Lesions resulted in degraded network performance, with "frontal" lesions producing greater decrements in network performance on letter cancellation tasks, whereas "parietal" lesions produced greater decrements in line bisection task performance. Lesions, however, produced some decrements in performance in the ipsilateral as well as contralateral hemispace on both tasks.

Study 5: Simulation of Extinction

Method A three-layer network was constructed employing a counter-propagation architecture (Hertz, Krogh, & Palmer, 1991). Using this architecture, the input layer accepted numerical data coded to represent either an X or O presented in either the left or right visual or tactile field. Employing an unsupervised, or Kohonen, learning algorithm, this layer and its connections with the next represents a pattern recognition device. The middle, or hidden, layer, fed pattern recognition information forward to four output units. These units were trained with a supervised learning algorithm to produce different numerical values when input sensory units were presented with digitized versions of an X, O, or no pattern (the processing layer). These layers thus functioned as a cognitive processing layer, accepting information about sensory patterns presented to the network and producing reduced output about the nature and position of those patterns.

The network was created and then trained as described above to a low level of error (mean squared error <0.001). The network was trained with examples using only one stimulus to one sensory field on any single learning trial. The network was then experimentally lesioned in several ways to simulate damage to fiber tracts or cortical areas as might occur in stroke. The network was assessed at different levels of lesioning (10, 25, or 50 percent of units or links) and with lesions in the areas simulating the right or left hemisphere. Both before and after lesioning, the network was presented with test stimuli simultaneously to both sensory fields to simulate its behavior under conditions of simultaneous bilateral stimulation. Outputs were recorded to assess the effects of site and extent of lesions (Ownby, 1997a, b)

Results The network was readily able to distinguish the two letters in sensory hemifields. Observation of the network showed that when the hidden layer contained the same number of elements as patterns, one element in the hidden layer was active for each distinct pattern. This result suggested that the pattern recognition portion of the network was appropriately trained. Outputs from the output layer after training were 100 percent accurate. For example, when pattern information for an X in the left hemifield was presented to it, the network consistently reported that an X was presented to the correct hemifield. This was true for all other possible combinations of pattern inputs and outputs. Presentation of bilateral inputs to the network reduced network accuracy. Rather than produce two correct outputs when presented with two stimuli, the network produced one correct output for each pattern, resulting in 50 percent accuracy.

Lesioning in both pattern recognition and supervised learning layers produced results consistent with inattention phenomena. Removal of small numbers of links (e.g., 10 percent) had little effect on network outputs. Removal of larger numbers, however, reduced network performances in both single and simultaneous bilateral presentation conditions. Bilateral simultaneous stimulation of lesioned networks showed that they were relatively more sensitive to the effects of this condition; their performance was degraded (to less than 50 percent correct) before lesions produced performance decrements in the same networks to unilateral presentation. Removal of larger numbers of links produced performance decrements in both conditions. As in the previous study, removal of large portions of the network on either side produced network outputs consistent with the clinical phenomenon of hemineglect. Lesions of the perceptual recognition layer were more likely to result in errors suggesting inattention of the contralateral hemispace, while errors in the processing layer resulted in both contralateral perceptual errors but also misrecognitions (e.g., reporting a O for an X).

DISCUSSION

These results show that a computational model based on the modular parallel distributed processing architecture of the anatomical network proposed by Mesulam can accurately simulate normal attention as well as some aspects of its disorders. These simple models demonstrate that a computational model can thus accurately simulate directed attention to either hemispace at different levels of exploratory effort and with different motivational saliences. It also shows how computational modeling can be used to investigate neuropsychological phenomena. Such modeling can thus shed light on the mechanisms affecting cognitive test performance in normal and disordered patients (see Cohen, Servan-Schreiber, Targ, et al., 1992, for example, for a discussion of modeling aspects of neuropsychological test performance in schizophrenia). The models' success lends at least indirect support for Mesulam and colleagues' proposed anatomical network that may underlie directed attention.

Enthusiasm for the successes of these elementary models in simulating attention, however, should be tempered by consideration of the things about attention that they do not simulate. For example, although the model simulates some aspects of normal and disordered performance on the CPT, it does not generate false-positive responses (when the person tested erroneously responds that the target is there when some other stimulus is present). The present model simulates reduced accuracy in detecting the target stimulus, false-negatives (one aspect of disordered performance on the CPT), but cannot reproduce the clinically observed converse. It can be speculated that impulsive false-positive responses may be generated by the interaction of a responding system that is unsuccessfully regulated by a detection and control system. Further development of the attentional model presented here might provide an improved simulation of false-positive responses in ADHD.

Another important aspect of attentional phenomena and its disorders that is not adequately explained by this model is the relatively greater importance of nondominant (usually, right) parietal cortex in the development of hemisensory neglect. It is widely assumed that this effect is the result of nondominant parietal cortex specialization for the perception and integration of spatial information. The present model implicitly assumes that the function of both right and left parietal cortex is the same; this assumption is clearly incorrect. Again, further development of the model may more adequately simulate the function of the anatomical network.

Yet another consideration in evaluating this model is the extent to which the network architecture chosen for it is appropriate. It may be more appropriate to simulate the parietal cortex element of the network by using a network architecture that is more suitable to simulation of the perceptual and integrative role of parietal cortex. As demonstrated in study 5 (simulation of sensory suppression or extinction), a self-organizing or Kohonen input layer (see Hertz et al. for a more detailed explanation) simulated the perceptual function implicit in the functioning of the parietal cortex. This sort of hybrid network may thus more accurately simulate the different functions of the different modules composing the network.

Given these limitations, it may seem surprising that this model works as well as it does in reproducing at least some of the phenomena associated with normal and disordered attention. As has been seen, it does a fairly good job at some things, and demonstrates how computational modeling can be used to address questions about neuropsychological phenomena. Further development of the model may address some of the model's failings and allow it to more accurately reproduce attention-related phenomena. This development is in progress.

REFERENCES

Cohen, J. D., Romero, R. D., Servan-Schreiber, D., & Farah, M. J. (1994). Mechanisms of spatial attention: The relation of macrostructure to microstructure in parietal neglect. *Journal of Cognitive Neuroscience, 6,* 377–387.

Cohen, J. D., Servan-Schreiber, D., Targ, E., & Spiegel, D. (1992). The fabric of thought disorder: A cognitive neuroscience approach to disturbances in the processing of context in schizophrenia. In D. Stein & J. Young (Eds.), *Cognitive science and clinical disorders* (pp. 99–126). New York: Academic Press.

Coslett, H. B., Bowers, D., Fitzpatrick, E., Haws, B., & Heilman, K. M. (1990). Directional hypokinesia and hemispatial inattention in neglect. *Brain, 113,* 475–486.

Gronwall, D. (1989). Cumulative and persisting effects of concussion on attention and cognition. In H. S. Levin, H. M. Eisenberg, & A. L. Benton (Eds.), *Mild head injury* (pp. 153–162). New York: Oxford University Press.

Heilman, K. M., Watson, R. T., & Valenstein, E. (1993). Neglect and related disorders. In K. M. Heilman & E. Valenstein (Eds.), *Clinical neuropsychology,* (3rd ed.). New York: Oxford University Press.

Hertz, J., Krogh, A., & Palmer, R. G. (1991). *Introduction to the theory of neural computation.* Reading, MA: Addison-Wesley.

Hinton, G. E., & Shallice, T. (1991). Lesioning an attractor network: Investigations of acquired dyslexia. *Psychological Review, 98,* 74–95.

Mesulam, M-M. (1981) A cortical network for directed attention and unilateral neglect. *Annals of Neurology, 10,* 309–325.

Mesulam, M-M. (1990). Large-scale neurocognitive networks and distributed processing for attention, language, and memory. *Annals of Neurology, 28,* 597–613.

Morecraft, R. J., Geula, C., & Mesulam, M-M. (1993). Architecture of connectivity within a cingulo-frontal-parietal neurocognitive network for directed attention. *Archives of Neurology, 50,* 279–284.

Ownby R. L. (1995). A computational model of stroke-related hemineglect: Preliminary development. Presented at the Workshop on Neural Modeling of Cognitive and Brain Disorders, University of Maryland Institute for Advanced Computing Studies, University of Maryland, College Park, MD.

Ownby, R. L. (1996a). A computational model of stroke-related hemineglect (abstract). *Journal of the International Neuropsychological Society, 9,* 38.

Ownby, R. L. (1996b). A computational model of attention-deficit/hyperactivity disorder (abstract). *Journal of the International Neuropsychological Society, 9,* 24.

Ownby, R. L. (1997a). A neural network model of sensory suppression. Presented at the annual meeting of the International Neuropsychological Society, Orlando, FL, February 1997.

Ownby, R. L. (1997b). Sensory neglect after stroke: A simulation. Presented at the annual meeting of the Cognitive Neuroscience Society, Boston, March 1997.

Rafal, R. D. (1997). Hemispatial neglect: Cognitive neuropsychological aspects. In T. E. Feinberg and M. J. Farah (Eds.), *Behavioral neurology and neuropsychology* (pp. 319–335). New York: McGraw-Hill.

Tippett, L. J., & Farah, M. J. (1994). A computational model of naming in Alzheimer's disease: Unitary or multiple impairments? *Neuropsychology, 8,* 3–13.

Zell, A., Mamier, G., & Vogt, M. (1996). Stuttgart Neural Network Simulator, user manual, version 4.1. Stuttgart, Germany: Institute for Parallel and Distributed High Performance Systems, University of Stuttgart. [The World Wide Web page on the simulator is available at: http://www.informatik.uni-stuttgart.de/ipvr/bv/projekte/snns/snns.html. The software is available for download at: ftp://ftp.informatik.uni-stuttgart.de/pub/SNNS.]

12 The Neural Basis of Lexical Retrieval

Daniel Tranel, Hanna Damasio, and Antonio R. Damasio

In neuropsychology, there is a long tradition of studies concerned with the question of which neural structures support the process whereby, in the course of speaking, writing, or thinking, we retrieve words denoting various entities, actions, and relationships. For many decades, the common answer to this question has focused on left hemisphere structures in and around the sylvian fissure, and in particular, on the Wernicke and Broca areas. This focus derives in large measure from studies in brain-damaged patients with aphasia, in whom word-retrieval (naming) defects are highly frequent. An assumption in this answer is that the classic language areas are activated directly by nonlanguage areas which support the concepts for which pertinent words are being retrieved; so, for example, the process of perceiving and recognizing a familiar face ("my mother"), supported by structures in occipital and occipitotemporal cortices, would in turn activate word-retrieval structures in the perisylvian language areas that would generate the appropriate name ("Virginia"). Based on new findings from lesion studies (H. Damasio, Grabowski, Tranel, et al., 1996; Tranel, Damasio, & Damasio, 1997a) and functional imaging studies (H. Damasio et al., 1996; Martin, Haxby, Lalonde, et al., 1995; Mazoyer, Tzourio, Frak, et al., 1993; Petersen, Fox, Posner, et al., 1988), as well as related work using electrophysiological techniques (Dehaene, 1995; Lesser, Gordon, & Uematsu, 1994; Nobre, Allison, & McCarthy, 1994; Nobre & McCarthy, 1995; Ojemann, 1991), we have proposed an alternative answer.

Specifically, we have proposed that although perisylvian structures (including early auditory and somatomotor cortices) are indeed involved in the transient reconstruction and explicit phonemic representation of word forms, additional neural sites mediate between the structures that support conceptual knowledge, and the perisylvian structures. These mediational structures thus trigger and conduct the process of word reconstruction (H. Damasio et al., 1996; Tranel et al., 1997a). Our account incorporates the notion that the retrieval of word forms depends on the transient reactivation of the phonemic and morphologic structure of given words within the appropriate early sensory cortices (e.g., auditory, somatosensory, visual) and motor-related structures (A. R. Damasio, 1990; A. R. Damasio & Damasio,

1992); the traditional Wernicke and Broca areas are partly contained within such sensory and motor structures. However, we propose that the phonemic-morphologic reactivation pertaining to a given word is directed from a variety of regions located in higher-order association cortices, but largely *outside* the early sensory and motor sites alluded to above, and, consequently, largely outside the traditional language areas. Those regions operate as "third-party" neural mediators between, on the one hand, the regions that support conceptual knowledge (which are distributed over varied association cortices), and, on the other, the sensorimotor regions in which the phonemic-morphologic structure can be transiently reconstructed during the word-recall process (e.g., naming), or instantiated during the perception of a word (e.g., reading).

We believe that for most persons, these regions are located in the left hemisphere, and are used as *lexical mediation units* (H. Damasio et al., 1996). Once activated by the evocation of a given concept, these units, which do not contain phonemic-morphologic information in explicit form, promote the activation of the linguistic information necessary to reconstruct a word form, momentarily, in sensorimotor terms. These units also promote activation of syntactic information necessary for the proper placement of a word in the phrases and sentences being planned. In schematic form then, this is a tripartite model in which mediational structures interlink between conceptual and implementation structures, in two directions: from conceptual structure to the word-form reconstruction required for language acts, and in reverse, from the perception of a word toward its usual conceptual structure correspondences. Our account is compatible with Levelt's (1989, 1992) proposal of lexical mediation units termed "lemmas," based on cognitive experiments in normal subjects, which has also been applied to retrieval of words for actions (Roelofs, 1993).

The general theoretical background for this proposal is the framework for synchronous retroactivation from convergence and divergence zones (A. R. Damasio, 1989a, b; A. R. Damasio & Damasio, 1994; see also Kosslyn, 1994). The framework posits that retrieval of concepts depends on the reconstruction of images or actions pertaining to characteristics and properties of entities. The images and movements themselves are reconstructed transiently in sectors of early sensory and motor structures. However, the reconstruction is directed from separate system components in higher-order association cortices, which contain dynamic regions which interlock feedforward and feedback projection neurons. Those regions, the convergence-divergence zones, thus hold a preferential but probability-driven and modifiable dispositional capacity to signal directly or intermediately to sensory or motor regions, whenever the zone receives appropriate signals.

Below, we review new work from our laboratory, which has dealt with several specific issues concerning word retrieval and the lexical mediation systems elaborated above. The first issue we addressed is whether the neural systems on which conceptual knowledge retrieval depends are separable from the neural systems on which word retrieval depends. Also, we tested the idea that lexical mediation systems would be located in the left hemisphere, and in particular, the question of whether the retrieval of words denoting concrete entities belonging to different conceptual categories would depend on relatively separable regions in higher-order cortices in the left temporal lobe. We also explored the hypothesis that different types of words—for instance, words for entities (nouns) vs. words for actions (verbs)—would depend on separate neural regions.

A few comments on terminology are in order. We use the designation *concrete entities* to refer to persons, animals, fruits and vegetables, tools and utensils, and other items that belong to varied conceptual classes, and that can be designated by an appropriately specific word (a proper or common noun). Concrete entities are mapped in the brain at different levels of *contextual complexity*. This permits us to classify a given entity along a dimension that ranges from *unique* (an entity belonging to a class with $N = 1$ and depending on a highly complex context for its definition), to varied *nonunique* levels (entities processed as belonging to classes with $N > 1$, having many members whose definition depends on less complex contexts). Also, as alluded to above, it is important to distinguish between retrieval of *conceptual* knowledge about entities, on the one hand, which relates to the traditional term *recognition* (i.e., "knowing" what an item is), and retrieval of the *word forms* for entities, which refers to the traditional term *naming*. In our experiments, we required subjects to recognize and to name unique entities (persons) at a *subordinate* level, and to recognize and to name nonunique entities at a *basic object* level (cf. Rosch, Mervis, Gray, et al., 1976).

The hypotheses were approached by studying patients with neurological lesions in various components of the large-scale neural system presumed to be related to the language lexicon. The demonstration of a defect in the retrieval of words relative to particular categories of entities was used as evidence for the relation between the putative system and the access to the lexicon for that particular conceptual category in the normal human brain. We also mention briefly some of our new work with functional imaging (positron emission tomography, PET).

RETRIEVAL OF WORDS FOR NONUNIQUE CONCRETE ENTITIES

Background

For over a decade, investigators in several laboratories have noted intriguing dissociations in naming ability in patients with and without aphasia (A. R. Damasio, Damasio, & Van Hoesen, 1982; Warrington & McCarthy, 1983; Hart Berndt, & Caramazza, 1985; Pietrini, Nertempi, Vaglia, et al., 1988; Basso, Capitani, & Laiacona, 1988; A. R. Damasio, 1990; Franklin, Howard, & Patterson, 1995; Goodglass & Budin, 1988; Goodglass, Wingfield, Hyde, et al., 1986; see also Small, Hart, Nguyen, et al., 1995). These observations suggested that, following a lesion, naming of items from various conceptual categories was not equally compromised across categories. The possibility was raised that there were different neural systems required for the retrieval of words for different classes of concepts.

One frequent finding has been that brain-damaged patients demonstrate greater impairment in naming living (natural, animate) entities, as compared to artifactual (nonliving, manmade, inanimate) ones (Basso et al., 1988; Hart & Gordon, 1992; Hillis & Caramazza, 1991; Pietrini et al., 1988; Satori & Job, 1988; Silveri & Gainotti, 1988). In a few cases, the defect for living entities has been reported as being disproportionately severe for one particular category—for instance, it has been found that either the category of animals (Hart & Gordon, 1992) or that of fruits and vegetables (Hart et al., 1985; Farah & Wallace, 1992) was relatively more affected. In some cases, such patterns have been reported in connection with name comprehension—that is, patients had disproportionate impairment in the comprehension of names of living entities, compared to comprehension of names of artifacts (McCarthy & Warrington, 1988; Warrington & McCarthy, 1987). A few cases have been reported in which the dissociation occurred in the other direction—that is, artifacts were disproportionately impaired, and living entities were relatively spared (Hillis & Caramazza, 1991; Sacchett & Humphreys, 1992; Tippett, Glosser, & Farah, 1996; Warrington & McCarthy, 1983). Other patterns of defects have also been reported, for example, disproportionate impairment of name comprehension for body parts (Goodglass & Budin, 1988), or relatively spared naming of body parts (Goodglass et al., 1986).

Dissociations between the ability to process abstract words vs. concrete words have also been reported. For example, patients may lose the ability to process concrete words, but remain capable of processing abstract words (A. R. Damasio & Tranel, 1990; A. R. Damasio, Damasio, Tranel, et al., 1990; Warrington, 1975, 1981; Warrington & Shallice, 1984). The reverse pattern has also been reported, that is, a patient whose defect in word retrieval was especially marked for abstract words, and who was less "anomic" for concrete words (Franklin et al., 1995).

Few of the studies cited above were hypothesis-driven, and most consisted of single-case reports. There was often incomplete sampling of the relevant categories. Another factor which hinders the interpretation of previous findings is the inconsistent use of *naming*, on the one hand, and *recognition*, on the other. These capacities are quite separable, and they are frequently dissociated in brain-damaged patients (see Tranel, Damasio, & Damasio, 1997b). Nonetheless, some investigators have used the two concepts interchangeably (e.g., Martin, Wiggs, Ungerleider, et al., 1996; Farah, Meyer, & McMullen, 1996; Riddoch & Humphreys, 1987; Sacchett & Humphreys, 1992), and it is therefore difficult to understand what was actually wrong with the patient or what process was actually being studied. (It should be acknowledged, however, that in normal subjects, recognition and naming may be difficult to dissociate, since the naming of an item that is shown for recognition cannot be voluntarily suppressed.)

The most important limitation in the extant literature as far as the neural basis of lexical retrieval is concerned, is that neuroanatomical data are quite limited. In most cases, the neuroanatomical status of the patient was mentioned only in passing, and the lesions were not analyzed systematically. Subjects were often grouped together because they shared some aspect of their cognitive profiles, regardless of their lesion status, and inspection of such groups frequently reveals the subjects to have lesions in many different areas of the brain, even different hemispheres.

We conducted a systematic study regarding word retrieval (A. R. Damasio et al., 1990; see also A. R. Damasio, 1990), in which the idea that there are separate neural systems involved in the naming performance for different lexical categories was supported. In another study, we were able to obtain postmortem evidence for selective involvement of left temporal cortices in a case of progressive loss of word retrieval for concrete entities (Graff-Radford, Damasio, Hyman, et al., 1990). Recent studies from our laboratory have confirmed and extended the initial findings (H. Damasio et al., 1996; Tranel, Logan, Frank, et al., 1997).

New Lesion Studies

We have added to previous findings on the breakdown of retrieval of words for nonunique entities by pursuing systematically their possible neural correlates (A. R. Damasio, 1992; A. R. Damasio, Brandt, Tranel, et al., 1991; A. R. Damasio & Damasio, 1992; A. R. Damasio, Damasio, Tranel, et al., 1990; A. R. Damasio & Tranel, 1990, 1993; H. Damasio et al., 1996; Tranel, 1991; Tranel et al., 1997a).

In the studies summarized below, we tested the following hypotheses: (1) retrieval of words denoting concrete entities depends on neural structures that are anatomically distinct from the neural structures on which concept retrieval (recognition) for the same entities depends; (2) retrieval of words related to separate conceptual categories of concrete entities (animals, fruits and vegetables, tools and utensils) is mediated by distinct neural systems.

Subjects

Brain-Damaged Subjects To address the hypotheses stated above, we conducted visual recognition and naming experiments in 127 brain-damaged subjects with single, unilateral lesions. Based on measurement with the Geschwind-Oldfield questionnaire, 115 subjects were right-handed, 6 were left-handed, and 6 had mixed-handedness. The subjects were selected from the division's patient registry so that as a group, they would permit us to sample the entire telencephalon. The subjects had lesions located in the left or right hemisphere, and in varied regions of the cerebral cortex, caused by either cerebrovascular disease (n = 106), herpes simplex encephalitis (n = 5), or temporal lobectomy (n = 16). All had IQs in the average range or higher; had a high-school education or higher; had been extensively characterized neuropsychologically and neuroanatomically; and had no difficulty with the attentive inspection of visual stimuli. None of the subjects had severe aphasia at the time of these experiments.

Control Subjects Normal control subjects (n = 55) were drawn from our visual recognition and naming studies described elsewhere (A. R. Damasio et al., 1990). They were matched to the brain-damaged subjects on age, education, and gender distribution. (Gender-related effects on visual recognition and naming are generally of fairly small magnitude [e.g., McKenna & Parry, 1994], with the most consistent finding being that women are better than men at naming fruits and vegetables, and men are better than women at naming animals. Hence, we used proportionate numbers of men and women in the brain-damaged and control groups, rather than analyzing the data separately by gender.)

Stimuli The stimuli for the study were 300 nonunique entities, comprising 161 of the black-and-white line drawings from the Snodgrass and Vanderwart set (1980), and 139 additional black-and-white and color photographs. Five categories are represented in the stimulus set: animals (n = 90), fruits and vegetables (n = 67), tools and utensils (n = 104), vehicles (n = 23), and musical instruments (n = 16). Here, we report results for the animals, fruits and vegetables, and tools and utensils categories.

Procedure The entities were depicted on slides and shown in random order one by one on a Caramate 4000 slide projector, in free field. For each, the subject was asked to tell the experimenter what the entity is ("What is this?"). If the subject produced a vague or superordinate-level response (e.g., "Some kind of animal"), the subject was prompted to "Be more specific; tell me exactly what you think that thing is." Time limits were not imposed. All responses were audiotaped.

Neuropsychological Data Quantification For each stimulus, the response of each brain-damaged patient was scored as correct if it matched the response of normal controls. For each experiment, we first determined which stimuli the patient *recognized* (see A. R. Damasio et al., 1990). In brief, a recognition response was scored as correct if either of two conditions was met: (1) the stimulus was named correctly (we accept this as unequivocal evidence of correct recognition; it should be noted that we have never found a subject who would produce a correct name and not recognize the stimulus that was named); or (2) the subject provided a specific description of the entity (e.g., "that's an animal that can store water in the hump on its back, lives in the desert, can go a long time without water, and can be ridden"). The number of stimuli the subject recognized correctly, divided by the total number of items in the category and multiplied by 100, constituted the *recognition score*.

The *naming score* was calculated by summing the number of correct naming responses *using only those stimuli for which the subject had produced a correct* recognition *response*. In other words, if a subject did not recognize a particular stimulus, that stimulus was not included in the naming score calculation. In this approach to data quantification, subjects are not penalized for failing to name stimuli that they also do not recognize. Scores were multiplied by 100 to produce final figures in terms of percent correct. This approach to data quantification separates clearly the recognition capacity of the subject from the naming capacity of the subject, and avoids mischaracterizing a subject with a naming defect as having a recognition defect. Scores from the brain-damaged subjects were compared with those of the controls, and scores that fell 2 or more SD below the mean of the control group were classified as defective.

Neuroanatomical Methods   The neuroanatomical analysis was based on magnetic resonance (MR) data, or in those subjects in whom MR imaging could not be obtained, on computezed tomography (CT) data, obtained at least three months post onset of lesion.

In most subjects, MR scans were obtained with an SPg sequence of thin (1.5 mm) and contiguous T_1-weighted coronal cuts. The resulting 124 slices were processed in Brainvox (H. Damasio & Frank, 1992) and a three-dimensional (3-D) reconstruction was obtained for each individual subject. In a few cases only a standard MR sequence was available with both axial and coronal T_1-weighted, 5-mm-thick slices. The anatomical description of the lesion and of its placement relative to neuroanatomical landmarks was performed with Brainvox. The results of the analysis were stored in relation to the standard brain segmentation used in our laboratory (H. Damasio & Damasio, 1989).

In a subsequent step, all lesions in this set were transposed and warped into a normal 3-D brain, so as to permit the determination of the maximal overlap of lesions relative to subjects grouped by neuropsychological defect. This technique, known as MAP-3, is carried out as follows: The normal 3-D brain is resliced so as to match the slices of the MR or CT of the subject and create a correspondence between each of the subject's MR or CT slices and the normal resliced brain. The contour of the lesion on each slice is then transposed onto the matched slices of the normal brain, warping it in relation to the available anatomical landmarks. The summation of these contours defines an "object" which represents, for each subject, the lesion in three dimensions placed in the normal reference brain. The final step consists of the detection of the intersection of the several "objects" in the reference brain, and the analysis of their placement in relation to the anatomical detail

Table 12.1 Retrieval of words and concepts: Means (SD)

| | Category* | | | | | |
| | Animals | | Fruits and Vegetables | | Tools and Utensils | |
	N	R	N	R	N	R
Group 1	*75.0*	90.9	*85.2*	91.7	*84.5*	95.7
(n = 10)	(15.0)	(3.7)	(16.4)	(3.4)	(8.9)	(2.8)
Group 2	*80.3*	*80.6*	*82.1*	*84.9*	*73.5*	*83.0*
(n = 12)	(20.6)	(15.3)	(17.5)	(12.5)	(21.9)	(9.7)
Group 3	94.7	*77.5*	94.6	*72.8*	95.7	94.8
(n = 21)	(3.2)	(8.0)	(4.9)	(19.7)	(3.3)	(3.4)
Normal controls	95.7	91.9	94.3	92.6	98.2	96.2
(n = 55)	(3.1)	(2.8)	(3.7)	(3.9)	(1.9)	(3.3)

N, percent correct naming; R, percent correct recognition.
Note: Italicized scores are defective.

of the reference brain. If the analysis is only concerned with the surface overlap of the lesions, we have designated it as MAP-2. In this instance, each view of the 3-D brain showing the lesion is matched, for each subject, with the corresponding view of the normal brain. The contour of the lesion is transposed from the subject's brain onto the normal brain taking into account its relation to sulcal and gyral landmarks.

Results Concerning Hypothesis No. 1 Retrieval of words vs. retrieval of concepts for the same concrete entities.

Neuropsychological Findings Table 12.1 presents neuropsychological results pertinent to the question of whether retrieval of conceptual knowledge and retrieval of words can be dissociated. So far, we have uncovered three different patterns of recognition and naming profiles, with respect to nonunique concrete entities: (1) group 1: defective naming accompanied by normal recognition; (2) group 2: defective naming accompanied by defective recognition (subjects have defective recognition and, in addition, have defective naming of items they can recognize); (3) group 3: normal naming but defective recognition (as defined for group 2), that is, subjects who could name correctly entities that they recognized, even though overall recognition was defective in one or more categories. Data from the normal controls are also presented.

Neuroanatomical Findings
Abnormal retrieval of words and normal retrieval of concepts (see table 12.1, group 1). The ten subjects in this group had lesions in the left temporal lobe, mostly overlapping in the middle and lateral inferior temporal (IT) region, and in the lateral aspect of the occipitotemporal parietal region.

Table 12.2 Word retrieval defects for animals and tools and utensils: means (SD)

Nature of Defect	Category*		
	Animals	Fruits and vegetables	Tools and utensils
Group 1: Animal	*66.6*	*70.6*	*74.9*
(n = 16)	(22.5)	(28.8)	(26.8)
Group 2: Animal only	*76.9*	90.3	92.3
(n = 7)	(8.7)	(4.6)	(3.1)
Group 3: Tool or utensil	74.1	73.7	*68.2*
(n = 16)	(26.8)	(29.2)	(23.5)
Group 4: Tool or utensil only	93.9	93.2	*76.9*
(n = 7)	(3.2)	(7.7)	(7.3)

Note: Italicized scores are defective.

Abnormal retrieval of words and concepts (see table 12.1, group 2).   The twelve subjects in this group showed lesions mainly in the left lateral temporo-occipital region, mostly overlapping at the temporo-occipitoparietal junction, at the posterior end of the superior temporal sulcus.

Normal retrieval of words and abnormal retrieval of concepts (see table 12.1, group 3).   Of the twenty-one subjects in this group, eleven had lesions in the right hemisphere, and ten in the left. The right unilateral lesions were concentrated in the inferior and mesial aspects of the occipital lobe. The main overlap of lesions was in the infracalcarine region (lingual gyrus), tapering anteroinferiorly in the posterior IT region. In the left hemisphere, there was an overlap of subjects in the anterior sector of the fusiform gyrus (see Tranel, Damasio, & Damasio, 1997b).

Results for hypothesis No. 2   Retrieval of words for concrete entities from separate conceptual categories.

Neuropsychological Findings   In table 12.2, the results are organized according to the category of naming impairment (collapsed across whether or not there was an accompanying recognition defect). In group 1, subjects had an animal-naming defect, irrespective of other naming impairments; in group 2 (a subset of group 1), the defect was *restricted* to the animal category. In group 3, subjects had a tool and utensil naming defect, irrespective of other naming impairments; in group 4 (a subset of group 3), the defect was *restricted* to the tool and utensil category.

We conducted statistical comparisons to confirm the reliability of the findings. Using *t*-tests, we compared the naming scores of defective groups with the naming scores of brain-damaged subjects who were not defective. The results supported the conclusion that there were significant differences between groups. For group 1, the animal-naming score differed significantly from the score of nondefective subjects ($t(125) = -4.79$, $P < .001$). For group 3, the tool-utensil–naming score differed significantly from the score of nondefective subjects ($t(125) = -4.56$, $P < .001$).

Neuroanatomical Findings

Abnormal retrieval of words for animals (see table 12.2, group 1). A defect in retrieval of words for animals was observed in sixteen subjects. In all but one, the lesions occurred in the left IT region. The maximal overlap was seen in the midanterior sector of the lateral and inferior aspect of the IT region. The overlap then tapered toward the anterior sector of the IT region and the temporal pole. With the exception of one subject, whose lesion was in the mesial left occipital region (in both supra- and infracalcarine regions), no lesions outside the IT region were associated with the defect.

Abnormal retrieval of words for tools and utensils (see table 12.2, group 3). Abnormal retrieval of words for tools and utensils was associated with damage in the left lateral temporal and occipital region and, to a lesser extent, in the left parietal region. (One subject had a lesion in the right temporal pole.) The maximal lesion overlap occurred in the left temporo-occipitoparietal junction.

Functional Imaging (PET) Studies

We recently completed a functional imaging study regarding retrieval of words for concrete unique and nonunique entities (A. R. Damasio, Grabowski, Damasio, et al., 1995; H. Damasio et al., 1996). We studied nine normal right-handed young adults, ranging in age from 22 to 49, all of whom were native English speakers. There were seven women and two men. The subjects engaged in three tasks: (1) naming unique persons from their faces; (2) naming animals; and (3) naming tools and utensils (results for the naming of unique familiar faces are reported below). In a control task, subjects were asked to decide and report whether unfamiliar faces were presented right side up or upside down.

The naming tasks were performed during a PET scanning session. Subjects performed each task twice, in random order. Task performance began 5 seconds after injection of $[^{15}O]H_2O$ into the antecubital vein and continued until 65 seconds after injection. Oral responses were recorded, and performance measures (accuracy, latency) were obtained. For each task, the stimuli were presented at set rates which pilot studies had shown to yield similar high but nonperfect performance accuracies, that is, rates at which subjects could perform well, but not at ceiling. Specifically, the familiar faces were presented one every 2.5 seconds, the tools and utensils were presented one every 1.8 seconds, and the animals were presented one every 1.5 seconds. These rates produced performance levels of about 90 percent correct for each task type. In a separate session, MR images of each subject's brain were obtained, and reconstructed in three dimensions using Brainvox (H. Damasio & Frank, 1992).

MR and PET data were coregistered a priori using PET-Brainvox (Grabowski, Damasio, Frank et al., 1995). This fit was corrected post hoc with automated image registration (AIR; Woods, Mazziotta, & Cherry 1993). PET data were subjected to Talairach transformation (Talairach & Szikla, 1967), based on analysis of the coregistered 3-D MR dataset. The data were analyzed with a pixelwise two-way, analysis of covariance (ANCOVA; estimated coefficients for global flow serving as the covariate), in which we compared adjusted mean activity in each of the three naming conditions with the control task (Friston, Fritch, Liddle, et al., 1991). Regions of statistically significant changes in normalized regional cerebral blood flow (rCBF) for each of the three naming tasks were searched for in the temporal polar (TP) area and in the IT cortices identified in the 3-D reconstructed MR scans of each subject.

When subjects named animals and tools and utensils, there were significant increases in rCBF in distinct loci in the posterior IT region in the left hemisphere. For the tools and utensils, the principal location of activation was in the posterolateral aspect of the left IT region, in the middle and inferior temporal gyri. Naming of animals produced activation which was mesial and anterior to that produced by naming tools and utensils, in the inferior and fourth temporal gyri. Most important, the areas of activation produced by naming animals and tools and utensils were not just separate, but also corresponded to the areas identified by the lesion studies as being crucial to these capacities. Our results are consistent with another recent PET study (Martin et al., 1995).

Conclusions

The data summarized above indicate that the neural systems required to retrieve conceptual knowledge for nonunique entities, and those required to retrieve the words for those entities, are separate, at least in part. The separation is most noteworthy for the animal category. For the tool and utensil category, the separation is less apparent; in fact, based on findings available thus far, it is not really possible to separate the systems. The results also address the status of the fruits and vegetables category. In nearly all of our subjects, the outcome for this category paralleled the outcome for the animals category. For example, in subjects with severely impaired animal recognition, recognition of fruits and vegetables was also severely defective in most cases (see group 3 in table 12.1). In fact, only two subjects out of a total of thirty-three (groups 2 and 3, table 12.1) had defective animal recognition but normal fruit and vegetable recognition. Also, in subjects who had naming defects in all three categories, the magnitude of impairment was comparable in the animals and fruits and vegetables categories (groups 1 and 3, table 12.2).

The data support the hypothesis that the neural systems required to retrieve words for nonunique entities are based nearly exclusively in *left* hemisphere regions. We only found one subject (out of 127) in whom defective word retrieval occurred with a lesion in the right hemisphere. The data also support the hypothesis that there are separable neural regions specialized for word retrieval related to entities from different conceptual categories. Abnormal retrieval of words for animals occurred in subjects with lesions that clustered in the anterior portion of the IT region. The maximal overlap occurred in lateral and inferior IT regions, in the anterior sector of the middle and inferior temporal gyri. Of importance with regard to the findings discussed in the next section, the temporal polar region was *not* included in the overlap. Abnormal retrieval of words for tools and utensils occurred in subjects whose lesions involved the posterior and lateral temporal cortices and the supramarginal gyrus; the maximal overlap occurred at the back end of the middle temporal gyrus and the anteroinferior sector of the supramarginal gyrus (a region we have designated as "posterior IT+").

It is interesting to note that the system segregation effects noted in our studies seem to obey consistent principles. Specifically, relative to the stream architecture of cortical projection neurons in the occipitotemporal region, (a) word retrieval defects for animals depend on damage to systems located anterior to those whose damage produces tool and utensil word-retrieval defects; and (b) in no instance was there a defect for word retrieval for animals caused by a lesion *posterior* to a lesion causing word-retrieval defects for tools and utensils.

In other studies, we have found category-related neuropsychological and neuroanatomical dissociations regarding the retrieval of *conceptual knowledge* for concrete entities, which parallel to some extent the dissociations described here for word retrieval (A. R. Damasio, 1990; A. R. Damasio et al., 1990; Tranel, Damasio, Damasio, et al., 1995; Tranel, Damasio, & Damasio, 1997b). For example, in a large-scale study of subjects with lesions throughout various sectors of the telencephalon, we found that damage centered in the right mesial and inferior occipitotemporal region, or centered in the left mesial occipital region, produced impairments in the retrieval of conceptual knowledge (recognition) for animals. Damage centered in the left posterior temporo-occipital and parieto-occipital regions produced impairments in the retrieval of conceptual knowledge for tools and utensils. These findings suggest that, as in the case of words, the recording and retrieval of conceptual knowledge of different domains depend on partially segregated neural systems (Tranel, Damasio, & Damasio, 1997b).

RETRIEVAL OF WORDS FOR UNIQUE CONCRETE ENTITIES

Background

The retrieval of words for unique, concrete entities (e.g., persons, places) may be disproportionately compromised relative to the retrieval of words for nonunique entities, and may in some cases constitute the only word-retrieval defect (Carney & Temple, 1993; Cipolotti, McNeil, & Warrington, 1993; Cohen, Bolgert, Timsit, et al., 1994; A. R. Damasio, 1990; Flude, Ellis, & Kay, 1989; Hittmair-Delazer, Denes, Semenza, et al., 1994; Lucchelli & De Renzi, 1992; McKenna & Warrington, 1978, 1980; McNeil, Cipolotti, & Warrington, 1994; Semenza & Zettin, 1988, 1989; Shallice & Kartsounis, 1993). However, most of these studies were conducted with little or no regard for neuroanatomical factors. This has produced a rather confusing array of findings, as far as understanding the neural basis of retrieval of words for unique entities is concerned. In fact, Hittmair-Delazer et al. (1994) concluded after reviewing this literature that it was not possible to provide a neuroanatomical basis for "proper name" retrieval. The authors provided a table showing the various lesion locations for the cases of "proper anomia" that have been reported to date, and concluded that the "relative pureness of all reported cases" and the observation of "quite distinctly located anatomical lesions" made it unlikely that an anatomical explanation would suffice. However, we believe this interpretation is a consequence of either insufficient precision of neuroanatomical analysis or inadequate assessment of naming compromise, or perhaps both.

In fact, we have findings obtained with careful neuroanatomical and neuropsychological investigations in a large series of patients, which point strongly and consistently to a specific neural correlate for retrieval of words for unique entities (A. R. Damasio et al., 1990; H. Damasio et al., 1996; Graff-Radford et al., 1990). The findings also suggest that access to words for unique entities depends on neural systems distinct from those that support access to words for nonunique entities (A.R. Damasio & Damasio, 1992; A. R. Damasio et al., 1991; A. R. Damasio et al., 1995; H. Damasio et al., 1996). Finally, the findings indicate that, as in the case of nonunique entities, the neural systems supporting retrieval of conceptual knowledge are partially segregated from those supporting the retrieval of words (Tranel, Damasio, & Damasio, 1997b).

New Lesion Studies

The main hypothesis we addressed in these experiments is that access to words for unique entities depends on neural systems distinct from the neural systems that support access to words for nonunique entities.

Subjects   We studied subjects with damage to varied sectors of the left or right hemisphere, as described in the previous section (n = 127). Fifty-five normal controls, described in the previous section, were also studied.

Method   Stimuli from two tests were utilized to measure naming of famous faces: seventy-seven items from the Iowa Famous Faces Test (Tranel, Damasio, & Damasio, 1995), and fifty-six items modified from the Boston Famous

Table 12.3 Retrieval of words for unique entities

Group	N	Mean	(SD)
Brain-damaged subjects			
Normal	114	89.3	(4.9)
Defective (all)	13	49.6	(23.1)
Defective (persons only)	7	63.4	(10.0)
Normal controls	55	92.3	(6.2)

Faces Test (Albert, Butters, & Levin, 1979). The stimuli are black-and-white slides depicting famous actors, politicians, and sports persons. The slides were shown one at a time, and for each the subject was asked to (1) indicate whether the face is familiar, and if so, to (2) indicate who the person is, and (3) supply the person's name.

Data Quantification The data were quantified in the same manner as described above for nonunique entities. Specifically, for each subject we first determined the stimuli for which the subject produced unequivocal *recognition* responses (using the same criteria as specified in the previous section). For example, for the pertinent stimulus, "Michael Jordan" and "famous basketball player who tried to play baseball; his team won more games than any other team during the season" would qualify as correct recognition responses, whereas "sports guy" and "basketball player" would not. Then, *for the stimuli that were recognized correctly*, we determined the *naming score* by dividing the number of correct naming responses by the number of correct recognition responses. The naming score was multiplied by 100 and compared with scores from controls; scores 2 or more SD below the control mean were considered defective.

Neuropsychological Results The results are summarized in table 12.3. There were thirteen subjects who had defective retrieval of names for persons. The mean performance in this group was significantly lower than that of the brain-damaged subjects who were not defective ($t(125) = -6.17$, $P < .001$). Of the thirteen defective subjects, seven had a defect that was exclusive for the person's category, that is, they had defective retrieval of words for person's, but normal retrieval of words for animals, fruits and vegetables, and tools and utensils. Also, it is important to reiterate that none of the thirteen subjects with defective retrieval of words for persons had defective *recognition* of persons. In fact, the average recognition performance in the thirteen subjects was 81.9 (SD = 9.8), which compares favorably with the control average of 75.7 (SD = 6.7).

Neuroanatomical Results The techniques for analysis were the same as those reported for the neuroanatomical results in the study above regarding retrieval of words for nonunique entities. In the seven subjects with a *pure* defect in retrieval of words for unique entities, damage was centered in the left TP region, in both the inferomesial and lateral aspects. When all subjects with a deficit in retrieval of words for persons were considered (n = 13), the site of maximal lesion overlap remained in the anterolateral and inferior sectors of the left TP region.

Functional Imaging (PET) Studies

The methods for the functional imaging study of proper naming were described in the previous section. When the nine normal subjects named familiar faces, there was an increase in normalized rCBF in the left TP but not in the left IT region. The left TP activation corresponds to the same region identified in the lesion study as being important for the retrieval of words for unique entities. There was also activation in the right TP area, which we interpret to reflect the *recognition* of the unique faces that would inevitably accompany the naming of the faces (the control task did not require recognition at a unique level). Again, this finding closely parallels results from lesion studies. The left TP activation associated with naming unique entities ·was distinctfrom the activation in IT associated with naming of nonunique entities. This finding provides convergent evidence for the existence of distinct anatomical systems supporting retrieval of words for unique vs. nonunique entities.

Conclusions

Our findings indicate that lesions to the left TP region were associated with defects in retrieval of words for unique concrete entities. None of these subjects, however, had a defect in retrieving the *concepts* of the persons for whom they could not retrieve the names, that is, recognition of identity was normal. We also found that lesions restricted to the left IT region, which did not involve the temporal pole, did not cause defects in retrieval of words for unique entities. Rather, as noted in the previous section, these subjects had impairments in word retrieval for nonunique entities.

We are intrigued that the findings continue to obey the principles described earlier in connection with our studies regarding word retrieval for nonunique entities. Specifically, word retrieval for unique entities depends on a system located *anterior* to the systems on which word retrieval for nonunique concrete entities depends. Of all the subjects with naming impairments (n = 30), there was never a violation of this principle. For example, there was never a case in which a naming defect for unique entities related to a lesion located posterior to a lesion that caused a defect in the naming of nonunique entities. Also, there was never a combination of a defect in naming unique entities with a defect in naming nonunique entities of the tool and utensil variety, without a defect in naming animals as well. In other words, we never found that a subject could have a defect in naming persons and in naming tools and utensils, but could be normal in naming animals.

In sum, impaired retrieval of words for concrete entities correlated with damage in higher-order cortices outside classic language areas. Impairments in various word categories were correlated in a consistent manner with separable neural sites—specifically, words for persons with TP lesions, words for animals with anterior IT lesions, and words for tools and utensils with posterior IT+ lesions. It is notable that two of these regions—TP and posterior IT+—are not contiguous, do not overlap cortically or subcortically, and are so distant as to make it virtually impossible for a single lesion to compromise them without also compromising the intervening region. This explains why a combined defect for persons and for tools and utensils never occurred in our sample.

RETRIEVAL OF WORDS FOR ACTIONS

Background

We have recently begun to study the neural correlates of retrieval of conceptual knowledge and words regarding *actions*. In one study (A. R. Damasio & Tranel, 1993), we reported a subject with a well-defined lesion in the left frontal operculum, involving both prefrontal and premotor cortex and underlying white matter. The subject had defective retrieval of words for actions, but *normal* retrieval of words for nonunique entities (animals, tools and utensils). This subject was contrasted with two other subjects, who had left IT lesions. Those two subjects had the reverse pattern—defective retrieval of words for concrete entities but normal retrieval of words for actions. Regarding the first subject and the other two, the lesions were nonoverlapping and the neuropsychological performances were quite distinct, and the result thus constituted a double dissociation relative to both naming performance and site of lesion.

This result hinted that the systems required for naming of entities and naming of actions are segregated in the human brain, at least in part, even if they normally operate in coordinated fashion. Our result came on a background of observations that patients can have disproportionate impairment of the ability to retrieve "nouns" or "verbs" (Breedin & Martin, 1996; Caramazza & Hillis, 1991; De Renzi & Pellegrino, 1995; McCarthy & Warrington, 1985; Miceli, Capasso, & Caramazza, 1994; Miceli, Silveri, Noncentini, et al., 1988; Miceli, Silveri, Villa, et al., 1984; Zingeser & Berndt, 1988, 1990). Two recent reports (Daniele, Givstolisi, Silveri, et al., 1994; Miozzo, Soardi, & Cappa, 1994) support the Damasio and Tranel (1993) study in three and one patients, respectively.

Another recent study compared syntactic constructions between patients with agrammatic (usually Broca's) aphasia and those with conduction aphasia

(Goodglass, Christiansen, & Gallagher, 1994). Consistent with previous studies of this type (e.g., Marin, Saffran, & Schwartz, 1976), the authors found that patients with agrammatic aphasia had a preponderance of nouns over verbs in running speech and in single-constituent utterances. This finding is consistent with our work (e.g., Damasio & Tranel, 1993), and with other studies reporting noun-verb discrepancies in word repetition (Katz & Goodglass, 1990) and written word retrieval (Baxter & Warrington, 1985; Caramazza & Hillis, 1991).

We have replicated and extended our initial finding in several additional cases, as summarized below.

New Lesion Studies

Subjects We have studied eighty-three subjects with lesions in the left premotor or prefrontal region, left temporal, parietal, or occipital cortices, or various right hemisphere regions. The subjects were drawn from our patient registry, and they conformed to the same inclusion criteria specified for the studies on concrete entities described earlier.

Experimental Task The task for measuring retrieval of words for actions was the Action Recognition and Naming Test recently developed in our laboratory (Fiez & Tranel, 1997). In brief, the test comprises 280 color photographs of various actions. The items elicit responses which vary along several dimensions, including (1) the inflection of the elicited response (gerundial forms [e.g., *eating*] vs. past-tense forms [e.g., *ate*]), (2) the frequency of the elicited verb per million words (Francis & Kucera, 1982), (3) the type of agent performing each action (person, animal, or object), and (4) compatibility with different argument structures; that is, some elicited responses can only be produced in a well-formed sentence as an intransitive verb (one-place predicate: e.g., "John RAN/IS RUNNING"), some only as a transitive verb (two-place predicate: e.g., "John HIT/IS HITTING the ball"; or three-place predicate: e.g., "John GAVE Mary a book), and some can be produced in either type of sentence. The items also represent a diverse range of conceptual categories (e.g., verbs of perception, motion, etc.). In the test, 75 percent of the stimuli are single pictures depicting an ongoing action, for which subjects are instructed to produce a single word which best describes what the person, animal, or object is doing (e.g., "walking"). The remaining 25 percent of the stimuli are picture pairs depicting some change in an object, and subjects are asked to produce a single word which best describes what was done to the object, or what the person or object did (e.g., "chopped").

Scoring and Data Quantification The Action Recognition and Naming Test was standardized in a series of experiments conducted in normal subjects (Fiez & Tranel, 1997). This yielded, for each item on the test, a naming

Table 12.4 Summary of action recognition and naming data (no. of subjects defective)

Lesion group	Total No.	Naming (and Recognition)	Naming Only
Left frontal	19	10	0
Left occipitotemporal	21	8	2
Right occipitotemporal	9	1	1
Other	34	2	1
Total	83	21	4

response (or in a few instances, two or three responses) which is considered correct. To quantify the performances of the brain-damaged subjects, we compared their responses with those of the standardization sample, and scored as correct those responses that matched those produced by the normal controls. A percent correct score was then calculated for each brain-damaged subject, and the score was classified as *defective* if it was 2 or more SD below the mean of the control group.

A hierarchical approach was used to classify the brain-damaged subjects into four different groups. First, we identified a group of nineteen subjects whose lesions included (but were not necessarily limited to) damage to any of the following left frontal areas: left frontal operculum, premotor region, rolandic region, basal ganglia. From the remaining sixty-four subjects, we next identified a group of twenty-one subjects whose lesions included (but were not necessarily limited to) damage to any of the following left occipitotemporal areas: infracalcarine cortex, supracalcarine cortex, the mesial temporo-occipital junction, the posterior portion of the middle temporal gyrus, the posterior portion of the IT gyrus. From the remaining forty-three subjects, we next identified a group of nine subjects whose lesions included (but were not necessarily limited to) damage to the mesial occipitotemporal areas in the right hemisphere. The remaining thirty-four subjects (whose lesions did not extend into any of the areas listed above) were not classified into specific neuroanatomical subgroups.

Results The results are presented in table 12.4. We found a number of subjects who had a defect in the retrieval of words for actions. It is interesting to note that in most cases, this impairment was accompanied by a defect in the retrieval of conceptual knowledge for actions (the "naming and recognition" group).

These findings provide a replication in ten additional subjects of our initial result regarding the association of defective retrieval of words for actions with damage to the left premotor or prefrontal region (Damasio & Tranel, 1993). Neuroanatomical analysis in these subjects revealed that the lesions clustered in the inferior motor and premotor regions, with the maximal lesion overlap occurring in the inferior frontal gyrus and the inferior sector of the precentral gyrus. The overlap tapered both into more anterior prefrontal regions, and posteriorly into the supramarginal gyrus.

The findings also suggest a strong association between recognition and naming, with regard to actions. In the brain-damaged subjects with defective naming, we found that there was a significant correlation between naming performance and the average conceptual retrieval (recognition) performance ($r = .55$, $P < .005$). Thus, recognition and naming tend to go together quite strongly with regard to actions. This contrasts with the frequent dissociations we have obtained between these two capacities with regard to concrete entities, especially persons and animals (although it is interesting to note that the tools and utensils category is more like the actions, inasmuch as naming and recognition tend to be disturbed concomitantly).

Functional Imaging (PET) Studies

There is a PET paradigm known as "verb generate," in which subjects are required to generate verbs (action words) (Petersen, Fox, Posner, et al., 1988, 1989; Raichle, Fiez, Videen, et al., 1994). We have conducted a PET study which replicates and extends the findings from the verb-generate studies (Grabowski, Frank, Brown, et al., 1996). We studied eighteen normal right-handed volunteers, who underwent both a 3-D MR study and a PET study, using the same methods described earlier. The subjects received injections of $[^{15}O]H_2O$ while performing the verb-generate task. In the task, subjects were presented common nouns visually at the rate of one word per 2 seconds, and for each, the subjects had to generate (and speak) a verb that went with the noun. Changes in rCBF associated with the task were analyzed using the same methods described earlier.

The strongest areas of rCBF increase associated with the verb-generate task were the left inferior frontal gyrus, left dorsolateral prefrontal cortex, and right cerebellum. These regions correspond closely to those reported in other PET studies using the same paradigm (Petersen et al., 1988, 1989; Raichle et al., 1994; see also Martin et al., 1995). Also, the finding of rCBF increases in the left premotor and prefrontal region during the PET studies is quite congruent with the findings from the lesion studies. Convergent evidence is also available from functional studies using other imaging modalities, such as functional MR imaging (Hinke, Stillman, Kim, et al., 1993).

Conclusions

The lesion studies support the idea that defective retrieval of words for actions is correlated with damage in the dorsolateral sector of the left frontal lobe, mostly in the inferior frontal gyrus, in premotor and prefrontal cortices. Functional imaging studies have produced findings consistent with this conclusion.

CONCLUDING REMARKS

The findings summarized in this chapter indicate that the retrieval of words which denote concrete entities depends on regions in higher-order association cortices in the left temporal region, and that the retrieval of words denoting actions depends on the left prefrontal and premotor region. We have suggested that these regions play an intermediary or mediational role in lexical retrieval (H. Damasio et al., 1996). For example, when the concept of a given animal is evoked (based on the activation of regions which support pertinent conceptual knowledge and promote its explicit representation in sensorimotor terms), an intermediary region becomes active and promotes (in the appropriate sensorimotor structures) the explicit representation of phonemic knowledge pertaining to the word form which denotes the given animal. A different intermediary region is engaged when a concept from another category—a tool, for example—is evoked. This process can operate in reverse to link word-form information to conceptual knowledge. We do not believe that the intermediary regions contain in explicit form the names for all entities; rather, we suggest that they hold knowledge about how to reconstruct a certain pattern (e.g., the phonemic structure of a given word) in explicit form, within the appropriate sensorimotor structures.

We have hypothesized that there are two main reasons why naming of different kinds of entities is correlated with different neural sites. One pertains to the overall physical characteristics of the entity being named, which determine the kind of sensorimotor mapping generated during interactions between an organism and the entity, and which are a key to the neural mapping of the corresponding conceptual knowledge. The other reason pertains to the fine physical characteristics and contextual linkages of an entity which permit the mapping of unique items such as familiar persons or places. We presume that the varied conceptual specification which results from factors such as physical characteristics and contextual complexity is the driving force and "principle" behind the differential and consistent neural placement of lexical intermediary regions. For instance, the multiple sensory channels (somatosensory, visual) and the hand motor patterns which are inherent in the conceptual description of a manipulable tool would be a driving force for the anatomical gravitation of the respective intermediary region toward a sector of cortex that is capable of receiving such multiple sensory signals, and is close to regions involved in visual motion and hand motion processing. The driving force for the intermediary region concerning names for persons comprises both the finer physical specification and contextual complexity necessary to define such unique items.

As far as the possible microstructure of the intermediary regions, we do not envision them as rigid "modules" or hard-edged "centers," because we see their structure and operation as being acquired and modified by learning. We suggest that an individual's learning experience of concepts of a similar kind (e.g., concepts of manipulable tools), and their corresponding words, leads to the recruitment, within the available neural architecture, of a critical set of spatially proximate microcircuits. We presume that the anatomical placement of the region within which the microcircuits are recruited for a certain range of items is not haphazard. Rather, it is the one best suited to permit the most effective interaction between the regions of cerebral cortex that subtend conceptual knowledge and those that can enact lexical knowledge. The findings in our studies suggest that distinct kinds of conceptual knowledge lead to the recruitment of distinct intermediary regions. We expect normal persons to develop, under similar conditions, a similar type of large-scale architecture, but we also predict ample individual variation of microcircuitry within each key region. We also expect that, at different times, the same individual will engage the same large-scale regions, but not necessarily the same microcircuitry within them.

In sum, the findings described here offer support for the idea that, in addition to the separation of the neural systems which support the retrieval of concepts for entities belonging to varied categories, there is a parallel regionalization for the systems which support the retrieval of the word forms corresponding to those entities.

ACKNOWLEDGMENT

Supported by NINDS Program Project Grant NS 19632 and ONR Grant N00014-91-J-1240. The authors thank Joan Brandt and Jon Spradling for technical help with the experiments, and Denise Krutzfeldt for help in scheduling the subjects.

REFERENCES

Albert, M. S., Butters, N., & Levin, J. A. (1979). Temporal gradients in the retrograde amnesia of patients with alcoholic Korsakoff's disease. *Archives of Neurology, 36*, 211–216.

Basso, A., Capitani, E., & Laiacona, M. (1988). Progressive language impairment without dementia: A case with isolated category-specific semantic defect. *Journal of Neurology, Neurosurgery, and Psychiatry, 51*, 1201–1207.

Baxter, D. M., & Warrington, E. K. (1985). Category-specific phonological dysgraphia. *Neuropsychologia, 23*, 653–666.

Breedin, S. D., & Martin, R. C. (1996). Patterns of verb impairment in aphasia: An analysis of four cases. *Cognitive Neuropsychology, 13*, 51–91.

Carammaza, A., & Hillis, A. (1991). Lexical organization of nouns and verbs in the brain. *Nature, 349*, 788–790.

Carney, A., & Temple, C. M. (1993). Prosopanomia? A possible category-specific anomia for faces. *Cognitive Neuropsychology, 10*, 185–195.

Cipolotti, L., McNeil, J. E., & Warrington, E. K. (1993). Spared written naming of proper names: A case report. *Memory, 1*, 289–331.

Cohen, L.. Bolgert, F., Timsit, S., & Chermann, J. F. (1994). Anomia for proper names after left thalamic infarct. *Journal of Neurology, Neurosurgery, and Psychiatry, 57*, 1283–1284.

Damasio, A. R. (1989a). Time-locked multiregional retroactivation: A systems-level proposal for the neural substrates of recall and recognition. *Cognition, 33,* 25–62.

Damasio, A. R. (1989b). Concepts in the brain. *Mind and Language, 4,* 24–28.

Damasio, A. R. (1990). Category-related recognition defects as a clue to the neural substrates of knowledge. *Trends in Neurosciences, 13,* 95–98.

Damasio, A. R. (1992). Aphasia. *New England Journal of Medicine, 326,* 531–539.

Damasio, A. R., Brandt, J. P., Tranel, D., & Damasio, H. (1991). Name dropping: Retrieval of proper or common nouns depends on different systems in left temporal cortex. *Society for Neuroscience Abstracts, 17,* 4.

Damasio, A. R., & Damasio, H. (1992). Brain and language. *Scientific American, 267* (September), 88–95.

Damasio, A. R., & Damasio, H. (1994). Cortical systems for retrieval of concrete knowledge: The convergence zone framework. In C. Koch (Ed.), *Large-scale neuronal theories of the brain* (pp. 61–74). Cambridge, MA: MIT Press.

Damasio, A. R., Damasio, H., Tranel, D., & Brandt, J.P. (1990). The neural regionalization of knowledge access: Preliminary evidence. *Quantitative Biology, 55,* 1039–1047.

Damasio, A. R., Damasio, H., & Van Hoesen, G. W. (1982). Prosopagnosia: Anatomic basis and behavioral mechanisms. *Neurology, 32,* 331–341.

Damasio, A. R., Grabowski, T. J., Damasio, H., Tranel, D., Frank, R. J., Spradling, J., Ponto, L. L. B., Watkins, G. L., & Hichwa, R. D. (1995). Separate lexical categories are retrieved from separate systems: A PET activation study. *Society for Neuroscience, 21,* 1498.

Damasio, A. R., & Tranel, D. (1990). Knowing that "Colorado" goes with "Denver" does not imply knowledge that "Denver" is in "Colorado." *Behavioural Brain Research, 40,* 193–200.

Damasio, A. R., & Tranel, D. (1993). Nouns and verbs are retrieved with differently distributed neural systems. *Proceedings of the National Academy of Sciences, 90,* 4957–4960.

Damasio, H., & Damasio, A. R. (1989). *Lesion analysis in neuropsychology.* New York: Oxford University Press.

Damasio, H., & Frank, R. (1992). Three-dimensional in vivo mapping of brain lesions in humans. *Archives of Neurology, 49,* 137–143.

Damasio, H., Grabowski, T. J., Tranel, D., Frank, R. J., Hichwa, R. D., & Damasio, A. R. (1996). A neural basis for lexical retrieval. *Nature, 380,* 499–505.

Daniele, A., Giustolisi, L., Silveri, M. C., Colosimo, C., & Gainotti, G. (1994). Evidence for a possible neuroanatomical basis for lexical processing of nouns and verbs. *Neuropsychologia, 32,* 1325–1341.

Dehaene, S. (1995). Electrophysiological evidence for category-specific word processing in the normal human brain. *NeuroReport, 6,* 2153–2157.

De Renzi, E., & Pellegrino, G. (1995). Sparing of verbs and preserved, but ineffectual reading in a patient with impaired word production. *Cortex, 31,* 619–636.

Farah, M. J., Meyer, M. M., & McMullen, P. A. (1996). The living/nonliving dissociation is not an artifact: Giving an a priori implausible hypothesis a strong test. *Cognitive Neuropsychology, 13,* 137–154.

Farah, M. J., & Wallace, M. A. (1992). Semantically-bounded anomia: Implications for the neural implementation of naming. *Neuropsychologia, 30,* 609–621.

Fiez, J. A., & Tranel, D. (1997). Standardized stimuli and procedures for investigating the retrieval of lexical and conceptual knowledge for actions. *Memory and Cognition, 25*, 543–569.

Flude, B. M., Ellis, A. W., & Kay, J. (1989). Face processing and name retrieval in an anomic aphasic: Names are stored separately from semantic information about familiar people. *Brain and Cognition, 11*, 60–72.

Francis, W. M., & Kucera, H. (1982). *Frequency analysis of English usage: Lexicon and grammar*. Boston: Houghton Mifflin.

Franklin, S., Howard, D., & Patterson, K. (1995). Abstract word anomia. *Cognitive Neuropsychology, 12*, 549–566.

Friston, K. J., Frith, C. D., Liddle, P. F., & Frackowiak, R.S.J. (1991). Comparing functional (PET) images: The assessment of significant change. *Journal of Cerebral Blood Flow and Metabolism, 11*, 690–699.

Goodglass, H., & Budin, C. (1988). Category and modality specific dissociations in word comprehension and concurrent phonological dyslexia. *Neuropsychologia, 26*, 67–78.

Goodglass, H., Christiansen, J. A., & Gallagher, R. E. (1994). Syntactic constructions used by agrammatic speakers: Comparison with conduction aphasics and normals. *Neuropsychology, 8*, 598–613.

Goodglass, H., Wingfield, A., Hyde, M. R., & Theurkauf, J. C. (1986). Category specific dissociations in naming and recognition by aphasic patients. *Cortex, 22*, 87–102.

Grabowski, T. J., Damasio, H., Frank, R., Hichwa, R. D., Boles-Ponto, L. L., & Watkins, G. L. (1995). A new technique for PET slice orientation and MRI-PET coregistration. *Human Brain Mapping, 2*, 123–133.

Grabowski, T. J., Frank, R. J., Brown, C. K., Damasio, H., Boles-Ponto, L. L., Watkins, G. L., & Hichwa, R. D. (1996). Reliability of PET activation across statistical methods, subject groups, and sample sizes. *Human Brain Mapping, 4*, 23–46.

Graff-Radford, N. R., Damasio, A. R., Hyman, B. T., Hart, M.N., Tranel, D., Damasio, H., Van Hoesen, G.W., & Rezai, K. (1990). Progressive aphasia in a patient with Pick's disease: A neuropsychological, radiologic, and anatomic study. *Neurology, 40*, 620–626.

Hart, J., Berndt, R. S., & Caramazza, A. (1985). Category-specific naming deficit following cerebral infarction. *Nature, 316*, 439–440.

Hart, J., & Gordon, B. (1992). Neural subsystems for object knowledge. *Nature, 359*, 60–64.

Hillis, A. E., & Caramazza, A. (1991). Category-specific naming and comprehension impairment: A double dissociation. *Brain, 114*, 2081–2094.

Hinke, R. M., Hu, X., Stillman, A. E., Kim, S.-G., Merkle, H., Salmi, R., & Ugurbil, K. (1993). Functional magnetic resonance imaging of Broca's area during internal speech. *NeuroReport, 4*, 675–678.

Hittmair-Delazer, M., Denes, G., Semenza, C., & Mantovan, M.C. (1994). Anomia for people's names. *Neuropsychologia, 32*, 465–476.

Katz, R. B., & Goodglass, H. (1990). Deep dysphasia: Analysis of a rare type of repetition disorder. *Brain and Language, 39*, 153–185.

Kosslyn, S. M. (1994). *Image and brain*. Cambridge, MA: MIT Press.

Lesser, R., Gordon, B., & Uematsu, S. (1994). Electrical stimulation and language. *Journal of Clinical Neurophysiology, 11*, 191–204.

Levelt, W. J. M. (1989). *Speaking: From intention to articulation*. Cambridge, MA: MIT Press.

Levelt, W. J. M. (1992). Accessing words in speech production: Stages, processes and representations. *Cognition, 42,* 1–22.

Lucchelli, F., & De Renzi, E. (1992). Proper name anomia. *Cortex, 28,* 221–230.

Marin, D. S. M., Saffran, E. M., & Schwartz, M. E. (1976). Dissociations of language in aphasia: Implications for normal function. *Annals of the New York Academy of Sciences, 280,* 868–889.

Martin, A., Haxby, J. V., Lalonde, F.M., Wiggs, C. L., & Ungerleider, L. G. (1995). Discrete cortical regions associated with knowledge of color and knowledge of action. *Science, 270,* 102–105.

Martin, A., Wiggs, C. L., Ungerleider, L., & Haxby, J. V. (1996). Neural correlates of category-specific knowledge. *Nature, 379,* 649–652.

Mazoyer, B. M., Tzourio, N., Frak, V., Syrota, A., Murayama, N., Levrier, O., Salamon, G., Dehaene, S., Cohen, L., & Mehler, J. (1993). The cortical representation of speech. *Journal of Cognitive Neuroscience, 5,* 467–479.

McCarthy, R. A., & Warrington, E. K. (1985). Category specificity in an agrammatic patient: The relative impairment of verb retrieval and comprehension. *Neuropsychologia, 23,* 709–727.

McCarthy, R. A., & Warrington, E. K. (1988). Evidence for modality-specific meaning systems in the brain. *Nature, 334,* 428–430.

McKenna, P., & Parry, R. (1994). Category specificity in the naming of natural and man-made objects: Normative data from adults and children. *Neuropsychological Rehabilitation, 4,* 255–281.

McKenna, P., & Warrington, E. K. (1978). Category-specific naming preservation: A single case study. *Journal of Neurology, Neurosurgery, and Psychiatry, 41,* 571–574.

McKenna, P., & Warrington, E. K. (1980). Testing for nominal dysphasia. *Journal of Neurology, Neurosurgery, and Psychiatry, 43,* 781–788.

McNeil, J. E., Cipolotti, L., & Warrington, E. K. (1994). The accessibility of proper names. *Neuropsychologia, 32,* 193–208.

Miceli, G., Capasso, R., & Caramazza, A. (1994). The interaction of lexical and sublexical processes in reading, writing and repetition. *Neuropsychologia, 32,* 317–333.

Miceli, G., Silveri, M. C., Nocentini, U., & Caramazza, A. (1988). Patterns of dissociation in comprehension and production of nouns and verbs. *Aphasiology, 2,* 351–358.

Miceli, G., Silveri, M. C., Villa, G. P., & Caramazza, A. (1984). On the basis for the agrammatic's difficulty in producing main verbs. *Cortex, 20,* 207–220.

Miozzo, A., Soardi, S., & Cappa, S. F. (1994). Pure anomia with spared action naming due to a left temporal lesion. *Neuropsychologia, 32,* 1101–1109.

Nobre, A. C., Allison, T., & McCarthy, G. (1994). Word recognition in the human inferior temporal lobe. *Nature, 372,* 260–263.

Nobre, A. C., & McCarthy, G. (1995). Language-related field potentials in the anterior-medial temporal lobe: II. Effects of word type and semantic priming. *Journal of Neuroscience, 15,* 1090–1098.

Ojemann, G. A. (1991). Cortical organization of language. *Journal of Neuroscience, 11,* 2281–2287.

Petersen, S. E., Fox, P. T., Posner, M.I., Mintun, M., & Raichle, M.E. (1988). Positron emission tomographic studies of the cortical anatomy of single-word processing. *Nature, 331,* 585–589.

Petersen, S. E., Fox, P. T., Posner, M. I., Mintun, M., & Raichle, M. E. (1989). Positron emission tomographic studies of the processing of single words. *Journal of Cognitive Neuroscience, 1,* 153–170.

Pietrini, V., Nertempi, P., Vaglia, A., Revello, H.G., Pinna, V., & Ferro-Milona, F. (1988). Recovery from herpes simplex encephalitis: Selective impairment of specific semantic categories with neuroradiological correlation. *Journal of Neurology, Neurosurgery, and Psychiatry, 51,* 1284–1293.

Raichle, M. E., Fiez, J. A., Videen, T. O., MacLeod, A.-M. K., Pardo, J. V., Fox, P. T., & Petersen, S. E. (1994). Practice-related changes in human brain functional anatomy during nonmotor learning. *Cerebral Cortex, 4,* 8–26.

Riddoch, M. J., & Humphreys, G. W. (1987). Visual object processing in optic aphasia: A case of semantic access agnosia. *Cognitive Neuropsychology, 4,* 131–185.

Roelofs, A. (1993). Testing a non-decompositional theory of lemma retrieval in speaking: Retrieval of verbs. *Cognition, 47,* 59–87.

Rosch, E., Mervis, C. B., Gray, W. D., Johnson, D. M., & Boyes-Braem, P. (1976). Basic objects in natural categories. *Cognitive Psychology, 8,* 382–439.

Sacchett, C., & Humphreys, G. W. (1992). Calling a squirrel a squirrel but a canoe a wigwam: A category-specific deficit for artefactual objects and body parts. *Cognitive Neuropsychology, 9,* 73–86.

Sartori, G., & Job, R. (1988). The oyster with four legs: A neuropsychological study on the interaction of visual and semantic information. *Cognitive Neuropsychology, 5,* 105–132.

Semenza, C., & Zettin, M. (1988). Generating proper names: A case of selective inability. *Cognitive Neuropsychology, 5,* 711–721.

Semenza, C., & Zettin, M. (1989). Evidence from aphasia for the role of proper names as pure referring expressions. *Nature, 342,* 678–679.

Shallice, T., & Kartsounis, L. D. (1993). Selective impairment of retrieving people's names: A category specific disorder? *Cortex, 29,* 281–291.

Silveri, M. C., & Gainotti, G. (1988). Interaction between vision and language in category-specific semantic impairment. *Cognitive Neuropsychology, 5,* 677–709.

Small, S. L., Hart, J., Nguyen, T., & Gordon, B. (1995). Distributed representations of semantic knowledge in the brain. *Brain, 118,* 441–453.

Snodgrass, J. G., & Vanderwart, M. (1980). A standardized set of 260 pictures: Norms for name agreement, image agreement, familiarity, and visual complexity. *Journal of Experimental Psychology: Human Learning and Memory, 6,* 174–215.

Talairach, J., & Szikla, G. (1967). *Atlas d'anatomie stéréotaxique du téléncephale.* Paris: Masson.

Tippett, L. J., Glosser, G., & Farah, M. J. (1996). A category-specific naming impairment after temporal lobectomy. *Neuropsychologia, 34,* 139–146.

Tranel, D. (1991). Dissociated verbal and nonverbal retrieval and learning following left anterior temporal damage. *Brain and Cognition, 15,* 187–200.

Tranel, D., Damasio, H., & Damasio, A. R. (1995). Double dissociation between overt and covert face recognition. *Journal of Cognitive Neuroscience, 7,* 425–432.

Tranel, D., Damasio, H., & Damasio, A. R. (1997a). On the neurology of naming. In H. Goodglass & A. Wingfield (Eds.), *Anomia: neuroanatomical and cognitive correlates* (pp. 65–90). New York: Academic Press.

Tranel, D., Damasio, H., & Damasio, A. R. (1997b). A neural basis for the retrieval of conceptual knowledge. *Neuropsychologia, 35,* 1319–1327.

Tranel, D., Damasio, H., Damasio, A. R., & Brandt, J. P. (1995). Separate concepts are retrieved from separate neural systems: Neuroanatomical and neuropsychological double dissociations. *Society for Neuroscience, 21,* 1497.

Tranel, D., Logan, C. G., Frank, R. J., & Damasio, A. R. (1997). Explaining category-related effects in the retrieval of conceptual and lexical knowledge for concrete entities: Operationalization and analysis of factors. *Neuropsychologia, 35,* 1329–1339.

Warrington, E. K. (1975). The selective impairment of semantic memory. *Quarterly Journal of Experimental Psychology, 27,* 635–657.

Warrington, E. K. (1981). Concrete word dyslexia. *British Journal of Psychology, 72,* 175–196.

Warrington, E. K., & McCarthy, R. A. (1983). Category specific access dysphasia. *Brain, 106,* 859–878.

Warrington, E. K., & McCarthy, R. A. (1987). Categories of knowledge: Further fractionations and an attempted integration. *Brain, 110,* 1273–1296.

Warrington, E. K., & Shallice, T. (1984). Category specific semantic impairments. *Brain, 107,* 829–854.

Woods, R. P., Mazziotta, J. C., & Cherry, S. R. (1993). MRI-PET registration with automated algorithm. *Journal of Computer Assisted Tomography, 17,* 536–546.

Zingeser, L. B., & Berndt, R. S. (1988). Grammatical class and context effects in a case of pure anomia: Implications for models of language production. *Cognitive Neuropsychology, 5,* 473–516.

Zingeser, L. B., & Berndt, R. S. (1990). Retrieval of nouns and verbs in agrammatism and anomia. *Brain and Language, 39,* 14–32.

IV Applications in Dementia

13 A Model of Human Memory Based on the Cellular Physiology of the Hippocampal Formation

Michael E. Hasselmo, Bradley P. Wyble, and
Chantal E. Stern

In recent years, the term *cognitive psychology* has given way to the term *cognitive neuroscience*, as researchers working on cognitive function embrace a range of new techniques. However, this change in terminology does not yet reflect a substantive change in the focus of cognitive psychology. Most researchers still appear to think in terms of step-by-step flow charts of cognitive function, seeking ever more finely tuned dissociations in behavior. The current use of brain-damaged subjects and neuroimaging techniques appears primarily to focus on mapping macroscopic brain structures to the superstructure of cognitive psychology. This approach still ignores the vast majority of neuroscience data, which are primarily obtained at the microscopic or molecular level. But effects at the cellular and receptor level clearly play a fundamental role in cognitive function—the range of memory effects of different drugs provides a good example. The work presented here attempts to bridge the gap between macroscopic behavior and microscopic function. In this chapter we present a detailed network model of the hippocampus which allows data on human memory function to be analyzed in terms of physiological and anatomical data at the cellular level. We demonstrate how the model has been used to simulate effects of drugs such as scopolamine and diazepam on memory function. In addition, we show how the model can be used to understand the effect of lesions of the hippocampal formation and the progression of cortical neuropathology in Alzheimer's disease.

Computational modeling is essential to bridging this gap. Here, detailed computational models of cortical networks are utilized to model human memory function. Though it addresses the same topic, this work contrasts with extensive previous work on models of human memory function. Previous memory modelers have frequently stated the eventual need to confront biological realism (Murdock, 1982), but most published work has utilized simple and abstract mathematical operations to model memory (Raaijmakers & Shiffrin, 1981; Metcalfe, 1993; Murdock & Kahana, 1993). These are sophisticated models which are useful for interpretation of behavioral data and specific hypotheses framed on a more intuitive level, but they are not true functional models. They do not address the actual brain mechanisms involved in memory. Because of this, the constraints applied to these models have been constraints of simplicity rather than biological validity. But it appears that the complex and often paradoxical data on human memory performance can only be explained by multiple overlapping systems. It will be important to constrain such multiple system models with biological data. Here we attempt to approach human memory function from a new perspective by drawing on extensive research and modeling of the hippocampal formation.

The wealth of data concerning the hippocampal formation provides an excellent opportunity to examine how theories developed at the behavioral level could be implemented using models incorporating detailed anatomical and physiological data. Behavioral data from humans suggest that the hippocampus mediates the learning of memories for specific episodes (Scoville & Milner, 1957; Penfield & Milner, 1958; Corkin, 1984; Zola-Morgan, Cohen, & Amaral, 1986). This includes work on patients with lesions due to surgical removal of large portions of the medial temporal lobe, such as patient H.M. (Scoville & Milner, 1957; Corkin, 1984), as well as patients with damage restricted to subregions of the hippocampus, as in patient R.B. (Zola-Morgan et al., 1986). Patients with damage to the hippocampus appear capable of retaining information for a short period without distraction—commonly displaying normal behavior in tests such as Digit Span (Corkin, 1984). In addition, they appear to retain most episodic information obtained prior to their lesion (Zola-Morgan, Cohen, & Squire, 1983; Zola-Morgan et al., 1986). However, they display severe anterograde amnesia—the inability to form new long-term memories. For example, in the paired-associates portion of the Wechsler Memory Scale, patient H.M. shows no recall of unrelated paired associates (Scoville & Milner, 1957). When tested three times sequentially on a list of ten unrelated paired associates, patient R.B. only recalled 3.7 pairs out of 30 (Zola-Morgan et al., 1986) and other hippocampal amnesiacs showed zero recall (Squire, Amaral, & Press, 1990), while controls recalled correct associations over twenty times. In tests of the free recall of ten words from the middle of a fifteen-word list, patient R.B. only recalled 10 percent of the words, whereas controls recalled about 40 percent (Graf, Squire, & Mandler, 1984). Similar striking differences between controls and patients with hippocampal lesions appear in tests of the free recall of information from a story—commonly a subtest of the Wechsler Memory Scale (Penfield & Milner, 1958; Zola-Morgan et al., 1986). These data support the specific significance of hippocampal subregions in storage of verbal information.

Animal data further support a role in episodic memory. Similar to human amnesiacs, monkeys with hippocampal lesions can retain information for short periods (under 10 seconds), but perform poorly at longer delays in a delayed-nonmatch-to-sample task (Alvarez-Royo, Zola-Morgan, & Squire, 1992). Lesions affecting hippocampal function have been shown to impair formation of "snapshot" memories (Gaffan & Harrison, 1989). Behavioral data from rats performing different tasks have led to a number of theories of hippocampal function. Sutherland and Rudy have proposed that the hippocampus is required for learning configural representations of stimuli which cannot be represented by simple links between preexisting concepts (Sutherland & Rudy, 1989; Rudy & Sutherland, 1989). Eichenbaum and colleagues have proposed that the hippocampus is essential for encoding of relations between multiple stimuli, but emphasize that these relational representations can be used in a more flexible manner for subsequent behavior than configural representations (Eichenbaum & Buckingham, 1990; Eichenbaum, Otto, & Cohen, 1994). Extensive work has focused on the role of the hippocampus in performing tasks requiring formation of spatial representations (McNaughton & Morris, 1987). These theories have been discussed in the context of neural network models, but they have not been explicitly simulated in a detailed manner.

Here, theories about the function of individual hippocampal cell populations are evaluated in the context of a full network simulation of hippocampal formation with specific behavioral function. This network simulation has been tested for the capability of forming rapid representations of sequentially presented "episodic" information. The model can be used to directly simulate cortical processes involved in performance of standard human memory tasks, including the cued recall of paired associates, and the free recall of lists of words. However, in contrast to previous models of human memory, the physiological detail of this model allows it to address questions at a biological level. These questions include patterns of physiological activity which might underlie memory function, and the cellular basis for drug effects on human memory. Here we illustrate the possible cellular mechanisms for the storage impairments associated with the drugs scopolamine and diazepam. In addition, this model can be used to address possible mechanisms for the initiation and progression of cortical neuropathologic changes in Alzheimer's disease.

SIMPLE OVERVIEW OF NEURAL NETWORKS

Most neural network papers assume too much knowledge on the part of their reader. Here a brief overview of biologically realistic neural network models is presented, based on the neural networks course taught by Michael Hasselmo at Harvard. Those who know this material can skip to the next section.

To understand the function of the model presented here, is it important to understand two basic types of neural network models: associative memories and self-organizing systems. These two basic functions appear in many subregions of the hippocampus simulation, and form the basis for the function of the simulation.

These neural network models always involve interacting populations of neurons, represented by the circles in figure 13.1. The populations of

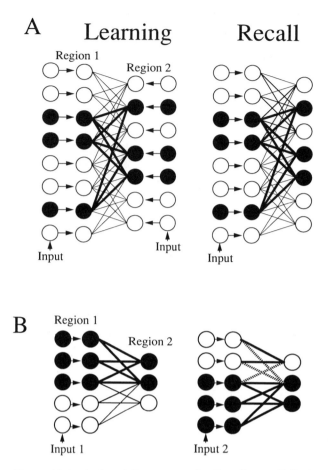

Figure 13.1 A, Associative memory function allows activity in region 1 to evoke an associated pattern in region 2. During learning (left), external input sets patterns of activity in region 1 and region 2 (shading represents active neurons). Hebbian synaptic modification strengthens connections between active units (thick lines represent strengthened connections). During recall (right), external input sets the pattern of activity in region 1. Activity spreads across strengthened connections to activate the previously associated pattern of activity in region 2. B, Self-organization allows patterns of activity in region 1 to evoke compressed or nonoverlapping representations in region 2. Dynamics are the same during learning and recall. External input is presented to region 1 but not region 2. The spread of activity across initially random synaptic connections from region 1 to region 2 activates specific neurons. Connections are then strengthened between active neurons in region 1 and active neurons in region 2, and weakened between active neurons and inactive neurons. This sets up region 2 representations of individual patterns or classes of patterns in region 1.

neurons interact via distributed connections or synapses, as represented by the lines connecting the circles in figure 13.1. Activity spreads from one neuron to another via these synapses using an activation rule. Learning involves changing the strength of connections. In the model presented here, learning will always use a Hebbian rule, that is, connections between two active neurons will be strengthened.

Associative Memory Function

In associative memory models, learning allows activity in one set of neurons to evoke an associated pattern of activity in another set of neurons. If the two sets of neurons are in the same region, this is referred to as "autoassociative" memory. If the two sets of neurons are in different regions, this is referred to as "heteroassociative" memory.

These models have two phases with different dynamics: a learning phase and a recall phase. During learning, external input sets the pattern of activity in each set of neurons, as shown on the left in figure 13.1A. Hebbian synaptic modification strengthens connections between active units, as shown by the thicker lines. Note that external input is the predominant influence on postsynaptic activity during learning.

During recall, external input is given to one set of neurons, but not to the other, as shown on the right in figure 13.1A. The activity then spreads across previously strengthened connections to activate the previously associated pattern of neurons.

This simple description applies to a wide range of models, including linear associative memories (Anderson, 1972), which involve a single step of recall, and attractor neural networks (Hopfield, 1984), which involve settling over many steps of activity during recall.

Note that external input is the predominant influence on postsynaptic activity during learning, but NOT during recall. Thus, associative memory function requires external mechanisms for suppressing transmission at modifiable synapses during learning (Hasselmo, 1994, 1995). In the model presented here, this can be provided by cholinergic suppression of synaptic transmission during learning. This could also be provided by suppression of synaptic transmission by activation of γ-aminobutyric acid type B ($GABA_B$) receptors (Tang & Hasselmo, 1994; Wallenstein & Hasselmo, 1997) or other receptors.

Self-Organization

In self-organizing systems, learning allows patterns of activity in one set of neurons to freely develop compressed or altered representations in another region, without any external guidance. These networks are often referred to as "competitive" neural networks, and are used to model the development of feature detectors and topographic maps.

During learning, external input sets different patterns of activity in one set of neurons, but not in the second set of neurons, as shown in figure 13.1B. This means that the second set of neurons responds on the basis of the spread of activity across the connections, which usually starts with a random distribution of strengths. Hebbian synaptic modification strengthens connections between active neurons in region 1 and neurons which happened to be active in region 2.

For self-organization, there must be some basis for competition between different units for synaptic weight. This can be obtained by weakening connections between an active unit and an inactive unit. This can also be obtained by normalization of synaptic strength, so the total sum of connection strength remains the same. This means that strengthening of one connection results in weakening of other connections. In most self-organizing systems, learning occurs during multiple presentations of many patterns. However, in the model presented here, sequential self-organization in response to single patterns is obtained.

During recall, external input sets particular patterns of activity in region 1. The activity spreads into region 2 via strengthened connections. The region 2 activity can be interpreted as a categorization or compressed representation of the patterns in region 1. For example, in the model presented here, highly overlapping patterns in region 1 representing a stream of episodic memories will be associated with nonoverlapping patterns with smaller numbers of active neurons in region 2. Note that in contrast to synapses involved in associative memory function, synapses involved in self-organization are the predominant influence on postsynaptic activity during learning. This might require suppression of the postsynaptic influence of other intrinsic synapses.

The self-organization function described here applies to a wide range of different models, most of which address the formation of feature detectors and topographic maps in the primary visual cortex (Miller, Keller, & Stryker, 1989).

A HIPPOCAMPAL MODEL OF FREE RECALL AND CUED RECALL

The network simulation of hippocampal function consists of interacting populations of neurons representing the activity of a number of different hippocampal subregions. Self-organization of input connections allows the formation of nonoverlapping, compressed representations of individual episodic memories. Associative memory function within and between regions allows input cues or context cues to evoke the stored patterns and send them back to neocortical structures.

Local Networks of Hippocampal Pyramidal Cells and Interneurons

This network simulation used simplified representations of individual neurons designed to mimic basic properties of hippocampal pyramidal cells and interneurons (Hasselmo & Stern, 1997; Hasselmo, Schnell, & Barkai, 1995). Each unit in the model had a variable representing membrane potential (relative to a resting potential of −60 to −70 mV). As in real neurons, this variable showed passive decay back to resting potential. Different models used either spiking neurons or continuous output neurons. In spiking neurons, the membrane potential would vary continuously until it reached a firing threshold, at which point a spike would be generated, and the potential would be reset to a lower value. Continuous output neurons were similar except that when the membrane potential reached firing threshold, the unit output would increase linearly in proportion to the amount by which activation exceeded the threshold.

Contrast with Connectionist Models

Simplifications are necessary in any model, but the simplifications present in this model differ considerably from most of the connectionist models you will find in this book. The models presented here can be more directly mapped to the neurophysiology of cortical regions. In contrast, many models still have physiologically unrealistic features. Three unrealistic features common to many connectionist models are (1) use of an explicit error signal to train the network; (2) use of sigmoid input-output functions; and (3) use of both positive and negative connections arising from a single unit.

1. Unrealistic supervised learning rules. Most connectionist models use supervised learning techniques—that is, techniques in which learning is regulated by an explicit comparison between actual output and desired output. The predominant technique is backpropagation of error. The explicit computation of error has not been demonstrated in cortical structures. Biologically realistic models commonly use learning rules dependent upon information available locally at individual synapses. For example, physiological data from the hippocampal formation support the existence of Hebbian synaptic modification (Kelso, Ganong, & Brown, 1986; Wigstrom, Gustafsson, Huang, et al., 1986).

2. Unrealistic sigmoid input-output functions. The sigmoid input-output function is used in most connectionist models of neocortex (Cohen & Servan-Schreiber, 1992) and hippocampus (Burgess, Recce, & O'Keefe, 1994; Gluck & Myers, 1993; McClelland, McNaughton, & O'Reilly, 1995; Myers & Gluck, 1994; Schmajuk & DiCarlo, 1992). In models with sigmoid input-output functions, the activity of individual units often gets very large, but the total output is constrained at a particular value (usually 1.0). However, cortical neurons almost never fire at the maximum firing rate dictated by intrinsic properties. Neurons can fire briefly at rates up to 200 Hz if driven very hard by current injection, but in awake behaving animals, the firing rates never go above 40 Hz in hippocampus (Ranck, 1973; Wiener, Paul, & Eichenbaum, 1989; Otto & Eichenbaum, 1992) or 100 Hz in neocortex (Hasselmo, Rolls, Baylis, et al., 1989). The shape of the sigmoid function is also wrong. The threshold in a sigmoid function is defined as the half-maximum, and the output of the neuron rises gradually below threshold as well. In contrast, intracellular recording from cortical pyramidal cells in brain slice preparations (Barkai & Hasselmo, 1994) shows that for the range of firing

frequencies observed in vivo (Schoenbaum & Eichenbaum, 1995), most neurons have a threshold linear input-output function.

3. Unrealistic combination of excitatory and inhibitory connections arising from individual units. In most connectionist models, individual units give rise to both positive and negative connections with other units (Gluck & Myers, 1993; McClelland et al., 1995; Myers & Gluck, 1994; Schmajuk & DiCarlo, 1992). This makes it easier to obtain complex functions with small numbers of units. However, it contrasts with physiological data showing a strict division between excitatory and inhibitory neurons in the cortex. The fast excitatory transmitter, glutamate, is usually released from the axon terminals of cortical pyramidal cells, which never release the fast inhibitory transmitter, GABA. In contrast, GABA is usually released from the axon terminals of cortical interneurons, which never release glutamate. Thus, there appears to be a strict division of cells causing fast excitatory potentials, and those causing fast inhibitory potentials. Co-release of transmitters with other modulatory substances has been observed, but these modulatory substances appear to have slower effects.

Connectivity Between Different Hippocampal Subregions

The basic circuit used to represent the activity in each hippocampal subregion is summarized in figure 13.2A. The network simulation of the hippocampal formation contained five subregions with different functions, including entorhinal cortex layers II and III, the dentate gyrus, hippocampal region CA3, region CA1, and entorhinal cortex layer IV. Local circuits representing these subregions were linked together to represent functional interactions within the hippocampal network. The anatomical structure of the hippocampus is summarized in figure 13.2B (see Amaral & Witter, 1989, for anatomical review), along with brief descriptions of the proposed function of individual hippocampal subregions.

Dynamics of Individual Subregions

Episodic memory function within the simulation required specific functional capabilities within the hippocampal subregions. Here the function of individual subregions is discussed in detail. The strength of individual connections is described in more detail in Hasselmo & Stern (1997).

Rapid Sequential Self-Organization in Dentate Gyrus   Self-organization of excitatory perforant path connections in the dentate gyrus formed new representations of each sequentially presented pattern. The manner in which this occurred involved the initial activation of a subset of dentate gyrus neurons due to the random initial strength of connections from the entorhinal cortex. Neurons which were active then developed stronger connections

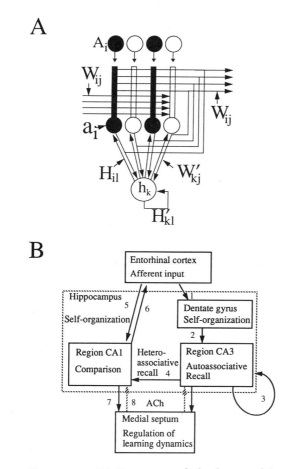

Figure 13.2 (A). Connectivity of a local circuit of the hippocampal model. Excitatory neurons with membrane potential a_i receive external input A_i and receive excitatory input from units within the region and in other regions via the connectivity matrix W_{ij}. These units also receive input from inhibitory interneurons via the connectivity matrix H_{il}. Inhibitory interneurons with membrane potential h_k receive input from excitatory neurons via connectivity matrix W'_{kj} and receive input from inhibitory neurons via the connectivity matrix H'_{kl}. (B) Proposed function of individual anatomical connections within the hippocampal formation. 1. Fibers of the perforant path connect entorhinal cortex layers II and III with the dentate gyrus. These undergo rapid self-organization to form new representations of patterns presented sequentially to entorhinal cortex. 2. The dentate gyrus projects to region CA3 via the mossy fibers. These connections pass the sparse representations on to region CA3 for autoassociative storage. 3. Longitudinal association fibers connect pyramidal cells within region CA3, mediating autoassociative storage and recall of CA3 patterns of activity. 4. The Schaffer collaterals connect region CA3 with region CA1 and mediate heteroassociative storage and recall of associations between activity in CA3 and the self-organized representations formed by entorhinal input to CA1 . 5. Perforant path connections also enter region CA1 from the entorhinal cortex. These undergo self-organization to form new representations of entorhinal cortex input for comparison with recall from CA3. 6. Projections back from region CA1 enter layer IV of the entorhinal cortex, either directly or via the subiculum. These store associations between CA1 activity and entorhinal cortex activity, allowing representations in CA1 to activate the associated activity patterns in entorhinal cortex layer IV. 7. Region CA1 can influence activity in the medial septum, either directly or via connections with the lateral septum, allowing a mismatch between recall and input to increase acetylcholine (ACh), and a match between recall and input to decrease ACh. 8. The medial septum (and the vertical limb of the diagonal band of Broca) provides cholinergic modulation to all hippocampal subregions.

with active neurons in entorhinal cortex, while connections with other inactive entorhinal cortex neurons became weaker due to the synaptic decay regulated by postsynaptic activity. In addition, connections between active entorhinal cortex neurons and inactive dentate gyrus neurons became weaker due to synaptic decay regulated by presynaptic activity. This caused a more selective pattern of connectivity between the active entorhinal cortex neurons and the neurons in the dentate gyrus forming a representation of this pattern.

At the same time as this occurred, synapses from the active inhibitory interneuron in the dentate gyrus to the active neurons in the dentate gyrus were also strengthened. This ensured that subsequently it would be more difficult to activate the dentate gyrus units which were members of this representation, ensuring that subsequent patterns of activity in entorhinal cortex would evoke different patterns of activity in the dentate gyrus. Without this feature, the network tended to lump all entorhinal cortex patterns into the same representation within the dentate gyrus.

Autoassociative Function of Recurrent Collaterals in CA3   Once individual dentate gyrus units became sufficiently active, the activity passed along one-to-one connections representing the mossy fibers and activated individual CA3 units. Initially, when cholinergic suppression was present, the pattern of activity was primarily determined by this afferent input rather than the strong recurrent excitation. This allowed selective strengthening of synapses between the neurons activated by the dentate gyrus. As these synapses became stronger, the activity in region CA3 increased, resulting in greater output to region CA1. As noted below, increased activity in region CA1 caused a decrease in cholinergic modulation throughout the network. This decreased modulation resulted in greater recurrent excitation in region CA3, such that the network entered a stable fixed point attractor pattern representing that stored memory.

This stable fixed point attractor was the main driving force for recall within the network. For example, when a cue pattern missing certain components of the previously stored input pattern was presented, it would more weakly activate individual neurons in the dentate gyrus. However, if the input was sufficient to activate a subcomponent of the CA3 representation, then the recurrent excitation would greatly strengthen this activity, pushing CA3 activity into the previously stored fixed point attractor state. Thus, considerably weaker input could elicit the same amount of CA3 output, thereby driving activity in region CA1 and entorhinal cortex layer IV.

Rapid Sequential Self-Organization in Region CA1   At the same time as sequential self-organization took place in the dentate gyrus, it also took place in region CA1 of the hippocampus. In this region, similar learning dynamics at excitatory and inhibitory connections mediated the formation of new representations. However, the considerably weaker input from the entorhinal cortex meant that this input alone could not strongly activate region CA1, but required conjoint input from region CA3. During learning, the perforant path and Schaffer collateral inputs would interact to form self-organized representations in region CA1. During recall, the pattern of activity in CA3 would elicit an associated pattern of activity in CA1, which would usually match the pattern of direct input from entorhinal cortex. When this match was sufficient, it would suppress cholinergic modulation and allow recall to be strongly driven by region CA3 output.

Heteroassociative Function of Schaffer Collaterals to CA1 As mentioned above, the output from region CA3 activated region CA1. During the initial learning of a novel pattern, the random initial connectivity of the Schaffer collaterals caused a distributed pattern of activity in region CA1, which would interact with the perforant path input to form a new self-organized representation. Subsequently, during recall, the perforant path input would initially have a stronger influence on activity in CA1. However, if the Schaffer collateral input matched the perforant path input sufficiently to cause reduction of cholinergic modulation, then the cholinergic suppression of synaptic transmission at the Schaffer collaterals would be removed. This allowed Schaffer collateral activity to dominate within region CA1, driving neurons strongly which had previously been associated with the particular activity pattern in region CA3.

Heteroassociative Feedback from Region CA1 to the Entorhinal Cortex Initially, during learning of a new pattern, the feedback from region CA1 would be suppressed by cholinergic modulation, allowing activity in entorhinal cortex layer IV to be dominated by the input coming via the one-to-one connections from layer II. This allowed storage of associations between the new pattern of activity in region CA1 and the simultaneous pattern of activity in entorhinal cortex. Subsequently, during recall, cholinergic modulation would be reduced (as described in the previous section), thereby removing the suppression of synaptic transmission at the feedback connections from region CA1. This allowed activity in region CA1 to effectively reactivate the previously associated pattern of activity in entorhinal cortex layer IV.

Feedback Regulation of Cholinergic Modulation from the Medial Septum The level of activity in region CA1 determined the level of cholinergic modulation from the medial septum. This allowed the network to respond initially to patterns with dynamics set by strong cholinergic modulation, suppressing the autoassociative and heteroassociative function of excitatory connections. This prevented associative recall at the Schaffer collaterals from interfering with effective self-organization of perforant path input to region CA1. In addition, this prevented previously stored representations from interfering with the storage of new associations at excitatory recurrent connections in region CA3, at the Schaffer collaterals connecting region CA3 and region CA1, and at the feedback connections from region CA1 to entorhinal cortex layer IV. When a sufficient level of activity in region CA1 was obtained, the cholinergic modulation would be reduced, allowing strong synaptic transmission to mediate associative recall at synapses in region CA3, region CA1, and entorhinal cortex layer IV. Thus, the feedback regulation of cholinergic modulation sets appropriate dynamics for learning and recall, though the cholinergic modulation goes through the same transition from high to low during presentation of each input pattern.

Modification of Synapses

Modifiable synapses in the model all utilized a similar Hebbian learning rule dependent upon postsynaptic and presynaptic activity, in keeping with experimental evidence on the Hebbian nature of long-term potentiation in the hippocampus (Levy & Steward, 1979; McNaughton, Douglas, & Goddard, 1978; Kelso et al., 1986; Wigstrom et al., 1986). This same learning rule provided self-organization of perforant path synapses from entorhinal cortex to dentate gyrus and region CA1, and associative memory function at the longitudinal association fibers in region CA3 and the Schaffer collaterals projecting to region CA1. The different functional properties did not arise from differences in the learning rule, but from the fact that cholinergic suppression of synaptic transmission during learning resulted in associative memory function, while the absence of suppression during learning allowed self-organization (Hasselmo, 1994, 1995). The simulation of both learning and recall within this model contrasts with other theoretical work on the hippocampus which assumes an initial pattern of connectivity and then focuses on the dynamics of recall (Treves & Rolls, 1994).

The rapid sequential self-organization of perforant path synapses in the dentate gyrus and region CA1 of the model also required decay of synaptic strength regulated by the amount of pre- and postsynaptic activity. Decay of synaptic strength can be taken as a representation of the phenomenon of long-term depression, as described in experimental preparations (Levy, Colbert, & Desmond, 1990). In most simulations, weights were clipped at specific values to maintain them within the region of stable attractor dynamics. Thus, the strength of modifiable connections did not exceed parameters termed W_{max}. The connections from inhibitory interneurons in the dentate gyrus and region CA1 were also modified. This selectively increased inhibition to units which responded strongly to an individual input pattern, making it more difficult for these same units to be activated by other patterns and ensuring their selectivity primarily for patterns closely matching the pattern to which they first responded.

Feedback Regulation of Cholinergic Modulation

The total output from units in region CA1 determined the level of cholinergic modulation within both region CA3 and region CA1. Increased region CA1 output caused decreased cholinergic modulation from the medial septum via activation of inhibitory neurons. This is consistent with experimental evidence suggesting that activity in region CA1 and region CA3 can inhibit activity in the medial septum, and thereby downregulate cholinergic modulation (McLennan & Miller, 1974). When levels of cholinergic modulation were high, there was strong suppression of synaptic transmission at the excitatory recurrent synapses in CA3, as demonstrated experimentally (Hasselmo et al., 1995), at the Schaffer collaterals projecting from region CA3 to CA1 (Valentino & Dingledine, 1981; Hasselmo & Schnell, 1994), and at projections from CA1 to entorhinal cortex layer IV. This prevented the spread of activity due to previous learning from interfering with self-organization. When levels of cholinergic modulation were decreased, the strength of synaptic transmission was increased, allowing associative recall to dominate. Simulations also included the suppression of inhibitory synaptic transmission (Pitler & Alger, 1992) in dentate gyrus, region CA3, and region CA1, and the suppression of excitatory input to inhibitory interneurons in region CA1. The cholinergic enhancement of excitatory synaptic modification (Burgard & Sarvey, 1990; Hasselmo & Barkai, 1995) was represented at all modifiable connections. Finally, cholinergic modulation caused direct depolarization of inhibitory and excitatory neurons in all regions (Barkai & Hasselmo, 1994; Benardo & Prince, 1982; Madison & Nicoll, 1984).

MEMORY FUNCTION IN THE MODEL

Basic features of human memory function were replicated in the model, using patterns of input in entorhinal cortex layer II as representations of the input during behavior, and using patterns of activity in entorhinal cortex layer IV as the output from the network. The function was analyzed in network models of the hippocampus using either spiking neurons or continuous output neurons. The spiking neuron simulations presented here have been demonstrated to perform cued recall for individual paired associates. The continuous output neuron simulations have been used to analyze learning and free recall of lists of items.

Modeling Cued Recall in a Spiking Model of Hippocampal Function

Learning and recall of paired associates was demonstrated in the network model of the hippocampus constructed from simulations of spiking neurons. An example of the function of this network is shown in figure 13.3. This figure shows the activity of neurons in different regions of the simulations

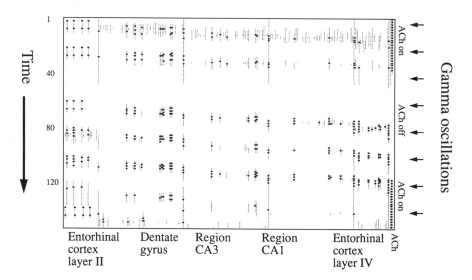

Figure 13.3 Network model of memory function in the hippocampus using spiking neurons. Activity of each of a population of neurons in each subregion of the model is represented by the width of black lines. Spiking appears as wide lines in each trace. Learning occurs when cholinergic modulation in the network is set at high levels (ACh modulation is plotted on the right-hand side). Input is presented as a pattern of activity in entorhinal cortex layer II. This forms rapid self-organized representations in the dentate gyrus, which are passed along to subsequent regions. Transmission delays between the different regions bridge the gap between sequential gamma oscillations, allowing activity on one cycle to be associated with activity on a subsequent cycle during learning. Recall occurs when cholinergic modulation in the network is at a low level. Presentation of a degraded version of the input pattern activates the previously formed representation in dentate gyrus. The spread of activity through the full loop reactivates the full representation in entorhinal cortex layer II.

(plotted horizontally) for each time step of the simulation (plotted vertically). Each black square represents a spike generated by the simulation.

As seen in the figure, a particular paired associate was presented to the model in the form of a distribution of spiking activity in entorhinal cortex layer II. Four neurons are activated on two consecutive gamma oscillations. This input was presented in the presence of cholinergic modulation (activity of cholinergic input is plotted on the far right). The activity then spreads through the network, activating a subset of dentate gyrus neurons, and then consecutively activating neurons in region CA3, region CA1, and entorhinal cortex layer IV. Synaptic modification during this activity results in storage of this self-organized representation in dentate gyrus, and associative memory function in CA3, CA1, and entorhinal cortex layer IV.

Later, the recall of the association is tested by presenting a degraded version of the input pattern to entorhinal cortex layer II, during the absence of cholinergic modulation. In the absence of cholinergic modulation, new representations are not formed, but the stronger synaptic transmission due to the absence of suppression allows strong activation of representations in CA3, CA1, and entorhinal cortex layer IV. The activity completes the full cycle and reactivates the full learned representation in entorhinal cortex layer II. This constitutes recall of the full pattern (and also allows further rehearsal of the pattern for better storage). In this framework, recall from the hippocampus requires transmission through the full trisynaptic loop, with the direct connections from entorhinal cortex to regions CA3 and CA1 providing a test of the validity of recall at each cycle. In this framework, recurrent connections within region CA3 are not the driving force for attractor dynamics, but could instead provide a mechanism for bridging between different loops, constituting links between different memories, or predictions about the next state of the environment.

Linking Episodic Memory Function to Physiological Data on Electroencephalographic and Single-Unit Recordings

Use of a spiking model of the hippocampus in evaluating episodic memory function allows this function to be discussed with direct reference to the available physiological data on hippocampal formation. Extensive recordings have been obtained from the hippocampus in awake behaving rats. Most recordings have been performed during exploration of the environment (Ranck, 1973; Wilson & McNaughton, 1993), but responses have also been analyzed during performance of various behavioral tasks (Ranck, 1973), including olfactory discrimination and delayed-nonmatch-to-sample (Otto & Eichenbaum, 1992). In addition, considerable research has focused on oscillatory dynamics within the hippocampal electroencephalogram (EEG). Low-frequency oscillations in the theta range (3 to 10 Hz) have been described extensively within the hippocampus during exploration of the environment (Ranck, 1973; Bland & Colom, 1993). And higher-frequency gamma oscillations have also been described (Chrobak & Buszaki, 1991). The firing of interneurons has been known to correlate with theta oscillations, leading to their initial designation as "theta cells" (Ranck, 1973; Stewart, Luo, & Fox, 1992). More recently, spiking of pyramidal cells has been proposed to maintain specific phase relations with the theta rhythm (O'Keefe & Recce, 1993). This allows the pattern of neuronal spike generation in the model to be discussed with regard to the pattern observed during electrophysiological experiments recording single-unit spiking activity or EEG field potentials.

Recently it has been proposed that hippocampal neurons should fire within individual gamma cycles, but only once during each theta cycle (Lisman & Idiart, 1995). This proposal may partly have arisen from the general report of very low average firing rates in hippocampal neurons. But these neurons actually show brief periods of high-frequency activity. In fact, pyramidal cells in the hippocampus are commonly referred to as "complex-spike" cells because of their tendency to emit bursts of action potentials due to an interaction of intrinsic conductances (Traub & Miles, 1991). These bursts could be ideal for driving the activity in CA3 into a particular attractor state corresponding to an individual memory since bursts result in repetitive output from a single neuron at intervals of only a few milliseconds, allowing several spikes within a single gamma oscillation. In addition to the generation of bursts, the neurons will fire at up to 30 to 40 Hz for brief periods of time, suggesting repetitive action within a single theta oscillation. This type of activity would be necessary if reverberatory activity occurs across gamma oscillations within the hippocampus.

The model presented above uses different time periods with cholinergic modulation present or absent. These changes in modulatory dynamics are particularly important with regard to the theta rhythm. It has been suggested that cholinergic modulation is important for induction of theta rhythm oscillations. This might be due to sustained cholinergic modulation inducing theta dynamics. If this is the case, it is unclear how both learning and recall can occur within the network, since the model presented above requires different dynamics for learning vs. recall. With regard to cholinergic modulation and theta rhythms, there are different possibilities.

1. Cholinergic activity follows the theta cycle. The levels of acetylcholine (ACh) within the hippocampus may rise and fall at the same rate as the theta rhythm, giving alternating cycles of learning and recall dynamics. Cholinergic neurons in the medial septum appear to fire in synchrony with theta cycles (Stewart et al., 1992), but the levels of ACh in the hippocampus have not been measured at such a fast time base. Microdialysis measurements of ACh levels are usually performed over a period of ten minutes (Inglis, Day, & Fibiger, 1994), preventing such a measurement. If this is the case, feedback regulation of modulation dependent upon the match of recall and input may set the amplitude of oscillations rather than changing a static level. However, recent data from this laboratory suggests that cholinergic effects are too slow for this—taking over a second to reach maximum amplitude, and decaying over many seconds (Fehlau and Hasselmo, unpublished data).

2. Cholinergic activity is tonic and sustained during the full period of theta dynamics. If this is the case, then changes between learning and recall dynamics must depend on other neuromodulators, since animals are clearly performing both learning and recall while they explore their environment. It is possible that cholinergic modulation sets a general activation tone during exploration, and then removal of this modulation results in sharp wave activity and consolidation, as proposed by Chrobak and Buszaki (1991). The continuum between learning and recall dynamics could instead be due to the activation of $GABA_B$ receptors on presynaptic terminals (Wallenstein and Hasselmo, 1997). Activation of these receptors causes suppression of synaptic transmission specific to connections arising from region CA3 pyramidal cells (Ault & Nadler, 1982; Colbert & Levy, 1992). The levels of GABA within the hippocampus clearly must change in time with the theta oscillation, since inhibitory interneurons are commonly phase-linked to theta oscillations (Skaggs et al., 1996; Fox et al., 1986). If this is the case, each

theta oscillation could constitute a shift between dynamics dominated by feedback and dynamics dominated by afferent input.

Modeling Paired Associate Learning in a Continuous Firing Rate Model

More extensive analysis of the storage of multiple patterns has been performed using a continuous firing rate representation of individual hippocampal neurons. This model has been used to replicate the learning and cued recall of a list of paired associates, as well as the learning and free recall of a list of single items.

For testing paired-associate memory, activity in the full hippocampal network was evaluated during sequential presentation of a series of highly overlapping activity patterns in the entorhinal cortex for 400 time steps each, followed by incomplete cues for each pattern. (The network activity was reset to zero between patterns.) This could be considered analogous to presentation of a list of paired associates, followed by presentation of one word from each pair for cued recall. Incomplete pattern cues were chosen so as to be unambiguous.

The network demonstrated the capability to store nine highly overlapping input patterns presented sequentially to the region representing entorhinal cortex layers II and III during steps 0 to 3600, followed by recall of these highly overlapping input patterns in response to incomplete cues during steps 3600 to 7200. The input and output of the simulation is shown in figure 13.4. Note that the output on the right side of the figure (entorhinal cortex layer IV) shows almost identical response to the nine incomplete cues as to the nine complete input patterns. This sequential storage and recall of highly overlapping patterns is interpreted as the capability to store episodic memories.

Figure 13.4 also shows the activity of individual neurons in the full hippocampal network during learning of the nine highly overlapping patterns of input activity. Each new pattern evoked a unique pattern of activity in the dentate gyrus, which was passed on to region CA3, where it was reinforced by recurrent excitation. The interaction of perforant path input from entorhinal cortex and Schaffer collateral input from region CA1 then activated a unique representation in region CA1, which was associated with the pattern of activity in entorhinal cortex layer IV. Sequentially presented patterns activated different representations, despite overlap between the stored patterns.

With no externally induced change in network dynamics, the network demonstrates the capability to recall stored patterns in response to incomplete cues, as shown in steps 3600 to 7200 in figure 13.4. Though the cues contain only 50 percent of the usual input activity, they sufficiently activate the previously stored representations in the dentate gyrus such that region CA3 enters the previously stored fixed point attractor state. This then activates the region CA1 representation and the associated full pattern in

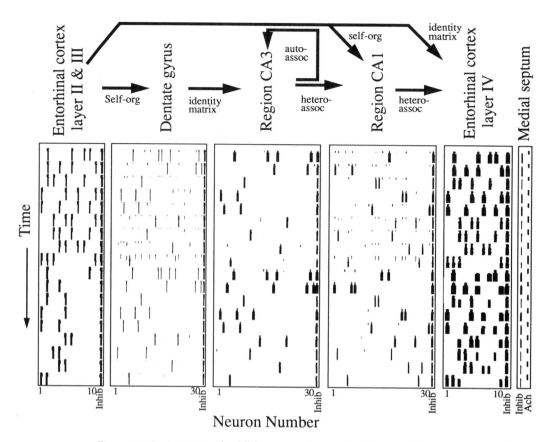

Figure 13.4 Activity in the full hippocampal network during paired-associate memory function (learning of sequentially presented overlapping input patterns). Horizontal width of black lines represents the output value of each neuron in the network during the full time period of the simulation. This includes ten excitatory neurons and one inhibitory neuron in entorhinal cortex layer II, thirty-one excitatory neurons and one inhibitory neuron in the dentate gyrus, region CA3, and region CA1, and ten excitatory neurons and one inhibitory neuron in entorhinal cortex layer IV. In addition, activity is shown for one inhibitory and one cholinergic basal forebrain neuron regulating cholinergic modulation. During the initial 3600 time steps, nine different patterns of activity are induced in entorhinal cortex layers II and III for 400 steps each. In response to each pattern, the network rapidly forms a self-organized representation of the pattern in the dentate gyrus and region CA1. The dentate gyrus pattern is autoassociated in region CA3, and associations are stored between the activity in CA3 and CA1 and between CA1 and entorhinal cortex layer IV. During steps 3600 to 7200, incomplete versions of each input pattern are presented to entorhinal cortex layers II and III. These evoke the previously formed self-organized representations in dentate gyrus, which induce recall activity in region CA3. This recall activity drives region CA1 along with the perforant path input, and the CA1 activity induces recall of previously stored patterns in entorhinal cortex layer IV. This allows the network to respond with activity in layer IV on steps 3600 to 7200 which matches the patterns learned on steps 0 to 3600.

entorhinal cortex layer IV. Comparison of the patterns in entorhinal cortex layer IV during steps 3600 to 7200 with those during steps 0 to 3600 show that the network has effectively recalled the nine stored patterns. However, note that the representations of each new pattern become more and more sparse as learning continues, resulting in weaker storage of memories stored later in the sequence. This detailed model of the hippocampus suggests a possible mechanism for the primacy effect observed in list learning. Separate simulations tested the capability of the network to respond to the incomplete cues when presented intermittently with the novel patterns to be stored. The network effectively set appropriate dynamics for storage and recall of the individual patterns without external regulation of network dynamics.

Extensive simulations demonstrated the breakdown of memory function in certain cases. Interference during recall could occur when the high degree of overlap between stored patterns resulted in recall cues being ambiguous (a cue with only two active lines would often result in recall of all patterns in which those two lines were active). This cue ambiguity could be overcome by ensuring that the cue only matched one stored pattern, or by adding an extra unambiguous input line. Interference during learning could also occur when a novel pattern matched a previously stored pattern by 75 percent of the input lines. In this case, the two patterns would be chunked together with units which initially formed the representation of the first pattern, and elements of either pattern would recall both patterns. This almost never occurred with patterns overlapping by 50 percent or less. Finally, as additional overlapping patterns were stored, the number of neurons available for forming new representations gradually decreased, resulting in sparser and sparser representations. In many cases, later patterns did not develop a stable representation, and could not be recalled with degraded cues.

Modeling Free Recall in a Continuous Firing Rate Model

Modeling free recall presents additional problems. In contrast to paired-associate learning, which has a distinct cue for each stored representation, free recall requires that a generic context associated with all items should be able to elicit recall of the individual items. This presents a difficult problem, but free recall was obtained in the model due to the attractor dynamics present in region CA3.

The structure of the model presented above was modified to allow separate attractor dynamics for context and item information. This required separate subpopulations in each hippocampal subregion to respond to the item information or to the context information. The dentate gyrus, CA3, and CA1 were all subdivided, with individual feedback interneurons for each subdivision mediating separate attractor dynamics for item and context. The function of this network is shown in figure 13.5. In region CA3, weak synaptic connections between the item and context information allowed weak

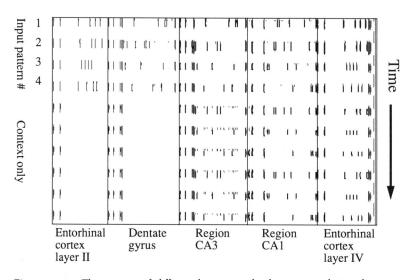

Figure 13.5 The activity of different hippocampal subregions is shown during storage and free recall of a set of four input patterns. Each region has been divided into subregions for item information and for context information, with an individual inhibitory interneuron for each subregion. There are weaker feedback connections between the context and item subregions in region CA3. The network forms rapid self-organized representations of each of the input patterns during learning. During recall, only the context portion of the input is presented to entorhinal cortex layer II. This activates the associated representation of context in the dentate gyrus and in region CA3. The context representation enters an attractor state in region CA3 which then drives recall of individual different items in the other portion of region CA3. Each attractor state in the network is terminated by the intrinsic adaptation properties of individual neurons. The persistence of adaptation currents within the neurons prevents the same pattern from being activated on sequential cycles. Note that the network sequentially recalls three of the stored items before starting a repetition of the full sequence.

associations to be formed between the context and each of the individual stored items. Subsequently, presentation of context only as a cue would evoke the attractor state associated with context. This attractor state would then activate one of the item attractor states.

Transitions between different attractor states in the free-recall model utilized an explicit model of the intrinsic adaptation properties of hippocampal pyramidal cells. The model contained representations of the buildup of intracellular calcium during firing activity, and of the calcium-dependent potassium current mediating adaptation in each pyramidal cell. This adaptation would build up during a period of activity, and eventually prevent further activity, terminating a particular attractor state. Persistence of the intracellular calcium levels in a previously recalled item attractor state would result in hyperpolarization, preventing previously recalled items from recurring on each recall cycle, but often items would appear repetitively over a longer cycle. As shown in figure 13.5, this network was capable of learning a set of items and then recalling individual items from the list.

Modeling the Effects of Scopolamine and Diazepam on Free Recall

This biologically detailed model of hippocampal memory function allows analysis of how the effect of drugs at a cellular level influences memory function. Drugs such as scopolamine and diazepam have been demonstrated to impair the learning of new information. These drugs do not affect the free recall of lists of words learned before injection of the drug, but they impair the recall of lists of words learned while under the influence of the drug (Ghoneim & Mewaldt, 1975; Peterson, 1977). The effects appear to be specific to long-term storage rather than short-term storage. For example, the ability to repeat a list of numbers forward and backward (digit span) is not affected by scopolamine (Drachman, 1978). In addition, immediate recall of the last few words in a list of words (the recency effect—Murdock, 1962) is not affected by scopolamine (Crow & Grove-White, 1973; Frith, Richardson, Samuel, et al., 1984). Thus, the recall of material stored without distraction is unaffected. However, once there is a period of distraction, even short-term storage is affected. Persistent activity in preexisting representations in the neocortex and hippocampus may mediate the retention of information for short periods without distraction. In contrast, retention of information for a period of seconds during distraction may require newly formed representations in the hippocampus. Retention of information for brief periods during distraction is tested by the Brown-Peterson task (Peterson & Peterson, 1959), in which consonant trigrams are presented before a distractor task. Scopolamine impairs recall of information in the Brown-Peterson task (Caine, Weingartner, Ludlow, et al., 1981; Beatty, Butters, & Janowsky, 1986).

The effect of scopolamine and diazepam on memory function is due to effects at specific receptors within the brain. Scopolamine (also known as hyocine) is a muscarinic cholinergic antagonist. That is, it selectively blocks the effects of ACh at a subtype of cholinergic receptor which is sensitive to muscarine (in contrast to nicotinic receptors). The effects of ACh at muscarinic receptors within cortical structures have been described extensively in brain slice and whole-animal preparations (Krnjevic & Phillis, 1963; Benardo & Prince, 1982; Madison & Nicoll, 1984; Hasselmo & Bower, 1992; Hasselmo & Schnell, 1994; Barkai & Hasselmo, 1994). As described above, these effects have been implemented in the model, allowing analysis of how their blockade impairs memory function.

Diazepam (Valium) is an agonist at the benzodiazepine receptor site of the $GABA_A$ receptor complex. The $GABA_A$ receptor protein contains a channel which allows passage of chloride ions. When activated by GABA, this channel has an inhibitory effect on cortical neurons. Activation of the benzodiazepine receptor site by diazepam enhances the conductivity of the channel, giving a stronger inhibitory effect. The enhancement of inhibitory effects within the model can be used to model the effects of diazepam on memory function.

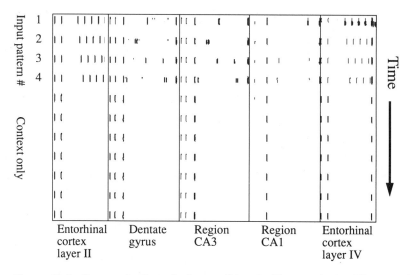

Figure 13.6 Storage of patterns for free recall impaired by scopolamine. The network shown in figure 13.5 was tested with decreased levels of cholinergic modulation during learning. The learning of new representations was impaired due to the absence of cholinergic depolarization and the slowed rate of synaptic modification. Only weak activity is elicited in response to the individual patterns presented to entorhinal cortex layer II. During recall, the context information does not elicit any item information within the network.

Figure 13.6 shows that partial blockade of cholinergic effects within the model interferes with the learning of new information for free recall, but does not interfere with the free recall of information learned before the administration of scopolamine. In this example, the impairment of learning is due to the loss of cholinergic depolarization of neurons, which prevents them from reaching activity levels sufficient for synaptic modification during learning. In addition, even when neurons do show some activity, the absence of the cholinergic enhancement of synaptic modification slows the process of learning. These effects prevent new learning, but because cholinergic suppression of synaptic transmission is also absent, the network can respond effectively to previously learned patterns.

The effects of diazepam differ considerably from those of scopolamine—they involve increasing the strength of inhibition throughout the network. However, the net effect of diazepam is similar—preventing activity sufficient for learning of new input patterns, but not preventing the recall of previously stored patterns.

A BREAKDOWN IN NETWORK FUNCTION AND ALZHEIMER'S DISEASE NEUROPATHOLOGY

If parameters are not balanced properly, the simulation undergoes a breakdown in function referred to as runaway synaptic modification (Hasselmo, 1994). Runaway synaptic modification results from synaptic transmission during synaptic modification causing an exponential growth in the strength of individual connections and the number of strengthened connections. In associative memory function, runaway synaptic modification can occur if the cholinergic suppression of synaptic transmission is insufficient to prevent recall of previously stored associations from interfering with the storage of new associations (Hasselmo, 1994). In self-organizing systems, runaway synaptic modification can occur if normalization or synaptic decay is not sufficiently strong enough to prevent activity from spreading to all neurons.

Runaway synaptic modification has been proposed to underlie the initiation and progression of neuropathologic changes in Alzheimer's disease (Hasselmo, 1994). This has been used to explain the apparent selective sensitivity of the hippocampal formation to the initial appearance of neurofibrillary tangles, and the eventual high density of neurofibrillary tangles found in this region (Braak & Braak, 1991). Because of its role in sequential storage of a large number of similar patterns, and its rapid rate of synaptic modification, the hippocampus is more sensitive to the phenomenon of runaway synaptic modification. The greatly increased demands on the metabolism and axonal transport mechanisms of a neuron strengthening a large number of individual synapses could result in the excessive production of the molecular markers of Alzheimer's disease, including the tau protein, which makes up a large component of neurofibrillary tangles.

In the hippocampal simulation, runaway synaptic modification can appear initially at the connections from entorhinal cortex layer II to the dentate gyrus if there is a reduction in the decay rate of connections to the dentate gyrus. Once this occurs, the breakdown in function can spread to other regions, owing to a sharp increase in the amount of overlap between different stored representations. Thus, the breakdown can spread to the feedback connections from region CA1 to entorhinal cortex layer IV, and via a similar mechanism can spread on into other neocortical regions.

If this breakdown in function reflects the actual progression of Alzheimer's disease, then the model can be used to generate predictions about the neuropsychological characteristics of Alzheimer's disease. In particular, it suggests that at an early stage, Alzheimer's disease should be characterized by a greater sensitivity to proactive interference. This prediction is being currently tested using a modification of the Brown-Peterson task focused on proactive interference. As the disease progresses, it will lead to a complete breakdown in episodic memory function, which is an extensively described feature of Alzheimer's disease. Other neuropsychological features of Alzheimer's disease have been discussed in the initial description of this theory (Hasselmo, 1994).

ROLE OF ACETYLCHOLINE IN NEOCORTICAL FUNCTION

So far, this chapter has focused on the hippocampus and memory function. However, the principles described here should apply to neocortical structures as well, since neocortical structures have also been demonstrated to have a capacity for Hebbian synaptic modification (Rauschecker, 1991), and the same effects of cholinergic modulation have been described within neocortical structures (Hasselmo & Cekic, 1995; Krnjevic and Phillis, 1963).

The common anatomical and physiological features of neocortical structures suggest that all neocortical regions share basic operating principles (Shepherd, 1988). Studies by neuropsychologists of the breakdown of cortical function can both contribute to and benefit from research focused on understanding the common processing characteristics of cortical structures. Research with physiologically realistic models is essential to this goal, because the wide range of cortical models which utilize connectionist architectures suffer from the failings described above—they do not sufficiently conform to physiological evidence to be mapped to the brain. As an alternative, some of the circuit properties described here might provide a means for obtaining the characteristics of error backpropagation within a more physiologically realistic framework.

Here the properties of a model of neocortical function are described, drawing on the associative attractor states, self-organizing interactions, and matching function described above. The basic unit of cortical function will be a conditional self-sustaining attractor state. Excitatory interactions within a local cortical region (such as a column) allow this self-sustained activity, similar to the sustained activity in the hippocampal model shown in figures 13.4, 13.5, and 13.6. These local excitatory loops will interact with other local circuits via self-organized connections.

The self-sustained attractor within a local circuit is conditional upon input from other regions, just as hippocampal activity is conditional upon a match between CA3 input and entorhinal cortex input to region CA1. This follows simple rules:

1. Input from another region initiates the loop, but must match the loop "recall" in order for the loop to become self-sustaining.

2. If there is no subsequent input, the loop will persist in activity for a period of time (working memory), but will eventually decay due to adaptation.

3. The loop will send output to other cortical regions via self-organized connections. These will initiate loops in other areas, which can interact either positively or negatively with the initiator.

4. It is possible for a loop to activate another loop which gives negative feedback, shutting off the first loop. This is not due to long-distance inhibitory connections, but to excitatory connections which do not match, and thereby act primarily through activation of local inhibition.

5. Positive feedback can result in metaloops which can progress through metasequences in which activation of step 2 loops shuts off step 1 loops.

6. When a particular input does not activate any previously established loop, then high levels of cholinergic modulation allow formation of a new

attractor state within the most active of columns. Formation of new attractors can occur across multiple columns, forming new global attractors.

7. In cases when multiple active loops are incompatible, the network will switch between different states until it finds a state that matches the incoming sensory constraints, or until new attractors are formed which can reconcile the conflicting attractor states.

8. This network can interact with a network containing representations of episodic memories, in order to arrive at a final consistent state without requiring repeated presentations of the individual conditions. Further development of this model of neocortical function will allow cognitive function to be directly linked to the dynamics of cortical physiology.

SUMMARY AND DISCUSSION

The simulation of the hippocampus presented here combines functional hypotheses about individual hippocampal subregions into a network capable of learning and recalling episodic memories. Simulations shown here have addressed the type of function required for paired-associate learning and free recall in tests of human memory function, and have demonstrated how the blockade of cholinergic effects by scopolamine may impair learning of new information. Within the hippocampal model, rapid self-organization of perforant path synapses in the dentate gyrus and region CA1 results in a pattern of synaptic connectivity which elicits sparse restricted patterns of activity. These patterns can be construed as representations of specific episodes (specific patterns of afferent input from the entorhinal cortex). These representations are distinct for each memory, allowing effective retrieval of missing elements of highly overlapping patterns.

The model presented here is not incompatible with another memory model focusing on different dynamics during theta rhythms and sharp waves (Buzsaki, 1989). In that theory, removal of synaptic suppression with much lower levels of ACh allows large-scale spread of excitatory activity from the hippocampus back into neocortical structures, as supported by physiological data (Chrobak & Buzsaki, 1994). That model focuses on contrasting storage of information in the hippocampus and consolidation of that information, that is, the transfer from hippocampus to neocortical structures (see McClelland et al., 1995). The model presented here focuses on the relative influence of previously stored representations or external input on the representations activated within the hippocampus by novel vs. familiar information. Consolidation has added in this network (Hasselmo et al. 1996).

The simulation presented here provides a detailed, explicit description of how hippocampal formation could mediate the formation of episodic memories. The loss of a structure which rapidly forms sparse representations of sequential input could result in the profound anterograde and partial retrograde amnesia observed in subjects such as patient H.M. (Scoville & Milner, 1957) and patient R.B. (Zola-Morgan et al., 1986). The sparing of remote episodic memory can be addressed in a simulation in which the stored hippocampal representations gradually cause the formation of discrete neocortical representations via feedback connections (Hasselmo et al., 1996; McClelland et al., 1995; Treves & Rolls, 1994). Further expansion of this model to include neocortical structures will allow simulation of a broader range of human memory data, including serial position effects in immediate free recall.

This simulation draws together hypotheses about individual hippocampal subregions, allowing analysis of the dynamic interaction of different regions. The dentate gyrus has frequently been proposed to form sparse, distributed representations of overlapping patterns in the entorhinal cortex (McNaughton, 1991; Treves & Rolls, 1994; O'Reilly & McClelland, 1994). However, sequential learning of separate self-organized representations is enhanced by the use of a novel mechanism presented here, in which inhibitory connections were strengthened in order to prevent previously formed representations from dominating learning in response to new representations. Region CA3 has frequently been proposed to have autoassociative memory function (McNaughton & Morris, 1987; Levy et al., 1990; Treves & Rolls, 1994), but this requires regulation of the strong influence of excitatory feedback. Here feedback inhibition is used to limit network activity (Hasselmo et al., 1995). In addition, excitatory feedback is prevented from interfering with new learning due to cholinergic suppression of synaptic transmission at recurrent synapses, similar to the mechanism proposed previously for piriform cortex (Hasselmo, Anderson, & Bower, 1992; Hasselmo, 1993, 1994). The Schaffer collaterals have been proposed to undergo either self-organization (Treves & Rolls, 1994) or heteroassociative memory function (McNaughton, 1991). The relative amount of these two functions depends upon how strongly the Schaffer collaterals influence activity in region CA1. If the Schaffer collaterals dominate postsynaptic activity in region CA1 during learning, then they will predominantly undergo self-organization, as proposed earlier. This must be assumed if no mechanism for modulation of synaptic transmission is incorporated in the models. However, with the cholinergic suppression of synaptic transmission at the Schaffer collaterals, the perforant path input can more strongly influence CA1 activity during learning, allowing heteroassociative memory function. This is necessary if the function of region CA1 is to provide a comparison between recall activity produced by region CA3 and direct input from entorhinal cortex, as proposed by some researchers (Eichenbaum & Buckingham, 1990). This comparison function will work most effectively if combined input from both entorhinal cortex and CA3 is necessary to cause region CA1 neurons to fire. In the simulations presented here, a comparison function of this type plays an important role in allowing cholinergic modulation to set appropriate dynamics for learning and recall.

ACKNOWLEDGMENTS

This chapter is supported by an Office of Naval Research Young Investigator Award N00014-93-1-0595 and an NIMH award R29 MH52732-01.

REFERENCES

Alvarez-Royo, P., Zola-Morgan, S., & Squire, L. R. (1992). Impairment of long-term memory and sparing of short-term memory in monkeys with medial temporal lobe lesions: A response to Ringo. *Behavioural Brain Research, 52,* 1–5.

Amaral, D. G., & Witter, M. P. (1989). The 3-dimensional organization of the hippocampal formation—A review of anatomical data. *Neuroscience, 31,* 571–591.

Anderson, J. A. (1972). A simple neural network generating an interactive memory. *Mathematical Biosciences, 14,* 197–220.

Ault, B., & Nadler, J. V. (1982). Baclofen selectively inhibits transmission at synapses made by axons of CA3 pyramidal cells in the hippocampal slice. *Journal of Pharmacology and Experimental Therapeutics, 223,* 291–297.

Barkai, E., & Hasselmo, M. E. (1994). Modulation of the input/output function of rat piriform cortex pyramidal cells. *Journal of Neurophysiology, 72,* 644–658.

Beatty, W. W., Butters, N., & Janowsky, D. S. (1986). Patterns of memory failure after scopolamine treatment: Implications for cholinergic hypotheses of dementia. *Behavioral and Neural Biology, 45,* 196–211.

Benardo, L. S., & Prince, D. A. (1982). Ionic mechanisms of cholinergic excitation in mammalian hippocampal pyramidal cells. *Brain Research, 249,* 333–344.

Bland, B. H., & Colom, L. V. (1993). Extrinsic and intrinsic properties underlying oscillation and synchrony in limbic cortex. *Progress in Neurobiology, 41,* 157–208.

Braak, J., & Braak, E. (1991). Neuropathological staging of Alzheimer-related changes. *Acta Neuropathologia, 82,* 239–259.

Burgard, E. C., & Sarvey, J. M. (1990). Muscarinic receptor activation facilitates the induction of long-term potentiation (LTP) in the rat dentate gyrus. *Neuroscience Letters, 116,* 34–39.

Burgess, N., Recce, M., & O'Keefe, J. (1994). A model of hippocampal function. *Neural Networks, 7,* 1065–1081.

Buzsaki, G. (1989). A two-stage model of memory trace formation: A role for "noisy" brain states. *Neuroscience, 31,* 551–570.

Caine, E. D., Weingartner, H., Ludlow, C. L., Cudahy, E. A., & Wehry, S. (1981). Qualitative analysis of scopolamine-induced amnesia. *Psychopharmacology (Berlin), 74,* 74–80.

Chrobak, J. J., & Buzsaki, G. (1994). Selective activation of deep layer retrohippocampal neurons during hippocampal sharp waves. *Journal of Neuroscience, 14,* 6160–6170.

Cohen, J. D., & Servan-Schreiber, D. (1992). Context, cortex and dopamine—A connectionist approach to behavior and biology in schizophrenia. *Psychological Review, 99,* 45–77.

Colbert, C. M., & Levy, W. B. (1992). Electrophysiological and pharmacological characterization of perforant path synapses in CA1: Mediation by glutamate receptors. *Journal of Neurophysiology, 68,* 1–7.

Corkin, S. (1984). Lasting consequences of bilateral medial temporal lobectomy: Clinical course and experimental findings in H.M. *Seminars in Neurology, 4,* 249–259.

Crow, T. J., & Grove-White, I. G. (1973). An analysis of the learning deficit following hyoscine administration to man. *British Journal of Pharmacology, 49,* 322–327.

Drachman, D. A. (1978). Central cholinergic system and memory. In M. A. Lipton, A. DiMascio, & K. F. Killam (Eds.), *Psychopharmacology: A generation of progress* (pp. 651–662). New York: Raven Press.

Eichenbaum, H., & Buckingham, J. (1990). Studies on hippocampal processing: Experiment, theory and model. In M. Gabriel & J. Moore (Eds.), *Learning and computational neuroscience: Foundations of adaptive networks* (pp. 171–231). Cambridge, MA: MIT Press.

Eichenbaum, H., Otto, T., & Cohen, N. J. (1994). Two functional components of the hippocampal memory system. *Behavioral and Brain Sciences, 17,* 449–518.

Fox, S. E., Wolfson, S., & Ranck, J. B. (1986). Hippocampal theta rhythm and the firing of neurons in walking and urethane anaesthetized rats. *Experimental Brain Research, 62,* 495–508.

Frith, C. D., Richardson, J. T. E., Samuel, M., Crow, T. J., & McKenna, P. J. (1984). The effects of intravenous diazepam and hyoscine upon human memory. *Quarterly Journal of Experimental Psychology, A, Human Experimental Psychology, 36,* 133–144.

Gaffan, D., & Harrison, S. (1989). Place memory and scene memory: Effects of fornix transection in the monkey. *Experimental Brain Research, 74,* 202–212.

Ghoneim, M. M., & Mewaldt, S. P. (1975). Effects of diazepam and scopolamine on storage, retrieval and organization processes in memory. *Psychopharmacologia, 44,* 257–262.

Gluck, M. A., & Myers, C. E. (1993). Hippocampal mediation of stimulus representation: A computational theory. *Hippocampus, 3,* 491–516.

Graf, P. A., Squire, L. R., & Mandler, G. (1984). The information that amnesic patients do not forget. *Journal of Experimental Psychology. Learning, Memory, and Cognition, 10,* 164–178.

Hasselmo, M. E. (1993). Acetylcholine and learning in a cortical associative memory. *Neural Computation, 5,* 32–44.

Hasselmo, M. E. (1994). Runaway synaptic modification in models of cortex: Implications for Alzheimer's disease. *Neural Networks, 7,* 13–40.

Hasselmo, M. E. (1995). Neuromodulation and cortical function: Modeling the physiological basis of behavior. *Behavioural Brain Research, 65,* 1–27.

Hasselmo, M. E., Anderson, B. P., & Bower, J. M. (1992). Cholinergic modulation of cortical associative memory function. *Journal of Neurophysiology, 67,* 1230–1246.

Hasselmo, M. E., & Barkai, E. (1995). Cholinergic modulation of activity-dependent synaptic plasticity in rat piriform cortex. *Journal of Neuroscience, 15*(10), 6592–6604.

Hasselmo, M. E., & Bower, J. M. (1992). Cholinergic suppression specific to intrinsic not afferent fiber synapses in rat piriform (olfactory) cortex. *Journal of Neurophysiology, 67,* 1222–1229.

Hasselmo, M. E., & Cekic, M. (1996). Suppression of synaptic transmission may allow combination of associative feedback and self-organizing feedforward connections in the neocortex. *Behavioural Brain Research, 79,* 153–161.

Hasselmo, M. E., Rolls, E. T., Baylis, G. C., & Nalwa, V. (1989). Object-centered encoding by face-selective neurons in the cortex in the superior temporal sulcus of the monkey. *Experimental Brain Research, 75,* 417–429.

Hasselmo, M. E., & Schnell, E. (1994). Laminar selectivity of the cholinergic suppression of synaptic transmission in rat hippocampal region CA1: Computational modeling and brain slice physiology. *Journal of Neuroscience, 14,* 3898–3914.

Hasselmo, M. E., Schnell, E., & Barkai, E. (1995). Learning and recall at excitatory recurrent synapses and cholinergic modulation in hippocampal region CA3. *Journal of Neuroscience, 15*(7), 5249–5262.

Hasselmo, M. E., & Stern, C. E. (1997). Linking LTP to network function: A simulation of episodic memory in the hippocampal formation. In M. Baudry & J. L. Davis (Eds.), *Long-term potentiation*, Vol. 3 (pp. 293–324). Cambridge, MA: MIT Press.

Hasselmo, M. E., & Wyble, B. P. (1998). Free recall and recognition in a network model of the hippocampus: Simulating effects of scopolamine on human memory function. *Behavioral Brain Research, 89*, 1–34.

Hesselmo, M. E., Wyble, B. P., & Wallenstein, G. V. (1996). Encoding and retrieval of episodic memories: Role of cholinergic and GABAergic modulation in the hippocampus. *Hippocampus, 6*, 693–708.

Hopfield, J. J. (1984). Neurons with graded responses have collective computational properties like those of two-state neurons. *Proceedings of the National Academy of Sciences, 81*, 3088–3092.

Inglis, F. M., Day, J. C., & Fibiger, H. C. (1994). Enhanced acetylcholine release in hippocampus and cortex during the anticipation and consumption of a palatable meal. *Neuroscience, 62*, 1049–1056.

Kelso, S. R., Ganong A. H., & Brown, T. H. (1986). Hebbian synapses in the hippocampus. *Proceedings of the National Academy of Sciences, 83*, 5326–5330.

Krnjevic, K., & Phillis, J. W. (1963). Acetylcholine-sensitive cells in the cerebral cortex. *Journal of Physiology, 166*, 296–327.

Levy, W. B., Colbert, C. M., & Desmond, N. L. (1990). Elemental adaptive processes of neurons and synapses: A statistical/computational perspective. In M. A. Gluck & D. E. Rumelhart (Eds.), *Neuroscience and connectionist theory*, (pp. 187–236). Hillsdale, NJ: Erblaum.

Levy, W. B., & Steward, O. (1979). Synapses as associative memory elements in the hippocampal formation. *Brain Research, 175*, 233–245.

Lisman, J. E., & Idiart, M. A. P. (1995). Storage of 7 ± 2 short-term memories in oscillatory subcycles. *Science, 267*, 1512–1515.

Madison, D. V., & Nicoll, R. A. (1984). Control of the repetitive discharge of rat CA1 pyramidal neurones in vitro. *Journal of Physiology, 354*, 319–331.

McClelland, J. L., McNaughton, B. L., & O'Reilly, R. (1995). Why are there complementary learning systems in the hippocampus and neocortex? Insights from the successes and failures of connectionist models of learning and memory. *Psychological Review, 102*, 419–457.

McLennan, H., & Miller, J. J. (1974). The hippocampal control of neuronal discharges in the septum of the rat. *Journal of Physiology, 237*, 607–624.

McNaughton, B. L. (1991). Associative pattern completion in hippocampal circuits: New evidence and new questions. *Brain Research. Brain Research Reviews, 16*, 193–220.

McNaughton, B. L., Douglas, R. M., Goddard, G. V. (1978). Synaptic enhancement in fascia dentata: Cooperativity among coactive afferents. *Brain Research, 157*, 277–293.

McNaughton, B. L., & Morris, R. G. M. (1987). Hippocampal synaptic enhancement and information storage within a distributed memory system. *Trends in Neurosciences, 10*, 408–415.

Metcalfe, J. (1993). Novelty monitoring, metacognition, and control in a composite holographic associative recall model: Implications for Korsakoff amnesia. *Psychological Review, 100*, 3–22.

Miller, K. D., Keller, J. B., & Stryker, M. P. (1989). Ocular dominance column development—analysis and simulation. *Science, 245*, 605–615.

Murdock, B. B. (1962). The serial position effect in free recall. *Journal of Experimental Psychology, 64,* 482–488.

Murdock, B. B. (1982). A theory for the storage and retrieval of item and associative information. *Psychological Review, 89,* 609–626.

Murdock, B. B., & Kahana, M. J. (1993). Analysis of the list-strength effect. *Journal of Experimental Psychology Learning, Memory, and Cognition, 19,* 689–697.

Myers, C. E., & Gluck, M. (1994). Context, conditioning and hippocampal rerepresentation in animal learning. *Behavioral Neuroscience, 108,* 835–847.

O'Keefe, J., & Recce, M. (1993). Phase relationship between hippocampal place units and the EEG theta rhythm. *Hippocampus, 3,* 317–330.

O'Reilly, R. C., & McClelland, J. L. (1994). Hippocampal conjunctive encoding, storage and recall: Avoiding a trade-off. *Hippocampus, 4,* 661–682.

Otto T., & Eichenbaum, J. (1992). Neuronal activity in the hippocampus during delayed nonmatch to sample performance in rats: Evidence for hippocampal processing in recognition memory. *Hippocampus, 2,* 323–334.

Penfield, W., & Milner, B. (1958). Memory deficit produced by bilateral lesions in the hippocampal zone. *Archives of Neurology and Psychiatry, 79,* 475–497.

Peterson, L. R. & Peterson, M. J. (1959). Short-term retention of individual verbal items. *Journal of Experimental Psychology, 58,* 193–198.

Peterson, R. C. (1977). Scopolamine induced learning failures in man. *Psychopharmacology, 52,* 283–289.

Pitler, T. A., & Alger, B. E. (1992). Cholinergic excitation of GABAergic interneurons in the rat hippocampal slice. *Journal of Physiology, 450,* 127–142.

Raaijmakers, J. G. W., & Shiffrin, R. M. (1981). Search of associative memory. *Psychological Review, 88,* 93–134.

Ranck, J. B. (1973). Studies of single neurons in dorsal hippocampal formation and septum in unrestrained rats. Part I. Behavioral correlates and firing repertoires. *Experimental Neurology, 41,* 461–531.

Rauschecker, J. P. (1991). Mechanisms of visual plasticity—Hebb synapses, NMDA receptors and beyond. *Physiological Reviews, 71,* 587–615.

Rudy, J. W., & Sutherland, R. J. (1989). The hippocampal formation is necessary for rats to learn and remember configural discriminations. *Behavioural Brain Research, 34,* 97–109.

Schmajuk, N. A., & DiCarlo, J. J. (1992). Stimulus configuration, classical conditioning, and hippocampal function. *Psychological Review, 99,* 268–305.

Schoenbaum, G., & Eichenbaum, H. (1995). Information coding in the rodent prefrontal cortex. 1. Single-neuron activity in orbitofrontal cortex compared with that in pyriform cortex. *Journal of Neurophysiology, 74,* 733–750.

Scoville, W. B., & Milner, B. (1957). Loss of recent memory after bilateral hippocampal lesions. *Journal of Neurology Neurosurgery and Psychiatry, 20,* 11–21.

Shepherd, G. M. (1988). A basic circuit of cortical organization. In M. S. Gazzaniga (Ed.), *Perspectives in memory research.* Cambridge, MA: MIT Press.

Skaggs, W. E., McNaughton, B. L., Wilson, M. A., & Barnes, C. A. (1996). Theta phase precession in hippocampal neuronal populations and the compression of thempSral sequences. *Hippocampus, 6,* 149–172.

Squire, L. R., Amaral, D. G., & Press, G. A. (1990). Magnetic resonance imaging of the hippocampal formation and mammillary nuclei distinguish medial temporal lobe and diencephalic amnesia. *Journal of Neuroscience, 10,* 3106–3117.

Stewart, M., Luo, Y. Q., & Fox, S. E. (1992). Effects of atropine on hippocampal theta-cells and complex-spike cells. *Brain Research, 591,* 122–128.

Sutherland, R. J., & Rudy, J. W. (1989). Configural association theory: The role of the hippocampal formation in learning, memory and amnesia. *Psychobiology, 17,* 129–144.

Tang, A. C., & Hasselmo, M. E. (1994). Selective suppression of intrinsic but not afferent fiber synaptic transmission by baclofen in the piriform (olfactory) cortex. *Brain Research, 659,* 75–81.

Traub, R., & Miles, R. (1991). *Neuronal networks of the hippocampus.* Cambridge, U.K.: Cambridge University Press.

Treves, A., & Rolls, E. T. (1994). Computational analysis of the role of the hippocampus in memory. *Hippocampus, 4,* 374–391.

Valentino, R. J., & Dingledine, R. (1981). Presynaptic inhibitory effect of acetylcholine in the hippocampus. *Journal of Neuroscience, 1,* 784–792.

Wallenstein, C. V., and Hasselmo., M. E. (1997). GABAergic modulation of hippocampal population activity: Sequence learning, place field development and the phase precession effect. *Journal of Neurophysiology, 78,* 393–408.

Wiener, S. I., Paul, C. A., & Eichenbaum, H. (1989). Spatial and behavioral correlates of hippocampal neuronal activity. *Journal of Neuroscience, 9,* 2737–2763.

Wigstrom, H., Gustafsson, B., Huang, Y.-Y., & Abraham, W. C. (1986). Hippocampal long-term potentiation is induced by pairing single afferent volleys with intracellularly injected depolarizing current pulses. *Acta Physiologica Scandinavica, 126,* 317–319.

Wilson, M. A., & McNaughton, B. L. (1993). Dynamics of the hippocampal ensemble code for space. *Science, 261,* 1055–1058.

Zola-Morgan, S., Cohen, N. J., & Squire, L. R. (1983). Recall of remote episodic memory in amnesia. *Neuropsychologia, 21,* 487–500.

Zola-Morgan, S., Squire, L. R., & Amaral, D. G. (1986). Human amnesia and the medial temporal region: Enduring memory impairment following a bilateral lesion limited to field CA1 of the hippocampus. *Journal of Neuroscience, 6,* 2950–2967.

14 Neural Network Modeling of Basal Ganglia Function in Parkinson's Disease and Related Disorders

Roderick K. Mahurin

The basal ganglia include the striatum (caudate, putamen, and ventral striatum), substantia nigra (pars reticularis and pars compacta), internal and external globus pallidus, subthalamic nucleus, and thalamic nuclei. Additional limbic and brain stem structures, including the amygdala, red nucleus, and reticular formation, frequently are classified as basal ganglia components. Recent studies have revealed function-specific cortico-subcortical pathways that course in parallel through the basal ganglia system (Alexander, 1995). These neural "circuits" maintain structural and functional segregation in cortex, basal ganglia, and thalamic regions. Additionally, they maintain consistent topographic mapping throughout striatothalamocortical pathways. The flow of information is of a feedforward reentrant nature, forming a series of closed loops between cortical and subcortical structures. These pathways have been designated broadly as *motor* (including oculomotor), *cognitive*, and *limbic* (Alexander, Crutcher, & DeLong, 1991; Alexander, DeLong, & Strick, 1986; Schell & Strick, 1984) (figure 14.1). Each of these neural circuits is discussed below with regard to structure, function, and clinical features.

The basal ganglia play a critical role in many neuropsychological functions, ranging from motor control and planning to attention and emotion. As subcortical structures, the basal ganglia receive information from widespread cortical sensorimotor and association regions. Information is channeled in parallel through anatomically discrete nuclei and projected back to the frontal cortex through thalamic relays. Within this structure, the basal ganglia form a network of processing centers vital to the initiation and regulation of goal-directed behavior. Certain biological attributes make the basal ganglia well suited to modeling by neural networks (Beiser, Hua, & Houk, 1997). These include (a) discrete, serially connected processing centers; (b) parallel pathways of information flow; (c) functional equivalence of processing stages for each pathway; (d) convergence of different types of information at each processing stage; (e) information flow through reentrant feedback-regulated processing loops; (f) dynamic adjustment of output based on changing spatiotemporal feedback; and (g) use of bias, or gain, to adjust overall output.

The following discussion emphasizes backpropagation networks (which are described in the first chapter of this book), but also presents several other

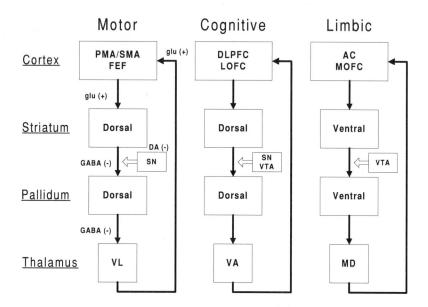

Figure 14.1 Three primary basal ganglia pathways. Note dorsal connectivity of motor and cognitive circuits, and ventral connectivity of limbic circuit. *Regions*: PMA/SMA, primary motor area/supplementary motor area; FEF, frontal eye fields; DLPC, dorsal lateral prefrontal cortex; LOFC, lateral orbitofrontal cortex; MOFC, medial orbitofrontal cortex; AC, anterior cingulate; SN, substantia nigra; VTA, ventral tegmental area; VL, ventral lateral; VA, ventral anterior; MD, medial dorsal. *Transmitters*: DA, dopamine; glu, glutamate; GABA, γ-aminobutyric acid.

important network models, including self-organizing feature maps and gated dipoles. The clinical focus is on motor control and Parkinson's disease (PD), with additional material on related neuropsychiatric disorders. The chapter concludes with a brief look at future directions in the field of computational modeling and neural network applications to basal ganglia studies.

MOTOR NETWORKS

The "motor" pathways originate in frontal motor regions, including the dorsal and ventral premotor areas, supplementary motor areas, and cingulate motor areas. Oculomotor circuits originate in cortical frontal and supplementary eye fields (Alexander & Crutcher, 1990). Target regions for motor pathways are principally in the putamen, which receives additional cortical input from postcentral somatosensory areas, as well as brainstem structures. These pathways are modulated by rich dopaminergic connections originating in the substantia nigra (Smith & Bolam, 1990). Output from the striatum to the pallidum is through two major pathways, the "direct" and the "indirect." The direct route involves the neurotransmitters γ-aminobutyric acid (GABA) and substance P, which act to inhibit output from the striatum to the internal globus pallidus, and from the internal globus pallidus to cortical output areas of the thalamus. Activation of this direct pathway facilitates movement by reducing thalamic inhibition, facilitating tonic excitation of cortical motor regions. The indirect pathway includes an additional pathway from the striatum to the internal globus pallidus, which projects to the subthalamic nucleus, the thalamus, and the cortex. This additional synaptic connection allows for a tonic inhibitory influence on the thalamus and its cortical projections. Under normal conditions, the direct basal ganglia pathway facilitates thalamic output, while the indirect pathway inhibits it (DeLong, 1990).

The basal ganglia projects to the frontal lobes via thalamocortical pathways, which terminate in regions from which cortical input originated. These connections complete frontal subcortical circuits of simple and complex motor processes, preserving somatotopic organization throughout the system (Hoover & Strick, 1993; Mushiake & Strick, 1993; Parent & Hazrati, 1993). Regardless of the original cortical sites, there are specific rostrocaudal target areas in the basal ganglia associated with distinct somatotopic areas, but with varying densities of dorsal vs. lateral innervation (Strick, Hoover, & Mushiake, 1993). A specific cortico-subcortical input channel may receive convergent information from several cortical sites, but this information is topographically segregated at smaller target zones within the basal ganglia themselves (Flaherty & Graybiel, 1993; Selemon & Goldman-Rakic, 1985).

PD is the most prevalent movement disorder associated with basal ganglia dysfunction, and study of the disorder has provided fundamental information on basal ganglia processes. Discovery of the essential role of degenerative changes in dopaminergic substantia nigra cells with resultant loss of input to the striatum, together with demonstrated improvement in PD following dopamine replacement therapy, has clarified the neurophysiological basis of the disorder (DeLong, 1990; Graybiel, 1984; Penney & Young, 1983). Primary clinical features of PD include bradykinesia, rigidity, and resting tremor, with associated features of postural instability, autonomic dysfunction, and oculomotor irregularities (Jankovic & Caine, 1987; Marsden, 1982, 1990). These motor symptoms often are accompanied by impairment in cognitive functioning (Cummings & Benson, 1992; Huber & Cummings, 1992; Mahurin, Feher, Nance, et al., 1993; Mayeux, 1990; Stern & Mayeux, 1986). Detailed studies of motor dysfunction consistently reveal slowness in limb movements, secondary to insufficient scaling of the force of the initial agonist impulse, resulting in several corrective agonist-antagonist iterations of decreasing velocity (Berardelli, Dick, Rothwell, et al., 1986; Evarts, Teravainen, & Calne, 1981). In addition, there is dampening of repetitive movements such as finger tapping, which progressively decrease in amplitude and velocity over time. PD patients also show disproportionate motor slowing when attempting to execute two motor programs either simultaneously or in sequential fashion (Benecke, Rothwell, Dick, et al., 1986). These and many other studies of motor function in PD have done much to elucidate the role of the basal ganglia in the initiation and maintenance of complex motor activity (Marsden, 1987).

Motor Control

The basal ganglia are essential to the planning, execution, and modification of goal-directed motor control. Artificial neural networks have proven to be valuable tools for modeling interactions between various cortical and subcortical structures vital to the production of such controlled motor behavior. Figure 14.2 illustrates a basic backpropagation network that effectively models elements of a self-correcting motor system. Output nodes represent motor commands to specific agonist and antagonist muscle groups, which pass from the basal ganglia to cortical motor areas, and then to the spinal cord and muscle effectors. The "goal state" represents a limb-target inter-

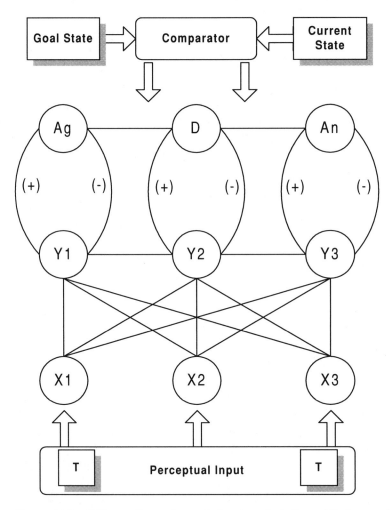

Figure 14.2 Self-correcting motor control system. A similar architecture can be applied to attention and goal-directed networks as described in the text. X, perceptual data; Y, inner layer; (+)/(−), connection weights; Ag, agonist; An, antagonist; D, displacement; T, time delay. (Adapted from Borrett, Yeap, & Kwan, 1993.)

section, and includes both temporal and spatial aspects. Input is acquired through visual, somatosensory, and proprioceptive receptors, and reflects "current state" information. The "comparator" calculates a temporal integration of output values over units of time, represented by consecutive passes of data through the network. The comparator function may represent the activity of prefrontal regions, basal ganglia centers, or ongoing interaction between cortical and subcortical areas (Tolkunov, Orlov, & Afanas'ev, 1997). Patterns of connection weights dynamically are sampled and self-adjust through backpropagation to minimize the difference value produced by the comparator. Movement precision can be enhanced by increasing the temporal resolution, increasing the quality or quantity of input data, or sharpening the signal-to-noise ratio through lateral competition (Miall, 1995).

Descriptions of PD and other movement disorders are based on the concept of disturbances in motor programming, in which stored action plans (schemas) are selected and carried out. However, motor programs per se have no obvious correlates in the activity of the nervous system itself. Borrett, Yeap, and Kwan (1993) designed a network that models the features of a motor program, but without the need for a central controller or programmer. The main feature of this model is an unsupervised relaxation of the network into one of three attractor states: fixed, periodic, or chaotic ("strange"). The last state is unpredictable, and represents tonic disturbance of the system under consideration. The model establishes a dynamic, recurrent network that extends the basic motor control system presented above by the addition of nodes for spatial displacement and a time delay (see figure 14.2). The time delay allows for reentrant input of the last output state as well as the next-to-last output. Synaptic (connection) weights are optimized through backpropagation to minimize the mean square error between the ideal limb trajectory (goal state) and the final output state produced by the network. This network can model both a simple ballistic movement and a repetitive movement about a single joint. Once the network is optimized, a generalized decrease in excitability of the inner layer of nodes can be introduced to mimic dopamine depletion in PD. This is accomplished by shifting the sigmoid transfer function to increase the threshold value. Final behavior of the network closely parallels that derived from quantitative evaluation of movements in PD patients (Borrett et al., 1993).

Pharmacologic Mechanisms

Several artificial network models have been developed to demonstrate the critical role of dopamine depletion in PD (Contreras-Vital & Stelmach, 1995; Kotter & Wickens, 1995). For example, Jamieson and colleagues (Jamieson, 1991) proposed a network approach to test several dopamine models of movement dysfunction in PD. Each of several base architectures was modified to simulate different neurophysiological interactions (figure 14.3). The

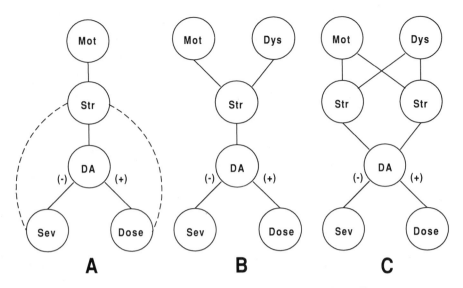

Figure 14.3 Pharmacologic network models developed to test levodopa effects on motor performance in Parkinson's disease. A, Direct vs. indirect input to striatum. B, Two output units. C, Two cross-connected output units. Mot, motor; Str, striatum; DA, dopamine; Sev, severity; Dys, dyskinesia. (Adapted in part from Jamieson, 1991.)

networks used a simplified model in which each node represented a neuronal population, drug effect, or treatment outcome. Two input nodes were utilized across all models: disease type and levodopa dosage. Disease type initially was assigned an inhibitory connection bias affecting the inner node of aggregate dopamine output (hypothetically from the pars compacta of the substantia nigra), while levodopa dosage was assigned an excitatory connection bias to the same dopaminergic node.

Input and output training data were obtained from a prior study by Mouradian, Juncos, and Fabbrinii (1988), which examined the pharmacological profiles of levodopa treatment of PD. Patients were grouped into four subsets: never treated, stable, wearing off, and on/off (fluctuating). A supervised backpropagation algorithm was used to optimize connection weights. The training goal was to produce an output pattern of motor learning (and, secondarily, dyskinesia) that accurately reflected experimentally derived reported dose-response data given one of the four levels of disease severity. Training was considered stabilized when the error term (total sum of squared error) between the model's dose response predictions and the experimental data was minimized.

Model A in figure 14.3 (solid lines) failed to predict treatment response as based on disease severity, suggesting that improvement in motor response does not directly act through serially connected dopaminergic and striatal units. However, modifications of model A employing direct connections between the striatal unit and either disease severity or levodopa dose units (dotted lines) satisfactorily modeled the experimental dose-response curves, suggesting direct mechanisms of action on the striatum. The remaining models were modified in an analogous manner, yielding additional information on treatment effects, dyskinesia, and potentially significant neuronal connection strengths (Jamieson, 1991).

Motor Maps

In backpropagation networks, specific node locations within a given layer have little effect on either input or output values, largely because each node within one layer is connected to every node in the adjoining layers. However, for "self-organizing" networks the spatial distribution of responses *within* a layer is of primary importance. The organization of intralayer connectivity is optimized to translate similarity of input signals into proximity of activated nodes. This allows for the creation of topographic maps, in which similar input values are translated into proximal spatial relationships among responding neurons in the network layer itself (Kohonen, 1982; Von der Malsburg, 1982; Willshaw & von der Malsburg, 1976). The assignment of values to lattice sites is modifiable to allow for new learning. Additionally, although the spatial arrangement of outputs within the map is critical, it can be a computational abstraction of real-world spatial mapping.

A critical characteristic of self-organizing networks is the incorporation of lateral inhibition (competitive learning) into the model. This feature was derived from neurophysiological mapping using single-unit recording of biological sensory systems, especially the visual and somatic systems (Hubel & Wiesel, 1962). In the most basic *feature map*, a single node is connected to each node immediately surrounding it. Through learning, connections from the most active node become excitatory to immediately surrounding nodes, and inhibitory to more remote nodes. Proximity to the active node also determines the strength of the connection weights, being inversely related to the distance between the primary (active) node and its neighbors. This creates a dynamic competition between nodes in the layer, with nodes that are remote to the "winning" node either having a weak signal, an inhibitory signal, or no signal at all. Such a system stabilizes so that only the node with the largest overall input value effectively propagates its signal to the next layer, or becomes an "attractor basin" within the feature map itself (Aleksander & Morton, 1995; Dayhoff, 1990; Freeman & Skapura, 1992).

Self-organizing *motor maps* represent an extension of sensory feature maps, allowing for the storage of output values for each matrix point. By including learning of output values, a self-organizing feature map can be designed to model motor control paradigms (Ritter & Schulten, 1987). In these models, control commands are mapped to two-dimensional locations of excitement, just as in sensory maps (Lemon, 1988). However, the formation of a map corresponds to the learning of a specific motor task. In contrast to the flat, two-dimensional feature map of sensory representations, movement occurs in a three-dimensional space. Thus, target aiming and manipulation require a three-dimensional matrix. This three-dimensional map does not necessarily conform to the flat microcolumnar topology of the cerebral cortex itself. Nevertheless, a three-dimensional grid can be flattened into a two-dimensional space without loss of original connectivity and organization of the excitatory nodes necessary for algorithmic representation (Ritter & Schulten, 1987).

Figure 14.4 illustrates the basic architecture of a sensory map and a motor map. The upper portion of the diagram depicts a topographic feature map for recognition of sensory input. The second layer forms a feature map based on lateral inhibition of competing input. The winning, or "active," node is depicted in black; proximal nodes are gray; and inhibited nodes are white. A learning step requires correspondence of an input vector and feature node. The lower portion of the diagram represents a topographic self-organizing motor map. The addition of the third layer allows for storage of an output value specific to a motor command. In this case, the learning step requires correspondence of the input vector, feature node, and output vector. The network utilizes selective enhancement of the motor signal through lateral inhibition in order to sharpen precision of motor control.

The biological instantiation of motor maps theoretically corresponds to neuronal populations, such as cortical microcolumns, rather than individual neurons (Goldman-Rakic, 1984; Mountcastle, 1957; Takeuchi & Amari, 1979). Associations among network connection patterns and motor cell assemblies are adjusted according to specific task demands. These associations initially are established through trial-and-error learning in the development of motor skills, but later refined through iterations of closed-loop associative learning. Using motor maps, basal ganglia activity can be modeled in terms of time-dependent visuomotor integration, with outputs to cortical and brainstem motor targets. These designs can be expanded to allow for multiple arrays, modeling increasingly complex motor processes (Morita, 1996). Output from motor maps can be scalar, vector, or linear transformations, giving great flexibility to the control process. The output values can specify torque, linear displacement, ballistic, or sustained force, allowing motor action to vary in nonlinear ways depending on the dynamic excitation of the feature layer.

Motor Learning

A self-organizing network also provides a mechanism for the learning and control of movement. Although biological equivalence is not assumed in these models, the basal ganglia provide a neuroanatomical substrate that could implement a self-organizing feature map. Neurophysiological studies have revealed convergence of inputs from motor and perceptual cortical association areas into the more spatially constrained architecture of striatal structures (Alexander et al., 1986; McGeorge & Faull, 1989). Within the striatum there appears to be a discrete functional organization of "domains"

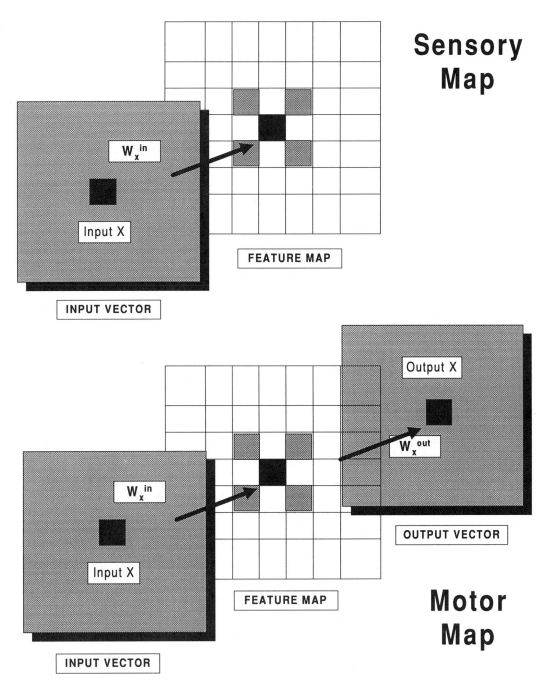

Figure 14.4 Self-organizing topographic networks. W, transfer function; black squares, active nodes; gray squares, weak nodes; white squares, inhibited nodes. (Adapted from Ritter & Schulten, 1987.)

Mahurin: Basal Ganglia Function in Parkinson's Disease

of spiny neurons corresponding to intersections of motor and sensory neo-cortical afferents (Rebec & Curtis, 1988; Selemon & Goldman-Rakic, 1985). Although the medium spiny cells in the striatum exhibit overlapping dendritic fields and local axonal aborization, neurotransmitter-dependent lateral inhibition has not directly been established between these elements. Therefore, it has been proposed that passive communication occurs within the striatal matrisome regions by way of direct electrotonic coupling (Connolly & Burns, 1995). In this manner, the firing frequency of the spiny cells codes gradient information corresponding to both the current feature state, and the next goal state in a motor sequence. Cortical neurons that project to the basal ganglia set the "boundary conditions" for competition within the feature map. Interactions between these striatal regions are hypothesized to be mutually inhibitory, with a spatial gradient function such as that for self-organizing feature maps (Wickens, Kotter, & Alexander, 1995). This type of architecture would allow for rapid computation over optimally short communication pathways, which in turn project back to the more sparsely coded cortical regions (Strick, 1985).

Maintenance of a network pattern within the striatum (i.e., relative weights of connectivity) potentially is implemented by elevations of spine calcium at corticostriatal synapses, which may persist for time intervals of up to a second (Wickens, 1988). Striatal dopamine is well established as fundamental to contingency-based learning in animals (e.g., experiments involving food, water, self-stimulation), and has been hypothesized to mediate a reward mechanism through brainstem afferents to the striatum, potentially reinforcing accurate sensorimotor behaviors (Hirata, Yin, & Mogenson, 1984). In addition, a high number of corticostriatal inputs terminate on dendritic spines that have convergent dopaminergic input from midbrain nuclei (Wickens, 1988). Striatal activity has been linked to local dopamine levels which are influenced by both cortical and limbic input (Kalivas, Churchill, & Klitenick, 1993). Approximately 40 percent of striatal spines are contacted by two boutons, one of cortical input, the other staining positively for dopamine (Freund, Powell, & Smith, 1984). Thus, an "effective" stimulus-response association (i.e., sensorimotor learning) can be strengthened at the synaptic level by time-dependent convergence of three striatal inputs: cortical sensory, cortical motor, and brain stem reinforcement (i.e., concurrent dopamine excitation) (Iriki, Pavlides, Keller, et al., 1991; Wickens, 1990; Wilson, 1995).

COGNITIVE NETWORKS

Neurophysiological studies indicate at least two primary "cognitive" striato-cortical pathways (Alexander & Crutcher, 1990). Both pathways originate in the prefrontal cortex, one in the dorsolateral area, and the other in the lateral orbitofrontal area. Both pathways have targets in the dorsal caudate nucleus. In contrast to the putamen, which is primarily involved in motor processes, the caudate nucleus is hypothesized to play a critical role in cognitive functions, including learning, memory, behavioral planning, perception, and language (Crosson, 1992; Cummings, 1990; Mayeux, 1990). A variety of networks have been constructed for modeling of cognitive processes, including those that involve the basal ganglia. Many of these networks emphasize cortical elements, and discussion of them can be found elsewhere in this book. One model, that of striatal-mediated spatial attention, is presented below.

Spatial Attention

Attentional dysfunction is a common feature of PD, in which both basal ganglia and cortical regions are closely concerned with the integration and allocation of spatial attention (Boller, Passafiume, Keefe, et al., 1984; Brown & Marsden, 1986; Hutton, Morris, Elias, et al., 1991; Levin, Llabre, Reisman, et al., 1991; Wright, Burns, Getten, et al., 1990). Frontoparietal connectivity has been described as underlying a large-scale attentional network with two major cortical components: (1) an "anterior" attention system (prefrontal and anterior cingulate) that selects (filters) incoming perceptual information and prepares goal-directed action sequences, and (2) a "posterior" attention system (parietal lobule, pulvinar, superior colliculus) that codes and transmits information regarding the spatial position of behaviorally relevant stimuli (Mesulam, 1990; Posner & Raichle, 1994). Anterior and posterior attention systems have reciprocal topological homology in their node-to-node connections, implying precise integration of spatial information (Goldman-Rakic & Friedman, 1991). In addinon, both systems synapse in the striatum in an alternating columnar architecture, allowing for integration within this region.

The basic mechanism of this attentional network is comparable to the motor control network depicted in figure 14.2 (Jackson & Houghton, 1995). However, in this instance the input to the "comparator" is that of a perceptual-attentional mismatch, rather than a limb-target mismatch. The trigger for the basal ganglia to propagate a signal is a match-mismatch comparison of inputs from the anterior and posterior attention systems. This comparison theoretically occurs either in prefrontal cortex or in the striatum itself (Schultz, Apicella, Romo, et al., 1991). When a match occurs (i.e., when the posterior spatial detection of the stimulus matches the anterior-determined positional goal state of the stimulus), the basal ganglia network is stabilized (i.e., optimized). This increases inhibition of thalamic output, and continues stabilization of the current system state. If, however, the intended and actual location states differ, the basal ganglia decrease inhibition of thalamic output, potentiating the flow of thalamofrontal information to initiate corrective motor activity (i.e., to readjust body or limb position relative to stimulus location) (Jackson & Houghton, 1995). This "tuning" of spatial attentional mechanisms through the basal ganglia is critical to proper movement, but may be disrupted in PD.

LIMBIC NETWORKS

The "limbic" corticostriatal pathway originates in, and returns to, regions of the anterior cingulate and medial orbitofrontal cortex. Subcortical targets of this pathway are in the ventral striatum, which has dopaminergic connections with the ventral tegmentum and nucleus accumbens. As discussed earlier, the cognitive and limbic pathways maintain a dorsal-ventral separation at both cortical and subcortical levels (Heimer, Alheid, & Alheid, 1993; Jayaraman, 1987) (see figure 14.1).

Contingency-based Learning

In conjunction with the limbic system, the basal ganglia underlie in the translation of motivationally relevant stimuli to adaptive behavioral responses (Kalivas et al., 1993; Mogenson, Brudzynski, Wu, et al., 1993). The limbic system itself regulates the recognition of salient goals, and monitors the outcome of behaviors directed toward achieving those goals. In turn, the basal ganglia carry out stored motor actions to obtain the limbic-generated goal states. Since most goals rarely are immediately present, a series of linked subgoals must be constructed and executed to temporally move the organism to where it can obtain each of a series of goal states (J. A. Gray, 1995a, b).

There is an extensive literature describing neostriatal mechanisms of behavioral leaning and goal-directed behavior. As with motor networks, several models of contingency-based learning hypothesize the formation of learned associations within the extended basal ganglia network (Wickens & Kotter, 1995). Coding by spiny neurons of interactions within specific dorsal cell assemblies may occur in the dorsal striatum (Rolls, 1995). Local connection weights thus are modified according to temporally dependent dopamine-mediated feedback from limbic (ventral) portions of the striatum. Progress toward proximate goals may not directly be monitored by the dorsal striatum, but by limbic structures, including the septohippocampal system and Papez circuit, including a loop from the subiculum via the mamillary bodies, anteroventral thalamus, and cingulate cortex (Totterdell & Smith, 1989). In this manner, dopamine-projecting neurons from the ventral tegmental area mediate a reward function via the nucleus accumbens, which interacts with the dorsal striatum in the selection and updating of appropriate motor actions (Oades, 1985; Young, Joseph, & Gray, 1992). Long-term memory storage of contingency-based information potentially is maintained in the septohippocampal system, with involvement of other regions such as cerebellar nuclei (J. A. Gray, 1995b; Lynch & Granger, 1992; O'Keefe & Nadel, 1978; Rawlins, Lyford, & Seferiades, 1991; Schmajuk & DiCarlo, 1991).

Based on these biological constraints, learning models have been proposed that use random associative networks for selection of appropriate actions by the basal ganglia (Rolls & Williams, 1987). Similar to motor and cognitive circuits, the striatocorticolimbic loop involves another "comparator" function. This function continually updates the organism regarding the match or mismatch between the network's current state and a motivationally salient goal state. The system also monitors the "success" or "failure" of each action in the goal gradient in approaching each subgoal. Based on this information, a backpropagation network dynamically updates the connection weights within the system. Comparator information is updated on a cyclic basis, corresponding to each "pass" of information through the limbic–basal ganglia loop (J. A. Gray, 1995b; Weiner, 1991). These contingency-based associations are mapped onto an associative network. This model requires temporal delay in the holding of information within the network, so that the "last-verified state of the world" can be held for comparison with the "current state of the world." In this manner the system can gauge progress toward each subgoal, as well as toward the final goal state (J. A. Gray, 1995b).

Neuropsychiatric Disorders

A variety of neuropsychiatric disorders are associated with basal ganglia dysfunction. For example, dysregulation of the contingency-based reward system has been associated with motivational deficits in schizophrenia, depression, and anxiety (F. Gray, Poirier, & Scaravilli, 1991; J. A. Gray, 1995b; Richfield, 1993; Swerdlow & Koob, 1987). Grossberg and colleagues (Grossberg, 1984) have developed network models for several basal ganglia–mediated neurologic and psychiatric disorders, including PD, schizophrenia, depression, and attention deficit hyperactivity disorder. These models employ the circuit-switching device of *gated dipoles*, an artificial instantiation of neural opponent processing found in biological systems. Excellent reviews of the gated dipole model can be found in several sources (Grossberg, 1984, 1991; Levine, 1991). Although the concepts of gated dipoles and opponent processing are discussed less frequently than backpropagation networks, they contain powerful features for modeling neuropsychological processes.

A schematized gated dipole model, adapted from the work of Grossberg (Grossberg, 1972a, b) is presented in figure 14.5. (for further discussion; see also Levine, 1991). Synaptic "transmitter" release at synapses W1 and W2 undergoes depletion secondary to tonic nonspecific arousal. Phasic activity temporarily increases the activity of pathway A, further depleting W1, and increasing inhibition to the output node. When this phasic input is removed, a competitive "rebound" occurs because of now greater signal strength in pathway B, increasing excitation to the output nodes. The cross-connected inhibitory pathways at A3 and B3 augment either effect. When system "arousal" is low, both the on-output and off-output channels exhibit abnormal properties. This output is determined by discontinuation of phasic activation of one input channel, in conjunction with enhancement of tonic activity from a second rebound channel once the input from the first channel is diminished or removed. Increased activity of one channel, therefore, is

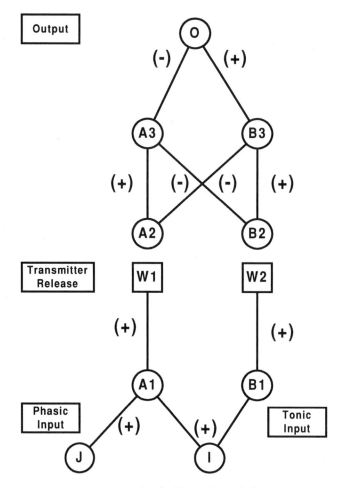

Figure 14.5 Diagram of a feedforward gated dipole network subsystem. I, chronic (non-specific) arousal; J, phasic arousal; A, B, network nodes (neurons); W1, W2, presynaptic nodes; O, output node. (Adapted from Grossberg, 1991.)

consequent to the cessation of phasic activity in the opponent channel. A gated dipole is able to compare current stimulus or reinforcement patterns with recent values of the same variables. The two channels are opposite in sign and "gate" signals based on the amount of computed "transmitter" values released at critical nodes.

The gated dipole can model such clinical features as bradykinesia, the "on/off" phenomenon, agitated depression, and manic-depressive mood swings (Grossberg, 1984). In these descriptions, the output of the gated dipole impinging on the basal ganglia depends on the interaction between context-specific time-limited activity (phasic arousal), and continuous nonspecific activity (tonic arousal). Monoamine levels theoretically determine tonic arousal. If nonspecific arousal is within a normal range, then normal behavior occurs. However, if nonspecific arousal is either above or below this normal range, pathological behavior occurs.

If tonic arousal is too low, the response threshold of phasic inputs is raised; that is, greater context-sensitive phasic arousal is required to activate these connections. Once the input threshold level is achieved, the system becomes hypersensitive to phasic input, consistent with symptoms of distractibility or inattentiveness in pathological states. As a slowly changing tonic mechanism, such switching is the hypothesized situation in attention deficit disorder, the "on/off" phenomenon in PD, and the mood swings between mania and depression. The tonic "gain" can be increased by administration to the system of an "activating" pharmacological agent, such as levodopa (carbidopa), amphetamine, methylphenidate, or a selective serotonin reuptake inhibitor (e.g., fluoxetine). A secondary effect of this intervention is a lowering of hypersensitivity.

In contrast, if tonic arousal is too high, the threshold for response to phasic input is reduced. However, once threshold is achieved, the system becomes relatively insensitive to changes in phasic input. This model of dopamine overactivation (tonic arousal) is consistent with two apparently contradictory symptoms of schizophrenic illness: positive symptoms (hallucinations, delusions, and conceptual disorganization) and negative symptoms (poverty of speech, motivation, movement, and affect). Too great an increase of an activating agent such as dopamine may result in schizophrenic-like symptoms (e.g., amphetamine psychosis). Overuse of drugs used to treat schizophrenia by lowering dopamine activity may have a contrasting effect, and induce parkinsonian side effects.

Another network model of basal ganglia–related psychopathology described by Hestenes and colleagues (Hestenes, 1991) attempts to account for interactions among the three primary monoamine neurotransmitters: dopamine (DA), serotonin (5-HT), and norepinephrine (NE). An example is manic-depressive illness. In this disorder, the site of dysfunction is ascribed to the nucleus accumbens, whose activity is influenced by both serotonergic and dopaminergic projections from brain stem nuclei. The nucleus accumbens, in turn, modulates motivational input arising from the limbic system and projecting to striatal targets (Deutch, Bourdelais, & Zahm, 1993). This modulation occurs secondary to the relative gain of both DA and 5-HT brainstem efferents to the nucleus accumbens (Swerdlow & Koob, 1987).

Evidence for this model is derived from several observations. DA pathways from the substantia nigra pars compacta project both to striatal and cortical regions (e.g., dorsolateral prefrontal cortex). PD-associated decrease in substantia nigra–produced DA is reflected in decreased receptor binding sites in the striatum, and is associated with decreased initiation and movement speed. Additional DA-modulated input arises from limbic structures, which are involved in expression of schizophrenia. In this model, tonic arousal is considered analogous to generalized DA-mediated system activation. NE is considered important for its regulation of attentional processes, particularly selective attention (phasic arousal), as well as limbic modulation of motivation, drive, and reinforcement. 5-HT is hypothesized to set a level of system-wide activity that facilitates pattern matching between different brain regions through specific and nonspecific inhibitory effects (Swerdlow & Koob, 1987).

Depression in Parkinson's Disease

PD is frequently accompanied by a persistent depressive state. It is unclear whether the degree of depression seen in PD parallels disease progression, suggesting a common pathological mechanism, or if depression is a reactive response to the debilitating aspects of PD, independent of disease severity (Ehmann, Beninger, Gawel, et al., 1990; Gotham, Brown, & Marsden, 1986; MacMahon & Fletcher, 1991; Marsden, 1990; Mayeux, Stern, Williams, et al., 1986). We approached this problem using neural network modeling of metabolic activity of brain regions involved both in PD and in major depression (Mahurin, Mayberg, Brannan, et al., 1996).

Three groups were studied: unipolar major depression (UD) (n = 25), PD with depression (PDD) (n = 12), and age-matched normal controls (NC) (n = 12). The glucose metabolic rate was measured with fluordeoxyglucose positron emission tomography (PET). Both depression groups showed similar degrees of depressive symptomatology (mean Hamilton Rating Scale for Depression = 29.4; SD = 6.9). Twelve regions of interest (ROIs) were included in the model, six previously shown to be affected in depression (dorsal anterior cingulate, ventral anterior cingulate, orbitofrontal cortex, caudate nucleus, anterior temporal region, and inferior parietal lobule) and six that had been shown to be unaffected (superior and inferior temporal gyri, posterior temporal region, hippocampus, thalamus, and striate cortex) (Mayberg, 1994; Mayberg et al., 1990).

Normalized PET counts for each of the 12 ROIs were input into a backpropagation network training model, with the three diagnostic groups representing unique output (classification) values (figure 14.6). Eight inner processing units were employed in the network architecture, characterized by weighted summation of input data (PET counts), a sigmoidal transfer function, and a 0 to 1 output value. Backpropagation recurrently adjusted the connection weights between the network units until the system relaxed into a fixed attractor state with a root mean square classification error of no greater than 5 percent.

The network was retested with a randomly preselected 10 percent of the original data set, again achieving the same level of diagnostic classification for depressed groups vs. controls. Addition of two cognitive measures to the model, the Stroop test and Trail Making test, increased the efficiency of both network classifications by a factor of 4. Once trained, the network was able to diagnosis an individual subject with a correct classification rate of 95 percent.

These findings support the hypothesis that a common neural substrate involving striatocortical interaction underlies both motor slowing and de-

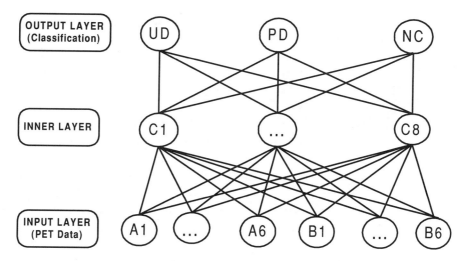

Figure 14.6 Network model for classification of Parkinson's disease and major depression. Input data, including values for basal ganglia, were derived from brain neuroimaging with positron emission tomography (PET). A, B, PET values; C, inner layer; UD, unipolar depression; PD, Parkinson's disease; NC, normal controls. (Adapted from Mahurin et al., 1996.)

pression in PD. An overlap of functional activity in depression and PD has been well documented by both clinical and neuroimaging studies (Mayberg et al., 1990). The locus of this deficit may be in the basal ganglia, frontal projection areas, or limbic regions. The described network model is consistent with clinical observations as to the difficulty in distinguishing "neurological" deficits in drive and motivation from "reactive" affective changes. This use of classification networks can be extended to more generalized models that relate cerebral, cognitive, and motor impairment in various neuropsychiatric and neurodegenerative disorders (Litran, 1996).

FUTURE DIRECTIONS

Although inspired by features of biological neurons, it should be emphasized that neural networks have varying levels of "biological equivalence" (i.e., fidelity to the anatomical systems they purport to model). "Weakly specified" computational networks can produce results identical to biological systems, but bear little resemblance in architecture to the biological system that is modeled. In contrast, "strongly specified" systems attempt to be faithful to the structure and connectivity of the biological system, as well as approximating experimentally derived relationships between input and output values. Although both types of networks are modeled on hypothesized neural connection weights, the latter cannot directly be measured between functioning neurons in the human brain. Rather, inferences are made based on the relationship between input strength or pattern and the resulting output (behavior or physiological change), similar to mapping the firing rate of the visual cortex as a function of visual signal frequency.

As suggested by Levine (1991), an effective method of modeling large-scale neural systems is to use interconnected subnetworks, in which the output of one (operation-specific) network functions as input for a second network, and so on. If connected, the output of the final subnetwork may be fed back into the first (or any of the middle networks), creating a large re-entrant system. Information flow is dynamic, self-correcting, and parallel. Further, an important aspect of multiple subnetworks is that they can be modified independently of the need to alter the overall architecture of the system.

Figure 14.7 presents a schematic of how interconnected subnetworks might be organized to model basal ganglia function. For clarity, certain critical intermediate structures, including pallidum, thalamus, substantia nigra, subthalamic nucleus, and brain stem nuclei, are not shown. Also, many aspects

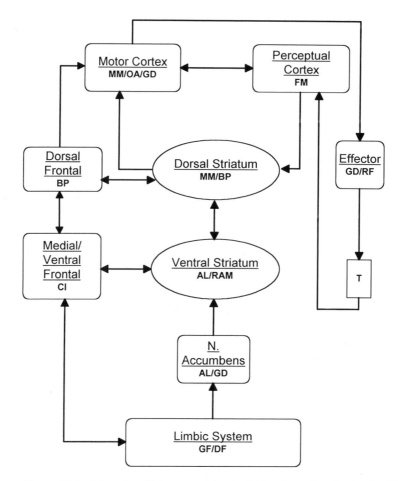

Figure 14.7 Schematic of interconnected potential basal ganglia subnetworks. *Networks*: MM, motor map; BP, backpropagation; FM, feature map; AL, associative learning; RAM, random associative memory; CI, competitive inhibition; GD, gated dipole; OA, outstar avalanche; RF, recurrent feedback; GF, gain function; DF, decay function; T, time delay.

of network architecture (e.g., cross-connections, convergence, transfer functions) have been omitted. The subnetworks include self-organizing feature mapping for perceptual analysis, associative learning for sensorimotor reinforcement, dipole gating for contingency learning, and backpropagation for programming and execution of complex motor sequences. Discussion of these networks can be found in this chapter and elsewhere throughout this book. With the addition of time-delayed feedback, and system-wide reinforcement, very complex models of basal ganglia function and disease are possible. The use of connected subnetworks is applicable to other aspects of cognition, and can be employed to model a wide range of neuropsychological disorders.

This chapter has focused on basal ganglia networks that provide goal-directed motor control and learning, with an emphasis on PD. Schizophrenia and depression were discussed as examples of neuropsychiatric disorders associated with basal ganglia dysfunction. However, networks have the potential to model other basal ganglia—related disorders, including attention deficit hyperactivity disorder, Tourette's syndrome, Huntington's disease, obsessive-compulsive disorder, and basal ganglia toxicity. Neuropsychological aspects of these disorders can be explored with the network components discussed above, including opponent processing, associative learning, lateral inhibition, and time-dependent feature analysis. New ways of viewing neuropsychological function will emerge in conjunction with new treatment strategies as clinicians become accustomed to thinking in terms of networked operations and processes. From this can arise a fundamental shift in cognitive test construction and interpretation based on anatomical and computational models of neural networking.

REFERENCES

Aleksander, I., & Morton, H. (1995). *An introduction to neural computing*, 2nd ed. New York: International Thomson Computer Press.

Alexander, G. E. (1995). Basal ganglia. In M. A. Arbib (Ed.), *The handbook of brain theory and neural networks* (pp. 139–144). Cambridge, MA: MIT Press.

Alexander, G. E., & Crutcher, M. D. (1990). Functional architecture of basal ganglia circuits: Neural substrates of parallel processing. *Trends in Neurosciences, 13,* 266–271.

Alexander, G. E., Crutcher, M. D., & DeLong, M. R. (1991). Basal ganglia—thalamocortical circuits: Parallel substrates for motor, oculomotor, "prefrontal" and "limbic" functions. *Progress in Brain Research, 85*(119), 145.

Alexander, G. E., DeLong, M. R., & Strick, P. L. (1986). Parallel organization of functionally segregated circuits linking basal ganglia and cortex. *Annual Review of Neuroscience, 9,* 357–381.

Beiser, D. G., Hua, S. E., & Houk, J. C. (1997). Network models of the basal ganglia. *Current Opinions in Neurobiology, 7,* 185–190.

Benecke, R., Rothwell, J. C., Dick, J. P. R., Day, B. L., & Marsden, C. D. (1986). Performance of simultaneous movements in patients with Parkinson's disease. *Brain, 109,* 739–757.

Berardelli, A., Dick, J. P. R., Rothwell, J. C., Day, B. L., & Marsden, C. D. (1986). Scaling of the size of the first agonist EMG burst during rapid wrist movements in patients with Parkinson's disease. *Journal of Neurology, Neurosurgery and Psychiatry, 49*, 1273–1279.

Boller, F., Passafiume, D., Keefe, N. C., Rogers, K., Morrow, L., & Kim, Y. (1984). Visuospatial impairments in Parkinson's disease: Role of perceptual and motor factors. *Archives of Neurology, 41*, 485–490.

Borrett, D. S., Yeap, T. H., & Kwan, H. C. (1993). Neural networks and Parkinson's disease. *Canadian Journal of Neurological Sciences, 20*, 107–113.

Brown, R. G., & Marsden, C. D. (1986). Visuospatial function in Parkinson's disease. *Brain, 109*, 987–1002.

Connolly, C. I., & Burns, J. B. (1995). A state-space striatal model. In J. C. Houk, J. L. Davis, & D. G. Beiser (Eds.), *Models of information processing in the basal ganglia* (pp. 163–177). Cambridge, MA: MIT Press.

Contreras-Vidal, J. L., & Stemlmach, G. E. (1995). A neural model of basal ganglia-thalamocortical relations in normal and parkinsonian movement. *Biological Cybernetics, 73*, 467–476.

Crosson, B. (1992). *Subcortical functions in language and memory.* New York: Guilford Press.

Cummings, J. L. (1990). *Subcortical dementia.* New York: Oxford University Press.

Cummings, J. L., & Benson, D. F. (1992). *Dementia: A clinical approach.* Boston: Butterworth-Heinemann.

Dayhoff, J. E. (1990). *Neural network architectures: An introduction.* New York: Van Nostrand Reinhold.

DeLong, M. R. (1990). Primate models of movement disorders of basal ganglia origin. *Trends in Neurosciences, 13*, 281–285.

Deutch, A. Y., Bourdelais, A. J., & Zahm, D. S. (1993). The nucleus accumbens core and shell: Accumbal compartments and their functional attributes. In P. W. Kalivas & C. D. Barnes (Eds.), *Limbic motor circuits and neuropsychiatry* (pp. 45–88). Boca Raton, FL: CRC Press.

Ehmann, T. S., Beninger, R. J., Gawel, M. J., & Riopelle, R. J. (1990). Depressive symptoms in Parkinson's disease: A comparison with disabled control subjects. *Journal of Geriatric Psychiatry and Neurology, 3*, 3–9.

Evarts, E. V., Teravainen, H., & Calne, D. B. (1981). Reaction time in Parkinson's disease. *Brain, 104*, 167–186.

Flaherty, A. W., & Graybiel, A. M. (1993). Two input systems for body representation in the primate striatal matrix: Experimental evidence in the squirrel monkey. *Journal of Neuroscience, 13*, 1120–1137.

Freeman, J. A., & Skapura, D. M. (1992). *Neural networks: Algorithms, applications, and programming techniques.* New York: Addison-Wesley.

Freund, T. F., Powell, J. F., & Smith, A. D. (1984). Tyrosine hydroxylase–immunoreactive boutons in synaptic contact with identified striatoniagral neurons, with particular reference to dendritic spines. *Neuroscience, 13*, 1189–1215.

Goldman-Rakic, P. S. (1984). Modular organization of prefrontal cortex. *Trends in Neurosciences, 7*, 419–429.

Goldman-Rakic, P. S., & Friedman, H. R. (1991). The circuitry of working memory revealed by anatomy and metabolic imaging. In H. S. Levin, H. S. Eisenberg, & A. L. Benton (Eds.), *Frontal lobe function and dysfunction.* New York: Oxford University Press.

Gotham, A., Brown, R. G., & Marsden, C. D. (1986). Depression in Parkinson's disease: A quantitative and qualitative analysis. *Journal of Neurology, Neurosurgery and Psychiatry, 49,* 381–389.

Gray, F., Poirier, J., & Scaravilli, F. (1991). Parkinson's disease and parkinsonian syndromes. In S. Duckett (Ed.), *The pathology of the aging human nervous system* (pp. 179–199). Philadelphia: Lea & Febiger.

Gray, J. A. (1995a). The contents of consciousness: A neuropsychological conjecture. *Behavioral and Brain Sciences, 18,* 659–676.

Gray, J. A. (1995b). A model of the limbic system and basal ganglia: Application to anxiety and schizophrenia. In M. S. Gazzaniga (Ed.), *The cognitive neurosciences* (pp. 1165–1176). Cambridge, MA: MIT Press.

Graybiel, A. M. (1984). Neurochemically specified subsystems in the basal ganglia. In D. Evered & M. O'Connor (Eds.), *Functions of the basal ganglia: CIBA Foundation Symposium 107* (pp. 114–144). London: Pitman.

Grossberg, S. (1972a). A neural theory of punishment and avoidance, l: Qualitative theory. *Mathematical Biosciences, 15,* 39–67.

Grossberg, S. (1972b). A neural theory of punishment and avoidance, ll: Quantitative theory. *Mathematical Biosciences, 15,* 253–285.

Grossberg, S. (1984). Some normal and abnormal behavioral syndromes due to transmitter gating of opponent processes. *Biological Psychiatry, 19,* 1075–1117.

Grossberg, S. (1991). A neural network architecture for Pavlovian conditioning: Reinforcement, attention, forgetting, timing. In M. L. Commons, S. Grossberg, & J. E. Staddon (Eds.), *Neural network models of conditioning and action* (pp. 69–122). Hillsdale, NJ: Erlbaum.

Heimer, L., Alheid, G. F., & Alheid, G. F. (1993). Basal forebrain organization: An anatomical framework for motor aspects of drive and motivation. In P. W. Kalivas & C. D. Barnes (Eds.), *Limbic motor circuits and neuropsychiatry* (pp. 1–43). Boca Raton, FL: CRC Press.

Hestenes, D. (1991). A neural network theory of manic-depressive illness. In D. S. Levine & S. J. Leven (Eds.), *Motivation, emotion, and goal direction in neural networks* (pp. 209–257). Hillsdale, NJ: Erlbaum.

Hirata, K., Yin, C. Y., & Mogenson, G. J. (1984). Excitatory input from sensory motor cortex to neostriatum and its modification by conditioning stimulation of the substantia nigra. *Brain Research, 321,* 1–8.

Hoover, J. E., & Strick, P. L. (1993). Multiple output channels in the basal ganglia. *Science, 259,* 819–821.

Hubel, D. H., & Wiesel, T. N. (1962). Receptive fields, binocular interaction, and functional architecture in the cat's visual cortex. *Journal of Physiology, 160,* 106–154.

Huber, S. J., & Cummings, J. L. (1992). *Parkinson's disease: Neurobehavioral aspects.* New York: Oxford University Press.

Hutton, J. T., Morris, J. L., Elias, J. W., & Varma, R. (1991). Spatial contrast sensitivity is reduced in bilateral Parkinson's disease. *Neurology, 41,* 1200–1202.

Iriki, A., Pavlides, C., Keller, A., & Asanuma, H. (1991). Long-term potentiation of thalamic input to the motor cortex induced by coactivation of thalamocortical and corticocortical afferents. *Journal of Neurophysiology, 65,* 1435–1441.

Jackson, S., & Houghton, G. (1995). Sensorimotor selection and the basal ganglia: A neural network model. In J. C. Houk, J. L. Davis, & D. G. Beiser (Eds.), *Models of information processing in the basal ganglia* (pp. 337–367). Cambridge, MA: MIT Press.

Jamieson, P. W. (1991). A computational model of levodopa pharmacodynamics in Parkinson's disease. *Clinical Neuropharmacology, 6*, 498–513.

Jankovic, J., & Caine, D. B. (1987). Parkinson's disease: etiology and treatment. In S. H. Appel (Ed.), *Current Neurology* (pp. 193–234). St. Louis: Mosby–Year Book.

Jayaraman, A. (1987). The basal ganglia and cognition: An interpretation of anatomical and connectivity patterns. In J. S. Schneider & T. I. Lidsky (Eds.), *Basal ganglia and behavior: Sensory aspects of motor functioning* (pp. 149–160). Bern: Hans Huber.

Kalivas, P. W., Churchill, L., & Klitenick, M. A. (1993). The circuitry mediating the translation of motivational stimuli into adaptive motor responses. In P. W. Kalivas & C. D. Barnes (Eds.), *Limbic motor circuits and neuropsychiatry* (pp. 237–287). Boca Raton, FL: CRC Press.

Kohonen, T. (1982). Self-organized formation of topologically correct feature maps. *Biological Cybernetics, 43*, 59–69.

Kotter, R., & Wickens, J. (1995). Interactions of glutamate and dopamine in a computational model of the striatum. *Journal of Computer Neurosciences, 2*, 195–214.

Lemon, R. (1988). The output map of the primate motor cortex: *Trends in Neurosciences, 11*, 501–506.

Levin, B. E., Llabre, M. M., Reisman, S., Weiner, W. J., Sanchez-Ramos, J., Singer, C., & Brown, M. C. (1991). Visuospatial impairment in Parkinson's disease. *Neurology, 41*, 365–369.

Levine, D. S. (1991). *Introduction to neural and cognitive modeling.* Hillsdale, NJ: Erlbaum.

Litvan, I., DeLeo, J. M., Hauw, J. J., Daniel, S. E., Jellinger, K., McKee, A., Dickson, D., Horoupian, D. S., Lantos, P. L., & Tabaton, M. (1996). What can artificial neural networks teach us about neurodegenerative disorders with extrapyramidal features? *Brain, 119 (Pt 3)*, 831–839.

Lynch, G., & Granger, R. (1992). Variations in synaptic plasticity and types of memory in cortico-hippocampal networks. *Journal of Cognitive Neuroscience, 4*, 189–199.

MacMahon, D. G., & Fletcher, P. (1991). Depression in Parkinson's disease. *Journal of Neurology, Neurosurgery and Psychiatry, 54*, 666.

Mahurin, R. K., Feher, E. P., Nance, M. L., Levy, J. K., & Pirozzolo, F. J. (1993). Cognition in Parkinson's disease and related disorders. In R. Parks, R. Zec, & R. Wilson (Eds.), *Neuropsychology of Alzheimer's disease and other dementias* (pp. 308–349). New York: Oxford University Press.

Mahurin, R. K., Mayberg, H. S., Brannan, S. K., Brickman, J. S., & Fox, P. T. (1996). Diagnostic utility of PET metabolic mapping and cognitive assessment in depression: A neural network model. *NeuroImage, 3(Pt 2)*, S78.

Marsden, C. D. (1982). The mysterious motor function of the basal ganglia: The Robert Wartenberg lecture. *Neurology, 32*, 514–539.

Marsden, C. D. (1987). What do the basal ganglia tell premotor cortical areas? In E. Bock, M. O. O'Connor, & J. Marsh (Eds.), *Motor areas of the cerebral cortex* (pp. 282–295). New York: Wiley.

Marsden, C. D. (1990). Parkinson's disease. *Lancet, 335*, 948–952.

Mayberg, H. S. (1994). Neuroimaging studies of depression in neurological disease. In S. E. Starkstein & R. G. Robinson (Eds.), *Depression in neurologic disease.* Baltimore: Johns Hopkins University Press.

Mayberg, H. S., Starkstein, S. E., Sadzot, B., Preziosi, T., Andrezejewski, P. L., Dannals, R. F., Wagner, H. N. J., & Robinson, R. G. (1990). Selective hypometabolism in the inferior frontal lobe in depressed patients with Parkinson's disease. *Annals of Neurology, 28*, 57–64.

Mayeux, R. (1990). Parkinson's disease: A review of cognitive and psychiatric disorders. *Neuropsychiatry, Neuropsychology, and Behavioral Neurology, 3*, 3–14.

Mayeux, R., Stern, Y., Williams, J. B. W., Sano, M., & Cote, L. (1986). Depression and Parkinson's disease. In M. D. Yahr & K. J. Bergmann (Eds.), *Advances in Neurology* (pp. 451–455). New York: Raven Press.

McGeorge, A. J., & Faull, R. L. M. (1989). The organization of the projections from the cerebral cortex to the striatum in the rat. *Neuroscience, 29*, 503–537.

Mesulam, M. M. (1990). Large-scale neurocognitive networks and distributed processing for attention, language, and memory. *Annals of Neurology, 28*, 597–613.

Miall, R. C. (1995). Motor control, biological and theoretical. In M. A. Arbib (Ed.), *The handbook of brain theory and neural networks* (pp. 597–600). Cambridge, MA: MIT Press.

Mogenson, G. J., Brudzynski, S. M., Wu, M., Yang, C. R., & Yim, C. C. Y. (1993). From motivation to action: A review of dopaminergic regulation of limbic-nucleus accumbens-ventral pallidum-pedunculopontine nucleus circuitries involved in limbic-motor integration. In P. W. Kalivas & C. D. Barnes (Eds.), *Limbic motor circuits and neuropsychiatry* (pp. 193–236). Boca Raton, FL: CRC Press.

Morita, M. (1996). Computational study on the neural mechanism of sequential pattern memory. *Brain Research and Cognitive Brain Research, 5*, 137–146.

Mountcastle, V. B. (1957). Modality and topographic properties of single neurons of cat's somatic sensory cortex. *Journal of Neurophysiology, 20*, 408–434.

Mouradian, M. M., Juncos, J. L., & Fabbrinii, G. (1988). Motor fluctuations in Parkinson's disease: Central pathophysiological mechanisms. Part II. *Annals of Neurology, 24*, 372–378.

Mushiake, H., & Strick, P. L. (1993). Activity of pallidal neurons during sequential movements. *Society for Neurosciences Abstracts, 19*, 1584.

Oades, R. D. (1985). The role of NA in tuning and DA in switching between signals in the CNS. *Neuroscience and Biobehavioral Review, 9*, 261–282.

O'Keefe, J., & Nadel, L. (1978). *The hippocampus as a cognitive map*. Clarendon, U.K.: Oxford University Press.

Parent, A., & Hazrati, L. N. (1993). Anatomical aspects of information processing in primate basal ganglia. *Trends in Neurosciences, 16*, 111–116.

Penney, G. R., & Young, A. B. (1983). Speculations of the functional anatomy of basal ganglia disorders. *Annual Review of Neuroscience, 6*, 73–94.

Posner, M. I., & Raichle, M. E. (1994). *Images of mind*. New York: Scientific American Library.

Rawlins, J. N. P., Lyford, G., & Seferiades, A. (1991). Does it still make sense to develop nonspatial theories of the hippocampal function? *Hippocampus, 1*, 283–286.

Rebec, G. V., & Curtis, S. D. (1988). Reciprocal zones of excitation and inhibition in the neostriatum. *Synapse, 2*, 633–635.

Richfield, E. K. (1993). Mesolimbic motor circuit in Parkinson's disease and other movement disorders. In P. W. Kalivas & C. D. Barnes (Eds.), *Limbic motor circuits and neuropsychiatry* (pp. 359–372). Boca Raton, FL: CRC Press.

Ritter, H., & Schulten, K. (1987). Extending Kohonen's self-organizing mapping algorithm to learn ballistic movements. In R. Eckmiller & E. von der Malsburg (Eds.), *Neural computers* (pp. 393–406). Heidelberg, Germany: Springer-Verlag.

Rolls, E. T. (1995). A theory of emotion and consciousness, and its application to understanding the neural basis of emotion. In M. S. Gazzaniga (Ed.), *The cognitive neurosciences* (pp. 1091–1106). Cambridge, MA: MIT Press.

Rolls, E. T., & Williams, G. V. (1987). Sensory and movement related neuronal activity in different regions of the primate striatum. In J. S. Schneider & T. I. Kidsky (Eds.), *Basal ganglia and behavior: Sensory aspects and motor functioning* (pp. 37–59). Bern: Huber.

Schell, G. R., & Strick, P. L. (1984). The origin of thalamic inputs to the arcuate premotor and supplementary motor areas. *Journal of Neuroscience, 2,* 539–560.

Schmajuk, N. A., & DiCarlo, J. J. (1991). Neural dynamics of hippocampal modulation of classical conditioning. In M. L. Commons, S. Grossberg, & J. E. Staddon (Eds.), *Neural network models of conditioning and action* (pp. 149–180). Hillsdale, NJ: Erlbaum.

Schultz, W., Apicella, P., Romo, R., & Scarnati, E. (1991). Context-dependent activity in primate striatum reflecting past and future behavioral events. In J. C. Houk, J. L. Davis, & D. G. Beiser (Eds.), *Models of information processing in the basal ganglia* (pp. 12–27). Cambridge, MA: MIT Press.

Selemon, L. D., & Goldman-Rakic, P. S. (1985). Common cortical and subcortical target areas of the dorsolateral prefrontal and posterior parietal cortices in the rhesus monkey. *Society of Neuroscience Abstracts, 11,* 323.

Smith, A. D., & Bolam, P. (1990). The neural network of the basal ganglia as revealed by the study of synaptic connections of identified neurones. *Trends in Neurosciences, 13,* 259–265.

Stern, Y., & Mayeux, R. (1986). Intellectual impairment in Parkinson's disease. In M. D. Yahr & K. J. Bergmann (Eds.), *Parkinson's disease* (pp. 405–408). New York: Raven Press.

Strick, P. (1985). How do the basal ganglia and cerebellum gain access to the cortical motor areas? *Behavioural Brain Research, 18,* 107–124.

Strick, P. L., Hoover, J. E., & Mushiake, H. (1993). Evidence for "output channels" in the basal ganglia and cerebellum. In N. Mano, I. Hamada, & M. R. DeLong (Eds.), *Role of the cerebellum and basal ganglia in voluntary movement* (pp. 171–180). Amsterdam: Elsevier.

Swerdlow, N. R., & Koob, G. F. (1987). Dopamine, schizophrenia, mania and depression: Toward a unified hypothesis of cortico-striato-pallidothalmic function. *Behavioral and Brain Sciences, 10,* 197–245.

Takeuchi, A., & Amari, S. (1979). Formation of topographic maps and columnar microstructures. *Biological Cybernetics, 35,* 63–72.

Tolkunov, B. F., Orlov, A. A., & Afanas'ev, S. V. (1997). Model of the function of the neostriatum and its neuronal activity during behavior in monkeys. *Neuroscience, Behavior, and Physiology, 27,* 68–74.

Totterdell, S., & Smith, A. D. (1989). Convergence of hippocampal and dopaminergic input onto identified neurons in the nucleus accumbens of the rat. *Journal of Chemistry and Neuroanatomy, 2,* 285–298.

Von der Malsburg, C. (1982). Outline of a theory for the ontogenesis of iso-orientation domains in the visual cortex. *Biological Cybernetics, 45,* 49–56.

Weiner, I. (1991). The accumbens–substantia nigra pathway, mismatch and amphetamine. *Behavioral and Brain Sciences, 14,* 54–55.

Wickens, J. (1988). Electrically coupled but chemically isolated synapses: Dendritic spines and calcium in a role for synaptic modification. *Progress in Neurobiology, 31,* 507–528.

Wickens, J. (1990). Striatal dopamine in motor activation and reward-mediated learning. *Journal of Neural Transmissions, 80,* 9–31.

Wickens, J., & Kotter, R. (1995). Cellular models of reinforcement. In J. C. Houk, J. L. Davis, & D. G. Beiser (Eds.), *Models of information processing in the basal ganglia* (pp. 188–214). Cambridge, MA: MIT Press.

Wickens, J. R., Kotter, R., & Alexander, M. E. (1995). Effects of local connectivity on striatal function: stimulation and analysis of a model. *Synapse, 20,* 281–298.

Willshaw, D. J., & von der Malsburg, C. (1976). How patterned neural connections can be set up be self-organization. *Proceedings of the Royal Society of London, Series B: Biological Sciences, 194,* 431–445.

Wilson, C. J. (1995). The contribution of cortical neurons to the firing pattern of striatal spiny neurons. In J. C. Houk, J. L. Davis, & D. G. Beiser (Eds.), *Models of information processing in the basal ganglia* (pp. 30–50). Cambridge, MA: MIT Press.

Wright, M. J., Burns, R. J., Geffen, G. M., & Geffen, L. B. (1990). Covert orientation of visual attention in Parkinson's disease: An impairment in the maintenance of attention. *Neuropsychologica, 28,* 151–159.

Young, A. M. J., Joseph, M. H., & Gray, J. A. (1992). Increased dopamine release in vivo in nucleus accumbens and caudate nucleus of the rat during drinking: A microdialysis study. *Neuroscience, 48,* 871–876.

15 Neural Network Modeling of Wisconsin Card Sorting and Verbal Fluency Tests: Applications with Frontal Lobe–Damaged and Alzheimer's Disease Patients

Randolph W. Parks and Daniel S. Levine

THEORETICAL MODELING OF FRONTAL LOBE FUNCTION

Several authors have developed neural network models of the effects of frontal lobe lesions on the performance of particular cognitive tasks (Bapi & Levine, 1994, 1997; Carter, Mintun, & Cohen, 1995; J. D. Cohen, Dunbar, McClelland, 1990; J. D. Cohen & Servan-Schreiber, 1992; Dehaene & Changeux, 1989, 1991; Kimberg & Farah, 1993; Leven & Levine, 1987; Levine & Prueitt, 1989; Monchi & Taylor, 1995; Parks & Cardoso, 1997; Parks, Levine, Long, et al., 1992). All these are models of selected classes of cognitive or behavioral data. They are based on approximations of neuroanatomy and general models of the functions of specific brain areas (Parks, Long, Levine, et al., 1991). The data modeled illustrate general themes about significant deficits that occur with frontal lesions. The modules and components of these networks typically illustrate general organizing principles that were designed to reproduce classes of cognitive data, and are based on structures that may be found in the brain. The reader is cautioned that the models emerging from our methodology are neither strict "localization" models, nor are they representative of an "equipotentiality" approach. The methods used in this chapter focus on the proportional contributions from multiple brain regions that work in concert to form cognitive networks or systems (Fuster, 1997; Luria, 1980; Parks, Crockett, & McGeer, 1989; Parks, Crockett, Tuokko, et al., 1989).

In this chapter, we focus on two tests commonly used by clinical neuropsychologists: the Wisconsin Card Sorting test (WCST) and the verbal fluency test (Spreen & Strauss, 1998). Both test the ability to follow dynamically changing instructions and to generate spontaneous, yet planned, behavior (Kolb & Whishaw, 1995). Performance on both tests is particularly impaired by damage to the dorsolateral prefrontal cortex (DLPFC); in the case of verbal fluency, it is especially left DLPFC lesions that impair performance (Heaton, Chelune, Talley, et al., 1993; Janowsky, Shimamura, Kritchevsky, et al., 1989; Mangels, Gershberg, & Knight, 1996; Perret, 1974; Robinson, Heaton, Lehman, et al., 1980). However, other researchers have suggested

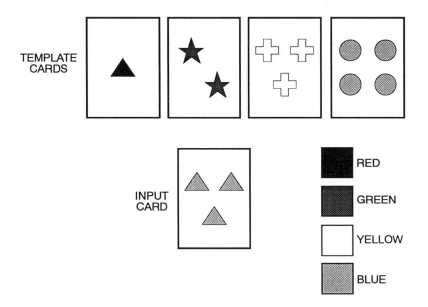

Figure 15.1 Visual Representation of the Wisconsin Card Sorting test used in clinical practice.

that the WCST and verbal fluency tests have only weak sensitivity to frontal lobe damage (for review, see Reitan & Wolfson, 1994).

In the WCST, the subject is given a sequence of 128 cards, each displaying a number, a color, and a shape, and asked to match each card to one of four template cards (one red triangle, two green stars, three yellow crosses, four blue circles; see figure 15.1). The clinician then says whether the match is right or wrong, without saying why. After ten correct color matches, the clinician switches the criterion to shape, without warning. After ten correct shape matches, the criterion is switched to number, then back to color, and so on. Milner (1963, 1964) showed that most patients with damage to the dorsolateral prefrontal cortex can learn the color criterion as rapidly as normals, but then cannot switch to shape.

There are several versions of verbal fluency tests used in clinical practice (Lezak, 1996; Spreen & Strauss, 1998). Two of the most frequently used versions include generating words in response to a letter or category in one minute. Three letters of the alphabet are used to obtain a total score over a three-minute period. The letters *F,A,S* is one version (Benton, 1968). An alternate form using the letters *C,F,L* or *P,R,W* is useful for retest assessments (Benton, Hamsher, & Sivan, 1994). Additional rules include not allowing proper names or repeating the same word with a slightly different ending. Our network is primarily concerned with phonemic or letter fluency using the letters *C,F,L*. This was done to avoid confusion with categorical fluency tests (e.g., names of animals, vegetables, and cities), which potentially have different regional cerebral network associations (Moscovitch, 1994; Troyer, Moscovitch, & Winocur, 1997).

The goal of our modeling, like that of some of the other authors in this book, is to create a network which, for different values of the network variables, can simulate both normal and frontally damaged behavior on these tests. Hence, we need to analyze which cognitive processes are involved in normal test performance. One characteristic set of defects caused by DLPFC lesions on both tests involves perseveration in a categorization that was formerly, but is no longer, rewarding or correct. Therefore, our networks need to include models of the process of categorization, selective attention, and formation of cognitive habits.

We take the approach of reducing these processes still further into smaller ones. These smaller processes, in different combinations, model a much wider range of cognitive and behavioral data, covering areas such as conditioning, decision making, and perception, as well as neuropsychological tasks. The component processes are modeled by principles that have been extensively studied mathematically and computationally. This approach was pioneered by Grossberg (1982, 1988; Hestenes, 1992, 1998; Levine, 1991; see also chapter 4 in this book).

NEURAL NETWORK PRINCIPLES

Each of the principles that we commonly use is designed for performance of a specific subfunction. These principles include

1. *associative learning,* to enable strengthening or weakening of connections between events based on contiguity or probable causality;

2. *lateral inhibition,* to enable choices between competing percepts, drives, categorizations, plans, or behaviors;

3. *opponent processing,* to enable selective enhancement of events that change over time;

4. *neuromodulation,* to enable contextual refinement of attention; and

5. *interlevel resonant feedback,* to enable reality testing of tentative classifications.

Most of these principles of network architecture were originally suggested by behavioral and cognitive data. These data were modeled using particular network dynamics that were analyzed mathematically. The mathematics often reflects generic relationships that can be manifested by an in-depth study of the experimental literature and theoretical conjecturing (Levine, 1991; Levine, Parks, & Prueitt, 1993; Rolls & Treves, 1998). The conjecturing has focused the theory and accounts for the specification of the neural network principles as follows:

• *Active representation.* Information is represented in a module by *stable activity patterns.*

• *Competitive selection.* Ambiguities and inconsistencies among module inputs are resolved by competition.

- *Associative learning.* Information is stored in modifiable synapses that encoded correlation between pre- and postsynaptic activities
- *Opponent processing* for rapid switches in pattern selection
- *Resonant coding and recognition.* New information is compressed and encoded by adaptive resonances. Recognition is a resonant matching process.

Often, neurobiological or neurochemical research will suggest improvements in the formulation of general principles that are descriptive of underlying ontology. For example, associative learning, discussed in a psychological context by Pavlov (1927) and Hull (1943), is thought to be based neurally on plasticity or modifiability of synaptic strengths. Synaptic plasticity was proposed by Hebb (1949) to explain Pavlovian conditioning data. Hebb proposed that such plasticity was based on physical growth of synaptic knobs. Subsequent experimental demonstrations of plasticity have been widespread, starting with Kandel and Tauc (1965), working in the sea slug, *Aplysia,* and Bliss and Lømo (1973), working in the rabbit hippocampus. These experimenters, however, did not find actual growth of synaptic knobs, but rather some more subtle changes in their electrochemical transmission properties. The other four principles likewise have undergone evolution as more experimental data have become available.

Lateral inhibition was first observed by psychologists studying vision (Hartline & Ratliff, 1957) who noted that bright spots were seen as brighter if closer to dark areas, and explained this in terms of inhibition between retinal or cortical reports for neighboring visual field positions. Gradually, this was generalized to other processes besides vision, such as categorization, motor control, and concept formation. In all these cases, models have been built on competitive inhibition between cell populations that code different stimuli or concepts of the same type (Amari, 1977; Grossberg, 1973; Von der Malsburg, 1973). Contrast enhancement results if the lateral inhibition is moderate, and selective attention to one component ("winner-take-all") results if the lateral inhibition is strong.

Opponent processing was developed by psychologists to explain shifts from one affect to the opposite affect with a change in the stimulus producing the emotional response (Solomon & Corbit, 1974). Grossberg (1972a,b) applied it to a network architecture which could process either novel stimuli or changes in external reinforcement. Grossberg suggested a biological basis for opponent processing that involved transmitter depletion at synapses, but a more plausible basis likely involves allosteric receptors that have been found more recently at postsynaptic membranes (Changeux, 1981).

Neuromodulation is a concept with a variety of meanings, but perhaps the best is given by Kaczmarek and Levitan (1987). These authors define *neuromodulation* as "the ability of neurons to alter their electrical properties in response to intracellular biochemical changes resulting from synaptic or hormonal stimulation" (p. 3). In networks, the idea of modulation is suggested by a large amount of cognitive data whereby contextual shifts influence what sensory features or stimuli are attended to by the organism. These contextual shifts could arise either externally, from changes in reinforcement contingencies, or internally, from changes in drive levels. Such attention shifts have suggested to many neural modelers (Dehaene & Changeux, 1989; Leven & Levine, 1987) the possibility that one neural signal can biochemically modulate the strength of another signal along a different pathway. This notion is instantiated both by the *synaptic triads* of Dehaene and Changeux's model, and the *bias nodes* of Leven and Levine's model; the latter is discussed below under Wisconsin Card Sorting Model.

Modulation is also suggested by a range of neurochemical data about the monoamine transmitters (norepinephrine, dopamine, and serotonin) and acetylcholine. Each of these substances is produced and released by a different midbrain nucleus, then sent out to broad areas of the cerebral cortex and limbic system. There is enough fragmentary evidence (Hestenes, 1992, 1998) to suggest network roles for all three of these transmitters (for norepinephrine, selective enhancement of novel or significant inputs; for serotonin, testing of match between two patterns; for dopamine, potentiation of reward signals).

Interlevel resonant feedback was introduced into a computational architecture by Carpenter and Grossberg (1987). The *adaptive resonance* model of Carpenter and Grossberg, which was one of the bases for our WCST model, was discussed in chapter 1. Basically, it includes two layers of network nodes, a feature and a category layer, which may correspond to two different levels of sensory processing. Arrays of feature patterns are classified into categories, and compared with previously stored prototypes (based on weighted averages of previous sensory inputs) to see if they are sufficiently close to the prototype patterns. If a new input pattern arrives that is unlike any prototype, it is assigned to a new category node.

Variations of these principles are introduced again, as needed, in the next two sections in the context of modeling the WCST and verbal fluency. These models include deficits on the WCST with dorsolateral prefrontal damage, and verbal fluency performance with prefrontal damage or different stages of Alzheimer's disease.

THE WISCONSIN CARD SORTING MODEL

Leven and Levine (1987) simulated the card sorting data using the network of figure 15.2. In this network, based on adaptive resonance theory (ART) (cf. figure 1.5 in chapter 1), the nodes in the layer F_1 code features, whereas the nodes in the F_2 code template cards determine categories. F_1 divides naturally into three parts that code colors, numbers, and shapes. (How these are abstracted out from the raw pattern is not considered in this network. There are numerous models of perceptual segmentation in the neural

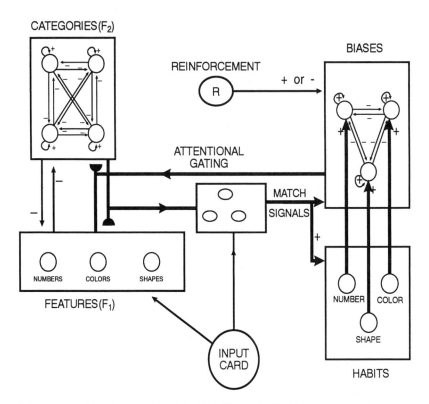

Figure 15.2 Neural network model of the Wisconsin Card Sorting test used to represent differences between frontal lobe patients and normal control subjects.

network literature, such as Grossberg and Mingolla, 1985.) Corresponding to each class of feature (color, number, shape) is a "habit node" and a "bias node." The habit nodes code how often classifications have been made, rightly or wrongly, on the basis of each feature. The bias nodes additively combine habit node activities with reinforcement signals (the experimenter's "right" or "wrong"). The bias nodes in turn modulate the excitatory signals from F_1 to F_2.

The network of figure 15.2 utilizes three of the network principles discussed in the last section. Lateral inhibition is used at the layer F_2, to allow decision between competing categorizations of an input card. Interlevel resonant feedback occurs between the two layers F_1 and F_2. This does not, however, involve long-term associative (Hebbian) learning, as in the classic applications of ART (Carpenter & Grossberg, 1987), for the connections are assumed only to be modified by the duration of the task. This short-term modification of weights is assumed to be handled by neuromodulation via connections from the bias nodes. Pennington (1994) has also suggested that there are connections to some parts of the frontal lobes that are not modifiable, in order to facilitate transient working memory storage.

Table 15.1 Results of frontal lobe modeling using the Wisconsin Card Sorting test with frontal lobe patients and control subject comparisons

	Criterion	Trial
α = 4 (Normal)	Color	13
	Shape	40
	Number	82
	Color (again)	96
	Shape (again)	115
α = 1.5 (Frontally damaged)	Color	13
	Thereafter, classified by color for all remaining trials	

Table 15.1 shows the results of simulating this network. A network parameter measuring the gain of reinforcement signals to bias nodes was varied. The network with high gain acted like Milner's normal subjects, whereas the network with low gain acted like Milner's frontal patients.

The interpretation of prefrontal damage as weak reward signals is supported by the findings of Nauta (1971), that the prefrontal cortex is the area of neocortex with strongest connections to motivational areas of the hypothalamus and limbic system. The separation of memories and habits is supported by results such as those summarized in Mishkin, Malamut, and Bachevalier (1984). These researchers showed that one neural system subserves memories of the reinforcement value of stimuli, and another system subserves motor habits regardless of reinforcement. The memory system includes the hippocampus and amygdala (part of the limbic system), and the habit system includes parts of the corpus striatum. Moreover, evidence reviewed in N. J. Cohen and Eichenbaum (1993) shows that hippocampally damaged amnesiacs with deficits in both semantic and episodic memory are far less impaired on implicit memory for specific motor procedures.

Besides the model of WCST introduced in Leven and Levine (1987) and Levine and Prueitt (1989), the other major neural network model of this task was developed by Dehaene and Changeux (1991). As discussed in Levine, Parks, and Prueitt (1993), there are striking parallels between the two models, even though they were developed independently: one primarily from the neural network principles section of this chapter, the other (Dehaene-Changeux) primarily from neurophysiological considerations.

Figure 15.3 shows the Dehaene-Changeux model. The analogies between the "input" and "memory" nodes of figure 15.3 and the "feature" and "category" fields of figure 15.2, and between their "rule-coding clusters" and our "bias nodes," are extremely close. As in our model, their rule clusters modulate synapses from input to memory nodes. Their equations demonstrate that their rule-coding clusters behave similarly to ours. In both models, the activity of rule clusters is an analog variable that can increase or decrease from

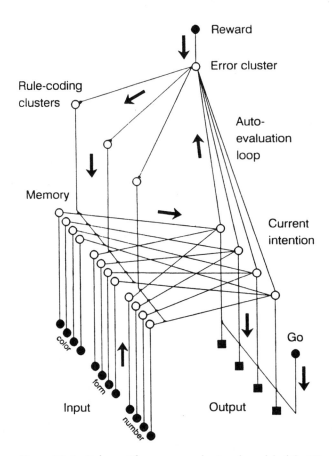

Figure 15.3 Dehaene-Changeux neural network model of the Wisconsin Card Sorting test.

one card presentation to the next. Our model also includes explicit lateral inhibition between rule clusters to enhance contrast, which theirs does not.

Dehaene and Changeux's model of the WCST goes through six stages of complexity, characterized by how they choose rules to make decisions. These choice strategies are described, in order, as (1) random; (2) random plus context; (3) random plus memory; (4) reasoning, no memory; (5) reasoning plus memory; (6) optimal. "Memory" refers to the episodic memory capacity (via an opponent-processing–like mechanism) mentioned above. "Reasoning" refers to rejecting all rules that would lead to the same incorrect response as would have been reached by the most recently rejected rule. The last two capabilities, reasoning and episodic memory, were not included in the WCST model of Leven and Levine (1987), mainly because the authors thought that the WCST was not sensitive enough to require such capabilities. However, Levine and Prueitt (1989) also use a similar network to model data (Pribram, 1973) showing enhanced reaction to novelty in monkeys with damage to the orbital prefrontal cortex. Levine and Prueitt included in the "novelty" model an opponent-processing mechanism which behaves similarly to Dehaene and Changeux's episodic memory.

DORSAL VS. ORBITAL PREFRONTAL CORTEX AND EXECUTIVE FUNCTION

The network of figure 15.2 does not deal with the distinctions between different parts of the prefrontal cortex. Petrides (1994) discussed relevant dissociations between dorsolateral (DLPFC) and medial and orbital (MOPFC) prefrontal cortex. After summarizing selected monkey and human lesion data on different cognitive tasks, Petrides suggested that tasks beyond a certain complexity, such as those where the concept of novelty is manipulated, seem to involve MOPFC. Petrides stated that tasks of still greater complexity, such as those that entail deductive reasoning, seem to involve the DLPFC.

The data, however, do not unequivocally support the notion that the main difference between those two regions is one of complexity. For example, the delayed response task, which is relatively simple, is impaired primarily by DLPFC lesions. From other data described by Petrides, the main reason for DLPFC involvement in delayed response seems to be the spatial nature of the task. That is, since the two objects are identical, in order to distinguish them the monkey must store their locations. Other tasks that are nonspatial are more dependent on MOPFC. In fact, on the delayed-matching-to-sample task, there seems to be a parcellation whereby dorsal cortex is involved if spatial cues are helpful, and orbital otherwise. Presumably, the importance of the DLPFC in spatial-related processing is related to the connections of this region with space-sensitive regions of the parietal cortex, whereas MOPFC modulates nonspatial processing through connections with object-sensitive regions of the inferior temporal cortex.

Another distinction between DLPFC and MOPFC is that the former is more involved in detailed cognitive processing, whereas the latter (via reciprocal connections with the amygdala and hypothalamus) is more involved in affective processing. In both the cognitive and affective subsystems, inhibition of inappropriate responses is important. Milner and Petrides (1984) noted that DLPFC is the most critical area for WCST, whose performance relies on inhibition of habitual responses when the context makes these responses inappropriate. Yet Damasio (1994) reported findings on patients with MOPFC lesions suffering lack of inhibition in socially inappropriate situations. Recent results of Dias, Robbins, and Roberts (1996) support such a functional dissociation of attentional and affective shifts at the prefrontal level.

Current efforts are underway (Levine, 1996) to integrate both the dorsal and orbital areas of the frontal lobes, and their connections to basal ganglia, thalamus, amygdala, and hippocampus, into an overall neural network theory of what has widely become known as *executive function* (Lezak, 1996; Luria, 1980). The term has been given many definitions, among them, "to maintain an appropriate problem-solving set for attainment of a future goal" (Welsh & Pennington, 1988, p. 201), and "to select the responses most advantageous for the organism in a complex social environment" (Damasio, 1991, p. 404).

Other researchers have suggested that executive functions also include insight, self-control, self-monitoring, and self-planning (Karpov & Haywood, 1998; McGlynn & Schacter, 1997; Rabbitt, 1998).

Many neuropsychologists have avoided the word "executive" for the frontal lobes because of its connotation of a single brain area with highly precise functions "controlling" the functions of the rest of the brain (Stuss, Shallice, & Alexander, 1995). However, we believe that the executive concept is a useful one for understanding the functional integration of many interdependent brain areas involved in cognitive function in complex environments. It is particularly useful if we think not of an executive *center* but of an executive *system*, in which different areas of the frontal lobes are playing dissociable but interconnected roles. In our laboratories, we have carried out an analysis of a range of cognitive data in humans and primates, with the assistance of R. Bapi, G. Bugmann, and J. Taylor, and have tentatively identified three principal subcomponents of executive functioning for modeling purposes. These are (1) establishing links between working memory representations, which could represent sensory stimuli, potential motor actions, rewards, or punishments (Goldman-Rakic, 1987, 1992; Kimberg & Farah, 1993); (2) creating, learning, and deciding among high-level schemas that embody repeatable, but often flexible action sequences (Grafman, 1994; Passingham, 1993); and (3) incorporating affective evaluations of sensory events or potential motor plans and using these evaluations to guide actions (Levine & Prueitt, 1989; Nauta, 1971).

In this regard, many symptoms that frontal lobe patients have (some dorsolateral and some orbital, though it is often difficult to locate the lesion exactly) are seen as disturbances of executive function (Lezak, 1996). Tranel, Anderson, and Benton (1994) summarized many tests of different aspects of executive function: these included the WCST, used to test flexibility in shifting between cognitive categories; verbal fluency, used to test both spontaneity and ability to follow instructions; and tests whose modeling is discussed in other chapters of this book, such as the Stroop test and Tower of Hanoi.

MODELING VERBAL FLUENCY

The model in Levine and Parks (1992) of frontal effects on verbal fluency is derived from a previous model of the WCST (Leven & Levine, 1987; Levine & Prueitt, 1989; Parks et al., 1992). While different in ways to be discussed, the verbal fluency test and WCST have enough in common to suggest that models of the two tests should share some features. For example, both tests involve sustained attention, shifting of cognitive set, perseveration, and category formation.

In the case of verbal fluency, there are at least three posslble effects by which frontal lobe damage can reduce the word count (Crockett, Bilsker, Hurwitz, et al., 1986). The model neural network of Levine and Parks (1992) is constructed in such a way that all three effects can be produced in the network by weakening of signals from the same node.

The first effect is perseveration, which is a common result of frontal lobe damage (for reviews, see Fuster, 1997, and Nauta, 1971). In the WCST, for example, the experimenter changes the reinforcement criterion in the middle of the task, from rewarding classifications based on the color of the cards to rewarding classifications based on the shape of the design on the cards. Normal subjects respond to the change in reinforcement by changing their choices, whereas frontally damaged subjects tend to perseverate in making color choices despite receiving error messages. Since the subjects are not receiving reinforcement during the verbal fluency test, perseveration here takes on different forms. For example, frontally damaged subjects are more likely to repeat words they have previously stated. Also, they are more likely to say words that begin with letters that experimenters asked them previously. For example, when they are successively asked to say words beginning with C, F, and L for one minute each, they might say C words when they are supposed to say F words.

The second effect is difficulty in following rules. Nauta (1971), for example, discussed several cases of frontal patients violating rules of games they were asked to play. In one game, subjects are asked to move a stylus horizontally or vertically across a board to go through a maze. Frontally damaged patients often try to take shortcuts by moving the stylus diagonally, which is against the rules. In the verbal fluency task, frontally damaged patients show a higher incidence than do normals of using proper names, which they have been told not to do.

The third effect is difficulty in paying attention to the task itself. Distractibility is a frequent effect of frontal lobe damage (Wilkins, Shallice, & McCarthy, 1987). This relates to the functions of the prefrontal cortex in linking events across time (Fuster, 1997) and in forming goal-directed sequences of behavior (Bapi & Levine, 1994). In the verbal fluency task, the minds of frontally damaged subjects could, for example, wander away from producing words beginning with the letter C toward other words or entirely irrelevant ideas. This task is particularly sensitive to distraction because it involves classification of words by a rule (opening letter) rather than by meaningful categories of experience (e.g., animals, dishes, parts of the body).

Figure 15.4 shows the neural network used to model frontal lesion effects on verbal fluency (Levine & Parks, 1992). The category nodes code the letters (C, F, and L) with which words begin. The Wisconsin Card Sorting network of Levine and Prueitt (1989) also included a feature layer, so that the feature and category nodes constituted a modified adaptive resonance module based on the ideas of Carpenter and Grossberg (1987). In the current network, however, the feature layer is omitted because the only feature of consequence (beginning letter) also defines the categories.

The node labeled "R," for reinforcement, has multiple effects in this network. As in the WCST model of figure 15.2, frontal damage corresponds to

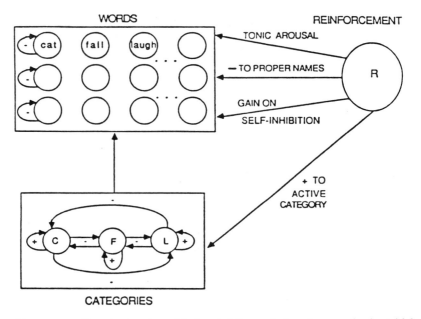

Figure 15.4 Neural network model of verbal fluency test performance for frontal lobe comparisons with normal control subjects.

weakened gain of signals from the reinforcement nodes to sensory (in this case, category and word) nodes. This is suggested by the fact that the frontal lobes are the main connecting link between sensory areas of the cortex and subcortical motivational areas of the limbic system and hypothalamus (Fuster, 1997; Nauta, 1971).

First, the reinforcement nodes provide tonic arousal in the form of random signals to all word nodes. The random signals are multiplied by a gain parameter, called α. If α is too small, background noise (external or internal to the network) tends to keep word node activation below the threshold necessary for words to be actually said, thus mimicking distractibility due to frontal lobe damage. However, some words are typically spoken even with frontal damage. To mimic that effect, we divided our word database into "easy" words, most of which had fewer than six letters, and "hard" words.

The same gain parameter α also determines the strength of the other three sets of signals from the reinforcement node. Two of these sets of signals go to word nodes, but are more specific in their effects. One set of signals is inhibitory of those nodes that represent proper names. The other consists of modulatory signals that influence the strength of self-inhibition at the word nodes. Such self-inhibition is activated once a word node has exceeded the threshold for speech, to prevent the same word node from getting reactivated by signals from the node for the currently active category. This mechanism mimics the operations of a widely used neural network called the *gated dipole field* (Carpenter & Grossberg, 1987; Levine & Prueitt, 1989), based on the principle of opponent processing, in which neurotransmitter depletion creates a tendency to disable previously active nodes.

The fourth and final set of signals from the reinforcement node goes to the node for the active category, as indicated by which of the three letters (in our simulations, C, F, and L) the experimenter has instructed the subject to concentrate on. The three category nodes compete via lateral inhibition. If the signal to the active node is too weak, there can be perseverative responses; for example, if the subject is asked to think of words beginning with C for one minute and then with F for another minute, the subject could continue to say some C words when he or she is supposed to say F words. Such a perseverative tendency is strengthened by positive feedback between category nodes and the corresponding *habit nodes*, which are similar to those utilized in the WCST model of figure 15.2.

The word count numbers may be varied, depending on the severity of the cognitive impairments, by changing the total number of words in the database beginning with each letter and the proportion of "easy" and "hard" words. For example, the "frontally damaged" network could be modeled to reproduce mild to severely impaired deficits in verbal fluency. Owing to the perseverative tendency caused by positive feedback between category and habit nodes, there were other parameter values for which frontal damage had an opposite effect. For those values, instead of reducing the word count, decreasing α to the "frontally damaged" range caused the network to say the same words over and over. Our earlier model (Levine & Parks, 1992) contained significant overestimations of the total number of words produced per minute for normal persons. However, the neural network model was successful overall, because it accurately reproduced the magnitude of differences between normals and frontal lobe–damaged patients. In other words, the frontal lobe patients' verbal fluency performance was severely impaired when compared with that of normal controls. In the next section, our new simulations between Alzheimer's disease patients and elderly controls was designed to mirror updated verbal fluency norms (Benton et al., 1994), which reflect adjustments for age. Moreover, the updated model contains new neuroanatomical and neurotransmitter computer nodes that enable us to model decline in verbal fluency performance as the patient passes through stages of the disease.

MODELING EFFECTS OF ALZHEIMER'S DISEASE WITH VERBAL FLUENCY

In this section we first explain selected neuromechanisms that underlie Alzheimer's disease (AD). Next, the rationale for the development of computer modules that reflect the neurotransmitter interactions with neuroanatomical regions such as the frontal and hippocampal areas are hypothesized. The computer model is then presented for verbal fluency that reflects decreases in word generation as a reflection of declining neural systems over a period of years.

Neurobiological and Neuroanatomical Aspects of Alzheimer's Disease

There is general agreement that the major neuropathological changes in AD are neurofibrillary tangles (NFT) and senile plaques (Solodkin & Van Hoesen, 1997). Hyman and associates (Hyman, Arriagada, Van Hoesen, et al., 1993) found from their anatomical studies that the hippocampal area is the first area to develop NFT, and that NFT accumulate in the association cortices as the clinical severity increases. A longitudinal positron emission tomography (PET) study of early neuropsychological and metabolic changes in AD suggested that degeneration and metabolic dysfunction first occur in the medial temporal area (Grady, Haxby, Horwitz, et al., 1988). This is followed by degeneration in the neocortical association regions (frontal, parietal, and lateral temporal regions). In the study by Grady et al., episodic memory tasks such as the delayed verbal memory aspects of the Wechsler Memory Scale (Russell, 1975) and the Buschke (1973) test become impaired one or more years before a decline in verbal fluency performance. Correspondingly, the AD subjects with initial impairment on the Wechsler Memory Scale and Buschke test were hypothesized to have initial metabolic dysfunction in the medial temporal area, even though the small size of the medial temporal area relative to the spatial resolution of the tomograph did not allow precise measurement. In summary, neuroanatomical and brain imaging studies imply that loss of hippocampal function proceeds at a more rapid rate than loss of frontal function in AD.

It is well known that AD dementia virtually always involves a deficit of cholinergic innervation from the midbrain nucleus basalis (Brioni & Decker, 1997; Hasselmo & Bower, 1992; Whitehouse, Price, Clark, et al., 1981). Therefore, we also add to our network a node representing cholinergic function. We assume that cholinergic innervation affects both the hippocampal and frontal nodes of our network, but that the effect of cholinergic innervation on hippocampal activation is faster. This is based on experimental results showing that the basal forebrain is the major source of cholinergic input to some areas of the central nervous system (CNS), such as to the frontal cortex from the nucleus basalis of Meynert (nBM) and to the hippocampus from the medial septum. It shares cholinergic input also with intrinsic neurons in the cortex and with the tegmental nuclei in the thalamus (Becker, 1991). There may be a differential loss of cholinergic input that could account for the differential effect on function. It is not known whether the accelerated loss of function in the hippocampus is secondary to loss of cholinergic innervation from the medial septum or due to a more rapid neural loss in the hippocampus than in the association cortices. Inferences from PET research suggest that different areas of the nBM degenerate at different rates, "resulting in the sequence of metabolic and cognitive deficits" (Grady et al., 1988, p. 592). More recent neuropathological studies have yielded evidence that hippocampus and entorhinal cortex show the earliest structural changes and dysfunction in AD, and that the frontal, parietal, and temporal areas follow as the disease progresses (Bancher, Braak, Fischer, et al., 1993; DeLacoste & White, 1993).

Computer Program Parameters for Verbal Fluency in Alzheimer's Disease

The details of cholinergic degeneration at the neuronal and synaptic level are modeled well in chapter 13. We concentrate instead on modeling at the system level, using simplified "frontal," "hippocampal," and "cholinergic" modules to simulate the effects of different stages of AD on verbal fluency. The decrease in word count is relatively mild in the early stages but becomes precipitous at the intermediate stages. The network used in our model of AD and verbal fluency is an extension of the network of figure 15.4 that includes these modules representing different brain areas.

To model the effect of AD on verbal fluency, we have split the function of the reinforcement node in figure 15.4 into "frontal" and a "hippocampal" components, with different time scales of activity. In our expanded network, shown in figure 15.5, the nonspecific arousal function previously attributed to the reinforcement node is now attributed to the hippocampal node. This is because the hippocampus is involved in setting the stage for the current situation, that is, orienting the organism to new stimuli (Teyler & DiScenna, 1986). The functions of rule generation are attributed to the frontal node. In the computer model of the verbal fluency performance, rule generation includes self-inhibition of nodes for previously stated words, inhibition of nodes for proper names, and excitation of nodes for the active letter (the one the clinican is currently asking for). Following a suggestion of Pennington (1994), based on an alternative connectionist model of Sloman and Rumelhart (1992), we propose that a part of the frontal cortex performs a "gating" or modulatory function on connections from this hippocampal node to stored semantic representations, in this case of previously learned words (based on the hippocampal indexing theory of Teyler and DiScenna, 1986). "Frontal" gating can either enhance or depress a "hippocampal" activation of a specific category or word node. The "frontal" node sends modulatory signals that are multiplied by the hippocampal signals. The frontal signal is a high number for the active category and a very low (much less than 1) number for word nodes representing proper names. Self-inhibitory signals at word nodes are used to prevent repetitions, as in the network of figure 15.4. The frontal cortex "decides" which word representations to gate positively or negatively.

Neuropsychological Implications

Memory tasks with the greatest hippocampal involvement should be affected the most in the early stages of AD. In particular, episodic memory is affected earlier in the course of the disease than is semantic memory (Zec,

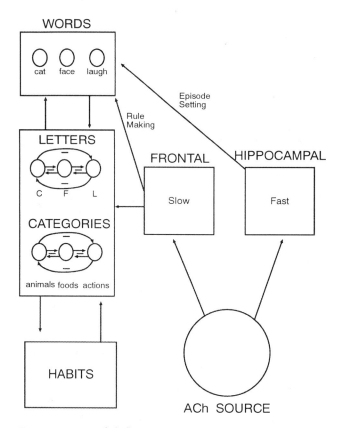

Figure 15.5 Verbal fluency test performance model for comparing Alzheimer's disease patients with elderly control subjects. It contains neuroanatomical computer nodes (frontal lobe and hippocampus) and neurotransmitter representation (cholinergic system). ACh source, acetylcholine source.

1993). Recall the distinction made by Tulving (1972): semantic memory involves recall of stored facts and relationships (e.g., "Springfield is the capital of Illinois"), whereas episodic memory (for review, see Wheeler, Stuss, & Tulving, 1997) involves recall of specific events (e.g., "I ate pizza for dinner yesterday"). While the verbal fluency test has one episodic component—remembering which letter the experimenter asked for—it is predominantly a semantic memory task.

The full network of figure 15.5 was designed to allow modifications for the possibility of modeling at least one task that primarily involves episodic memory. The task is the Rey Auditory Verbal Learning test, which involves recall from a list of fifteen words presented five times (Powell, Cripe, & Dodrill, 1991; Spreen & Strauss, 1998). Our laboratory is currently working on the Rey Auditory Verbal Leaning test model that uses a similar database as seen for verbal fluency performance in table 15.2. Preliminary versions of our episodic task model include intrusion errors (words totally unrelated to the list recall), in addition to perseveration errors.

Table 15.2 Partial representative word database showing initial letter and semantic category

Semantic Category	C words	F words	L words
Foods	cheese cherry ...	fish fig ...	lettuce lobster ...
Body parts or clothes	chin coat ...	foot face ...	leg lip ...
Animals	cat cow ...	frog fox ...	lamb lion ...
House objects	chair cup ...	floor fan ...	lamp light ...
Actions	call clap ...	fall file ...	laugh leap ...
Adjectives	cold creepy ...	famous fatal ...	long lame ...
Proper names	Carl Cindy ...	France Fred ...	Lisa Larry ...

Representative simulation of verbal fluency results are shown in figure 15.6. The "deterioration" parameter measures the amount of loss of cholinergic function, so that the abscissa describes progressive stages of AD. Note that verbal fluency declines more gradually for mild AD, then drops precipitously at an intermediate stage of the "disease." Verbal fluency is impaired in some studies comparing elderly controls to patients with mild AD (Barr & Brandt, 1996; Hart, Smith, & Swash, 1988; Miller, 1984; Ober, Dronkers, Koss, et al., 1986). Moreover, verbal fluency is sensitive to impairments seen in other clinical groups such as Huntington's disease (Monsch, Bondi, Paulsen, et al., 1994). Other research has suggested that categorical fluency discriminates patient groups better than the letter fluency test used in our experiments (for review, see Salmon & Chan, 1994).

Depending on the severity of patients' neuropathologic changes, both frontal lobe and AD patients have deficits in executive functions when compared with control groups. More specifically, these patients have difficulty with concurrent manipulation of information such as set shifting and self-monitoring (Baddeley, Sala, Papagno, et al., 1997; Bondi, Monsch, Galasko, et al., 1994; Lafleche & Albert, 1995; Parks, Zec, & Wilson, 1993; Salmon, 1997; Zec, Parks, Gambach, et al., 1992). Caution should be used as to rigid use of the neural network model presented here. We modeled some of the more obvious behaviors, neuropathologic findings, and neurochemical systems. Important aspects of human functioning were not fully addressed, namely the role of motor networks and visuospatial integration. On the positive side, a careful analysis of various human biological systems has accurately reproduced selected cognitive functions with the assistance of innovations in computer programming.

ACKNOWLEDGMENTS

The information in this chapter contains significant adaptations and reproductions from "Parallel Distributed Processing and Neuropsychology: A Neural Network Model of Wisconsin Card Sorting and Verbal Fluency" by Parks et al., 1992, *Neuropsychology Review*, Plenum Publishing Corporation, used with permission. A representation of a psychological test used in this

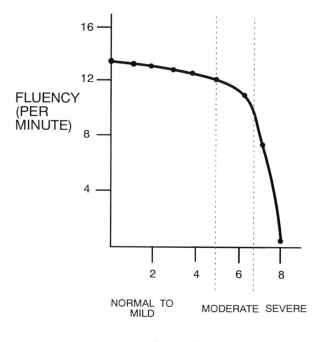

Figure 15.6 Decline in verbal fluency test performance model over a period of years in Alzheimer's disease patients. This graph shows the various stages of the disease progression and cholinergic dysfunction (ACh).

chapter was reproduced by special permission of the publisher, Psychological Assessment Resources, Inc., 16204 North Florida Avenue, Lutz, FL 33549, from the Wisconsin Card Sorting test and the *Wisconsin Card Sorting Test Manual* by Dr. Robert Heaton, et al., copyright 1981. Further reproduction is prohibited without permission of Psychological Assessment Resources, Inc. Code for the Wisconsin Card Sorting and verbal fluency models is being made available at http://www.uta.edu/psychology/faculty/levine.

REFERENCES

Amari, S.-I. (1977). Dynamics of pattern formation in lateral-inhibition type neural fields. *Biological Cybernetics, 27,* 77–87.

Baddeley, A., Sala, S. D., Papagno, C., & Spinnler, H. (1997). Dual-task performance in dysexecutive and nondysexecutive patients with a frontal lesion. *Neuropsychology, 11,* 187–194.

Bancher, C., Braak, H., Fischer, P., & Jellinger, K. A. (1993). Neuropathological staging of Alzheimer lesions and intellectual status in Alzheimer's and Parkinson's disease patients. *Neuroscience Letters, 162,* 179–182.

Bapi, R. S., & Levine, D. S. (1994). Modeling the role of the frontal lobes in performing sequential tasks. I. Basic structure and primacy effects. *Neural Networks, 7,* 1167–1180.

Bapi, R. S., & Levine, D. S. (1997). Modeling the role of the frontal lobes in performing sequential tasks. II. Classification of sequences. *Neural Network World, 1(97),* 3–28.

Barr, A., & Brandt, J. (1996). Word-list generation deficits in dementia. *Journal of Clinical and Experimental Neuropsychology, 18,* 810–822.

Becker, R. E. (1991). Therapy of the cognitive deficit in Alzheimer's Disease: The cholinergic system. In R. Becker & E. Giacobini (Eds.), *Cholinergic basis for Alzheimer therapy* (pp. 1–24). Boston: Birkhäuser.

Benton, A. L. (1968). Differential behavioral effects in frontal lobe disease. *Neuropsychologia, 6,* 53–60.

Benton, A. L., Hamsher, K., & Sivan, A. B. (1994). *Multilingual aphasia examination,* 3rd ed. Iowa City: AJA Associates.

Bliss, T. V. P., & Lømo, T. (1973). Long-lasting potentiation of synaptic transmission in the dentate area of the anaesthetized rabbit following stimulation of the perforant path. *Journal of Physiology (London), 232,* 331–356.

Bondi, M. W., Monsch, A. U., Galasko, D., Butters, N., Salmon, D. P., & Delis, D. C. (1994). Preclinical cognitive markers of dementia of the Alzheimer Type. *Neuropsychology, 8,* 374–384.

Brioni, J. D., & Decker M. W. (Eds.). (1997). *Pharmacological treatment of Alzheimer's disease.* New York: Wiley-Liss.

Buschke, H. (1973). Selective reminding for analysis of memory and learning. *Journal of Verbal Learning and Verbal Behavior, 12,* 543–550.

Carpenter, G. A., & Grossberg, S. (1987). A massively parallel architecture for a self-organizing neural pattern recognition machine. *Computer Vision, Graphics, and Image Processing, 37,* 54–115.

Carter, C. S., Mintun, M., & Cohen, J. D. (1995). Interference and facilitation effects during selective attention: An H2 15O PET study of Stroop task performance. *Neuroimage, 2,* 264–272.

Changeux, J.-P. (1981). The acetylcholine receptor: An allosteric membrane protein. *Harvey Lectures 75,* 85–254.

Cohen, J. D., Dunbar, K., & McClelland, J. L. (1990). On the control of automatic processes: A parallel distributed processing account of the Stroop effect. *Psychological Review, 97,* 332–361.

Cohen, J. D., & Servan-Schreiber, D. (1992). Context, cortex and dopamine: A connectionist approach to behavior and biology in schizophrenia. *Psychological Review, 99,* 45–77.

Cohen, N. J., & Eichenbaum, H. (1993). *Memory, amnesia, and the hippocampal system.* Cambridge, MA: MIT Press.

Crockett, D. J., Bilsker, D., Hurwitz, T., & Kozak, J. (1986). Clinical utility of three measures of frontal lobe dysfunction in neuropsychiatric samples. *International Journal of Neuroscience, 30,* 241–248.

Damasio, A. R. (1991). Concluding comments. In H. S. Levin, H. M. Eisenberg, & A. L. Benton (Eds.), *Frontal lobe function and dysfunction* (pp. 401–407). New York: Oxford University Press.

Damasio, A. R. (1994). *Descartes' error: Emotion, reason, and the human brain.* New York: Grosset Putnam.

Dehaene, S., & Changeux, J-P. (1989). A simple model of prefrontal cortex function in delayed-response tasks. *Journal of Cognitive Neuroscience, 1,* 244–261.

Dehaene, S., & Changeux, J-P. (1991). The Wisconsin card sorting test: Theoretical analysis and modeling in a neural network. *Cerebral Cortex, 1,* 62–79.

DeLacoste, M., & White, C. L. (1993). The role of cortical connectivity in Alzheimer's disease pathogenesis: A review and model system. *Neurobiology of Aging, 14,* 1–16.

Dias, R., Robbins, T. W., & Roberts, A. C. (1996). Dissociation in prefrontal cortex of affective and attentional shifts. *Nature, 380*, 69–72.

Fuster, J. M. (1997). *The prefrontal cortex: Anatomy, physiology, and neuropsychology of the frontal lobe.* 3rd ed. New York: Raven.

Goldman-Rakic, P. S. (1987). Circuitry of primate prefrontal cortex and regulation of behavior by representational memory. In F. Plum (Ed.), *Handbook of physiology*, Vol. 5 (pp. 373–417). Bethesda, MD: American Physiological Society.

Goldman-Rakic, P. S. (1992). Working memory and the mind. *Scientific American*, September, 73–79.

Grady, C. L., Haxby, J. V., Horwitz, B., Sunadaram, M., Berg, G., Schapiro, M. B., Friedland, R. P., & Rapoport, S. I. (1988). Longitudinal study of early neuropsychological and cerebral metabolic changes in dementia of the Alzheimer type. *Journal of Clinical and Experimental Neuropsychology, 10*, 576–596.

Grafman, J. (1994). Alternative frameworks for the conceptualization of prefrontal lobe functions. In F. Boller & J. Grafman (Eds.), *Handbook of neuropsychology*, Vol. 9, (pp. 187–201). Amsterdam: Elsevier.

Grossberg, S. (1972a). A neural theory of punishment and avoidance. I. Qualitative theory. *Mathematical Biosciences 15*, 39–67.

Grossberg, S. (1972b). A neural theory of punishment and avoidance. II. Quantitative theory. *Mathematical Biosciences 15*, 253–285.

Grossberg, S. (1973). Contour enhancement, short term memory, and constancies in reverberating neural networks. *Studies in Applied Mathematics 52*, 213–257.

Grossberg, S. (1982). *Studies in mind and brain.* Dordrecht, Netherlands: Reidel.

Grossberg, S. (1988). *Neural networks and natural intelligence.* Cambridge, MA: MIT Press.

Grossberg, S., & Mingolla, E. (1985). Neural dynamics of perceptual grouping: Textures, boundaries, and emergent segmentations. *Perception and Psychophysics, 38*, 141–171.

Hart, S., Smith, C. M., & Swash, M. (1988). Word fluency in patients with early dementia of Alzheimer type. *British Journal of Clinical Psychology, 27*, 115–124.

Hartline, H. K., & Ratliff, F. (1957). Inhibitory interactions of receptor units in the eye of *Limulus*. *Journal of General Physiology, 40*, 351–376.

Hasselmo, M. E., & Bower, J. M. (1992). Cholinergic suppression specific to intrinsic not afferent fiber synapses in rat piriform (olfactory) cortex. *Journal of Neurophysiology, 67*, 1222–1229.

Heaton, R. K., Chelune, G. J., Talley, J. L., Kay, G. G., & Curtiss, G. (1993). *Wisconsin Card Sorting test manual: Revised and expanded.* Odessa, FL: Psychological Assessment Resources.

Hebb, D. O. (1949). *The organization of behavior.* New York: Wiley.

Hestenes, D. O. (1992). A neural network theory of manic-depressive illness. In D. S. Levine & S. J. Leven (Eds.), *Motivation, emotion, and goal direction in neural networks* (pp. 209–257). Hillsdale, NJ: Erlbaum.

Hestenes, D. O. (1998). Modulatory mechanisms in mental disorders. In D. J. Stein & J. Ludik (Eds.), *Neural networks in psychopathology* (pp. 132–164). Cambridge, U.K.: Cambridge University Press.

Hull, C. L. (1943). *Principles of behavior.* New York: Appleton.

Hyman, B. T., Arriagada, P. V., Van Hoesen, G. W., & Damasio, A. R. (1993). Memory impairment in Alzheimer's Disease: An anatomical perspective. In R. W. Parks, R. F. Zec, & R. S. Wilson (Eds.), *Neuropsychology of Alzheimer's Disease and other dementias* (pp. 138–150). New York: Oxford University Press.

Janowsky, J. S., Shimamura, A. P., Kritchevsky, M., & Squire, L. R. (1989). Cognitive impairment following frontal lobe damage and its relevance to human amnesia. *Behavioral Neuroscience, 103*, 548–560.

Kaczmarek, L. K., & Levitan, I. B. (1987). *Neuromodulation: The biochemical control of neuronal excitability.* New York: Oxford University Press.

Kandel, E. R., & Tauc, L. (1965). Heterosynaptic facilitation in neurones of the abdominal ganglion of *Aplysia depilans. Journal of Physiology (London), 181*, 1–27.

Karpov, Y. V., & Haywood, H. C. (1998). Two ways to elaborate Vygotsky's concept of mediation. *American Psychologist, 53*, 27–36.

Kimberg, D. Y., & Farah, M. J. (1993). A unified account of cognitive impairments following frontal lobe damage: The role of working memory in complex, organized behavior. *Journal of Experimental Psychology: General, 122*, 411–428.

Kolb, B., & Whishaw, I. Q. (1995). *Fundamentals of human neuropsychology*, 4th ed. New York: W. H. Freeman.

Lafleche, G., & Albert, M. S. (1995). Executive function deficits in mild Alzheimer's disease. *Neuropsychology, 9*, 313–320.

Leven, S. J., & Levine, D. S. (1987). Effects of reinforcement on knowledge retrieval and evaluation. In *IEEE first international conference on neural networks*, Vol. 2 (pp. 269–279). San Diego: IEEE/ICNN.

Levine, D. S. (1991). *Introduction to neural and cognitive modeling.* Hillsdale, NJ: Erlbaum.

Levine, D. S. (1996). Modeling dysfunction of the prefrontal executive system. In J. Reggia, E. Ruppin, & R. Berndt (Eds.), *Neural modeling of brain disorders.* (pp. 413–439). River Edge, NJ: World Scientific.

Levine, D. S., & Parks, R. W. (1992). Frontal lesion effects on verbal fluency in a network model. In *International Joint Conference on Neural Networks, Baltimore*, Vol. 2 (pp. 39–44). Piscataway, NJ: IEEE.

Levine, D. S., Parks, R. W., & Prueitt, R. S. (1993). Methodological and theoretical issues in neural network models of frontal cognitive functions. *International Journal of Neuroscience, 72*, 209–233.

Levine, D. S., & Prueitt, P. S. (1989). Modeling some effects of frontal lobe damage: Novelty and perseveration. *Neural Networks, 2*, 103–116.

Lezak, M. (1996). *Neuropsychological assessment*, 3rd ed. New York: Oxford University Press.

Luria, A. R. (1980). *Higher cortical functions in man*, 2nd ed. New York: Basic Books.

Mangels, J. A., Gershberg, F. B., & Knight, R. T. (1996). Impaired retrieval from remote memory in patients with frontal lobe damage. *Neuropsychology, 10*, 32–41.

McGlynn, S. M., & Schacter, D. L. (1997). The neuropsychology of insight: Impaired awareness of deficits in a psychiatric context. *Psychiatric Annals, 27*, 806–811.

Miller, E. (1984). Verbal fluency as a function of a measure of verbal intelligence and in relation to different types of cerebral pathology. *British Journal of Clinical Psychology, 23*, 53–57.

Milner, B. (1963). Effects of different brain lesions in card sorting. *Archives of Neurology 9*, 90–100.

Milner, B. (1964). Some effects of frontal lobectomy in man. In J. M. Warren & K. Akert (Eds.), *The frontal granular cortex and behavior* (pp. 313–334). New York: McGraw-Hill.

Milner, B., & Petrides, M. (1984). Behavioral effects of frontal-lobe lesions in man. *Trends in Neurosciences, 7*, 403–407.

Mishkin, M., Malamut, B., & Bachevalier, J. (1984). Memories and habits: Two neural systems. In G. Lynch, J. McGaugh, & N. Weinberger (Eds.), *Neurobiology of learning and memory* (pp. 65–77). New York: Guilford Press.

Monchi, O., & Taylor, J. G. (1995). A model of the prefrontal loop that includes the basal ganglia in solving the recency task. In *World congress on neural networks*, Washington, DC, Vol. 3 (pp. 48–51). Hillsdale, NJ: Erlbaum.

Monsch, A. U., Bondi, M. W., Paulsen, J. S., Brugger, P., Butters, N., Salmon, D. P., & Swenson, M. (1994). A comparison of category and letter fluency in Alzheimer's disease and Huntington's disease. *Neuropsychology, 8,* 25–30.

Moscovitch, M. (1994). Cognitive resources and dual-task interference effects at retrieval in normal people: The role of the frontal lobes and medial temporal cortex. *Neuropsychology, 8,* 524–534.

Nauta, W. J. H. (1971). The problem of the frontal lobe: A reinterpretation. *Journal of Psychiatric Research, 8,* 167–187.

Ober, B., Dronkers, N. D., Koss, E., Delis, D. C., & Friedland, R. P. (1986). Retrieval from semantic memory in Alzheimer-type dementia. *Journal of Clinical and Experimental Neuropsychology, 8,* 75–92.

Parks, R. W., & Cardoso, J. (1997). Parallel distributed processing and executive functioning: Tower of Hanoi neural network model in healthy controls and left frontal lobe patients. *International Journal of Neuroscience, 89,* 217–240.

Parks, R. W., Crockett, D. J., & McGeer, P. L. (1989). Systems model of cortical organization: Positron emission tomography and neuropsychological test performance. *Archives of Clinical Neuropsychology, 4,* 335–349.

Parks, R. W., Crockett, D. J., Tuokko, H., Beattie, B. L., Ashford, J. W., Coburn, K. L., Zec, R. F., Becker, R. E., McGeer, P. L., & McGeer, E. G. (1989). Neuropsychological "systems efficiency" and positron emission tomography. *Journal of Neuropsychiatry and Clinical Neurosciences, 1,* 269–282.

Parks, R. W., Levine, D. S., Long, D. L., Crockett, D. J., Dalton, I. E., Weingartner, H., Fedio, P., Matthews, J. R., Coburn, K. L., Siler, G., & Becker, R. E. (1992). Parallel distributed processing and neuropsychology: A neural network model of Wisconsin Card Sorting and verbal fluency. *Neuropsychology Review, 3,* 213–233.

Parks, R. W., Long, D. L., Levine, D. S., Crockett, D. J., Dalton, I. E., Zec, R. F., Coburn, K. L., Siler, G., Nelson, M. E., Bower, J. M., Becker, R. E., McGeer, E. G., & McGeer, P. L. (1991). Parallel distributed processing and neural networks: Origins, methodology and cognitive functions. *International Journal of Neuroscience, 60,* 195–214.

Parks, R. W., Zec, R. F., & Wilson, R. S. (Eds.). (1993). *Neuropsychology of Alzheimer's disease and other dementias.* New York: Oxford University Press.

Passingham, R. E. (1993). *The frontal lobes and voluntary action.* Oxford, U.K.: Oxford University Press.

Pavlov, I. P. (1927). *Conditioned reflexes* V. Anrep (trans.). London: Oxford University Press.

Pennington, B. F. (1994). The working memory function of the prefrontal cortices: Implications for developmental and individual differences in cognition. In M. Haith, J. Benson, R. Roberts, & B. F. Pennington (Eds.), *Future oriented processes in development* (pp. 243–289). Chicago: University of Chicago Press.

Perret, E. (1974). The left frontal lobe of man and the suppression of habitual responses in verbal categorical behavior. *Neuropsychologia, 12,* 323–330.

Petrides, M. (1994). Frontal lobes and working memory: Evidence from investigations of the effects of cortical excisions in nonhuman primates. In F. Boller & J. Grafman (Eds.), *Handbook of neuropsychology*, Vol. 9, (pp. 59–82). Amsterdam: Elsevier.

Powell, J. B., Cripe, L. I., & Dodrill, C. B. (1991). Assessment of brain impairment with the Rey Auditory Verbal Learning Test: A comparison with other neuropsychological measures. *Archives of Clinical Neuropsychology, 6*, 241–249.

Pribram, K. H. (1973). The primate frontal cortex: Executive of the brain. In K. H. Pribram & A. R. Luria (Eds.), *Psychophysiology of the frontal lobes* (pp. 293–314). New York: Academic Press.

Pribram, K. H. (1991). *Brain and perception: Holonomy and structure in figural processing.* Hillsdale, NJ: Erlbaum.

Rabbitt, P. (1998). *Methodology of frontal and executive function.* Bristol, PA: Taylor & Francis.

Reitan, R. M. & Wolfson, D. (1994). A selected and critical review of neuropsychological deficits and the frontal lobes. *Neuropsychology Review, 4*, 161–198.

Robinson, A. L., Heaton, R. K., Lehman, R. A. W., & Stilson, D., W. (1980). The utility of the Wisconsin Card Sorting Test in detecting and localizing frontal lobe lesions. *Journal of Consulting and Clinical Psychology, 48*, 605–614.

Rolls, E., & Treves, A. (1998). *Neural networks and brain function.* New York: Oxford University Press.

Russell, E. W. (1975). A multiple scoring method for the assessment of complex memory functions. *Journal of Consulting and Clinical Psychology, 43*, 800–809.

Salmon, D. P. (1997). Neuropsychological features of Alzheimer's disease. In J. D. Brioni, & M. W. Decker (Eds.), *Pharmacological treatment of Alzheimer's disease: Molecular and neurobiological foundations* (pp. 129–147). New York: Wiley-Liss.

Salmon, D. P., & Chang, A. S. (1994). Semantic memory deficits associated with Alzheimer's disease. In L. S. Cermak (Ed.), *Neuropsychological explorations of memory and cognition: Essays in honor of Nelson Butters* (pp. 61–76). New York: Plenum Press.

Sloman, S. A., & Rumelhart, D. E. (1992). Reducing interference in distributed memories through episodic gating. In A. F. Healy, S. M. Kosslyn, & R. M. Shiffrin (Eds.), *From learning theory to connectionist theory: Essays in honor of William K. Estes* (pp. 227–248). Hillsdale, NJ: Erlbaum.

Solodkin, A., & Van Hoesen, G. W. (1997). Neuropathology and functional anatomy of Alzheimer's disease. In J. D. Brioni, & M. W. Decker (Eds.), *Pharmacological treatment of Alzheimer's disease* (pp. 151–177). New York: Wiley.

Solomon, R. L., & Corbit, J. D. (1974). An opponent-process theory of motivation: I. Temporal dynamics of affect. *Psychological Review, 81*, 119–145.

Spreen, O., & Strauss, E. (1998). *A compendium of neuropsychological tests* 2nd ed. New York: Oxford University Press.

Stuss, D. T., Shallice, T., & Alexander, M. P. (1995). A multidisciplinary approach to anterior attentional functions. *Annals of the New York Academy of Sciences, 769*, 191–211.

Teyler, T. J., & DiScenna, P. (1986). The hippocampal memory indexing theory. *Behavioral Neuroscience, 100*, 147–154.

Tranel, D., Anderson, S. W., & Benton, A. (1994). Development of the concept of "executive function" and its relationship to the frontal lobes. In F. Boller & J. Grafman (Eds.), *Handbook of neuropsychology*, Vol. 9, (pp. 125–148). Amsterdam: Elsevier.

Troyer, A. K., Moscovitch, M., & Winocur, G. (1997). Clustering and switching as two components of verbal fluency: Evidence from younger and older healthy adults. *Neuropsychology, 11,* 138–146.

Tulving, E. (1972). Episodic and semantic memory. In E. Tulving & M. Donaldson (Eds.), *Organization of memory* (pp. 381–403). New York: Academic Press.

Von der Malsburg, C. (1973). Self-organization of orientation sensitive cells in the striate cortex. *Kybernetik 14,* 85–100.

Welsh, M. C., & Pennington, B. F. (1988). Assessing frontal lobe function in children: Views from developmental psychology. *Developmental Neuropsychology, 4,* 199–230.

Wheeler, M. A., Stuss, D. T., & Tulving, E. (1997). Toward a theory of episodic memory: The frontal lobes and autonoetic consciousness. *Psychological Bulletin, 121,* 331–354.

Whitehouse, P. J., Price, D. L., Clark, A. W., Coyle, J. T., & Delong, M. R. (1981). Alzheimer disease: Evidence for selective loss of cholinergic neurons in the nucleus basalis. *Annals of Neurology, 10,* 122–126.

Wilkins, A. J., Shallice, T., & McCarthy, R. (1987). Frontal lesions and sustained attention. *Neuropsychologia, 25,* 359–365.

Zec, R. F. (1993). Neuropsychological functioning in Alzheimer's disease. In R. W. Parks, R. F. Zec, & R. S. Wilson (Eds.), *Neuropsychology of Alzheimer's Disease and other Dementias* (pp. 3–80). New York: Oxford University Press.

Zec, R. F., Parks, R. W., Gambach, J., & Vicari, S. (1992). The executive board system: An Innovative approach to cognitive-behavioral rehabilitation in patients with traumatic brain injury. In C. J. Long & L. K. Ross (Eds.), *Handbook of head trauma: Acute care to recovery* (pp. 219–230). New York: Plenum Press.

16 Semantic Network Abnormalities in Patients with Alzheimer's Disease

Agnes S. Chan, David P. Salmon, and Nelson Butters

The semantic network model assumes that our general fund of knowledge is organized as a complex network consisting of concepts or representations that are related through serial or parallel associations or both (Collins & Quillian, 1969; Rumelhart & McClelland, 1986). Within the network, concepts that share many attributes are more highly associated, or more closely related, than those that share few attributes (Collins & Loftus, 1975). For example, the concept *dog* is strongly associated with the concept *cat* because they share such attributes as being living creatures, four-legged animals, domestic pets, meat eaters, furry, and relatively small in size. In contrast, the concepts *dog* and *sky* are only weakly associated, at most, since they do not share any obvious salient attributes. Psychological evidence for the associative nature of semantic knowledge has been provided by numerous studies using such diverse tasks as sentence verification (Collins & Quillian, 1969; Collins & Loftus, 1975; Anderson, 1983), semantic priming (Meyer & Schvaneveldt, 1975), typicality ranking (Rips, Shoben, & Smith, 1973), and analogies (Rips et al., 1973).

Although the semantic network model provides a functional view of how knowledge may be organized in the human mind, it does not provide a clear model of how semantic memory might be represented in the brain. Some progress has been made over the past decade, however, in developing neural network models of semantic memory by studying the effects of brain damage on the integrity of semantic knowledge (e.g., Shallice, 1988). Studies of patients with progressive anomia and impaired word comprehension, for example, suggest that semantic knowledge is stored in a distributed fashion in the association cortex of the temporal, frontal, and parietal lobes (McCarthy & Warrington, 1988, 1990; Warrington & Shallice, 1984). This hypothesis has been supported by studies of other neurologic patient populations (e.g., semantic dementia: Hodges & Patterson, 1995) and by analogous studies in nonhuman primates (see Fuster, 1995, for a comprehensive review).

A neural network model that postulates that semantic knowledge is stored in a distributed fashion in the cortical association areas has important implications for the expected nature of the cognitive impairment associated with Alzheimer's disease (AD). AD is a progressive dementing disorder that is characterized by neuron loss, synapse loss, and the development of characteristic neuropathological abnormalities (e.g., neurofibrillary tangles, neuritic plaques, amyloid deposition), primarily in the hippocampal formation and the cortical association areas of the frontal, temporal, and parietal lobes (Terry & Katzman, 1983; Terry, Masliah, Salmon, et al., 1991). Because the disease prominently affects those brain regions that are thought to be integrally involved in the neural network underlying semantic knowledge, a disorganization of this knowledge might be expected as the disease progresses.

Consistent with this notion, one of the primary clinical manifestations early in the course of AD is a language impairment that some investigators have attributed to a loss of semantic knowledge and a breakdown in the organization and structure of semantic memory. Evidence for this disruption includes AD patients' particularly poor performance on verbal fluency tasks in which they must generate exemplars from a specific semantic category (Butters, Granholm, Salmon, et al., 1987), a propensity to produce semantic errors on tests of confrontation naming (Bayles & Tomoeda, 1983; Hodges, Salmon, & Butters, 1991), and consistency in producing errors for a particular semantic concept regardless of the mode of access and output (e.g., naming, sorting by category, word-picture matching: Chertkow & Bub, 1990; Hodges, Salmon, & Butters, 1992). These deficits in semantic memory become more pronounced over time (e.g., Hodges, Salmon, & Butters, 1990), presumably as the pathological abnormalities of AD progress and the neocortical association areas become more involved (Braak & Braak, 1991).

In this chapter we describe a number of recent studies that have directly explored the impact of AD on the integrity of the semantic network. These studies employed various multidimensional, graphic scaling techniques (Romney, Shepard, & Nerlove, 1972; Shepard, Romney, & Nerlove, 1972; Tversky & Hutchinson, 1986) to model the organization of semantic memory in AD patients to see how this organization might be altered by the neocortical deterioration that occurs in the disease. The underlying hypothesis for these studies was that deterioration of the neocortical sites of storage of semantic representations and associations would lead to a gradual alteration of the associative network. This hypothesized relationship between cortical degradation and semantic network deterioration in AD is reminiscent of the observed effects of artificial "lesions" imposed on computational neural network models. As Rumelhart and McClelland (1986) stated, "performance is characterized by a kind of graceful degradation in which the system's performance gradually deteriorates as more and more neural units are destroyed ... This kind of graceful degradation is characteristic of such global degenerative syndromes as Alzheimer's disease ..." (p. 134).

THE SEMANTIC NETWORK IN PATIENTS WITH ALZHEIMER'S DISEASE

Over the past five years, a number of studies from our laboratory have used multidimensional graphic scaling analyses to explore the underlying structure of data generated by AD patients on various semantic memory tasks. In general, these data analysis techniques generate a graphic representation of the data based on some measurement of the relative degree of association (i.e., closeness or proximity) between concepts in semantic memory. The resulting models embed the concepts under study within a coordinate space where the distances between points are assumed to reflect the psychological *proximity* between the respective items in an internal *semantic network* or *cognitive map* (Collins & Quillian, 1969; Collins & Loftus, 1975; Anderson, 1983).

In an initial study (Chan, Butters, Paulsen, et al., 1993a), we compared the organization of the semantic networks for the category "animals" in AD patients and elderly normal control (NC) subjects. In addition, we examined the semantic networks of patients with Huntington's disease (HD), a progressive dementing disorder that predominantly affects subcortical (i.e., the basal ganglia), rather than cortical, brain structures. The proximity between concepts was estimated for each subject from the sequence of their responses on a category fluency task in which they generated names of animals for one minute. It was assumed that through spreading activation within the semantic network (Collin & Loftus, 1975; Meyer & Schvaneveldt, 1975), highly associated animals would tend to be produced closer together within a subject's sequential responses than those that are not highly associated. Therefore, the number of items that intervene between two target words, corrected for the number of words produced, provided an estimate of the semantic proximity of the target words. The proximity scores were subjected to multidimensional scaling (MDS) and clustering analyses which generated a model of the organization of semantic knowledge for each group of subjects.

Although MDS analyses resulted in cognitive maps for all three groups that were best represented by two dimensions, *domesticity* and *size* (figure 16.1), the cognitive map of the AD patients differed considerably from those of the NC subjects and HD patients in terms of the classification of individual exemplars. For example, in the cognitive map of AD patients, but not NC or HD subjects, *bear* appeared in the space representing domestic animals, and *zebra* appeared in the space representing small animals. In addition, the cluster analyses revealed two global clusters for the NC subjects and HD patients which were interpretable as *wild* and *domestic*, whereas three essentially uninterpretable clusters were derived for the AD patients.

The close similarity in the cognitive maps and clusters of animal names generated for HD patients and NC subjects is of particular interest because the HD patients produced as few exemplars in the fluency task as the AD

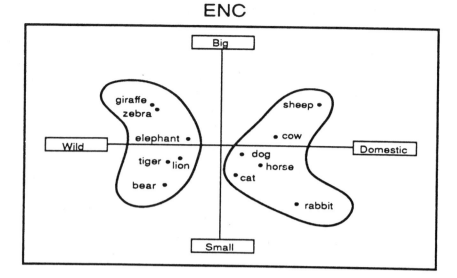

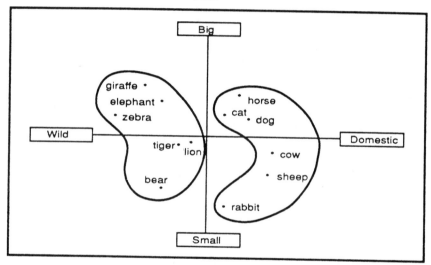

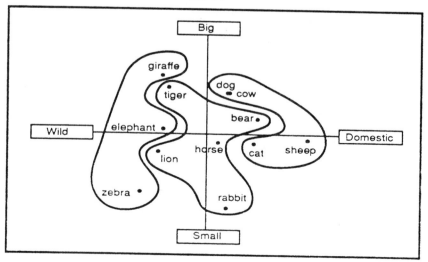

subjects. This result is consistent with previous studies that suggest that the poor fluency performance of HD patients is due to a general retrieval deficit rather than to a breakdown in the organization of semantic memory (Butters et al., 1987), and indicates that the abnormal cognitive maps of the AD patients are not likely to be an artifact of poor fluency performance per se.

The study described above was the first to demonstrate with MDS techniques that the organization of semantic knowledge becomes abnormal as a consequence of AD, a cortical degenerative brain disorder. However, methodological limitations of this study precluded a full exploration of the effects of AD on the semantic network. Specifically, the salience of a particular dimension for categorizing concepts and individual differences in the semantic network could not be examined with the data from the verbal fluency task because of the variance in the total number of responses produced by each subject. To circumvent these deficiencies, we conducted a second study using a more systematic procedure to measure the proximity between concepts (Chan, Butters, Salmon, et al., 1993b).

In this second study, the proximity (i.e., strength of association) between concepts was estimated by a triadic comparison task in which subjects chose from among three concepts (i.e., animals) the two that are most alike. A sample of twelve high-frequency animal names served as the concepts in this task and every combination of three animal names was presented for a total of 220 trials. This procedure produced a proximity score reflecting the strength of association for each pair of animals in relation to all of the other animal names; that is, how frequently those two animals were chosen as most alike. The proximity scores were subjected to an MDS analysis which produced cognitive maps for AD patients and elderly NC subjects. In addition to the cognitive maps for the two groups, the proximity data were used to calculate for each individual subject a quantitative measure of the relative importance of the various dimensions for categorizing concepts (i.e., dimension weights) and a measure of the degree of reliance on one or more of the dimensions (i.e., skewness index).

The cognitive maps of AD and NC subjects revealed with this analysis were best represented by three dimensions that appeared to correspond to domesticity (i.e., wild vs. domestic), predation (herbivore vs. carnivore), and size (large vs. small) (figure 16.2). Although a three-dimensional solution provided the best spatial representation of the semantic network of both AD and NC subjects, several significant alterations were evident in the semantic network of the AD patients.

Figure 16.1 The cognitive maps of elderly normal control (ENC) subjects, patients with Huntington's disease (HD), and patients with dementia of the Alzheimer type (DAT) obtained from multidimensional scaling and clustering analyses performed on data from a verbal fluency task. The position of each animal name is determined by multidimensional scaling; animals in the same cluster are encircled together. (Adapted from Chan et al., 1993a.)

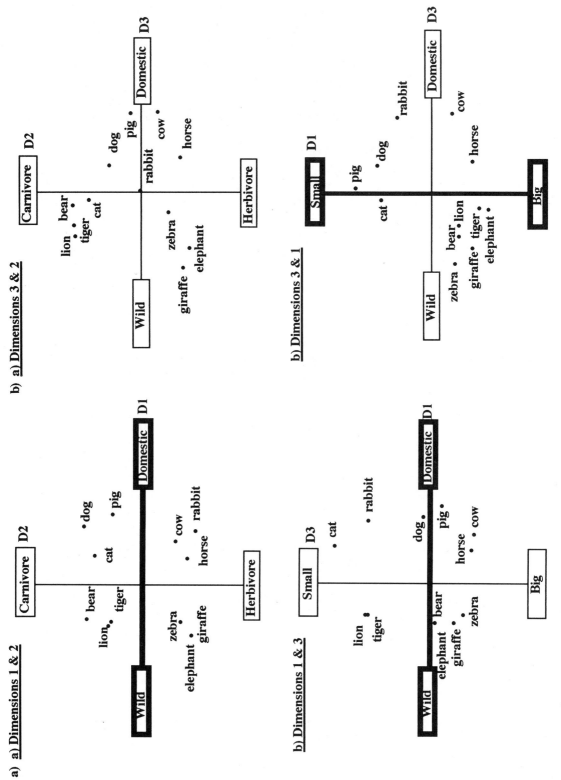

a) a) Dimensions 1 & 2

b) a) Dimensions 3 & 2

b) Dimensions 1 & 3

b) Dimensions 3 & 1

Figure 16.2 The cognitive maps of thirteen elderly normal control subjects (left panel) and thirteen patients with Alzheimer's disease (right panel) generated with multi-dimensional scaling analyses. The most salient dimension subjects used to categorize concepts is represented in bold boxed type. (Adapted from Chan et al., 1993b.)

First, AD patients focused primarily on concrete conceptual information (i.e., size) in categorizing animals, whereas control subjects stressed abstract conceptual knowledge (i.e., domesticity). Second, a number of animals that were highly associated and clustered together for NC subjects were not strongly associated for patients with AD. Third, patients with AD had significantly lower skewness indices than the NC subjects, indicating that they were less consistent in utilizing the various attributes of the animals (predation, domesticity, and size) for categorization. It should be noted that these results are not likely to be a consequence of random responding by the AD patients (due to a lack of attention or an inablity to follow instructions), because virtually identical results were obtained when the patients were tested again with the same procedures five to seven days later.

The semantic networks of the AD patients and NC subjects were further explored by performing Pathfinder analyses (Dearholt & Schvaneveldt, 1990) on the triadic comparison task data generated from the Chan et al. (1993b) study (Chan, Butters, Salmon, et al., 1995). The Pathfinder analysis is more effective than MDS for examining the number and strength of the associations constituting the semantic network. This analysis systematically constructs a model of the semantic network that consists of nodes representing concepts, and links representing the connections between concepts. It has been proposed that persons who possess sufficient knowledge in a particular domain to evaluate the degree of association between concepts will develop a clear and concise network composed only of relevant connections, whereas those who never developed this degree of knowledge, or who have lost knowledge they once possessed, will tend to organize concepts in a relatively chaotic way with many unnecessary adjunct connections. When the Pathfinder-generated cognitive maps of the AD patients were compared with those of the NC subjects, they were characterized by abnormal strength of association between usually weakly related concepts and a large number of unnecessary adjunct links (figure 16.3).

In contrast to the cognitive maps generated for the AD patients, the semantic network models generated by MDS and Pathfinder analyses for HD patients and patients with a circumscribed amnestic syndrome did not differ significantly from those of their age-matched control subjects in terms of the number of dimensions employed, the strength of associations, or the number of common links between concepts. These results provide further evidence that factors such as general cognitive decline, deficiencies in retrieval processes, or impaired episodic memory have little impact on the nature of the cognitive map generated by these multidimensional analyses of data from semantic memory tasks. Thus, the distorted cognitive map of the AD patients most likely reflects semantic memory disruption that may arise from extensive damage to the association cortices (McCarthy & Warrington, 1988; 1990; Warrington & Shallice, 1984).

a)

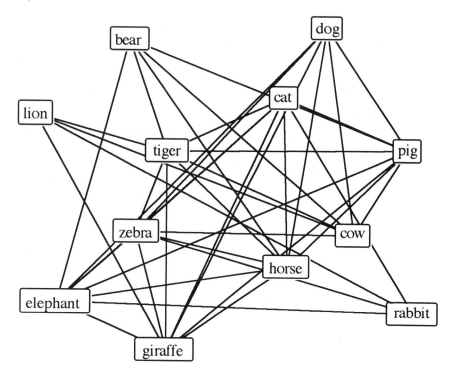

b)

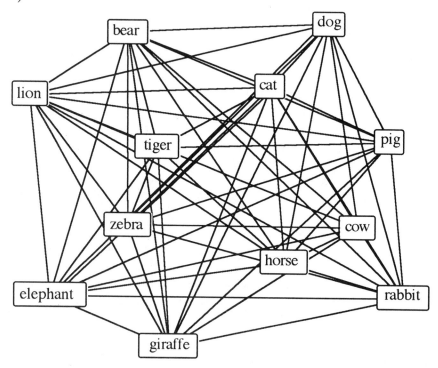

Figure 16.3 The semantic networks of thirteen elderly normal control subjects (a) and thirteen patients with Alzheimer's disease (b) generated with the Pathfinder analysis. (Adapted from Chan et al., 1995.)

DETERIORATION OF THE SEMANTIC NETWORK OF ALZHEIMER'S DISEASE PATIENTS OVER TIME

While the studies reviewed above provide compelling evidence that the structure of semantic knowledge is disrupted in patients with AD, little is known about how semantic networks are altered as the disease progresses. Because AD is a progressive degenerative disorder in which the neocortical association areas become increasingly degraded (Braak & Braak, 1991), we hypothesized that AD patients' semantic networks would become more and more disorganized over time. To explore this hypothesis, we recently examined the relationship between semantic network deterioration and the severity of global dementia in patients with AD (Chan, Butters, & Salmon, 1997), assuming that the severity of global cognitive impairment is a reflection of the degree of pathological abnormality.

In this study, a standard semantic network for animals was generated, based on triadic comparison task data, for a group of elderly NC subjects using an MDS analysis. A semantic network generated for each AD patient was then evaluated against this standard network and a goodness-of-fit measure was calculated based on the percentage of variance in the AD patient's semantic network that could be accounted for by the standard network. When the goodness-of-fit measure was related to severity of dementia as measured by the Dementia Rating Scale (DRS; Mattis, 1976), a significant negative correlation was observed indicating that the integrity of the semantic network decreases as dementia progresses. Furthermore, qualitative assessment of the results of the MDS analysis demonstrated that AD patients tended to rely less on abstract attributes (e.g., domesticity), and more on perceptual attributes (e.g., size), in categorizing animals as they became more demented, and the primary dimension used to classify animals on the triadic comparison task became less salient as the severity of dementia increased.

An examination of the relationship between dementia severity and the semantic network model generated with the Pathfinder analysis in this study indicated that the complexity of the network and the strength of association between concepts changes with disease progression. The complexity of the semantic network was evaluated by comparing the number of links in the standard semantic network of a group of elderly NC subjects with the number in group networks generated for mildly, moderately, and severely demented AD patients. The Pathfinder-generated networks of all three AD groups contained more links than that of the NC subjects (but the difference between the NC and mildly demented AD subjects only approached significance) and the AD groups differed significantly from each other, with more links being evident as the severity of dementia increased. This increase in the complexity of the semantic network with increasing dementia was confirmed by a correlational analysis which demonstrated a significant negative correlation between the number of links in each AD patient's network and his or her score on the DRS.

To further explore the relationship between the integrity of the semantic network and the severity of dementia, we calculated a *similarity index* for each AD patient based on the number of links that his or her Pathfinder network had in common with the standard control network. The higher the similarity index for a given patient, the more intact the semantic network. A correlation analysis revealed that the integrity of the semantic network (i.e., the similarity score) was correlated with the level of dementia as measured by the DRS scores of the AD patients. This finding suggests that the AD patients' understanding of the relative association among concepts is altered throughout the course of the disease and the organization of their semantic knowledge becomes more and more abnormal as the disease progresses.

Another recent study demonstrated that the integrity of the semantic network can predict the subsequent rate of global cognitive decline in AD patients (Chan, Salmon, Butters, et al., 1995). A highly significant correlation was found between AD patients' similarity indices generated from Pathfinder analyses as described above, and their subsequent global cognitive decline as measured by changes over one year in their scores on the DRS (figure 16.4). Given that semantic knowledge may be stored in a distributed fashion within

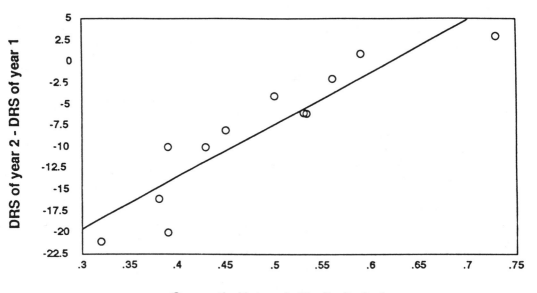

y = 61.852x - 38.145, r-squared = .84

Figure 16.4 The semantic network similarity index of twelve patients with Alzheimer's disease plotted as a function of rate of cognitive decline as measured by the difference between the Dementia Rating Scale (DRS) scores obtained near the time of semantic knowledge testing (year 1) and approximately one year later (year 2). (Adapted from Chan et al., 1995.)

the association cortices (Warrington & Shallice, 1984), this result suggests that early evidence of semantic memory dysfunction in AD patients may serve as a marker for the susceptibility of these cortical regions to further deterioration and a resulting increase in the severity of global dementia.

CONCLUSIONS

The results of the studies reviewed in this chapter indicate that network models of the organization of semantic knowledge are abnormal in patients with AD. While the source of this abnormality remains somewhat controversial (Bonilla & Johnson, 1995), the models may reflect a deterioration in the organization of semantic memory, or an actual loss of semantic knowledge, in patients with AD. This degradation of semantic memory may arise from the gradual deterioration of the neocortical association areas in which semantic knowledge is thought to be stored (McCarthy & Warrington, 1988, 1990). It should be noted, however, that semantic memory is not totally destroyed in AD. Even in the later stages of their disease, the semantic networks of AD patients remain grossly intact with interpretable dimensions and some normal associative links between concepts. It is the change in the number and quality of these associations, and changes in the salience of the dimensions characterizing concepts, that differentiate them from NC subjects.

The normal semantic network models generated for HD and amnestic patients suggest that the disorganization seen in the AD patients' networks are not due to nonspecific factors such as global cognitive impairment, episodic memory impairment, or a deficiency in retrieval processes. The patients with HD that took part in the studies described above were as severely demented as the AD patients in most cases, and a general retrieval deficit has been proposed as a primary characteristic of their dementia syndrome (see Heindel, Salmon, & Butters, 1993). Similarly, the amnestic patients' episodic memory deficits were as severe as those of the AD patients. It is also important to note that of these three patient groups, only AD patients develop semantic memory dysfunction, and only AD patients develop significant neuropathological changes in the cortical association areas.

ACKNOWLEDGMENTS

Dr. Butters passed away before the publication of this book. We dedicate this chapter to his memory. The preparation of this chapter was supported in part by NIA grant AG-05131 and NIMH grant MH-48819 to the University of California at San Diego.

REFERENCES

Anderson, J. R. (1983). *The architecture of cognition.* Cambridge, MA: Harvard University Press.

Bayles, K. A., & Tomoeda, C. K. (1983). Confrontation naming impairment in dementia. *Brain and Language, 19,* 98–114.

Bonilla, J. L., & Johnson, M. K. (1995). Semantic space in Alzheimer's disease patients. *Neuropsychology, 9*, 345–353.

Braak, H., & Braak, E. (1991). Neuropathological staging of Alzheimer-related changes. *Acta Neuropathologica, 82*, 239–259.

Butters, N., Granholm, E., Salmon, D., Grant, I., & Wolfe, J. (1987). Episodic and semantic memory: A comparison of amnesic and demented patients. *Journal of Clinical and Experimental Neuropsychology, 9*, 479–497.

Chan, A. S., Butters, N., Paulsen, J. S., Salmon, D. P., Swenson, M. R., & Maloney, L. T. (1993a). An assessment of the semantic network in patients with Alzheimer's disease. *Journal of Cognitive Neuroscience, 5*, 254–261.

Chan, A. S., Butters, N., & Salmon, D. P. (1997). The deterioration of semantic networks in patients with Alzheimer's disease: A cross-sectional study. *Neuropsychologia, 35*, 241–248.

Chan, A. S., Butters, N., Salmon, D. P., Johnson, S. A., Paulsen, J. S., & Swenson, M. R. (1995). Comparison of the semantic networks in patients with dementia and amnesia. *Neuropsychology, 9*, 177–186.

Chan, A. S., Butters, N., Salmon, D. P., & McGuire, K. A. (1993b). Dimensionality and clustering in the semantic network of patients with Alzheimer's disease. *Psychology and Aging, 8*, 411–419.

Chan, A. S., Salmon, D. P., Butters, N., & Johnson, S. A. (1995). Semantic network abnormality predicts rate of cognitive decline in patients with probable Alzheimer's disease. *Journal of the International Neuropsychological Society, 1*, 297–303.

Chertkow, H., & Bub, D. (1990). Semantic memory loss in dementia of Alzheimer's type. *Brain, 113*, 397–417.

Collins, A. M., & Loftus, E. F. (1975). A spreading activation theory of semantic processing. *Psychological Review, 82*, 407–428.

Collins, A. M., & Quillian, M. R. (1969). Retrieval time from semantic memory. *Journal of Verbal Learning and Verbal Behavior, 8*, 240–247.

Dearholt, D. W., & Schvaneveldt, R. W. (1990). Properties of Pathfinder networks. In R. W. Schvaneveldt (Ed.), *Pathfinder associative networks: Studies in knowledge organization* (pp. 1–30). Norwood, NJ: Ablex.

Fuster, J. M. (1995). *Memory in the cerebral cortex: An empirical approach to neural networks in the human and nonhuman primate.* Cambridge, MA: MIT Press.

Heindel, W. C., Salmon, D. P., & Butters, N. (1993). Cognitive approaches to the memory disorders of demented patients. In P. B. Sutker & H. E. Adams (Eds.), *Comprehensive handbook of psychopathology*, 2nd ed., (pp. 735–761). New York: Plenum Press.

Hodges, J. R., & Patterson, K. (1995). Is semantic memory consistently impaired early in the course of Alzheimer's disease?: Neuroanatomical and diagnostic implications. *Neuropsychologia, 33*, 441–459.

Hodges, J. R., Salmon, D. P., & Butters, N. (1990). Differential impairment of semantic and episodic memory in Alzheimer's and Huntington's diseases: A controlled prospective study. *Journal of Neurology, Neurosurgery and Psychiatry, 53*, 1089–1095.

Hodges, J. R., Salmon, D. P., & Butters, N. (1991). The nature of the naming deficit in Alzheimer's and Huntington's disease. *Brain, 114*, 1547–1558.

Hodges, J. R., Salmon, D. P., & Butters, N. (1992). Semantic memory impairment in Alzheimer's disease: Failure of access or degraded knowledge? *Neuropsychologia, 30*, 301–314.

Mattis, S. (1976). Mental status examination for organic mental syndrome in the elderly patient. In L. Bellack & T. Karasu (Eds.), *Geriatric psychiatry*. New York: Grune & Stratton.

McCarthy, R. A., & Warrington, E. K. (1988). Evidence for modality-specific meaning systems in the brain. *Nature, 334*, 428–430.

McCarthy, R. A., & Warrington, E. K. (1990). The dissolution of semantics. *Nature, 343*, 599.

Meyer, D. E., & Schvaneveldt, R. W. (1975). Meaning, memory structure, and mental processes. In C. N. Cofer (Ed.), *The structure of human memory* (pp. 54–89). San Francisco: Freeman.

Rips, L. J., Shoben, E. J., & Smith, E. E. (1973). Semantic distance and the verification of semantic relations. *Journal of Verbal Learning and Verbal Behavior, 12*, 1–20.

Romney, A. K., Shepard, R. N., & Nerlove, S. B. (1972). *Multidimensional scaling: Theory and applications in the behavioral sciences*, Vol. 2. New York: Seminar Press.

Rumelhart, D., & McClelland, J., & the PDP Research Group (1986). *Parallel distributed processing: Explorations in the microstructure of cognition, Vol. 1: Foundations*. Cambridge, MA: MIT Press.

Shallice, T. (1988). *From neuropsychology to mental structure*. Cambridge, U. K.: Cambridge University Press.

Shepard, R. N., Romney, A. K., & Nerlove, S. B. (1972). *Multidimensional scaling: Theory and applications in the behavioral sciences*, Vol. 1. New York: Seminar Press.

Terry, R. D., & Katzman, R. (1983). Senile dementia of the Alzheimer type. *Annals of Neurology, 14*, 497–506.

Terry, R. D., Masliah, E., Salmon, D. P., Butters, N., DeTeresa, R., Hill, R., Hansen, L. A., & Katzman, R. (1991). Physical basis of cognitive alterations in Alzheimer's disease: Synapse loss is the major correlate of cognitive impairment. *Annals of Neurology, 30*, 572–580.

Tversky, A., & Hutchinson, J., W. (1986). Nearest neighbor analysis of psychological spaces. *Psychological Review, 93*, 3–22.

Warrington, E. K., & Shallice, T. (1984). Category specific semantic impairments. *Brain, 107*, 829–854.

17 Parallel Distributed Processing Models in Alzheimer's Disease

Lynette J. Tippett and Martha J. Farah

Much of the research on cognitive impairments in Alzheimer's disease (AD) has been aimed at identifying the underlying locus or loci of processing impairments within the cognitive architecture. Cognitive neuropsychologists commonly use two types of experimental strategy to localize the underlying impairment in persons with AD or other forms of brain damage. The first involves the analysis of error types made on tasks. For example, if the errors in a naming task are visual, in the sense that the name produced belongs to a different but visually similar object, then researchers infer that the locus of processing impairment is visual. Similarly, semantic errors suggest breakdowns at semantic stages, and so on. The second main approach to inferring the locus of processing impairment is the selective manipulation of the difficulty of individual task components. For example, if the difficulty of lexical retrieval in a naming task is increased by selecting objects with low-frequency names, and this manipulation disproportionately affects AD patients' naming performance, then researchers infer that the locus of processing impairment is lexical. Alternatively, if a person is disproportionately affected by reducing the visual quality of a stimulus, this suggests an impairment in the visual stages of processing. These strategies provide straightforward means of investigating functional impairments in brain-damaged persons and drawing conclusions from the results.

In this chapter we explore alternative ways of interpreting the performance of persons with AD, making use of the concepts and tools of parallel distributed processing (PDP) (Rumelhart, McClelland, & the PDP Research Group, 1986). The PDP approach can lead to very different conclusions concerning the underlying loci of impairment in persons with brain damage (Farah, 1994). In the first part of the chapter, we review the results of research aimed at identifying the locus of damage responsible for the confrontation naming deficit in AD. According to the traditional types of reasoning just described, the effects of selective manipulations of difficulty in confrontation naming have seemed to implicate both visual and lexical impairments in AD. We then demonstrate by simulation that these results are consistent with an impairment confined to semantic memory, assuming representations that are distributed and interactive. In the second part of the chapter we provide an alternative interpretation for naming errors that seem, according to traditional means of neuropsychological inference, to imply that semantic knowledge of categories and exemplars is separate and that AD primarily affects the latter. Again using a simulation of confrontation naming, we show how an undifferentiated semantic memory store would, when damaged, lead to preserved knowledge of categories because of the greater degree of initial learning for knowledge of categories in distributed representations.

NAMING IMPAIRMENTS IN ALZHEIMER'S DISEASE: SEMANTIC, VISUAL, OR LEXICAL LOCUS OF DAMAGE?

The first question we addressed with a PDP approach emerged from attempts to localize the functional locus of impairment of the naming difficulty in AD. Difficulty in naming objects is an early and consistent sign associated with AD, which typically worsens as the disease progresses. Despite the vast amount of data collected in studies with AD participants, the functional deficit underlying the naming problem is not well understood. One explanation is that it results from impaired semantic memory. According to this view persons with AD cannot name objects because their semantic memory knowledge about them is impoverished. One source of evidence for this comes from the qualitative nature of errors made in naming tasks. Typical kinds of errors include calling an object either by the name of its superordinate category (e.g., animal instead of cat) or by the name of a semantically related object (e.g., lettuce for asparagus) (e.g., Bayles & Tomoeda, 1983; Hodges, Salmon, & Butters, 1991; Martin & Fedio, 1983). These errors suggest that the available semantic representations are degraded or underspecified. In addition to evidence from naming tasks themselves, evidence from other experimental paradigms also implicates semantic memory as a major locus of cognitive impairments in AD (e.g., Chan, Butters & Salmon, 1997; Hodges, Patterson, Graham, et al., 1996; Ralph, Patterson & Hodges, 1997; also see Nebes, 1989, 1992, for reviews). As a result of both sources of evidence, impaired semantic memory is currently the predominant explanation for the naming deficit in AD.

Nevertheless, there remain two alternative accounts, each of which appears to be supported by direct evidence from AD subjects' performance on naming tasks. One account is based on the finding that AD subjects are disproportionately affected by reduction of the visual quality of the stimulus to be named (e.g., line drawings vs. objects; e.g., Kirshner, Webb, & Kelly, 1984; Shuttleworth & Huber, 1988), suggesting a deficit of visual perception. The second account arises from the finding that AD subjects are differentially impaired at naming objects whose names are low-frequency words, relative to objects whose names occur with high frequency (e.g., Barker & Lawson, 1968; Skelton-Robinson & Jones, 1984; Shuttleworth & Huber,

1988), which suggests a deficit of lexical access. Furthermore, phonemic cuing has been reported to improve AD subjects' naming (e.g., Martin & Fedio, 1983; Neils, Brennan, Cole, et al., 1988), again implicating lexical or phonological retrieval as the locus of impairment.

This range of results appears to implicate three different loci of impairment underlying the naming deficit in AD, namely, semantic, visual, and lexical. This multiloci account may be valid, either as a result of heterogeneity of impairments between different persons with AD, or because individual subjects may have multiple loci of impairment. An alternative view, however, is that a semantic memory impairment alone is sufficient to account for the data directly implicating semantic memory as the locus of impairment, and for the apparently conflicting findings implicating visual perceptual and lexical factors. This alternative view rests on two key ideas from PDP: *distributed representation* and *interactivity*. In a highly interactive and distributed system of representation, different parts, or components, of the system are in a constant give-and-take relationship, continuously updating each other with the partial, intermediate results of their processing. Each part of an item's representation (e.g., visual, semantic, and lexical) depends on other parts for input to become activated, so that damage confined to one part of the system will render all parts less able to attain their proper activation states. In such a system, manipulations of difficulty that are targeted to nondamaged parts of the system would have an increased effect, because the functioning of the nondamaged parts is nevertheless compromised. Thus, if AD patients have a deficit of semantic memory, reducing the quality of the visual input may affect naming performance more than in persons with intact semantic memory because their visual systems are deprived of some of the normal support from semantics. Similarly, producing words that occur with low frequency may be more vulnerable to damage to semantic memory than producing words that occur with high frequency. Providing additional activation to the lexical or phonological components in the form of phonological cuing may facilitate activation of the correct name, regardless of whether there is damage in the lexical component.

These ideas have their roots in the last century, when neurologists pointed out the interactive nature of brain organization, and the resultant possibility that widespread changes in functioning could follow a localized lesion (e.g., Ferrier, 1886). Some modern neurologists (e.g., Kinsbourne, 1977) have also championed an interactive conception of neural information processing. Goodglass (1980) has specifically raised the possibility of a close interaction between semantics and lexical access, suggesting that "inadequate activation of a concept prevents retrieval of its name." Caramazza, Berndt, and Brownell (1982) and Bayles and Tomoeda (1983) have also emphasized the interaction between strictly perceptual and strictly lexical processes in confrontation naming. Hinton and Shallice (1991) and Plaut and Shallice (1993) have documented the effects of interactivity between vision and semantics on errors in reading, confirming that error type is not always transparently diagnostic of the underlying locus of damage. What has been lacking, however, are studies that explicitly investigate these general ideas of interactivity among perceptual, semantic, and lexical components of confrontation naming in order to interpret the effects of visual and lexical difficulty on naming performance in AD. We attempted to do just this by implementing a PDP model of confrontation naming in AD.

Specifically, we trained an interactive neural network to produce "name" patterns when presented with "visual" patterns by way of an intermediate set of "semantic" patterns, thus simulating confrontation naming. We then investigated the claim that damage to the "semantic" component will result in enhanced vulnerability to manipulations affecting nondamaged components, specifically the quality of "visual" inputs, frequency of training of patterns, and effects of phonological cuing (Tippett & Farah, 1994).

The Model

In PDP models, representations consist of a pattern of activation over a set of highly interconnected neuron-like units. The extent to which the activation of one unit causes an increase or decrease in the activation of a neighboring unit depends on the "weight" of the connection between them; positive weights cause units to excite each other and negative weights cause units to inhibit each other. For the network to learn that a certain name representation goes with a certain visual stimulus representation, the weights among units in the network are adjusted so that presentation of either the visual pattern in the visual units or the name pattern in the name units causes the corresponding other pattern to become activated. Upon presentation of the input pattern to the input units, all of the units connected with those input units will begin to change their activation under the influence of two kinds of constraints: the activation value of the units to which they are connected and the weights of the connections. These units might in turn connect to others, and influence their activation levels in the same way. In recurrent, or attractor, networks, such as the model to be presented here, the units downstream will also begin to influence the activation levels of the earlier units. Eventually, these shifting activation levels across the units of the network settle into a stable pattern, or attractor state. The attractor state into which a network settles is determined jointly by the input pattern (stimulus) and the weights of the network (stored knowledge).

Figure 17.1 shows the architecture of the model. There are five pools of units. The 16 "visual units" subserve visual representations of objects. The 32 "semantic units" subserve representations of the semantic knowledge that can be activated either by "visual inputs," or by "name inputs." The 16 "name units" subserve the representation of names associated with objects. The model is trained to associate the patterns of activity between these three layers. The learning of these associations is assisted by the presence of the remaining two unit pools, the "hidden units" (Rumelhart, Hinton, & Williams,

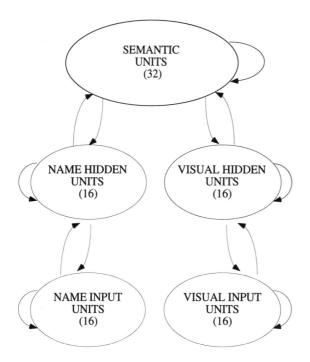

Figure 17.1 Functional architecture of model of confrontation naming.

1986). These are located between the visual and semantic layers (the "visual hidden units") and the name and semantic layers (the "name hidden units"). All units within each layer are connected to each other, and all connections, both between and within layers, are bidirectional. Thus, there is a high degree of interconnectivity in the model, which allows for extensive interaction among the different components in the course of naming. In addition to weights between units, there are bias weights for each unit, which encode the relative likelihood of each unit being activated over all trained patterns.

Twenty patterns consisting of patterns in the visual layer, semantic layer, and name layer, were generated. Visual representations and names of objects are represented by randomly generated patterns of activity (-1's and $+1$'s) over the 16 units in each pool. Similarly, the semantic knowledge activated by these inputs is represented by a random pattern of activity over the pool of 32 units in the semantic layer. The representations are distributed, in the sense that an object is represented by a pattern of activation over visual, semantic, and name units, and in the sense that within each of these pools of units all of the units participate in representing all of the known patterns. Each unit encodes information that represents some "microfeature" (Hinton, McClelland, & Rumelhart, 1986), but there is no attempt to assign units to specific easily labeled microfeatures (e.g., "red" or "round" for a visual representation). Of course, there is nothing intrinsically visual, semantic, or verbal about these pools of units, aside from the fact that their patterns of mutual connectivity conform to the general notion that semantic

Tippett & Farah: PDP Models in Alzheimer's Disease

representations must be accessed in order to mediate between visual and name representations.

Units in this model can take on continuous activation values between -1 and $+1$. The weights on the connections between units can take on any real values. Activation levels are updated according to a nonlinear activation function (a hyperbolic tangent). The network was trained to correctly associate the patterns of activity between the three layers, such that when an input pattern was presented to one of the layers (e.g., the visual layer), it was able to produce the correct patterns of activity at the other two layers (the semantic layer and the name layer). During training, as well as testing, inputs were soft-clamped, that is, their activation values were not fixed, but were the result of input activation along with activation from other units to which they were connected. Noise was injected into each layer to facilitate robustness of learning. To assess the generality of the results, multiple networks were trained with the same patterns but with different random starting weights. The learning procedure used during training was the contrastive Hebbian learning (CHL) algorithm (Movellan, 1990). Note that we are using CHL as a means of setting the weights in the network to enable it to perform naming; we are not concerned with the psychological reality of the training procedure as a model of learning.

Confrontation naming was simulated by presenting just the visual pattern to the visual input layer, allowing the network to settle, then looking at the pattern of activation on the name units to see which of the 20 name patterns it matched most closely. The degree of pattern match was simply the number of units whose values ($+1$ and -1) matched. It was therefore, a forced choice between the twenty patterns representing names.

Damage to semantic memory was simulated by removing randomly chosen subsets of the semantic units. Four levels of damage were used, to explore the effects of increasingly severe damage: 2 units, 4 units, 6 units, and 8 units, or 6.25 percent, 12.5 percent, 18.75 percent and 25 percent of the semantic layer. Although the neuropathological changes in AD are more complex than a simple loss of cells, we chose this means of lesioning the network because it was the simplest and most straightforward. Furthermore, Patterson, Seidenberg, and McClelland (1989) compared the effects on network performance of deleting units, deleting weights, and adding noise, and found them similar. Not all changes to a network necessarily have comparable effects: In their neural network simulation of AD, Chan and associates (Chan, Marshall, Butters, et al., 1992) found distinctive effects of selectively lesioning inhibitory connections. Nevertheless, the issues of interest in this study could be addressed by this more generic form of damage.

Simulations of Naming Deficit in Alzheimer's Disease

The first question of interest was the claim that if the components underlying naming are highly interactive, damage to semantics could render the system more sensitive to manipulations of the visual quality of the stimulus. This was investigated by testing trained undamaged and damaged networks on the production of the correct name patterns with normal visual inputs and impoverished visual inputs. Five undamaged trained networks were used. Twenty different random lesionings at each level of damage were then carried out for each network.

Visual impoverishment of the input patterns was simulated by reducing the inputs of a randomly chosen 50 percent of the units in the input pattern. For example, if part of the pattern was +1 +1 −1 −1, then the impoverished input might be +.5 +1 −1 −.5. Two levels of visual impoverishment were used for both damaged and undamaged networks. The first was used so that the naming task was as difficult as possible for the intact network without resulting in any errors. The second level of visual impoverishment used was selected so that the intact network made at least one error. These levels were motivated by the observation that normal subjects make few or no errors in naming impoverished stimuli.

While it was expected that damage to the semantic layer would impair network performance on the naming task overall, the question of interest was whether the damaged networks would show enhanced vulnerability to impoverished visual inputs relative to the intact networks. The results showed that although the amount of interaction between visual impoverishment and damage becomes smaller at increasing levels of damage, there is a highly consistent and significant interaction at all levels for the first level of impoverishment (figure 17.2) and for sixteen out of twenty of the damaged networks at the second level of impoverishment (figure 17.3) (see Tippett & Farah, 1994, for further details). In other words, the effect of visual degradation was greater on networks with semantic damage than on intact networks.

In our simulations, normal performance is at or near ceiling. This raises the possibility that the appearance of increased sensitivity to visual impoverishment in the damaged networks is due to a ceiling effect in the intact networks. Of course, the same point can be made about the empirical data from AD subjects and normal controls: normal subjects invariably perform at or near 100 percent in confrontation naming, even with the presentation of impoverished visual stimuli (e.g., see data of Kirshner et al., 1984). We do not think the high performance of normal subjects undermines the logic of the experiments using visual impoverishment, for the following reason. These studies were cast within the traditional framework of assumptions of discrete stage models (e.g., Sternberg, 1969) in which processors (such as a visual processor) transfer the results of their processing to further stages only after successful completion of that stage of processing. Using these assumptions, if it were true that AD patients have normal perception, then they should be just as much at ceiling in the visual processing of stimuli as normal controls. Therefore, with respect to those manipulations of visual processing difficulty for which normal subjects were at ceiling, AD patients should be just as immune, by virtue of the same ceiling effect. If this were the

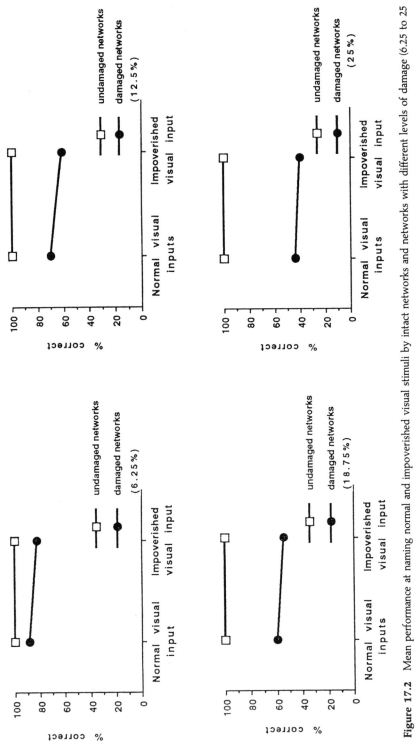

Figure 17.2 Mean performance at naming normal and impoverished visual stimuli by intact networks and networks with different levels of damage (6.25 to 25 percent) to the semantic units.

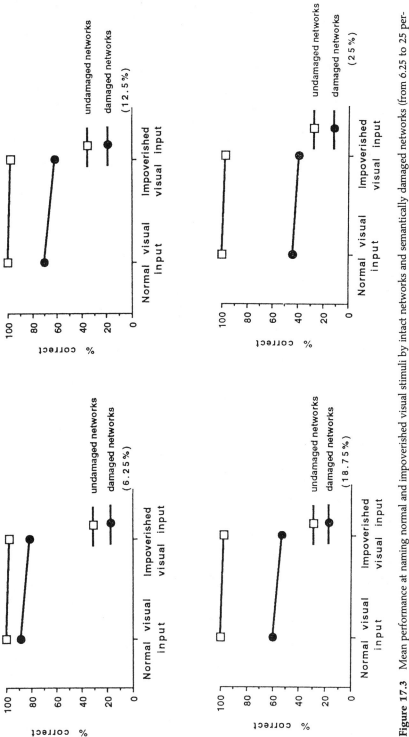

Figure 17.3 Mean performance at naming normal and impoverished visual stimuli by intact networks and semantically damaged networks (from 6.25 to 25 percent), when the level of impoverishment causes each intact network to make an error.

case, there would be no interaction caused by visual impoverishment, and AD patients' generally lower performance on all confrontation naming would be due to problems downstream, such as semantic memory.

Of course, if a system were highly interactive, such logic would not apply. As we demonstrated in this simulation in a highly interactive network, manipulations of difficulty (visual impoverishment) at one level can interact with impairment of a component at another level (semantic damage), while these same manipulations of difficulty have little or no effect on networks with intact semantics.

The second question of interest is the prediction that a naming system with highly interactive components will have more difficulty producing the names of items that have occurred with lower frequency during learning than those that occurred with higher frequency, after damage to the semantic component. This is based on the claim that in an interactive system, items trained with lower frequency will be less robustly represented, and therefore more vulnerable to damage in any component of the system. The investigation was carried out by training a series of twelve networks with stimulus items presented at different frequencies, that is, ten of the stimulus items were presented at a lower frequency than the other ten items. Six networks were trained with an item-frequency ratio of $4:1$ and six networks with an item frequency ratio of $3:1$. Networks were then damaged by removing randomly selected units in the semantic layer and were tested on the full set of items used in training. Each network was subjected to ten different random lesions at each of four levels of damage.

As predicted, more errors were made in the production of names for items trained at *low frequency*, compared with items trained at *high frequency* for networks trained on each of the two ratios and at each level of semantic damage from 6.25 percent to 25 percent (see figure 17.4 for results of networks trained at the $4:1$ ratio). With no damage, all the networks produce all names for the low- and high-frequency items without error. With damage in the semantic layer, networks make differentially more errors producing names for the low-frequency items. These findings were significant on twenty-two out of twenty-four tests that compared the effects of the four levels of semantic damage on naming the high frequency items versus the low frequency items in networks trained at the ratio of $4:1$. For the six networks that were trained at the ratio of $3:1$, sixteen out of twenty-four tests were significant.

These data support the hypothesis that lower-frequency items will suffer disproportionately after damage to semantics in an interactive naming system. However, in this simulation the frequency manipulation involved different amounts of training for the visual and semantic, as well as the lexical, levels of representation. In effect, our lexical frequency manipulation was confounded with other types of frequency. However, the same is undoubtedly true, on average, for the concrete nouns used in confrontation naming tasks, even though the degree of correlation among lexical, semantic, and

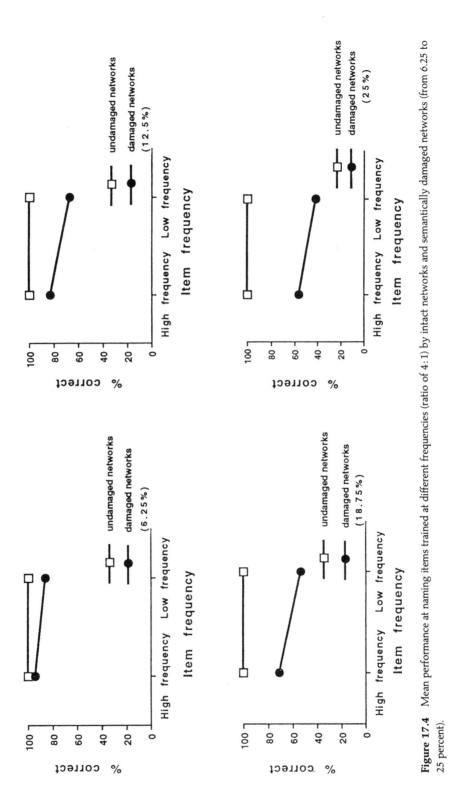

Figure 17.4 Mean performance at naming items trained at different frequencies (ratio of 4:1) by intact networks and semantically damaged networks (from 6.25 to 25 percent).

Table 17.1 Effectiveness of "phonemic cuing" on networks with damage in the semantic units: Mean percentage of correct name responses on previously failed items

	Level of Damage			
	6.25%	12.5%	18.75%	25%
Sample of 10 lesioned networks	$M = 67.6\%$ $SD = 32.40$	$M = 81.5\%$ $SD = 12.15$	$M = 73.5\%$ $SD = 15.93$	$M = 71.2\%$ $SD = 7.24$
	range 0%–100% (0/1–2/2)	range 60%–100% (3/5–7/7)	range 50%–100% (3/6–9/9)	range 58%–83.3% (7/12–10/12)

visual frequency would be less perfect in reality than it was in our simulation. In fact, without controlling for some nonlexical measure of familiarity, the lexical frequency manipulation cannot be used to implicate a specifically lexical locus of impairment, even in a discrete-stage architecture. For this reason, the results of phonemic cuing with AD patients seem a more decisive form of evidence favoring a lexical locus of impairment.

If a phonemic cue helps a patient produce the name of an object, it is generally inferred that the locus of naming impairment is lexical, as opposed to semantic. The final manipulation applied to this model was to test the validity of this inference. Will the naming performance of an interactive system, with damage confined to the semantic layer, be facilitated by presentation of a partial "phonemic" pattern, just as the naming of objects by AD patients is facilitated by the provision of a phonemic cue? A random sample of ten damaged networks from the first simulation was tested, using only those items on which they made errors. For each such item, the network was given a "phonemic cue." This was accomplished by soft-clamping 25 percent of the name units with the correct name pattern while the visual pattern was presented to the visual units, thus simulating, for example, saying "br" to facilitate the naming of a picture of a broom.

For networks at all levels of damage, phonemic cuing frequently enabled correct naming performance on those items that had previously been failed. Table 17.1 provides a summary of the mean percentage of correct name responses produced following cuing. The efficacy of cuing ranged from a mean of 67.6 percent for networks with 6.25 percent damage to the semantic units, to 81.5 percent for networks with 12.5 percent damage. At the highest level of damage to the semantic units (25 percent) the mean improvement was 71.24 percent. These findings demonstrate that an unambiguously lexical or phonological manipulation is effective in a semantically damaged system.

In summary, these simulations were undertaken to attempt to reconcile apparently conflicting data in the literature about the underlying impairment of the naming deficit in AD. In an interactive PDP model, it was possible to demonstrate that if one component of the system is damaged, in this case the semantic component, the remaining components were impaired in their functioning, if only to the extent of being more easily taxed by difficulty manipulations such as visual impoverishment. Similarly, when processing in one component was bolstered by additional external input, as in phonemic cuing, this helped a system whose damage was in another component. The findings are consistent with the view that a single locus of impairment in AD, namely in semantic memory, is sufficient to account for a wide variety of data related to naming tasks, including those thought to implicate other loci of impairment. Of course, this does not imply that there is always only one locus of impairment in AD. Schwartz and Stark (1990) have reviewed a large body of evidence on the clinical and pathological course of AD, and conclude that there is considerable variability in the systems affected, and in the stage of illness at which they are affected.

These findings clearly do not support the general strategy of inferring the locus of cognitive impairment on the basis of sensitivity to manipulations which selectively affect the processing of one component at a time. The model demonstrates that this approach is not reliable in highly interactive systems, since both visual and phonemic manipulations yielded positive results in our model when the damage was confined to semantics. This suggests that the analysis of patients' cognitive impairments will have to make use of more fine-grained measures such as distributions of error types, and converging operations among experimental tasks, perhaps in conjunction with computational modeling.

Preservation of Categorical Knowledge in Alzheimer's Disease

A second question that we addressed with the use of neural network models relates to the nature of the semantic memory impairment in AD. A common observation is that in persons with AD, semantic knowledge of exemplars often appears disproportionately impaired relative to knowledge of superordinate categories. The dissociation between exemplar and category knowledge can be seen in various measures of semantic memory, including confrontation naming (e.g., naming a desk as "furniture" or "a chair") category and attribute verification, picture-name matching, and category fluency (e.g., Bayles & Tomoeda, 1983; Chertkow, Bub, & Seidenberg, 1989; Hodges et al., 1991; Hodges, et al., 1996; Huff, Corkin, & Growdon, 1986; Martin, 1987; Martin & Fedio, 1983; Ober, Dronkers, Koss, et al., 1986; Tröster, Salmon, McCullough, et al., 1989 but see Cox, Bayles & Trosset, 1996 for a counter finding).

The most transparent interpretation of these observations is that the brain honors the distinction between different levels of a hierarchical, categorical knowledge system, and that AD primarily affects the neural systems subserving exemplar knowledge. The principles of PDP give rise to a second interpretation of the dissociation found in AD, however, which does not involve separate systems for representing these two kinds of knowledge. In

PDP systems, knowledge representation is widely distributed, with a many-to-many mapping of things represented and things (units) doing the representing. In other words, many units are involved in a representation, and individual units are involved in many representations. Because of this, semantic memory may be conceptualized as a distributed system of knowledge representation, in which the same physical substrate represents both categorical and exemplar information. The relative preservation of category knowledge is a consequence of the greater robustness of the category attributes (i.e., those attributes shared by all or most members of a category) compared to exemplar-unique attributes. This greater robustness is a direct consequence of the increased frequency of learning of category attributes resulting from the more inclusive nature of categories. In other words, the category attributes of a semantic pattern are learned and activated each time a member of that category is presented or encountered. In contrast, exemplar-unique attributes become active only when that particular exemplar is presented.

Simulations of Preserved Category Knowledge in Alzheimer's Disease

We tested and confirmed the computational adequacy of this hypothesis in two computer simulations (Tippett, McAuliffe & Farah, 1995). We trained the same interactive network described above (see figure 17.1), to associate patterns in pools of "visual" units with patterns in "semantic" and "lexical" units. As before, there is nothing intrinsically visual, semantic, or verbal about these pools of units, aside from the fact that their patterns of mutual connectivity conform to the general notion that semantic representations must be accessed in order to mediate between visual and name representations.

In these simulations the twenty patterns in the semantic layer were constructed so that four categories were represented, each with five individual exemplars. Half of each semantic pattern, that is, 16 of the 32 units of the semantic representation, represented the properties shared across exemplars within a category. This portion of the pattern was therefore identical across the five exemplars. The other 16 units represented the individual exemplar knowledge for each item and overlapped with other exemplars within the category by only 8 of the 16 units. An example is provided in figure 17.5, which shows the semantic patterns of the five members of categories 1 and 2. The other categories were constructed in a similar manner except that they shared different sets of 16 units. Specifically, the category portion of the semantic patterns for category 1 involved semantic units 1 though 16, category 2 involved semantic units 9 through 24, category 3 involved semantic units 17 through 32, and category 4 involved semantic units 1 through 8 and 24 through 31. Thus, all semantic units functioned equally often to represent category and exemplar knowledge. There is no division of labor, within the semantic layer, for category vs. exemplar knowledge.

CATEGORY 1

SEMANTIC UNITS	1 - 8	9-16	17-24	25-32
	+-+-+-+-	+-+-+-+-	++++++++	++++++++
	+-+-+-+-	+-+-+-+-	--------	++++++++
	+-+-+-+-	+-+-+-+-	++++----	++++----
	+-+-+-+-	+-+-+-+-	----++++	++++----
	+-+-+-+-	+-+-+-+-	+-+-+-+-	-+-+-+-+

CATEGORY 2

SEMANTIC UNITS	1 - 8	9-16	17-24	25-32
	++++++++	-++--++-	-++--++-	++++++++
	--------	-++--++-	-++--++-	++++++++
	++++----	-++--++-	-++--++-	++++----
	----++++	-++--++-	-++--++-	++++----
	+-+-+-+-	-++--++-	-++--++-	-+-+-+-+

Figure 17.5 Semantic patterns of the five members of category 1 and the five members of category 2. Note that units 1–16 carry the category information for category 1, and units 9–24 carry the category information for category 2.

Ten networks were trained to associate twenty patterns of activity on the visual, naming, and semantic layers. Each network was trained with the semantic patterns described above, but the visual and naming patterns were different for each of the ten networks. As before, damage to semantic memory was simulated by removing randomly chosen subsets of the semantic units. Four levels of damage were used to explore the effects of increasingly severe damage: 2 units, 4 units, 6 units, and 8 units, or 6.25 percent, 12.5 percent, 18.75 percent, and 25 percent of the semantic layer. At each of these levels of damage, each network was lesioned in twenty different ways, that is, with twenty different random patterns of semantic units eliminated.

The results of this simulation are summarized in table 17.2. After damage, the system showed a stronger tendency to within-category errors than between-category errors, as do persons with AD, even though the damaged representations do not separately implement category and exemplar knowledge. While appearing to confirm our hypothesis as to the greater robustness of category-level knowledge to damage, in fact the reason for these results is ambiguous. It is well known that similar patterns may be confused with one another after network damage (e.g., Hinton & Shallice, 1991; Plaut & Shallice, 1993). Therefore, it is possible that this finding simply reflects the greater similarity among exemplars within a category than among exemplars of different categories, rather than being a result of the greater robustness of the category-level knowledge.

Table 17.2 Average number of multiple-choice naming errors out of twenty, at four levels of damage, showing expected and observed within-category errors

Level of Damage to Semantic Layer (%)	Average Overall Errors	Expected Within-Category Errors	Observed Within-Category Errors	Significance Level (Binomial Test)
6.25	2.5	0.53	0.79	0.001
12.50	5.58	1.17	1.76	0.001
18.75	7.97	1.68	2.39	0.001
25.00	10.64	2.24	2.91	0.001

Table 17.3 Average number of erroneous unit activation values per pattern in category and exemplar portions of semantic patterns at four levels of damage

Level of Damage to Semantic Layer (%)	Category Unit Errors	Exemplar Unit Errors	Significance Level (Binomial Test)
6.25	0.20	0.24	0.001
12.50	0.48	0.59	0.001
18.75	0.80	0.88	0.001
25.00	1.04	1.12	0.001

In order to check this possibility we carried out a second simulation to assess directly the state of category and exemplar knowledge after semantic layer damage. Instead of looking at the names produced by the damaged network, we looked at the semantic layer itself and compared the relative accuracy of the category vs. exemplar portions of the patterns. Table 17.3 shows the average error in category and exemplar portions of the patterns in ten different networks after twenty different random lesionings at each level of damage. There is a consistent tendency for the categorical information to be more robust to damage than the exemplar-unique information, even though errors in category and exemplar units should be equally likely by chance. In other words, in this simulation the preservation of categorical and exemplar-unique semantic knowledge is assessed directly, without the confounding influence of the greater number of similar and hence confusable patterns within a category than between categories on our error measure. The results support the claim that categorical information is robust to damage because of the greater degree of training enjoyed by categorical information.

This simulation illustrates that observed neuropsychological dissociations do not invariably and transparently reflect the structure of the underlying cognitive architecture (Farah, 1994; Shallice, 1988), particularly in the case of single dissociations, in which two abilities may rely on the same architectural component, but one may be more resistant to damage than the other

(Teuber, 1955). In the case of the dissociation between category and exemplar knowledge observed in AD, it is not necessary to hypothesize that semantic memory is compartmentalized into category-level knowledge and exemplar knowledge. In very general terms, our explanation is an instance of the type of explanation noted by both Teuber (1955) and Shallice (1988), in which the relatively impaired ability is simply "easier" or more "robust" than the relatively spared ability. "Easy" and "robust" are not mechanistic terms, however; rather they are descriptive labels in an incomplete explanation. The advantage of the computational approach is that it directly tests these rather nonspecific concepts, and in so doing provides an explicit, mechanistic account of the phenomena.

In these simulations, there are two features of neural network computation which are particularly relevant to the explanation of preserved category knowledge in AD, namely, distributed representation and graded learning. With distributed representations of knowledge, the category is implicitly represented by the attributes shared by all or most members of the category (see figure 17.5). The categorical portion of each exemplar's representation is therefore encountered more frequently, during learning, than the exemplar-unique portions. Because learning is not all-or-none in connectionist networks, but a matter of degree which depends on, among other factors, frequency of training, category knowledge is more overlearned in a trained network than exemplar knowledge.

IMPLICATIONS FOR CLINICAL NEUROPSYCHOLOGY

Do findings from these PDP models have implications for the practice of clinical neuropsychology? Indeed they do. In our view, these findings have both specific implications for understanding cognitive impairment in AD, and general implications for the clinical assessment of cognitive impairments of individuals with various types of brain damage.

Neuropsychological assessment of cognitive impairment in persons either suspected of, or with, a diagnosis of probable or possible AD is challenging because of the variability in the cortical regions affected and in the stage of illness at which they are affected, and the consequent variability in cognitive deficits. An increase in knowledge about impairments most consistently present during the early to middle stages of the disease, such as semantic memory, will assist the clinician in selecting tests appropriate for assessing critical areas of cognitive functioning. The findings from our PDP models support other research suggesting that semantic memory is a locus of impairment in most patients with AD. In addition, they have shown that in an interactive system a semantic impairment alone can account for patterns of performance that might at first glance appear to indicate another type of cognitive deficit (e.g., the sensitivity of AD patients to phonemic cuing on naming tasks).

The brain has long been viewed as a complex interactive system by many academic and clinical neuropsychologists. Nevertheless, applying this general principle in a meaningful way to our understanding of the consequences of damage to specific components of the cognitive architecture has been very difficult, and instead interpretation of patient performance has tended to be much more literal. Sensitivity to visual factors in tasks, or the production of visual errors, has, for example, been interpreted as indicating impairment in the visual stage of processing. In other words, for want of any clear specific alternative, there has been a tendency to interpret impaired neuropsychological performance as if brain and cognition operate as discrete stage systems, rather than as interactive systems. The advent of connectionist theory and PDP models, however, provides an alternative: PDP models provide a means to reason about the complex relations between interactive systems and behavior and the effects of damaging such a system. Importantly the approach also allows us to test in explicit mechanistic terms such reasoning. Thus, for example, the PDP models described in this chapter have shown that differential sensitivity to manipulations of visual factors on naming tasks does not reliably indicate a deficit at the visual stage of processing in highly interactive systems. The relation between results of such manipulations and the locus of impairment in the damaged cognitive system is much less transparent.

Such findings clearly have implications for interpreting cognitive performance in brain-damaged individuals generally. Interpretation of patients' cognitive impairments must make use of more fine-grained measures such as distributions of error types and converging evidence from a variety of tasks. Many clinical neuropsychologists are well practiced at looking at patterns of performance across tasks, so the adaptation required may be less one of procedural change, and more one of the reasoning about, and interpretation of, performance.

WHERE TO FROM HERE?

We have used two examples to illustrate the application of computational modeling, in this case PDP models, to questions emerging from the neuropsychological literature on cognitive impairments in AD. These simulations have allowed us to test, in an explicit and mechanistic manner, general claims made about the properties of interactive systems. One of the major criticisms of computational models, however, is that they are post hoc; they account for old data without making new contributions or predictions. For this reason we believe it is important that novel predictions emerging from these models be tested with AD subjects. This is important both from the point of view of checking the validity of the computational model and from our need to extend further our knowledge and understanding of the impairments experienced by persons with AD. In this way the relation between computational modeling and empirical work with persons with brain damage assumes the properties of an interactive system: both components in a constant give-and-take relation, continually updating each other with the partial, intermediate results of their processing.

ACKNOWLEDGMENTS

This research was supported by a University of Auckland Research Committee grant awarded to L. J. T., and Alzheimer's Association Pilot Research Grant PRG-93-153, ONR grant N00014-93-I0621, NIMH grant R01 MH48274, and NSF STC grant to the Institute for Research in Cognitive Science at the University of Pennsylvania, University of Pennsylvania Research Research Foundation, awarded to M. J. F.

REFERENCES

Barker, M., & Lawson, J. (1968). Nominal aphasia in dementia. *British Journal of Psychiatry, 114*, 1351–1356.

Bayles, K. A., & Tomoeda, C. K. (1983). Confrontation naming impairment in dementia. *Brain and Language, 19*, 98–114.

Caramazza, A., Berndt, R. S., & Brownell, H. H. (1982). The semantic deficit hypothesis: Perceptual parsing and object classification by aphasic patients. *Brain and Language, 15*, 161–189.

Chan, A. S., Butters, N., & Salmon, D. (1997). The deterioration of semantic networks in patients with Alzheimer's disease: A cross-sectional study. *Neuropsychologia, 35*, 241–248.

Chan, A. S., Marshall, S., Butters, N., & Salmon, D. (1992). *Understanding semantic memory in Alzheimer's disease patients: A computational approach*. Presented at the fourth annual convention of the American Psychological Society, San Diego, June 1992.

Chertkow, H., Bub, D., & Seidenberg, M. (1989). Priming and semantic memory loss in Alzheimer's disease. *Brain and Language, 36*, 420–446.

Cox, D. M., Bayles, K. A., & Trosset, M. W. (1996). Category and attribute Knowledge deterioration in Alzheimer's disease. *Brain and Language, 52*, 536–550.

Farah, M. J. (1994). Neuropsychological inference with an interactive brain. *Behavioral and Brain Sciences, 17*, 43–104.

Ferrier, D., (1886). *The functions of the brain*. London: Smith, Elder.

Goodglass, H. (1980). Disorders of naming following brain injury. *American Scientist, 68*, 647–655.

Hinton, G. E., McClelland, J. L., & Rumelhart, D. E. (1986). Distributed representations. In D. Rumelhart, J. L. McClelland, & the PDP Research Group (Eds.), *Parallel distributed processing: Explorations in the microstructure of cognition*, Vol. 1 (pp. 77–109). Cambridge, MA: MIT Press.

Hinton, G. E., & Shallice, T. (1991). Lesioning an attractor network: Investigations of acquired dyslexia. *Psychological Review, 98*, 74–95.

Hodges, J. R., Patterson, K., Graham, N., & Dawson, K. (1996). Naming and knowing in dementia of Alzheimer's type. *Brain and Language, 54*, 302–325.

Hodges, J. R., Salmon, D. P., & Butters, N. (1991). The nature of the naming deficit in Alzheimer's and Huntington's disease. *Brain, 114*, 1547–1558.

Huff, J. F., Corkin, S., & Growdon, J. H. (1986). Semantic impairment and anomia in Alzheimer's disease. *Brain and Language, 28,* 235–249.

Kinsbourne, M. (1977). Hemi-neglect and hemispheric rivalry. In E. A. Weinstein and R. P. Friendland (Eds.), *Hemi-inattention and hemispheric specialization* (pp. 41–49). New York: Raven Press.

Kirshner, H. S., Webb, W. G., & Kelly, M. P. (1984). The naming disorder of dementia. *Neuropsychologia, 22,* 23–30.

Martin, A. (1987). Representation of semantic and spatial knowledge in Alzheimer's patients: Implications for models of preserved learning in amnesia. *Journal of Clinical and Experimental Neuropsychology, 9,* 191–224.

Martin, A., & Fedio, P. (1983). Word production and comprehension in Alzheimer's disease: The breakdown of semantic knowledge. *Brain and Language, 19,* 124–141.

Movellan, J. (1990). Contrastive Hebbian learning in the continuous Hopfield model. In D. S. Touretzky, G. E. Hinton, & T. J. Sejnowski (Eds.), *Proceedings of the 1989 connectionist models summer school* (pp. 10–17). San Mateo, CA: Morgan Kaufman.

Nebes, R. D. (1989). Semantic memory in Alzheimer's disease. *Psychological Bulletin, 106,* 377–394.

Nebes, R. D. (1992). Cognitive dysfunction in Alzheimer's disease. In F. I. M. Craik & T. A. Salthouse (Eds.), *The handbook of aging and cognition* (pp. 373–446). Hillsdale, NJ: Erlbaum.

Neils, J., Brennan, M. M., Cole, M., Boller, F., & Gerdeman, B. (1988). The use of phonemic cuing with Alzheimer's disease patients. *Neuropsychologia, 26,* 351–354.

Ober, B. A., Dronkers, N. F., Koss, E., Delis, D. C., & Friedland, R. P. (1986). Retrieval from semantic memory in Alzheimer-type dementia. *Journal of Clinical and Experimental Neuropsychology, 8,* 75–92.

Patterson, K., Seidenberg, M. S., & McClelland, J. L. (1989). Connections and disconnections: Acquired dyslexia in a computational model of reading processes. In R. G. M. Morris (Ed.), *Parallel distributed processing: Implications for psychology and neurobiology* (pp. 131–181). Oxford: Oxford University Press.

Plaut, D. C., & Shallice, T. (1993). Perseverative and semantic influences on visual object naming errors in optic aphasia: A connectionist account. *Journal of Cognitive Neuroscience, 5,* 89–117.

Ralph, M. A. L., Patterson, K., & Hodges, J. R. (1997). The relationship between naming and semantic knowledge for different categories in dementia of Alzheimer's type. *Neuropsychologia, 35,* 1251–1260.

Rumelhart, D. E., Hinton, G. E., & Williams, R. J. (1986). Learning internal representations by error propagation. In D. Rumelhart, J. L. McClelland, & the PDP Research Group (Eds.), *Parallel distributed processing: Explorations in the microstructure of cognition, Vol. 1: Foundations* (pp. 318–362). Cambridge, MA: MIT Press.

Rumelhart, D., McClelland, J. L., & the PDP Research Group (1986). *Parallel distributed processing: Explorations in the microstructure of cognition, Vol. 1: Foundations.* Cambridge, MA: MIT Press.

Schwartz, M. F., & Stark, J. A. (1990). Clinicopathological models of Alzheimer's disease and senile dementia: Unraveling the contradictions. In M. F. Schwartz (Ed.), *Modular deficits in Alzheimer-type dementia* (pp. 61–82). Cambridge, MA: MIT Press.

Shallice, T. (1988). *From neuropsychology to mental structure.* Cambridge, U. K.: Cambridge University Press.

Shuttleworth, E. C., & Huber, S. J. (1988). The naming disorder of dementia of Alzheimer type. *Brain and Language, 34,* 222–234.

Skelton-Robinson, M., & Jones, S. (1984). Nominal dysphasia and the severity of senile dementia. *British Journal of Psychiatry, 145,* 168–171.

Sternberg, S. (1969). The discovery of processing stages: Extension of Donder's method. *Acta Psychologia, 30,* 276–315.

Teuber, H. L. (1955). Physiological psychology. *Annual Review of Psychology, 6,* 267–296.

Tippett, L. J., & Farah, M. J. (1994). A computational model of naming in Alzheimer's disease: Unitary or multiple impairments? *Neuropsychology, 8,* 3–13.

Tippett, L. J., McAuliffe, S., & Farah, M. J. (1995). Preservation of categorical knowledge in Alzheimer's Disease: A computational account. *Memory, 3,* 519–533.

Tröster, A. I., Salmon, D. P., McCullough, D., & Butters, N. (1989). A comparison of category fluency deficits associated with Alzheimer's and Huntington's disease. *Brain and Language, 37,* 500–513.

Index